Biological surveys of estuaries and coasts

Estuarine and brackish-water sciences association handbook

Biological surveys of estuaries and coasts

Edited by

J. M. BAKER
Field Studies Council, Preston Montford, Shrewsbury, England

W. J. WOLFF
Rijksinstituut voor Natuurbeheer, Den Burg, Texel, The Netherlands

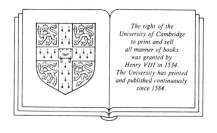

CAMBRIDGE UNIVERSITY PRESS
Cambridge
London   New York   New Rochelle
Melbourne   Sydney

Published by the Press Syndicate of the University of Cambridge
The Pitt Building, Trumpington Street, Cambridge CB2 1RP
32 East 57th Street, New York, NY 10022, USA
10 Stamford Road, Oakleigh, Melbourne 3166, Australia

First published 1987

Printed in Great Britain by the University Press, Cambridge

British Library cataloguing in publication data
Biological surveys of estuaries and coasts.
1. Coastal ecology   2. Estuarine ecology
I. Baker, J. M.   II. Wolff, W. J.
574.5′2636   QH541.5.C65

ISBN 0521 324076 hard covers
ISBN 0521 311918 paperback

Contents

Contributors

J. M. Baker, Field Studies Council, Preston Montford, Shrewsbury, England

L. A. Bouwman, Instituut voor Bodemvruchtbaarheid, Haren, The Netherlands

J. H. Crothers, Field Studies Council, The Leonard Wills Field Centre, Williton, Taunton, England

D. H. Dalby, Department of Pure and Applied Biology, Imperial College, London, England

B. Dicks, Field Studies Council Oil Pollution Research Unit, Orielton Field Centre, Pembroke, Wales

R. H. L. Disney, Field Studies Council, c/o Department of Zoology, University of Cambridge, England

G. D. Floodgate, School of Ocean Sciences, University College of North Wales, Menai Bridge, Gwynedd, Wales

J. P. Hartley, BP Petroleum Development Ltd., Dyce, Aberdeen, Scotland

K. Hiscock, Field Studies Council Oil Pollution Research Unit, Orielton Field Centre, Pembroke, Wales (now at Nature Conservancy Council, Northminster House, Peterborough, England)

N. A. Holme, Marine Biological Association of the U.K., The Laboratory, Citadel Hill, Plymouth, England

E. B. G. Jones, Department of Biological Sciences, Portsmouth Polytechnic, England

C. S. Lloyd, Nature Conservancy Council, 17 Rubislaw Terrace, Aberdeen, Scotland

D. Nichols, Department of Biological Sciences, University of Exeter, England

G. W. Potts, Marine Biological Association of the U.K., The Laboratory, Citadel Hill, Plymouth, England

A. J. Prater, Royal Society for the Protection of Birds, S.E. England Office, Shoreham-by-Sea, West Sussex, England

P. J. Reay, Department of Biological Sciences, Plymouth Polytechnic, England

P. B. Tett, SMBA Research Fellow, School of Ocean Sciences, University College of North Wales, Menai Bridge, Gwynedd, Wales

W. J. Wolff, Rijksinstituut voor Natuurbeheer, Den Burg, Texel, The Netherlands

Preface

Recent years have seen a growth in demand for biological surveys for a variety of practical purposes, such as environmental impact assessment and surveillance, management of amenity, and identification of sites for conservation priority. Biological surveys are concerned with investigating the distribution and abundance of organisms. They involve decisions about location of sampling sites; types, numbers, and sizes of samples; equipment; and data processing. They also usually include the collection of physical and chemical data as aids to interpretation. From the scientific point of view, Harper (1982) warns against 'excessive preoccupation with the distribution of taxa (cartography for taxomists)' but recognizes that it is natural that the first stages in the growth of any science should consist of the description and ordering of the material for study. Much estuarine and coastal biology is still at this stage.

For the purpose of this book, estuaries are defined as semi-enclosed and coastal bodies of water that have free connections with the open sea and within which sea water is measurably diluted with fresh water derived from land drainage (Cameron & Pritchard, 1963). Coasts are defined as the zone where estuary or sea water meets the land. They include the intertidal zone, nearshore waters and subtidal areas, and cliffs rising directly from the shore. The book is intended to give an introduction to techniques (together with their advantages and limitations) for these different habitats and the main groups of organisms to be found in them. The material is mainly European but should be relevant to many parts of the world (excluding specifically tropical features such as mangroves and coral reefs). It is hoped that the bringing together in one volume of techniques for a great diversity of organisms and habitats will be useful for those planning broadly based surveys and may also encourage some cross fertilization of methodology between different specializations.

The editors would like to thank the Estuarine and Brackish-Water Sciences Association, Cambridge University Press, and the contributors for their patience during the long gestation period of this book, all the referees for their constructive comments, and Dr. R. Mitchell for his invaluable assistance in planning the book. J. M. Baker would like to thank the Winston Churchill Memorial Trust and the Field Studies Council for making possible study periods at the early planning and crescendo stages of the book respectively.

References
Cameron, W. M. & Pritchard, D. W. (1963). Estuaries. In *The Sea*, vol. 2, ed. M. N. Hill, pp. 306–24. New York: John Wiley and Sons.
Harper, J. L. (1982). After description. In *The Plant Community as a Working Mechanism*, ed. E. I. Newman, pp. 11–25. Oxford: Blackwell Scientific Publications.

J. M. Baker and W. J. Wolff

1

Planning biological surveys

J. M. BAKER, J. P. HARTLEY, and B. DICKS

Why do biological surveys?
Biological surveys of estuaries and coasts may be carried out for
a variety of reasons including the following.

Scientific research
The survey may be exploration of a new area, part of a wider study leading
to (for example) energy flow modelling for a whole estuary, or a prelude
to experimental work aimed (for example) at understanding the distribution
of a single species.

Education
Estuaries and coasts are favourite biological training grounds. There is a
rich variety of organisms and communities, and gradients (e.g., of salinity,
wave exposure, and tidal emersion time) are easily available for studies
relating the distribution of organisms to physical and chemical variables.

Conservation
Choice of priority sites for conservation arises from a ranking process
which in turn requires site descriptions. A variety of criteria may be used
for ranking purposes, e.g., diversity, uniqueness, or representativeness.
Conservation concerns may also be at the root of environmental impact
assessments, biological surveillance, and contingency plans.

Exploitation of natural resources
Survey information (e.g., concerning fish, shellfish, or algae) allows
evaluation of the potential of an area. Surveillance or monitoring are
prerequisites of effective action against over-exploitation.

Management of amenity
The recreational use of the shore and nearshore waters (e.g., for boating, fishing, including bait digging, and diving) is a particular type of exploitation of natural resources, with similar survey requirements.

Environmental impact assessments (EIAs)
Environmental impact assessments are now required by law for industrial and other developments in many countries. Examples of such developments are barrages, land reclamation, oil production in nearshore waters, and desalination plants.

Biological surveillance or monitoring
Surveillance and monitoring imply the use of a repeated protocol for the detection of temporal change. Choice of components for monitoring is best based upon an initial survey which reveals which organisms and communities are present in the area of interest. A baseline survey is a different concept – its purpose is to provide information against which subsequent monitoring data may be compared.

The terms surveillance and monitoring are sometimes used interchangeably; however, Holdgate (1976) restricted 'monitoring' to those cases where change is measured with a defined goal or standard in mind (whether or not it is mandatory).

Contingency plans
Murphy's Law states that (1) if it is possible for something to go wrong, sooner or later it will and (2) it is impossible to make any system foolproof because fools are so ingenious (Holdgate, 1976). Contingency plans are a response to Murphy's Law and have probably been best developed with regard to oil spill response. An essential feature of contingency plans is identification and mapping of vulnerable areas, and consideration 'before the event' of priorities for protection.

Damage assessment
After accidents such as spills of toxic chemicals it may be necessary to describe which organisms or communities have been affected, and over what area. Settlement of compensation claims may rest upon this information. It is also possible to do 'one-off' surveys around chronic discharges, e.g., sewage works outfalls, to find the spatial distribution of sedentary organisms and so estimate the area affected by the discharge.

Thinking around the problem

A survey is a way of tackling a problem. A common mistake is to spend insufficient time thinking about the problem (i.e., how to fulfil the aims of the survey) and consequently to plunge too soon into inappropriate survey routines. Deliberate use of a rational decision-making process helps (after Open University, 1983):

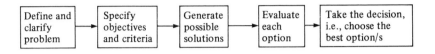

Setting objectives and criteria

It is essential that thinking about the problem leads to clear objectives and criteria as these influence all subsequent aspects of the planning and execution of the work. Several objectives may emerge from each problem. See Table 1.1 for some examples of specific objectives.

Criteria may be both scientific and operational, as illustrated by the following examples.

Must yield quantitative data, with a pre-defined level of precision.
Must be carried out during August:
    So that results are comparable with those of a previous survey.
    To take into account the seasonal behaviour of species X.
Must cost less than £10 000.

Table 1.1. *Examples of survey objectives*

Problem (how to fulfil the aims of the survey)	Specific objectives
How to find the best site for a tidal barrage taking into account the conservation value of salt marshes	Carry out an aerial reconnaissance plus colour and false colour infrared aerial photography Select sites from the photographs and visit them to collect 'ground truth' information on vegetation Prepare maps showing distribution of salt marshes and main vegetation types
How to map the national distribution of conspicuous species of the shallow subtidal zone	Develop identification guides and recording cards suitable for use by amateur divers Publicise scheme among diving clubs and enlist support Develop computer-based data-handling system

Options

The central box of the decision-making process illustrated above is concerned with the generation of solutions or options. This stage in particular benefits from discussion with colleagues. Brain storming or lateral thinking techniques (Open University, 1983) may be useful here, though they do not seem to have been much used for survey planning purposes.

Example:

Objective: To delimit the area of effect of an effluent discharge flowing over a rocky shore.

Options include:

Ignore biology altogether, use tracer dyes combined with aerial photography, or salinity measurements, at different stages of the tide.

Colour and false colour infrared photography of shore at low tide from nearby cliff top.

Walk around the shore and make notes and a sketchmap.

Grid the shore (parallel transects); at grid stations record abundance of:

All taxa to species level if possible, or

Selected taxonomic groups, or

Functional groups, e.g., producers/herbivores/carnivores.

As above but just record presence/absence at grid stations.

Planning considerations

Levels of planning

Planning is commonly required on different levels, those of (1) the estuary or coast, (2) the habitat, community, or population, and (3) the sample. A different dimension is (4) the amount of time required. For any survey a time budget should be developed, including data processing and reporting. Thus one may have hierarchies of objectives, criteria, and options.

Estuary/coast

Examples of planning considerations:

What area is to be included?

What is known already about this area?

Can local people help with information?

What components (e.g., subtidal macrobenthos, salt-marsh invertebrates, bacteria, birds) are to be included?

Will remote sensing further the aims of the survey?

How is it possible to travel within the area?
What restrictions on working time are imposed by tidal conditions?
Is it necessary to obtain permission in advance to visit any parts of the area?
What hazards may be expected and what safety precautions should be taken?

Habitat/community/population
Examples of planning considerations:
What access points are available (e.g., to rocky shores)?
How will time of year affect the population distribution/species present/size of organisms? Should a series of surveys be carried out at different times of year?
How should sampling sites be located?

Samples
Examples of planning considerations:
How will the sample be taken (e.g., quadrat, corer, grab, suction sampler)?
What is the optimum size for the sample?
How many replicates should be taken? Could the sample comprise pooled sub-samples?
What degree of taxonomic discrimination or classification scheme is appropriate?
How will the taxa be recorded (presence/absence, abundance scale grade, density, biomass, etc.)?
What size taxa will be recorded (e.g., anything over 0.5 mm, less than and greater than 5 mm shell length, comprehensive size-frequency classes)?
Should the sample (e.g., a quadrat of vegetation) be recorded photographically as a supplement to or substitute for detailed field recording?
Which physical and chemical variables should be recorded in the sampling area?
Should the sampling area be permanently marked (e.g., with a wooden post or pat of concrete) to facilitate future surveys/surveillance?
How will the data be processed?

Location of sites and stations

The different chapters of this book contain information relevant to specific habitats or groups of organisms. The purpose of this section is to highlight important considerations of general relevance.

A strategy provides a rationale for the location of sites and stations, and it should be based on as much pre-existing information (e.g., maps, aerial photographs) as possible. The term 'site' refers to the locations within the estuary or along the coast at which the work is being carried out, and the term 'station' refers to the division of the site into survey or sampling units. Strategies for major components of the estuarine or coastal system are usually considered separately, and this is reflected in the structure of this book.

Options

The options for site and/or station selection can be represented in the form of a decision tree (Fig. 1.1).

Total/partial. The need for choosing sites is eliminated with those survey approaches that give total coverage, e.g., aerial photography; walking along an entire shoreline and recording main habitat types on a map. Conversely, if taxonomic and/or quantitative detail are required, attention must be focused on small parts (sites) of the general area of interest.

Objective/subjective. A site may be chosen on subjective grounds (e.g., because it looks representative or because someone is worried about its conservation status) or objectively (e.g., because it is at an intersection on a national cartographic grid).

Different objective approaches. Systematic location of sites or stations, usually along transects or using a grid system, is appropriate for distribution/mapping studies, or in cases where environmental (including pollutant) gradients are suspected. Random location (using random numbers) is necessary if the requirement is for quantitative data with the maximum potential for parametric statistical analysis. In practice many surveys employ a stratified random strategy – sites are located systematically or

Fig. 1.1. Decision tree for site/station location.

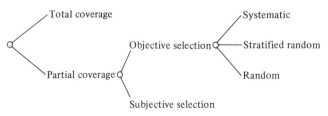

with respect to predetermined divisions of the area into different environmental categories, but replicate stations at each site are randomized.

Examples

1. Stratified random strategy

Quantification (density estimates) of organisms on a tidal flat (Fig. 1.2). The three strata (based on a preliminary inspection) are mud, poorly sorted sediments, and the mussel bed. Each stratum is considered separately for the random location of sampling stations. The optimum number and size of samples (see next section) will probably be different for each stratum.

If the area to be considered is very large then two levels of stratification could be considered before randomization. Primary strata would be the mud, poorly sorted sediments, and mussel bed, as before; secondary strata could be systematic grids imposed separately on each primary stratum. Sampling stations would then be randomized within each square of each grid.

2. 'Complex' strategy

Rocky shore survey of a large bay (description of the distribution and abundance of macroflora and macrofauna) (Fig. 1.3).

The rocky shores are located using maps, photographs, and preliminary

Fig. 1.2. Tidal flat sampling in three strata: (1) mud; (2) poorly sorted sediments; (3) mussel bed.

inspection. This amounts to 'stratification' of the bay into two components – rocky shores and the rest. Rocky shore sites for detailed survey are chosen using a 'modified' systematic approach, i.e., the sites are as evenly distributed round the bay as possible bearing in mind the two main constraints of rocky shore distribution and safe access. The final choice of site may be partly subjective in that it may be chosen, on the basis of a rapid inspection of a relatively large area, to be representative of the area.

At each site a belt transect is established and the abundance of organisms assessed systematically, e.g., at regular vertical height intervals along the transect. Each transect may be a stratified random sampling scheme in itself, with regular placement of transect stations combined with random quadrats, e.g., for limpet density, at each station.

Further examples of survey strategies are given elsewhere in this book, for example, see Chapter 5 for benthic sampling grids and Chapter 8 for a variety of rocky shore transect strategies.

Fig. 1.3. Distribution of rocky shore survey sites in Bantry Bay, Eire. After Baker & Hiscock, 1984.

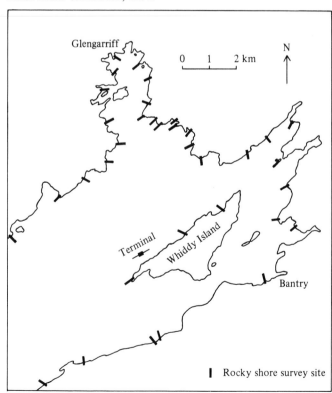

Sizes and numbers of samples

A sample is the unit of investigation at a survey station. On a large scale, countries or regions can be sampled (on the ground or using aerial photographs or satellite-derived imagery) for habitat types or other major environmental features. More usually, a sample is the unit within which organisms are listed and their abundance assessed. Examples of such units are:

A measured 50 m along a rocky shore, within which the presence or absence of one rare species of particular interest is recorded.

A 1 m² quadrat on salt-marsh vegetation, within which percentage cover of the different species is estimated.

A photograph of a quadrat, with percentage cover estimates worked out from the photograph in the laboratory.

A 15 cm wide × 20 cm deep core on a mud flat, with subsequent sieving and counting of the different species.

A timed trawl for large epibenthic organisms on subtidal sediments.

A timed haul of a plankton net.

A count of shore birds at a high-tide roost.

In practical terms, there is an obvious trade-off between sample size and the numbers of samples possible at any particular survey site. The first example above is of a large sampling area where replication would not be necessary – one would move on to another length of shore, i.e., another survey site. The second example could easily be replicated and this would be essential if the aim were to quantify salt-marsh organisms. Large or rare organisms will not be detected if the total sample area is too small, whilst several small randomized replicates are best for estimates of populations of common or widely distributed organisms.

If the main purpose of a study is to obtain an idea of the species richness of a site for comparison with other sites, the *minimum sampling area* needs to be considered. Minimum area curves and their interpretation are described in most texts on ecological methods, e.g., Mueller-Dombois & Ellenberg (1974) and Shimwell (1971). Hawkins & Hartnoll (1980) provide a critical review (with particular reference to rocky shores) and further methods based on probability theory for the extrapolation of minimum-area curves. The basic technique used to obtain a curve is to plot the cumulative number of species present against increasing sample area (e.g., from a number of quadrats). The point at which a 'satisfactory' proportion of the total number of species present in a community is collected is arbitrary. It has been usual to select a point along the curve at which an increase of 10% of the total sample area yields only 10% or 5% more species of the total number recorded. However, this method is greatly affected by the slope of the curve. Another approach which can be taken is to determine the mean increase in species number between quadrats, tabulate the percentage increase in species numbers per sample increment, and make an arbitrary determination of the point at which the majority are included. Drew (1971) suggests that a suitable point to select as a minimal area is that at which a 100% increase in area yields only 10% or perhaps 5% more species.

If it is required to obtain information on the quantity of a species for comparison either with other sites or for following temporal change in the abundance of that species, an *optimum number of samples* will need to be determined. Inevitably it will only be possible to calculate mean abundance within reasonable statistical limits for a small number of species in a community, unless enormous numbers of samples are to be taken. The acceptable statistical limits thus have to be set in an arbitrary fashion. Plotting a running mean for the quantity of a species present is a rapid way of assessing the adequacy of a sample number (see, e.g., Kershaw, 1973). A method based on probability statistics is given on p. 207.

For further reading on sampling, see the excellent handbook by Green (1979) on sampling design and statistical methods for environmental biologists. A useful statistical checklist on sampling (by Jeffers) is available from the Publications Officer, Institute of Terrestrial Ecology, Monks Wood Experimental Station, Abbots Ripton, Huntingdon, Cambridgeshire, U.K.

Comparability and reproducibility

If spatial and/or temporal differences between sites are to be identified, it is crucial to employ standardised and adequate methods, and to give good descriptions of the methods employed. This may seem blindingly obvious, but consider the conclusions of Nichols (1973) and D. H. Dalby (personal communication). Nichols reviewed about 20 studies of the benthos of San Francisco Bay carried out since 1912 (the majority since 1950). Despite the considerable expenditure of resources, it was concluded that there were few reliable quantitative data with which to compare future assessments of the benthos of the area, because of the range of methods used to collect and treat the benthic samples, coupled with subsequent incomplete or erroneous species identification. Dalby identified five different recording schemes used during a ten year period on a single intertidal monitoring study.

One means of cross-checking methods is to undertake laboratory intercalibration exercises. Recent literature on this subject indicates that

Table 1.2. *Worker variability with lichen percentage cover estimates*

	'Objective' estimate of percentage cover, based on 563 point quadrats (14 February 1979)	13 February 1979					14 February 1979							
		1	2	3	4	5	6	7	8	9	10	11	12	13
Bare rock	48.3	53	60	35–40	40	48	73–78	63	64	40	75	88	39	74
White lichen	9.8	12	5	15	5	7	5–10	10	8	20	8	4	11	10
Yellow lichen	18.6	15	15	25	20	18	15	15	20	30	12	6	23	14
Green lichen	23.3	20	20	20–25	35	27	2	12	8	10	5	2	27	2

Survey conditions: 13 February – rain, rock wet; 14 February – occasional snow showers, rock comparatively dry. Over two days 13 observers (all with previous rocky shore experience) independently assessed, by eye, the percentage cover of three lichen species within a marked rock area at Porlock (Bristol Channel coast, U.K.). Estimates varied considerably, however one of the sources of variation appeared to be weather conditions. In particular the estimates for green lichen were greater when the rock was wet. The lichen changed colour when wet, becoming much greener and more obviously visible.

statistically significant differences in results may occur even when closely related sampling methods are used. Ankar *et al.* (1979) compared several aspects of sampling and sample treatment methodology between a Swedish and a Finnish laboratory using two designs of the Van Veen grab. They concluded that the probable reasons for the differences in results were the design of the grabs, the sieving techniques, and possibly also the sorting and preservation methods used.

Even when exactly the same methods are used (as prescribed in detailed written instructions) it is necessary to take *worker variability* into account. Differences between workers are most understandable when 'by eye' estimates are required (Table 1.2) but also occur with 'objective' quantitative methods (Table 1.3).

These results highlight the importance of field work teams training together and having practice sessions with comparison and discussion of individual results. Moreover, continuity between one survey and the next should be maximized by using the same staff as far as possible.

Table 1.2 also illustrates the fact that perceptions may be altered by weather conditions; moreover, the poor performances indicated in Table 1.3 could result from the extreme cold and snow showers at the time of the test.

There is little point in using statistical tests to find if a species density at site A is significantly different from the density at site B if the data have been collected by two workers who perform differently.

The time dimension

Any one survey is a snapshot in time. For a 'one-off' survey one particular time of year may be best, depending on the species involved and their seasonal behaviour. For example, phytoplankton 'bloom' in the

Table 1.3. *Worker variability with counting* Littorina *in seaweed*

Counts (arranged lowest → highest)									
16	17	18	25	28	32	32	34	41	48

x̄ 29.1
s.e. 3.3

Thirty-nine *Littorina obtusata* were put into a marked area (50 × 100 cm) of fucoid algae previously cleared of *Littorina*, at Watchet (Bristol Channel coast, U.K.). Observers 1–10 were asked to count the number of individuals within the marked area. Some workers appeared to miss the animals among the algae, others appeared to replace and inadvertently re-count them.

x̄, mean.

s.e., standard error.

spring (see Chapter 11) and many European estuaries receive influxes of wading birds in the winter (see Chapter 13).

For the investigation of seasonal and longer-term changes it is important to be able to relocate sites accurately, and ways of doing this appropriate to the different habitats are described in different chapters in this book. Photography is an invaluable general aid to site relocation.

Some types of temporal change can be detected retrospectively. On the one hand it may be possible to obtain useful information from the past, e.g., aerial and other photographs and fisheries statistics. On the other, it may be possible to carry out an age-class analysis on a population, e.g., for fish, using scale or otolith growth rings (see Chapter 12).

The physical and chemical environment

In practice, most biological surveys go hand in hand with physical and chemical measurements. Techniques for these are described in two other handbooks sponsored by the Estuarine and Brackish-Water Sciences Association, namely *Estuarine Hydrography and Sedimentation* (Dyer, 1979) and *Practical Estuarine Chemistry* (Head, 1985). Other useful references are *Practical Procedures for Estuarine Studies* (Morris, 1983) and *Methods for the Study of Marine Benthos* (Holme & McIntyre, 1984). The former contains chapters on sampling and analysis of physical features and measurement of chemical distributions and processes; the latter has a chapter on sediment analysis. Both also deal with a variety of biological methods and are accordingly referenced elsewhere in this handbook.

Data handling and presentation

Classification schemes

Depending on survey objectives, there are numerous possible classification schemes which can be used for organizing information. Examples are:

Habitats identifiable on aerial photographs, e.g., the categories used in a study of Maplin Sands (Table 1.4).

Shore exposure grades (see Chapter 8).

'Environmental sensitivity' grades, e.g., the index of vulnerability to oil pollution proposed by Gundlach & Hayes (1978) (Table 1.5).

Identification of organisms to species level.

Intraspecific classification, e.g., into size or shape classes.

Life form (see, example, Raunkiaer, 1934).

Trophic status.

Reproductive strategy.

Table 1.4. *Categories of information on Maplin Sands habitat maps*

Salt marsh	Reclaimed marsh	Other items
Zostera species	Unimproved ungrazed marsh	Intertidal flats (limited by low water mark)
Large beds of green algae	Unimproved grazed marsh	Sand/shell/shingle accumulations
	Semi-improved pasture	Oyster pits
Pioneer salt marsh	Improved pasture	Degraded salt marsh
Aster tripolium	Seasonally flooded wetland	Sea embankments
Salicornia species	Arable and other land usage	Nature reserves
Spartina species	Drainage channels	Boating facilities
		Caravan sites
Mature salt marsh		Chalet sites
Youthful *Puccinellia*		Railways
Wet *Puccinellia*		Roads and tracks
Grazed *Puccinellia*		Rubbish dumps
Trampled *Puccinellia*		Sewage works
Species rich (salt pan)		Gravel pits
Eroded marsh		Streams and rivers
Runnels		
Agropyron pungens,		
Limonium spp. and		
Halimione portulacoides		
In combination with above		
Reeds		

From Institute of Terrestrial Ecology (1977).

Table 1.5. *Environmental classification in order of increasing vulnerability to oil spill damage*

Vulnerability index	Shoreline type	Comments
1	Exposed rocky headlands	Wave reflection keeps most of the oil offshore. Clean-up frequently unnecessary.
2	Eroding wave-cut platforms	Wave-swept. Most oil removed by natural processes within weeks.
3	Fine-grained sand beaches	Oil does not usually penetrate far into the sediment, facilitating mechanical removal if necessary. Otherwise, oil may persist several months.
4	Coarse-grained sand beaches	Oil may sink and/or be buried rapidly making clean-up difficult. Under moderate to high energy conditions, oil will be removed naturally within months from most of the beachface.
5	Exposed, compacted tidal flats	Most oil will not adhere to, nor penetrate into the compacted tidal flat. Clean-up is usually unnecessary, except to prevent the oil from going elsewhere.
6	Mixed sand and gravel beaches	Oil may undergo rapid penetration and burial. Under moderate to low energy conditions, oil may persist for years.
7	Gravel beaches	Same as above. Clean-up should concentrate on high-tide swash area. A solid asphalt pavement may form under heavy oil accumulations.
8	Sheltered rocky coasts	Areas of reduced wave action. Oil may persist for many years. Clean-up is not recommended unless oil concentration is very heavy.
9	Sheltered tidal flats	Areas of low wave energy and high biological productivity. Clean-up is not recommended unless oil accumulation is very heavy. These areas should receive priority protection by using booms or oil sorbent materials.
10	Salt marshes	Most productive of aquatic environments. Oil may persist for years. Cleaning of salt marshes by burning, cutting or stripping should be undertaken only if heavily oiled. Protection by booms or sorbent material should receive first priority.

After Gundlach & Hayes (1978).

Identification of all organisms to species level can be extremely time consuming. It does, however, offer the greatest potential for retrospective analysis of the data using other classification schemes. If the only reason for identification of all organisms is to obtain a measure of diversity using some kind of diversity index, then it is not, of course, necessary for each species to be fully *named*; a 'label' such as *Gammarus* sp. 1 will suffice.

Identification literature is detailed in Chapter 14.

Recording data

In many cases, standardised recording forms, cards, or check lists can be used with advantage. Examples are given in Chapters 4, 8 and 9. Otherwise, data obtained whilst sampling should be entered in waterproof ink or pencil in a field notebook, which should preferably be pocket sized, made of good quality paper with a sewn binding, and tolerant of immersion in sea or rain water. For very wet conditions, plastic 'paper' or laminated plastic writing boards are useful (see p. 209). Upon return to the laboratory, data should be transcribed to station record sheets. These data should include station details, including time of sampling, weather, and a reference to any samples whose analyses will be recorded elsewhere. Some values will not immediately be available, and some will later be corrected, but notes should be entered concerning, for example, water samples stored for later precision measurement of salinity.

Such station records serve several purposes. They duplicate the field notebooks, which might be lost on the next sampling trip. They can resolve the ambiguities that easily arise when recording data under poor conditions at sea. Also, they eventually bring together data on many of the variables, including those that are not determined until later.

Many of these records, and much of the subsequent work of analysis, can be computerized. Microcomputers are now widely available and are suitable for this task unless the amount of data collected is very large. The microcomputer should have a heavy-duty typewriter-style (and perhaps also numeric) keyboard, at least 48 kilobytes of internal memory, and an 80-column upper- and lower-case display. It should be equipped with two floppy disk drives each capable of storing at least 100 kilobytes, a printer, and a graph plotter.

The amount of storage required depends on the type of data and the format adopted. Species lists, for example, may be numerically coded and packed into a small amount of memory. But it is advantageous to use an open format and names rather than codes, and the string-handling facilities of many implementations of PASCAL allow for this. Given this approach, one disk is likely to hold data corresponding, for example, to the species composition analysis of about 100 plankton samples or about the same number of station record sheets. It is likely that one disk drive will contain a disk with the operating system and data-analysis programs, and the second drive used for data. It is feasible to build up a large library of disks so long as data analysis can proceed sequentially. Problems arise, however, when the system must be searched for particular data whose location is unknown. If there are more than a few hundred kilobytes of data to be examined, search times become unacceptably long, and a larger computer is required.

Statistical treatment of results

Most survey results will require some form of statistical analysis. Non-parametric statistics (see Siegel, 1956) require few assumptions about data quality but allow the presentation of results only as frequencies or ranks. To use parametric statistical techniques, such as the comparison of means through their standard errors, or the linear regression of a dependent upon an independent variable, it is necessary to examine the quality of and, if necessary, to transform the raw data (Sokal & Rohlf, 1981). To test the qualitatitive aspect of the sampling, simple cumulative species/area curves can be drawn for all stations sampled (see p. 9). In theory the curve approaches a straight line representing the total species complement of the area. In practice diverse communities require very large numbers of samples to provide a complete description.

Variance and standard error

Variance and standard error estimate variability other than that sought. This other variability may be called noise or ascribed to the effects of natural variation, patchiness, or measurement error. Its effect is to confuse interpretation of the results. For example, is the difference in bacterial 'viable count' numbers (Chapter 10) observed between two stations meaningful and thus perhaps the result of a sewage discharge at one station, or is it spurious, due to faulty measurements or to sampling from a patchy distribution of bacteria? For sets of replicate samples a mean and variance can be calculated, and a plot of log variance against log mean used to determine if and how the data should be transformed. For example, in many cases plankton data cluster about a slope of 2, indicating the need for logarithmic transformation of the raw data.

Once any necessary transformation has been carried out an average sampling variance should be computed for each variable. If there are n sets of m replicates of variable x, the average variance of x is given by:

$$\bar{s}^2 = \frac{1}{\mathrm{df}} \sum_n \sum_m (x_{(n,\,m)} - \bar{x}_n)^2$$

where $\bar{x}_n$ is the mean of replicate set n, and $x_{(n, m)}$ is an individual value (after transformation, if necessary). Degrees of freedom are given by:

$$df = \sum_n (m-1)$$

This approach assumes that the sampling and measurement errors remain constant throughout the survey, which need not be true.

In the simplest forms of graph the standard error derived from this variance can be used to draw an error bar for each point, or it can appear in parenthesis in a table. If the value of x quoted or plotted is the mean of i individual values, then the standard error of this mean is:

$$\text{s.e.} = \sqrt{\frac{\bar{s}^2}{i}}$$

The error bar is 1 s.e. on either side of the point. Only if x is plotted on a scale that reflects its transformation will the error bars be symmetrical.

Diversity and dominance indices

A wide range of diversity indices have been proposed which summarise voluminous floral and faunal data from a station in a single value by integrating the two components of the diversity of an area, viz., species richness and the relative abundance of the species. The various indices have been subjected to a number of comparative reviews (e.g., Heip & Engels, 1974; Addy, 1979) which have suggested that the Shannon–Wiener Index (Shannon & Weaver, 1963) provides one of the best measures of community diversity. Although the Shannon–Wiener Index has been criticised both on theoretical grounds (e.g., Hurlbert, 1971; Goodman, 1975) and for practical reasons (Nichols, 1973), it continues to be widely used as a method for community description and provides a useful method for inter-station comparison within surveys. A number of formulae exist for calculating the Shannon–Wiener Index, e.g.:

$$H(S) = -n_i \sum_{i=1}^{S} n_i \log_2 n_i$$

where S is the total number of species, and n_i is the number of individuals in the ith species (Shannon & Weaver, 1963). A simplified formula was proposed by Lloyd, Zar & Karr (1968) for calculation by hand:

$$H(S) = \frac{C}{N}(N\log_{10} N - n_i \sum_{i=1}^{S} \log_{10} n_i)$$

S and n_i are as above, N is the total number of individuals, and C is 3.321928 (constant to convert log 2 to log 10).

Pielou (1966) proposed a measure (J) of the evenness with which the individuals were distributed amongst the species. This is derived by dividing the observed value of the Shannon–Wiener Index by the theoretical maximum value:

$$J = \frac{H(S)}{H(S)_{max}}$$

where $H(S)_{max} = \log S$ (S is the number of species recorded).

Another useful index is Simpson's Index of dominance (c) which gives an indication of the degree of numerical domination by individual taxa. This index is calculated using the formula given by Simpson (1949):

$$c = \sum_{i=1}^{S} \frac{n_i^2}{N}$$

where n is the number of individuals in the ith species and N is the total number of individuals.

As mentioned earlier, diversity indices are useful in summarising voluminous biological data and can be very useful in identifying areas of reduced or enhanced faunal diversity. However, they should not be used or quoted in isolation; as a minimum, the faunal density and number of species recorded should be given for each station and whenever possible the original data should be included.

Rarefaction

Another way of illustrating and comparing diversity is the rarefaction methodology of Sanders (1958), which has the advantage of allowing direct comparison between samples of different sizes. The rarefaction technique has been improved by Hurlbert (1971) and Sanders (1977) published revised curves from his 1958 study. A program for calculating Sanders's improved rarefaction curves is given by Simberloff (1978). Rarefaction curves can be particularly useful for comparing diversities between areas, and a large amount of comparative information is available for subtidal sediment faunas, e.g., Gage (1972) and Eagle (1973).

The rarefaction method also gives the opportunity to present the data as 'number of species per 100 individuals' (or 200, 500, 1000, etc). This allows representation of rarefaction data on a map.

Numerically dominant species

It is often useful to list the numerically dominant species at each station as an aid to comparison of results between stations and between surveys. The definition of numerically dominant species is rather arbitrary and a number of criteria have been used. Buchanan, Sheader & Kingston (1978) listed the ten top-ranked species from each of three benthic stations characteristic of faunal associations identified by ordination. We normally define numerically dominant species as those top-ranked species contributing to the first 50% of the number of individuals at a station, and thus the length of the list is dependent on the level of domination of the fauna by species.

Multivariate analyses

In recent years multivariate analyses have become standard analytical methods in community ecology. These techniques have been developed to reveal groupings or gradients in the data and are referred to as classification and ordination, respectively. These analyses may be fairly simple and carried out by hand, e.g., the polar ordination of Bray & Curtis (1957) or trellis diagram classification such as that used by Sanders (1960) and Lie & Kelley (1970). More complex techniques involving the use of computers are described and discussed in texts such as Sneath & Sokal (1973), Clifford & Stephenson (1975), and Gauch (1982).

A hierarchical classification of data produces a branching diagram (dendrogram) of stations or species divided on the basis of an index of similarity or dissimilarity. Bloom (1981) concluded that Czekanowski's Quantitative Index (see Bloom, 1981, p. 125) was the best of the commonly used similarity indices, and this formula is given in Bray & Curtis (1957) and Field & McFarlane (1968). There are various clustering strategies used to produce dendrograms which are reviewed by Sneath & Sokal (1973). One of the more widely used procedures is the group average sorting method of Lance & Williams (1967).

Ordination analyses produce a series of axis scores for each station (or species); the number of axes desired can be specified but it is usual to restrict the analyses to the first five axes since little additional information accrues from subsequent axes. For each axis an Eigen value is calculated which is proportional to the variation accounted for by that axis (which roughly equates to the relative importance of the axis).

The correlation of an axis with an environmental variable in ordinations of this kind is intuitive (Kershaw, 1973). Methods for presenting the results of ordinations in three dimensions have been described by Kershaw (1973).

More recently faults have been found with all ordination techniques currently in use (Hill & Gauch, 1980); these faults, although not rendering existing methods useless, call for caution in the interpretation of results. Hill & Gauch (1980) prepared an improved technique – detrended correspondence analysis – to overcome these faults, and this program is now widely available on university computers.

Estimation of community structure using the log-normal method
Preston (1948) put forward the hypothesis that the distribution of individuals among the species of a community followed a log-normal pattern.
Assuming a full description of a community has been made, the species
recorded can be arranged into geometric classes according to the number
of individuals found per species. If the community follows the log-normal
model, then the histograms of numbers of species against geometric class
will be bell shaped, i.e., a normal distribution. Preston (1948) found that
usually the whole community had not been sampled, resulting in a
truncated log-normal distribution.

   More recently 'applied' use of the log-normal distribution has been
made in pollution monitoring studies. Nagasawa & Nuorteva (1974),
examining bird survey data from various localities in Finland, noted that,
in contrast to the other areas studied, the data from a city centre did not
fit the log-normal distribution and they suggested that this lack of fit might
be an indication of environmental disturbance. This idea has been
developed in relation to marine communities by Gray (1979, 1981) and
Gray & Mirza (1979).

   Once the survey data have been arranged into geometric classes,
histograms of number of species per class are drawn to see if the data
follow the expected truncated normal distribution. When the number
of species per class is plotted on a cumulative percentage frequency basis
on a probability axis, a straight-line relationship would result if the data
fit a log-normal distribution. As noted above, Gray (1979, 1981) has
developed the hypothesis that deviation from the log-normal may be a
sensitive indicator of perturbation effects in marine benthic communities,
and the method does seem to be effective in cases of organic enrichment.
In a number of cases involving oil pollution, the log-normal method does
not appear to provide useful results, e.g., Dauvin (1982) and Hartley
(1979).

Correlation tests
To establish statistically significant relationships between measured physical
and chemical variables and faunal results, correlation tests are required.

   There are a large number of tests available and the tests chosen are
essentially dictated by the nature of the available data. Information on the
selection of suitable tests and their calculation can be found in Snedecor
& Cochran (1967), Lehmann (1975), and Sokal & Rohlf (1981).

Presenting the results

The spatial distribution of organisms may be visualized by contour mapping (e.g., Fig. 3.3) or by drawing diagrams where information is illustrated to heighten proportional differences. Such methods include proportional circles (Fig. 1.4), proportional squares (see Wilson, Crothers & Oldham, 1983 for a boulder shore example), bar histograms, and graphs on three-dimensional paper and have recently been discussed by Crothers (1981). For proportional circle diagrams the organism densities, etc. may be converted to circle radii using the simple formula:

$$r = \frac{N}{C}$$

where r is the radius of circle, N is the organism density, and C is the constant calculated from

$$C = \frac{N_{max}}{r_{max}^2}$$

where N_{max} is the maximum density and r_{max} is the maximum desired

Fig. 1.4. The distribution of *Scoloplos armiger* in the Beatrice Oilfield, 1980. The distribution shows a natural gradient in relation to sediment type. Published with the kind permission of Britoil PLC (formerly BNOC).

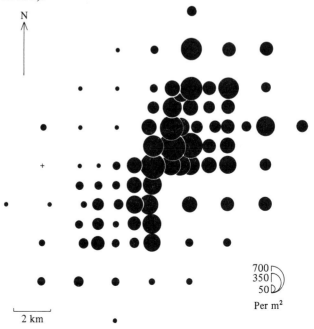

circle radius. Thus in these diagrams the area of the circle drawn is proportional to the recorded value of the variable.

Another effective method for visualising differences over the survey area is graphing the variable against distance; examples of this are SAB (species/abundance/biomass) curves (see Pearson & Rosenberg, 1978), although other variables can be included, e.g., Eh (redox potential) (Pearson & Stanley, 1979). Sections are useful for water column communities (e.g., plankton) where data are often shown in relation to depth (see Chapter 11).

The value of a subjective appraisal of survey results should not be underestimated since it is an exception rather than a rule for more sophisticated analyses to reveal groupings or trends in the data which were not picked out subjectively.

Acknowledgements

The authors would like to thank Dr D. H. Dalby, Dr R. S. K. Barnes, and Dr P. B. Tett for their assistance during the preparation of this chapter.

References

Addy, J. M. (1979). 'Some Studies of Benthic Communities in Areas of Oil Industry Activity'. Ph.D. thesis, University of Wales, Swansea.

Ankar, S., Andersin, A.-B., Lessig, J., Norling, L. & Sandler, H. (1979). Methods for studying benthic macrofauna. An intercalibration between two laboratories in the Baltic Sea. *Finnish Marine Research*, **246**, 147–160.

Baker, J. M. & Hiscock, K. (1984). Predicting the impact of oil terminal development on the in-shore marine environment: retrospective analysis. In *Planning and Ecology*, ed. R. D. Roberts & T. M. Roberts, pp. 422–38. London: Chapman and Hall.

Bloom, S. A. (1981). Similarity indices in community studies: potential pitfalls. *Mar. Ecol. Prog. Ser.* **5**, 125–8.

Bray, J. R. & Curtis, J. T. (1957). An ordination of the upland forest communities of southern Wisconsin. *Ecol. Monog.* **27**, 325–49.

Buchanan, J. B., Sheader, M. & Kingston, P. F. (1978). Sources of variability in the benthic macrofauna off the south Northumberland coast, 1971–1976. *J. mar. biol. Ass. U.K.* **58**, 191–209.

Clifford, H. T. & Stephenson, W. (1975). *An Introduction to Numerical Classification*. New York: Academic Press.

Crothers, J. H. (1981). On the graphical presentation of quantitative data. *Field Studies*, **5** (3), 487–511.

Dauvin, J.-C. (1982). Impact of *Amoco Cadiz* oil spill on the muddy fine sand *Abra alba* and *Melinna palmata* community from the Bay of Morlaix. *Estuar. Coast. Shelf. Sci.* **14**, 517–31.

Drew, E. A. (1971). Botany. In *Underwater Science*, ed. J. D. Woods & J. N. Lythgoe, pp. 25–68. Oxford University Press.

Dyer, K. R. (ed.) (1979). *Estuarine Hydrography and Sedimentation*. Estuarine and Brackish-Water Sciences Association Handbook. Cambridge University Press.

Eagle, R. A. (1973). Benthic studies in the southeast of Liverpool Bay. *Estuar. Coast. Mar. Sci.* **1**, 285–99.

Field, J. G. & McFarlane, G. (1968). Numerical methods in marine ecology. 1. A quantitative 'similarity' analysis of rocky shore samples in False Bay, South Africa. *Zool. Afr.* **3**, 119–37.

Gage, J. (1972). Community structure of the benthos in Scottish sea-lochs. 1. Introduction and species diversity. *Mar. Biol.* **14**, 281–97.

Gauch, H. G. (1982). *Multivariate Analyses in Community Ecology*. Cambridge University Press.

Goodman, D. (1975). The theory of diversity-stability relationships in ecology. *Q. Rev. Biol.* **50**, 237–66.

Gray, J. S. (1979). Pollution-induced changes in populations. *Phil. Trans. R. Soc. Lond. B.* **286**, 545–61.

Gray, J. S. (1981). Detecting pollution-induced changes in communities using the log-normal distribution of individuals among species. *Mar. Pollut. Bull.* **12**, 173–6.

Gray, J. S. & Mirza, F. B. (1979). A possible method for the detection of pollution-induced disturbance on marine benthic communities. *Mar. Pollut. Bull.* **10**, 142–6.

Green, R. H. (1979). *Sampling Design and Statistical Methods for Environmental Biologists*. New York: Wiley.

Gundlach, E. R. & Hayes, M. O. (1978). Vulnerability of coastal environments to oil spill impacts. *Mar. Tech. Soc. J.* **12**, 18–27.

Hartley, J. P. (1979). Biological monitoring of the seabed in the Forties Oilfield. In *Proceedings of Conference on Ecological Damage Assessment*, Society of Petroleum Industry Biologists, Arlington, Virginia, pp. 215–53.

Hawkins, S. J. & Hartnoll, R. G. (1980). A study of the small-scale relationship between species number and area on a rocky shore. *Estuar. Coast. Mar. Sci.* **10**, 201–14.

Head, P. C. (ed.) (1985). *Practical Estuarine chemistry*. Estuarine and Brackish-Water Sciences Association Handbook. Cambridge University Press.

Heip, C. & Engels, P. (1974). Comparing species diversity and evenness indices. *J. mar. biol. Ass. U.K.* **54**, 559–63.

Hill, M. O. & Gauch, H. G. (1980). Detrended correspondence analysis: an improved ordination technique. *Vegetatio*, **42**, 47–58.

Holdgate, M. W. (1976). Closing summary. In *Marine Ecology and Oil Pollution*, ed. J. M. Baker, pp. 525–34. Barking: Applied Science Publishers.

Holme, N. A. & McIntyre, A. D. (eds) (1984). *Methods for the Study of Marine Benthos*. Oxford: Blackwell Scientific Publications.

Hurlbert, S. H. (1971). The nonconcept of species diversity: a critique and alternative parameters. *Ecology*, **52**, 577–86.

Institute of Terrestrial Ecology. (1977). *Ecology of Maplin Sands and the Coastal Zones of Suffolk, Essex and North Kent.* Cambridge: ITE.

Kershaw, K. A. (1973). *Quantitative and Dynamic Plant Ecology.* London: Edward Arnold.

Lance, G. N. & Williams, W. T. (1967). A general theory of classificatory sorting strategies. I. Hierarchical systems. *Comp. J.* **9**, 373–80.

Lehmann, E. L. (1975). *Non-Parametrics – Statistical Methods Based on Ranks.* San Francisco: Holden Day Inc.

Lie, U. & Kelley, J. C. (1970). Benthic infauna communities off the coast of Washington and in Puget Sound: identification and distribution of the communities. *J. Fish. Res. Bd. Can.* **27**, 621–51.

Lloyd, H., Zar, J. H. & Karr, J. R. (1968). On the calculation of information – theoretical measures of diversity. *Am. Mid. Nat.* **79**, 257–72.

Morris, A. W. (ed.) (1983). *Practical Procedures for Estuarine Studies.* Plymouth: Natural Environment Research Council, Institute for Marine Environmental Research.

Mueller-Dombois, D. & Ellenberg, H. (1974). *Aims and Methods of Vegetation Ecology.* New York: Wiley.

Nagasawa, S. & Nuorteva, P. (1974). Failure of survey data to conform to mathematical population models as an indicator of environmental disturbance. *Ann. Zool. Fennici,* **11**, 244–50.

Nichols, F. H. (1973). A review of benthic faunal surveys in San Francisco Bay. *Geol. Survey Circ.* No. 677.

Open University. (1983). *Open Business School P670 Course Book 1.* Milton Keynes: Open University.

Pearson, T. H. & Rosenberg, R. (1978). Macrobenthic succession in relation to organic enrichment and pollution of the marine environment. *Oceanogr. Mar. Biol. Ann. Rev.* **16**, 229–311.

Pearson, T. H. & Stanley, S. O. (1979). Comparative measurement of the redox potential of marine sediments as a rapid means of assessing the effects of organic pollution. *Mar. Biol.* **53**, 371–9.

Pielou, E. C. (1966). The measurement of diversity in different types of biological collections. *J. theor. Biol.* **13**, 131–44.

Preston, F. W. (1948). The commonness and rarity of species. *Ecology,* **29**, 254–83.

Raunkiaer, C. (1934). *The Life Forms of Plants and Statistical Plant Geography.* Oxford: Clarendon Press.

Sanders, H. L. (1958). Benthic studies in Buzzards Bay. I. Animal–sediment relationships. *Limnol. Oceanogr.* **3**, 245–58.

Sanders, H. L. (1960). Benthic studies in Buzzards Bay. III. The structure of the soft-bottom community. *Limnol. Oceanogr.* **5**, 138–53.

Sanders, H. L. (1977). Evolutionary ecology and the deep-sea benthos. In *Changing Scenes in Natural Sciences, 1776–1976,* ed. C. E. Goulden. Special Publication No. 12. Philadelphia: Academy of Natural Sciences.

Shannon, C. E. & Weaver, W. (1963). *The Mathematical Theory of Communication.* Urbana: University of Illinois Press.

Shimwell, D. W. (1971). *The Description and Classification of Vegetation.* London: Sidgwick & Jackson.

Siegel, S. (1956). *Non-Parametric Statistics for the Behavioural Sciences.* Kogakusha, Tokyo: McGraw-Hill.

Simberloff, D. (1978). Use of rarefaction and related methods in ecology. In *Biological Data in Water Pollution Assessment: Quantitation and Statistical Analysis*, ed. K. L. Dickson, J. Cairns & R. L. Livingstone, pp. 105–65. Philadelphia: American Society for Testing and Materials.

Simpson, E. H. (1949). Measurement of diversity. *Nature*, **163**, 688.

Sneath, P. H. A. & Sokal, R. R. (1973). *Numerical Taxonomy. The Principles and Practices of Numerical Classification.* San Francisco: Freeman.

Snedecor, G. W. & Cochran, W. G. (1967). *Statistical Methods*, 6th ed Ames: Iowa State University Press.

Sokal, R. R. & Rohlf, R. F. (1981). *Biometry*, 2nd edn. San Francisco; W. H. Freeman.

Wilson, C. M., Crothers, J. H. & Oldham, J. H. (1983). Realized niche: the effects of a small stream on sea-shore distribution patterns. *J. biol. Ed.* **17**, 51–8.

2

Remote sensing

D. H. DALBY AND W. J. WOLFF

Introduction

Remote sensing techniques are those in which properties of the earth's surface are assessed from a distance, mainly from aircraft or satellites. Good introductions are provided by Schanda (1976), Lillesand & Kiefer (1979), Barrett & Curtis (1982), and Curran (1985). Two broad categories may be recognised: aerial photography (a so-called analogue system, because information sensed is expressed in an analogue form as a photographic image) and digital systems (where the information is expressed in digital form directly ready for computer processing).

Examples of possible applications for biological surveys in coastal areas are:

> Aerial photography – specially suitable for smaller-scale studies with finer ground resolution, such as the distribution of particular types of salt-marsh vegetation, intertidal seagrasses, or mussel beds, and the recording of shoals of fish or flocks of birds.

> Digital remote sensing – environmental features and conditions such as water depth, suspended sediments in coastal waters, sea surface temperatures, and major effluent plumes. Examples are given by Gierloff-Emden (1977, 1982) and the National Remote Sensing Centre (1984). Such information is valuable in the broad planning of biological surveys and in interpreting some kinds of survey data on a large scale geographically.

Remote sensing from aircraft may also be in a digital form (see, e.g., Dennert-Möller & Dörjes, 1977). So far however aerial photography is the main system used widely for biological surveys of coastal areas (e.g., Grimes & Hubbard, 1971; Steffensen & McGregor, 1976; Coulson *et al.*, 1980; Michaelis, Ragutzki & Ramm, 1982; Wieland, 1984). Michaelis *et al.* (1982) compared both systems and concluded that digital systems did not add any new information to their interpretation of aerial photographs but, instead, confirmed them. Barrett & Curtis (1982) strongly recommend that visual interpretation of small data sets (using aerial photographs, VDU displays, etc.) should be preferred initially because of their speed and low cost. More sophisticated techniques may follow later if they can be justified. Nevertheless, it may be that as remote sensing systems become more widely used and their ground resolution improves, the balance of opinion may shift more to favour digitised systems. Whatever the type of image, it should be used in conjunction with field observations ('ground truth') to identify unknown features on the images and to check the identity of recognised features. A combination of remote sensing and field work can greatly improve the efficiency of some types of survey; for example, Michaelis *et al.* (1982) compared a survey of a large tidal-flat area in the Federal Republic of Germany by means of false colour photography with their earlier surveys without aerial photography and concluded that the use of this method reduced their field work from 4 or 5 summer seasons to only 2 summers. On the basis of photographs and field work, they could distinguish 27 different types of habitat. Interpretation problems mainly arose with the separation of mud flats from mixed sand–mud flats.

Aerial photography
Film
In aerial photography four main film types are used:

Panchromatic: a black and white film sensitive for the visible part of the spectrum

Black and white infrared: a black and white film not only sensitive for the visible part of the spectrum, but also for a part of the infrared spectrum

Full colour: a colour film sensitive for the visible part of the spectrum, giving 'true colour' images

False colour: a colour film in which the red layer has been made sensitive for a part of the infrared spectrum and the other colours have shifted, with blue being cut off entirely by a yellow filter

Panchromatic film has been used for a very long time in aerial photography for map making, and countless examples have been published. However, detail is not always good enough for many biological purposes. For tidal flats the only easily identifiable features are likely to be the marsh–tidal flat boundary, the tidal flat–tidal channel boundary, megaripples, dried-out sand banks, and mussel beds (Fig. 2.1). Vegetation characteristics are less easy or even impossible to observe (Grimes &

Hubbard, 1971; Steffensen & McGregor, 1976). Moreover, different shades of grey occurring on large parts of the photographs appear to reflect mainly differences in the amount of water on and in the sediment, a feature known to change in relation to weather conditions and time since tidal immersion. Black and white infrared film gives good land–water contrast, but it has no particular advantages for other ecological work.

Full colour and false colour film give much more detail, especially with respect to algal and seagrass vegetation (Grimes & Hubbard, 1971; Steffensen & McGregor, 1976; Michaelis *et al.*, 1982). Some authors strongly recommend false colour but Steffensen & McGregor (1976) point out that even a thin covering of water can have a marked influence on the tone of the colour. The latter authors recommend a combination of full and false colour. Full colour film is very sensitive to haze and this decreases the number of days suitable for flights. False colour is insensitive to blue so cuts through haze and gives a sharper image. However it has narrow limits for temperature and light amount. False colour photography is also much more expensive than panchromatic pictures, and it is more difficult to obtain extra copies of the same quality. The properties of some films used in aerial photography are given in Schanda (1976, Chapter 2). Coulson *et al.* (1980) describe the use of Kodak colour Infrared Type 3443 (the only film available at the time of their work suitable for infrared

Fig. 2.1. Aerial photograph of tidal flats showing mussel beds.

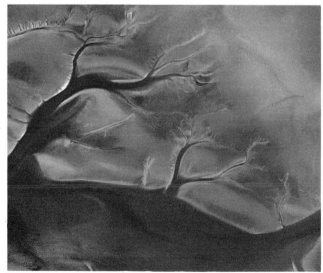

ssel bed ⟶

↑
mussel bed

survey work) in a project covering salt marshes and mud flats in Chichester Harbour.

Constraints

Cost

The commissioning of professional aerial photography is expensive, although it is not always necessary to rely on this technique. It is advisable to check initially on whether suitable aerial cover already exists (see section on sources of information). For example, Dijkema (personal communication) was able to map the entire Wadden Sea in Denmark, the Federal Republic of Germany, and the Netherlands (8000 km²) from existing photographs. For some areas as many as five different sets of photographs could be obtained. If new photographs are required, a hand-held camera operated from a small plane may produce the required kind of information in some cases, though it is not of course possible to obtain true vertical photographs (for accurate mapping) in this way. In other instances oblique photographs taken from tall chimney stacks or cliffs may be useful.

Scale requirements

The scale of the final map is determined by the detail to be shown, and this in turn determines flight height and the number of photographs to be taken. Hubbard & Grimes (1972) point to the problems of flying too low, with too many photographs showing too much detail. They suggest a scale of 1:7500 as being suitable for many vegetation surveys; the Nature Conservancy Council preferred one at 1:5000 for Chichester Harbour (Coulson *et al.*, 1980) and this scale may be regarded as generally acceptable for biological mapping in most areas. Scales of 1:10000 to 1:25000 are suitable for more general surveys of large estuaries.

Season

Optical and vegetational characteristics vary with the season, providing difficulties (though also some advantages) in comparing photographs taken at different times of year (Grimes & Hubbard, 1971).

Weather and time of day

Colour film is best exposed during the middle of the day avoiding low sunshine and haze and mist. Note that even on an apparently clear sunny day, there can be enough water vapour in the atmosphere to render ordinary colour photographs taken from as low as 100 m almost useless.

State of the tide

If the map is to represent creek shapes and patterns at a particular tide height (e.g., mean sea level or low water springs) then the flight must be timed precisely to coincide with this, as the passage of only a few minutes can bring about drastic changes in the position of the water line on flat shores. Tide and weather together can have severe effects for this demanding kind of aerial photography. Coulson *et al.* (1980) describe how out of 14 theoretically suitable days available in August 1978, only one proved ideal, and similar events occurred in 1979.

Photogrammetry

The general principles of photogrammetry, the preparation of maps from aerial photographs, are given by, e.g., Moffitt (1967) and Ellis (1978).

Maps are normally made using specialised stereoscopic plotters working from standard format stereo pairs of photographs. These can be used to draw in contours directly, even at 1–m intervals on salt marshes and mud flats. Lower-quality maps can be drawn from single photographs (but without contours) provided one has access to equipment with corrections for tilt. Such corrections (rectification) require ground control using points whose angular relationships are known and which are clearly visible in the photograph. Ranwell (1964) used such a technique in a study of *Spartina* colonisation in Bridgwater Bay.

It is not always necessary to have precise control for scale and orientation, and obliques may give enough information for projects not relying upon accurate mapping.

Photointerpretation

False colour film can provide a sensitive method for distinguishing between different plant species and vegetation types. The colour layers in this film show a shift in colour sensitivity compared with ordinary colour film, with visual red in the film representing the wide range of invisible infrared radiation from about 700 to 900 nm (see outline discussion in Coulson *et al.*, 1980). Plants reflect widely in the infrared, so the different species appear as various reds and browns (with further modifications according to how much background shows between the plants). A table showing the colour and textural criteria for this recognition in Chichester Harbour is given as Table II in Coulson *et al.* (1980) but with the warning that time of year, height of sun, etc. can all modify these diagnostic colours further still, so that 'an interpreter has to consider every set of photographs as a separate identification task'.

Because of the close relationship between photointerpretation and base map production (especially when both make use of the same diapositives), Coulson *et al.* (1980) favour the photointerpreter himself learning the techniques of photogrammetry so that he can insert the vegetation cover on his own map with the minimum discrepancy.

Interpretation of black and white photographs is more difficult than for colour since one must work entirely from texture, tone on a grey scale, etc. with essential assistance from ground truth data. A good general account of the principles involved in the context of salt marshes is given by Hubbard & Grimes (1972).

Digital systems
Principles and general information

These most recent techniques are based on the transmission of digital data from scanning spectroradiometers (carried, for example, on the LANDSAT satellites or by aircraft) recording the intensity of reflected radiation over specific spectral bands, the band positions and widths being controlled by appropriate filters. Instrumentation is being rapidly developed and it is certain that these sophisticated techniques will become increasingly used in coastal survey work. Most of the operational digital systems provide two types of products, viz.,:

> In the form of preprocessed analogue images: either black and white negatives of single-band images or false colour composite diapositives. The user can apply photographic processing techniques.

> In the form of computer compatible tapes (CCT) that can be processed in any way.

Vegetation studies so far have mainly made use of sensing in the visible spectrum and the near infrared, but other methods using, e.g., longer-wave thermal infrared (as a measure of surface temperatures), side-looking radar, etc. are being used in other connections.

Multispectral scanners (MSS) sense unit areas on the earth's surface in each radiation band; the unit area sensed instantaneously is called a ground resolution cell, and its corresponding coded imagery (picture element) is called a pixel. The area represented by each pixel is largely responsible for the final resolution of the imagery, hence the progressive trend towards smaller resolution cells. However, the computer capacity required increases with decreasing pixel size.

Some characteristics of the American LANDSAT and French SPOT satellites and their imagery are given in Tables 2.1–2.3. Note that the multispectral scanners in these two systems are very different instruments;

the latter has fewer bands but has the ability to look obliquely for stereoscopic viewing.

Photographic prints and computer compatible tapes (CCT) for specified areas can be obtained through the addresses listed in Table 2.4. The National Points of Contact maintain 'quick-look' indexes of black and white photographic prints for the approximate identification of areas available with MSS or (thematic mapper) TM. Each area, known as a scene, is identified by path (orbit) and row numbers, and documentation includes the satellite number, scanner used, acquisition date, proportion of cloud cover, and the latitude and longitude of the scene centre.

LANDSAT MSS imagery makes use of radiation bands equivalent to those of false colour film, so false colour composites can be prepared by

Table 2.1. *Operation dates and scanners carried by LANDSAT, NIMBUS and SPOT satellites*

Satellite	Launched	Ceased operation	Scanner type
LANDSAT 1	22 July 1972	6 January 1978	MSS
LANDSAT 2	22 January 1975	25 February 1982[a]	MSS
LANDSAT 3	5 March 1978	31 March 1983[b]	MSS
LANDSAT 4	16 July 1982	operational	MSS, TM
LANDSAT 5	1 March 1984	operational	MSS, TM
LANDSAT 6	proposed 1988		
LANDSAT 7	proposed 1991		
NIMBUS 7	24 October 1978	September 1984	CZCS[c]
SPOT 1	22 February 1986	operational	SPOT-MSS
SPOT 2	proposed 1988		SPOT-MSS

[a] Suspended 5 November 1979 to 6 June 1980.
[b] Suspended 17 December 1980 to 13 April 1981.
[c] Coastal Zone Colour Scanner.

Table 2.2. Scene and ground resolution cell data for LANDSAT and SPOT satellites

	LANDSAT MSS	LANDSAT TM	SPOT-MSS
Scene size (km)	185 × 185	185 × 185	60 × 60
Ground resolution cell (pixel size) (m)	56 × 79	30 × 30	20 × 20 – multispectral mode
			10 × 10 – panchromatic mode

combining bands 4, 5, and 7. These are equivalent to false colour photographs and can be interpreted in the same way. The LANDSAT TM uses narrower bands, designed to be more useful to vegetation scientists. Budd & Milton (1982) give a description of ground-level tests on salt-marsh vegetation using a hand-held radiometer (Milton, 1980) sensing at similar wavelengths. As with aerial photography, these newer remote sensing techniques require precise ground truth which, in practice, becomes increasingly difficult to relate to the imagery as distance and/or resolution coarsens. For such reasons each new generation of scanner is designed to sense smaller areas of ground surface. TM imagery and simulated SPOT-MSS (multispectral scanner) imagery show a remarkable improvement over data from LANDSAT MSS, but at present the airborne thematic mapper (Daedalus ATM) flown by the Hunting Group and the Natural Environment Research Council in the United Kingdom is vastly more useful in coastal survey work.

Constraints

We have come across very few examples where ecologically meaningful subdivisions of tidal flats or salt marshes have been made using satellite-based digital systems, though the potential for this must increase as the size of the ground resolution cells decreases. Moreover, there are certain difficulties in interpretation which are special to intertidal areas. Natural processes such as displacement of the water line over the flats and

Table 2.3. *Band characteristics of the LANDSAT and SPOT multispectral scanners*

Scanner	Band no.	Band position and width (μm)	Colour
MSS	4	0.5–0.6	green
	5	0.6–0.7	red
	6	0.7–0.8	red–near infrared
	7	0.8–1.1	near infrared
TM	1	0.45–0.52	blue green
	2	0.52–0.60	green
	3	0.63–0.69	red
	4	0.76–0.90	near infrared
	5	1.55–1.75	mid infrared
	6	10.4–12.5	thermal infrared
	7	2.08–2.35	mid infrared
SPOT-MSS	1	0.50–0.59	green
	2	0.61–0.68	red
	3	0.79–0.89	near infrared

the vertical migration of benthic microalgae have a time-scale such that a change of the phenomena can be occurring while the sensor system works on data acquisition (Gierloff-Emden, 1980, 1982). This may cause blurred boundaries. Another problem is that low tides and clear skies required for the data acquisition only seldom coincide with the passage of the right type of satellite. A third problem is that in large areas low tide does not occur everywhere at the same time, so that different satellite pictures are required.

Digital processing of analogue imagery

Digitally transmitted signals (coded between 0–63 for MSS and 0–255 for TM and SPOT-MSS per band per pixel) can be processed rapidly by computer, and it is here that the main power of the digital

Table 2.4. Addresses where information on satellite scenes, prints, and computer compatible tapes is available

USA	NOAA/NESDIS Landsat Customer Service, Mundt Federal Building, Sioux Falls, SD 57198, USA
Austria	Austrian Space & Solar Agency-ASSA, Garnisongasse 7, A-1090 Vienna
Belgium	Institut Géographique National-IGN, 13 Abbaye de la Cambre, B-1050 Brussels
Denmark	Electromagnetic Institute, DTH-Building 348, DK-2800 Lyngby
France	GDTA; Centre Spatiale de Toulouse, 18 Av. Edouard Belin, F-31055 Toulouse
Germany	DFVLR Hauptabteilung, Raumflugbetrieb, D-8031 Oberpfaffenhofen, Post Wessling
Ireland	National Board for Science & Technology, Shelbourne House, Shelbourne Road, Dublin 4
Italy	Telespazio, Via Bergamini, 50, I-00158 Roma
Netherlands	National Aerospace Laboratory-NLR, Anthonie Fokkerweg 2, NL-1059 CM Amsterdam
Norway	Tromsö Telemetry Station, P.O. Box 387, N-9001 Tromsö
Spain	CONIE, Pintor Rosales 34, E-Madrid 8
Sweden	Swedish Space Corporation, Tritonvägen 27, S-17154 Solna
Switzerland	Bundesamt für Landestopographie, Seftigenstrasse 264, CH-3084 Wabern
United Kingdom	National Remote Sensing Centre, Royal Aircraft Establishment, Farnborough, Hants, GU14 6TD
Other European countries:	European Space Agency, Earthnet Programme Office, User Services, Via Galileo Galilei, 00044 Frascati, Italy
Other countries:	see USA

method is to be found. The computer operator can apply many types of selection or enhancement to the data set, including contrast stretching, density slicing (reducing the 64 or 256 scale units to a much smaller number), and the identification and display of all pixels with certain specified reflectance properties. This last-mentioned facility enables particular vegetation types to be isolated and mapped automatically. However, this is only feasible when differences in vegetation type correspond clearly to differences in reflection characteristics, an ideal situation occurring rarely in reality.

Few institutions possess the equipment for digital processing and few survey workers will have access to suitable digital imagery of their ground areas, but it is possible to scan photographs (the preferred analogues are the original negatives rather than prints) to set them into compatible digital form. Apart from the considerable loss of detail, they can then be processed by the full range of computer programs referred to above. These techniques will become more familiar as more types of digital sensing equipment appear on the market.

Acknowledgements

The authors are grateful to Dr D. Spitzer and Dr D. van der Zee who commented upon earlier drafts of the manuscript.

References

Barrett, E. C. & Curtis, L. F. (1982). *Introduction to Environmental Remote Sensing*. London: Chapman & Hall.

Budd, J. T. C. & Milton, E. J. (1982). Remote sensing of salt marsh vegetation in the first four proposed thematic mapper bands. *Int. J. Remote Sensing*, **3**, 147–61.

Coulson, M. G., Budd, T. T. C., Withers, R. G., Nicholls, T. T. C. (1980). Remote sensing and field sampling of mudflat organisms in Langstone and Chichester Harbours, Southern England. In *The Shore Environment*, vol. 1: *Methods*, ed. J. H. Price, D. E. G. Irvine & W. P. Farnham. London: Academic Press.

Curran, P. J. (1985). *Principles of Remote sensing*. Harlow: Longmans.

Dennert-Möller, E. & Dörjes, J. (1977). *Multispektrale Klassifizierung von Wattgebieten. Symposium Flugzeugmessprogramm* Hannover, 29–31 August 1977, ed. J. Albertz & M. Schroeder, pp. 143–51. Hannover: Technische Universität Hannover.

Ellis, M. Y. (ed.) (1978). *Coastal Mapping Handbook*. Washington: United States Government Printing Office.

Gierloff-Emden, H. G. (1977). *Orbital Remote Sensing of Coastal and Offshore Environments – A Manual of Interpretation*. Berlin: De Gruyter.

Gierloff-Emden, H. G. (1980). Timescale as interface of satellite data acquisition systems against coastal water and tidal region processes. *Int. Archs Photogrammetry*, **23**, suppl.

Gierloff-Emden, H. G. (1982). Interest of remote sensing in coastal lagoon research. *Oceanologica Acta 1982: Actes du Symposium International Surles Lagunes Cotières*, Bordeaux, 8–14 Sept. 1981, ed. P. Laserre & H. Postma, pp. 139–49. Paris: Gauthier-Villars.

Grimes, B. H. & Hubbard, J. C. E. (1971). A comparison of film type and the importance of season for interpretation of coastal marshland. *Photogrammetic Rec.* **7**, 213–22.

Hubbard, J. C. E. & Grimes, B. H. (1972). The analysis of coastal vegetation through the medium of aerial photography. *Med. Biol. Illustration*, **22**, 182–90.

Lillesand, T. M. & Kiefer, R. W. (1979). *Remote Sensing and Image Interpretation*. Chichester: John Wiley.

Michaelis, H., Ragutzki, G. & Ramm, G. (1982). Sedimentologische und biologische Untersuchung der Watten des Jadebusens. *Intermaritec* **82**, 738–48.

Milton, E. J. (1980). A portable multiband radiometer for ground data collection in remote sensing. *Int. J. Remote Sensing*, **1**, 153–65.

Moffitt, F. M. (1967). *Photogrammetry*, 2nd ed. Scranton: International Textbook Company.

National Remote Sensing Centre (1984). *U.K. National Remote Sensing Centre.* Farnborough: NRSC.

Ranwell, D. S. (1964). *Spartina* salt marshes in Southern England. III. Rates of establishment, succession and nutrient supply. Bridgwater Bay, Somerset. *J. Ecol.* **52**, 95–105.

Schanda, E. (ed.) (1976). *Remote Sensing for Environmental Sciences.* Ecological Studies no. 18. Heidelberg: Springer Verlag.

Steffensen, D. A. & McGregor, F. E. (1976). The application of aerial photography to estuarine ecology. *Aquat. Bot.* **2**, 3–11.

Wieland, P. (1984). Fernerkundung als Hilfsmittel in der Wattenforschung. *Die Küste* **40**, 91–106.

3

Salt marshes

D. H. DALBY

Introduction

Salt marshes are defined by Chapman (1960) as 'areas of land bordering on the sea, more or less covered with vegetation and subject to periodic inundation by the tide'. They normally develop along sheltered coasts where fine sediments can accumulate, the fine material being derived initially from land but sometimes secondarily from shallow-water offshore sediments. Sedimentation is limited upwards by the level of high tides, and laterally by constraints offered by water movement, and on each marsh there is a balance between deposition and erosion. This dynamic component makes salt-marsh survey work particularly difficult when observations are continued over months or years; it also has major consequences for both the marsh flora and fauna. Angiosperms usually show a vertical zonation of species, following partly from such factors as frequency in tidal cover, variations in salinity and development of a stable soil profile, and partly from the varied interactions with and between the plants themselves. The salt-marsh fauna at lower levels is largely influenced by the nature of the substratum and by frequency of water cover, but at higher levels the physical structure of the flowering-plant cover plays an increasingly important role. It appears that physical and chemical factors control the main sedimentation processes in estuaries, with plants and animals being secondary in importance. Microscopic algae are now understood to assist in stabilising sediment surfaces, whilst further sediment accumulates after being washed from stems and leaves by rain and by release when these organs die and collapse.

Accounts of salt marsh ecology (with particular emphasis on vegetation and topography) appear in Tansley (1949), Chapman (1960), Ranwell (1972), Beeftink (1976, 1977), and Long & Mason (1983). The salt-marsh fauna is discussed by Daiber (1976). Wider aspects are included in Jefferies & Davy (1979) and Price, Irvine & Farnham, (1980).

Planning the survey

Salt-marsh survey techniques are as diverse as the marshes themselves are varied. They range from very detailed studies (perhaps on single plants) through to broad views of entire salt-marsh systems, and no single method could ever be suitable for all sites and all purposes. If the reader feels that of the examples considered none is really suited to his purpose, there is ample scope for uninhibited invention – the purpose of the study is all-important. Two extremes of approach are outlined below by reference to actual examples.

As part of the environmental monitoring programmes carried out in conjunction with oil developments in Shetland, the writer was required to check the 'health' of very small salt marshes around Sullom Voe (Fig. 3.1) and for this purpose attention was directed (Dalby 1981, 1982) towards the performance of the dominant grass of the marshes, *Puccinellia maritima*, on which the physical existence of the salt marshes appears to depend. Annual stolon extension and shoot density were assessed along short marked transects, and rates and densities were compared on a year-to-year basis, using appropriate statistical tests. Choice of the single

Fig. 3.1. Narrow salt-marsh fringe with scattered *Puccinellia maritima* at the lower edge, Garth's Voe, Shetland.

species was determined by (a) the limited flowering-plant species composition of the northern marshes, (b) the need to represent the 'health' of the marshes by a restricted number of measurements to keep financial expenditure as low as possible, (c) the need to provide for a factual assessment of change that could be judged by statistical tests of significance, and finally (d) to be able to initiate localised, more detailed studies if the overall annual surveys suggest that they are needed.

In contrast to such very small-scale studies, one may quote the wider investigations carried out by the Institute of Terrestrial Ecology (ITE, 1977) in connection with plans for the third London airport on the Maplin Sands. Although the study was initiated as a response to airport construction, its objectives of assessment of resources and threats to these resources, and management policy for substitute sites are equally suited to any other large-scale development in the area. The results obtained provide a comprehensive background against which detailed studies may be set. The ITE team of ten scientists cooperated with 21 other organisations and nearly 200 individual workers over a period (for the main project) of three and a half years. The project covered the preparation of large-scale habitat maps; distributional studies of *Zostera* spp. on tidal flats; and distributional and composition studies on salt-marsh vegetation, the vegetation of reclaimed salt marshes, the size and distribution of the fauna of the soft sediments, and the abundance and diversity of waders, wildfowl, and brent geese. Obviously the various components of this exercise involve very different field study methods. The financial outlay is also obviously much greater than for the Shetland study outlined above.

We still know rather little about the detailed autecology of many salt-marsh species, yet we use these species in survey and monitoring programmes. I feel that specially tailored programmes should (a) be freed from any traditional restraints on 'how they should be done', and (b) should be associated with closely related research projects when these are helpful in filling gaps in our ecological knowledge.

Delimiting the working area

At the start of any survey the limits of the working area will be defined either by the terms of reference or by biological or topographical properties of the site itself. In practice, arbitrary decisions of detail very often have to be made.

Upper limits

Salt marshes are generally well delimited upwards by land boundaries (often coinciding with sea-walls), reflecting both ownership and the differing uses to which tidal and non-tidal lands are put. Natural transitions to grassland or woodland are now much less common than in the past. Much attention has been given to the definition of the tide mark in the United States in recent years as a result of federal government proposals for definition and protection of tidal salt marshes. These are discussed in Clark (1977, pp. 582ff and pp. 738–40) and Frenkel, Eilers & Jefferson (1981). Some states employ indicator species such as the salt bushes *Baccharis halimifolia* and *Iva frutescens* in their definitions (see Silberhorn, Dawes & Barnard, 1974). No method is ideal however; Frenkel *et al.* (1981) write 'Despite the proliferation of methods for distinguishing wetlands from uplands, the problem of how the administrator and wetlands manager can establish a defensible *line* within a transitional *belt* remains paramount'. In many parts of western Europe the biological boundary is more clear-cut because of the higher salinity of the offshore water, but there are problems on coastlines (such as those of the Baltic) fronting waters of lower salinity. Purely natural boundaries involving transitional communities between salt-marsh and terrestrial vegetation in fact do form a linear habitat of small overall area, and they deserve more attention in salt marsh survey work than their total area may suggest.

Lower limits

The lower limits to salt marshes may often be set rather artificially, at least from the ecological point of view, since the vegetated marsh merges into the lower silt and sand flats via the marsh creek system, and because there is increasingly open ground between plants at the lower edge of the vegetated marsh. The observed lower limits for perennial species such as *Spartina anglica* and *Puccinellia maritima* are fixed because of the interaction between accretion and succession. Furthermore, in Europe at least, the beds of *Enteromorpha* and *Zostera* spp. should still be considered in close association with the salt marsh ecosystem, even if there is a case for regarding the seagrass communities of lower latitudes as being rather different entities (see Mann, 1982).

Composite treatments

In estuary systems where there are several salt marshes at intervals away from the sea, it is often useful to treat these separate marshes together in one study as done by Beeftink (1975) for the Delta area in the Netherlands, Dalby (1970) for Milford Haven, and Gray & Bunce (1972) for Morecambe Bay. This approach draws attention to possible large-scale gradients in salinity, water pollution, or other factors and provides a background for understanding patterns of bird movement and plant distribution. Such a method might take the form of a single transect from each marsh, or sampling could be weighted locally in proportion to, say, marsh areas.

Markers and reference points

Sampling areas, permanent quadrats, and local datum points for levelling need to be relocated on later occasions. This is done using maps, measured compass bearings, and photographs based on permanent local features such as church towers or other tall buildings, or sometimes less permanent features such as trees, telegraph poles, navigation marks, pans, and angles of creeks on the marsh itself. These are usually augmented by specially inserted markers on the marsh surface.

Photography

Ground-level photographs of salt marshes can be very uninformative when interpreted on site. Salt-marsh surfaces are usually flat and relatively featureless (especially in diffuse lighting under cloud), and small changes in slope rarely photograph clearly. Distinctive creek shapes change rapidly with water level, and location photographs taken from nearby high ground may be difficult to relate to the marsh surface itself. The most helpful photographs will however include local features which can be recognised again, such as marker pegs, creek and pan edges, stones, and so on. Sometimes photography in low evening light will exaggerate small changes in slope, and printing on high-contrast grade paper may have an equivalent effect.

Markers

The size and nature of artificially placed markers has to be decided for each study in the face of possibly conflicting objectives such as stability, permanence, and conspicuousness.

Stability

Posts must be stout enough to survive the drag forces exerted by water currents on wrack and other entangled debris, and the casual impacts from people and animals on the marsh (and from boats when it is water covered). Many animals will deliberately seek out posts to rub against. For maximum stability one should use sharpened wooden posts (between 5 and 10 cm across), perhaps sunk in the ground with the help of a post-hole corer. Repeated driving with a sledge hammer tends to split the post tops. An alternative is to use similarly placed metal angle-irons. Surveyors' metal earth anchors have feet which splay out at the desired depth; these are stable but are also much more expensive.

For shorter-term studies small pegs (down to 2 cm across) can be used but they are less stable. On very stony ground (as may be found on some sediment-poor salt marshes), markers can be difficult to insert at a precise position as they may be deflected by buried stones.

Marker posts must protrude sufficiently for them to be relocated after subsequent sediment accretion or growth of vegetation. On cattle-grazed marshes care should be taken to have them high enough to avoid possible damage to the feet of animals. A. J. Gray (personal communication) has used deeply buried angle-irons with their tops protruding by about 15 cm, but there can be no fixed rule for this.

Permanence

Iron markers will corrode in time, whilst wooden posts and pegs (though lasting better than in non-saline situations) are subject to fungal decay. Treatment with a preservative is desirable for wooden control posts intended to last *in situ* for a number of years.

Conspicuousness

In conflict with the need for stability is the need not to attract sheep, cattle, and passers-by. Children in particular will often search over an area out of curiosity after survey work has been completed. Paradoxically there are times when very prominent stakes are less vulnerable than more modest ones: they withstand trivial disturbance better and they quickly become accepted as part of the scenery. A. J. Gray (personal communication) has totally buried angle-irons and subsequently attempted to relocate them with metal detectors, but he writes that he had only moderate success on a highly unstable low marsh, and that other markers nearby were also needed.

Very low markers, flush with the marsh surface or only a few centimeters high, are prone to being buried by moving sediment or by the accumulation of plant material (this is particularly true for the Festucetum where leaf litter is not removed annually by natural processes). Thin coatings of mud encourage the growth of algae, and these in turn accelerate mud accumulation.

In very dense *Spartina* stands where there are virtually no topographical features it can be easier to locate even tall posts by their position in relation to access routes than by reference to any other points.

If reference points are located on rocks, stone walls, or other hard permanent features, record the exact site photographically, and note that intertidal rock surfaces (even if cleared artificially) can be obscured by fucoid growth within a season or so.

Recommendations

For the reasons given above, it is not possible to recommend a single 'ideal' method for marking salt-marsh survey sites, but emphasis should be given to the following.

1. Posts for survey control points and other major reference points should be very securely inserted, and where possible hard bedrock features or stone sea-walls should be used.
2. The location of reference points by horizontal or vertical measurement should be to unambiguous topographical features.
3. Photographic records must be prepared with care in the field, and must be amply annotated.
4. Quadrat corners may often be marked by quite small pegs, relying on their general invisibility, but they should be related to more substantial stakes nearby. Triangulation using compass bearings from two such stakes may be helpful.

Trampling effects

Like all wetland sites, salt marshes are very prone to damage by trampling, and repeated access to sites can cause intense local damage from which it may take several years to recover. Student transects across salt marshes in Milford Haven remain conspicuously disturbed for the whole summer after only one or two visits early in the season, and trampling lines in dense *Spartina anglica* have become semi-permanent features. Permanent pathways across saltings to boats and fishing areas are a familiar feature of many marshes. When planning repeated visits to salt marshes, one should decide at the outset whether access is to be by the same route at all time or whether the impact is to be spread (it cannot be avoided) over a larger area.

At the study site itself there must be provision for the observer to stand or kneel whilst making observations, and damage in this peripheral zone to surrounding tall vegetation might modify air movement and illumination in the study site. Continued local pressure produces hollows which hold water after rain or tidal cover. The severity of these and other effects depends of course on the softness of the sediments and the frequency of visits. To avoid the surface depression and crushing of vegetation when it is knelt upon, Dalby (1981) has used a cushioned board about 20 cm × 45 cm to spread the weight adequately on rather firm salt marshes in Shetland, but a larger board might be preferable in softer situations. M. Wilson (personal communication) has described a framework that he has constructed for making density observations in quadrats on a very soft salt marsh in Bridgwater Bay. This framework consists of two parallel wooden rails, about 3 m long and separated by about 3 m, supported at their ends and centres on 1.35-m uprights driven into the mud. A ladder is placed across the two rails and the observer lies on a foam-padded board about 45 cm × 60 cm placed on the ladder. The uprights were of such a length above the mud that the observer, when resting on the ladder and board, could just reach the ground; this distance proved critical in easing fatigue. All the wood used in the framework was about 10 cm × 10 cm in section and was treated so as to be decay-resistant.

Whilst human disturbance is alien to the natural salt-marsh ecosystem and should be limited or controlled wherever possible, the local trampling damage caused by cattle, horses, and sheep is a biotic effect which may or may not be acceptable according to site management policy. Animal-disturbed upper marshes are beneficial to certain local species (such as *Spergularia marina* and perhaps *Puccinellia rupestris* and *P. distans*) which thrive where niches are opened up in otherwise closed vegetation.

Preparation of base maps

This section is concerned with the preparation of base maps upon which may be plotted distributions of species, communities, or other items of interest. A map is a fundamental tool in survey work: it 'is a method which planners and politicians are accustomed to using and if conservationists can also set their interests on a map, then one has an excellent medium for communication' (Dahl, 1973). Even if one does not share Dahl's optimism about politicians, maps remain as indispensable vehicles for communicating information visually.

Only very rarely in salt-marsh studies will any suitable detailed base map be available on which the field worker can enter his observations; almost always one must make (or have made) a base map *de novo*. A common experience is that of Coulson *et al.* (1980) who found that existing maps of Chichester Harbour did not show the details of creeks and mud banks at a suitable scale because no one had ever required these details previously.

Mapping small areas

Very small areas (e.g., individual salt-marsh pans or quadrats) are best mapped by laying out an accurate orthogonal grid with squares of, say, 10- or 20-cm sides, and then transferring observed features by eye to a corresponding but smaller grid on paper. The following problems relate to matters of accuracy – effort put into overcoming them must be balanced against the purpose of the study.

Parallax
The map is to be a vertical projection of the area observed, so the mapper must look vertically down upon the field grid.

Ambiguous or indeterminate topographical features
Whilst for example stones on the salt-marsh surface will have sharply defined outlines, many commoner features (degraded erosion cliffs, sloping edges to creeks and pans) do not, and it then becomes a matter of personal judgement where to enter them in the drawn grid. If change with time is to be assessed in this manner, then considerable uncertainty may be introduced. The edges of vegetation stands offer particular problems when outliers are present, or where marginal plants send out stolons reaching beyond the general stand limit.

Poor draughtsmanship
However well-defined the features to be mapped, the result will be of little value if one is unable to draw on paper what one sees in the field.

Site location
If the map is to be used for entering field data on later occasions to display changes, then it must be located accurately in relation to field markers. These need not be within the mapped area itself, but there must be some provision for precise re-location.

Site disturbance
Intensive work at one position will cause serious disturbance from standing or kneeling, so take the necessary care (see above, Trampling effects).

Photographic cover of small areas
A photographic approach to mapping very small areas may seem to offer a way of avoiding most of the problems outlined above, but a series of new problems will be encountered.

Size and distance restrictions
A 35-mm camera with a standard 50-mm lens will have a frame length equivalent to about 1.25 m at a distance of 2.0 m.

Empirical tests by the writer suggest that 50-mm lenses are the best compromise between availability, degree of distortion (all lenses distort), and working area in relation to working distance. If the study area is larger than this, the operator can no longer use the view finder when standing at ground level, and the camera must be elevated in some way. J. M. Baker (personal communication) used a small scaffold tower in Milford Haven, and various devices have been suggested by field workers (though apparently not usually tested in practice) such as elevation on a cantilever frame, and suspension by kite or balloon. All remote methods of this kind present difficulties in locating the correct field of view, and some would obviously fail in strong wind.

Horizontal control
The film plane should be horizontal, though geometrical corrections could be applied provided that at least four reference points whose angular and distance relationships are known on the ground appear in the photograph.

Optical distortion
Provided the area mapped does not reach to the extreme edge of the field of view, distortion of a plane surface will be slight and will probably come within the scale of mapping errors. A natural area of marsh surface is, in reality, never truly plane, and parallax errors will inevitably be present, especially evident for stems and leaves which ascend towards the camera and so become slightly exaggerated in size. Stems and leaves ascending vertically at the edge of the field of view will photograph as seen slightly from one side. The best advice here is to work with the camera as far away as possible and to keep the study area in the centre of the field of view.

Lighting
Lighting needs care even if it cannot be controlled, since brilliant low sunlight can give harsh shadows to pan edges, below leaves, and so on with detail obscured by darkness. Even illumination (as from overcast cloudy skies) however removes visual clues for interpreting such features as subtle gentle slopes.

Ground truth
Even a small-area photograph needs its own 'ground truth', that is, an interpretation of the photographic image in terms of the subject being photographed. This must be done at the time of taking the photograph, perhaps by way of an annotated field sketch showing which way the ground

slopes, which species are which, and so on. The absolute necessity for this becomes evident when one tries to interpret the photographs later on, but is denied information beyond that in the photograph itself.

Mosaics

A somewhat larger area may be mapped using a series of overlapping photographs on a grid basis; the regions of overlap are those most affected by parallax distortion, and these are excluded when the prints are assembled into a mosaic. In virtually all instances the edges of the central areas still will not match exactly and some subjective adjustment will be necessary.

Transport to site

The larger and more complicated the equipment, the more difficult it becomes to transport to the site, and a balance has to be achieved between portability and quality of the final photographs.

Instrument mapping of larger areas

A one-off survey will almost certainly not justify the expense and time involved in an instrument survey, but it will probably be essential if the base map is to cover a large area and is to be used for the plotting of detail on future occasions. It is not possible to consider here all aspects of field mapping – the reader should consult a book such as Pugh (1975) for an outline of accepted practice in field survey techniques. In addition, there are many technical publications covering the use of instruments, accuracy limits, and the interpretation of data. However, some important points follow.

1. Decide on the smallest detail to be plotted by way of field observation, since the magnitude and cost in effort of the whole survey is determined by this minimum detail.

2. Orient the map to a national grid north, or to true or magnetic north.

3. Establish a baseline on flat ground with uninterrupted visibility between two permanent control points. This distance should be measured with the maximum accuracy possible according to available equipment – with a nylon-coated steel tape under standard tension it should be possible to measure to within 5 mm over a distance of 100 m.

4. Set up a network of control points, again all marked permanently, and with their angular and distance relationships determined as accurately as is convenient or necessary.

5. Add fine detail using a theodolite, plane table, or compass bearings, in order of preference. The general rule is to work from the most accurate observations (the baseline) through to the least accurate (final detail).

6. Check all observations as the survey progresses.

If heights are to be included, these must be related to some known datum level – this could be part of a national geodetic network (in mainland Britain, that of the Ordnance Survey) – or to an arbitrary local datum which may or may not be tied in with the main geodetic network at some future date. Any such local datum must be recorded and identified unambiguously and as accurately as possible. As reference datum points are often several kilometers from the marsh, it may be necessary to establish a number of local levelled points, each photographed for record purposes and set on permanent structures such as the tops of rocks. The relating of these levelled reference points to the datum level is done by spirit levelling. If contours are to be added over an extensive or inaccessible area, it is best to prepare them from aerial photographs using stereo pairs.

Spirit levelling

Spirit levelling can be carried out accurately over a distance of several kilometres, especially if one has access to a modern self-aligning level rather than a quickset model, since the former is so much more rapid in use. In general, make sure that the distance between tripod and staff is about equal during each leg of the survey, and that it does not exceed about 70 m. Levelling data must be entered meticulously with headings to all the columns of numbers in a log book, and it is recommended that the reader of the level check each reading after entering it in the book before moving on to the next position. Those unused to reading levels should take particular care not to confuse the upper and lower stadia lines with the main horizontal line in the field of view. It is sometimes suggested that one should enter heights corresponding to the stadia lines as well (even if they are not to be used further) as a check to eliminate confusion.

Staff and tripod stability can be a serious problem on soft sediment shores and marshy ground, where the equipment may sink slightly under its own weight and the surveyor himself may cause local disturbance. Circumstances vary, but the staff may be placed on local areas of firmer ground; on a domed bolt head protruding through the upper surface of a 20–30 cm square metal or wooden plate (a bolt head is recommended because a simple flat board will almost certainly not lie truly horizontally, but the bolt head will allow the staff to be easily adjusted until it is vertical; similarly the staff can be rotated through 180° for the next leg of the survey and still be exactly positioned on the domed bolt); on the top of a length of metal or wood driven well into the ground; or it can be held by a surveyor's metal 'crows foot' to assist stability. There is little alternative for the tripod however except to stand it on firm ground, and then take great care when walking or standing close to it, and never to use the tripod (even momentarily) for one's own support. The staff-holder could use boards for his own support.

A serious problem, for which there is no solution, is vibration in the tripod during very strong winds. If this is met with, there is no alternative to suspending survey work until the wind subsides.

Tide heights as local datum levels

At times it may be possible to have access to a recording tide gauge within close distance of the working area (as in the Wadden Sea, Netherlands, or Milford Haven, Wales), but this is not a common situation. Enquiries should be made however to local water authorities, drainage boards, and civil engineering firms engaged in local work, as they often make short-term tidal height studies.

Local water levels can differ by many centimetres over a few kilometres as a result of wind and tidal currents, so survey heights based on such levels can never be more than approximations and cannot replace spirit-level-derived heights from known datum points. Sometimes however approximate heights will be sufficient; the local datum level should then be based on as many low and high waters as possible. Individual tide heights differ from those predicted in tide tables as a result of wind and air pressure perhaps operating some distance away, as happens with tidal surges in the North Sea, and tidal predictions for shallow water areas are always somewhat unreliable.

Tidal heights are predicted for a number of primary ports in the Admiralty Tide Tables in the British Isles, and elsewhere in national tide tables, together with predictions for secondary ports. These latter are derived from the former by making time and height corrections (sometimes by interpolation) and are not expected to be so accurate. Note that secondary ports are not in fact always ports, but may instead be useful places for coastal navigation. Using the published predictions, it is often possible to make estimates for one's own working area, but be aware of the following problems.

    1. There is no accurate correction that can be made for each individual combination of wind speed, wind direction, and atmospheric pressure.

2. Local seiche effects (up to 5 cm or more) can follow from strong winds persisting along narrow sea inlets.
3. Double-peaked tide curves are more common than one might expect.
4. The tide curve is usually much distorted in areas of shallow water.
5. On a small scale (such as an individual salt marsh) tidal flow may be quite irregular, with the pattern of small creeks lateral to the main creeks producing short-term water velocity surges (Pethick, 1980).

The correlation of heights along a shore is better made by instrument survey rather than by using tidal strand lines. Different sizes of drift may float at different depths, wave environments differ along the shore, and maximum water levels are not necessarily the same because of local surges.

In summary: predictions for time are far more reliable than predictions for height; all predictions are subject to error; instrumentally derived local datum levels are more reliable than those based on short-term local tidal observations; if one is forced to use such tides, then employ as many as possible and state the nature of the data on which one's local datum level is based.

Microtopography

Small variations in surface height can lead to major differences in the rate of drainage of tidal water from the marsh surface. Topographical patterns can often be related to the distribution patterns shown by different species. Boorman & Woodell (1966) describe a piece of equipment, the topograph, derived initially from a points quadrat frame and designed for detecting surface irregularities in salt-marsh communities.

Small differences in height along short transects in Shetland have been measured by spirit levelling, using a staff made from clearly marked metre rules with scale units at 1 mm intervals (Dalby, 1981).

Vegetation mapping

Once a base map has been prepared, it may be used for entering the distribution of vegetation units or individual species, together with other environmental information if appropriate. In general the purpose of a map is to display information visually, when it becomes a powerful tool for assisting the non-specialist or the layman. For a general discussion of vegetation maps, their presentation and interpretation, see Küchler (1967, 1973), whilst for a summary of the suitability of different scales (from

1:50000000 to 1:10000000 for global mapping, through to 1:10000 or 1:1000 or even larger scale) see Clapham (1980).

Irrespective of the origin of mapping data (e.g., photointerpretation of infrared false colour film, or by direct observation through a small grid laid on the ground surface), there are some general points to be made.

1. Vegetation units frequently have diffuse edges, and the cartographer must make arbitrary decisions as to where to place boundaries, adopting a compromise between mapping scale and the width of transitional areas.

2. Do not use dispersed letters or symbols (as was done on many early salt marsh vegetation maps) to represent the scattered distribution of a single species if this could lead to the misinterpretation of such letters or symbols standing for the precise location of individual specimens.

3. Bounding lines should be drawn around dots or other symbols with great caution, for once such lines are drawn, the eye interprets the pattern of dots in terms of those lines, and the overall distribution is given an apparent form which may not match reality.

4. Tone should be added mechanically where possible, using diagonal or transverse hatching of different line thicknesses as well as directions, and overall dots of differing sizes and spacings. The purpose of such tones or tints is to distinguish individual areas immediately, without the viewer having to search each in turn analytically to see how it differs from its neighbours in line direction or thickness.

5. Dots and other symbols should be unambiguous and large enough to read after reduction, and should not conflict with other symbols on the map. When used to represent a graded sequence (such as plant density), their size or form should relate logically to that sequence.

6. Colour printing can improve legibility (provided its density does not obscure base map detail), but at the penalty of greatly increased costs. Colours should be chosen wherever possible so as to reflect ecological gradients.

7. Successful map production involves the use of many conventions which are the solution to restrictions of scale, uncertainty of mapped features, and so on; consultation with cartographers is recommended. Some relevant information is also in Dalby & Dalby (1980).

Measures of plant abundance

Surveys often take into account the actual quantities of the plant species present (i.e., their abundance) as well as their spatial distribution.

Quadrat studies

It must always be clear whether abundance measures relate to the whole study area or merely to some selected parts; it is generally best to make observations on samples rather than the whole with the assumption that these samples are in act representative of the whole area. The truth of this is influenced by both the spatial pattern of the species in question, and the method of laying out the sampling area. Whether or not the sampling areas (quadrats, plots) should be chosen to be vegetationally homogeneous depends entirely on the purpose of the study – strong views are held here by different workers.

Quadrat shape

It is customary to use square quadrats, though there is theoretical support for using elongated rectangles which increase the probability of bridging the components of the vegetation mosaic and so reduce the variance of the data. See Clapham (1932) and Cain & Castro (1971) for general comments. Rectangular quadrats may also be particularly suitable for sampling linear communities such as on creek levees and along drift lines. Milner & Hughes (1968) favour circular quadrats, although they could not refer to experience with their use in very varied grassland types. Circular quadrats are also difficult to maintain physically undistorted.

Quadrat size and number

Optimal size and numbers are influenced by properties of the vegetation itself (e.g., evenness of distribution, clump size), and by the methods used subsequently for analysis or display. In theory one should use minimal-area curves derived from a preliminary survey (see Kershaw, 1964) to determine the optimal size, but in reality these often suggest impracticably large quadrats through the curves not flattening out.

Gray & Bunce (1972) used 2 m × 2 m squares in Morecambe Bay; Milner & Hughes (1968) quote 50 cm × 50 cm for natural and montane grasslands; Gillner (1960) employed various sizes in SW Sweden but mostly used 25 cm × 25 cm, and Dalby (1981) used 14 cm × 14 cm squares (subdivided for very species-poor marshes) in Shetland (Fig. 3.2). Quadrats within this size range will be suitable for most purposes, without any rigid recommendations being possible.

With regard to quadrat numbers, it is also not possible to provide any approved standards. If placing is by the intersections of a regular grid, then its dimensions determine quadrat numbers; if the placing is to be random, then numbers are most likely to be controlled by time available in the field. Rough estimates of plant parameters such as density may be obtained by plotting means for increasingly large numbers of quadrats and observing where the curve for these successive means levels off. Milner & Hughes (1968) quote a method for use in the International Biological Programme (IBP) studies, where a 10% error in the mean would be acceptable, which may be summarised as follows.

First obtain mean ($\bar{x}$) and standard error (s) for say 10 trial quadrats. Then N, the number needed, is given by

$$N = \frac{t \cdot s}{D \cdot \bar{x}}$$

where D is the level of accuracy specified (for an accuracy of 10%, $D = 0.1$), and t is obtained from statistical tables. It should be noted that this formula refers to quantitative parameters; it is obviously not suitable for determining optimal or minimal quadrat sizes in purely floristic studies.

Fig. 3.2. Recording species frequencies with a small subdivided quadrat on a heavily sheep-grazed salt-marsh turf, Houb at Sullom, Shetland.

Qualitative estimates

For quick and necessarily subjective recording, the DAFOR scale may be used:

D, dominant

A, abundant

F, frequent

O, occasional

R, rare

These terms are defined and applied anew at each site, with a considerable amount of personal bias. The absence of precise definition prevents the scale being used for any study where abundance data is processed mathematically. The scale is similarly unsuitable for rigorous mapping purposes. It is possible to give the terms satisfactory definitions however; see, for instance, Dicks (1976) who employed a similar scale (with the terms

Fig. 3.3. Distribution of *Spartina anglica* recolonising Fawley marsh, Southampton Water, following an effluent improvement programme, August 1983. 1 and 2 are refinery effluents. Abundant: Most shoots less than 50 cm apart, and often very close together.
Common: Most shoots between 50 cm and 1 m apart. There may be small denser clumps in this category, or small patches of less-dense vegetation.
Rare: Shoots more than 1 m apart, and may be very widely scattered.
Map by B. Dicks, published with the kind permission of Esso Petroleum Co. Ltd.

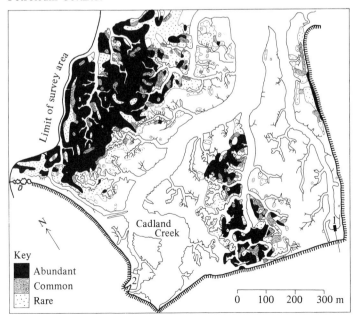

Abundant, Common, and Rare defined by reference to distances between plants) in a study of an effluent-damaged salt marsh (Fig. 3.3). He adds that the categories are arbitrary, 'and were chosen for speed of use and to fit with the observed plant distributions'. In this study, the marsh (1.25 km across) was very difficult to traverse, and the scale adopted concentrated attention on plant density, fundamental in an examination of recolonisation.

Combined cover–abundance scales (such as those of Domin and Braun-Blanquet referred to below) also have a subjective element; this does not seem to offer many problems in practice once one is used to their application, but there may be some subsequent theoretical problems concerning numerical data processing.

Quantitative measures

These methods are essential if tests of statistical significance are to be applied; they should also be used if, for example, mean scores are to be calculated, or if work is to be continued by other individuals on a later occasion.

Density

The simplest concept is the number of plants, flowering shoots, clumps, etc. per unit area. The concept is much favoured by zoologists dealing with discrete animals which can be counted, but it presents serious difficulties for botanists seeking to count individual plants in dense stands of vegetation where shoots may be connected by buried stolons or rhizomes. Many zoological diversity indices are based on numbers of individuals; these need modification before they can be applied in a botanical context. Density figures should be expressed as actual counts per specified unit area, or by using a ranking scale such as

    1 (or A), 1–10 individuals
    2 (or B), 11–100 individuals
    3 (or C), 101–1000 individuals

The class numerals or letters have no meaning without their corresponding numerical definitions. The numerical equivalents for the classes may proceed upwards in an arithmetic sequence (e.g., 10, 20, 30...) or in an exponential (geometric) manner (e.g., 1, 10, 100...). The former scaling gives equal weight to all values, the latter is a simple transformation giving more weight to low values in contrast to high ones. Note that exponential scales can never reach zero and have to be curtailed arbitrarily at some specified value. Most scales will regard zero as a unique class, and so some compensating adjustment is needed in the next class following. Biologists often feel that exponential scales have more 'meaning' than arithmetic scales, but many workers would still recommend actual counts in the field subsequently followed by transformation if this was felt appropriate. Data grouped into classes is particularly suitable for visual display purposes where the gain in clarity more then compensates for some loss of information through grouping.

Frequency

Frequency is the term applied to the number of quadrats or other sampling units containing a given species, recorded on a presence or absence basis. Relative and percentage frequencies refer to the same measure expressed as a proportion or percentage, respectively, of the total number of quadrats in the study. Frequency figures are probability estimates: if a species occurs in 7 quadrats out of 10, its relative frequency is 0.7, its percentage frequency is 70%, and there is a 7 in 10 probability that a randomly placed quadrat placed in the study area will contain that species.

Frequency measures give poor estimates of abundance because they are much influenced by quadrat size and plant pattern. In particular they exaggerate the contribution made by evenly spaced plants of little overall cover (such as grass stems and leaves). The lower and upper constraining values (zero and unity for relative frequency) prevent the use of parametric statistical tests being applied to the unmodified data; the angular or arcsin transformation (Sokal & Rohlf, 1981) is often acceptable. If there are many very high or very low values, then this transformation is not appropriate and non-parametric methods must be employed.

Cover

Cover (the vertical projection of all above-ground plant organs onto a horizontal plane) has been widely used in quantitative plant ecology. Relative or percentage cover may be estimated by eye, but even with experience one must accept a possible error of up to 10%. Greater error may be encountered when working in dense grasslands because of the virtual impossibility of integrating by eye the numerous and often minute cover elements offered by narrow and inclined stems and leaves. Tests with students have shown enormous differences in cover estimates (e.g., between 15% and 40% for the same area), and data obtained by different workers should only be combined after field tests to confirm the comparability of their visual judgement.

Cover–abundance scales

Combined scales weighted towards density at the lower end and towards cover at the higher end are very much used in phytosociological studies; they can also be used for strictly numerical work provided certain assumptions are made. The properties and application of the Braun-Blanquet and Domin scales are discussed fully by Westhoff & van der Maarel (1978). A related scale used especially in salt marsh studies in the Netherlands is that of Doing Kraft (1954) which makes use of arithmetic cover classes, but with the division of the less than 5% cover class into four subjective classes (r, *raro*; p, *paupulum*; a, *amplius*; m, *multum*). Beeftink (1975) gives precise definitions in terms of numbers of individuals for these four classes.

Objections to the use of cover–abundance scales are based on the fact that their classes are actually ranks, and ordinal data should not be processed by the normal rules of arithmetic. Nevertheless, the ordinal equivalents of the classes have been used on many occasions in multivariate studies without calamity; this is probably because the mean class-cover values increase in an approximately exponential manner. The matter is discussed by Bannister (1966), who provides cover equivalents for each of the Domin classes.

Support for the use of cover–abundance scales comes from their wide usage in many countries, and from their fundamental contribution to the methodology of the international phytosociological approach.

Point sampling

This is the most accurate method for assessment of cover in the field, making use of contacts with a vertical pin or wire or with the vertical projection downwards by eye of a cross-wire intersection. Various sampling frames and devices have been described (see, e.g. Woodell & Boorman 1966). The following are major difficulties with the method.

1. It is difficult to handle sampling frames in tall vegetation (3-m-high *Spartina cynosuroides* in the eastern United States would seem to be intractable; even the more common *S. alterniflora* would scarcely be more amenable).

2. Every contact must be identified, yet this cannot normally be done without some disturbance in order to reveal contacts with lower strata in the vegetation. In grazed salt-marsh turfs *Puccinellia maritima* and *Festuca rubra* can look very similar and can be separated only by examination of leaf base and ligule characters (Dalby, 1970; Gray & Scott, 1977).

3. A compromise has to be reached between pin diameter and

robustness; thinner pins are preferable theoretically, yet are easily distorted.

4. Point sampling using a frame of spaced points (often ten) is equivalent to a plot with ten regularly spaced quadrats; the result is a measure of local frequency and does not yield ten independent scores.

5. Since leaves do not generally spread strictly horizontally, some workers prefer to incline their sampling pins, but the angle that is optimal must vary from species to species according to its leaf and shoot architecture.

6. Point sampling takes much time, and it may be rejected for this reason alone. A realistic trial study will show whether it is worth the effort required.

Some (though not all) of these difficulties can be overcome by the use of colour slides projected onto a predrawn grid of lines or randomly placed intersections. D. H. Dalby (unpublished) has found this method satisfactory for short Puccinellietum, but the photographs must be taken in diffuse lighting since it is impossible to distinguish living from dead foliage in the harsh shadows cast by strong sunshine. This technique is of very limited value in tall vegetation with several canopy layers.

Local frequency

This is perhaps the best compromise between time taken in recording and final information yielded. A fairly large number (i.e., 50–100) of small squares are recorded on a presence/absence basis within each larger quadrat. A serious problem (as with all frequency measures) is the exaggeration of scores for species of low cover but even spread (such as grasses). Dalby (1981) has used squares 14 cm × 14 cm divided into 49 smaller squares each 2 cm × 2 cm in forb (non-grassy) salt marshes in Shetland, but whilst they were well suited to unexpanded rosettes of *Plantago maritima* and *Armeria maritima* in early May, they were clearly too large for scattered *Puccinellia maritima* interspersed with them.

Cover repetition

If the points contact method is extended to include the total number of times that each pin touches each species, the measure obtained is cover repetition. It is a better measure of total biomass than any method so far discussed, but it is extremely sensitive to sampling disturbance. It is also impossible to apply by optical sighting in dense vegetation as there are no physical contacts that can be checked by looking obliquely.

Small algae

Microscopic algae, conspicuous in quantity but invisible in the field when scarce, offer special problems. Almost all methods tried in salt-marsh studies make use of local frequency in small quadrats (e.g., 2 cm × 2 cm) within larger quadrats (de Jonge, 1976; Nienhuis, 1978). Kitchenside (1981) took samples 2 mm thick and 4 mm diameter from 25 points on a regular grid within a larger square 0.5 m × 0.5 m. Each sample was dispersed under a large cover glass, and ten random fields (1 mm diameter) examined on a presence/absence basis under a microscope.

Polderman (1980b) used representative samples from each unit visible in the field, and continued microscope searching until no new species were found. Sampling that involves searching under the microscope can be exceedingly time consuming, yet this searching is essential if the data obtained are to be in any way realistic. Problems in identifying some algae (especially if preserved) should be mentioned here, diatom frustules being particularly troublesome.

Further information is given in Chapter 4.

Sampling stands of mixed age and structure

Measures of abundance such as cover lose some of their value when applied to stands with mixed age-classes, since the survival potential of seedlings is not proportional to their cover when considered simultaneously with mature plants. Density measures are probably the most appropriate in this case. A selection of species at the seedling stage, from salt marshes in SW Wales, is illustrated in Dalby (1970).

Little attention has been given to variation in vegetation structure of salt-marsh communities, although the diversity introduced when tall and short vegetation alternate in a mosaic must provide increased habitats for the salt-marsh fauna. In dense vegetation there are spaces and passageways for animals on the mud surface and below the stems and foliage canopy, whilst the considerable accumulation of dead leaves and stems in the Festucetum has few equivalents at lower levels on the salt marsh. Special habitats are also available for the smaller algae; for example, on the stems of *Halimione portulacoides* and within the basal leaf sheaths of *Triglochin maritima*.

Plant performance

Salt marshes are essentially grassland communities, and the techniques described by Milner & Hughes (1968) for the International Biological Programme (IBP) studies, should generally be applicable to salt-marsh habitats.

Indirect methods

These methods of estimating performance are generally non-destructive and involve measurements made *in situ* which are regarded as being significantly correlated with overall growth. Examples include the number of leaves per shoot and the height to the top of the inflorescence in *Spartina anglica* (Goodman, 1960), and stolon length in *Puccinellia maritima* (Dalby, 1981).

Direct methods

Estimates of biomass using fresh weight, ash-free weight, or dry weight (oven dried, or air dried for some weeks to constant weight) are essential when investigating productivity and energy-flow relationships. Linthurst & Reimold (1978) compared five different methods for estimating net aerial production in a range of North American salt marsh species and found tenfold differences in the extreme values obtained.

The partitioning of resources between root and shoot have been investigated by Gray & Scott (1977) in *Puccinellia maritima* and by Smith, Good & Good (1979) in *Spartina alterniflora* who found just 11% of total biomass located in the shoot, and about 89% in the underground portions of the plant. Note that on shores with high sedimentation rates, there will be considerable amounts of silt adhering to stem and leaf surfaces (often sufficient to colour the plants grey), and this may be difficult to remove.

In field experiments, access routes and places where observers stand should be planned to ensure that areas of vegetation which will need to be sampled at a later date are not damaged. Special studies require special strategies however, thus Ranwell (1961) harvested sub-plots within larger field plots using different sets of random coordinates on different occasions. This permitted some to be harvested twice, the aim of the study being to simulate light grazing.

According to Mann (1982), over 90% of the studies on salt-marsh energetics have been carried out in the United States (mostly on the extensive eastern *Spartina alterniflora* marshes), with the paper by Teal (1962) occupying a central place. More recent work (putting earlier studies into perspective) includes that by Long & Woolhouse (1979), Wiegert (1979), Nixon (1980), and Pomeroy & Wiegert (1981).

Pattern studies

In addition to changes in performance during the development of a salt marsh, many species show changes in density associated with the transition from early immigration through to the equilibrium of the mature marsh sward. Brereton (1971) used covariance analysis of data from contiguous

10 cm × 10 cm quadrats along three transects in a study of *Puccinellia maritima* and *Salicornia europaea*. Ranwell (1964*b*) showed that the growth of *Spartina anglica* is inversely related to litter accumulation and that other species (such as *Atriplex hastata*) are only able to establish in dense *Spartina* swards in areas where *Spartina* drift is deposited in large amounts and then decomposes *in situ*. Chater & Jones (1957) measured the rates of radial growth in *Spartina anglica* tussocks to distinguish growth rates on different substrata. Note here that the number of readily distinguishable tussocks per unit area falls with time as tussocks fuse to form a sward.

Remote sensing studies
Remote sensing techniques would appear to be potentially useful for estimating salt-marsh biomass, but Budd & Milton (1982) report that there is very poor correlation between dry weight of *Spartina anglica* and its reflectance properties using a ground-based radiometer sensing in the four bands of the Landsat thematic mapper (TM); they discuss reasons for this, but do not offer any full explanation. Rather better results were obtained for *Fucus vesiculosus* and *Zostera marina*, and Jensen (1980) obtained estimates within 10% of direct ground measurements for *Halimione portulacoides* stands on the Skallingen marsh in Denmark.

Marking individual specimens in the field
It is often necessary to mark individual specimens so that they can be located on a future occasion. This marking may be direct (where a marker is attached to the plant) or indirect (where the plant is located by reference to some external marker).

Direct marking
Plastic or metal rings may be attached directly to a plant, generally by fastening around the stem. Problems are:
1. The markers must not disintegrate in sea water or rain.
2. They must not be conspicuous.
3. They must not be so heavy or bulky as to constrict or bend the plant, nor must they tangle with floating drift material.
4. They must not slide down the stem.

An alternative could be to punch holes in leaves in such a way as not to damage the plant significantly; this technique is used satisfactorily with algae and seagrasses.

Indirect marking

Individuals may be relocated by reference to other plants, to stones or pegs inserted in the ground, or by photographic recording. A possible problem is that sometimes growth may be faster than expected between visits (low-marsh *Salicornia* plants which start erect frequently become decumbent with maturity and their overall appearance changes drastically), and what was originally obvious becomes ambiguous at a later date.

Formal classification of salt-marsh plant communities

If vegetation units (communities in a broad sense) are to be mapped, they must first be recognised and defined. 'Classification has one very practical function, as a basis of inventory and mapping, either as an objective in itself or as a basis of management' (Greig-Smith, 1980).

Vegetational units may be structurally based using, for example, the Fosberg system (Fosberg, 1967; Clapham, 1980; see also Beard, 1978; Kirkpatrick & Glasby, 1981) or floristically based using species composition. Physiognomic approaches are generally unsuitable for salt marshes because of the limited range of life forms represented, and floristic systems generally prove to be much more informative.

Subjective floristic approach

Communities defined by subjective impressions of dominance (such as the Puccinellietum maritimae of Tansley, 1949) have been traditionally used in descriptive studies. Their main advantages are:
1. Speed of application;
2. Lack of need for comparisons with other sites.
Disadvantages are serious and are listed below.
1. Similarly named communities in different sites may differ in botanical detail.
2. In species-rich communities there can be much variation in secondary species hidden under the blanket name of the dominant, and many of these may carry information on edaphic or other environmental factors.
3. The lack of precision in the community descriptions makes them useless in the context of monitoring programmes.

International phytosociological approach

This takes the form of a hierarchical classification of plant communities based on features of floristic composition, with the categories being known as syntaxa (analogous to taxa in biological classifications).

The framework is controlled by an international code (see Barkman, Moravec & Rauschert, 1976) and provides for detailed descriptions of the various syntaxa with which new communities can be compared. If found necessary, extra syntaxa can be added to those already described. The description of communities should follow established practice – see Westhoff & van der Maarel (1978) for a full discussion of methodology and basic philosophy. Major virtues of the approach are as follows.

1. Descriptions of communities are standardised between workers.
2. As the phytosociological framework is extended, so the inter-relationships between floristics and environment are better understood.
3. Provision is made for syntaxa of low order to cover local variants, such as those with special edaphic preferences.

Problems include the following.

1. An element of subjective selection is necessary in choosing the positions for relevés (the floristically homogeneous quadrats used in phytosociological survey work) when working in the field.
2. As with biological classifications, the higher categories (e.g., classes) are less precisely defined than the lower ones (e.g., associations), so the full synsystematic placing of individual relevés and syntaxa may depend on personal judgement.
3. Northern salt-marsh communities are very poor in species compared with their counterparts at lower latitudes, making them hard to place if most of the character species are missing.

Salt-marsh taxa from north-west Europe are outlined by Beeftink (1977), which should be read in conjunction with the account by Westhoff & van der Maarel (1978) on phytosociological methodology. See also Adam (1981).

Proposals for mapping units for coastal vegetation, including the salt marshes, in Scandinavia are summarised by Clapham (1980, Appendix 5).

Applying equivalent principles to algal communities, Polderman (1979) describes 11 algal formations from the Netherlands and in a second paper (1980a) explains his philosophical criteria for delimiting these syntaxa.

A comprehensive interactive FORTRAN program, TABORD, has been introduced by van der Maarel, Janssen & Louppen (1978), and 'is considered a numerical elaboration of the intuitive table sorting procedure according to the Braun-Blanquet method'. It requires a certain amount of visual sorting at the end to remove aberrant relevés or to rearrange certain columns or rows in the final table. TABORD is however not the only program which is based on manual hand-sorting of data, and readers should check with computer centres for programs that are now available to them.

Objective numerical approach

This section considers numerical methods of analysis where, once the field data have been obtained, subsequent processing follows along lines that can be defined in such a way as to yield identical results in the hands of different workers. Objective units (in this sense) can be extracted from quadrat data using various types of clustering programs (such as the CLUSTAN package (Wishart, 1982) or smaller programs equivalent to portions of that package). These programs produce hierarchical classifications that leave the user to select his own cluster levels to suit his purpose. It must not be assumed that the vast number of computer programs available free the user from making personal decisions during the processing, nor must it be assumed that every cluster picked out numerically will have biological or phytosociological significance – personal judgement must again be exercised. It must also be appreciated that classification analyses are often unsuited to intergrading zonations (as are so commonly met with on salt marshes). Finally, the cluster sequence obtained is often very sensitive to the clustering algorithm employed.

For examples of salt-marsh communities defined by computer analysis of quadrat data, see Lausi & Feoli (1979) for Europe in general, Kortekaas, van der Maarel & Beeftink (1976) for *Spartina*-dominated communities, and Gray & Bunce (1972) for salt-marsh communities in Morecambe Bay, England. General references to numerical classifications are Sneath & Sokal (1973) and Goodall (1978).

Transect studies

Because tidally controlled environmental factors are graded in their effects up the shore, salt-marsh floras and faunas are similarly graded and certain species groups make up zones at different levels. A suitable method for studying this zonation is the line transect, accompanied by studies on correlations between species abundances and appropriate environmental factors. Some general points may be made:

1. It is helpful to include a levelled transect profile, choosing a ratio of between 1:4 and 1:8 for vertical:horizontal ranges on the final figure.
2. It is also helpful to enter levels corresponding to tide levels such as mean high water springs or extreme high water springs, and it is useful to relate the vertical scale to local Chart Datum if possible.
3. Pans and creeks may be added to scale, even if they do not appear at regular levelling stations.
4. Vegetation may be added as histograms or lines indicating the ranges of individual species or plant communities.

5. Similarly, environmental measures (such as soil salinity, organic content, etc.) may be added to assist visual interpretation.
6. Transect studies emphasise the correlation between species distributions and environmental factors; these correlations may need testing experimentally to determine whether or not they are causal. Note the close relationship between correlation and regression analysis, and the need to use model II methods, that is, where there is random error associated with both variables (in model I methods such error is restricted to the dependent variable and the independent variable is assumed to be measured without error; see Sokal & Rohlf, 1981). Laws & Archie (1981) draw attention to this in relation to field observations.

A simple floristic transect diagram is given as Fig. 7 in Dalby (1970) and a transect with histograms for soil particle size and loss of weight on ignition is given by Packham & Liddle (1970).

Accretion measurements

Fine sediment brought to the salt marsh by tidal movements is deposited either directly onto the mud surface, or it first adheres to plant stems and leaves from which it is washed free by rain or falls on drying. Ranwell (1972) notes that 'True accretion is the depth of sediment deposited in unit time minus the reduction in thickness of the accreted layer due to settlement factors'. It is not always easy to decide whether one is measuring true or apparent accretions because settlement operates continuously down to depths well below those involved in contemporary processes. Below are various techniques used for measuring sedimentation rates.

1. Bamboo canes pushed well into soft mud and protruding about 15 cm were used by Ranwell (1964a) on fast-accreting marsh in Bridgwater Bay, England. Accretion was estimated by measuring the successive differences between mud surface and cane tops. The narrowness of the canes prevented there being significant tidal scouring effects around their bases.
2. Inglis & Kestner (1958) cored out holes in the surface of sand flats in the Wash, eastern England, and filled the holes with a creamed suspension of silica flour which they also spread locally over the sand surface. When erosion dominated over accretion, they found the silica flour cores to have been cut down. They note the effects of the cores differing slightly in consistency from the surrounding sand – obviously it would be preferable if they were identical.

3. A commonly used method is to lay a thin layer of distinctly coloured sand or equivalent material and then to cut through the subsequently accreted sediment to locate the original layer. This method, apparently invented by Nielsen (1935) for work on the Danish coast, has been followed, for example, by Coles (1979) in studies in the Wash. The sediment often peels easily at the critical level making its recognition easy. Dalby (1982) reports on the use of this method in Shetland, where it was found that on several marshes all trace of sand had been lost; it seems that alternative techniques are needed for these small and dynamically active marshes where there is appreciable erosion and recycling of material.

4. Direct measurement of elevation by levelling in relation to nearby datum marks has been used by Dalby (1982) in Shetland. Using a staff marked in millimetres and levelling over distances not exceeding about 10–15 m, the error in the vertical measurements is less than that due to the difficulty in relocating the exact levelling stations on steep shores with small stones being shifted around by water action between surveys.

5. In contrast to artificially laid sand, Clymo (1967) was able to measure accretion over natural sand layers blown over mud from nearby sand dunes at known dates at Blakeney, England. Ranwell (1964a) has determined annual sediment increments from seed-rich horizons in salt-marsh deposits.

6. For a more sophisticated (and expensive) method, see DeLaune, Patrick & Buresh (1978), who cut sediment cores into short sections and determined ^{137}Cs levels in each. The first significant ^{137}Cs fall-out occurred in 1954 with the peak year being 1963; these two dates can be used to calibrate the sections.

7. A range of sediment traps are used in marine benthic studies (see e.g., Hargrave & Burns, 1979); some of these might be adaptable for use in the salt marsh environment.

8. For studies on seasonal aspects of accretion on salt marshes, see Ranwell (1964a) and Richard (1978).

Sampling the salt-marsh fauna

Practically all the techniques available to the terrestrial ecologist for sampling animals have been used in salt-marsh studies (though perhaps in modified form). A classification of field sampling methods, which specifically includes those for animals, is given in Eberhardt (1976, pp. 41–3), whilst general summaries are provided by Seber (1973) and

Southward (1978). Note that monographs for particular groups often include sections on appropriate sampling methods. Comprehensive accounts of the salt-marsh fauna are given in Nicol (1935), Heydemann (1967, 1979), Macdonald (1969), Kraeuter & Wolf (1974) and Daiber (1976). Critical discussions of field techniques are given by Paviour-Smith (1956); techniques for working in *Spartina alterniflora* marshes are given by Barnes (1953) and Davis & Gray (1966). In these extensive *Spartina* stands, ants and grasshoppers were found more frequently on sunny days, whilst the animal groups showed differing responses to sweeping: grasshoppers escape from the sweep net but plant hoppers do not, and *Littorina irrorata* fell off the grass leaves and crushed other specimens in the net. An approach to rapid surveys for ranking sites is given in the appendix. The following account concentrates on general problems in sampling.

Tidal cover

The marsh, unless behind a sea-wall, is regularly covered by the tide, and apparatus or equipment left for more than one tidal exposure period may be inundated (check whether successive tides are rising or falling, and remember that tides during the night are often higher than those during the day). Heydemann (1967) describes a pitfall trap which cannot be flooded.

Adhering salt and silt

Dry vegetation frequently carries quantities of salt crystals (partly derived from evaporated sea water, partly tissue exudates of similar compositions), and these hygroscopic crystals fall into sweep nets making them sticky and difficult to handle. Even a little moisture damages the delicate wings of Homopteran plant bugs if they attempt to fly free. In addition to salt, there are usually silt particles that will also fall into nets.

Humidity near the ground

Apart from the uppermost few millimetres, salt-marsh sediments never wholly dry out, and conditions are always wet close to the bases of erect stems, under sheets of algae, etc.

Fauna of soft sediments

Salt-marsh creeks and pans (and the open ground between plants in sparsely vegetated areas) have an affinity with the silt and sand flats seaward of the vegetated marsh proper. Chapters 4, 6, and 7 should be consulted for relevant soft sediment techniques.

Fauna of the sediment surface

A distinctive fauna is present in the few millimetres of unconsol-idated surface sediment that is disturbed by water currents during tidal movements even on sheltered shores. This is, especially if slightly muddy, a productive habitat for Foraminifera. Murray (1979) suggests sampling the top centimeter (perhaps over 10 cm × 10 cm) and he summarises methods for utilising their upwards movements on the vertical sides of containing vessels or leaving them to adhere to the under surface of filter paper laid on the sediment. If the sample is to be preserved, it can be fixed in 50% ethanol (Murray, 1979) or neutral formalin (Phleger, 1965). Animals can be hand-picked; they can be recognised because their cyto-plasm appears brownish in an unstained sample (Hofker, 1977). Visual contrast may be improved however by staining with rose bengal.

Extraction from loose organic soils

Berlese funnel techniques are suitable for extracting animals from the more organic and looser-textured soils of the upper marsh. Polderman (1974) took soil cores 10 cm diameter and 5 cm deep and, after cutting them into pieces, dried them on a Berlese funnel without heating. When extracting oribatid mites, the process takes 2–3 weeks.

Animal behaviour

Many salt-marsh animals are active when under water but hide away when the tide is out (and when most biologists visit the marsh). There is much scope for observations during the period of tidal cover, perhaps using shallow-draught boats with glass panels or buckets with glass bottoms. Dare & Edwards (1981) using underwater television, studied the very active movements by the crab *Carcinus maenas* during rising and falling tides in the Menai Straits, Wales. Their report is some guide to the potential for such studies. Most of the terrestrial components of the salt-marsh fauna move to safety to avoid cover by the rising tide, but a number of specialist species cling to stems, in the angles of petiole bases and amongst algal mats, enclosed in air bubbles.

Local migration

It is sometimes difficult to separate the resident component of the marsh fauna from temporary visitors. Crabs and fish move extensively during tidal cover; spiders and dragonflies normally living at or above the strand line may search the marsh surface for food at low tide; and various insects visit the flowers of species such as *Limonium vulgare*, *Aster tripolium*, and *Armeria maritima*. Some birds recorded from salt marshes are likely to be no more than casuals. Packham & Liddle (1970), for instance list species 'which apparently fed, landed on or swam over' the Cefni salt marsh in north Wales.

Problems in identification

Some groups of animals, important because of their abundance, may prove very difficult to identify. Examples are the Nematoda, some Crustacea, Homoptera, and Acarina. One may have to adopt a working taxonomy that is based on the degree of specialist assistance available and subject to further problems due to the presence of immature forms. Identification literature is detailed in Chapter 14.

Indicator species

The concept of indicator species has not been followed very far in salt-marsh studies, but there is some potential for their use as indicators of present environmental conditions or of post management history. Clark (1977, p. 72) writes in connection with the assessment of coastal ecosystem health 'we believe that examination of the presence and condition of certain rooted aquatic plants represents a promising approach, and it would seem useful to explore the possibility of using such plant indicators in coastal zone ecosystem management programs'. Detailed knowledge of environmental preferences is essential, yet this is only rarely available, and

Table 3.1. *Selected salt-marsh species and their possible use as indicators of environmental conditions*

Species	Environmental conditions
Scirpus maritimus ⎫ *Triglochin palustris* ⎬ *Agrostis stolonifera* ⎭	freshwater influence
Puccinellia maritima ⎫ *Triglochin maritima* ⎭	locally wetter areas with longer-standing salt water after tide cover
Halimione portulacoides	possibly indicates drying of marsh surface in some sites
Spartina maritima	old marsh surface not disturbed by human activity, in SE England
Limonium vulgare	'unpolluted marsh' (Boorman, 1967)
Plantago coronopus	locally sandy substratum
Spergularia marina	grazed and trodden marsh surface
Dominance of *Ameria maritima*, *Plantago maritima*, and *Limonium* spp.; paucity of grasses	upper marsh soils low in nitrogen and exposed to hyper-salinity in summer (Jefferies, 1977); forb salt marsh (Dalby, 1970)

sometimes the evidence seems contradictory. The indicator concept only has value if species have narrow ranges of tolerance in relation to the total range available in the study area, and the absence of a species always means less than its presence because absence can be due to so many diverse causes. The environmental factor apparently 'indicated' by a particular species may not actually be the causal factor; salinity, oxygen status, nutrient uptake rates, and so on interact and are themselves partially controlled by tidal cover, freshwater irrigation, and topography. A further restriction in the application of the indicator species concept is that certain common species (e.g., *Agrostis stolonifera* and *Festuca rubra*) have ecotypes that have more precise environmental requirements than the species as a whole and so the presence of the species *sensu lato* has reduced value as an environmental indicator.

Table 3.1 contains tentative suggestions for angiosperms on northern and western salt marshes in the British Isles – they will certainly need to be modified with further knowledge.

The various diagnostic taxa used in phytosociological studies are employed initially to characterise particular syntaxa, but their very success in this respect implies that they may be used as indicators of corresponding combinations of environmental factors. Westhoff & van der Maarel (1978) emphasise that groups of species may be more reliable than individual species, and that dominance alone has no indicator value.

High faunal diversity is probably generally associated with high structural diversity in the vegetation, and this is most likely to be encountered in salt marshes with low sedimentation rates. Sites with high species diversity are generally considered to have high conservation value.

Site evaluation

Survey work on salt marshes is often associated with the assessment of their conservation value in relation to proposals for various kinds of development. We do not intend to argue the case for preservation of salt marshes here, but to outline the criteria that may be used in reaching a decision. Before any value judgements can be made, there must be an inventory of the characteristics of the sites in question on a comparable basis. This approach is part of the United States federal regulations relating to the approval of individual state coastal management programmes (see, e.g., Clark, 1977, pp. 800ff), is used by the Nature Conservancy Council in the United Kingdom, and was employed in the International Biological Programme (Clapham, 1980).

The Nature Conservancy Council (Ratcliffe, 1977) list criteria regarded as having paramount importance throughout the whole range of coastal

habitats in the British Isles in assessing conservation value. These criteria
are:

1. area;
2. physiographic and ecological diversity;
3. breeding and winter bird populations;
4. freedom from disturbance.

Within the series of salt-marsh sites, a full zonation from pioneer
communities through to non-saline grassland, and the presence of numerous
creeks and pans are specified as being major components in item 2 above.

Beeftink (1977) suggests the following criteria for the assessment of the
scientific value of salt marshes:

1. area;
2. habitat and species diversity;
3. rarity of habitats and species;
4. naturalness;
5. potential for natural replacement if lost.

Some of these criteria can be judged on a purely factual basis during
field survey work (such as area, and species diversity) but others, such as
items 4 in both lists, are much more subjective. North American assessments
are likely to include more society-orientated aspects, such as aesthetic value
(see Clark, 1977, pp. 557–62), which are difficult to score objectively.

Whilst the inventory approach has much to commend it, and the ranking
of each attribute in a local or national context is a necessary step in the
procedure, any extension that sums these scores to give a single number
of site 'value' is misleading and logically indefensible. A site achieving 10
is not to be understood as being twice as valuable as one scoring 5, since
it is not possible to equate say x units of rarity value with x units of
diversity value. As Siegel (1956, p. 3) writes, one may not add ranked scores
without introducing distortion. From the conservation point of view,
low-scoring sites may still justify protection yet their low scores invite
planners to put them forward preferentially for development. There is also
the danger that such scores may be used to assess financial value for sites.

Acknowledgements

I would like to thank Dr W. J. Wolff and Dr A. Gray for their helpful
comments on a draft of this chapter.

APPENDIX 3.1

Rapid surveys of arthropods and the ranking of sites in terms of conservation value
R. H. L. *Disney*

In the light of our present, inadequate knowledge of the invertebrate faunas of different habitat types, the problem of estimating the relative conservation values of different sites is essentially a problem of finding repeatable procedures for ranking the sites in terms of species diversity. With regard to the survey of arthropods of estuaries and coasts, the problem is that comprehensive surveys of the species that are present at a particular site require sampling at several seasons over several years, using a variety of collecting methods. Therefore, for rapid surveys one must be deliberately selective. One must be selective in both method employed and time involved.

For rapid surveys one needs to employ a method that produces standardised, replicated, quantified samples. The method employed (e.g., pitfall traps, white-water traps, baited funnel traps) will vary according to whether one is sampling spiders or hoverflies, carabid beetles or aphids. For each group one should select the method that gives the best return for the least effort. Even an inefficient method of sampling, however, can produce interesting results provided one obtains simultaneous, replicated, quantitative samples. For example, pitfall traps are very inefficient at catching Sepsidae or Phoridae (Disney *et al.*, 1982) and yet a pitfall trap survey of 42 sites over the same period revealed interesting differences (Disney, Coulson & Butterfield, 1981; Randall, Coulson & Butterfield, 1981).

To compare sites one must employ the same trapping method at the same time at the different sites. One can then compare the means per trap for each site, it being reasonable to assume that these means are a function of the actual diversity at each site. These means can then be compared with those from the other sites. The significance of the differences can be determined using standard statistical procedures. The sites can then be ranked in terms of the means. If one of the sites surveyed has been subjected to attempts at a comprehensive survey, one can assess the general validity of one's findings for this site by expressing the number of species obtained in the rapid survey as a percentage of the species recorded in the comprehensive survey. This can then provide a measure of the selectivity of one's rapid survey of the several sites as a whole.

In rapid surveys of the Diptera of several sites simultaneously, the following procedures have been adopted. Ten white-water traps are laid at each site and are left for a minimum of 24 hours. The data for each site are recorded in the following manner:

Site	Dates (period of trapping)										
FAMILY	Number of species in trap number										No. spp. in all 10 traps
	1	2	3	4	5	6	7	8	9	10	
TOTALS											

From these data the mean number of species per trap is calculated for each site and then the results for each site entered in a table in descending order of the mean number of species (where two sites produce the same mean, the site with the highest total number of species is entered first). The results table is as follows:

SITE	Total no. spp. in 10 traps	Mean no. spp. per trap	Range	p value	Rank
				–	1

The p (probability) values are calculated by use of the Mann–Whitney U-test (Siegel, 1956; Elliott, 1977) (this test actually compares the median values). Starting at the bottom of the results table, each site is compared with the one above. In the column headed 'Rank', starting from the top of the table, the sites are sequentially numbered 1, 2, 3, etc. When a p value ≥ 0.05 is encountered, the site is given the same rank as that of the site immediately above it in the table.

With regard to the effort required on a rapid survey, this can only be assessed in terms of the results. One can increase the number of traps at each of the ten trap points (thus one may have three traps at each trap point, but these are aggregated to still give ten samples only) and/or extend the period of trapping or repeat the exercise at a later date, until the cumulative totals are adequate for the performance of the necessary statistical procedures involved in the analysis of the findings. The essential point is that the same number of traps must be employed over the same period of time if one is to make meaningful comparisons. If at a later date one wishes to survey a different set of sites, one can compare this later survey with the earlier by including at least one of the previously surveyed sites in this later survey. Ideally at least one site selected for a re-survey should be the key site that has been subject to a comprehensive survey. The more frequently this key site is used as the basis for comparison in rapid surveys of other sites in the same region, the more likely one is to ensure that the comprehensive survey of the key site is indeed comprehensive.

The development of suitable trapping procedures for the rapid survey of estuarine and coastal habitats is a priority requirement for the evaluation of the conservation value of such sites in terms of arthropods.

References

Adam, P. (1981). The vegetation of British salt marshes. *New Phytologist*, **88**, 143–96.

Bannister, P. (1966). The use of subjective estimates of cover-abundance as the basis for ordination. *J. Ecol.* **54**, 665–74.

Barkman, J. J., Moravec, J. & Rauschert, S. (1976). Code of Phytosociological Nomenclature. *Vegetatio*, **32**, 131–85.

Barnes, R. D. (1953). The ecological distribution of spiders in non-forest maritime communities at Beaufort, North Carolina. *Ecol. Mono.* **23**, 315–37.

Beard, J. S. (1978). The physiognomic approach. In *Classification of Plant Communities*, ed. R. H. Whittaker, pp. 33–64. The Hague: Dr. W. Junk.

Beeftink, W. G. (1975). The ecological significance of embankment and drainage with respect to the vegetation of south-west Netherlands. *J. Ecol.* **63**, 423–58.

Beeftink, W. G. (1976). The coastal salt marshes of western and northern Europe: an ecological and phytosociological approach. In *Wet Coastal Ecosystems*, ed. V. J. Chapman, pp. 109—55 Amsterdam: Elsevier.

Beeftink, W. G. (1977). Salt-marshes. In *The Coastline*, ed. R. S. K. Barnes, pp. 93–121. London: John Wiley and Sons.

Boorman, L. A. (1967). *Limonium vulgare* Mill. and *L. humile* Mill. Biological Flora of the British Isles. *J. Ecol.* **40**, 217–27.

Boorman, L. A. & Woodell, S. R. J. (1966). The topograph, an instrument for measuring microtopography. *Ecology*, **47**, 869–71.

Brereton, A. J. (1971). The structure of the species populations in the initial stages of salt-marsh succession. *J. Ecol.* **59**, 321–38.

Budd, J. T. C. & Milton, E. J. (1982). Remote sensing of salt marsh vegetation in the first four proposed thematic mapper bands. *Int. J. Remote Sensing*, **3**, 147–61.

Cain, S. A. & Castro, G. M. de O. (1971). *Manual of Vegetation Analysis*. New York: Hafner Publishing Company.

Chapman, V. J. (1960). *Salt Marshes and Salt Deserts of the World*. London: Leonard Hill.

Chater, E. H. & Jones, H. (1957). Some observations of *Spartina townsendii* H. & J. Groves in the Dovey Estuary. *J. Ecol* **45**, 157–67.

Clapham, A. R. (1932). The form of the observational unit in quantitative ecology. *J. Ecol.* **20**, 192–7.

Clapham, A. R. (ed.) (1980). *The IBP Survey of Conservation Sites: an Experimental Study*. International Biological Programme 24. Cambridge University Press.

Clark, J. R. (1977). *Coastal Ecosystem Management*. New York: John Wiley & Sons.

Clymo, R. S. (1967). Accretion rate in two salt marshes at Blakeney Point, Norfolk. *Trans. Norfolk and Norwich Naturalists Soc.* **21**, 17–18.

Coles, S. M. (1979). Benthic microalgal populations on intertidal sediments and their role as precursors to salt marsh development. In *Ecological Processes in Coastal Environments*, ed. R. L. Jefferies & A. J. Davy, pp. 25–42. Oxford: Blackwell.

Coulson, M. G., Budd, J. T. C., Withers, R. G. & Nicholls, D. N. (1980). Remote sensing and field sampling of mudflat organisms in Langstone and Chichester Harbours, Southern England. In *The Shore Environment*, vol. 1: Methods, ed. J. H. Price, D. E. G. Irvine & W. F. Farnham. Systematics Association special volume no. 17(a). London: Academic Press.

Dahl, E. (1973). P. 10 in Marker, E. (ed.), *IBP/CT-Symposium om Vegetasjonsklassifisering og Vegetasjonskartlegging*, 27–28 September 1972, Ås, Norge. IBP i Norden No. 11.

Daiber, F. C. (1976). Salt-marsh animals: distributions related to tidal flooding, salinity and vegetation. In *Wet Coastal Ecosystems*, ed. V. J. Chapman, pp. 79–108. Amsterdam: Elsevier.

Dalby, C. & Dalby, D. H. (1980). Biological illustration. *Field Studies*, **5**, 307–21.

Dalby, D. H. (1970). The salt marshes of Milford Haven, Pembrokeshire. *Field Studies*, **3**, 297–330.

Dalby, D. H. (1981). The salt marshes of Sullom Voe. *Proc. R. Soc. Edinb.* **80B**, 191–202.

Dalby, D. H. (1982). Report to SOTEAG on salt marsh monitoring around Sullom Voe in 1981. Unpublished report to the Shetland Oil Terminal Environmental Advisory Group.

Dare, P. J. & Edwards, D. B. (1981). Underwater television observations on the intertidal movements of shore crabs, *Carcinus maenas*, across a mudflat. *J. mar. biol. Ass. U. K.* **61**, 107–16.

Davis, L. V. & Gray, I. E. (1966). Zonal and seasonal distribution of insects in North Carolina salt marshes. *Ecol. Monog.* **36**, 275–95.

DeLaune, R. D., Patrick, W. H. Jr, & Buresh, R. J. (1978). Sedimentation rates determined by ^{137}Cs dating in a rapidly accreting saltmarsh. *Nature*, **275**, 532–3.

Dicks, B. (1976). The effects of refinery effluents: the case history of a salt marsh. In *Marine Ecology and Oil Pollution*, ed. J. M. Baker, pp. 227–45. Barking: Applied Science Publishers.

Disney, R. H. L., Coulson, J. C. & Butterfield, J. (1981). A survey of the scuttle flies (Diptera: Phoridae) of upland habitats in northern England. *Naturalist*, Hull, **106**, 53–66.

Disney, R. H. L., Erzinçlioğlu, Y. Z., Henshaw, D. J. de C., Howse, D., Unwin, D. M., Withers, P. & Woods, A. (1982). Collecting methods and the adequacy of attempted fauna surveys, with reference to the Diptera. *Field Studies*, **5**, 607–21.

Doing Kraft, H. (1954). L'analyse des carrés permanents. *Acta Botanica Neerlandica*, **3**, 421–4.

Eberhardt, L. L. (1976). Quantitative ecology and impact assessment. *J. Environ. Manag.* **4**, 27–70.

Elliott, J. M. (1977). *Some Methods for the Statistical Analysis of Samples of Benthic Invertebrates*. Scientific Publication 25. Ambleside: Freshwater Biological Association.

Fosberg, F. R. (1967). A classification of vegetation for general purposes. In *Guide to the Check Sheet of IBP Areas*, IBP Handbook No. 4, ed. G. F. Peterken, pp. 73–120. Oxford: Blackwell.

Frenkel, R. E., Eilers, H. P. & Jefferson, C. A. (1981). Oregon coastal salt marsh upper limits and tidal datums. *Estuaries*, **4**, 198–205.

Gillner, V. (1960). Vegetations- und Standortsuntersuchungen in den Strandweisen der schwedischen Westküste. *Acta Phytogeographica Suecica*, **43**.

Goodall, D. W. (1978). Numerical classification. In *Classification of Plant Communities*, ed. R. H. Whittaker, pp. 247–86. The Hague: Dr. W Junk.

Goodman, P. J. (1960). Investigations into 'die-back' in *Spartina townsendii* agg. II. The morphological structure of the Lymington sward. *J. Ecol.* **48**, 711–24.

Gray, A. J. & Bunce, R. G. H. (1972). The ecology of Morecambe Bay. VI. Soils and vegetation of the salt marshes: a multivariate approach. *J. Appl. Ecol.* **9**, 221–34.

Gray, A J. & Scott, R. (1977). The ecology of Morecambe Bay. VII. The distribution of *Puccinellia maritima, Festuca rubra* and *Agrostis stolonifera* in the salt marsh. *J. Appl. Ecol.* **14**, 229–41.

Greig-Smith, P. (1980). The development of numerical classification and ordination. *Vegetation*, **42**, 1–9.

Hargrave, B. T. & Burns, N. M. (1979). Assessment of sediment trap collection efficiency. *Limnol. Oceanogr.* **24**, 1124–35.

Heydemann, B. (1967). *Die biologische Grenze Land-Meer im Bereich der Salzwiesen*. Wiesbaden: Franz Steiner Verlag.

Heydemann, B. (1979). Responses of animals to spatial and temporal environmental heterogeneity within salt marshes. In *Ecological Processes in Coastal Environments*, ed. R. L. Jefferies & A. J. Davy, pp. 145–63. Oxford: Blackwell.

Hofker, J. (1977). The Foraminifera of Dutch tidal flats and salt marshes. *Neth. J. Sea Res.* **11**, 223–96.

Inglis, C. C. & Kestner, F. J. T. (1958). Changes in the Wash as affected by training walls and reclamation works. *Proc. Inst. Civil Engineer.* **11**, 435–66.

Institute of Terrestrial Ecology (1977). *Ecology of Maplin Sands and the Coastal Zones of Suffolk, Essex and north Kent.* Cambridge: ITE.

Jefferies, R. L. (1977). Growth responses of coastal halophytes to inorganic nitrogen. *J. Ecol.* **65**, 847–65.

Jefferies, R. L. & Davy, A. J. (eds) (1979). *Ecological Processes in Coastal Environments.* Oxford: Blackwell.

Jensen, A. (1980). Seasonal changes in near infrared reflectance ratio and standing crop biomass in a salt marsh community dominated by *Halimione portulacoides* (L.) Aellen. *New Phytologist,* **86**, 57–68.

Jonge, V. N. de (1976). Algal vegetations on salt-marshes along the western Dutch Wadden Sea. *Neth. J. Sea Res.* **10**, 262–83.

Kershaw, K. A. (1964). *Quantitative and Dynamic Ecology.* London: Edward Arnold.

Kirkpatrick, J. B. & Glasby, J. (1981). *Salt Marshes in Tasmania.* Occasional Paper 8. Hobart: Dept. of Geography, University of Tasmania.

Kitchenside, J. R. (1981). 'Some Studies on Salt Marsh Algae'. Unpublished D.I.C. thesis, Imperial College, University of London.

Kortekaas, W. M., Maarel, E. van der & Beeftink, W. G. (1976). A numerical classification of European *Spartina* communities. *Vegetatio,* **33**, 51–60.

Kraeuter, J. N. & Wolf, P. L. (1974). The relationship of marine macroinvertebrates to salt marsh plants. In *Ecology of Halophytes,* ed. R. J. Reimold & W. H. Queen, pp. 449–62. New York: Academic Press.

Küchler, A. W. (1967). *Vegetation Mapping.* New York: Ronald Press.

Küchler, A. W. (1973). Problems in classifying and mapping vegetation for ecological regionalization. *Ecology,* **54**, 512–23.

Lausi, D. & Feoli, E. (1979). Hierarchical classification of European salt marsh vegetation based on numerical methods. *Vegetatio,* **39**, 171–84.

Laws, E. A. & Archie, J. W. (1981). Appropriate use of regression analysis in marine biology. *Mar. Biol.* **65**, 13–16.

Linthurst, R. A. & Reimold, R. J. (1978). An evaluation of methods for estimating the net aerial primary production of estuarine angiosperms. *J. Appl. Ecol.* **15**, 919–31.

Long, S. P. & Mason, C. F. (1983). *Salt Marsh Ecology.* Glasgow: Blackie & Son Ltd.

Long, S. P. & Woolhouse, H. W. (1979). Primary production in *Spartina* marshes. In *Ecological Processes in Coastal Environments,* ed. R. L. Jefferies & A. J. Davy, pp. 333–52. Oxford: Blackwell.

Maarel, E. van der, Janssen, J. G. M. & Louppen, J. M. W. (1978). Tabord, a program for structuring phytosociological tables. *Vegetatio,* **38**, 143–56.

Macdonald, K. B. (1969). Quantitative studies of salt marsh faunas from the North American Pacific coast. *Ecol. Monog.* **39**, 33–60.

Mann, K. H. (1982). *Ecology of Coastal Waters, a Systems Approach.* Oxford: Blackwell.

Milner, C. & Hughes, R. E. (1968). *Methods for the Measurement of the Primary Production of Grasslands.* IBP Handbook No. 6. Oxford: Blackwell.

Murray, J. W. (1979). *British Nearshore Foraminiferids.* London: Academic Press.

Nicol, E. A. T. (1935). The ecology of a salt marsh. *J. Mar. Biol. Ass. U.K.* **20**, 203–61.

Nielsen, N. (1935). Eine Methode zur exakten Sedimentationsmessung. Studien über die Marschbildung auf der Halbinsel Skalling. *Medd. Skall. Lab.* **1**, 1–97.

Nienhuis, P. H. (1978). Dynamics of benthic algal vegetation and environment in Dutch estuarine salt marshes, studied by means of permanent quadrats. *Vegetatio*, **38**, 103–12.

Nixon, S. W. (1980). Between coastal marshes and coastal waters – a review of twenty years of speculation and research on the role of salt marshes on estuarine productivity and water chemistry. In *Estuarine and Wetlands Processes*, ed. P. Hamilton & K. Macdonald. New York: Plenum.

Packham, J. R. & Liddle, M. J. (1970). The Cefni salt marsh, Anglesey, and its recent development. *Field Studies*, **3**, 331–56.

Paviour-Smith, K. (1956). The biotic community of a salt meadow in New Zealand. *Trans. R. Soc. N.Z.* **8**, 525–54.

Pethick, J. S. (1980). Velocity surges and asymmetry in tidal channels. *Estuar. Coast. Mar. Sci.* **11**, 331–45.

Phleger, F. B. (1965). Patterns of marsh foraminifera, Galveston Bay, Texas. *Limnol Oceanogr*, **10**, R169–84.

Polderman, P. J. G. (1974). The Oribatida (Acari) of saline areas in the western part of the Dutch Wadden sea. *Neth. J. Sea Res.* **8**, 49–72.

Polderman, P. J. G. (1979). The salt marsh community in the Wadden area, with reference to the distribution and ecology in N.W. Europe I. The distribution and ecology of the algal communities. *J. Biogeog.* **6**, 225–66.

Polderman, P. J. G. (1980a). The salt marsh community in the Wadden area, with reference to the distribution and ecology in N. W. Europe. III. The classificatory and semantic problems of saltmarsh algal communities. *J. Biogeog.* **7**, 115–26.

Polderman, P. J. G. (1980b). The permanent quadrat method, a means of investigating the dynamics of salt marsh algal vegetation. In *The Shore Environment*, vol. 1: Methods, ed. J. H. Price, D. E. G. Irvine & W. F. Farnham, pp. 193–212. London: Academic Press.

Pomeroy, L. R, & Wiegert, R. G. (eds) (1981). *The Ecology of a Salt Marsh.* New York: Springer-Verlag.

Price, J. H., Irvine, D. E. G. & Farnham, W. F. (eds.) (1980). *The Shore Environment*, 2 volumes. London & New York: Academic Press.

Pugh, J. C. (1975). *Surveying for Field Scientists.* London: Methuen.

Randall, M., Coulson, J. C. & Butterfield, J. (1981). The distribution and biology of Sepsidae (Diptera) in upland regions of northern England. *Ecol. Entomol.* **6**, 183–90.

Ranwell, D. S. (1961). *Spartina* salt marshes in southern England. I. The effects of sheep grazing at the upper limits of *Spartina* marsh in Bridgwater Bay. *J. Ecol.* **49**, 325–40.

Ranwell, D. S. (1964a). *Spartina* salt marshes in Southern England. II. Rate and seasonal pattern of sediment accretion. *J. Ecol.* **52**, 79–94.

Ranwell, D. S. (1964b). *Spartina* salt marshes in Southern England. III. Rates of establishment, succession and nutrient supply at Bridgwater Bay, Somerset. *J. Ecol.* **52**, 95–105.

Ranwell, D. S. (1972). *Ecology of Salt Marshes and Sand Dunes*. London: Chapman & Hall.

Ratcliffe, D. A. (ed.) (1977). *A Nature Conservation Review*, vol. I. Cambridge University Press.

Richard, G. A. (1978). Seasonal and environmental variations in sediment accretion in a Long Island salt marsh. *Estuaries*, **1**, 29–35.

Seber, G. A. F. (1973). *The Estimation of Animal Abundance and Related Parameters*. London: Griffin.

Silberhorn, G. M. Dawes, G. M. & Barnard, T. A., Jr (1974). *Coastal Wetlands of Virginia*. Interim report no 3. Virginia Institute of Marine Science, Gloucester Point, Virginia.

Siegal, S. (1956). *Nonparametric Statistics for the Behavioural Sciences*. International Student edition. New York & Kogakusha, Tokyo: McGraw-Hill.

Smith, K. K., Good, R. E. & Good, N. F. (1979). Production dynamics for above and below ground components of a New Jersey *Spartina alterniflora* tidal marsh. *Estuar. Coast. Mar. Sci.* **9**, 189–201.

Sneath, P. H. A. & Sokal, R. R. (1973). *Numerical Taxonomy*. San Francisco: W. H. Freeman & Company.

Sokal, R. R. & Rohlf, R. F. (1981). *Biometry*, 2nd edn. San Francisco: W. H. Freeman.

Southwood, T. R. E. (1978). *Ecological Methods*, 2nd edn. London: Chapman & Hall.

Tansley, A. G. (1949). *The British Islands and their Vegetation*, vol. II. Cambridge University Press.

Teal, J. M. (1962). Energy flow in the salt marsh ecosystem of Georgia. *Ecology*, **43**, 614–24.

Westhoff, V. & Maarel, E. van der (1978). The Braun-Blanquet approach. In *Classification of Plant Communities*, ed. R. H. Whittaker, pp. 287–397. The Hague: Dr W. Junk.

Wiegert, R. G. (1979). Ecological processes characteristic of coastal *Spartina* marshes of the south-eastern U.S.A. In *Ecological Processes in Coastal Environments*, ed. R. L. Jefferies & A. J. Davy, pp. 467–90. Oxford: Blackwell.

Wishart, D. (1982). *Clustan User Manual*, 3rd edn. Program Library Unit. University of Edinburgh.

Woodell, S. R. J. & Boorman, L. A. (1966). A light, sturdy, inexpensive point quadrat frame. *Ecology*, **47**, 870–1.

4

Flora and macrofauna of intertidal sediments

W. J. WOLFF

Introduction

Intertidal sediments form beaches and tidal flats – usually gently sloping areas without erect vegetation. The upper limit of flats often forms the lower limit of salt marshes (Chapter 3). Along tidal waters of high salinity in Europe and the west coast of North America, this boundary more or less coincides with mean high water level, but along the east coast of North America and in the low salinity reaches of estuaries, the salt marsh–tidal flat transition normally occurs close to mid tide level. The lower limit of flats is usually not accompanied by a clearly recognizable feature. Hence, mean low tide level or a similarly defined boundary is normally adopted as the lower limit. So, tidal flats border on subtidal sediments (Chapter 5).

Beaches are normally sandy and may occupy the entire intertidal zone; there is usually also a dry zone above high tide level which may be backed by dunes or cliffs. At its lower limit the wet beach usually borders on subtidal sediments (Chapter 5).

Sand and mud flats are the most extensive intertidal habitat in the majority of the north-west European countries, occupying, for example, over 2000 km² in Great Britain, about 1500 km² in the Netherlands, and about 2000 km² in the Federal Republic of Germany. Smit (1980) estimates that in Europe and north-west Africa north of the distribution limit of mangroves, about 7000 km² of tidal flats occur. Flats also cover extensive areas elsewhere in the world. Within estuaries they may occur all the way along the salinity gradient.

Beaches and tidal flats are affected by both vertical and horizontal gradients. Factors varying vertically include duration of emergence and submergence, influence of weather, and sediment composition. Horizontal gradients, more important for tidal flats, run from the open shore into the

81

estuary and include salinity, wave exposure, sediment composition, and tidal amplitude.

The ecology of tidal flats and beaches has been described by Perkins (1974), Barnes (1977), Day (1981), and McLachlan & Erasmus (1983, particularly in McLachlan, 1983).

It is important to realize that most studies of beach tidal flat ecology have been carried out during low tide. However, the differences that come with the flood should not be forgotten. Some aquatic predators migrate with the flood-and-ebb rhythm; they feed on the flats during high tide and retreat to the channels at ebb. Such species will be missed in surveys during low tide. Similarly, species occurring in the top sediment layers at high tide may retreat to much deeper layers at low tide (Vader, 1964).

Beaches and tidal flats are important to people for many reasons. Beaches have a large amenity value, but also play a part in coastal protection. Tidal flats can be very important as nurseries for species of fish and crustaceans (Zijlstra, 1972), but also support their own fisheries for shellfish and invertebrates for bait. Tidal flats also have a high conservation value because they serve as feeding grounds for millions of shorebirds (Smit, 1980). Notwithstanding these values, tidal flats and, to a lesser extent, beaches are threatened in many areas by over-exploitation, pollution, and embankment for land reclamation.

Mapping

Mapping of the biological features of beaches and tidal flats is in many ways comparable to salt-marsh mapping (Chapter 3). In some cases Ordnance Survey maps or nautical charts may be used as base maps, but the representation of intertidal areas on charts is often inaccurate, out of date, or both. For example, the latest (1978) edition of the Danish chart of the Horns Rev area still shows the intertidal topography of 1911 for the Wadden Sea. In some countries (e.g., Federal Republic of Germany, The Netherlands) government agencies have detailed and up-to-date bathymetric maps of all coastal waters, including intertidal areas, which are suitable as base maps. If no suitable base map can be obtained, one must make such a map before the biological survey.

Some biological features (e.g., mussel beds, seagrass beds) may be mapped from aerial photographs (see Chapter 2). Other features have to be mapped in the field. The mapping of large areas of intertidal sediment is facilitated by the use of grids or regularly spaced transects; for example, Wolff & de Wolf (1977) mapped the tidal flats of the Grevelingen estuary using transects 200 m apart. Along each transect, samples were taken at 200 m intervals, and in between sampling stations any conspicuous changes in the visible benthos were recorded. The data were used to prepare species distribution maps and the results were synthesized in maps of the major benthic communities (Fig. 4.1). Such maps are liable to bias, however, because information is more readily available for species easily recognizable at the surface, e.g., *Zostera* or *Arenicola*, than for those living in the sediment without signs at the surface.

Qualitative surveys

Qualitative biological surveys essentially record the presence or absence of species. The simplest approach is to visit the coast at regular distances and to note down what may be observed at each locality. Without taking samples to be sorted in the laboratory this procedure gives information on the distribution of only a limited number of species with conspicuous features at the surface of the sediment, e.g., *Arenicola marina* (casts), *Heteromastus filiformis* (casts), *Lanice conchilega* (tubes), *Carcinus maenas*, *Cerastoderma edule*, *Mytilus edulis*, *Littorina littorea*, and species of *Zostera*. Results may be presented as distribution maps, examples of which are given in Fig. 4.2. If samples are taken to find what infauna

Fig. 4.1. Distribution of intertidal communities in the Grevelingen estuary, The Netherlands. (1) salt marshes; (2) *Corophium* community; (3) *Scoloplos* community; (4) *Mya* community; (5) Soft muds; (6) mussel beds; (7) seagrass (*Zostera*) beds; (8) *Scolelepis* community; (9) shell ridges; (?) not investigated. After Wolff & De Wolf (1977).

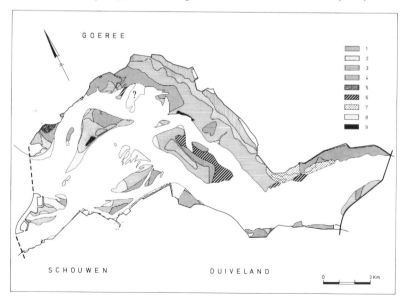

species are present, particular attention should be paid to sample size – see Chapter 1 and McIntyre, Elliott & Ellis (1984) on species – area relationships.

Qualitative procedures may be standardised by using checklists of all expected and macroscopically recognizable biota in the area. These may take the form of field cards as devised by the UK South West Marine

Fig. 4.2. Distribution of *Orchestia gammarella* and *O. cavimana* (Amphipoda) in the estuarine area of the rivers Rhine, Meuse, and Scheldt, The Netherlands. Dots, tidal locations; triangles, non-tidal locations. After den Hartog (1963).

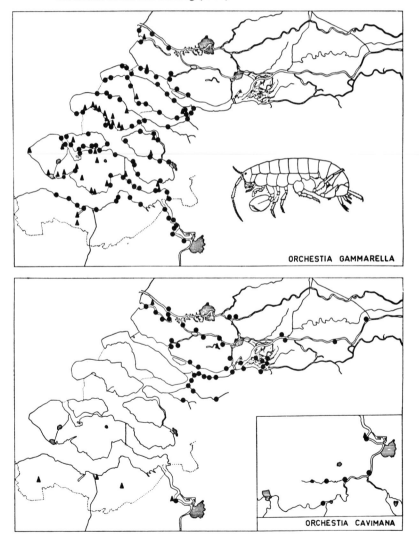

ORCHESTIA GAMMARELLA

ORCHESTIA CAVIMANA

Biology Study Group (Holme & Nichols, 1980). The rationale behind the compilation of field cards has been outlined in Chapter 8. The principal difficulty arises from the specific identification of the infauna, and co-ordinators of surveys of particulate shores must expect less in the way of fauna lists than will normally be returned on rocky shore cards. The sandy shore card is illustrated in Fig. 4.3. The number of cards used on any particular shore is entered along with the part of the shore that the card refers to. This underlines the fact that a particular shore may have conspicuously different areas, due to local sedimentary conditions, and a single card for an extensive shore may be wholly inappropriate.

Then the card seeks information on the dominant and secondary types of sediment present. Other physical details requested are slope, wave exposure, surface details such as ripples and sand banks, consistency, depth of black layer beneath the surface, and drainage.

Surface evidence of animal and plant life is assessed in four sections, one for surface-living organisms such as algae and mussels, one for lugworm activity, one for holes into sub-surface burrows, and one for tubes. A section follows on burrowing animals, identified to major group only; and then there is a section on drift material left behind on the shore. The last three sections are similar to those of the rocky shore card, namely, activity that may have an effect on the shore, such as feeding birds, digging for bait, fishing, collecting cockles or clams, field studies or recreation, and a subjective assessment of species richness and number of individuals. As

Fig. 4.3. Sandy shore field card, from Holme & Nichols (1980).

serial no. S	SANDY Shore Field Card S. W. Marine Biology Study Group	Coastal Area:
Date: .... / .... / .... Time: .... to .... Time of L.T.: .... hrs Predicted tide ht.: .... m at: .... Distance HW to LW: .... m	Observer: .... Pollution (if any):	Locality: Grid Ref.: ☐ ☐ Designation: Access:

Coast: cliff ☐ 1 low ☐ 2 dunes ☐ 3 estuary/inlet ☐ 4 ....

Cards; total no.	whole shore ☐ 5 upper ☐ 6 mid ☐ 7 lower ☐ 8 low-tide flat ☐ 9 ....
1. Dominant type	pebbles ☐ 10 granules ☐ 11 sand ☐ 12 silt & clay ☐ 13 | comparator ☐ 14 calcareous ☐ 15 ....
2. Secondary ftrs.	reefs ☐ 16 boulders ☐ 17 cobbles ☐ 18 pebbles ☐ 19 granules ☐ 20 sand ☐ 21 silt & clay ☐ 22 ....
3. Slope	moderate ☐ 23 gentle ☐ 24 flat ☐ 25 irregular ☐ 26 ....
4. Wave exposure	v. exp. ☐ 27 exp. ☐ 28 shelt. ☐ 29 v. shelt. ☐ 30 ....
5. Detail	ripples ☐ 31 sand waves ☐ 32 banks ☐ 33 wave/current disturbed ☐ 34 none ☐ 35 ....
6. Consistency	firm ☐ 36 shallow sink ☐ 37 deep sink ☐ 38 mobile ☐ 39 powder ☐ 40 ....
7. Black layer	under 2 cm. ☐ 41 2-10 cm. ☐ 42 over 10 cm. ☐ 43 indistinct grey ☐ 44 absent ☐ 45 ....
8. Drainage	good ☐ 46 standing water ☐ 47 pools ☐ 48 S. W. stream ☐ 49 F. W. stream ☐ 50 ....
9. Surface life	algae ☐ 51 eel grass ☐ 52 mussels ☐ 53 other ☐ 54 ....
10. Lugworm casts	plentiful ☐ 55 scattered ☐ 56 local ☐ 57 scarce ☐ 58 absent ☐ 59 ....
11. Holes	over 10 mm. ☐ 60 3-10 mm. ☐ 61 under 3 mm. ☐ 62 | plentiful ☐ 63 scat. ☐ 64 scarce ☐ 65 absent ☐ 66 ....
12. Tubes	sand ☐ 67 shell ☐ 68 mud ☐ 69 other ☐ 70 | large ☐ 71 small ☐ 72 detached ☐ 73 ....
13. Burrowers	anemones ☐ 74 worms ☐ 75 crustacea ☐ 76 bivalves ☐ 77 urchins ☐ 78 sand eels ☐ 79 ....
14. Drift	mollusc shells ☐ 80 crab shells ☐ 81 egg cases ☐ 82 algae ☐ 83 eel grass ☐ 84 ....
15. Activity	birds ☐ 85 bait ☐ 86 fishing ☐ 87 food collection ☐ 88 field studies ☐ 89 recreation ☐ 90 ....
16. Numbers spp.	plants: high ☐ 91 med. ☐ 92 low ☐ 93 | animals: high ☐ 94 med. ☐ 95 low ☐ 96 ....
17. Numbers indivs.	plants: high ☐ 97 med. ☐ 98 low ☐ 99 nil ☐ 100 | animals: high ☐ 101 med. ☐ 102 low ☐ 103 nil ☐ 104 ....

1978S

Fig. 4.4. Photographs of sampling stations in the German Wadden Sea. Courtesy Dr. H. Michaelis, Norderney.

with the rocky shore card, a detailed instruction sheet accompanies the card.

Any survey should be accompanied by photographs of the sites studied (Fig. 4.4), especially for reference purposes during the analysis of the data.

The results of qualitative surveys of intertidal sediments described so far are likely to be biased. The data must be influenced by the observers' interpretation of the area being sampled; transition zones are unlikely to be recognized and sampled, some species will almost certainly be under-sampled or even missed completely depending on the observers' experience, and the fauna and flora will appear to be more discontinuous than in reality. Nevertheless, qualitative surveys may be useful for primary surveys and for planning subsequent quantitative sampling more effectively (McGrorty, 1973).

Several of these problems can be remedied by a systematic sampling scheme, which is appropriate when the aims of the survey are concerned with identifying the species composition of an area and detecting the pattern of species distributions. The ideal arrangement of sample sites on a relatively undifferentiated area like a large tidal flat is a rectangular grid with equidistant spacing in both directions. The size of the grid should be based in the first place on the number of samples that can be processed in the time available (McGrorty, 1973).

Quantitative surveys

Sampling strategies

In quantitative biological surveys the major aim is to estimate the numbers of one or more species or another parameter (e.g., biomass) per unit area from a series of samples taken from the populations within a defined area. Important problems encountered are the often heterogeneous nature of tidal flats and beaches and the usually aggregated distribution patterns of benthic organisms.

The heterogeneity of tidal flats and beaches can be tackled by using stratified sampling schemes. The heterogeneous area to be investigated is divided into homogeneous sub-areas, and each sub-area is investigated using an adequate number of samples. Aerial photography (see Chapter 2) greatly facilitates the division into sub-areas.

Most benthic organisms show aggregated distribution patterns. An appropriate sampling scheme involves random distribution of the samples in an area or sub-area and a large number of samples. Because of the applicability of the central-limit theorem at sample numbers over 30, Elliott (1977) advises at least 30 and if possible more than 50 randomly placed samples in an area. This allows the calculation of a mean value within reasonably close confidence limits for species with an aggregated distribution pattern. For species with a Poisson type of distribution (*Arenicola marina* and *Macoma balthica* often show this type) a smaller number of samples may be used. For further information see Chapter 1 of this book, Elliott (1977), and McIntyre *et al.* (1984).

There are many ways of achieving randomly located samples, but the following has been tried and has worked successfully on many intertidal flats (McGrorty, 1973). The largest scale map of the area to be sampled should be chosen and divided into the smallest possible grid (e.g., overlaid with millimetre graph paper). Each grid line is numbered. Pairs of numbers are taken from random number tables to give co-ordinates that locate the sampling stations on the map by pinpricks through the overlay. The stations are located on the ground by pacing the distance along a compass bearing from a recognizable landmark (see p. 100). If the procedure is rigidly followed, the sample stations will have been randomly selected.

Beukema (1976) in a survey of the Dutch Wadden Sea grouped the stations for his sampling scheme in randomly chosen transects, thus reducing transport problems.

When a large number of samples is required, the smallest acceptable sample size (see Chapter 1) is advantageous to reduce the amount of labour involved in sample processing. Since densities of different species of benthic organisms (e.g., *Arenicola* and *Hydrobia*) differ widely (often by a factor of 1000 or more), different sample sizes may save labour. Large, relatively rare, deep-living species may be sampled with a large-size sampler, whereas small, abundant, surface-living species may be investigated with small samplers. Separate large and small samples are to be preferred over sub-samples from large samples, since sub-sampling tends to introduce extra variance.

Intertidal benthic organisms show a distinct seasonality in temperate and colder climates. Generally numbers are larger and weights are heavier during summer. For this reason annual surveys that have to be compared should be made at the same time of the year. In planning surveys it should be realised that the highest abundance of many benthic species occurs after the breeding season, i.e., in summer. Summer samples, therefore, may have statistical advantages because of the large numbers of specimens, but practical disadvantages because of the sorting time required.

Microflora
Bacteria and fungi are dealt with in Chapter 10.

Strategies for microalgae

Microalgae are usually present in large numbers on mud and sand flats, but their true abundance is very difficult to judge in the field and nearly always requires more detailed, usually laboratory-based, analysis. The main associations of benthic microalgae can be recognised by the micro-habitat in which they occur. They are best considered in two groups. First there are the algae that are attached to relatively immobile substrata; examples are the microalgae growing attached to macroalgae and higher plants. The second group, of greater importance on sand and mud flats, are the microalgae that live on soft or mobile inorganic substrata. In this second group two main categories can be recognised: the epipelic microalgae which are mobile and free living on the sediments and the epipsammic microalgae which grow attached to sand grains. In any area where the substratum is muddy, epipelic microalgae predominate; their motility makes them well adapted to life in such habitats and they often exhibit rhythmic vertical migrations in phase with the tidal cycle (rhythms that may remain for some days under laboratory conditions, when the tidal cycle is removed). In sandy areas epipelic/epipsammic ratios may vary considerably even at one locality during the year (Cadée & Hegeman, 1974).

The predominant microalgae living on soft sediments are almost invariably pennate diatoms and the only others likely to be found in large numbers are blue-green algae and certain euglenoid flagellates. In most surveys it is unlikely that time will be spent on identifying individual species, as these are numerous and there are many unresolved taxonomic problems. However, even if only the major groups of algae are recognised, the results may be of ecological significance; for example, blue-green algae are generally rare on many mud flats but may be abundant in areas of pollution.

Benthic microalgae have been neglected in the past and methods need further testing. Some of the main problems result from heterogeneity associated with sediment characteristics, and variability with time. The propagation time of some species may be as short as a few hours under ideal conditions. Sampling needs to be more comprehensive than is usually necessary for phytoplankton, but a 'one-off' survey, however intensively carried out, is of limited value. A useful compromise is to confine sampling to a series of permanent quadrats placed in areas representing different microhabitats or zones. They may only need to be about 1 m² but should, as far as possible, only cover areas uniform in appearance. Intensive sampling on a randomized basis and at regular time intervals can then be carried out within these quadrats. The methods for estimation of microalgal populations clearly depend on the aims of the survey, and a useful guide is given by Round & Hickman (1984). Van den Hoek *et al.* (1979) discuss various approaches to estimating phytobenthos biomass and productivity in the Wadden Sea area, whereas Planti-Cuny (1978) gives an extensive review of methods used by many authors. Species identification is discussed in Chapter 14.

Any sampling scheme must be preceded by tests to estimate the number of samples required for the desired level of accuracy. Most observations of microalgae are concerned with generations, or change in abundance of 100%; therefore an accuracy of $\pm 50\%$ is usually quite adequate (Lund, Kipling & le Cren, 1958). There are two main approaches for estimating populations: direct counts, and chemical extraction of the photosynthetic pigments from the sediments followed by their estimation. Neither approach is the one method appropriate for all circumstances. Counting enables species abundance to be estimated and permits size of a population and its growth to be followed in terms of division rate, where that is applicable. However, since cell sizes vary widely in populations of microbenthic algae and since chlorophyll content per cell is related to the light intensity under which growth has occurred, cell number does not provide a good basis on which to standardise results of productivity or photosynthesis determinations. In these latter cases the chlorophyll density of the microbenthic population is a better measure; moreover, chemical methods of estimating populations have the advantage that measurements can be made on relatively large samples, thus avoiding some of the small-scale variability in any community. However, sample separation from the sediment may lead to gross underestimation, and extraction straight from the sediment is likely to lead to contamination. Counting techniques need not be too arduous and can have several advantages (Lund *et al.*, 1958), including the reduction in errors due to extraneous matter and the information gained on the species composition of the algal populations.

Further considerations are that the lens tissue technique mentioned below has been found to recover up to about 90% of the microbenthic algal population, but percentage recovery depends on the vertical migration behaviour of the cells, which in turn is related to both presence of light and to the tidal cycle. Thus if it is wished to compare different sites, sampling must be standardised with regard to duration and time relative to tidal cycle. By contrast, the chlorophyll extraction techniques is carried out on a core of sediment as deep as the operator wishes to take and so is independent of the migratory behaviour of the cells.

At least the migration of cells for the lens tissue techniques ensures that, in general, only living cells are counted while, depending on the precise details of the pigment extraction techniques used, this latter method may include greater or lesser amounts of chlorophyll-breakdown products, which may be abundant in dead cells and plant detritus. There is also dispute about extraction technique details, since different solvents may modify slightly the absorption properties of the extracted pigments. In general, replicate cores give wide variation in pigment amounts estimated so that in sampling a population it is necessary to take several cores and find the mean value.

Separation and counting

Methods for estimating populations of benthic microalgae are more difficult than those for phytoplankton due to the presence of sediment, and many methods involve separating the algae. Epipsammic algae can be separated by shaking the sand in filtered water, decanting the detrital material and epipelic algae, and then separating the algae from the sand by ultrasonic vibration. Epipelic algae can be separated by placing a coverslip or a piece of lens tissue on the surface of the sediment. The algae migrate onto these and can be lifted off (Eaton & Moss, 1966). De Jonge (1979) developed a method to separate living microalgae from dead material by centrifugation over a density gradient. If such methods are used, preliminary tests must be carried out to find their efficiency.

The following procedure (S. Eden, personal communication) is a guide to a simple counting method with a minimum of specialised apparatus, suitable for estimating the populations of epipelic microalgae on muddy substrata. Processing can be carried out in the field, but it is easier if cores of mud are brought back to the laboratory. The cores should be kept cool and under conditions of natural lighting until they can be processed. The cores should be exposed to light for 1–2 hours before sampling, to allow the algae to migrate to the surface of the sediment (a colour change is usually visible); the sampling time should correspond to the timing of low tide from the area in which they were collected. The surface sediment with the algae is then removed from a small known surface area (such an area can be easily marked out using an open-ended box made of coverslips joined together). The sediment and algae are scraped off the area to a depth of about 1.5 mm using a coverslip.

This method has the advantage of removing as many algae as possible but as little sediment as possible. The sediment and algae are then made up in a known volume of liquid, of sufficient volume to allow the algae to be clearly visible in a counting chamber (usually some form of haemocytometer). Lugol's iodine provides a suitable temporary preservative. (It is made up of 10 g pure iodine, 20 g KI, 200 ml distilled water, and

20 g glacial acetic acid added a few days prior to using; it should be stored in dark glass bottles.) If a more permanent preservative is required, a few drops of formalin can be added. A useful additive is a few drops of 1% rose bengal; this stain makes the algae more readily visible among the sediment. Dispersion of the sediment in the liquid is helped by adding small (2-mm diameter) glass beads to the mixture before shaking. A double-celled modified Fuchs Rosenthal haemocytometer is a suitable haemocytometer, but one with a metallised chamber is essential, as the sediment can otherwise mask the lines.

Pigment extraction and estimation
One pigment extraction approach that has been found successful is described below. It is important to realize, however, that other approaches may give different readings and the method may play as great a part as any underlying biological phenomenon in explaining different values from pigment estimations by different authors.

Individual core samples are taken to obtain sediment that can be ground and extracted. These core samples need not be large, although they will need much replication. Simple core samplers can be made from 10-ml disposable plastic syringes. The end of the syringe to which the needle is normally attached is sawn off with a hacksaw to give a plastic cylinder open at one end, but with the plunger in the other end. To take a sample, the open end is pushed into the sediment to the desired depth, using the plunger to avoid trapping air over the sediment. The open end of the corer can then be sealed with a microbiological test-tube cap and on return to the laboratory the complete sampler containing the core sample can be deep frozen until required for extraction.

Many such cores may be needed to characterise microbenthic chlorophyll levels of a particular locality or habitat. One technique (M. Wilkinson, personal communication) is to divide the shore to be sampled into a number of transect lines. Stations are then established corresponding approximately to mean high water neap, mid tide, and mean low water neap levels. At each station on each transect a minimum of nine core samples is taken, within a 25 cm × 25 cm quadrat. The minimum of nine cores was found to be statistically acceptable for some studies on British estuarine tidal flats (M. Wilkinson, personal communication). The detailed placing of the quadrat and the selection of the core sites should be random except that care must be taken to avoid interfering factors such as *Vaucheria* mats (which may be embedded in the sediment), other macro-algae, and atypical areas such as standing water. Experience indicates that a large difference may not necessarily be found between areas of sediment coloured by microbenthic algae at the surface and those areas not so coloured.

When extraction is to be carried out, the frozen core is allowed to thaw for up to 30 minutes. The still rigid core is pushed out of the core sampler and a portion of it is cut off with a sharp knife. It is usual to work with either the top 0.5 cm or top 1.0 cm of the core. This part of the core, which corresponds to a known surface area of sediment related to the internal diameter of the corer, is then ground up for 3 minutes using a mortar and pestle with 5 ml of 90% acetone neutralized with magnesium carbonate. The extract is decanted into a graduated glass centrifuge tube fitted with a ground glass stopper. The solvent volume is made up to exactly 10 ml with rinsings from the mortar and the tube is then stoppered. The tube is allowed to stand overnight in the dark in a refrigerator or cold room to complete the extraction. After standing, it is shaken and centrifuged at 3000 rpm for 5 minutes in a bench centrifuge. The absorption of the supernatant is read in a spectrophotometer at certain wavelengths. The wavelengths used depend on the particular equations being employed to calculate the chlorophyll level. In the case described here equations of Lorenzen (1967) are used requiring measurements at wavelengths of 665 and 750 nm. After the absorption has been read the extract is acidified with 2 drops of 1 M hydrochloric acid and the absorption read again at the same two wavelengths.

Measurement before and after acidification allows correction to be made for absorption by pheopigments so that 'active' chlorophyll can be distinguished from that in detrital plant material. The measurement at 750 nm is a turbidity blank and is subtracted from the corresponding reading at 665 nm so that the latter more truly represents absorption by pigments.

The following equations are applied:

$$\frac{\text{chlorophyll } a}{\text{(in mg m}^{-2})} = \frac{26.7\ (665_0 - 665_A) \cdot 10V}{s \cdot l}$$

$$\frac{\text{pheopigments}}{\text{(in mg m}^{-2})} = \frac{26.7\ [1.7\ (665_A) - 665_0] \cdot 10V}{s \cdot l}$$

where 665_0 is the absorption at 665 nm before acidification minus that at 750 nm

665_A is the absorption at 665 nm after acidification minus that at 750 nm

V is the volume of extractant used (in ml)

s is the surface area of sediment sampled

l is the path length of the spectrophotometer cells used (in cm)

It is stressed that only one possible method has been described above. Other solvents may be used, e.g., methanol; other equations may be used; fluorimetric rather than spectrophotometric determinations may be carried out. Accessory pigments such as chlorophylls b and c and carotenes may be estimated and might possibly be used to distinguish particular abundances of those algal groups which contain large amounts of these particular pigments. Further information on these other methods can be found in Strickland & Parsons (1972); Morris (1983); and Parsons, Maita & Lalli (1984). The reader should be warned that almost all handbooks describing pigment estimation methods for marine microalgae deal with phytoplankton and it is necessary to make slight arithmetical changes to the formulae presented to convert from water volume sampled to sediment surface area.

It is beyond the scope of this book to discuss the measurement of marine primary productivity. It may however be a useful measure of a microbenthic algal community to estimate its rate of photosynthesis, either *in situ* in the field or as potential production under standardised incubation conditions in the laboratory. This can be done by measurements of oxygen exchange or of ^{14}C uptake. Further information can be found in UNESCO (1973) and Morris (1983).

Macroflora
Seagrasses

Seagrasses occur in widely varying densities on European tidal flats. Usually only one or two species of *Zostera* occur, but in brackish situations *Ruppia* and even *Potamogeton* may be found. Dense intertidal seagrass beds can be surveyed using aerial photography as described in Chapter 2, but more scattered plants should be treated as outlined in the sections on sampling strategy (p. 87) and macrofauna (p. 95), since such occurrences tend to be overlooked on photographs.

Biomass samples can be taken either using corers or by removing all plant material within a square or circular frame of suitable size, e.g., 0.25 m². Above- and below-ground biomass can usefully be determined separately. Cover can be determined within sample plots using point quadrats; in some cases it has been useful to photograph plots and subsequently estimate cover using grids of points on the photographs (J. Baker, personal communication).

Further information can be obtained from Phillips & McRoy (1980).

Macroalgae

The distribution of macroalgae is very variable. They may be absent from large areas and may form dense extensive beds in others. Their initial growth usually depends on some form of relatively firm substratum, but in sheltered areas drift algae can collect and continue growing as loose mats lying on the sediments or suspended as masses of algae transported to and fro by the tidal currents. The most abundant species are generally members of the Chlorophyceae (e.g., *Ulva* and *Enteromorpha* spp.), which are fast-growing ephemeral species. The sections on sampling strategy (p. 87) and macrofauna sampling (below), and some of the rocky shore methods described in Chapter 8 are applicable to the algae of intertidal flats, but precautions are necessary when interpreting the results. Populations of such fast-growing ephemeral species can fluctuate very rapidly and whole populations of even attached plants can be removed by a single storm. These rapid changes emphasise the need for repeated sampling. Even then it is difficult to predict future yields in the same area because the nature of the substratum can change. If gross changes in distribution of beds of algae over large areas are to be measured, it is worth considering aerial photography, as described in Chapter 2.

Identification to genera of the seaweeds on intertidal flats is fairly easy, but nevertheless requires microscopical examination, as several species may occur together as dense wefts of fine filaments. Difficulties beyond the generic level arise because many of the groups have not yet been investigated thoroughly and there are no up-to-date floras, although this latter difficulty should diminish over the next few years. Available literature is detailed in Chapter 14.

Macrofauna

Macrofauna is usually defined as all invertebrate animals retained by a sieve with a mesh size of 0.5 or 1.0 mm. This boundary of 0.5–1.0 mm is used mainly for practical reasons, since macrofauna on the one hand and meio- and microfauna on the other hand have to be studied by different methods. The exact position of this boundary derives mainly from the particle size distribution of coastal and estuarine sediments, since macrofauna samples are usually sieved using a mesh size that is passed by most of the sediment and retains a major part of the fauna.

The choice of sampling method(s) should be determined by the aims of the survey, the sediment composition, and the financial resources (including the amount of time available), hence there exists no standard method for all macrofauna surveys.

Some species may be sampled by visual inspection; for example, lugworm densities may be obtained from counts of casts within random quadrats. Such non-destructive sampling is particularly useful for long-term surveillance, however, de Wilde & Berghuis (1979) show that considerable underestimation may result because not all animals are active all the time.

If destructive sampling is appropriate for the project, estimates of densities and biomass may be obtained by driving a square sheet-metal (steel) frame of, for example, 0.1 or 0.25 m² into the sediment to a depth of about 30 cm. The contents can be dug out with a spade (Warwick, 1983; Eleftheriou & Holme, 1984). However, the use of a spade may result in relatively many damaged specimens, especially for the larger species.

Cylindrical corers are also widely used (Fig. 4.5). These can be made from various materials, e.g., Perspex, PVC, or stainless steel, and commonly have a cross-sectional area of 0.01–0.02 m². Grange & Anderson (1976) used a corer with an area of 0.1 m². Corers are open at the bottom end and the lower edge may be sharpened. In small corers (0.0005–0.001 m²) used in moist sediment, the top end may be open as well. In larger corers and especially in those used in relatively wet sediments, the top end has to be closed, e.g., with a rubber bung. For convenience of handling, the length of the corer should be about 1 m. It is also helpful to have a centimetre or decimetre scale on the outside of the corer with the zero value at the lower edge.

Fig. 4.5. Macrofauna sampling apparatus in use by the Netherlands Research Institute for Nature Management.

The corer is pushed vertically into the sediment with the top open. When the required depth in the sediment is reached, the top is closed and the corer is pulled out. In some sediments and with large corers this may be difficult, and the corer should be dug out with a spade or a fork. Usually, the sediment core will remain in the corer until the top is opened, but very wet sediments and very dry sands tend to run out. In these cases the corer may be held horizontally once it is free from the sediment, although this disturbs the layering of the core.

Coring depth in the sediment may vary according to the survey requirements. It should be at least 40 cm if it is wished to obtain the few, but large deep-living bivalves and polychaetes. Otherwise, 20–25 cm will be sufficient for most species and 10 cm may be adequate if one is interested only in shallow living species, such as cockles and small polychaetes. The most suitable sampling depth may be established in a small pilot investigation.

The type of sampling described in the preceding paragraphs is best done by two or three persons. 'Wet' and 'dry' jobs should be separated; e.g., one person uses the corer and does the sieving (see Chapter 6) whereas

Fig. 4.6. Mode of operation of the flushing sampler designed by van Arkel & Mulder (1975). The sampler is pushed into the sediment whilst a small inboard pump flushes a sediment and water mixture into a collecting bag mounted halfway.

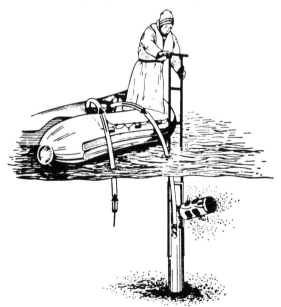

another one determines the position (see below), does the writing, and takes photographs.

The methods described so far are designed for work on the shore at low tide. If the tidal range is sufficiently large, samples can also be taken from ships during high tide by the methods described in Chapter 5 and by Eleftheriou & Holme (1984) and Warwick (1983). Van Arkel & Mulder (1975; see also Mulder & van Arkel, 1980) developed a suction sampler for tidal flats that can be operated from a small boat at high tide and they used it successfully in the Ems estuary with a tidal range of about 3 m (Fig. 4.6). Muus (1967) developed a small hand-operated grab to be used from a boat in Danish lagoons (Fig. 4.7). A drawback common to all equipment to be used from a boat is that no impression is obtained of the character of the tidal flat habitat. Diver-operated suction samplers are probably relatively inefficient over large submerged flats, and any diving work is

Fig. 4.7. Hand-grab to be operated from a boat in shallow water. After Muus (1967).

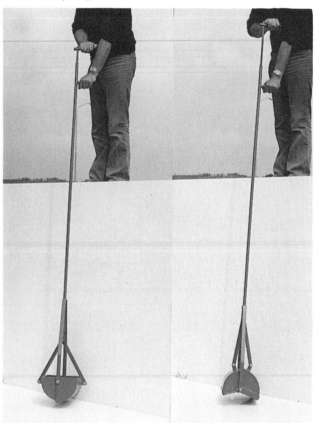

likely to be complicated by the strong tidal flows and the poor visibility in such areas.

Some habitats require modified sampling programmes. For example, animals living under flotsam and driftwood on the beach may be sampled by collecting by hand for a fixed period of time or by using pitfall traps. For specific programmes, specially designed samplers and methods may be developed, e.g., De Vlas (1982), in a survey of cockle densities, used an aluminium frame 0.1 m² with a rake or shovel (Fig. 4.8). After pushing the sediment aside, the cockles could be counted *in situ*. In combination with radio transmission of the figures to an accompanying ship this method resulted in an extremely high working speed with a minimal input of manpower.

Any sampling programme will profit from photographs taken of the sampling stations (Fig. 4.4), especially for reference purposes during the analysis of the data.

The further treatment of macrofauna is described in Chapter 6. Identification is discussed in Chapter 14.

Position fixing

If a good map is available and if an intertidal area has sufficient conspicuous features, the position of a sampling station may be fixed on

Fig. 4.8. Cockle-counting apparatus designed by Dr J. de Vlas (Research Institute for Nature Management, Texel, The Netherlands.

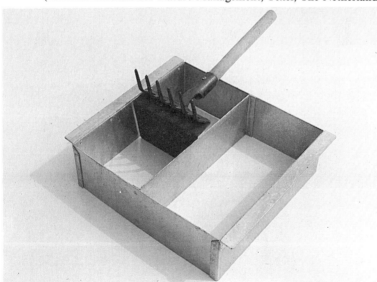

the map with little trouble. However, tidal flats are usually rather featureless and at least two compass bearings to coastal landmarks or fixed structures in the adjacent area of water are needed to determine the position of a station. Subsequent station positions may be determined in the same way, but it is also possible to rely on measuring distances along a chosen bearing for a limited number of subsequent positions. This can be done with a measuring tape, but it may be more convenient to appoint one person of the sampling party as a 'pacer'. Her or his pace is checked against a standard measure on site. The number of paces required to reach the next sampling station is calculated and the pacer proceeds along the correct compass bearing for the appropriate distance. When setting out transects, canes or piles of sediment can be placed at intervals to help keep a straight line if there is no convenient object on the horizon to line up with the first sampling station. This method of site location may appear inaccurate, but has been found to work well, even in difficult conditions. After some of the stations have been set out, the exact position should be determined again by taking compass bearings on two or more landmarks (McGrorty, 1973; Wolff & de Wolf, 1977).

If a ship with radar is available nearby this can also be employed to determine station positions. The ship should be at anchor at an exactly known position. On the shipboard radar the sampling party can be followed on the tidal flat when a suitable radar reflector is used. A metal sieve, for example, gives a conspicuous echo on the radar screen. By radio or a visual signalling code, the sampling party indicates when a sampling station is reached and this is then plotted on a map on board ship from the radar system. More information on position fixing by ships is given in Chapter 5.

If a station has to be visited more than once, a marker can be used. This can be a wooden post of 60–80 cm driven into the sediment to 40–50 cm depth. Although on sheltered flats such markers may last for years, they tend to disappear rapidly from sandy flats and beaches exposed to strong water movements. Ice on the flats is also very efficient in removing wooden posts. A better method, therefore, is the use of long iron rods (e.g., iron used for reinforcing concrete). These may be driven into the sediment to a depth of 1–2 m, with the length above the sediment about 0.5 m.

Markers should be conspicuous enough to be seen from a few hundreds of metres distance by somebody looking for them, but on the other hand should not attract attention from passers-by too easily. More than once people have been observed to dig for bait between the posts of a permanent quadrat because they expected to obtain a higher yield in such a marked place. One method of preventing this is to locate the sampling at the intersection of two lines, each marked by two or three posts. The same kinds of problems have been encountered and to some extent solved in salt marshes (Chapter 3).

Transport

Transport of people, equipment, and samples on intertidal flats often poses problems. When it is necessary to walk to the survey stations, having light weight equipment and samples leads to greater efficiency of field-work. Examples of ways to reduce weight are smaller samples, a PVC corer instead of a metal one, and polythene bags instead of glass or plastic jars.

Fig. 4.9. Traditional mud-sledge used in the border region of the Federal Republic of Germany and the Netherlands.

When distances become larger a simple hand-drawn cart (Fig. 4.5) can be useful. Because of the combined effect of salt water, sand, and mud, all moving parts should be constructed simply and robustly and be well protected. In very muddy areas some type of mud-sledge is often indispensable; Warwick (1983) recommends an old-fashioned tin bath but the traditional mud-sledges still in use in some mud flat areas may also be used (Fig. 4.9).

For very large distances mechanized transport, e.g., tractor, hovercraft, or helicopter, might be a solution. However, wheeled transport always runs the risk of getting stuck in soft sediments and subsequently being covered by the tide, whereas hovercraft and helicopters are expensive and noisy. A very different solution is transport and sampling from a boat during high tide (van Arkel & Mulder, 1975; Mulder & van Arkel, 1980).

Measurement of environmental factors

Common measurements of abiotic environment factors in intertidal field-work are those of sediment particle size distribution, salinity, level in relation to tidal levels, redox potential, organic carbon content of sediment, and temperature. Several others are measured less frequently.

Measurement of sediment particle size distribution is discussed in Chapter 5; see also Dyer (1979). Chemical methods are detailed in Head (1985).

Methods to determine heights and levels in relation to tidal levels are discussed in Chapter 3.

Wave exposure is not easily measured, but may be inferred from local topography (e.g., the amount of open sea around a locality; P. G. Baardseth, personal communication), sediment composition, and the biota of nearby rocky shores (see Chapter 8).

Acknowledgements

This chapter has been partly based on written contributions by Drs B. E. Barnett, S. M. Eden, S. McGrorty, N. A. Holme, D. Nichols, and M. Wilkinson. Many other people have read and criticized the various drafts of the manuscript. The help of all of them is gratefully acknowledged; any fault in the interpretation of their contributions is entirely the responsibility of the final author.

References

Arkel, M. A. van & Mulder, M. (1975). A device for quantitative sampling of benthic organisms in shallow water by means of a flushing technique. *Neth. J. Sea Res.* **9**, 365–70.

Barnes, R. S. K. (1977). *The Coastline.* Chichester: Wiley.

Beukema, J. J. (1976). Biomass and species richness of the macro-benthic animals living on the tidal flats of the Dutch Wadden Sea. *Neth. J. Sea Res.* **10**, 236–61.

Cadée, G. C. & Hegeman, J. (1974). Primary production of the benthic microflora living on tidal flats in the Dutch Wadden Sea. *Neth. J. Sea Res.* **8**, 260–91.

Day, J. H. (1981). *Estuarine Ecology, with Particular Reference to Southern Africa.* Rotterdam: Balkema.

Dyer, K. R. (ed.) (1979). *Estuarine Hydrography and Sedimentation.* Cambridge University Press.

Eaton, J. W. & Moss, B. (1966). The estimation of numbers and pigment content in epipelic algal populations. *Limnol. Oceanogr.* **11**, 584–95.

Eleftheriou, A. & Holme, N. A. (1984). Macrofauna techniques. In *Methods for the Study of Marine Benthos*, 2nd edn, ed. N. A. Holme & A. D. McIntyre, pp. 140–216. Oxford: Blackwell.

Elliott, J. M. (1977). *Some Methods for the Statistical Analysis of Samples of Benthic Invertebrates.* Scientific Publication 25. Ambleside: Freshwater Biological Association.

Grange, K. R. & Anderson, P. W. A soft-sediment sampler for the collection of biological specimens. *Rec. N.Z. Oceanogr. Inst.* **3**, 9–13.

Hartog, C. den (1963). The amphipods of the Deltaic region of the rivers Rhine, Meuse, and Scheldt in relation to the hydrography of the area. II. The Talitridae. *Neth. J. Sea Res.* **2**, 40–67.

Head, P. C. (ed.) (1985). *Practical Estuarine Chemistry.* Cambridge University Press.

Hoek, C. van den, Admiraal, W., Colijn F. & Jonge, V. N. de (1979). The role of algae and seagrasses in the ecosystem of the Wadden Sea: a review. In *Flora and Vegetation of the Wadden Sea*, ed. W. J. Wolff, pp. 9–118. Rotterdam: Balkema.

Holme, N. A. & Nichols, D. (1980). *Habitat Survey Cards for the Shores of the British Isles.* Occasional Publication No. 2. London: Field Studies Council.

Jonge, V. N. de (1979). Quantitative separation of benthic diatoms from sediments using density gradient centrifugation in the colloidal silica Ludox – TM. *Mar. Biol.* **51**, 267–78.

Lorenzen, C. J. (1967). Determination of chlorophyll and phaeopigments: spectrophotometric equations. *Limnol. Oceanogr.* **12**, 343–6.

Lund, J. W. G., Kipling, C. & le Cren, E. D. (1958). The inverted microscope method of estimating algal numbers and the statistical basis of estimations by counting. *Hydrobiologia*, **11**, 143–70.

McGrorty, S. (1973). A guide to the sampling of intertidal flat macro-invertebrate faunas. *Coastal Ecology Research Paper* 6. Colney, Norfolk: Institute of Terrestrial Ecology.

McIntyre, A. D., Elliott, J. M. & Ellis, D. V. (1984). Introduction: design of sampling programmes. In *Methods for the Study of Marine Benthos*, 2nd edn, ed. N. A. Holme & A. D. McIntyre, pp. 1–26. Oxford: Blackwell.

McLachlan, A. (1983). Sandy beach ecology. A review. In *Sandy Beaches as Ecosystems*, A. McLachlan & T. Erasmus, pp. 321–80. the Hague: Junk.

McLachlan, A. & Erasmus, T. (1983). *Sandy Beaches as Ecosystems*. The Hague: Junk.

Morris, A. W. (ed.) (1983). *Practical Procedures for Estuarine Studies*. Plymouth: Institute for Marine Environmental Research.

Mulder, M. & Arkel, M. A. van (1980). An improved system for quantitative sampling of benthos in shallow water using the flushing technique. *Neth. J. Sea Res.* **14**, 119–22.

Muus, B. J. (1967). The fauna of Danish estuaries and lagoons. Distribution and ecology of dominating species in the shallow reaches of the mesohaline zone. *Medd. Danmarks Fisk. Havundersog. N.S.* **5**(1), 1–316.

Parsons, T. R., Maita, Y. & Lalli, C. M. (1984). *A Manual of Chemical and Biological Methods for Seawater Analysis*. Oxford & New York: Pergamon Press.

Perkins, E. J. (1974). *The Biology of Estuaries and Coastal Waters*. London: Academic Press.

Phillips, R. C. & McRoy C. P. (1980). *Handbook of Seagrass Biology, an Ecosystem Perspective*. New York: Garland.

Planti-Cuny, M. R. (1978). Pigments photosynthetiques et production primaire des fonds meubles neritiques d'une region tropicale (Nosy Be, Madagascar). *Trav. Doc. O.R.S.T.O.M.* **96**, 1–359.

Round, F. E. & Hickman, M. (1984). Phytobenthos sampling and estimation of primary production. In *Methods for the Study of Marine Benthos*, 2nd edn, ed. N. A. Holme & A. D. McIntyre, pp. 245–83. Oxford: Blackwell.

Smit, C. J. (1980). The importance of the Wadden Sea for estuarine birds. In *Birds of the Wadden Sea*, ed. C. J. Smit & W. J. Wolff, pp. 280–9. Rotterdam: Balkema.

Strickland, J. D. H. & Parsons, T. R. (1972). *A Practical Handbook of Seawater Analysis*. Fisheries Research Board of Canada Bulletin 167, 2nd edn. Ottawa.

UNESCO (1973). A guide to the measurement of marine primary production under some special conditions. *Monographs on Oceanographic Methodology* 3. Paris: UNESCO.

Vader, W. J. M. (1964). A preliminary investigation into the reactions of the infauna of the tidal flats to tidal fluctuations in water level. *Neth. J. Sea Res.* **2**, 189–222.

Vlas, J. de (1982). *De effecten van de kokkelvisserij op de bodemfauna van Waddenzee en Oosterschelde*. RIN-rapport 82/19: Texel: Research Institute for Nature Management.

Warwick, R. M. (1983). Sampling and analysis of benthic communities. In *Practical Procedures for Estuarine Studies*, ed. A. W. Morris, pp. 185–212. Plymouth: Institute for Marine Environmental Research.

Wilde, P. A. W. J. de & Berghuis, E. M. (1979). Laboratory experiments on growth of juvenile lugworms, *Arenicola marina*. *Neth. J. Sea Res.* **13**, 497–502.

Wolff, W. J. & Wolf, L. de (1977). Biomass and production of zoobenthos in the Grevelingen estuary, The Netherlands. *Estuar. Coast. Mar. Sci.* **5**, 1–24.

Zijlstra, J. J. (1972). On the importance of the Wadden Sea as a nursery area in relation to the conservation of the Southern North Sea fishery resources. In *Symposia of the Zoological Society of London*, Vol. 29, ed. R. W. Edwards & D. J. Garrod, pp. 233–258. London: Academic Press.

5

Macrofauna of subtidal sediments using remote sampling

J. P. HARTLEY and B. DICKS

Introduction

This chapter is concerned with strategies and methods for studying the abundance and distribution of benthic organisms in soft sediments, to assess both natural distributions and the effects of human influences. Emphasis has been placed on the assessment of pollution damage in view of increasing concern over the effects of discharges to the marine environment.

Many of the sampling and laboratory methods that have been employed in macrobenthic studies of soft sediments have been dealt with comprehensively elsewhere, notably in Stirn (1981) and Holme & McIntyre (1984). Wherever possible, overlap with these publications has been avoided and we have limited ourselves to techniques that work particularly well or have not been previously reported in detail. Particular attention has been given to sampling strategies and the way in which the aims of the studies influence methods.

The chapter covers soft sediments from the low-water mark to the edge of the continental shelf. Deep ocean sediments and intertidal sediments are omitted although some overlap of strategies and methods does occur, especially with the latter. Like Holme & McIntyre (1984), we deal chiefly with the macrofauna living within the sediment, i.e., the macro-infauna. There is some disagreement on the minimum size of macrofauna, but generally organisms retained by a 0.5-mm or 1.0-mm mesh screen are regarded as macrofauna. However, any size classification is arbitrary and in most studies mesh sizes are selected to suit objectives and the communities found (see Chapter 6).

Soft sediments support a wide range of community types and standing crops and have long been recognized as valuable feeding areas for commercial fish. Soft sediments also act as sinks for a variety of contaminants, especially oil, organic and inorganic particulates, and heavy metals. Many benthic organisms are effectively sessile and, with time, act as integrators of the effects of the various kinds and levels of environmental stress and of pollutants; studies of the sea-bed have proved particularly useful in monitoring or gauging pollution effects in many areas (e.g., Pearson, 1975; Addy, Levell & Hartley, 1978; Gray & Mirza, 1979; Sharp *et al.*, 1979). There may be considerable natural fluctuations in the density and distribution of organisms, and methods for study must be selected to enable such natural variation to be measured and, where necessary, differentiated from pollution-induced change.

As well as the value of macrobenthic organisms as indicators of sea-bed pollution effects, their dependence on the overlying water column for food, oxygen, and, in many cases, the early development of larvae make them useful as indicators of natural or pollution-induced change in water quality. Thus in many areas it may be inferred that if benthic communities remain largely stable or unaffected, the same is likely to be true of organisms of the water column.

Aims and objectives

The broad aims of macrobenthic surveys are likely to fall within one or more of the categories listed in Chapter 1. More specific objectives can often be expressed as simple questions, e.g.:

1. What are the main community types in an area, how are they distributed spatially, and what environmental factors influence their distribution?
2. How do they change with time?
3. What causes observed change?

However, answering these questions may not be simple and can be further complicated by additional requirements of detecting and delimiting pollution-induced effects. Many recent studies of the macrobenthos have been conducted in relation to discharges of pollutants (e.g. sewage, refinery effluent, pulp mill wastes, etc.) to determine:

1. The extent and form of biological changes caused by the operations.
2. How that situation changes with time.
3. Whether changes become sufficiently serious to be regarded as damage requiring corrective action.

Additionally, the survey results may be used to assess conservation value and the sensitivity of habitats to pollutants, and to make environmental impact predictions, as in the case of the Severn Barrage feasibility study and many recent industrial developments.

Macrobenthic studies as part of a pollution monitoring scheme are particularly useful where:

1. Contaminants naturally end up in the sediment of the area.
2. Communities are more or less uniform over the area.
3. Sediments are easily sampled and organisms quantified.

They are less useful where sediments are:

1. Highly mobile (e.g., in strong currents/wave action) and support impoverished communities or accumulate contaminants poorly.
2. Patchily distributed and thus variable in community type.
3. Difficult to sample, e.g., because of hard-packed sands or the presence of stones.

The physical nature of the site under study (water depth, range of sea conditions, and sediment type) will determine requirements for sampling vessels and sampling equipment. The nature of discharges and the volumes, dispersion, and ultimate fate of contaminants are especially relevant to the selection of sample station locations and spatial extent of sampling. Changes in pollution load or observed natural biological changes will influence the frequency of sampling, and the desired degree of sensitivity with which change may be detected will influence sample size, replication, and the selection of appropriate sieve mesh sizes. Ultimately, all are under the constraints of time, costs, and the availability of equipment and expertise – in most cases compromises must be made.

To relate cause to effect, it is important that natural variables such as sediment type, organic content, water depth, currents, salinity, temperature, and turbidity are recorded and taken into account in the interpretation of results. Equally important are chemical analyses for contaminants; these analyses should be carefully chosen in relation to the actual or expected inputs to the site. Without such information the differentiation of pollution effects from natural variation becomes very difficult.

Sampling strategies
Standardisation of methods

The importance of using standardised and adequate methods is emphasised on p. 10. In the short term, appropriate data and data treatment are essential to the early detection of pollution effects. On a longer time-scale comparable results are necessary if faunal change over a wide area is to be convincingly demonstrated; an example of this is the study indicating that eutrophication has occurred in the Baltic Sea over the past 20 years (Cederwall & Elmgren, 1980). Recommendations for standard methods for use in the Baltic Sea have been published (Dybern, Ackefors & Elmgren, 1976), and such recommendations for soft-sediment monitoring strategies in other areas are long overdue.

The International Council for Exploration of the Seas (ICES) are investigating standardisation of methods/strategies for North Sea benthic studies. Although standardisation is a desirable objective, site-to-site variation requires the retention of flexibility both in equipment and strategy.

In spite of such problems, strategies employed in many studies have been remarkably similar, and the relative merits of various published approaches will be dealt with in following sections.

With regard to the nature of the data to be collected, Moore (1971) suggested that a qualitative approach might be appropriate for pollution-monitoring studies, extrapolating from the results of a kelp holdfast study on the north-east coast of Britain. However, since chronic pollution effects are initially manifested by changes in abundance rather than extinction of species in a community, and since it requires almost as much effort to generate accurate qualitative as opposed to quantitative data from soft-bottom samples, we believe that Moore's approach is too restrictive. For these reasons we generally recommend that quantitative data be collected. In addition to the collection of data on the number of species and individuals present it is often useful to estimate the biomass of the fauna (see Chapter 6; also Dybern *et al.*, 1976; Holme & McIntyre, 1984).

Spatial distribution of sampling stations
General considerations
The distribution of samples over a survey area should be made in relation to the objectives of the programme. A primary concern is whether the survey is to define natural distribution of organisms at a site or to estimate such natural gradients in addition to the effects of pollution. Random sampling may be inappropriate where a strong natural or pollution gradient is known or suspected or where a point source discharge occurs. In such areas sampling stations are best arranged with reference to the gradient or gradients. This may be a single transect line of sample stations with the main axis along the suspected gradient, or a series of transect lines across a gradient. Where the direction of a gradient is largely unknown (or gradients are weak or absent), regular grids of stations may be preferable. If stations are arranged systematically in transect lines or grids, and a number of random replicate samples are taken at each station, then this constitutes a stratified random strategy (p. 6). This has many advantages if there is a requirement to analyse statistically the relationships between the different stations.

Where variation in sediment type is considerable, some habitat types may be badly under-sampled unless the stations on the grid are very close together. The value of a preliminary survey to determine sediment/habitat variability before planning the main survey is obvious, but a preliminary survey may be prohibitively costly in some areas, or may take too long in cases where urgent action is required (e.g., during or after oil spills). Some rapid techniques for identifying distribution of habitat types can be used on some occasions, e.g., aerial surveillance/photography in clear water to locate reefs, seagrass beds, etc. The number of stations sampled is largely a function of time and cost, but it is preferable in a first survey to over-sample, subsequently reducing numbers in the light of accumulated information rather than finding that the number of sample stations has been inadequate to provide interpretable data.

The area over which sampling is carried out may be limited by topographical constraints, but where it is necessary to delineate areas of human influence or pollution effects, it should be defined in relation to the likely direction of spread of contaminants. A useful approach is to arrange the sampling stations at increasing distances from the source so that those at the periphery of the survey area are (or may reasonably be expected to be) largely beyond the influence of pollution and therefore act as reference stations. It is then possible to define both naturally occurring and pollution-induced gradients and to distinguish natural community change from pollution effects.

The ability to define the extent of changes is related to the closeness and distribution of stations. Closely spaced stations allow precise definition of gradients or pollution effects and an estimation of rate of spatial spread by means of resurveys. Transect lines necessarily leave areas unsampled whereas grids allow the delineation of effect in any direction from a source.

In general, the greater the number of sample stations, the greater the precision in defining effects. However, a greater number of samples will increase the time required for laboratory sorting and analysis unless unlimited manpower and facilities are available. The speed with which results are required may need to be taken into account in survey planning and, subsequently, in deciding the sequence in which samples are sorted/analysed.

Examples

The following examples illustrate some approaches used in various coastal waters.

> *Milford Haven.* Studies presently underway on the soft-sediment macrobenthos of Milford Haven (D. Rostron, unpublished data) in relation to oil industry activities have employed a regular sampling grid of 135 stations (Fig. 5.1). The high number of sample stations was necessary partly as a result of strong natural gradients in wave exposure, water movements,

and salinity, which had been shown to cause considerable variation in benthic sediments and communities, and partly to identify areas of influence of oil industry activities from which more detailed monitoring schemes could be designed. In addition, previously observed distributions of hydrocarbons in Haven sediments (Dicks & Hartley, 1982) were to be further investigated.

Southampton Water. Studies in Southampton Water (Levell, 1976) described the biological communities of the estuary in relation to sediment type and major inputs of a variety of industrial and urban effluents (Fig. 5.2). Subsequently, an intensive survey grid was employed to characterise the distribution of organisms around a single refinery/petrochemical effluent discharge at Fawley.

Botany Bay. Bottom sediments were surveyed and analysed by Jones (1981) in relation to a programme of dredging and land reclamation. Three hundred fifty-two stations along series of transect lines were sampled for particle size analysis (Fig. 5.3*a*). Subsequently, to establish the effects of dredging, biological sampling was carried out by comparing fauna in dredged and undredged areas (Jones & Candy, 1981). A total of 90 stations randomly located within a stratified grid were sampled (Fig. 5.3*b*).

North Sea oilfields. In offshore oilfields, platforms may be regarded as point sources of pollution contamination or disturbance. At

Fig. 5.1 The locations of benthic sample stations in Milford Haven, 1982 (D. Rostron, unpublished data).

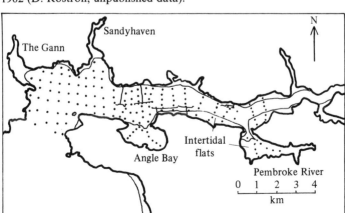

Fig. 5.2. Sample site locations in Southampton Water in 1975/76 (Levell, 1976) and an intensive grid around the discharge point of two refinery effluents (sampled in 1979, 1980, 1981, and 1982). Published with the kind permission of Esso Petroleum Co Ltd.

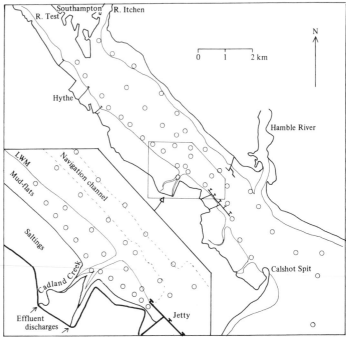

Fig. 5.3. Sea-bed sampling stations in Botany Bay. Redrawn from Jones (1981) and Jones & Candy (1981). (a) Sediment sampling stations in relation to areas of dredging (shaded); (b) Biological sampling in nine strata (A–I) in relation to areas of dredging; ten samples were taken per stratum.

present, information regarding the extent of effects resulting from presence and operation of platforms, information on which to plan the necessary areal extent of a sampling progamme, is limited but steadily increasing. Two studies that have demonstrated effects around oilfield installations indicate that the effects may extend from about 100 m (Wolfson *et al.*, 1979) to 3000 m (Addy *et al.*, 1978). It is likely that small-scale changes such as those detailed by Wolfson *et al.* (1979) occur around every offshore production platform, and we feel that monitoring should concentrate on the potentially more serious effects. The predicted increase of discharges of oily production water in oilfields over a long period of oil production (Read & Blackman, 1980) should be borne in mind when planning areal

Fig. 5.4. Combined grid and transect sampling strategy, Thistle Oilfield, North Sea. Published with the kind permission of Britoil PLC (formerly BNOC).

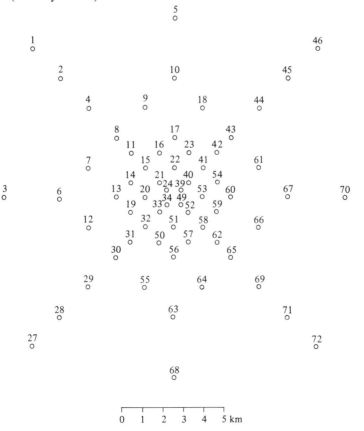

extent of sampling. The discharge of drill cuttings contaminated with oil-based drilling muds during exploration and production drilling has produced dramatic effects in a restricted area around a number of oilfields (see Dicks, 1982; Hartley, 1982a,b; Addy, Hartley & Tibbetts, 1984; Davies et al., 1984). Although drilling is likely to be of limited duration in the development of each oilfield, the relatively large amounts of material, the probable persistence of the oil base, and both toxic and organic enrichment processes will require continued localised monitoring around many platforms.

Radiating transects from a point source of pollution with regularly spaced stations have the advantage that the sampling is concentrated near the source, facilitating the detection of gradients of effect. Such an arrangement has been used successfully in the Ekofisk Field (Dicks, 1976; Addy et al., 1978). A combination of grids and transects may be employed usefully around defined point sources as in the Thistle Field (Oil Pollution Research Unit, Field Studies Council, unpublished data; Fig. 5.4).

Frequency of resurvey

Frequency of resurvey is closely related to the aims and objectives of the work. Where population dynamics or life histories of species, seasonal cycles, or short-term changes are being studied, sampling will need to be frequent and must be determined by the expected rates of change. In an ideal situation, staff time and costs are irrelevant to sampling programme design, but in practice very frequent sampling can produce vast numbers of samples for analysis; therefore a compromise must be reached between sorting/analysis time and costs, number of sample stations, and frequency of resurvey.

Monitoring studies may be concerned with the population dynamics of individual species, but many studies designed to monitor the effects of human activities are concerned with community composition and spatial relationships. The numerical composition of a macrobenthic community may change with time (both seasonally and from year to year) and these variations must either be measured or avoided as far as possible, if the task of detecting pollution effects is to be simplified. Benthos shows considerable numerical variability over a year due to larval recruitment and mortality (Mileikovsky, 1974; Buchanan, Sheader & Kingston 1978). The results of repeated surveys are more easily compared if they are carried out at the same time of year. Different species have different larval settlement times but the work of Buchanan et al. (1978) suggests that, at least for the North Sea, the best time to sample in order to avoid the largely ephemeral larval recruitment is the first six months of the year. The winter weather of the North Sea effectively curtails the sampling period to April, May, and June for offshore areas.

Examination of the success of larval recruitment to an area in relation to pollution discharges may be suggested as a way of including an element of early warning in a monitoring programme. Whilst this may be the case, there are a number of potential drawbacks; for example, if recruitment was sporadic or patchy, cause-and-effect relationships would be extremely difficult to demonstrate. Similarly, interpretative problems would arise from the different settling times of the larvae of different species, the difficulties of identification of juveniles, and the natural occurrence of irregular settlement patterns (as was shown for *Echinocardium cordatum* off Northumberland by Buchanan, 1967). For these reasons we feel that monitoring by subsequent survey of the adult populations is more rewarding.

Frequency of sampling also depends upon the scale and nature of pollution, changes in pollution input or distribution, and the rate at which changes may be expected or observed to occur in communities. Frequency of sampling may, of course, be changed following several surveys in the light of findings. Pearson (1975), when monitoring a pulp mill discharge to Loch Eil, initially surveyed five times per year but subsequently reduced this to twice yearly. In pollution monitoring studies, we would generally recommend surveying annually, although, where seasonal changes are to be followed, more frequent surveying will be necessary. Frequency may be reduced following initial surveys once areas of effect and approximate rates of change have been defined. Where effects are found to be minimal, surveying may be necessary only infrequently or not at all. If effects are found to spread rapidly or substantial changes are made to effluent discharges that may result in rapid biological change, sampling must be more frequent and the methods and survey design amended to cope with the problems of larval recruitment and numerical variability.

Sample replication

The number of samples that should be taken at a station has been discussed by McIntyre, Elliott & Ellis, (1984) and this is influenced by the objectives of the work. The taking of a limited number of samples per station is a practical necessity that results in only a proportion of the total species complement of the community being recorded at each station. However, if each station is sampled at the same intensity and the samples are treated in the same way, then it is possible to make comparisons over the survey area. Since it is difficult, or may be impossible, to provide a complete community description at each station, the objective of the sampling should be to provide statistically adequate estimates of the abundance of the fauna. Longhurst (1959) noted that there is usually less inter-sample variation of the total number of species or individuals than there is of the number of individuals of each species, and this was supported by evidence given by McIntyre *et al.* (1984). In samples of diverse communities the majority of species will be uncommon and therefore not suited to tests of the adequacy of the density estimates. Priority should thus be given to obtaining acceptable estimates of the densities of the more abundant species. In our experience the five 0.1 m² replicate samples recommended by Longhurst (1959) and McIntyre *et al.* (1984) are usually sufficient to provide adequate data.

More recently, consideration has been given to strategies for the most effective location of limited sampling resources. Saila, Pikanowksi & Vaughan, (1976), working in the New York Bight, discussed the advantages of stratified sampling and suggested a method for optimum allocation of resources. They found that there was considerable variation in the number of replicates per station (1–3) and stations per stratum (7–34) required to provide adequate estimates of density of individual species, despite setting a comparatively low precision threshold ($\pm 50\%$ of the mean with a 90% probability). Cuff & Coleman (1979), in a retrospective examination of data from a stratified random sampling survey of the macrobenthos in Westernport Bay, Australia, reported that substantial gains in precision could have been made by increasing the number of stations at the expense of the number of replicates per station. Indeed they suggested that the optimum number of grab samples per station was only one. This suggestion is interesting *but* it does require further consideration. Cuff & Coleman (1979) noted that of 572 species found during the survey, only 18 species were numerically dominant. Instead of conducting the analyses on these species, they combined the data to give just three variables: the number of polychaete, crustacean, and molluscan individuals per station. This step has a major bearing on the results obtained because, as noted earlier, counts of groups of organisms may be less variable than those of a single species.

Hartley (1982*a*), using the results of a North Sea benthic survey, calculated the number of replicates required to give a desired degree of precision (standard error of 20% of the mean) for selected monospecific taxa and for data grouped in the manner of Cuff & Coleman (1979). The results indicated that considerably fewer replicates were needed to obtain adequate estimates of the densities of the grouped taxa than for the non-grouped taxa. These results are not unexpected (see Longhurst, 1959), but emphasise the need for further comparative quantitative studies involving non-grouped taxa to identify optimum levels of replication.

Size of samples

There is a size spectrum of benthic animals from microorganisms to megafauna and, in general, faunal densities increase with decreasing organism size. This presents problems in the choice of sample size to provide adequate data for a wide range of species. For macrofauna (extracted using a 1-mm mesh size) a sample size of 0.1 m² has been widely used and seems to be appropriate. However, when sieve meshes of less than 1 mm are to be employed, the use of samplers with an area of less than 0.1 m² (e.g., Van Veen grabs with an area of 0.04 m²) is worth investigating. Sieve mesh size helps determine the number of animals retained, and may thus have a bearing on the accuracy of the estimates of individual species. Regardless of the area of the sample, a minimum penetration of 5 cm is recommended to ensure the collection of a sizeable proportion of the faunal density. Penetration of 15 cm or more is desirable.

Meiofauna and smaller macrofauna have been sampled with a variety of core sizes (2–20 cm diameter) taken either with specialised corers or sub-sampled from grabs. For a fixed sampling effort, the taking of large numbers of smaller samples may offer statistical advantages for counts of the smaller fauna but may not provide adequate information for the larger, more widely scattered organisms.

Sampling equipment

A number of excellent publications deal with sampling equipment and procedures. Holme & McIntyre (1984) provide an invaluable guide to the range of equipment for studies of marine benthos. Further useful information on sediment sampling can be found in Buller & McManus (1979) and Stirn (1981). We have restricted our approach mainly to quantitative samplers, although such equipment can, of course, be used qualitatively. Some techniques and pieces of equipment that have been found useful in sampling in European waters are described below.

In all cases, sampling equipment must be selected to suit the objectives of the sampling programme, but especially to suit the sea-bed conditions (biological, community, and sediment type) at the survey site. Where sea-bed conditions are unknown, a selection of equipment should be taken to ensure that appropriate samplers are available. Samplers should also be duplicated in case losses or damage occur – it is very frustrating to lose equipment and have to return to port if weather is ideal for sampling. In general, towed equipment (dredges, sleds, trawls) is more liable to loss or damage than raised/lowered equipment (grabs, corers).

Sampling boats and gear for handling sampling equipment

Boats must be selected with several factors in mind. The two most important are:

1. Boat size should be adequate to cope with the weather conditions and sea states likely to be encountered. Much time can be wasted sailing to and from the sample area in response to changes in weather conditions.

2. Boat size should be suitable for the size of equipment to be handled. Considerable difficulty may be experienced in handling heavy or bulky gear from small ships.

Winches, davits, booms, A-frames, and ropes or wire cables should be of suitable safe-working load for the equipment used, bearing in mind the sometimes considerable force needed to extract a full sampler from the sea-bed or that trawls occasionally fill with substantial weights of sediment when towed too slowly or across patches of mud or stones. Winches should be selected for raising or lowering speeds at which equipment operates most efficiently (premature triggering of grabs during lowering and washing-out of sediments during too-rapid raising are common problems). The master and drawings of the ship should be consulted to make sure that there are no underwater obstructions (e.g., bilge keels) on which gear being raised or lowered can foul.

Sample station location and relocation

To accurately plot and interpret data gained from sea-bed sampling, the positions of sampling stations must be precisely known in relation to each other and to other features (e.g., coastal features, offshore platforms, sewage outfalls, etc.). If stations are to be resampled at intervals, it is important that these can be accurately relocated. This is particularly important where community distributions may be patchy and a particular community is to be resampled. Traditional and electronic navigation techniques are comprehensively dealt with in Bowditch (1977) and Sonnenberg (1978). Brief notes on the uses of traditional methods and electronic navigators are given below.

Sightings and triangulation

Compass bearings to coastal landmarks, fixed beacons, or offshore platforms can be very accurate provided a good pair or more of readings can be taken for a particular station. Accuracy decreases with distance from the landmarks. Many areas of coast may appear more or less featureless from the sea, and offshore no structures may be available. Poor visibility may prevent sighting even where landmarks exist. In such cases electronic aids should be employed. Buoys or other anchored structures should not be used as reference points as they may move considerably in position in response to wind, currents, and tide.

Radar

Radar can be useful in poor visibility or where visible landmarks are not readily available. Many systems can be used to provide a range and bearing to a coastal feature or fixed structure, but errors increase with distance. In systems on most vessels, accuracies of greater than + 200 m are unlikely except at ranges of less than 3–5 km. Some high-precision radars are available and manufacturers need to be consulted for details. In general, radar is particularly useful close inshore or in estuaries.

Electronic navigators, land-based

These may be extremely useful offshore. Main Chain Decca Navigator is available for many European waters, though the accuracy of location/relocation depends upon obtaining a good 'cross' on at least two of the three channels available. Accuracy can be as good as ± 30 m in ideal conditions but varies with time of day, atmospheric conditions, etc. In some nearshore areas, small inherent errors in the Decca system may be amplified by coastal features such as steep cliffs, thus making it unsuitable for use.

Higher-resolution systems such as 'Pulse 8' and Decca 'Hifix' are available at greater cost than Main Chain Decca. Accuracy is greatly improved in these systems (to within ± 1 m) and they are available for many European waters. Data plotting systems (track plotters) that give a pictorial representation of ship's position can be linked in, which makes station relocation simpler. Hooper (1979) provides a summary of these systems.

Satellite navigation systems.

The SatNav system uses a series of eight satellites on fairly low polar orbits on paths that parallel lines of longitude. The satellites orbit in a fixed relationship to each other and receive 'ground traffic' information from three land-based transmitting stations. Orbit time is about 90 minutes. At the poles, all eight satellites pass overhead in sequence and are available for position-fixing continuously. At any point on the equator a strong signal will be received from one or perhaps two satellites for about 30 minutes every 90 minutes. In the North Sea about five satellites are available.

Shipboard computer instrumentation receives information from the satellites as well as from the ship's gyro compass, doppler log, water speed indicator, and any other navigation aids onboard. On receiving a satellite signal the computer takes about 12 minutes to calculate a position fix in latitude/longitude accurate to less than 30 m (may be as good as 1–2 m in optimum conditions). Subsequently, information from the ship's logging systems updates the ship's position in relation to its speed until the next satellite signal is received. After receiving satellite signals for about $1\frac{1}{2}$ hours the system will be 'tuned-in' to local water movements, etc., and be able to continuously compute position to within at least 30 m for a moving vessel and normally closer than that for a stationary vessel. Track plotters facilitate station re-location because they provide a continuous visual display of ship's position.

A great advantage of these systems, apart from their accuracy, is that they are more or less independent of weather conditions, since only the most severe tropical electric storms upset satellite reception. Other radio transmission equipment onboard ship can interfere with reception. It is currently possible to purchase units for small boats relatively cheaply (about £1,500). These units are accurate to within about 20 m.

Three further general points should be made about position-fixing:

1. Once a station is relocated, subsequent ship movements (which effectively randomize remote sampling at any one station at which replicate grabs are taken) must be taken into account. Movement of a vessel at anchor can be of the order of several hundreds of metres in deep water.

2. Position-fixing is usually made in relation to the position of the signal-receiving or -measuring equipment on board; on a large ship this may be 30 m or more from the location of sampling equipment, thus introducing a further potential station location error.

3. Wherever possible, different position-fixing methods should not be used for different parts of a survey area. Problems can be encountered in matching positions obtained by different methods.

Qualitative samplers – dredges and trawls

In some cases qualitative samples may provide useful data, especially where a preliminary survey is to be carried out to obtain information on sediment type and distribution quickly as an aid to planning the main survey programme. Dredges, especially simple ones, e.g. a pipe dredge or an anchor dredge, are very suitable. The costs of obtaining such data must be weighed against information gained.

Neither grabs nor dredges provide adequate samples of the larger, widely distributed, or more mobile epifauna. Although difficult to quantify, these organisms can often be qualitatively sampled relatively easily in deeper water by timed trawls at constant towing speeds using single- or double-sided trawls such as beam trawls or Agassiz trawls. Such samples provide useful additions to species lists and may provide a variety of larger species for tissue analysis for contaminants such as oil or heavy metals. Commercial fishing equipment can also be employed to obtain such samples but it is much more bulky and difficult to use. In shallow water small Agassiz trawls (1 m or less in width) may be operated from shallow-draught boats, and in wading-depth water push nets may be used.

Quantitative samplers – grabs and corers
Very shallow water (less than 2 m) close to the low tide mark

Where wading is possible, some of the techniques employed in intertidal regions may be applicable, particularly if the water is clear (see Chapter 4). The full suite of remote sampling techniques from larger vessels (see below) are applicable at high tide if water depth is sufficient for boat access without excessive sediment disturbance. At slightly greater depths, snorkelling or SCUBA diving may be appropriate, with sampling done with hand corers or suction samplers (see Chapter 9). Where turbidity, water movements, or softness of the sediments make such alternatives impractical, it may be possible to use hand-operated grab samplers or corers (often miniaturised from existing designs) from shallow-draught boats (see, e.g., Buller & McManus, 1979; Elliott & Drake, 1981). Sediment sampling may be impossible in some locations or at certain times as a result of high current speeds during tidal ebb or flow or because of sediment type. Few hand-operated samplers work well in medium or coarse gravels or where substantial numbers of stones are present (see Elliott & Drake, 1981). Heavier equipment may not be a viable alternative in small boats because of a lack of suitable davits or winching facilities.

Nearshore waters, 2–20 m in depth

It has been established by a number of studies (e.g., Massé, Plante & Reys, 1977) that in shallow water (realistically less than 20 m for intensive sampling), diver-operated suction samplers provide the most accurate samples of soft-bottom benthos, since contiguous samples of uniform size and depth may be consistently obtained (see Chapter 9). In areas of strong currents or high turbidity, however, it may be preferable to resort to remote sampling (see below). In some cases remote sampling may be quicker or cheaper than diving, and the relative merits of each must be carefully assessed.

Waters deeper than 20 m

Although theoretically suction samplers might be used in deeper water offshore either by divers using mixed-gas techniques or by manipulation from submersibles, in practice the costs of such undertakings would be prohibitive, and in deeper water remote sampling is currently standard practice. A great variety of remote samplers are available in two principal types, grabs and corers.

Grabs for macrofaunal sampling usually cover an area of 0.1 m² and have a limited depth of penetration. In many substrata there are deep-burrowing infaunal animals such as *Ensis*, *Lutraria*, and *Lanice* which would be missed by a shallow-biting grab. The omission of deep-burrowing species from samples is unlikely to significantly influence results in terms of numerical abundance of the fauna but if biomass were being studied, a large proportion would not have been included (which could influence the results of production or energy flow studies). Two solutions to this problem are (1) to increase the size and weight of the grab, e.g., the Campbell grab sampling 0.55 m² to a depth of about 30 cm and weighing 410 kg, or (2) to employ a heavy (750 kg) box corer such as the Reineck corer which samples an area of 0.96 m² to a depth of 45 cm (Eleftheriou & Holme, 1984). Such heavy pieces of equipment require special handling gear and are generally unsuitable for use from small boats. In shallow water the use of suction samplers overcomes the problem, but in deeper water there is currently no alternative to using the heavier equipment.

The difficulty of sampling the deeper-burrowing forms has a number of implications. Salzwedel (1979), in a study of *Tellina fabula*, found that for a large number of samples the mean shell length of the longest animal taken was related to the depth of penetration of the grab. He reported that at an offshore sampling station (in 26 m) grab penetration of at least 10 cm was necessary to catch the largest animals. The maximum penetration of most grabs is 10–15 cm although this is only realised on comparatively soft sediments. This, in addition to differences in bite profiles between grabs, emphasises the need to use corers either routinely or to estimate the under-sampling error if using a grab during population studies of even relatively shallow-burrowing infaunal species.

A large number of grabs have been designed for obtaining quantitative samples of the sea-bed since the first modern grab was described by Petersen (1918), and the majority of these have been reviewed by Eleftheriou & Holme (1984). The following grabs can be recommended as being simple and easy to handle; they penetrate the sea-bed to a sufficient depth to provide adequate samples for most sediment types.

The *Day* grab (Fig. 5.5) was developed as a simplified and stronger

Fig. 5.5. The Day grab.

version of the Smith–McIntyre grab by the NERC Research Base at Barry, Wales. Its operation is based on mechanical leverage without spring assistance, and handling therefore presents fewer hazards than spring-loaded grabs. The pyramid-shaped frame supporting the mechanism is very robust, making the grab difficult to damage and very unlikely to fall on its side.

The *Smith–McIntyre* grab is mechanically similar to the Day grab but employs springs, which need tensioning, to assist initial penetration of the buckets into the sediment. Its framework is less robust and somewhat taller than that of the Day grab and it is more prone to toppling.

The *Van Veen* grab is the simplest of the three and it has no supporting framework. Its simplicity and relative lightness make it particularly useful from small boats, but also mean it works best in softer sediments. It is somewhat prone to misfiring, taking incomplete samples, or toppling onto its sides in rough seas.

The problems of sample volume varying with sediment type can be overcome to a certain extent by adjusting the amount of weight added to the grab. Where this is inadequate, heavy grabs may need to be used (see above).

One aspect of the comparative efficiencies of grabs that has not received much attention is the effect of the pressure wave produced by the descent of the grab. Smith & McIntyre (1954) noted that their new sampler captured nearly twice as many amphipods as did a Van Veen grab and suggested that this might be due to differences in intensity of the pressure waves, since their grab had gauze covering the tops of the jaws which would allow water to pass through on descent. The pressure wave of a Van Veen grab has been observed by Wigley (1967) and Ankar (1977) to sweep away loose surface sediment from under the grab, and it is likely that the pressure wave from a Day grab would have a similar effect. Few studies have been carried out on the vagile benthos and hyperbenthos (see Oug, 1977) and thus the potential effects of the pressure wave on the sample taken are difficult to assess. This is regarded as an important area for investigation with particular reference to pollution-monitoring studies since many small crustaceans live at the sediment/water interface, and various amphipods have recently been shown to be sensitive to oil pollution, e.g., after the *Amoco Cadiz* spill (Chassé, 1978; Cabioch *et al.*, 1981) and the *Florida* spill (Sanders *et al.*, 1980). Similarly sediment levels of hydrocarbons may be seriously underestimated if the loose surface material is not included in the samples. Sedimentation has recently been shown to be an important pathway in the removal of oil from the water column (Johansson, 1980; Johansson, Larsson & Boehn, 1980), and it may take some time before the material is incorporated into more compact sediments whilst having biological impact from an early stage.

The following practical problems concerning the operation of grab samplers are worth noting. Small samples may result from sampling in rough weather, particularly with grabs of the Van Veen-type action, since the rise and fall of the vessel causes the grab to be snatched off the sea-bed before a full bite has been taken. A similar problem may result from clumsy winch operation (Ursin, 1954). Endless warps seem to improve Van Veen performance in heavy seas (W. J. Wolff, personal communication). When the sediment contains stones or large shells, these may become wedged in the jaws resulting in a loss of sediment due to washing out. It is important for the reproducibility of samples that such samples are discarded. It is the responsibility of the biologist conducting the sampling to keep a careful check on the quality of the samples being obtained.

Remote sensing techniques
Aerial photography

Where the water is clear, aerial photography from helicopters or light aircraft may prove useful for rapid survey of the distribution of rock reefs, seagrass beds, or areas of sediment. It may also be used in mapping distribution of sediments discharging from river mouths to nearshore areas. For further information see Chapter 2.

Linescan systems

Linescan imagery relies on aircraft-mounted cameras that scan a narrow band across the line of flight, successive bands building an image of ground conditions along the flight path. This technique is used most commonly to record infrared radiation, but can be used with other light frequencies. In certain infrared frequencies it can provide useful data in tracking of heated effluent plumes for correlation with biological data.

Satellite imagery

This technique can provide useful information on distribution of, e.g., river outfalls, plankton blooms, and reef systems for large areas of the coastline. As the resolution of the systems improves, usefulness to survey planners will also improve.

All the remote sensing techniques noted above must be accurately calibrated by 'ground truth' surveys so that locations of sampling stations may be accurately determined.

For further information see Chapter 2.

Correlative measurements

Although the prime concerns of the biologist will be the assessment of spatial and temporal biological change, the attribution of recorded change to a cause will require a number of correlative measurements, as mentioned earlier. These include natural variables that affect organism distribution (e.g., sediment particle size distribution, water depth, temperature, salinity, dissolved oxygen, suspended solids, Eh, organic carbon content of sediment, currents, wave action) as well as pollutant inputs (e.g., hydrocarbons, heavy metals, organic nutrients, suspended solids). Measured variables must be selected in relation to the area under survey and the objectives of the programme, but a fundamental analysis is that of sediment particle size distribution.

The subject is dealt with comprehensively by Buchanan (1984) and Buller & McManus (1979). The quantification of mud particles (less than 63 μm diameter), which correlates well with organic distribution and with the occurrence of many pollutants, especially oil and heavy metals, has been of particular value to many studies. Simple dry-sieving techniques such as the rapid method of Buchanan (1984) provide only limited information on these muds, which at some sites form more than 95% of marine sediments, e.g., in muddy areas of Southampton Water. They may be characterised in detail by pipette analysis or Coulter Counter (see, e.g., Buller & McManus, 1979; Little, Staggs & Woodman, 1984). The relative merits of the two techniques are discussed in Buller & McManus (1979) and McCave (1979). The two key contrasts between the methods are that pipette analysis requires little specialist equipment but is extremely time consuming, especially for the very fine particles, whereas Coulter Counter analysis is rapid and accurate but requires relatively costly equipment. Where routine analysis of large numbers of samples with substantial clay content is necessary, Coulter Counter analysis is the preferable technique.

Techniques for the analysis of other variables are dealt with in detail in a range of publications and the reader is referred to these as follows: hydrography, suspended solids, sedimentation rates, organic carbon, salinity, current, and temperature are dealt with in Dyer (1979); chemical analysis of seawater in Strickland & Parsons (1972) and Parsons, Maita & Lalli (1984); and estuarine chemistry in Head (1985).

Publications that deal with the measurement of pollutants in marine habitats are numerous and since detailed consideration of analytical techniques is outside the scope of this chapter, the following references may be useful as starting points for further reading: hydrocarbons and petrochemicals, Malins (1977), CONCAWE (1979), and CONCAWE (1982); heavy metals, Bryan (1976); pesticides, Addison (1976); and sewage and organic nutrients, Strickland & Parsons (1972) and MAFF (1981).

Many modern techniques rely on various types of electronic equipment. For example, hydrocarbon analysis utilises infrared or ultraviolet spectrometry and gas chromatography/mass spectrometry; heavy metal analysis utilises atomic absorption spectrometry; and pesticide analysis utilises electron capture gas chromatography. Manufacturers of equipment can provide much useful guidance and advice.

References

Addison, R. F. 1976. Organochlorine compounds in aquatic organisms: their distribution, transport and physiological significance. In *The Effects of Pollutants on Aquatic Organisms*, ed. A. P. M. Lockwood, pp. 127–45. Cambridge University Press.

Addy, J. M., Hartley, J. P. & Tibbetts, P. J. C. (1984). Ecological effects of oil-based mud drilling in the Beatrice oilfield. *Mar. Pollut. Bull.* **15**, 429–35.

Addy, J. M., Levell, D. & Hartley, J. P. (1978). Biological monitoring of sediments in the Ekofisk oilfield. In *Proceedings of Conference on Assessment of Ecological Impacts of Oil Spills*. American Institute for Biological Sciences, June 1978, Keystone, Colorado, pp. 514–39.

Ankar, S. (1977). Digging profile and penetration of the Van Veen grab in different sediment types. *Contrib. Askö Lab. Univ. Stockholm*, **16**, 1–22.

Bowditch, N. (1977). *American Practical Navigator*, vol. I. Defense Mapping Agency Hydrographic Center, Publication No. 9. Washington.

Bryan, G. W. (1976). Some aspects of heavy metal tolerance in aquatic organisms. In *The Effects of Pollutants on Aquatic Organisms*, ed. A. P. M. Lockwood, pp. 7–34. Cambridge University Press.

Buchanan, J. B. (1967). Dispersion and demography of some infaunal echinoderm populations. *Symp. zool. soc. Lond.* **20**, 1–11.

Buchanan, J. B. (1984). Sediment analysis. In *Methods for the Study of Marine Benthos*, ed. N. A. Holme & A. D. McIntyre, pp. 41–65. Oxford: Blackwell Scientific Publications.

Buchanan, J. B., Sheader, M. & Kingston P. F. (1978). Sources of variability in the benthic macrofauna off the south Northumberland coast, 1971–1976. *J. mar. biol. Ass. U.K.* **58**, 191–209.

Buller, A. T. & McManus, J. (1979). Sediment sampling and analysis. In *Estuarine Hydrography and Sedimentation*, ed. K. R. Dyer, pp. 87–130. Cambridge University Press.

Cabioch, L., Dauvin, J. C., Gentil, F., Retière, C. & Rivain, V. (1981). Perturbations induites dans la composition et le fonctionnement des peuplements benthiques sublittoraux, sous l'effet des hydrocarbures de l' *Amoco Cadiz*. In *Amoco Cadiz: Fate and Effects of the Oil Spill*, pp. 513–27, Paris: CNEXO.

Cederwall, H. & Elmgren, R. (1980). Biomass increase of benthic macrofauna demonstrates eutrophication of the Baltic Sea. *Ophelia*, Suppl. 1, 287–304.

Chassé, C. (1978). The ecological impact on and near shores by the Amoco Cadiz oil spill. *Mar. Pollut. Bull.* **9**, 298–301.

CONCAWE (1979). *The Environmental Impact of Refinery Effluents*. Report No. 5/79. Den Haag: CONCAWE.

CONCAWE (1982). *Approaches to the Characterization of Aqueous Effluents from the Oil Refining Industry*. Report No. 9/82. Den Haag: CONCAWE.

Cuff, W. & Coleman, N. (1979). Optimal survey design: lessons from a stratified random sample of macrobenthos. *J. Fish Res. Board Can.* **36**, 351–61.

Davies, J., Addy, J., Blackman, R., Ferbrache, J., Moore, D., Somerville, H., Whitehead, A. & Wilkinson, T. (1984). Environmental effects of oil-based mud cuttings. *Mar. Pollut. Bull.* **15**, 363–70.

Dicks, B. (1976). Offshore biological monitoring. In *Marine Ecology and Oil Pollution*, ed. J. M. Baker, pp. 325–440. Barking: Applied Science Publishers.

Dicks, B. (1982). Monitoring the biological effects of North Sea platforms. *Mar. Pollut. Bull.* **13**, 221–7.

Dicks, B. & Hartley, J. P. (1982). The effects of repeated small oil spillages and chronic discharges. *Phil. Trans. R. Soc. London B*, **297**, 285–307.

Dybern, B. I., Ackefors, H. & Elmgren, R. (eds) (1976). Recommendations on methods for marine biological studies in the Baltic Sea. *Baltic Marine Biologists, Publ.* **1**, 1–98.

Dyer, K. R. (ed.) (1979) *Estuarine Hydrography and Sedimentation*. Estuarine and Brackish-Water Sciences Association Handbook. Cambridge University Press.

Eleftheriou, A. & Holme, N. A. (1984). Macrofauna techniques. In *Methods for the Study of Marine Benthos*, ed. N. A. Holme & A. D. McIntyre. Oxford: Blackwell Scientific Publications.

Elliott, J. M. & Drake, C. M. (1981). A comparative study of four dredges used for sampling benthic macroinvertebrates in rivers. *Freshwater Biol.* **11**, 245–61.

Gray, J. S. & Mirza, F. B. (1979). A possible method for the detection of pollution-induced disturbance on marine benthic communities. *Mar. Pollut. Bull.* **10**, 142–6.

Hartley, J. P. (1982*a*). 'Benthic Studies in Two North Sea Oilfields.' Unpublished Ph.D. thesis, University of Wales, Bangor.

Hartley, J. P. (1982*b*). Methods for monitoring offshore macrobenthos. *Mar. Pollut. Bull.* **13**, 150–3.

Head, P. C. (ed.) (1985). *Practical Estuarine Chemistry*. Estuarine and Brackish-Water Sciences Association Handbook. Cambridge University Press.

Holme, N. A. & McIntyre, A. D. (eds) (1984). *Methods for the Study of Marine Benthos*. Oxford: Blackwell Scientific Publications.

Hooper, D. J. (1979). Hydrographic surveying. In *Estuarine Hydrography and Sedimentation*, ed. K. R. Dyer, pp. 41–56. Cambridge University Press.

Johansson, S. (1980. Impact of oil on the pelagic ecosystem. In *The Tsesis Oil*

Spill, ed. J. J. Kineman, R. Elmgren & S. Hansson, pp. 61–80. United States Department of Commerce, National Oceanic and Atmospheric Administration Report No. PB80-226285. University of Stockholm.

Johansson, S., Larsson, U. & Boehn, P. (1980). The *Tsesis* oil spill. *Mar. Pollut. Bull.* **11**, 284–93.

Jones, G. (1981). Effects of dredging and reclamation on the sediments of Botany Bay. *Aust J. Mar. Freshwater Res.* **32**, 369–77.

Jones, G. & Candy, S. (1981). Effects of dredging on the macrobenthic infauna of Botany Bay. *Aust. J. Mar. Freshwater Res*, **32**, 379–98.

Levell, D. (1976). *Southampton Water Benthic Surveys, 1975 and 1976*. Limited circulation report: Oil Pollution Research Unit, Field Studies Council, Pembroke.

Little, D. I., Staggs, M. F. & Woodman, S. S. C. (1984). Sample pretreatment and size analysis of poorly-sorted cohesive sediments by sieve and electronic particle counter. In *Transfer Processes in Cohesive Sediment Systems*, ed. W. R. Parker & D. J. J. Kinsman, pp. 47–74. New York: Plenum.

Longhurst, A. R. (1959). The sampling problem in benthic ecology. *Proc. N. Z. Ecol. Soc.* **6**, 8–12.

McCave, I. N. (1979). Suspended sediment. In *Estuarine Hydrography and Sedimentation*, ed. K. R. Dyer, pp. 131–85. Cambridge University Press.

McIntyre, A. D., Elliott, J. M. & Ellis, D. V. (1984). Design of sampling programmes. In *Methods for the Study of Marine Benthos*, ed. N. A. Holme & A. D. McIntyre, Oxford: Blackwell Scientific Publications:

MAFF (1981). *The Analysis of Agricultural Materials*. Report No. RB247. London: H.M.S.O.

Malins, D. C. (ed.) (1977). *Effects of Petroleum on Arctic and Subarctic Marine Environments and Organisms*, vol 1: *Nature and Fate of Petroleum*. New York: Academic Press.

Massé, H., Plante, R. & Reys, J. P. (1977). Etude comparative de l'efficacité de deux bennes et d'une suceuse en fonction de la nature de fond. In *Biology of Benthic Organisms*, ed. B. F. Keegan, P. O. Ceidigh & P. J. S. Boaden, pp. 465–74. Oxford: Pergamon Press.

Mileikovsky, S. A. (1974). On predation of pelagic larvae and early juveniles of marine bottom invertebrates by adult benthic invertebrates and their passing alive through their predators. *Mar. Biol.* **26**, 303–11.

Moore, P. G. (1971). Ecological survey strategy. *Mar. Pollut. Bull.* **2**, 37–9.

Oug, E. (1977). Faunal distribution close to the sediment of a shallow marine environment. *Sarsia*, **63**, 115–21.

Parsons, T. R., Maita, Y. & Lalli, C. M. (1984). *A Manual of Chemical and Biological Methods for Seawater Analysis*. Oxford & New York: Pergamon Press.

Pearson, T. H. (1975). The benthic ecology of Loch Linnhe and Loch Eil, a sea-loch system on the west coast of Scotland. IV. Changes in the benthic fauna attributable to organic enrichment. *J. exp. mar. Biol. Ecol.* **20**, 1–41.

Petersen, C. G. J. (1981). *The Sea Bottom and its Production of Fish Food.*

Report of the Danish Biological Station to the Board of Agriculture (Ministry of Fisheries) No. 25, Copenhagen.

Read, A. D. & Blackman, R. A. A. (1980). Oily water discharges from offshore North Sea installations: a perspective. *Mar. Pollut. Bull.* **11**, 44–67.

Saila, S. B., Pikanowski, R. A. & Vaughan, D. S. (1976). Optimum allocation strategies for sampling benthos in the New York Bight. *Estuar. Coast. Mar. Sci.* **4**, 1199–28.

Salzwedel, H. (1979). Reproduction, growth, mortality and variations in abundance and biomass of *Tellina fabula* (Bivalvia) in the German Bight in 1975/76. *Veröff. Inst. Meeresforsch. Bremerh.* **18**, 111–202.

Sanders, H. L., Grassle, J. F., Hampson, G. R., Morse, L. S. Garner-Price, S. & Jones, C. C. (1980). Anatomy of an oil spill: long-term effects from the grounding of the barge *Florida* off West Falmouth, Massachusetts. *J. Mar. Res.* **38**, 265–380.

Sharp, J. M., Appan, S. G., Bender, H. E., Linton, T. L., Reish, D. J. & Ward, C. H. (1979). Natural variability of biological community structure as a quantitative basis for ecological impact assessment. In *Proceedings of Conference on Ecological Damage Assessment* (Arlington, Virginia), pp. 257–84. Society of Petroleum Industry Biologists.

Smith, W. & McIntyre, A. D. (1954). A spring-loaded bottom sampler. *J. mar. biol. Ass. U.K.* **33**, 257–64.

Sonnenberg, G. J. (1978). *Radar and Electronic Navigation*, 5th edn. London: Butterworths.

Stirn, J. (1981). Manual of methods in aquatic environment research. Part 8 of *Ecological Assessment of Pollution Effects*. Technical paper no. 209, Food and Agricultural Organisation, Rome.

Strickland, J. D. H. & Parsons, T. R. (1972). *A Practical Handbook of Seawater Analysis*, Fisheries Research Board of Canada Bulletin 167, Ottawa.

Ursin, E. (1954). Efficiency of marine bottom samplers of the Van Veen and Petersen types. *Meddr. Danmarks Fisk. Havundersog N. S.* **1**, 3–8.

Wigley, R. L. (1967). Comparative efficiencies of Van Veen and Smith-McIntyre grab samples as revealed by motion pictures. *Ecology*, **48**, 168–9.

Wolfson, A., Van Blaricom, G., Davis, N. & Lewbel, G. C. (1979). The marine life of an offshore oil platform. *Mar. Ecol. Prog. Ser.* **1**, 81–9.

6

Processing sediment macrofauna samples

J. P. HARTLEY, B. DICKS, and W. J. WOLFF

Introduction

The processing techniques for macrofauna samples from intertidal surveys (Chapter 4) and subtidal surveys (Chapters 5 and 9) have many features in common, and so have been combined in this chapter.

Extraction of fauna from sediments

On board research vessels

After removal from the grab, samples for faunal analysis should be washed using sea water on the selected screen size to remove unwanted fine sediments and small organisms. A washing hopper along the lines of that described by Holme (1959) is useful and may be used with an integral water line or with a hand-held hose. Once the whole sample is sieved, the residue should be carefully backwashed to a corner of the sieve and transferred into storage jars, and backwashing should be repeated until no further material remains. Any organisms adhering to the sieve mesh should be picked off and added to the sample. Problems associated with sample sieving include washing for too-long periods or at too high a pressure, thus allowing or forcing organisms (generally the soft-bodied forms that would normally be retained) to pass through the mesh. If possible the duration and intensity of sieving of each sample should be as gentle as possible and approximately equivalent. The use of a ship's sea-water hose system for washing samples may result in the appearance of pelagic organisms such as hyperiid amphipods in the samples, particularly when working at night. Such organisms may justifiably be excluded from data analysis although alternative explanations for their appearance in the samples cannot be discounted. A better solution to this problem is to filter the water before use.

Where stiff clay or silt sediments are encountered, sieving and hosing at sea may do little to reduce sample volume, and the physico-chemical method of Barnett (1980) for faunal extraction may be employed (see below).

On tidal flats

Some types of sampling apparatus, e.g., that designed by van Arkel & Mulder (1975; see also Mulder & van Arkel, 1980 and Chapter 4), produce samples that have already been freed from sediment. In other cases the macrofauna has to be extracted from the sediment after sampling. Field processing reduces problems of storage and transportation but generally leads to less accurate results than laboratory procedures, especially in bad weather conditions and when sampling small animals.

Sieving on a tidal flat can be done in natural puddles, creeks, or holes specially dug for the purpose. It is best to work down the shore as the tide recedes and the flat drains, so that a suitable place for sieving is never difficult to find. On extensive tidal flats this is safer as well.

After sieving, the residue consisting of animals, shell fragments, and detritus may be removed from the sieve using a spoon and a laboratory squeeze bottle filled with sea water.

In the laboratory

The same sieving techniques as employed in the field may be used. Estuary or sea water should be used whenever possible as this will result in animal specimens of better quality.

Additional laboratory techniques for the separation of fauna from sediments include a freezing and Calgon technique for stiff clays described by Barnett (1980). The procedure comprises four steps: (1) storage in formalin for some days to fix the animals: (2) deep-freezing and subsequent thawing; (3) elutriation (see below); and (4) if necessary, the remaining sediment is treated with a water-softening agent (Calgon) and thoroughly shaken; after 24 hours this remainder is sieved. Kleef (1984) describes a method to sort *Corophium volutator* from detritus-rich sediment based on the swimming behaviour of the animals. Sea water is led over the sample carrying all emerging *Corophium* into a collecting sieve.

Various elutriation baths have been designed (e.g., Lauff et al, 1961; Eleftheriou & Holme, 1984) for the separation of macrofauna from sediment, although these have received little comparative evaluation or widespread use in surveys. Certainly the idea of a piece of equipment that quickly separates fauna from sediment is very attractive, but in practice the amount of time saved may be much less than expected. Elutriation may float off light organic debris from which the fauna have to be separated, and the sediment residue would have to be carefully checked for heavy-shelled molluscs, sipunculans inhabiting old shells, and small animals inhabiting large or heavy tubes. However, elutriation may be particularly useful and time saving when sorting fauna of a limited size range, e.g., animals passing through a 1-mm mesh but retained on a 0.5-mm mesh. Elutriation is usually carried out following preservation (see next section), in which case tap water may be used. Estuary or sea water should be used if the samples are processed before preservation.

Another laboratory technique is flotation using liquid of higher density than water (Eleftheriou & Holme, 1984). In general surveys flotation appears to offer little improvement on the techniques already described, but it may be useful for studies of one or a few species. For example, juvenile shore crabs could be sorted very quickly by using zinc sulphate (Klein Breteler, personal communication).

Size of sieve mesh

The sieve mesh used is undoubtedly one of the most important variables in the processing of benthic samples (Reish, 1959; Eleftheriou & Holme, 1984; Rees, 1984). Benthic organisms range in size from bacteria to very large molluscs, crustaceans, and echinoderms. The use of a sieve to screen benthic samples places an arbitrary cut-off on the size spectrum of the animals which has little taxonomic or ecological justification. Sieving is carried out to reduce samples to manageable portions both in terms of the number of animals present and the amount of sediment retained from which the animals need to be picked out. The lower size limit of macrofauna is usually regarded as 0.5 or 1 mm although the juvenile stages of macrofaunal animals may be much smaller than this. In the final analysis the size of mesh chosen should provide adequate information to answer the questions in hand; a few examples are given below.

Although some standardisation of mesh size is desirable to promote comparability of results, flexibility needs to be retained to cater for differing objectives and particular habitats. By way of example, Willems *et al.* (1982) used a 250-μm mesh to study the abundant interstitial fauna of an offshore gravel bank where large macrofauna was comparatively scarce. Haaland & Schram (1982), studying the larval development of the polychaete *Gyptis rosea*, used a range of sieves from 1 mm down to 0.063 mm. Buchanan & Warwick (1974), in an investigation of macrofaunal dynamics and productivity, conducted bimonthly sampling and used a 0.5-mm mesh. Meshes that are 0.5 and 1.0 mm have been widely used in tidal flat work. Pollution monitoring surveys tend to be carried out on a longer time-scale, e.g., annual sampling, and in these cases a 1-mm mesh is generally regarded as adequate. The use of a 1-mm mesh has been vindicated by the detection of pollution effects in a number of areas, e.g., Rosenberg (1973), Pearson (1975), and Addy, Levell & Hartley (1978), and for monitoring purposes we regard it as the most cost-effective compromise between ease of sorting and information gained.

For some surveys, the combination of large samples sieved through a coarse mesh for the study of large but relatively uncommon animals, plus small samples sieved through a fine mesh for studying abundant but small animals, will be helpful, since the time needed for sorting may be reduced considerably.

Sieves (Fig. 6.1) can be made of perforated or woven stainless steel or brass, or woven nylon. All of these can give satisfactory results, though some workers have found that woven sieves are more liable to damage which may bias the results. A sieve may be rectangular or circular. Rectangular sieves of about 40 cm × 60 cm, with a vertical side of 10–15 cm, are practical for tidal work, especially when the sieve is strong enough to be used as a stool as well. Circular sieves may have a diameter of about 50 cm. It is helpful if sieving in a puddle on the flats if the vertical sides of the sieve are perforated as well as the base. During sieving the movement should be up and down rather than back and forth, to reduce

Fig. 6.1. Different types of sieve. *Left*, perforated stainless steel; *right*, woven brass gauze.

abrasion of animals. To facilitate removal of the sample, all angles on the inner side of the sieve should be rounded.

Preservation of unsorted samples

Prior to preservation the organisms may be relaxed using a 7% solution of magnesium chloride in sea water. This is not general practice but has been recommended by Fauchald (1977), who reports that it results in a greatly increased proportion of identifiable polychaetes. The technique may be particularly useful if sampling in poorly studied areas where specimens in good condition are essential for identification.

It is essential that benthic samples are initially preserved with a formalin solution to fix the soft-bodied animals and soft parts. Soft-bodied animals preserved with ethyl alcohol rapidly become unusable and post-fixation of alcohol-preserved material does not work (Fauchald, 1977). The use of alcohol as an initial preservative has a number of other disadvantages, notably the problem of ensuring that adequate concentrations reach all parts of the sieved sample. In addition, alcohol frequently causes the separation of bivalve soft parts from their shells. The strength of formalin solution used varies considerably between workers (see Ankar, 1976), but it seems advisable to err on the side of strength, particularly since Self & Jumars (1978) noted that solutions of less than 20% formalin did not adequately fix tubicolous ampharetid polychaete specimens, albeit for a detailed study of gut contents. Unless the sieved sample residue contains much shell gravel or calcareous material, the acidic formalin solution should be neutralised to prevent dissolution or etching of shells or other calcareous structures. Buffering of formalin solution is usually achieved with borax, hexamine, or marble chips (Eleftheriou & Holme, 1984), and Ankar (1976) gives details of suitable hexamine concentrations (200 g/l of 40% formaldehyde).

It has been established in a number of studies that bulk staining of samples greatly facilitates quick and accurate sorting (Starling, 1971; Williams, 1974; Williams & Williams, 1974). This staining is most easily carried out in the field with the stain included in the preserving fluid. The most commonly used stain is rose bengal, although others such as eosin are employed.

All samples should be stored in plastic or glass containers or jars, which should be marked in waterproof ink stating all relevant details. The jar itself should bear the marking rather than the lid since lids may be exchanged. A plastic or paper label marked with pencil or waterproof ink should be added inside the jar – it is often useful to prepare the labels beforehand. Jars with watertight seals (e.g. Kilner jars) are desirable to prevent spillage of formalin during transport and subsequent storage of samples.

Deep-freezing of fresh samples as a storage method is not recommended, since without pre-fixing, deep-frozen samples yield animals in very poor condition which are difficult to process and identify.

Sample sorting and analysis
Sorting methods

Sample sorting has recently received some attention in the literature (Ankar, 1976; Barnett, 1979; Coleman, 1980), and the results of the latter two studies suggest that sorting may be a major source of error. Eleftheriou & Holme (1984) describe various methods for sample sorting, although the most common practice is to spread out the sample in a white tray, cover it with water, and sort by eye. With diligence, great accuracy can be achieved following this procedure when sorting samples sieved on a 1-mm mesh. Coleman (1980) reports that sorting samples twice increased the number of species recorded from a three-replicate station by about 13%, and that most of the species found by resorting were polychaetes and crustaceans. This source of error can be reduced or removed by the adoption of the following method described by Eleftheriou & Holme (1984). The samples are divided into two fractions by the repeated addition of water followed by agitation and pouring the supernatant onto a 1-mm mesh. This separates the small fauna (notably crustaceans and polychaetes) and organic debris from the larger or heavy-shelled forms and sediment. Both fractions are sorted separately and the fine material is checked under a binocular microscope. This may appear an elaborate process but the rewards in increased accuracy more than justify the additional sorting time. If samples have been screened on meshes of less than 1 mm, it is essential that sorting is carried out using a binocular microscope to ensure accuracy.

The advantages of bulk-staining the samples to facilitate the laboratory separation of animals from sediment are clear, but a cautionary note must be that not all organisms stain or stain the expected colour. An example of this is young *Arctica islandica* in which the periostracum does not stain and the shell is comparatively thick and opaque, thus obscuring the colour of the stained soft tissues.

If fresh sieved samples that have not been fixed are kept cool (e.g., in a refrigerator at 0–5 °C), most of the animals will stay alive for at least several hours. Sorting of live animals has two advantages: moving animals are easier to find, and live animals are usually in good condition for identification. Some oligochaete taxa can only be fully identified when alive. Sea or estuary water has to be available to sort the animals in.

Samples preserved in formalin must be thoroughly rinsed in tap or sea water before sorting to avoid health risks (see Chapter 15).

Identification

Identification literature is detailed in Chapter 14.

Age classes

In many species age-classes may be distinguished, either based on growth marks on some hard part of the animal or on size-frequency distributions. Growth marks are known from mollusc shells, jaws of polychaetes, and tests of sea-urchins. Crisp (1984) and Warwick (1984) give more detailed information.

Biomass

Biomass may be expressed in various ways, e.g., wet weight of organisms, dry weight, ash-free dry weight, total nitrogen content, and calorific value. Ash-free dry weight is often considered as a reasonable compromise between usefulness of information and amount of labour. The following procedure may be used for the determination of ash-free dry weight, although Crisp (1984) lists several alternatives.

1. Dry sample at 90 °C until constant weight. Normally 40 hours will be sufficient.
2. Put dried sample in desiccator and allow to cool.
3. Weigh sample.
4. Incinerate the sample at about 550 °C (in a muffle furnace for 2–4 hours). At higher temperatures calcium carbonate decomposes.
5. Allow muffle furnace temperature to drop to 80–90 °C. Transfer sample to desiccator for further cooling.
6. Weigh sample.
7. Subtract weight in step 6 from weight in step 3.

Molluscs may be removed from their shells by submersion in boiling water for a few seconds before step 1 of the procedure is started.

Preservation of reference specimens

After sorting and identification, it is recommended that a reference collection of specimens be made and maintained. Such collections are invaluable should taxonomic queries arise.

Specimens sorted and identified alive should be fixed in 3–5% formalin for a few days. Afterwards these specimens as well as those preserved in formalin before sorting may be stored in either 5% formalin or 90% ethyl alcohol. In the case of formalin, care should be taken to neutralise the preservative as described on page 135. A label, either pencil or waterproof ink on paper or plastic, should be put inside the container.

References

Addy, J. M., Levell, D. & Hartley, J. P. (1978). Biological monitoring of sediments in the Ekofisk oilfield. In *Proceedings of Conference on Assessment of Ecological Impacts of Oil Spills*, pp. 514–39, American Institute Biological Sciences, June 1978, Keystone, Colorado.

Ankar, S. (1976). Final report from the Benthic Macrofauna Group. Baltic Sea expert meeting on intercalibration of biological and chemical methods, Asko, June 8–15, 1974. *Contrib. Asko Lab. Univ. Stockholm*, **12**, 1–27.

Arkel, M. A., van & M. Mulder. (1975). A device for quantitative sampling of benthic organisms in shallow water by means of a flushing technique. *Neth. J. Sea Res.* **9**, 365–70.

Barnett, B. E. (1979). Sorting benthic samples. *Mar. Pollut. Bull.* **10**, 241–2.

Barnett, B. E. (1980). A physico-chemical method for the extraction of marine and estuarine benthos from clays and resistant muds. *J. mar. biol. Ass. U.K.* **60**, 225.

Buchanan, J. B. & Warwick, R. M. (1974). An estimate of benthic macrofaunal production in an offshore mud off the Northumberland coast. *J. mar. biol. Ass. U.K.* **54**, 197–222.

Coleman, N. (1980) More on sorting benthic samples. *Mar. Pollut. Bull.* **11**, 150–2.

Crisp, D. J. (1984). Energy flow measurements. In *Methods for the Study of Marine Benthos*, 2nd ed, ed. N. A. Holme & A. D. McIntyre, pp. 284–372. Oxford: Blackwell.

Eleftheriou, A. & Holme, N. A. (1984). Macrofauna techniques. In *Methods for the Study of Marine Benthos*, 2nd edn, ed. N. A. Holme & A. D. McIntyre, pp. 140–216. Oxford: Blackwell.

Fauchald, K. (1977). The polychaete worms. Definitions and keys to the orders, families and genera. *Natural History Museum of Los Angeles County, Science Series*, **28**, 1–190.

Haaland, B. & Schram, T. A. (1982). Larval development and metamorphosis of *Gyptis rosea* (Malm) (Hesionidae: Polychaeta). *Sarsia* **67**, 107–18.

Holme, N. A. (1959). A hopper for use when sieving bottom samples at sea. *J. mar. biol. Ass. U.K.* **38**, 525–9.

Kleef, H. L. (1984). A simple and time-saving method for quantitative collection of *Corophium volutator* (Crustacea: Amphipoda) from plankton samples rich in detritus. *Hydrobiol. Bull.* **18**, 47–50.

Lauff, G. M., Cummins, K. W., Enksen, C. H. & Parker, M. (1961). A method for sorting bottom fauna samples by elutriation. *Limnol. Oceanogr.* **6**, 462–6.

Mulder, M. & Arkel, M. A. van (1980). An improved system for quantitative sampling of benthos in shallow water using the flushing technique. *Neth. J. Sea Res.* **14**, 119–22.

Pearson, T. H. (1975). The benthic ecology of Loch Linnhe and Loch Eil, a sea-loch system on the west coast of Scotland. IV. Changes in the benthic fauna attributable to organic enrichment. *J. exp. mar. Biol. Ecol.* **20**, 1–41.

Rees, H. L. (1984). A note on mesh selection and sampling efficiency in benthic studies. *Mar. Pollut. Bull.* **15**, 225–9.

Reish, D. J., 1959. A discussion of the importance of the screen size in quantitative marine bottom samples. *Ecology*, **40**, 307–9.

Rosenberg, R. (1973). Succession in benthic macrofauna in a Swedish fjord subsequent to the closure of a sulphite pulp mill. *Oikos*, **24**, 1–16.

Self, R. F. L. & Jumars, P. A. (1978). New resource axes for deposit feeders? *J. mar. Res.* **36**, 627–41.

Starling, C. C. (1971). Handpicking macroinvertebrates. Three methods compared. *Proc. Ann. Conf. S. E. Assoc. Game Fish. Comm.* **25**, 622–26.

Warwick, R. M. (1984). Sampling and analysis of benthic communities. In *Practical Procedures for Estuarine Studies*, ed. A. W. Morris, pp. 185–212. Plymouth: Institute for Marine Environmental Research.

Willems, K. A., Vanosmael, C., Claeys, D., Vincx, M. & Heip, C. (1982). Benthos of a sublittoral sandbank in the southern bight of the North Sea: general considerations. *J. mar. biol. Ass. U.K.* **62**, 549–57.

Williams, G. E., III (1974). New technique to facilitate handpicking macrobenthos. *Trans. Amer. Micros. Soc.* **93**, 220–6.

Williams, D. D. & Williams, N. E. (1974). A counterstaining technique for use in sorting benthic samples. *Limnol. Oceanogr.* **19**, 152–4.

7

Meiofauna

L. A. BOUWMAN

Introduction

The meiofauna comprises animals intermediate in size between microfaunal organisms such as ciliates, amoebas, and foraminiferans, and macrofaunal organisms such as gastropods, bivalves, and polychaetes. It is usually defined as benthic metazoa that can pass through a sieve with a mesh size of 0.5 or 1.0 mm. The smaller mesh size excludes small and larval macrofauna more effectively, however, larger meiofauna may also be retained. The meiofauna consists mainly of various types of microscopic worms and crustaceans.

Warwick (1984) studied the size distribution of animal species in various marine benthic communities. In the histograms obtained he observed a trough between numbers of meio- and macrobenthic species at a body weight of 45 μg (dry weight), as the meiofaunal mode occurred at c. 0.6 μg and the macrofaunal mode at c. 3 mg. This gap probably separates an interstitial and a burrowing mode of life and is thus of real ecological importance. The mentioned gap is widened by the fact that larval stages of most macrofauna live pelagically. It seems that the numerical under-representation of small macrofauna could be responsible for the conjectured lack of flux of biomass from meio- to macrofauna.

In the marine environment, the fundamental biological processes of primary production and of decomposition are largely performed by microscopic algae and bacteria, whereas metazoa thrive on these micro-organisms, directly or indirectly. However, although metazoa are not essential to the basic processes, they accelerate or slow down the process rates. In the benthic environment meiofauna consume unicellular organisms such as bacteria, microscopic algae, and protozoa; in turn, meiofauna are consumed by macrofaunal organisms such as shrimps, gobies, and juvenile flatfish. Moreover, in nearly all meiofaunal associations, internal predation also occurs. Johannes (1965) proposed the hypothesis that grazing nematodes and other meiofauna play a major role in benthic nutrient recycling by keeping microorganisms in an active state and thus preventing them from becoming senescent bottle-necks in the energy flow of benthic ecosystems. Also Gerlach (1978) emphasised the role of meiofaunal organisms as gardeners of the microflora and -fauna. Meiofaunal organisms, because of their feeding habits and minute size, are intimately bound to the microbenthos; thus, these animals reflect characteristics of the microflora and -fauna, such as abundance and diversity, in terms of their own density and wealth of species. Therefore, the study of meiofauna may also provide insights on the microbenthos and consequently on the entire biological system.

Meiofaunal organisms occur in nearly all benthic biotopes: abyssal, sublittoral, littoral, and supralittoral; in all types of sediment; in surface layers and down to depths of 30 cm, and in some places even deeper; in oxygenated and anoxic habitats; in physically exposed and in sheltered sediments. In coarse sediments the organisms live in the interstitial spaces without altering these, and in muds they move as burrowers. Most meiofaunal organisms do not actively leave the sediment as they cannot swim However, many species of harpacticoid copepods and turbellarians commute between the sediment surface and the overlying water; consequently, these organisms are more vulnerable to predation than permanently interstitial species.

On average, densities of meiofaunal organisms in coastal areas amount to several millions of individuals per square metre and biomasses are up to 2 g of carbon m^{-2} (see also Table 7.1). Species numbers in the various habitats range from a dozen to several hundreds. Highest densities and lowest species numbers occur in sheltered estuarine habitats and lowest densities in wave-exposed and in abyssal surroundings. Highest diversities are observed in subtidal fully marine sediments.

Generation times take from a few days up to one year, but the majority of meiofaunal organisms complete life cycles in a few weeks or months. Most species reproduce sexually and produce up to about 100 offspring. Other modes of reproduction and larger numbers of offspring are not rare, however, and occur in particular among opportunistic species. McIntyre (1969), Gerlach (1971), and Warwick & Price (1979) estimated meiofaunal annual turnover rates to be 8 to 10 and thus an order of magnitude larger than the turnover rate of macrofauna. Although, in general, biomass of meiofauna is small compared with macrofaunal biomass, the metabolic activity of the meiofauna often equals the activity of the macrofauna as was demonstrated by Warwick & Price (1979) for an estuarine mud flat.

Table 7.1. *Abundance, biomass, and taxonomic composition of meiofauna in some offshore, shallow subtidal, exposed, and sheltered intertidal sediments*

	Offshore			Coastal: shallow subtidal		Intertidal		
	(1)	(1)	(1)	(2)	(3)	(4)	(5)	(2)
Number of organisms m⁻² (×10⁶)	0.3	0.6	0.025	2.5	4.0	4.0	6.0	2.0
						1–12	2–20	0.5–4.2[a]
Biomass as grams m⁻² (dry weight)				1.1	0.8		2.5	0.6
Relative proportion (%) of the various taxa:								
nematodes	65	90	87	61	96	86	95	47
harp. copepods	15	4	6	17	3	4	1	25
turbellarians	2	+	+	8		4	1	10
oligochaetes	0.5	0.5	1	0	+		3	2
others	+	+	+	+	+	+		+
Water depth in metres	400	800	4000	0–7	35	tidal	tidal	tidal
Type of sediment	fine sand	silt	silt	fine sand	very fine silty sand	silt /clay	very fine silty sand	medium sand

$\quad$Number of organisms m⁻² $(\times 10^6)$

(1) Atlantic Ocean – North Carolina, USA (Coull *et al.*, 1977).
(2) Atlantic Ocean – Loch Ewe, West Coast, Scotland (McIntyre & Murison, 1973).
(3) North Sea – Helgoland, German Bight, Federal Republic of Germany (Juario, 1975).
(4) Atlantic Ocean – Bristol Channel, Cardiff area, UK (Rees, 1940).
(5) North Sea – Ems estuary, Dollart, The Netherlands (Bouwman *et al.*, 1984).
[a] For the intertidal areas the minimum and maximum densities are also given.

Tietjen (1969), Skoolmun & Gerlach (1971), Bouwman (1983), and Bouwman, Romeyn & Admiraal (1984) showed that meiofaunal associations fluctuate seasonally with respect to density, biomass, and species composition in shallow waters, intertidal areas, and estuaries; in deeper, subtidal waters, however, Warwick & Buchanan (1971) and Juario (1975) observed no seasonal fluctuations. When seasonal fluctuations occur, densities generally increase in spring following the low winter levels; sometimes a second rise is observed in autumn. The various species and higher taxonomic categories do not fluctuate synchronously and may peak at different times of the year.

The following taxa, in sequence of numerical abundance and extent of distribution, constitute the meiofauna: Nematoda, Copepoda harpacticoida, Turbellaria, Oligochaeta, Ostracoda. Taxa of minor significance are: Nemertini, Tardigrada, Kinorhyncha, Gastrotricha, Rotatoria, Archiannelida, Halacarida, Priapulida, Tanaidacea, small Polychaeta, and, finally, larval stages of macrofauna. Nematodes occur in almost all marine habitats: abyssal, sublittoral, shallow sublittoral, exposed and sheltered intertidal, on the surface of marine macrophytes, and in the deeper sediment layers. They dominate meiofaunal species associations numerically and with respect to biomass and species diversity. The success of nematodes as a group is due to their shape which is particularly adapted to the interstitial labyrinth, to their ability to exploit all types of microorganisms as food, to their diverse methods of reproduction, and to their resistance to almost all types of physico–chemical stress. Whereas a particular nematode species may demand specific environmental conditions, the variation within the taxon of nematodes is so wide that for every environment a number of adapted species is available. Harpacticoid copepods rank second in abundance among marine meiofauna. Most other groups of meiofaunal organisms are less ubiquitous, though in particular environments turbellarians, oligochaetes, or ostracods may constitute important components of the meiofauna. In exposed coastal areas turbellarians comprise almost as many species as the nematodes, and in sheltered estuarine surroundings oligochaetes, ostracods, and turbellarians may be almost as numerous as the nematodes although their wealth of species is always considerably less. With regard to species diversity, Wolff & Dankers (1981), for example, listed the following numbers of species for the Wadden Sea: Nematoda, $c.\,300$; Turbellaria, $c.\,300$; Copepoda harpacticoida, $c.\,150$; Ostracoda, $c.\,30$; Oligochaeta, $c.\,20$; Archiannelida, 6; Nemertini, 4; Tardigrada, 3. It may be assumed that these numbers of species are underestimates of the real numbers but they demonstrate the order of magnitude of the species richness in a certain area. For the

North Sea area altogether more than 700 nematode species and 500 harpacticoid species were listed by Heip, Herman & Vincx (1983).

Although from the evolutionary viewpoint estuarine and intertidal meiofauna is mainly of marine origin, this meiofauna differs considerably from the fauna in offshore waters, and a few species of freshwater origin may also occupy dominant positions. In parallel with decreasing salinity, strictly marine species vanish and densities of marine species adapted to brackish-water conditions increase; simultaneously, the total number of different species and higher taxonomic entities decreases.

Aims of meiofauna surveys

Biological surveys of estuaries and coasts deal with species and species associations that have occurred there for a certain period. Consequently, the species associations sampled at a certain date are determined by the environmental conditions in the preceding period of time, and one should know these conditions, in particular the extreme events such as storms, occurrences of ice, freshwater floods, and desiccation of the sediment. These extreme impacts are able to destroy or remove entire meiofaunal associations and the species of the successive pioneer association may be quite different.

Aims of surveys concerning meiofauna can be ranged under the same categories as biological surveys in general (Chapter 1.) The following aims are of particular relevance.

1. Scientific research concerning the (aut)ecology of a species or a higher taxonomic category. Investigations of distribution and ecology of a particular species or of higher categories are generally carried out by meiofauna specialists. Often this type of research is of a fundamental scientific character. However, when a survey shows that a particular species or higher taxonomic category is indicative for particular environmental conditions, the significance of the study of that species goes beyond the species concerned. In particular the performance (population dynamics, growth, production) of a species in a certain habitat may have wider implications.

2. Scientific research concerning the role of meiofauna in the functioning of marine ecosystems. For example, in budget studies quantitative information is needed; therefore, in such studies densities of meiofaunal organisms and their distribution have to be surveyed, either as total numbers or as numbers of organisms per species or higher taxonomic category. A transformation of numbers into wet or dry weights or into grams of carbon m^{-2} is

usual. Biomass figures may be used for calculations of annual meiofaunal productivity. This is often based on data from the literature, but it is sometimes completed with data from one's own laboratory experiments on metabolic rates. Production estimates should be based on actual species compositions, densities expressed as grams of carbon m^{-2}, respiration figures for the various component species, and the annual course of the temperature. Recent figures on metabolic activity of nematodes from an estuarine intertidal mud flat are presented by Warwick & Price (1979). They determined respiration rates of 16 dominating nematode species and calculated the total annual respiration of the nematode association from their study site in the Lynher estuary by combining the data from the respiration rates measured in the laboratory with field data on population structure, size frequency, and mean monthly water temperatures. The average population of 12.5×10^6 nematodes m^{-2} (2.0 g dry weight; 0.8 g carbon) respired annually 28 l O$_2$ m^{-2} (11.2 g carbon) and produced annually 6.6 g carbon m^{-2}.

3. Education. Because of their diversity and manifold ecological adaptations, meiofauna may be particularly suitable to illustrate ecological principles to students. Many species of estuarine and coastal nematodes and harpacticoids can be reared under laboratory conditions and due to their relatively short generation times, yield much information on their biology in the course of a few months.

4. Biological surveillance. Meiofauna may be used to monitor the state of a marine or estuarine ecosystem. A first step towards this is usually a survey and the development of a protocol for the detection of temporal change. As knowledge on the ecology of individual species is limited, presence or absence of a species in a particular area in general cannot be fully explained; consequently, at the present state of knowledge individual meiofaunal species do not seem to be very useful for monitoring ecosystems. Thus, indices of biomass, diversity, and presence or absence of higher taxonomic categories offer the better parameters.

5. Assessment of damage. Pollution in coastal and estuarine areas may be of chemical (organic waste, heavy metals, etc.) or physical (turbidity, heat, etc.) origin. Surveys of meiofauna aimed at investigating pollution effects are very difficult because of the natural variability and the spatial and temporal variations within meiofaunal associations. Thus, to unravel the effects of pollution,

knowledge of these variations is essential, as is the knowledge of the meiofauna in a comparable unpolluted area. This information is not easily collected as has been demonstrated by Eskin & Coull (1984).

Planning considerations

In principle, when designing a sampling programme for meiofauna one has to deal with the same problems as designing a macrofauna survey; however, the scale is centimetres instead of metres. Distribution of meiofaunal organisms in the sediment is aggregated for total numbers as well as for individual species. Thus, replication of samples and samplings is necessary to determine the variance between sites and dates and to allow statistical evaluation of differences. The number of replicates to be taken depends on the aims of the survey, the required level of accuracy, and the available resources. For the obligate benthic nematodes, patches with diameters of 1–6 cm have been observed by Arlt (1973), Findlay (1981), and Eskin & Coull (1984); these nematode patches probably cover aggregated food organisms. Many harpacticoid copepods, however, commute between the sediment surface and the overlying water and thus their aggregated distribution should also be due to microhydrographic and microtopographic factors. Also, on a larger scale, meiofauna changes qualitatively as well as quantitatively. This is the case towards coasts and the heads of estuaries in parallel with salinity gradients, but also vertically down into the sediment and in certain cases over time.

Research into meiofauna is very time consuming and one has to decide at an early stage either to investigate species or higher taxonomic categories. When studying species, much expertise on taxonomy and methods of handling particular taxa has to be recruited before a sample programme can be started. One must also realize that the size and shape of most meiofaunal species is very variable, depending on the environmental conditions; thus, the within-species variability may hamper the identification by inexperienced investigators.

Meiofauna studies may be qualitative (presence/absence of species or higher taxonomic entities at various sites or dates), semi-quantitative (relative composition of the meiofauna at the level of species or higher taxonomic entities), or quantitative (absolute numbers, densities of species, or numbers of organisms belonging to different meiofaunal groups). For quantitative studies far more replicates are needed than for qualitative studies. The survey programme has to compromise between limited time and sampling facilities and the questions to be answered. Sampling at sea will generally have to accommodate to programmes designed for other purposes; for shore sampling special meiofauna programmes may be carried out with more ease.

The main factor to be taken into account when locating the sample stations is the occurrence of gradients in the area investigated. These gradients may be of natural origin (physical, chemical, sedimentological, hydrographical, biological) and of human origin (pollution, hydraulic interventions). Presence, direction, and trend of all possible gradients in the survey area should be known if possible, consequently it must be decided which gradient(s) are probably relevant to the aims of the survey and these have to be taken into account when setting out the sample stations. Most gradients run parallel or at right angles to the coast line but directions from point source discharges may be different, depending on hydrographical conditions.

A pre-sampling programme is likely to give information invaluable for designing the final programme. Preliminary insight into densities, distribution patterns, diversities, and gradients in meiofaunal associations will indicate the size and number of replicate samples to be taken. Sampling a homogeneous area without measurable gradients is simple, stations being located by means of a grid or at random. Usually, however, gradients have to be taken into account and sample stations have to be located along transects parallel to the gradient(s). The number of stations depends on the steepness of the gradient. When, for example, sampling is carried out along a salinity gradient running from fresh water to fully marine conditions, from the biological point of view at least six stations should be investigated; these stations should be located within the ranges of < 0.5, 0.5–5, 5–10, 10–20, 20–30, and $> 30\%_0$ S (total salinity).

The appropriate number of replicates depends on the aims of the survey and the density and distribution of the organisms to be sampled. For a survey of one species, one sample per station may suffice, and the chosen sample size should depend on the expected density of that species; the frequency of sampling should depend on the rate at which the life cycle of the investigated species proceeds. This also applies for a qualitative survey of a certain taxonomic entity such as the nematodes or the harpacticoids. For a semi-quantitative survey of a higher taxonomic category, the required number of replicates will depend on the relative species diversity; in meiofauna research, diversity is usually expressed by means of the Shannon-Wiener index of diversity (see Chapter 1). With respect to nematodes, these being the most diverse and numerically predominant taxon, Bouwman (1983) indicates that three replicates generally suffice for associations with a high diversity and at least two replicates are needed for the characterisation of associations with low diversity. For quantitative surveys more replicates are needed; for numerical studies of meiofauna a high degree of precision requires at least 30 and preferably 50 small samples per station (Elliott, 1977). Slight increases in sample numbers do not repay the extra time necessary for processing the samples. Thus, generally one has to accept the lowest level of precision with respect to the aims of quantitative studies, otherwise processing will be too time consuming.

With respect to sampling frequency, one has to bear in mind that the dominating nematodes and copepods in offshore associations do not change very much throughout the year, whereas in intertidal and shallow subtidal coastal and estuarine sediments, the associations change seasonally. For stable, subtidal associations, one sampling in the warmer season and one in the colder season are probably sufficient; in dynamic intertidal and shallow waters, stations should preferably be sampled monthly, but at least four times per year.

In case a preliminary sampling programme at sea is not feasible, one should locate the stations along probable hydrographic gradients. Because steepness of the gradients and diversity and variability of the meiofauna are not known, it is recommended to have larger numbers of stations and of samples per station than usual.

Sampling methods

Patchiness in the horizontal plane is a matter of centimetres for meiofaunal organisms. Yet the sharpest gradients in the abundance and species composition of meiofauna occur vertically in the sediment: several different biotopes, each with its own characteristic meiofauna, may be distinguished over a depth of one or a few centimetres. A device to sample thin (1 mm) sections of sediment cores is described by Joint, Gee & Warwick (1982). Because of this small-scale horizontal patchiness and layering in the vertical plane, meiofaunists generally analyse small entire samples. Sub-sampling from larger volumes is not recommended because of the increased chance of the introduction of inaccuracies.

For quantitative sampling, Perspex tubes 1.0–2.5 cm in diameter and 10–30 cm in length should be used to take the large number of required sediment cores, both at sea and on the shore. For qualitative sampling, small numbers of larger samples should be taken with 2.5–4.0 cm diameter tubes. For sampling at sea, larger sample cores are often taken to reduce the number of replicates and investigators such as Tietjen (1969) and Coull (1969) therefore used tubes with a diameter of 3.5 cm. Special corers are necessary to carry out the sampling from aboard a ship. The Craib corers, described by Craib (1965) and Holme & McIntyre (1984) and developed by the Scottish Marine Biological Association, are considered to serve best for sampling the meiofauna of subtidal sediments. McIntyre (1971) demonstrated that sub-sampling from larger samples taken for other purposes by a grab or a dredge is not quantitatively reliable; besides, these samplers also disturb or destroy the vertical structure of the sample. However, the use of such samplers may be the only thing possible to fit with other survey work. Sampling by means of SCUBA diving (see Chapter 9) is as reliable as the use of a Craib corer.

In view of the vertical faunal gradients, it is recommended to slice the core as soon as possible after sampling. The thickness of the slices will depend on the steepness of the vertical sediment gradients as well as on changes in the packing of the core, easily visible through the transparent tube. The length of the sampled core and the chosen thickness of the slices may also be chosen following preliminary analyses of the vertical distribution of meiofaunal organisms and associations; generally short cores (5–15 cm) should be taken in muddy sediments and long cores (20–30 cm) should be taken in sandy sediments.

In the case of sampling harpacticoids, one has to sample also a small volume of the overlying water, otherwise a large proportion of the organisms will be missed.

Sample processing

Samples (core slices) are generally preserved in 4% formaldehyde before further processing the organisms. However, for soft meiofauna such as gastrotrichs and turbellarians, fresh samples should be studied. These may be stored temporarily at 4 °C. Also, for observations on hard meiofauna such as nematodes and copepods, living animals may provide information that disappears during fixation (pigments, eye spots, etc.). The addition of the protein stain rose bengal to the sample increases the visibility of the organisms during sorting.

For separation of meiofauna from sediments, the choice of method depends on the aims of the research and the type of sediment. For qualitative purposes, suspension of up to 15 cm³ of sediment in c. 800 ml water (height c. 30 cm) and decantation of the supernatant through a sieve (30–60 μm mesh size) after a short period of settlement (30–60 sec) generally suffices to obtain sufficient numbers of organisms; this method is applicable to coarse as well as fine sediments. For quantitative isolation of organisms from coarse sediments, the procedure of suspension, decantation, and sieving is also effective, but it has to be repeated up to seven times. Therefore in this case the use of an elutriator, such as that developed by Boisseau (1957) or Oostenbrink (1960), is recommended when large numbers of samples have to be processed. For quantitative isolation of organisms from fine sediments, the Ludox-flotation method of de Jonge & Bouwman (1977) seems to be most appropriate. In this procedure sediment samples are suspended in the colloidal silica Ludox-TM (Du Pont, 1973) in which organisms and light detritus float at the surface while sediment particles sink to the bottom in about 12 hours time. Then the supernatant Ludox is poured through a sieve on which the organisms are rinsed with distilled water (sea/estuary water if it is required to isolate living animals from fresh samples) to remove the Ludox and small detritus. The procedure is accelerated considerably by 7 minutes centrifugation at 6000 rpm instead of standing overnight (Holme & McIntyre, 1984). For some heavier organisms such as ostracods the method is not appropriate as these organisms also sink in the Ludox. Ostracods should be isolated by means of a method such as that described by Barnett (1968). With this method the sample is put on a horizontal trough, 90 cm long and 2 cm wide. Tapwater (or sea/estuary water if it is required to isolate living animals from fresh samples) is allowed to run over the sample for half an hour and the sediment is periodically stirred with the aid of a siphon; meiofaunal organisms, including 100% of the ostracods, are collected on a sieve.

Mesh sizes larger than 45 μm may be used, in particular for silty sediments, to prevent clogging of the sieve when pouring out the supernatant or the overflow from the elutriator. However, increasing mesh size decreases efficiency; for example, McIntyre (1964) found that only 60% of the nematodes were retained on a 76 μm sieve.

For the isolation of and observations on living meiofauna, the organisms should be anaesthetised with magnesium chloride isotonic with sea water; this treatment is recommended because living animals often adhere strongly to sand grains and thus, during separation, also sink to the bottom.

A review on isolation methods is given by Uhlig, Thiel & Gray (1973). However, since the introduction of the Ludox-flotation method, most other methods appear to be rendered out of date.

For sub-sampling from larger samples, the separated organisms are put into a certain volume of water that is vigorously agitated by means of bubbling while at the same time the sub-sample of known volume is sucked up with a pipette. Then the organisms are sorted and counted under a binocular microscope and, if necessary, identified to species level under a high-power microscope.

For identification the hard meiofauna can be mounted as permanent slides in glycerol after a gradual substitution of water (via alcohol) by glycerol (Seinhorst, 1959). Special requirements for the examination of the various higher taxonomic categories are given by Hulings & Gray (1971).

The dry weight of heavier organisms can be determined directly on an electrobalance sensitive to c. 0.1 μg, whereas for lighter species or life stages, weights may be estimated from volume determinations. For nematodes an estimate of the volume can be obtained by measuring body length and maximum body width; calculation methods used by Andrássy (1956) have been modified by Warwick & Price (1979). Volume is transformed to dry weight by assuming a specific gravity of 1.13 and a dry weight/wet weight ratio of c. 0.25; the carbon content amounts to 40–50% of the dry weight, according to Jensen (1984). Warwick & Gee (1984) developed a method for estimating copepod body volumes. They distinguished eight types of body form, which cover the variety that may be found in samples, and determined conversion factors for each form. Biomass of all organisms in a sample can be determined directly by means of combustion in a total-carbon analyser; small individual organisms may be analysed rapidly in the carbon analyser developed by Salonen (1979). Dry weight figures for nematode species (individuals) range from c. 0.1 to 2.0 μg (Warwick & Price, 1979) and for harpacticoids from c. 0.5 to 14.0 μg (Goodman, 1980). For the oligochaetes, turbellarians, and ostracods the same range of dry weights occurs (0.1–14.0 μg).

Data processing and interpretation

Table 7.2 shows a framework of options for meiofauna surveys of increasing completeness, ranging from an occasional survey of one species to frequent samplings of the entire meiofauna during several years. Surveys of a meiofaunal species or a higher taxonomic category may produce information on spatial and temporal distribution and on the performance along gradients or in a particular area. These data should be related to the environmental parameters measured to find out which parameter(s) primarily control distribution and other characteristics of that species or higher taxonomic category. In wave-exposed beaches, physical parameters probably are of predominant importance, whereas in sheltered areas, crowded with small macrofauna, biological parameters may be dominating. In polluted areas, chemical conditions may be of prime importance, as has been discussed by Hulings & Gray (1976). Survey data should be compared with literature data from similar areas to qualify or quantify their relative significance.

Distribution and performance of a particular species or higher taxonomic category may be indicative of some environmental condition. Obviously, easily perceptible macrofaunal species can generally be better used as environmental indicators than microscopic meiofaunal species. However, such macrofaunal species do not occur in all habitats; moreover, meiofaunal organisms may in particular be indicative of interstitial conditions. For example, members of the marine nematode family of the Comesomatidae inhabit muddy sediments, often in high densities (Jensen, 1981). The

Table 7.2. *Framework for meiofauna survey*

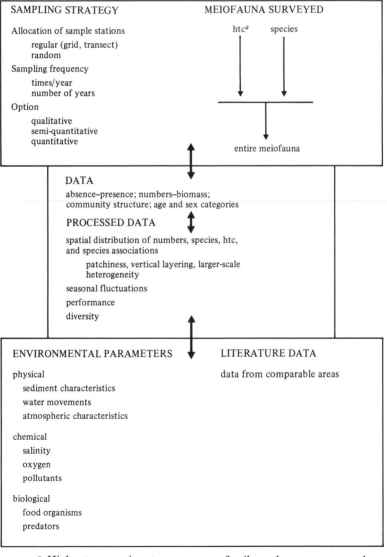

SAMPLING STRATEGY   MEIOFAUNA SURVEYED

Allocation of sample stations   htc[a]   species
   regular (grid, transect)
   random
Sampling frequency
   times/year
   number of years
Option
   qualitative
   semi-quantitative
   quantitative   entire meiofauna

DATA
absence–presence; numbers–biomass;
community structure; age and sex categories

PROCESSED DATA

spatial distribution of numbers, species, htc,
and species associations
   patchiness, vertical layering, larger-scale
   heterogeneity
seasonal fluctuations
performance
diversity

ENVIRONMENTAL PARAMETERS   LITERATURE DATA

physical   data from comparable areas
   sediment characteristics
   water movements
   atmospheric characteristics

chemical
   salinity
   oxygen
   pollutants

biological
   food organisms
   predators

[a] Higher taxonomic category; genus, family, order, or groups such as nematodes and oligochaetes.

comesomatid species *Sabatieria pulchra* often predominates in the nematode fauna of north-west European estuarine muds, in the intertidal as well as the subtidal zones. The favoured microenvironment of this species is the redox potential discontinuity layer; this sediment layer is located a few millimetres to a few centimetres deep, between the oxygenated upper and the anaerobic deeper layers. Bouwman (1978) observed that this nematode species disappeared while at the same time the discontinuity layer diminished as an effect of an increased load of fresh organic waste-water. The disappearance of the nematode probably was caused primarily by the reduction of its microhabitat but the disappearance may have been enhanced by a change to adverse salinity. The example illustrates a generality, namely that indicators of pollution effects should preferably have narrow amplitudes of distribution, and that they should occur in considerable densities in clearly defined habitats. At present, too little is known about the eco-physiology of common meiofaunal species for them to be of much use as indicators of environmental conditions.

For higher taxonomic categories the same comments apply as for individual species: genera, families, orders, and entire groups such as harpacticoids and ostracods have their own, characteristic, more-or-less extensive area of distribution. For a group (such as the nematodes) that is abundant in nearly all biotopes, families or even orders may be characteristically distributed. For example, one of the five important marine nematode orders, the Desmodorida, is quite numerous (numbers and species) under fully marine conditions and nearly absent under reduced salinity conditions. Because areas of distribution of higher taxonomic categories are generally wider than those of most individual species, surveys of their distribution may render information on a larger scale. However, for the study of meiofaunal performance, the use of higher taxonomic categories could be too complicated, and for these studies individual species probably offer better opportunities.

For the further study of higher taxonomic categories, the isolated specimens may be identified to species level, age category, and sex categories. In this way faunal associations may be distinguished and temporal dynamics, spatial distribution, diversity, and productivity may be calculated. A comparison with literature data from similar areas may indicate whether the meiofauna of the surveyed area is relatively diverse or uniform, productive or unproductive, in equilibrium or not.

References

Andrássy, I. (1956). Die Rauminhalts- und Gewichtsbestimmung der Fadenwürmer (Nematoden). *Acta Zoologica Acadaem. Scientiarum Hungaricae* **2**, 1–15.

Arlt, G. (1973). Vertical and horizontal microdistribution of the meiofauna in the Griefswalder Bodden. *Oikos*, Suppl. **15**, 105–111.

Barnett, P. R. O. (1968). Distribution and ecology of harpacticoid copepods of an intertidal mud flat. *Internationale Revue der Gesamten Hydrobiologie*, **53**, 177–209.

Boisseau, J. P. (1957). Technique pour l'étude quantitative de la faune interstitielle des sables. *Comptes Rendus du Congrès des Sociétés Savantes de Paris et des Départements*, 117–19.

Bouwman, L. A. (1978). Investigation on nematodes in the Ems-Dollart estuary. *Anns. Soc. r. zoo. Belg.* **108**, 103–5.

Bouwman, L. A. (1983). A survey of nematodes from the Ems estuary. II. Species assemblages and associations. *Zoo. Jb., Systematik, Oekologie und Geographie der Tiere* **110**, 345–76.

Bouwman, L. A., Romeyn, K. & Admiraal, W. (1984). On the ecology of meiofauna in an organically polluted estuarine mudflat. *Estuar. Coast. Shelf Sci.* **19**, 633–53.

Coull, B. C. (1969). Shallow water meiobenthos of the Bermuda platform. *Oecologia* (Berl.) **4**, 325–57.

Coull, B. C., Ellison, R. L., Fleeger, J. W., Higgins, R. P., Hope, W. D., Hummon, W. D., Rieger, R. M., Sterrer, W. E., Thiel, H. & Tietjen, J. H., (1977). Quantitative estimates of the meiofauna from the deep sea off North Carolina, USA. *Mar. Biol.* **39**, 233–40.

Craib, J. S. (1965). A sampler for taking short undisturbed cores. *Journal du Conseil Permanent International pour l'Exploration de la Mer* **30**, 346–53.

Du Pont (1973). *Ludox Colloidal Silica.* Product Information Bulletin, E. I. Du Pont de Nemours & Co. (Inc.), Industrial Chemicals Department, Wilmington, Delaware, U.S.A.

Elliott, J. M. (1977). *Some Methods for the Statistical Analysis of Samples of Invertebrates*, 2nd edn. Scientific Publications 25 (2nd ed.). Ambleside: Freshwater Biological Association.

Eskin, R. A. & Coull, B. C. (1984). A priori determination of valid control sites: an example using marine meiobenthic nematodes. *Mar. environ. Res.* **12**, 161–172.

Findlay, S. E. G. (1981). Small-scale spatial distribution of meiofauna on a mud- and sandflat. *Estuar. Coast. Shelf Sci.* **12**, 471–84.

Gerlach, S. A. (1971). On the importance of marine meiofauna for benthos communities. *Oecologia* (Berl.) **6**, 176–90.

Gerlach, S. A. (1978). Food-chain relationships in subtidal silty sand marine sediments and the role of meiofauna in stimulating bacterial productivity. *Oecologia* (Berl.) **33**, 55–69.

Goodman, K. S. (1980). The estimation of individual dry weight and standing crop of harpacticoid copepods. *Hydrobiologia* **72**, 253–9.

Heip, C., Herman, R. & Vincx, M. (1983). Subtidal meiofauna of the North Sea: a review. *Biologisch Jaarboek Dodonaea*, **51**, 116–70.

Holme, N. A. & McIntyre, A. D. (eds) (1984) *Methods for the Study of Marine Benthos.* IBP Handbook 16. Oxford: Blackwell Scientific Publications.

Hulings, N. C. & Gray, J. S. (1971). A manual for the study of meiofauna. *Smithsonian Contrib. Zool.* **78**, 1–84.

Hulings, N. C. & Gray, J. S. (1976). Physical factors controlling abundance of meiofauna on tidal and atidal beaches. *Mar. Biol.* **34**, 77–83.

Jensen, P. (1981). Species, distribution and a microhabitat theory for the marine mud dwelling Comesomatidae (Nematoda) in European waters. *Cahiers de Biologie Marine* **22**, 231–41.

Jensen, P. (1984). Measuring carbon content in nematodes. *Helgoländer wissenschaftliche Meeresuntersuchungen* **38**, 83–6.

Johannes, R. E. (1965). Influence of marine protozoa on nutrient regeneration. *Limnol. Oceanogr.* **10**, 434–42.

Joint, I. R., Gee, J. M & Warwick, R. M. (1982). Determination of fine-scale distribution of microbes and meiofauna in an intertidal sediment. *Mar. Biol.* **72**, 157–64.

Jonge, V. N. de & Bouwman, L. A. (1977). A simple density separation technique for quantitative isolation of meiobenthos using the colloidal silica Ludox-TM. *Mar. Biol.* **42**, 143–8.

Juario, J. V. (1975). Nematode species composition and seasonal fluctuation of a sublittoral meiofauna community in the German Bight. *Veröffentlichungen Institut für Meeresforschung Bremerhaven* **15**, 283–337.

McIntyre, A. D. (1964). Meiobenthos of sublittoral muds. *J. mar. biol. Ass. U.K.* **44**, 665–74.

McIntyre, A. D. (1969). Ecology of marine meiobenthos. *Biol. Rev. Camb. phil. Soc.* **44**, 245–90.

McIntyre, A. D. (1971). Deficiency of gravity corers for sampling meiobenthos and sediments. *Nature* (Lond.) **231**, 260.

McIntyre, A. D. & Murison, D. J. (1973). The meiofauna of a flatfish nursery ground. *J. mar. biol. Ass. U.K.* **53**, 93–118.

Oostenbrink, M. (1960). Estimating nematode populations by some selected methods. In *Nematology*, ed. J. N. Sasser & W. R. Jenkins, pp. 196–205. Columbia: University of North Carolina Press.

Rees, C. B. (1940). A preliminary study of the ecology of a mudflat. *J. Mar. biol. Ass. U.K.* **24**, 185–99.

Salonen, K. (1979). A versatile method for the rapid and accurate determination of carbon by high temperature combustion. *Limnol. Oceanog.* **18**, 306–10.

Seinhorst, J. W. (1959). A rapid method for the transfer of nematodes from fixative to anhydrous glycerine. *Nematologica*, **4**, 67–9.

Skoolmun, P. & Gerlach, S. A. (1971). Jahreszeitliche Fluktuationen der Nematodenfauna im Gezeitenbereich des Weser-Ästuars (Deutsche Bucht). *Veröffentlichungen Institut für Meeresforschung Bremerhaven* **13**, 119–38.

Tietjen, J. H. (1969). The ecology of shallow water meiofauna in two New England estuaries. *Oecologia* (Berl.) **2**, 251–91.

Uhlig, G. H., Thiel, H. & Grey, J. S. (1973). The quantitative separation of meiofauna. A comparison of methods. *Helgoländer wissenschaftliche Meeresuntersuchungen* **25**, 173–95.

Warwick, R. M. (1984). Species size distribution in marine benthic communities. *Oecologia* (Berl.) **61**, 32–41.

Warwick, R. M. & Buchanan, J. B. (1971). The meiofauna off the coast of

Northumberland. II. Seasonal stability of the nematode population. *J. mar. biol. Ass. U.K.* **51**, 355–62.

Warwick, R. M. & Gee, J. M. (1984). Community structure of estuarine meiobenthos. *Marine Ecology – Progress Series* **18**, 97–111.

Warwick, R. M. & Price, R. (1979). Ecological and metabolic studies on free-living nematodes from an estuarine mud-flat. *Estuar. Coast. Mar. Sci.* **9**, 257–71.

Wolff, W. J. & Dankers, N. (1981). Preliminary checklist of the zoobenthos and nekton species of the Wadden Sea. In *Invertebrates of the Wadden Sea; final report of the Marine Zoology section of the Wadden Sea Working Group*, ed. N. Dankers, H. Kühl & W. J. Wolff, pp. 29–60. Rotterdam: Balkema.

8

Intertidal rock

J. M. BAKER and J. H. CROTHERS

Introduction

Rocky shores, with their obvious zonation of plants and animals, are attractive for both research and educational projects. Moreover, in recent years there has been an upsurge of interest from two other points of view: the need to identify areas of conservation importance (part of a wider movement towards the establishment of marine reserves), and the need to assess the effects of coastal industrial operations. General consideration of reasons for doing surveys is given in Chapter 1. This present chapter describes a range of survey techniques for rocky shores and gives some conclusions regarding applicability for different objectives. Good introductions to rocky shore ecology are provided by Lewis (1964) for the British Isles, Stephenson & Stephenson (1972) for shores worldwide, and Carefoot (1977) for Pacific shores. Moore & Seed (1985) is a recent well-illustrated and comprehensive work of international relevance.

Planning considerations

General planning considerations including the importance of clear decisions about aims and objectives are covered in Chapter 1 which includes some rocky shore examples. Some points of particular relevance to rocky shores follow.

Time available on the shore

Budgetary restrictions, or the necessity to complete a project within, for example, one particular week of spring tides, necessitate tight planning. In many cases it is essential to complete discrete sections of work, e.g., a transect at location X, between two successive high tides (in which case a maximum time of about 8 hours is available) or between high tide and low tide (4 hours maximum). The latter approach may leave time for another transect at a nearby location Y to be studied immediately afterwards between low tide and high tide. Working time is likely to be restricted in winter when more low spring tide periods occur in the dark.

Delimiting the working area
Vertical zonation

Vertical zonation (dependent upon tidal submersion/emersion times) needs to be considered from the outset in defining the survey area. At the upper limits, does one start at the top of the splash zone (maybe 20 m up a precipitous cliff), the top of the yellow lichen zone, the high water spring tide level, or at some other datum? Similarly, datum points on the lower shore may include the top of the kelp zone, the mean low water spring tide mark, or the extreme low water mark. Decisions will be based on survey objectives, safety considerations, and knowledge of tidal behaviour during the survey period. Surveys are usually timed to coincide with spring tide periods (see national tidal predictions) so that a greater extent of lower shore can be examined.

Whatever upper and lower limits are set on the survey area, it is necessary to stick to them if spatial or temporal comparisons are being made. Obviously, if transect 1 does not include the zone between mean low water spring tide mark and extreme low water mark, and transect 2 does, there is a good chance of finding more species on transect 2.

Horizontal variation

There is biological variation along the shore depending upon gradients of exposure to wave action, salinity, and turbidity. This has to be borne in mind when defining the horizontal limits of the survey area, particularly on irregular coasts with many bays and promontories, and in estuaries. The implication for survey and monitoring work is that if one wishes to compare like with like, it is necessary to measure these horizontal variables. One cannot, for example, describe oil spill effects on a moderately exposed shore by reference to an adjacent unpolluted sheltered shore – the reference or 'control' site has to be moderately exposed. In the case illustrated in Fig. 8.1, are limpet density and size affected by an exposure gradient or an effluent gradient?

Microhabitats

Rocky shores are often greatly complicated by cracks and crevices, rock pools and overhangs, boulders, and variations in slope, aspect, and rock type. Decisions on how to cope with this variety depend upon the aims of the survey. If the aim is to assess the shore for conservation value, then it is important to include the full range of microhabitats in the survey protocol because they will probably contribute greatly to the total species richness. In contrast, if one is interested in studying main zonation patterns, or in surveillance of 'key' organisms (p. 183), then transects or permanent quadrats can be located as far as possible on unbroken, evenly sloping bedrock. This makes subsequent quantitative work much easier.

Fig. 8.1. The relationship between limpet density, limpet size, and distance from an effluent discharge pipe. After Petpiroon *et al.* (1982).

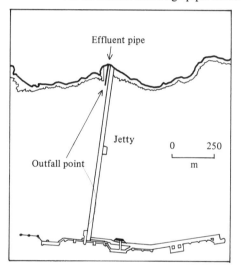

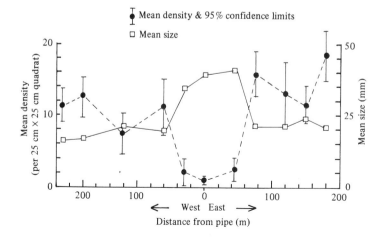

Markers and reference points
Markers

Working areas may be relocated using a permanent datum point on the upper shore. This could be a wooden post hammered into a crack, a paint mark (touched up as necessary), or a small pat of concrete set into an irregular rock surface for maximum adhesion. Absolute values of height above Chart Datum for the permanent datum points may be obtained by reference to tide gauge readings or (from the landward side) features such as the UK Ordnance Survey bench-marks.

The following techniques are useful for marking transect stations or permanent quadrats:

1. With some rock types, it may be possible to hammer masonry nails or pitons into cracks.
2. Brass screws set into drill holes using Araldite have been used by Crothers (1983*a*). He used a hand brace and masonry bit for drilling.
3. A hammer and chisel (or preferably a star-drill) can be used to make small pits in the rock.
4. Drills powered from SCUBA cylinders (Hawkins & Hartnoll, 1979).

Photography

Photographs are invaluable for relocating:

1. Working areas, with reference to features such as distinctive rocks, or buildings above high tide level.
2. Transects, which should be photographed with tape measures in place along the transect lines and with station markers (e.g., chalk marks on rocks).
3. Permanent quadrats, with reference to features such as cracks in the rock.

A time series of such photographs also records gross biological changes, so photography is a useful surveillance technique.

Trampling effects

It is inevitable that people walking on the shore will crush barnacles under foot, dislodge occasional limpets and winkles, and tear some algae from their holdfasts. Every effort should be made to minimise these effects. Regular visits to permanent transects or quadrats will produce trodden pathways of varying degrees of visibility. This should be remembered when recording, and unsampled border zones or 'safety areas' should be left around permanent quadrats. There is a real risk of damaging the community by over-frequent examination (Hawkins & Hartnoll, 1983a).

Worker variability

The concept of worker variability is introduced in Chapter 1 together with some rocky shore examples. It is important that field work teams train together and have practice sessions with comparison and discussion of individual results. Continuity between one survey and the next should be maximised by using the same staff as far as possible.

Safety

Many people have lost their lives on rocky shores. Please consult Chapter 15 for safety precautions.

Factors affecting shore communities

Exposure to wave action

Lewis (1964) describes factors influencing wave size. Fetch (the uninterrupted distance over which the wind can blow across the water) is of greatest importance, but other factors that need to be considered are the open angle of the shore to the sea, and coastal topography. For example, in west Wales, Ballantine (1961) listed 'extremely exposed' shores open over 67° to fetches of more than 2000 miles, 'very exposed' shores open over 40–50° to fetches of more than 2000 miles, and so on to 'very sheltered' shores open to fetches of less than 10 miles over less than 60°. Lewis (1964) describes how the flatter and more irregular the shore profile, the more gentle the conditions will be, due to the dissipation of wave energy against the seaward edge of the shore. Information about the nature of the sea-bed beyond the shore is also useful; rocky shores that extend into a shallow bay will have different characteristics from those that extend as steeply sloping rock below low water level, even if the intertidal areas have similar aspects and profiles.

The communities on any one shore reflect the cumulative effect of waves striking that shore over a period of many years. There have been numerous attempts to measure wave action but it is not one simple environmental factor; on the contrary, it encompasses many correlated and interacting components such as wave pressures, drag forces, abrasion by water-borne particles, and severity of desiccation.

Physical measurements of wave action

Direct measures have included:

> Wave height (e.g. waves may be viewed against a marked cliff).
> See also Southward (1953).
>
> Wave pressures, using pressure transducers fixed to a range of
> shores (Wright, 1981), or the simple dynamometer of Denny
> (1983).
>
> Drag forces, using a drogue attached to a spring balance in turn
> attached to the shore by means of a flexible coupling (Jones &
> Demetropoulos, 1968). See also Palumbi (1984).
>
> Erosion rates of plaster of Paris (Muus, 1968; Doty, 1971).

In principle, the direct measurement of forces experienced by shore biota
is an obvious approach. In practice, there are two main problems: direct
measurements are difficult to conduct for the long period of time necessary

Fig. 8.2. Measurements used in calculation of modified maximum
fetch (Wright, 1981). *MF*, maximum fetch (km); *SH*, angle subtended
by sea horizon; *MW*, minimum width of channel to outer coast (km);
DIST, distance to outer coast (km); *D*, maximum depth offshore
(fathoms) within 1 mile perpendicular to the shore. (D_{max} is the
maximum value for *D* encountered in the whole of the survey area; it
was 60 in the case of Wright's Shetland study.)

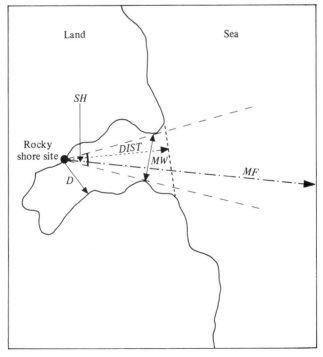

to fully describe any one site, and the measurements do not necessarily reflect the complex physical interactions to which the shore biota actually respond.

Indirect measurements rely upon data such as fetch and open angle of the shore to the sea (see example above from Ballantine, 1961). A great advantage of this approach is that in many cases the data can be obtained quickly from pre-existing maps and charts.

Wright (1981) describes his study of 83 sites in Shetland. He found highly significant correlation (correlation coefficient $= -0.834*$) between the following 'modified maximum fetch' and biological estimates of wave exposure (see Fig. 8.2 for definitions).

modified maximum fetch
$$= MF \cdot (SH + 180)/180 \cdot MW/(DIST + MW) \cdot D/D_{max}$$

This equation is reproduced here as an example of how indirect physical measurements can be used – it is not intended to be definitive.

A different approach to the same topic is given by Thomas (1986).

Biological indicators of exposure

By their very survival the communities on any rocky shore represent an integration of the complex variables comprising 'exposure', and this suggests measurement of the biota for indicating exposure grades. The first biological exposure scale was described by Ballantine (1961) for a number of shores in west Wales. It allows ranking of shores according to the differential abundance of indicator species, using abundance categories developed by Crisp & Southward (1958). The most obvious limitation (as pointed out by Ballantine from the outset) is that the scale is based on a circular argument: a shore is judged to be exposed because it has a certain community pattern, but it has that community pattern because it is exposed. This does not invalidate the scale but it does mean that independent physical measurements of some kind are necessary if it is required to 'calibrate' biological exposure scales for different geographical areas (see previous section).

There are other problems. Shores on the middle points of the scales tend to change with time due to cyclical biological events. Shores on the Isle of Man have changed from exposure grades 3 to 4 to 5 to 3 and keep on changing depending on the balance of fucoids and barnacles (S. J. Hawkins, personal communication; see also Hawkins & Hartnoll, 1983*a*). On shores already affected by pollution, the communities may be so altered as to invalidate exposure grade estimates.

* Note that the value is negative because high wave action equates with low values on the biological exposure scales.

When Ballantine applied his scale to a few sites on the coasts of Norway and Spain, he found it unsatisfactory since it suggested that there were no exposed shores in that part of Norway and no sheltered ones in Spain. He explained this as being the result of latitudinal changes in the flora and fauna, together with the possibility that some wide-ranging species showed different environmental preferences in different regions. In using his scale, it is important to record the abundance of as many of the indicator species as possible. Dependence on one or two may be misleading. *Alaria esculenta*, for example, is an excellent indicator of truly exposed shores in south-west Wales; but it is absent further south, and it is widespread on all but the most sheltered shores in Faroe. Geographical variations such as these have stimulated the development of other exposure scales: Lewis (1965) for British shores, Wright (1981) for Shetland, and Dalby *et al.* (1978) for western Norway.

Ballantine's scale cannot be used in its original form on the east coast of North America. *Patella* limpets are absent and their place as controlling herbivore is taken by *Littorina littorea* on the middle shore and the urchin *Strongylocentrotus droebachiensis* on the lower shore. Grazing pressure is thus greatest on sheltered shores, and these are often devoid of algae, especially at the lower levels. Exposed shores, in contrast, are fucoid dominated, with *Ascophyllum* (an indicator of shelter in Britain) often the most conspicuous species.

Notwithstanding the problems, biological exposure scales (calibrated using some form of physical measurement) remain a useful method for classifying or ranking rocky shore communities.

Individual species may also serve as indicators of exposure. The best known are as follows:

> The dog-whelk *Nucella lapillus*. Shells of *Nucella lapillus* (L.) are short and squat on exposed shores but become progressively more elongated with increasing shelter. This variation appears to be under genetic control as populations breed true (Crothers, 1977) but it is also maintained by stabilizing selection. Information on different geographical areas is given in a series of papers listed in the references and summarised by Crothers (1985). There are a number of problems; for example, in the Severn Estuary there is a very elongated form of *Nucella* that does not show any relationship with exposure (Crothers, 1974) and in the Shetland Islands the form usually associated with sheltered shores extends onto all but the most exposed shores (Crothers, 1979). Information for *Nucella emarginata* on the Pacific coast of North America is given by Crothers (1984).

Algal morphology. The morphology of some species of algae clearly varies with shore exposure, as has been observed by many workers, e.g., Lewis, 1964. For example, *Fucus vesiculosus* tends to have fewer vesicles on more exposed shores. For more information, see Appendix 8.1.

Height of the black lichen zone. The relationship between height of the black lichen zone and exposure has been described for two European areas by Dalby *et al.* (1978). The zone is usually conspicuous on the upper shore and is characterised by the black epilithic lichen *Verrucaria maura*, accompanied by other lichen species. Blue-green algae may be present (and may dominate this zone in some parts of the world). The height of the top of this zone increases with increasing exposure to wave action.

Secondary physical factors

When physical factors other than wave action become extreme, they may have an overriding influence on shore ecology as follows:

Aspect

In the northern hemisphere, north-facing slopes are likely to be relatively shady, damp, and cool, and thus to favour organisms such as red algae. Conversely, where southern species are near the northern limits of their geographical distribution, they may be more abundant on south-facing slopes, as reported for *Chthamalus* in Caithness (Lewis, 1964).

Slope

A steep shore will concentrate the force of the waves and appear (biologically) to be more exposed than might be expected from other factors such as fetch.

Rock type

The sea-walls of the Netherlands, built of various materials including granite, basalt, concrete, and limestone, are ideal for studying the effects of rock type in otherwise standardised conditions. Nienhuis (1969) concluded that on these walls a relatively soft and rough substratum shows a more complete algal zonation pattern than a hard, smooth surface, and that the position of algal belts with regard to mean high water level is strongly influenced by the physical characteristics of the substratum.

Cracks and crevices

Cracks and crevices provide protection from waves and from desiccation, and (depending on size and number) will increase species richness of a shore and the abundance of some species. For an example, see Raffaelli & Hughes (1978) on the effects of crevice size and availability on populations of two species of *Littorina*.

Stones and boulders

As the numbers of stones increase, the mobility of the substratum increases, which may cause a reduction in the flora and fauna through abrasion. Large boulders, however, will be moved only rarely in winter storms and at their bases may protect areas of sediment and small pools which are rich in species.

Rock pools

Rock pools provide relatively sheltered microhabitats at all levels on the shore, and support many organisms such as delicate algae which could not survive on the open shore surface. Thus the presence of rock pools increases the species richness of the shore.

Appendix 8.2 is an example of a data sheet for secondary physical factors. It is not intended to be definitive, but merely to introduce some useful recording ideas, e.g., the shore 'roughness ratio' of Wright (1981):

$$\frac{\text{length of tape over rocks (m)}}{\text{length of tape stretched tight (m)}}$$

Water quality

Salinity

Salinity may affect the distribution of shore species over large areas, e.g., Bassindale (1943) has described the salinity conditions of the Tees and Severn estuaries, and has related the distribution of shore amphipods to salinity (Bassindale, 1942). However, in most estuaries salinity changes are accompanied by changes in the suspended sediment, and the distribution of some species is likely to be affected by both these factors. Also wave action decreases up estuaries. Unattached proliferating forms of fucoid algae (e.g., *Ascophyllum nodosum* f. *mackaii*) are found where conditions are both sheltered and of relatively low salinity (e.g., Scottish sea lochs, Norwegian fjords, and the Baltic Sea). The salinity-dependent distribution of algae in estuarine areas of Icelandic fjords has been described by Munda (1978). On a smaller scale, freshwater streams (and effluents containing fresh water) may debouche over rocky shores and affect local distribution patterns. An example from West Somerset, UK is provided by Wilson, Crothers & Oldham (1983). In this case a grid survey showed that *Enteromorpha* spp. and the mussel *Mytilus edulis* were positively associated with fresh water. *Enteromorpha* is known to be tolerant of very low salinities but a freshwater stream is hardly the optimum niche for *Mytilus edulis*. It was concluded that the stream was the only portion of the species' potential niche that could be realised because it offered a refuge from dog-whelk (*Nucella lapillus*) predation. Laboratory experiments showed the dog-whelk to be inactive in the low salinities of the stream discharge area.

For methods of salinity measurement, see Kjerfve (1979).

Other water quality parameters
Temperature, suspended sediment, and chemical composition of the water may all be important in interpreting rocky shore biology. See Kjerfve (1979) for temperature measurement, McCave (1979) for suspended sediment techniques, and Head (1985) for a handbook on chemical methods.

Temporal changes
Diurnal changes
Many rocky shore animals are more active during periods of emersion if these fall during the comparative coolness and dampness of the middle of the night. Limpts and winkles are more likely to move around grazing at this time, and crustaceans come out of their hiding places. The same effect may be noticed sometimes during the daytime on a shady shore that the tide has just left. Shore animals are also active during periods of submersion. The numbers of mobile animals (e.g., species of *Littorina* and *Patella*) within fixed quadrats may therefore vary tremendously within 24-hour periods, though of course *Patella* home scars will not vary. For a relevant review on grazing of intertidal algae by marine invertebrates, see Hawkins & Hartnoll (1983b).

Weather conditions (e.g., sunshine, rain, humidity) can cause major variations in counts of highly mobile organisms such as *Anurida* and *Hyale*. Disturbance is likely to have a similar effect, so it is important to try and 'standardise' disturbance during surveys – especially where botanists and zoologists are working on the same shore.

Seasonal changes
Most algae show seasonal changes in growth which are reflected in changes of cover (see Fig. 8.3 for an example), and many are ephemeral species

which may 'bloom' at different times. Thus if a shore is being surveyed annually, it is important that visits are made at the same time each year. In late summer if the weather is hot and sunny, algae may be extensively bleached (see Hawkins & Hartnoll, 1985).

In the spring, dog-whelks cluster into breeding groups, and limpet and barnacle larvae settle on the shore, sometimes in very high numbers which decrease through natural wastage as the year proceeds. Winter storms may tear algae from rocks and low temperatures may kill shore invertebrates. Ice formation on northern shores leads to scouring of the rocks and anything attached to them.

Detailed examples of seasonal changes recorded on the shores of Anglesey, UK have been published (Jones *et al.*, 1980). The full data from the Anglesey surveillance programme are available in the annual reports of the Coastal Surveillance Unit, archived at the School of Ocean Sciences, Menai Bridge, Gwynedd, Wales.

Long-term changes

Many biological surveys are 'one-off', and without the perspective of time-series data, they may be misleading. A cautionary tale has been told by Bowman (1978) to illustrate the pitfalls of instant assessment. In this case, a survey to assess oil spill effects in northern Scotland revealed a 'classic' loss of limpets with consequent algal bloom. Pre-spill data are, however, available for this site and show that the loss of limpets was caused by overheating during the summer of 1976, before the oil spill.

Extremely hot summers, extremely cold winters, and spills of toxic materials are all events that may kill key organisms and so modify shore communities for many years. 'Red tides' (toxic dinoflagellate blooms) may have a similar effect (Cross & Southgate, 1980).

Long-term surveillance has its own pitfalls. Mass mortalites and their

Fig. 8.3. Percentage cover of *Palmaria palmata* at monthly intervals in a permanent quadrat at Porthyrysgaw, Anglesey. Redrawn from Jones *et al.*, 1979.

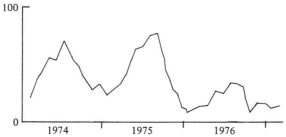

knock-on effects are relatively easy to follow, but most changes are difficult to interpret because they reflect the net result of all the physical and biological events of the preceding 5–20 years or more (the range of potential life spans of key species). The paper by Lewis (1976) is recommended for those embarking upon surveillance programmes. One of Lewis' points (with considerable planning implications) is that understanding of change will almost certainly involve a wide geographical scale of operations. This is necessary for distinction between local and more general events; moreover, the more widely distributed the change, the greater the probability that it is a response to climatic or natural hydrographic conditions.

Biological interactions

Changes in community structure are often caused by fluctuations in recruitment of interacting species. In particular, changes on shores of intermediate exposure are associated with the balance between limpets/ barnacles and fucoid algae. For example, a dominant cohort of limpets can reduce juvenile recruitment and then cause a drastic reduction in grazing control of fucoids when the old limpets die (Hawkins, Southward & Barrett, 1984). Stands of fucoid algae of the same size and age prevent subsequent settlement of sporelings in two ways: directly, by sweeping, and indirectly, by harbouring high densities of grazers (Hawkins & Hartnoll, 1983a, b). Dense settlement of barnacles (Barnes & Powell, 1950) can lead to hummocks and clumps which will eventually be wrenched from the rock by wave action. Because of cyclical biological events such as these, shores on the middle points of biological exposure scales tend to change rank with time (see p. 163).

Abundance scales

Abundance scales are often used for extensive surveys or transect surveys. They were developed by Crisp & Southward (1958) and subsequently used by Ballantine (1961) in his work on exposure. Modifications have been made by Crapp (1973) and by Hiscock (Table 8.1).

Den Hartog (1959) used the Braun-Blanquet cover-abundance scale for investigating epilithic algal communities along the coast of the Netherlands. This scale (used mainly by terrestrial botanists) is discussed fully by Westhoff & van der Maarel (1978).

Abundance scales are relatively quick to use and have the advantage of 'evening out' or integrating small-scale patchiness. They are not, of course, quantitative so are not suitable for some purposes (e.g., recording small-scale changes). If used on transect surveys, the transect should be a belt as wide as possible; it will be obvious from some of the abundance categories (e.g., when rare is less than 1 m^{-2}) that the scales are not suitable for narrow (e.g., 0.5 m) transect stations or small (e.g., 0.25 m^2) quadrats.

Table 8.1. *Abundance scales for rocky shore organisms*

1. ALGAE
E. more than 90% cover
S. 60–90% cover
A. 30–59% cover
C. 5–29% cover
F. less than 5% cover but zone still apparent
O. scattered plants, zone indistinct
R. only one or two plants present

2. LICHENS, *Lithothamnion*
E. more than 80% cover
S. 50–79% cover
A. 20–49% cover
C. 1–19% cover
F. large scattered patches
O. widely scattered patches, all small
R. only one or two small patches present

3. BARNACLES, SMALL WINKLES
E. 500 or more 0.01 m^{-2}
S. 300–499 0.01 m^{-2}
A. 100–299 0.01 m^{-2}
C. 10–99 0.01 m^{-2}
F. 1–9 0.01 m^{-2}
O. 1–99 m^{-2}
R. less than 1 ms^{-2}

4. LIMPETS, LARGE WINKLES
E. 20 or more 0.1 m^{-2}
S. 10–19 0.1 m^{-2}
A. 5–9 0.1 m^{-2}
C. 1–4 0.1 m^{-2}
F. 5–9 m^{-2}
O. 1–4 m^{-2}
R. less than 1 m^{-2}

5. *Balanus perforatus*

E. 300 or more 0.01 m^{-2}
S. 100–299 0.01 m^{-2}
A. 10–99 0.01 m^{-2}
C. 1–9 0.01 m^{-2}
F. 1–9 0.1 m^{-2}
O. 1–9 m^{-2}
R. less than 1 m^{-2}

6. DOGWHELKS, TOP-SHELLS, ANEMONES
E. 10 or more 0.1 m^{-2}
S. 5–9 0.1 m^{-2}
A. 1–4 0.1 m^{-2}
C. 5–9 m^{-2}, locally sometimes more
F. 1–4 m^{-2}, locally sometimes more
O. less than 1 m^{-2}, locally sometimes more
R. always less than 1 m^{-2}

7. MUSSELS, PIDDOCKS (score holes)
E. more than 80% cover
S. 50–79% cover
A. 20–49% cover
C. 5–19% cover
F. small patches, covering less than 5% of rock
O. 1–9 individuals m^{-2}: no patches
R. less than 1 individual m^{-2}

8. TUBE WORMS *Pomatoceros*
A. 50 or more tubes 0.01 m^{-2}
C. 1–49 tubes 0.01 m^{-2}
F. 1–9 tubes 0.1 m^{-2}
O. 1–9 tubes m^{-2}
R. less than 1 tube m^{-2}

E, extremely abundant.   C, common.   O, occasional.
S, superabundant.   F, frequent.   R, rare.
A, abundant.

There are limitations with data processing and statistical analysis. In particular it should be remembered that abundance categories are actually ranks, and ordinal data should not be processed by the normal rules of arithmetic. It is unacceptable to number the ranks R–E in Table 8.1 as 1–7 and then to add or find means of these numbers. However, anything that can be ranked can be analysed using non-parametric statistical techniques; see Siegel (1956), Hawkins (1985), and Chalmers & Parker (1986).

Arithmetic scales (e.g., 1–10% cover, 11–20%, 21–30%, etc.) or logarithmic scales give greater scope for statistical analysis but do not seem to have been used much. This is probably because the human eye can discriminate well between small differences in cover/abundance near the zero and 100% cover ends of the scale but less well in the middle. The scales in Table 8.1 reflect, in fact, what the eye can discriminate with relative ease.

Extensive descriptive surveys
Primary surveys
Primary surveys concentrate on outline descriptions of habitats and assessments of selected organisms, in an attempt to evaluate a large area for further work. For example, following publication of the UK report on Marine Wildlife Conservation (Natural Environment Research Council, 1973), a group of biologists formed the South West Marine Biology Study Group, principally to assess the biological potential of habitats in the littoral zone in Devon and Cornwall. As a first step, the group designed and tested the field cards described below, on which volunteers could record, in standard form, the main features of any shore site they visited. Some interest in these cards has been shown by groups elsewhere, and it is possible that other stretches of coastline may be recorded and assessed by techniques similar to those initiated in south-west Britain. A card for sandy shores is described in Chapter 4.

Remote sensing information, particularly aerial photographs, may be useful when planning primary surveys and for complementing the field work data. See Chapter 2.

A field card for rocky shore habitats, D. Nichols and N. A. Holme
The printed face of the card is given in Fig. 8.4. The reverse side of the card is plain and can be used for extra details. The cards are printed on waterproof paper (Wiggins Teape 'Goatskin' parchment, 120 g) so that they can be used in all weathers and will also stand accidental immersion in sea water. The paper will take most writing materials, even when wet.

The front face of the card is divided into three sections, the largest of which is devoted to physical and biological features. Information is sought on the coastal features adjacent to the shore, such as cliffs and dunes, the dominant rock features and secondary pebbles or other particulate substrata of the shore, habitats such as turnable stones and crevices, slope of the shore, its degree of exposure, and the type of rock pools present.

Of the plant cover, the card seeks entries about fucoids, *Pelvetia*, *Ascophyllum*, kelp, and '*Lithothamnion*', and in particular whether distinct zones are present. To an experienced eye this can give valuable information about the type of shore and its biological potential.

The categories for shore animals are also reduced to those groups that are common and easily recognised, and that give the fullest picture of the type of shore to the experienced assessor. As with the plants, species are not distinguished. The categories here are limpets, barnacles, top-shells, periwinkles, and mussels.

There is an item called 'activity' that records information on animal and human influences. The final two categories are admittedly subjective; one seeks an assessment of the number of species of plants and animals on that particular shore, and the other seeks the number of plant and animal individuals. Trials so far suggest that a recorder can quickly acquire a useful, if personal, scale for each of these categories, and the problem for the co-ordinator becomes akin to that of an examination board who must apply factors for 'strictness' or 'leniency' to each examiner in reaching a final assessment.

The instruction sheet is also printed on waterproof paper, so that it can

Fig. 8.4. Rocky shore field card, from Holme & Nichols (1980).

serial no. R	ROCKY Shore Field Card S. W. Marine Biology Study Group	Coastal Area:
Date: .... / .... / .... Time: .... to .... Time of L.T.: .... hrs Predicted tide ht.: .... m at: .... Distance HW to LW: .... m	Observer: .... Pollution (if any):	Locality: Grid Ref.: [ ][ ] Designation: Access:

Coast: cliff ☐1 low ☐2 dunes ☐3 estuary/inlet ☐4 ....

1.	Dominant type	continuous reefs ☐5 interrupted reefs ☐6 boulders ☐7 ....
2.	Secondary ftrs.	boulders ☐8 cobbles ☐9 pebbles ☐10 granules ☐11 sand ☐12 silt & clay ☐13 sand-scour ☐14 ....
3.	Habitats	turnable rocks ☐15 shaded ☐16 crevices ☐17 chalk ☐18 limestone ☐19 ....
4.	Slope	steep ☐20 med. ☐21 gentle ☐22 flat ☐23 irreg. ☐24 ....
5.	Wave exposure	v. exp. ☐25 exp. ☐26 less exp. ☐27 mod. shelt. ☐28 v. shelt ☐29 ....
6.	Pools	u. sh:dp. ☐30 mod ☐31 sh. ☐32 comn. ☐33 sc. ☐34 | l. sh:dp. ☐35 mod. ☐36 sh. ☐37; comn. ☐38 sc. ☐39
7.	Fucoid cover	u. sh. ☐40 mid. sh. ☐41 lower sh. ☐42 | well mkd. zones ☐43 ....
8.	Pelvetia	distinct zone ☐44 scattered ☐45 scarce ☐46 absent ☐47 ....
9.	Ascophyllum	distinct zone ☐48 scattered ☐49 scarce ☐50 absent ☐51 ....
10.	Kelps	distinct zone at L. W. ☐52 scattered ☐53 scarce ☐54 absent ☐55 ....
11.	'Lithothamnion'	ext. cover ☐56 scattered patches ☐57 in pools ☐58 scarce ☐59 absent ☐60 ....
12.	Limpets	plentiful ☐61 scattered ☐62 patchy ☐63 scarce ☐64 absent ☐65 ....
13.	Barnacles	plentiful ☐66 good cover locally ☐67 patchy ☐68 scarce ☐69 absent ☐70 ....
14.	Top shells	u. sh:pl. ☐71 scat. ☐72 sc. ☐73 abs. ☐74 | m. & l. sh:pl. ☐75 scat. ☐76 sc. ☐77 abs. ☐78 ....
15.	Periwinkles	u. sh:pl. ☐79 scat. ☐80 sc. ☐81 abs. ☐82 | m. & l. sh:pl. ☐83 scat. ☐84 sc. ☐85 abs. ☐86 ....
16.	Mussels	plentiful ☐87 scattered ☐88 scarce ☐89 absent ☐90 ....
17.	Activity	birds ☐91 bait ☐92 fishing ☐93 food collecting ☐94 field studies ☐95 recreation ☐96 ....
18.	Numbers spp.	plants: high ☐97 med. ☐98 low ☐99 | animals: high ☐100 med. ☐101 low ☐102 ....
19.	Numbers indivs.	plants: high ☐103 med. ☐104 low ☐105 | animals: high ☐106 med. ☐107 low ☐108 ....

1978R

be referred to in the field. It amplifies and explains where necessary the very abbreviated categories on the card, and gives actual figures for more accurate assessment of certain features. For instance, when referring to rock pools, 'deep' means 'over 30-cm depth', and 'very shallow' means 'less than 5-cm depth'.

The item for which this is particularly necessary is that under 'Secondary features' of the substratum, in which the categories are listed according to the Wentworth scale (Wentworth, 1922); these categories can be read off from a grain-size comparator such as the disc type designed by the Sedimentology Unit of the Institute of Oceanographic Sciences (Kirby, 1973). The instruction sheet is reproduced in full by Holme & Nichols (1980).

During the formulation of the card, various trials were carried out (Holme & Nichols, 1980) using, in some cases, recorders of varying experience and careful instruction, and in others, inexperienced recorders with no instruction. The results amply confirm that verbal instruction, plus the issue of a full instruction sheet to accompany the card, are necessary for reliable and standardised results to be obtained. One trial, using 12 mainly professional or in-training biologists with little or no instruction, showed that no single category received ticks from every recorder, meaning that the subdivisions were not sufficiently clear-cut or unambiguous to evoke a uniform response from all those taking part. On the other hand, a trial using 11 recorders, experienced in shore work but not in the use of this particular card, produced, when working with the instruction sheet, as nearly standardised results as one could hope to achieve. The principle difficulties were encountered, as one would expect, when recorders were required to distinguish between, for instance, 'good cover locally' and 'scattered patches', and only further experience by the same people can tune out differences in somewhat subjective assessments like these.

Detailed extensive surveys

Detailed extensive surveys are appropriate for assessing and comparing the nature conservation interest of sites. Details of methods used by the UK Nature Conservancy Council (NCC) (developed in association with the Scottish Marine Biological Association/Marine Biological Association Intertidal Survey Unit and the Field Studies Council) are given by Lumb (1985; see also Knight & Mitchell, 1980), and are summarised below (from Lumb, 1985).

Within a survey area sites are pre-selected to include as wide a range of habitats as possible and to give a good geographic coverage. The precise location of survey sites and the habitats recorded are determined on the shore by the survey team. A systematic shore survey is carried out in accordance with the following instructions produced by Hiscock (1984).

Instructions to survey team

1. On reaching the shore, the team leader should decide what sort of survey will be carried out. Normally a systematic description of the abundance of species in the main communities present at different heights on the open shore will be completed and descriptions of the communities in other major habitats present will be made. For some shores where time does not permit a full survey or where the shore is very similar to one previously surveyed, a brief description is made. Where some important subsidiary habitat such as rock pools, underboulder or cave areas requires detailed survey, this may take precedence over the open-shore survey.

2. For open-shore surveys the botanist and zoologist agree on the line of the survey belt. Using the tidal height predictions they establish the height of sea level above chart datum and starting at $+0.0$ m station near sea level, level up the shore with a cross-staff level (see p. 176), marking each interval with chalk. The botanist and zoologist should then agree on the location of each of the distinctly different communities they are to survey, which will normally be on the Lower Shore (LS), Lower Midshore (LMS), Midshore (MS), Upper Midshore (UMS), Upper Shore (US) and Splash Zone (Spl.).

   Record the abundance of all of the algae and animals which can be seen in each of the agreed areas, surveying across a *c.* 5 m width of shore. The quantity of each species is recorded according to the appropriate abundance scale.

3. For surveys of other habitats, describe the species present and give an estimate of their abundance.

4. Take photographs of the shore with views up and down the shore, from the side (as far as possible with the sea and sky on the left), and of each community present. Also, take photographs of some of the main species present. Three photographs are taken of each subject.

5. Make a sketch of the site location and of the site profile or of any other features felt to be important (such as the distribution of species in rock pools).

Site and habitat information is recorded on the NCC rocky shore recording sheet (Lumb, 1985). This is along the same lines as the field card described above (see Fig. 8.4) but is more detailed. Species check-lists are completed for each habitat/community/ zone sampled, and abundance scale assessments recorded (see Lumb, 1985; also Table 8.1).

A computer-based data storage and processing system is used. Assessment of the nature conservation value of sites is based on the criteria outlined by Ratcliffe (1977).

A single visit to a shore places constraints upon the information collected; both long-term and seasonal variations in species abundance can markedly influence the shore communities. Nevertheless, the characteristic pattern and extent of many of these fluctuations is known and can be taken into account, both when planning surveys and when analysing results for nature conservation interest.

The use of experienced workers is important to ensure that all the major habitats are surveyed and that comprehensive species records are compiled. Experience is also required for the analysis of results and assessment of the nature conservation interest, when judgement is often based on a wider knowledge.

The use of single visits, unmarked transects, and semi-quantitative abundance estimates, inherent in this type of extensive survey, precludes the use of data for detecting other than gross changes in shore communities.

Transect surveys

Transect surveys are appropriate if it is desired to sample the whole range of communities from low to high water levels. There are many possible transect methods, ranging from abundance scale estimates at stations along broad belt transects (suitable for general shore descriptions and comparisons, or conservation assessment as described above) to quantitative measures at stations along narrow permanent transects (suitable for following seasonal changes or longer term surveillance).

A variety of methods have been described in the literature; see e.g., Crapp (1973), Myers, Cross & Southgate (1978), Jones (1980), and Jones et al. (1980). A number of different approaches are described below together with their advantages and disadvantages. Other possibilities will no doubt spring to mind, but it should be pointed out that long-running surveillance schemes have to be 'locked' into the original methodology to ensure comparability of data from year to year.

Levelling

Spirit levelling

Spirit levelling as described in Chapter 3 may be suitable for large areas with relatively gentle slopes, as may the use of a Cowley (builders') level. The following two methods are more practical on steep, irregular shores.

Cross-staff method

The cross-staff, as developed by Moyse & Nelson-Smith (1968) and Crapp (1970) is illustrated in Fig. 8.5. It has been commonly used for setting out stations along transects, the vertical height intervals between stations equalling the length of the cross-staff leg. A convenient leg length to use (which results in all of the main zonal communities usually being included) is one tenth of the spring tide range of the survey area, and cross-staffs with interchangeable legs of different lengths may be used anywhere.

Fig. 8.5. Cross-staff (after Crapp, 1970). Height measured is $X + Y + Z$. Other heights are possible with leg adjustments.

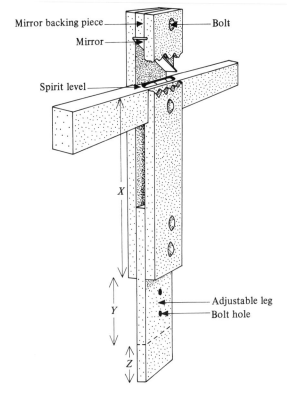

The surveyor sights along the cross piece and can observe when this is horizontal by means of the angled mirror.

Bottle and tube method
A plastic bottle full of water and a long flexible transparent plastic tube (Fig. 8.6) form a cheap and accurate levelling device with wide applications (including sighting round corners!).

Datum points
Sea-level itself can be used as a datum point, preferably on calm days only! For example, a transect can be set out with reference to low tide mark on a particular day, and the height of that tide can be obtained from tidal predictions (or better, if available, from a nearby tide gauge). It should be stressed that actual tidal heights may vary from predictions depending upon factors such as atmospheric pressure and winds, so predicted height should not be taken as an absolute value.

If transects are to be revisited it is useful to be able to relocate them using a permanent datum point (see p. 160).

Transect techniques
Abundance scale assessment of interrupted belt transect
The following technique was originated by Moyse & Nelson-Smith (1963) and variations have been used over a wide geographical area. The following procedure is described by Little (1985). It has been used by the Field Studies Council for shore surveys, including shores that are resurveyed at intervals for the detection of broad patterns of change.

A tape is laid down the shore. In the case of surveillance schemes, the tape is laid from a permanent concrete datum point, along exactly the same

Fig. 8.6. Use of plastic bottle and tube for levelling. The tube is filled with water by syphoning, and the end X then closed (e.g., with the thumb).

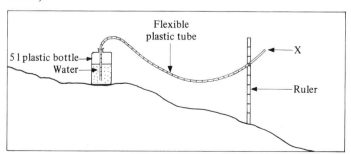

line as previously surveyed using a combination of existing station marks, site photographs, sketches, and compass bearings for relocation. Stations are at vertical intervals of approximately one tenth of the tidal range, established using a cross-staff (see p. 176).

The abundance of plants and animals on a check-list is surveyed and recorded in a strip 3 m wide × 30 cm deep at each station (Fig. 8.7). The abundance scales used are given by Little (1985); see also Table 8.1.

For each species on the check-list, abundance is estimated by one of the following methods:

1. Small winkles and barnacles: counts of numbers in three to five 0.01 m² quadrats, depending on variability.
2. Larger animals, e.g., limpets, dog-whelks: counts of numbers in three to five 0.1 m² quadrats, depending on variability.
3. Lichens, algae, and encrusting animals: subjective assessment of the cover with the aid of 0.1 m² quadrats.

Where organisms are present only in cracks, shade, pools, or under overhangs, they are simply recorded as present (p) with suffix to denote where found: p^c, present in crevices; p^p, present in pools; p^{uo}, present under overhangs; p^{ot}, present off transect; p^l, present on limpets; p^d, present in the damp.

In the margins of the recording sheets, notes are made of anything unusual or interesting, and of weather and rock surface conditions, to assist with the interpretation of records such as lichen cover estimates and numbers of littorinids. Some lichens and some gastropods are very difficult to see when the rock surface is wet. Under the same conditions some littorinids usually found in crevices may be out on the open rock surface.

This technique is relatively quick and it is possible for experienced teams to complete two transects during one tidal cycle. The separation of stations by vertical height intervals means that the technique is suitable for

Fig. 8.7. Interrupted belt transect, showing survey area (stippled) and cross-staff for setting out stations.

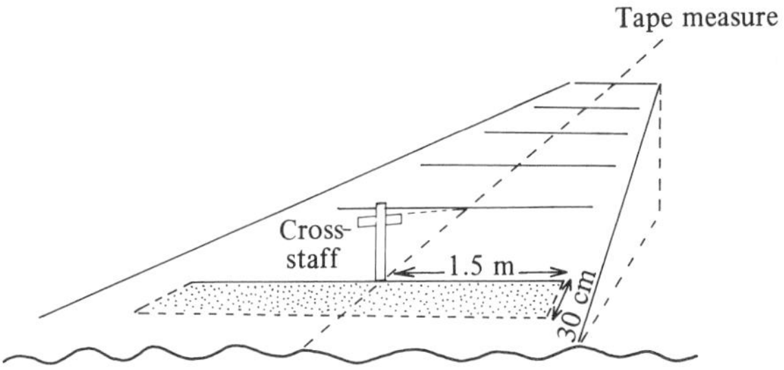

comparing shores of different slopes, and it can, to some extent, accommodate stony and irregular shores. These features are its main strengths.

The rectangular sampling area is useful for both cutting across small-scale mosaics laterally, and keeping within a narrow biological zone vertically. The disadvantages of the method stem from the shortcomings of abundance scales (see section on abundance scales). Moreover, it could be argued that abundance scales could be more useful on belts of shore more than 3 m wide. Ten-metre belts have in fact been used for some projects but shore irregularities are often so great that suitable 10-m wide sites cannot be found. They are to be preferred wherever they are possible because narrower belts are inadequate to assess realistically some of the larger and irregularly distributed species.

Quantitative assessment of continuous belt transect
The technique described below was developed by the Coastal Surveillance Unit (University College of North Wales) for monthly recordings of sites round Anglesey. The aim was to record seasonal changes and long-term or cyclic changes. Details have been given by Jones *et al.* (1980) and may be summarised as follows (Barnet, 1985).

A tape is laid down the shore, accurately relocated by reference to holes drilled in the rock, and fitted with marker tags. For zoological recording, 0.5 m × 0.5 m quadrats (area 0.25 m²) are laid contiguously down the transect. All species are recorded as total number in quadrat except:

1. barnacles (including dead barnacles), mussels, and *Polydora ciliata* holes; these are recorded as percentage cover per quadrat;
2. hydroids, bryozoans, and spirorbids occurring on algae in rockpools; these are recorded as present or absent; and
3. sponges; these are recorded using the following abundance scale:
   1, rare: spot only
   2, occasional: patch or several spots
   3, frequent: scattered patches
   4, common: 5–19% cover
   5, abundant: greater than 20% cover

Due to difficulties or potential inaccuracies with identification in the field, *Patella* species, *Littorina obtusata* and *L. mariae*, *Chthamalus montagui* and *C. stellatus*, and *Pomatoceros triqueter* and *P. lamarckii* are placed, respectively, in generic categories.

Three groups (or groups of species) are recorded according to the following size classes:

Patella species: 2–4 mm, 4–6 mm, 6–8 mm, 8–10 mm, greater
than 10 mm

Nucella lapillus: less than 3 mm, 3–5 mm, 5–10 mm, greater than
10 mm

Littorina obtusata/mariae: less than 2 mm, 2–5 mm, 5–10 mm,
greater than 10 mm

Carcinus maenas is recorded as 'adult', 'juvenile', or 'recently metamor-
phosed'. All other species are recorded as 'adult' or 'juvenile' where
appropriate or, for example in the case of *Actinia equina*, as 'recently
settled'. No size limits are given for these distinctions.

Barnacle settlement is recorded in several ways:

1. percentage cover of cyprids or recently settled juvenile barnacles
   per quadrat – for very heavy settlements;
2. total number of cyprids or recently settled juvenile barnacles per
   quadrat – for lighter settlements;
3. as two categories: the number of cyprids or recently settled
   juvenile barnacles per square inch (i.e., 6.45 cm^2; this size was
   chosen for practical convenience) with an estimate of the percentage area of the quadrat over which this density was observed –
   this method is used to record very patchy settlements.

For some studies it is convenient to assess barnacle settlement separately
in pre-scraped settlement squares (Bennell, 1981; Hawkins & Hartnoll,
1982).

This variety of methods for recording barnacle settlements was designed
for ease of use in the field, but analysis of such data has proved very
complex. Anglesey data have been converted to total numbers of barnacles
(adults and recently settled individuals) and cyprids, based on the estimated
area occupied by an adult barnacle, a young barnacle, and a cyprid. This
enables direct comparison of settlements from different sites and different
years.

For botanical recording, a sliding frame with cross-wires is used (Fig.
8.8). This covers the same area (0.25 m^2) as the zoological quadrat. All algal
and lichen species observed beneath each cross-wire are recorded to give
an estimate of cover. The condition of algal species is also recorded, e.g.,
fruiting plants, young plants, plants observed in rock pools, bleached
plants, and battered plants. 'Young fucoids' are generally placed in one
category until identifying characteristics become apparent. Other features
such as presence of bare rock, sand, silt, shells, barnacles, and limpets are
also recorded.

The method is suitable for rocky shores that have a reasonably uniform
surface and that are intact from high-water to low-water marks. However,

the gentler the slope, the longer the transect, and the longer the recording time necessary. A 50-cm-wide transect may not be representative of the shore at any particular level.

The quantitative data allow the precise description of changes on the transects and are amenable to a wide range of statistical tests and analysis by computer (see Jones *et al.* 1980). However, the quantity and complexity of time-series data may be so great that even computer analysis is likely to be very time consuming (Barnet, 1985).

Quantitative assessment of permanent representative quadrats in main zones
This technique was developed to provide baseline data for the Moray Firth, Scotland, against which effects of oilfield operations could be assessed. The transects are recorded at least once a year. The following summary is from Terry *et al.* (1985).

The transect marker is usually a patch of concrete embedded into the rock, or some distinctive feature of the upper shore. The line of transect is re-established at each visit from a compass bearing taken from the origin. A number of fixed quadrat locations (usually five or six) are established along the transect line with replication of quadrats at each level. The location of the quadrats is such that as flat a surface as possible, excluding rock pools, is used to give sampling points representative of the major communities present on the particular shore. For example, mid-shore quadrats cover areas dominated by barnacles and/or fucoids or heavily grazed regions, while the low-shore quadrats can cover species-rich areas or areas of mussel domination, depending on local conditions. The positions of the permanent quadrats are found by reference to the distance along the transect line from the origin, by reference to prominent local features, and by reference to photographs taken on previous visits. The

Fig. 8.8. A 100-point sliding frame used for estimating cover of algal and lichen species. Redrawn from Jones *et al.*, 1980.

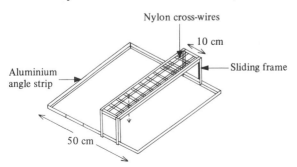

photographs are of particular importance in re-positioning the quadrats exactly, although in some places nails or chisel marks are placed to aid quadrat alignment. Metal grids 1 × 0.25 m in size are used as the basic quadrat area, with subdivisions of 5 × 5 cm.

The following procedure is adopted once the quadrat has been positioned:

1. Colour print and transparency photographs are taken of the location of each quadrat or group of quadrats and the whole of the quadrat; close-ups are taken of the left- and right-hand sides of each quadrat separately.

2. Cover is estimated for algae and sedentary animals such as barnacles and mussels by recording occurrence under grid intersections.

3. Selected quadrats are used to monitor fluctuations in the abundance of *Semibalanus balanoides*. Close-up transparencies are taken and these are analysed using a Hewlett-Packard 86 microcomputer with plotter and graphics tablet. The transparencies are projected via a mirror onto the horizontally placed tablet. Separate counts are made of the number of adults and juveniles in randomly selected 5 × 5 cm squares of the quadrat using the digitising pen of the tablet in response to a menu of prompts from the computer. The program calculates statistics (mean and standard deviation) for the data and calculates the estimated number of both adults and juveniles per square metre. A standard Hewlett-Packard graphics package generates histograms of these populations.

4. Photographs are taken of limpets, together with a scale marker, for computer analysis of population structure from selected areas (see above). (These analyses could, of course, be done 'by hand' if computer facilities are not available).

The method is suitable for most rocky shores that have large enough areas of stable substratum on which to place the quadrats. The limitation of the transect to representative quadrats means that it can be recorded relatively quickly. There is of course a greater subjective element in the location of quadrats than is the case with the other methods described. This does not matter when the aim (as in the Moray Firth) is to provide long-term records of change in selected areas, but such quadrats would not be suitable for the objective description of shore communities. The importance of photography in the methods may be a disadvantage during bad weather, but photographic records may be re-analysed if there are queries about change, and are always a help in communicating results to the non-specialist.

Quantitative assessment of multiple random quadrats at different levels
This method is suitable for bedrock shores with fairly uniform surfaces. A transect is established with stations at fixed vertical intervals, and multiple random quadrats are sampled at each level. The quadrats may be located by using random numbers along tapes laid at right angles to the transect line. In Orkney, Jones (1980) used vertical intervals of 30 cm (one tenth of the mean spring tidal range), with a minimum of three and a maximum of five quadrats at each level. Trials demonstrated that on fucoid shores, a 1-m² quadrat was the minimum size that yielded reliable results, but on barnacle-dominated shores a 0.1-m² quadrat could be used; wherever possible 1-m² quadrats were used on all shores. Algae and barnacles were determined as percentage cover using a point quadrat method, while other animals were determined as densities by counting.

Further information on sizes and numbers of quadrats is given by Hartnoll & Hawkins (1980, 1985); see also p. 9.

A great advantage of quantitative assessments within random quadrats is that a measure of variability is obtained. However, if the shore has much horizontal patchiness, an impracticably large number of quadrats may be necessary to achieve an acceptable variance. Microhabitat variation can be circumvented to some extent, for example, by ignoring pools and crevices and concentrating on open-rock communities.

Quadrat surveys

Multiple random quadrats for the assessment of abundance
This technique has not been sufficiently evaluated but seems to merit further investigation. Hartnoll & Hawkins (1985) have pointed out that where the aim of an exercise is to quantify the abundance of selected species within a defined area and to determine whether there have been any statistically significant changes, the use of multiple random quadrats has much to recommend it in theory. However, on rocky shores there are many practical restraints arising from vertical and horizontal environmental gradients, and patchy species distribution resulting from intra- and interspecific interactions. See also the above section on multiple random quadrats at different levels.

Permanent quadrats for surveillance
Permanent quadrats have been used generally to investigate changes in the major species in selected shore zones or communities, following the 'fixed site/key species' approach advocated by Lewis (1976). Permanent quadrats are in some cases arranged in transects, so some ideas on recording may be gained from the section on transects. Other variations

have been published; see, e.g., Hartnoll & Hawkins (1980) and Hawkins & Hartnoll (1983a).

These authors used the following technique for even, gently sloping shores in the Isle of Man (quoted from Hawkins & Hartnoll, 1985).

Quadrats 2 m × 1 m are located at three levels on the shore. For sampling, each quadrat is subdivided into eight half-metre-sided sub-quadrats marked by holes drilled in the rock. The half-metre quadrat frame is located precisely by fitting the spikes on its corners into these holes (see Fig. 8.9). In each sub-quadrat the percentage canopy cover of fucoids, the percentage substratum cover of under-storey algae, ephemeral algae, and *Semibalanus balanoides*, and the percentage of bare rock are assessed. *Actinia equina*, *Nucella lapillus*, and *Patella vulgata* are counted, and the number of limpets recorded in each 10 cm × 10 cm division of the sub-quadrat. Limpets with shell lengths below and above 15 mm are counted separately, this roughly distinguishing the more mobile juveniles from the larger specimens with home sites. *Nucella* below and above 10 mm length are separated, to distinguish first year from older individuals; as well as being counted in the quadrat, they are counted in the surrounding half-metre-wide band, to give a total sample area of 2 m × 3 m.

Percentage canopy cover of fucoids is estimated with a 26-point sighting frame (the points being the intersections of the divisions of the quadrat frame), the proportion of points coincident with a particular species being expressed as a percentage. The marginal

Fig. 8.9. Permanent quadrat technique used by Hawkins & Hartnoll (1983a).

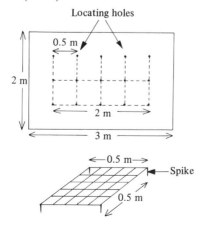

points are used, as well as the internal ones, to allow individual treatment of each sub-quadrat. This means that marginal points on the common side of adjacent sub-quadrats are counted twice; however, this does not affect estimates for the whole quadrat, as both presence and absence are equally weighted. Substratum cover is estimated subjectively, using the 10 cm × 10 cm subdivisions of the frame as a guide (each representing 4% cover). One complication with fucoids is that as young plants they are substratum cover, but with growth they become canopy cover. The transition is deemed to occur once they become recognisable, at about 10–15 cm length. For recording both seasonal and longer term changes, four recording sessions per year are probably the minimum, and six to eight times is adequate. More frequent sampling will not yield information of much higher grade, and may be counterproductive because of trampling damage.

Quadrat samples for community analysis

Russell (1980) sampled 273 quadrats on the shores of the north Irish Sea. Quadrat locations were unbiased by any prior opinions on the zonal structure. Algal cover abundance was assessed on a five-point scale, and a number of simple classification and ordination techniques were used to analyse the data. Such techniques have been used relatively little by rocky shore ecologists, but they could be a valuable way of objectively identifying communities and examining their relationships. However, careful attention needs to be given to quadrat size in relation to the scale of patchiness within a community. If the quadrat size is too small, the survey results will be very difficult to interpret. Moreover, if distribution patterns on rocky shores are clear to the eye, then classification and ordination techniques will generally not add much that is not obvious and will require considerable effort (Hawkins & Russell, 1981).

Artificial substrata

Standardised artificial substrata offer the advantage of eliminating variability resulting from small-scale patchiness in rock type, roughness, crevicing, and pre-existing biota. They can be used over wide areas, e.g., to investigate latitudinal variations in recruitment of barnacle species. They can also be used repeatedly in local surveillance studies, for the detection of change. Examples of materials used for artificial substrata are given below.

Laminate squares used as settlement plates for recruitment studies (slates have also been used but chthamalid barnacles do not settle readily on these). The plates are bolted to the shore or to jetty piles and subsequently brought back to the laboratory for analysis.

Nylon mesh pan scourers used for surveillance of cryptofauna (Myers & Southgate, 1980).

Structures such as sea-walls, piers, and jetty piles can be viewed as artificial substrata particularly suitable when surveying localised gradients, e.g., effluent gradients associated with point-source discharges.

Concrete blocks placed on the outside of Plymouth breakwater have been used in studies of succession by Hawkins *et al.* (1984).

Identification

Identification literature is detailed in Chapter 14.

Problems may be caused by morphological variation; lack of adequate field characteristics (as opposed to internal anatomical characteristics); juvenile forms and encrusting growths, e.g., on limpet shells. Some commonly encountered problem species in north-west Europe are given below.

Fucoid algae. It is often impossible to differentiate between young plants of different species of the genus *Fucus.* Mature *Fucus vesiculosus* f. *linearis* and non-spiralling *F. spiralis* on moderately exposed shores can be distinguished by the sterile margins on the fruiting bodies of the latter.

Verrucaria *species.* It is usually easy to differentiate *Verrucaria maura* (a black lichen of the upper shore) if the weather is fine. Under dry conditions a network of cracks over the lichen surface can be seen with a hand lens. Under wet conditions it may be difficult to differentiate *V. maura* from other *Verrucaria* species.

Limpets. Shell shape and foot colour are used as field characteristics in some guides (e.g., Fretter & Graham, 1976) but experience suggests that shell shape is variable and cannot reliably be used by most people in differentiating the species. S. J. Hawkins (personal communication) estimates that 3–5 years of experience are needed before limpets can be reliably identified from external characteristics. The foot colour of *Patella aspera* is distinctive, but tremendous damage will be caused by removal of these dominant grazers for identification purposes. Limpets do not often survive removal and rarely re-attach successfully. Further confusion is added by young small limpets that may be present in large numbers and that are virtually impossible to tell apart. Encrusting algal growths may also be a problem, particularly when distinguishing species of *Acmaea*, for which shell colour is a field characteristic.

Littorina. Winkles, the commonest group of rocky shore gastropods, present the greatest problems for the shore surveyor because the features used to separate taxa in one area at one season may not apply in a different area at a different season. For example:

1. Juvenile *L. littorea* are heavily ridged and are easily confused with rough winkles – especially as they may appear on shores from which the adults are absent.

2. Juvenile and immature flat winkles (*L. obtusata* and *L. fabalis = L. mariae*; see Smith, 1982) cannot be easily separated. Size, colour, and position on the shore can be used in some places, but these characteristics are not to be relied upon in an unfamiliar area.

3. The shell characters used to separate the upper shore rough winkles (*L. arcana* and *L. saxatilis*) are not consistent from shore to shore, and juveniles are virtually indistinguishable anyway.

4. *L. neglecta* is usually pale in colour, banded, or tessellated. In most places it can be easily separated from the midnight blue *L. neritoides*. In some places, e.g., Shetland, *L. neglecta* is black and separation in the field is unreliable.

Barnacles. Experience has shown that reliable separation of *Chthamalus* species is difficult in the field; some individuals are readily identified, others (especially distorted ones in crevices) are not.

Faced with these (and many other) taxonomic problems, the surveyor should resist the temptation to identify species from their position on the shore or from any preconceived idea about which animals and plants 'ought' to be present on a shore of that exposure. It cannot be assumed that the vertical and horizontal distribution of a species is the same throughout a large geographical area. The field surveyor is advised to become a 'lumper' when necessary, using categories such as 'young fucoids', 'black lichens', 'little black winkles', 'red encrusting algae', and so on. To some this practice appears unscientific but the reverse is the case: to apply a specific name when the organism has not been reliably identified to species is misleading.

Table 8.2. Summary of the survey techniques appropriate to different survey objectives

Survey Objectives	Visual assessment of shore by experienced scientist and general photographs	Species listing with or without abundance notations	Abundance scales to record species present at marked sites	Quantitative recording using marked areas at selected vertical heights			Manipulative studies/settlement plates/transplants	Allied research			
				All conspicuous species	Selected species	Quantitative recording by replicated random sampling		Morphological studies	Physiological studies	Cell biology studies	Reproductive studies
Description of the communities present on a shore	1	1	2[a]	2[a]	2	2	3	3	3	3	3
Description of gross change	1	1	1	1	1	1	3	3	3	3	3
Detection of a gradient from point-source discharge	2	2	2	1	1	1	1	2	2 / not tested	2	2
Description of subtle change	3	3	3	1	1	1	2	2	2	2	2
Distinction of effects of low-level chronic pollution	—	3	3	1	1	1	1	1	1	1	1

(none of these is fully tested and the scale relates to potential)

Conclusions

Conclusions concerning survey techniques appropriate for different survey objectives are given in Table 8.2. It is also concluded that methods need to be developed for surveying stone/boulder shore communities. For example, it might be feasible to take say 10–20 samples of stones of a particular size and look at the organisms associated with them. Stones could be compared in this way from shore to shore, and the technique would overcome the problems of using quadrats on this shore type. Pitfall traps could possibly be used to catch mobile organisms.

Acknowledgements

We would like to thank the following people who made invaluable comments on a draft of this chapter: Ms E. Barnet, Dr R. S. Hartnoll, Dr S. Hawkins, Dr. K. Hiscock, Dr W. E. Jones, Mr. C. Lumb, Prof. D. Nichols, Dr. L. Terry, and Dr. R. Wright. A rocky shore survey and monitoring workshop organized by Dr K. Hiscock (Field Studies Council) and Dr K. Goodman (British Petroleum International Ltd.) in May 1984 was a fruitful source of information and ideas. However, final responsibility for the chapter lies with the authors.

APPENDIX 8.1

Variation in algal morphology with shore exposure

The morphology of some species of algae clearly varies with shore exposure, e.g., the mean lamina base angle of *Laminaria digitata* increases with decreasing exposure (Wright, 1981); with *Fucus vesiculosus* fewer vesicles are observed on smaller plants as the location becomes more exposed (see Fig. 8A.1). The number of vesicles is partly determined by plant size, which must therefore be taken into account. In Wright's study, the fresh weight of plants was chosen as the easiest measure of size. Ten plants were sampled from each of three sites and were selected at random from the middle of the zone of maximum abundance. In the laboratory, the plants were shaken to remove surface water and littorinids before being weighed. The vesicles on each plant were then counted. Fig. 8A.1 shows the number of vesicles on each plant plotted against its fresh weight, with linear regressions put through the points. With normal linear regressions, the value of the intercept was very small for the samples from Clubb of Mulla and Aith Voe (0.840 and 2.170 respectively), while the intercept was a high positive value (62.1) for the sample from Clousta. Since there was no possibility of 62 bladders with no fresh weight, the regression lines of samples from all the sites were forced through the origin for comparison. The regressions were as follows:

Clubb of Mulla $Y = 1.56\ X$
Aith Voe $Y = 2.46\ X$
Clousta $Y = 2.97\ X$

where Y is the number of vesicles and X is the fresh weight of the plant. Using a t test (described in most statistics textbooks, e.g., Sokal & Rohlf, 1981; Chalmers & Parker, 1986), it was found that these regression lines are significantly different at a probability of 0.1%.

Fig. 8A.1. Number of vesicles versus fresh weight of *Fucus vesiculosus* from three Shetland sites. Inset: slope of regression line versus exposure grade. From Wright (1981).

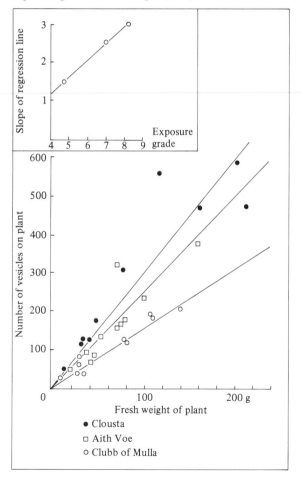

As an inset to Fig. 8A.1, the slopes of the regression lines have been plotted against exposure grade (a Shetland modification of the Ballantine exposure grade system). For the three sites from which samples were taken, there is a relationship between exposure grade and morphological change in *Fucus vesiculosus*, demonstrating that the exposure scale and changes in morphology are related to wave action in a similar way.

This preliminary study is described here as an example of quantitative work on algal morphology and exposure, an example that could be followed elsewhere, and (with modifications) using other species and morphological features.

APPENDIX 8.2

Example of data sheet for secondary factors, completed for a shore in Shetland (from Wright, 1981)

SITE NAME/No: BURRA VOE, YELL SH18	OS MAP REF: NU 530 798	PHOTO No: 28,29,30

Aspect: 198°	Angle of slope of shore: 12°

Rock Type: Schist & Gneiss

Surface Texture
(Depressions counted are those over 1 cm in width and depth along six parallels equally spaced in 0.1 m² quadrat (each parallel approx 30 cm long)).

	Field	Lab	Final
1. Very smooth flat surface			
2. Globular surface, similar to coarse-grained granite, few depressions greater than 1 cm width or depth			
3. Rough surface, but less than 50 depressions/180 cm length	3	3	3
4. Rough surface, 50 - 150 depressions/180 cm length			
5. Very rough surface, with more than 150 depressions/180 cm			

Degree of Fissuring

	Field	Lab	Final
1. Less than 0.1 m / 0.1 m²			
2. 0.1 - 0.5 m / 0.1 m²			
3. 0.5 - 1.0 m / 0.1 m²	3	3	3
4. 1.0 - 1.5 m / 0.1 m²			
5. More than 1.5 m / 0.1 m²			

Roughness of Shore

			Roughness Ratio	Mean Roughness Ratio
1. Length of tape over rocks (m) 9.4 / Length of tape stretched tight(m) 8.0	=		1.18	
2. Length of tape over rocks (m) 9.8 / Length of tape stretched tight(m) 8.8	=		1.11	1.14
3. Length of tape over rocks (m) 9.2 / Length of tape stretched tight(m) 8.1	=		1.14	

Mobility of Substrate

% transect stones up to 5 cm: –   % transect silt: –

Approx.density of stones larger than 5 cm: Top Shore: – / m²
Middle Shore: – / m²
Low Shore: – / m²

References

Ballantine, W. J. (1961). A biologically-defined exposure scale for the comparative description of rocky shores. *Field Studies*, **1**, 1–19.

Barnes, H. & Powell, H. T. (1950). The development, general morphology and subsequent elimination of barnacle populations, *Balanus crenatus* and *B. balanoides*, after a heavy initial settlement. *J. Anim. Ecol.* **19**, 175–9.

Barnet, E. A. (1985). Survey methods used by the Coast Surveillance Unit. In *Rocky Shore Survey and Monitoring Workshop*, ed. K. Hiscock, pp. 45–50. London: BP International.

Bassindale, R. (1942). The distribution of amphipods in the Severn Estuary and Bristol Channel. *J. Anim. Ecol.* **11**, 131–44.

Bassindale, R. (1943). A comparison of the varying salinity conditions of the Tees and Severn estuaries. *J. Anim. Ecol* **12**, 1–10.

Bennel, S. J. (1981). Some observations on the littoral barnacle populations of North Wales. *Mar. environ. Res.* **5**, 227–40.

Bowman, R. (1978). Dounreay oil spill: major implications of a minor incident. *Mar. Pollut. Bull.* **9**, 269–73.

Carefoot, T. (1977). *Pacific Seashores: A Guide to Intertidal Ecology.* Vancouver: J. J. Douglas.

Chalmers, N. & Parker, P. (1986). The OU project guide: fieldwork and statistics for ecological projects. *Occasional Publication of the Field Studies Council* No. 9. London: Field Studies Council.

Crapp, G. B. (1970). '*The Biological Effects of Marine Oil Pollution and Shore Cleansing.*' Unpublished Ph.D thesis, University of Wales, University College, Swansea.

Crapp, G. B. (1973). The distribution and abundance of animals and plants on the rocky shores of Bantry Bay. *Irish Fish. Invest.* (*B*), **9**, 1–35.

Crisp, D. J. & Southward, A. J. (1958). The distribution of intertidal organisms along the coasts of the English Channel. *J. mar. biol. Ass. U.K.* **37**, 157–208.

Cross, T. F. & Southgate, T. (1980). Mortalities of fauna of rocky substrates in south-west Ireland associated with the occurrence of *Gyrodinium aureolum* blooms during autumn 1979. *J. mar. biol. Ass. U.K.* **60**, 1071–3.

Crothers, J. H. (1973). On variation in *Nucella lapillus* (L): shell shape in populations from Pembrokeshire, South Wales. *Proc. Malac. Soc. Lond.* **40**, 319–27.

Crothers, J. H. (1974). On variation in *Nucella lapillus* (L.): shell shape in populations from the Bristol Channel. *Proc. Malac. Soc. Lond.* **41**, 157–70.

Crothers, J. H. (1975). On variation in *Nucella lapillus* (L.): shell shape in populations from the Channel Islands and north-western France. *Proc. Malac. Soc. Lond.* **41**, 499–502.

Crothers, J. H. (1977). Some observations on the growth of the common dog-whelk, *Nucella lapillus*, in the laboratory. *J. Conch.* **29**, 157–62.

Crothers, J. H. (1979). Variation in the shell of the dog-whelk *Nucella lapillus* (L.) from Sullom Voe and other parts of the Shetland Islands. *Mar. Environ. Res.* **2**, 311–27.

Crothers, J. H. (1983*a*). Field experiments on the effects of crude oil and dispersant on the common animals and plants of rocky sea shores. *Mar. Environ. Res.* **8**, 215–39.

Crothers, J. H. (1983*b*). Some observations on shell-shape variation in North American populations of *Nucella lapillus* (L.) *Biol. J. Linnean Soc.* **19**, 237–74.

Crothers, J. H. (1984). Some observations on shell shape variation in Pacific *Nucella*. *Biol. J. Linnean Soc.* **21**, 259–81.

Crothers, J. H. (1985). Dog whelks: an introduction to the biology of *Nucella lapillus* (L.). *Field Studies*, **6**, 291–360.

Crothers, J. H. & Cowell, E. B. (1979). On variation in *Nucella lapillus* (L.): shell shape in populations from Fensfjorden, Norway: an applied example. *J. Moll. Stud.* **45**, 108–14.

Dalby, D. H., Cowell, E. B., Syratt, W. J. & Crothers, J. H. (1978). An exposure scale for marine shores in western Norway. *J. mar. biol. Ass. U.K.* **58**, 975–96.

Denny, M. W. (1983). A simple device for recording the maximum force exerted on intertidal organisms. *Limnol. Oceanogr.* **28**, 1269–74.

Doty, M. S. (1971). Measurement of water movement in reference to benthic algal growth. *Botanica Marina*, **14**, 32–5.

Fretter, V & Graham, A. (1976). The Prosobranch Molluscs of Britain and Denmark. Part I. Pleurotomariacea, Fissurellacea and Patellacea. *J. Moll. Stud.*, Suppl. **1**, 1–37.

Hartnoll, R. G. & Hawkins, S. J. (1980). Monitoring rocky shore communities: a critical look at spatial and temporal variation. *Helgol. Meeresunters.* **33**, 484–94.

Hartnoll, R. G. & Hawkins, S. J. (1985). The use of multiple random quadrats for the assessment of the abundance of rocky shore organisms. In *Rocky Shore Survey and Monitoring Workshop*, ed. K. Hiscock, pp. 73–74. London: BP International.

Hartog, C. den (1959). The epilithic algal communities occurring along the coast of the Netherlands. *Wentia* **1**, 68.

Hawkins, S. J. (1985). Simple statistical methods for used in surveys and monitoring of rocky shores. In *Rocky Shore Survey and Monitoring Workshop*, ed. K. Hiscock, pp. 105–117. London: BP International.

Hawkins, S. J. & Hartnoll, R. G. (1979). A compressed air drill powered by SCUBA cylinders for use on rocky shores. *Estuar. Coast. Mar. Sci.* **9**, 819–20.

Hawkins, S. J. & Hartnoll, R. G. (1982). Settlement patterns of *Semibalanus balanoides* (L.) on the Isle of Man (1977–1981). *J. exp. mar. Biol. Ecol.* **62**, 271–83.

Hawkins, S. J. & Hartnoll, R. G. (1983*a*) Changes in a rocky shore community: an evaluation of monitoring. *Mar. environ. Res.* **9**, 131–81.

Hawkins, S. J. & Hartnoll, R. G. (1983*b*). Grazing of intertidal algae by marine invertebrates. *Oceanogr. Mar. Biol. Ann. Rev.* **21**, 195–282.

Hawkins, S. J. & Hartnoll, R. G. (1985). The use of fixed quadrats in monitoring rocky shore communities. In *Rocky Shore Survey and Monitoring Workshop*, ed. K. Hiscock, pp. 68–72. London: BP International.

Hawkins, S. J. & Russell, G. (1981). Some comments on aims and methods in rocky shore ecology. *Br. Phyc. J.* **16**, 136.

Hawkins, S. J., Southward, A. J. & Barrett, R. L. (1984). Population structure of *Patella vulgata* during succession on rocky shores in south-west England. *Acta Oceanologica*, special no., 103–7.

Head, P. C. (ed.) (1985). *Practical Estuarine Chemistry*. Estuarine and Brackish-Water Sciences Association Handbook. Cambridge University Press.

Hiscock, K. (1984). *Rocky Shore Surveys of the Isles of Scilly*. Unpublished report to the Nature Conservancy Council.

Hiscock, K. (ed.) (1985). *Rocky Shore Survey and Monitoring Workshop*, 1–4 May 1984. London: BP International.

Holme, N. A. & Nichols, D. (1980). *Habitat Survey Cards for the Shores of the British Isles*. Occasional Publication, London: Field Studies Council.

Jones, A. M. (1980). Monitoring studies associated with an oil reception terminal. *Rapp. P.-v. Reun. Cons. int. Explor. Mer*, **179**, 194–200.

Jones, W. E. & Demetropoulos, A. (1968). Exposure to wave action: measurements of an important ecological parameter on rocky shores on Anglesey. *J. exp. mar. Biol. Ecol.* **2**, 46–63.

Jones, W. E., Bennell, S., Beveridge, C., McConnell, B., Mack-Smith, S., Mitchell, J. & Fletcher, A. (1980). Methods of data collection and processing in rocky intertidal monitoring. In *The Shore Environment*, vol. 1: *Methods*, ed. J. H. Price, D. E. G. Irvine & W. F. Farnham, pp. 137–70. Published for the Systematics Association by Academic Press, London.

Jones, W. E., Fletcher, A., Bennell, S. J., McConnell, B. J., Richards, A. V. L. & Mack-Smith, S. (1979). Intertidal surveillance. In *Monitoring the Marine Environment*, ed. D. Nichols, pp. 1–23. London: Institute of Biology.

Kirby, R. (1973). The U.C.S. grain-size comparator disc. *Mar. Geol.* **14**, M11–M14.

Kjerfve, B. (1979). Measurement and analysis of water current, temperature, salinity and density. In *Estuarine Hydrography and Sedimentation*, Estuarine and Brackish-Water Sciences Association Handbook, ed. K. R. Dyer, pp. 186–216. Cambridge University Press.

Knight, S. J. T. & Mitchell, R. (1980). The survey and nature conservation assessment of littoral areas. In *The Shore Environment*, vol. 1: *Methods*, ed. J. H. Price, D. E. G. Irvine & W. F. Farnham, pp. 303–21. Published for the Systematics Association by Academic Press, London.

Lewis, J. R. (1964). *The Ecology of Rocky Shores*. London: Hodder and Stoughton.

Lewis, J. R. (1976). Long-term ecological surveillance: practical realities in the rocky littoral. *Oceanogr. Mar. Biol. Ann. Rev.* **14**, 371–90.

Little, A. (1985). Abundance scale techniques for the surveying of rocky shores. In *Rocky Shore Survey and Monitoring Workshop*, ed. K. Hiscock, pp. 38–44. London: BP International.

Lumb, C. M. (1985). Survey for the assessment of nature conservation importance of sites. In *Rocky Shore Survey and Monitoring Workshop*, ed. K. Hiscock, pp. 24–32. London: BP International.

McCave, I. N. (1979). Suspended sediment. In *Estuarine Hydrography and Sedimentation*, Estuarine and Brackish-Water Sciences Association Handbook, ed. K. R. Dyer, pp. 131–85. Cambridge University Press.

Moore, P. G. & Seed, R. (eds) (1985). *The Ecology of Rocky Coasts.*
Sevenoaks: Hodder & Stoughton.

Moyse, J. & Nelson-Smith, A. (1963). Zonation of animals and plants on rocky
shores around Dale, Pembrokeshire. *Field Studies* **1**, 1–31.

Munda, I. M. (1978). Salinity dependent distribution of benthic algae in
estuarine areas of Icelandic fjords. *Botanica Marina* **21**, 451–68.

Muus, B. J. (1968). A field method for measuring 'exposure' by means of
plaster balls. A preliminary account. *Sarsia*, **34**, 61–8.

Myers, A. A., Cross, T. F. & Southgate, T. (1978). *Bantry Bay Survey. First
Annual Report.* Cork: University College.

Myers, A. A. & Southgate, T. (1980) Artificial substrates as a means of
monitoring rocky shore cryptofauna. *J. mar. biol. Ass. U.K.* **60**,
963–75.

Natural Environment Research Council (1973). *Marine Wildlife Conservation.*
NERC Publications, Series B, No. 5. Swindon: NERC.

Nienhuis, P. H. (1969). The significance of the substratum for intertidal algal
growth on the artificial rocky shore of the Netherlands. *Int. Revue ges.
Hydrobiol.* **54**, 207–15.

Palumbi, S. R. (1984). Measuring intertidal wave forces. *J. exp. mar. Biol. Ecol.*
81, 171–9.

Petpiroon, S., Dicks, B., Iball, K. & Crump, R. (1982). Environmental effects of
a refinery effluent and its use for teaching purposes. *Field Studies* **5**,
623–41.

Raffaelli, D. G. & Hughes, R. N. (1978). The effects of crevice size and
availability on populations of *Littorina rudis* and *Littorina neritoides.*
J. Anim. Ecol. **47**, 71–83.

Ratcliffe, D. A. (ed.) (1977). *A Nature Conservation Review*, vol. 1. Cambridge
University Press.

Russell, G. (1980). Applications of simple numerical methods to the analysis of
intertidal vegetation. In *The Shore Environment*, vol. 1: *Methods*, ed.
J. H. Price, D. E. G. Irvine & W. F. Farnham, pp. 171–92. Published
for the Systematics Association by Academic Press, London.

Siegel, S. (1956). *Non-Parametric Statistics for the Behavioural Sciences.*
Kogakusha, Tokyo: McGraw-Hill.

Smith, S. M. (1982). A review of the genus *Littorina* in British and Atlantic
waters. (Gastropoda: Prosobranchia). *Malacologia*, **22**, 535–9.

Sokal, R. R. & Rohlf, R. F. (1981). Biometry, 2nd edn. San Francisco:
W. H. Freeman.

Southward, A. J. (1953). The ecology of some rocky shores in the south of the
Isle of Man. *Proc. Trans. Lpool biol. Soc.* **59**, 1–50.

Stephenson, T. A. & Stephenson, A. (1972). *Life between Tidemarks on Rocky
Shores.* San Francisco: W. H. Freeman.

Terry, L. A., Sell, D., Ralph, R. & Addy, J. M. (1985). Survey methods used in
the Moray Firth. In *Rocky Shore Survey and Monitoring Workshop*,
ed. K. Hiscock, pp. 51–54. BP International, London.

Thomas, M. L. H. (1986). A physically derived exposure index for marine
shorelines. *Ophelia*, **25**, 1–13.

Wentworth, C. K. (1922). Grade and class terms for clastic sediments. *J. Geol.* **30**, 377–92.

Westhoff, V. & Maarel, E. van der. (1978). The Braun-Blanquet approach. In *Classification of Plant Communities*, ed. R. H. Whittaker, pp. 287–397. The Hague: Dr. W. Junk.

Wilson, C. M., Crothers, J. H. & Oldham, J. H. (1983). Realized niche: the effects of a small stream on sea-shore distribution patterns. *J. Biol. Ed.* **17**, 51–8.

Wright, R. A. D. (1981). 'Wave Exposure Studies on Rocky Shores in Shetland.' Unpublished Ph.D thesis, University of London (Imperial College of Science and Technology).

9

Subtidal rock and shallow sediments using diving

K. HISCOCK

Introduction

Observations and sampling in sublittoral rocky areas can only be carried out effectively *in situ*, and free diving (SCUBA) is usually employed. Diving is also used to observe and sample the fauna of sediments where the area is unsuitable for remote sampling or where precision is required in the relative positioning of different stations. This chapter describes techniques for survey and sampling on nearshore rock and sediments using diving.

During the past 12 years, considerable advances have been made in developing techniques and equipment and in testing different survey strategies for biologists using self-contained diving apparatus. For instance, techniques for descriptive surveys have been extensively developed and used in a large number of surveys carried out in the British Isles to assess the nature conservation value of sites, whilst in Scandinavia the use of underwater stereophotography is now a standard practice for monitoring fluctuations in rocky subtidal species and communities. Other techniques such as suction sampling for collecting rocky subtidal epibiota are well developed from the point of view of equipment but not sampling strategy.

Diving requires good training, particularly where the work is to be carried out in conditions of low underwater visibility, darkness, or cold. In Britain, biologists using diving are required by the government to be qualified to a certain standard, and a high degree of competence is required before the biologist can expect to carry out survey work of even a low degree of complexity. Inevitably, the time taken to train can be long and the cost of training can be high. Most biologists start training with a sport diving club and this considerably reduces the cost. There are other major problems in using diving. The physiological limitations of diving mean that speed and efficiency are essential in carrying out work underwater. Also, the problems involved in mobilising boats and equipment, getting kitted up, filling air bottles, and often having only a short period of slack water in which to work, all lead to a lot of preparation for a very small amount of survey or sampling time. However, the individual researcher or the head of a department faced with establishing a diving facility should not be discouraged. There is no other way of adequately describing and sampling sublittoral hard substrata, and much work remains to be done in an ecosystem about which we know very little.

Strategy
General planning

I have discussed the planning of surveys in a previous paper (Hiscock, 1979) but, for the sake of completeness, include some of that material here.

The first requirement in planning all surveys is to understand what questions are to be answered. Having established what the objective of the survey is, the location of sampling sites and the techniques most appropriate to the requirements of the survey can be decided. The project director should also consider whether diving is really the most efficient or effective means of achieving the aims of the survey or whether remote observation or sampling could be used. At this stage, it is also necessary to consider the methods that will be used to analyse the data so that the information can be collected in a suitable form.

A minimum of two divers will be required in any survey, with a third person to act as supervisor/boat coxswain. The divers work either as a pair or with one acting as a stand-by diver. In some cases it is more efficient for a diver to work alone; a partner can easily stir up sediment so that work at one site becomes impossible, dislodge equipment, or distract the working diver when contact has to be ensured in poor visibility. There are many other problems and a competent field-worker can, on entering cold turbid water, become forgetful and incompetent. Also, the worker cannot be sure of remembering everything seen during a dive when there are many things to be thought about associated with the dive other than just the survey task. Therefore, the work to be carried out should be designed to take account of the many difficulties of working underwater and the experience of the staff. The following factors should be considered at the planning stage:

1. Account should be taken of the experience of the divers – in diving, in species recognition (for descriptive surveys), and in the work to be carried out. The absence of general guides to the identification of sublittoral species and the lack of formal education

at university in rocky sublittoral ecology in particular will make the description of communities more difficult because personnel are usually inexperienced. In surveys of species distribution, the worker should not be expected to learn recognition as he or she goes along and some days should be devoted to training, before or after the start of the survey. The individual skills of each worker should be used to greatest effect.

2. The sea-water temperature and likely tolerance of workers to cold need to be taken into account. The efficiency of divers working in wet-suits drops considerably at temperatures below about 12 °C, although this depends on experience, enthusiasm, and individual tolerance. Dry-suits make comfortable, warm working conditions possible in cold water and are now used extensively.

3. When operating in depths greater than 9 m, the time available on the sea-bed before decompression becomes necessary, and the number of dives possible in one day in relation to decompression schedules should be borne in mind. Also, nitrogen narcosis and anxiety make tasks more difficult with increasing depth.

4. The safety procedures appropriate to diving and boating need to be taken into account during planning (see Chapter 15).

5. Problems of access to sites for shore-based parties and problems of launching facilities for small boats should be considered.

6. The times and duration of slack water at proposed sites should be noted. Admiralty Coastal Pilots and Charts include information on slack-water times.

7. The exposure of coasts to wave action should be taken into account; exposed coasts should be surveyed as soon as weather conditions permit and each day's work should be made complete, so that usable information is obtained even if adverse winds prevent further work at that site.

8. The limitations that poor visibility and/or poor light will impose on the survey should be considered. Work becomes difficult in a horizontal visibility of less than about 3 m or where a torch is required. This is particularly the case where habitats or stations have to be located or where divers are working together.

9. Provision should be made for adequate briefing before each dive to ensure, for instance, that pairs of divers know what each is supposed to be doing underwater or to ensure that (in descriptive surveys) a botanist and zoologist are recording in the same habitats at the same site.

10. The ease of relocation of stations where surveys are to be carried

out at the same site over several days or where monitoring is the aim should be borne in mind. It might be necessary to allow time for the laying of guide lines or other site marks.

11. Account should be taken of the variation in species abundance through the year and from year to year. The abundance and range of species of algae and some animals varies greatly from summer to winter. Surveys of several locations aimed at comparing differences in species composition should be carried out at, or as near as possible, the same time of year to minimise the possibility of seasonal changes producing the differences. In monitoring a site from year to year, surveys should be made, as far as possible, at the same time in each year.

12. In monitoring studies, it is prudent to consider whether surveying will be possible at set intervals or whether flexibility will be required because of variable environmental conditions that might make diving or the required work impossible (e.g., turbidity or wave action).

13. An assessment should always be made of the time available to sort and identify collected material or to transcribe data both during the survey and afterwards. There is no value in diving if the data or samples collected are not properly written up or identified.

Survey and sampling units

The project director must determine the survey or sampling units to be investigated and the range of species that are to be included to satisfy the aims of the work. Selection of survey or sampling units or the definition of the main units to be studied will be based on, e.g.:

1. The main biotic zones or subzones with depth – the sublittoral fringe, upper infralittoral, lower infralittoral, upper circalittoral, lower circalittoral.

2. Particular habitats or substrata, e.g. whole *Laminaria hyperborea* plants, *L. hyperborea* holdfasts, leaves of *Zostera marina*, upward-facing unbroken rock surfaces, sediment plains.

The range of species to be studied or sampled and the detail in which records are to be made must also be decided. Choice of the range of species includes:

1. 'All' species (from the large widely dispersed species to small undergrowth species larger than 0.5 mm).

2. Conspicuous species easily recognised *in situ*.

3. Undergrowth species requiring collection for identification.

4. Key, characteristic, or 'indicator' species.

5. Species groups (e.g., foliose algae, kelp, Bryozoa/Hydrozoa).
6. Species within taxonomic groups (e.g., algae, coelenterates, sponges).
7. Single species.

The detail in which records are to be made will be based on:

1. Quantitative samples or measurements (carefully collected random or systematic samples or measurements from a known area expressed as density, percentage cover, or weight).
2. Semi-quantitative samples or records (collections from roughly delimited area, estimates or rough counts of density or percentage cover).
3. Qualitative (presence/absence) records.

Location of sites and stations

The question of where to locate sites has exercised the minds of many marine ecologists who must weigh the benefits of systematic or random placing of sites (see Chapter 1) against the fact that such techniques will almost certainly miss some important habitats or communities that the experienced worker 'knows' are there, or will make the survey difficult for practical reasons. Extensive descriptive surveys are usually carried out based on the experience of the project leader who, by inspection of maps, charts and coastal pilots, will select a number of sites to provide situations exposed to widely different environmental conditions. Intensive surveys aimed at the accurate tracing of gradients in species distribution or frequency of occurrence of species or habitats will require systematically or randomly placed sites. The methods for undertaking such selections are described in Chapter 1.

Determining depth intervals at which survey stations should be placed must be based on a preliminary knowledge of the communities present. Thus, for instance, a 2-m vertical depth interval in the clear waters of southern Ireland would result in a multitude of basically similar stations in the kelp forest that is very extensive there, whilst in parts of the Bristol Channel the worker would entirely miss the transition between kelp communities at 0 m and animal communities with virtually no algae present at -2 m. Whatever the sampling interval, supplementary stations located according to depth might be needed in areas of rapid community change. The main sublittoral sub-zones in which distinctively different communities occur have been described by Hiscock & Mitchell (1980). The most economical method for descriptive survey is to locate stations in each of these main sub-zones. Hiscock & Mitchell (1980) also describe the main habitat types that have distinctly different communities and, in

Table 9.1. *Number of animal species recorded by different methods and the approximate time taken for data/sample analysis by experienced staff using familiar techniques*

Survey/sample method	Number of recorded taxa (mostly identified to species)	Number of taxa not recorded in quantitative samples (for *in situ* survey and photographs) or by *in situ* survey and photographs together (for quantitative sampling)	Time taken for collection	Time taken for identification and/or transcription and analysis	Notes
In situ descriptive survey of conspicuous species over whole of port side of wreck.	39	14	Diving including preparation: 5 hours (combined with photography) (1 day total)	3 hours	Taxa not recorded in samples were mostly large, widely dispersed species.
Photography of 22 contiguous quadrats of 0.03 m². Photographs analysed to determine percentage cover of colonial or foliose species. Solitary species counted.	29	4	Diving including preparation: 5 hours (combined with photography) (1 day total)	2 hours	This technique also excluded some large, widely distributed species. Percentage cover of colonial or foliose species could be accurately determined.
Quantitative sampling of seven 0.1 m² quadrats placed at random grid co-ordinates using a suction sampler fitted with a 0.5-mm mesh.	161	127	Diving including preparation carried out at 20 m below sea-level on a 'no-stop' decompression schedule (3 days total)	Sorting: 2 days/sample. Identification and counting: 3 days/sample (35 days total)	The species that were recorded only from quantitative samples were mostly small annelids, Crustacea, and Mollusca. Numbers of specimens of particular species were much higher than those recorded in photographs. This sample sorting took considerably longer than sorting samples from sediments because of the presence of tangled branching species.

This work was carried out in 1980 on the wreck of the *MV Robert* off Lundy at a depth of 15 m below chart datum.

surveys aimed at comparing communities and sites, different stations should be established in each different habitat or the work should be restricted to one particular habitat, e.g., 'upward-facing bedrock'. The most recent classification of sublittoral habitats likely to hold distinctly

Fig. 9.1. Habitat recording sheet developed by the Marine Conservation Society/Field Studies Council/Nature Conservancy Council for sublittoral areas.

SITUATION (TICK ONE ONLY)		WAVE EXPOSURE (SURFACE) (TICK)		ROCK TYPE (TICK)	
OPEN SEA (> 1 km offshore)	1	VERY EXPOSED (prevailing wind and swell)	30	IGNEOUS	50
				LIMESTONES	51
OPEN COASTLINE–ROCK (>30° deep-water window to open sea)	2	EXPOSED (prevailing wind)	31	HARD SAND./MUDSTONES	52
				SOFT SAND./MUDSTONES	53
		SEMI-EXPOSED (strong wind frequent)	32	HARD SLATE/SHALES	54
OPEN COASTLINE–SEDIMENT (>30° deep-water window to open sea)	3			FRIABLE SLATE/SHALES	55
		SHELTERED (strong wind rare)	33	NOT KNOWN	56
ENCLOSED COASTLINE–ROCK (<30° deep-water window to open sea)	4	VERY SHELTERED (fetch <20 km)	34	OTHER (tick and note below)	57
		EXTREMELY SHELTERED (fetch <3 km)	35		
ENC. COASTLINE–SEDIMENT (<30° deep-water window to open sea)	5	MAX. TIDAL STREAM STRENGTH (TICK)		SITE INFORMATION (TICK)	
		VERY STRONG (6 k+)	36	MNR, NNR, LNR, SSSI NEARBY	65
COASTAL TYPE (TICK)		STRONG (3–6 k)	37	SEWAGE/INDUSTRIAL OUTFALL NEAR	66
HEADLAND	6	MOD. STRONG (1–3 k)	38	
'LINEAR COAST'	7	WEAK (<1 k)	39	OTHER SOURCES OF DISTURANCE (tick & note below)	67
BAY	8	VERY WEAK (negligible)	40	
SPIT/BAR	9	SALINITY (TICK)		
OFFSHORE SM. ISLAND	10	NORMAL (around 34°/oo)	41	
AMONGST ROCKS/ISLETS	11	VARIABLE (30°/oo+)	42	OTHER DATA RECORDED	
SOUND/NARROWS	12	LOW (<30°/oo)	43	PHOTOGRAPHS: SURF	80
SHALLOW RAPIDS	13	SALINITY MEASURED (TICK)	44	W–A	81
SEA LOCH	14	NOT KNOWN	45	C–U	82
ESTUARY/MARINE INLET	15			WATER ANALYSIS	83
COASTAL LAGOON	16	WATER STRATIFICATION (TICK)		SEDIMENT ANALYSIS	84
HARBOUR	17	THERMOCLINE	46	SPECIMENS COLLECTED	85
SEA CAVE	18	HALOCLINE	47	ALGAL CHECKLIST	86
WRECK	19	NOT STRATIFIED	48	ANIMAL CHECKLIST	87
OTHER (tick and note below)	20	NOT KNOWN	49	OTHER (tick and note below)	88

different communities is included in the habitat recording sheet shown in Fig. 9.1. Vastly different amounts of time will be required for different survey and sampling methods. Table 9.1 gives one set of estimates for a fairly straightforward survey and sampling programme. Clearly, the

Fig. 9.1 (*cont.*)

UNDERWATER DATA

SITE NO.

DEPTH ZONE (OPEN ROCK) (TICK ONE)		STN./HABITAT 1 2 3 4 5 6	OVERALL INCLINATION (TICK ONE)		STN./HABITAT 1 2 3 4 5 6
SUBLITTORAL FRINGE	100		OVERHANG	170	
UPPER INFRALITTORAL	101		VERTICAL (80-100°)	171	
LOWER INFRALITTORAL	102		V. STEEP (40-80°)	172	
UPPER CIRCALITTORAL	103		STEEP (20-40°)	173	
LOWER CIRCALITTORAL	104		SHALLOW (<20°)	174	
NOT KNOWN	105		HORIZONTAL	175	

DEPTH BAND (m) BELOW CD (TICK ONE)		1 2 3 4 5 6	ROCK FEATURES (SCORE 1-3)		1 2 3 4 5 6
<0	106		OUTCROP	176	
0-5	107		(UNBROKEN ROCK	177	
5-10	108		(BROKEN ROCK	178	
10-20	109		(TERRACES .	179	
20-30	110		(LEDGES	180	
>30	111		ROCK WALLS	181	
			OPEN GULLIES	182	
SUBSTRATUM (SCORE 1 = RARE, 2 = SECONDARY, 3 = PREDOMINANT		1 2 3 4 5 6	(STEEP-SIDED GULLIES (MAN)	183	
			LARGE FISSURES/CREV. (ARM)	184	
BEDROCK	112		(SMALL FISSURES/CREV. (FINGER)	185	
LG. BOULDERS (500 mm+)	113		LARGE CAVE (SWIM IN)	186	
SM. BOULDERS (256-500 mm)	114		SMALL CAVE (PUT HEAD IN)	187	
LG. COBBLES (128-256 mm)	115		POTHOLES	188	
LG. SLATES (128-256 mm)	116		ROCKMILLS	189	
SM. ANGULAR COBBLES (64-128 mm)	117		(BOULDER INTERSTICES	190	
SM. ROUND COBBLES (64-128 mm)	118		(COBBLE INTERSTICES	191	
SM. SLATES	119		(PEBBLE INTERSTICES	192	
V. LG. & LG. ANG. PEBBLES (16-64 mm)	120		STABLE BOULDER SLOPE	193	
V. LG. & LG. ROUND PEBBLES (16-64 mm)	121		SCREE	194	
MED. & SM. PEBBLES (4-16 mm)	122		MOBILE COBBLES	195	
CLEAN GRAVEL (2-4 mm)	123		SCOURED ROCK	196	
MUDDY GRAVEL (2-4 mm)	124		SAND ON ROCKS	197	
MAERL GRAVEL	125		THIN SILT ON ROCKS	198	
CLEAN SHELL GRAVEL	126		THICK/FLOC. SILT ON ROCKS	199	
MUDDY SHELL GRAVEL	127		OTHER (tick & note/score below)	200	
COARSE SAND (0.5-2 mm)	128				
FINE CLEAN SAND	129				
FINE MUDDY SAND	130		SEDIMENT FEATURES (SCORE 1-3)		1 2 3 4 5 6
SANDY MUD	131		FIRM	220	
MUD	132		SOFT	221	
MIXTURE OF TYPES IN HABITAT	133		SMOOTH	222	
KELP PLANTS	134		WORKED	223	
WHOLE SHELLS	135		RIPPLED	224	
TREE BRANCHES	136		MOUNDS	225	
OTHER (score & note type below)	137		BURROWS	226	
			SHELLS (INTACT)	227	
ARTIFICIAL SUBSTRATUM (SCORE 1-3)		1 2 3 4 5 6	OTHER (tick & note/score below)	228	
METAL	150				
CONCRETE	151				
WOOD	152				
OTHER (tick & note/score below)	153		SEDIMENT COVER (SCORE 1-3)		1 2 3 4 5 6
			SEAGRASS BED	240	
ROCK COVER (SCORE 1-3)		1 2 3 4 5 6	ALGAL MEADOW	241	
KELP CANOPY			ALGAL TURF	242	
ALGAL MEADOW			ALGAL MAT	243	
ALGAL TURF			UNATTACHED ALGAE	244	
ALGAL CRUST			LIVE MAERL BED	245	
FAUNAL TURF			FAUNAL BED	246	
FAUNAL BED					

project leader must consider carefully the usefulness of the extra information that would be obtained by the usually much more time-consuming quantitative sampling. Later sections describing the different methods of survey should assist in determining the techniques to be used in any one survey with relation to the experience of personnel and the aims of the study.

Sample size

For both *in situ* recording and for collection of samples, it is necessary to obtain at least some idea of the size of the study area or sample size required to fulfil the aims of the survey. Methods for determining sample size are described and discussed in Chapter 1. However, little work has yet been carried out in the north-east Atlantic to provide any general guide-lines regarding sampling areas necessary for different types of survey on sublittoral rocks.

Previous attempts to answer questions regarding minimum sampling area on sublittoral hard substrata have mainly been directed at algae. Boudouresque (1971) considered that a sampled area of only 100 cm² was adequate to list all of the algae present in shallow shaded areas whilst 250 cm² was required in the coralligenous zone of the circalittoral in the Mediterranean. Similar results were obtained by Coppejans (1980). Larkum, Drew & Crossett (1967) used 400 cm² as the minimum sampling area required for algal vegetation off Malta but noted that, because of patchiness within communities, the eight samples usually taken at each station may not have given a completely reliable picture of the vegetation. For algal populations in British waters, it seems likely that a much larger sample needs to be taken than for Mediterranean areas. S. Hiscock (personal communication) collected samples of algae from six 0.25 m² quadrats at three depths and three sites off Skomer Island in west Wales. On doubling the sample area from 0.5 to 1.0 m², increases of between 7% and 200% in the number of species recorded were obtained. From 1.0 to 1.5 m², the number of species increased by between 7% and 50%. Maggs (1984), studying seasonal changes in communities of algae attached to maerl, used species–area curves to determine the volume of sample necessary in this three-dimensional habitat and concluded that a sample size of 300 cm³ was required.

Much less work has been undertaken on animal communities. Based on data collected from 0.25 m² quantitative samples of animal communities on sublittoral rocks at Lough Ine and Lundy, Hiscock (1979) suggested that 0.5 m² was not an adequate sampling area and that 1 m² might have been preferable to collect a reasonably high percentage of the species present. D. M. Rostron & K. Hiscock (unpublished data), working on a highly homogeneous animal community on the side of a wreck, found that the point beyond which an additional 0.1 m² quadrat provided less than 5% more species was at 0.6 m². However, the point at which a 100% increase in sample area would yield a 10% increase in species was at 1.5 m². Actual and extrapolated species numbers were 152 (0.6 m²), 159 (0.7 m²), 189 (1.5 m²), and 209 (3.0 m²).

If it is required to obtain information on the quantity of a species present for comparison either with other sites or for following temporal change in the abundance of that species, an optimum sample size will need to be determined. This is the sample size required to provide quantitative information on the abundance of certain species. Inevitably, it will only be possible to calculate mean abundance within reasonable statistical limits for a small number of species in a community unless enormous samples are to be taken. Plotting a running mean for the quantity of a species present is a rapid way of assessing the adequacy of sample number (Chapter 1). If probability statistics are used, the analysis takes longer but provides more accurate results. D. M. Rostron & K. Hiscock (unpublished data) considered a 95% probability of a standard error equal to 20% of the mean to be a reasonable level of accuracy to aim for and found that of the 152 non-colonial species that were counted from 14 0.1 m² samples, ten species could be adequately sampled within the above statistical limits in ten 0.1 m² samples. By extrapolation, it was found that 26 species required 20 0.1 m² sample units to achieve the desired accuracy but that, for a standard error of 10% of the mean, only four species were described adequately by 20 sample units.

Data compatibility

Several different techniques that result in a mixture of semi-quantitative and quantitative data will be outlined in succeeding sections. For detailed data analysis, counts of organisms, measures of percentage cover, or measures of wet weights clearly provide the most accurate basis for the analysis. However, a mixture of quantitative and semi-quantitative data is difficult to cope with, and the worker inevitably finds it necessary to resort to some semi-quantitative method to provide a comparative score for species measured by the different methods. Analysis is most easily accomplished if any scale of abundance follows a mathematical sequence (for instance, an exponential or logarithmic increase from notation to notation). Table 9.2 has been prepared to reflect the range of organisms found underwater in the north-east Atlantic, their form, and the amounts they are generally found in.

Table 9.2. *A scale of abundance for obtaining compatible abundance grades for species with widely different growth forms and quantities*

Species category	per station c. 100 m²			per 10 m²			per 1 m²			per 0.1 m²			per 0.01 m² or % cover or g/0.1 m²						
	1–2	3–5	6–9	1–2	3–5	6–9	1–2	3–5	6–9	1–2	3–5	6–9	1–2	3–5	6–9	10–20	21–50	51–99	100+
1	1	2	3	4	5	6	7	8	↑										
2		←	1	2	3	4	5	6	7		↑								
3		←	1		2	3			3		→								
4						←1		2	4	5		6		5		8	↑		|8
5						←1	2	3	4	8		7		6	6			7	|8
6						←1	2	3	←1	5		4		6	7	8	↑		8	
7		←	←1	←1				3		4	5	5		6	7	7		8	↑
8						2		3		4	<0.1% 1	<1% 2	3		6		8	8	↑
9				1 = a few sprigs			2 = 0.1 to 1.0 g/0.1 m²						3	4	5	6	7	8	↑↑
10				1 = 1 or 2 patches or sprigs,			3 = several small patches,		6 = present on most suitable surfaces,			8 = present on all suitable surfaces				7	8	↑↑

* 1. Large solitary or clumped species usually present in small numbers (e.g., some echinoderms, massive sponges, hydroid clumps).
2. Large solitary or clumped species often present in large numbers. (e.g. some echinoderms, massive sponges, hydroid clumps).
3. Small but easily visible species (e.g., cup corals, anemones, nudibranchs, some ascidians, large non-clumped hydroids).
4. Small conspicuous species sometimes in very large numbers (e.g. barnacles).
5. Small species generally visible only in collected samples but never present in large numbers (e.g., some Annelida, small Crustacea, small Mollusca).
6. Small species generally visible only in collected samples and present in large numbers (e.g. some Annelida, small Crustacea, small Mollusca).
7. Crustose, foliose and turf-forming species observed *in situ*.
8. Crustose, foliose and turf-forming species only recorded as % cover.
9. Turf-forming species collected in samples and recorded as g/0.1 m².
10. Hydrozoa and Bryozoa encrusting on other species.
Note: vertical lines indicate the limits for categories 3,4 and 7.

General equipment and methods

Some methods or items of equipment are used in several types of survey and are therefore described here. I have included only the techniques or equipment widely available or easily constructed. Thus, the use of underwater laboratories or submersibles is not described.

Basic aids to observation and collecting

The diving biologist's basic item of equipment is the laminated plastic writing pad and graphite pencil. Where systematic observations are being made, a check-list of species or tasks on the board is important if the worker is to be sure of remembering everything that needs to be searched for. Plastic 'paper' can also be used, particularly if large amounts of information are to be noted. For many surveys, the diver will find it useful to have several numbered self-sealing plastic bags. These are most conveniently held in loops of elastic on an arm band. Site details can be noted for the bag number in which samples are placed. Filled bags should be deposited in a net bag with a closing top.

Photography

Photographs can be used to aid later description of sites or communities, to illustrate reports, to enable measurements to be made in comfort with no restriction on time, or to follow changes at the same location. Guides to underwater photographic methods and equipment are given in Glover, Harwood & Lythgoe, (1977), Turner (1982), and Rowlands (1983). The use of photography in underwater biological surveys is described by several authors in George, Lythgoe & Lythgoe (1985).

A wide variety of cameras are available in waterproof housings, including 6 cm × 6 cm and 35-mm format cameras. The Nikonos is a small, waterproof, and very versatile 35-mm camera that does not require a housing. Television and cinematography have been used mainly for remote surveys or for illustration. The quality of underwater video equipment has increased greatly in recent years and offers the possibility of extensive survey and recording, including use by non-biologist divers.

Tape recorders and communications equipment

Where a great deal of information needs to be collected in a short period of time, there are very considerable advantages to be gained by tape-recording observations underwater. Fig. 9.2 shows an underwater tape recorder that is easy to use and, when employed in conjunction with a mouth mask or full-face mask, has good word clarity. A smaller unit is described by Byers (1977). An on/off switch operated by the diver keeps to a minimum the time required for transcription of the tape. However, if the push switch is unreliable or if a time-base for observations is useful, an on/off switch is best mounted on the lid of the unit and switched on just before the diver enters the water. Ready-constructed cases are available into which appropriate controls can be fitted, and at least one 'off-the-shelf' underwater tape recorder is marketed. Tape recordings can take a lot of time to transcribe and further time is needed to organise the transcribed data. Diver-to-surface telephone communication systems are also useful inexpensive means of transmitting information, and conversation can be tape-recorded or written down by a surface operator. The telephone requires that the diver is connected to the surface, and is particularly useful where a towed hydroplane is being used during a drift dive or where the diver is working in one place. Ultrasonic (wireless) diver-to-diver communication systems are available, but good word clarity is found only in the expensive models. Many of the problems involved in communication between divers underwater or between the diver and surface staff can be reduced by good briefing and liaison before the dive, and in many

Fig. 9.2. Underwater tape recorder. Full face mask not shown.

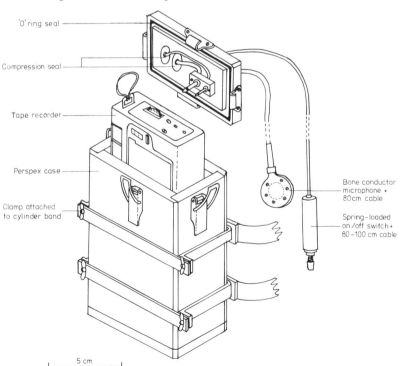

situations this is preferable to the problems of setting up and maintaining electronic equipment.

Towing systems including hydroplanes and underwater tugs

Where a large area of fairly unbroken sea-bed is to be surveyed, some system of towing rather than swimming will greatly increase the distance covered in one dive. The simplest way to achieve this is for the diver to hold a rope towed at a speed of about 1 knot by the surface boat. Communication by a telephone or through-water communication system is very important if the most suitable speed is to be achieved, safety assured, and stops made where required. Hydroplanes have been developed to provide support and manoeuvrability for the diver (Fig. 9.3). Larger towed vehicles are used, and Main & Sangster (1978) describe a towed wet submersible used for fisheries research. Up to about 1 km of sea-bed can

Fig. 9.3. Towed underwater sledges. (*a*) Port Erin marine biology station sledge. (*b*) Redrawn from Erwin (1977). (*c*) Redrawn from Sigl *et al.* (1969).

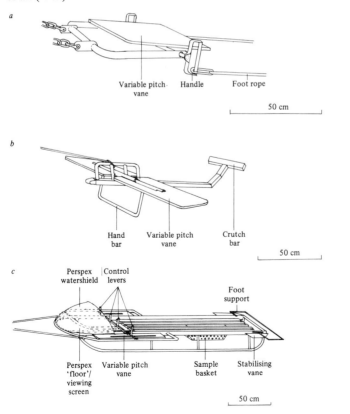

be covered in 30 minutes using a simple towed hydroplane. Hydroplanes are not usually sufficiently manoeuvrable to avoid objects more than 1 m high and cannot safely be used in a visibility of less than 3 m. The diver must be able to abandon the hydroplane quickly. Underwater tugs are electrically driven and the diver has direct control over speed, stopping, starting, and manoeuvring. Tugs are therefore more suitable than hydroplanes for use in areas of very irregular topography. Battery capacity generally limits time on the sea-bed to about two hours. Woods & Lythgoe (1971) illustrate a tug adapted to carry samples.

During swimming, using a hydroplane or tug, a calibrated flowmeter mounted ahead of the diver will indicate distance covered and provide a means of recording location along the direction of travel, although account must be taken of prevailing currents.

Lines and grids

Lines and grids are laid to determine the location of survey stations, to provide a means of re-finding stations, or to act as a basis for measuring. Non-floating or weighted lines are most efficiently laid by a diver swimming with a free-running reel along the appropriate compass bearing or depth contour near the sea-bed. If the diver laying the line is also carrying out the survey, he or she can swim back reeling up the line whilst surveying or sampling each station as it is reached (the method used in the Shetland survey described by Earll, 1977). Tape measures should be of fibreglass and in open aluminium, brass, or wooden reels. Atkinson (1974) describes how a grid 10 m × 10 m divided into squares with 100-cm sides was floated on the surface over a site and lowered to the sea-bed by four divers, one at each corner, holding the grid taut. The grid was then squared up on the sea-bed. Mullett & Mullett (1980) describe the laying of a 50 m × 50 m grid. However, grids are difficult to lay successfully even in calm weather, particularly in poor visibility.

Fixing equipment to the sea-bed

The methods used to fix equipment to the sea-bed will depend on the degree of permanence and the accuracy of location required. If the apparatus is to survive winter storms, the fixings will have to be extremely firm. If no regular spacing is required, polythene bags filled with a mixture of cement and sand can be jammed into irregular crevices, and a bolt, metal or plastic plugs, or whatever is appropriate can be embedded in the concrete. The bag is then punctured to allow sea-water in, and the concrete is allowed to set. Strong nails or pitons can be hammered into crevices.

Metal augers can be screwed into some sediments to provide a firm fixing for grids or lines. Heavy concrete blocks also provide firm anchorages.

For regular spacing of markers or for fixing quadrats onto rock, it may be necessary to drill holes and fix expanding bolts, resin-embedded bolts, plastic plugs and screw fittings, or plastic studs. Drilling of small holes in some rocks may be possible with a hand drill. Lundalv (1971) used a pneumatic drill and compressed air cylinders to drill 10-mm-diameter holes in granite. Such drills use at least 1.3 m³ of air per minute and therefore the number of holes that can be drilled in one dive is small. Another system using a compressed-air drill for such work, described by Hawkins & Hartnoll (1979), can also be used underwater. The air drill is about the size of a domestic electric drill and uses good-quality tungsten-tipped drill bits up to 8 mm in diameter. However, underwater the diver needs to push or pull against something such as a rock ledge for the drill to penetrate hard rock, and attempts to drill granite sufficiently deep to take a plastic plug have sometimes been unsuccessful. A Cox gun fires a bolt into rock to make a hole and a fixing can then be inserted in the hole and held in place with epoxy resin. A nail gun might be used to fix apparatus, but the fixings will corrode.

Location and relocation of sites

When return is intended or features are being mapped, accurate relocation will be essential. Adjacent to a rocky shore, position can often be determined within a few metres by reference to prominent topographical features and careful marking on large-scale maps. A marker, such as a small paint mark or pat of concrete on the rocks above high-water level, or photographs showing the alignment of topographical features on land will add to the ease of location. Offshore, accuracy in location is more difficult. Navigation systems such as the Decca transponder chain or satellite navigation systems (see Chapter 5) will enable fairly accurate location offshore to c. 30 m in optimum conditions. For some studies, a series of transponders might be especially established to give accuracy within a few metres. The visual alternative is the use of transit markers selected or established on the shore that can be lined up to position the boat over a site. A sighting compass can be used to obtain bearings on objects on the shore shown on maps or placed before the survey. Greater accuracy is achieved if a sextant can be used, but this is difficult in a small boat and where there are few shore features. An echo sounder can be used over a steeply sloping sea-bed by recording depth and correcting for tidal differences; position can then be relocated by motoring along a transit line until the recorded depth is reached. None of these methods can be expected to put a diver exactly on the correct spot offshore, and guide lines along the sea-bed radiating from the site location or crossing it will be needed. Thus the diver can, for instance, be dropped in shallower water than the site and swim down the slope until he or she encounters the guide line. Underwater 'pingers' and transponders provide an easily used method of locating an underwater site, though battery life of pingers is limited to about three months.

Mapping profiles underwater

Rock profiles are sometimes shown as background to description of vertical zonation patterns. The technique of mapping is simple and requires the use of a calibrated depth gauge, tape measure, and writing board (Fig. 9.4). The tape reel is allowed to float and the tape fixed to the base of the rock slope. The tape can either be stretched from prominent feature to prominent feature while swimming along a bearing at right angles to the shore or can be fixed to the profile with clips attached to organisms before surveying. The length along the tape and the depth at each gully, pinnacle, or interval along the tape are recorded. The eventual plotting of the profile can be considerably aided by a sketch made while

Fig. 9.4. Method for mapping a rock profile.

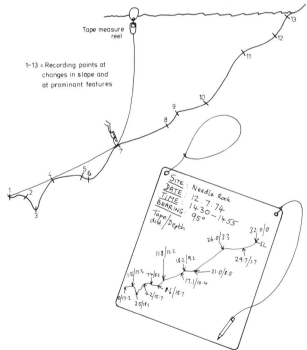

surveying. Using this technique, a steeply sloping rock surface such as that illustrated in Fig. 9.4 can be mapped in one dive.

Describing habitats

The description of environmental conditions at a site and the habitats present at each survey station are important information for the interpretation of biological data. Several different check-lists have been developed to record site characteristics and the most recent is shown in Fig. 9.1. Most such check-lists will be accompanied by a written description of the depth, substrata, and main cover organisms at each station.

Recording of conspicuous species

The methods described in this section are for *in situ* survey of taxa that can be recognised underwater. Where such work involves the description of communities, it requires that the diver is able to recognise most of the conspicuous species present. Often it will be necessary to carry out reconnaissance before detailed work to compile check-lists so that each species that is likely to occur is searched for during systematic survey. Hiscock & Mitchell (1980) recommend recording from separate habitats during descriptive surveys of communities of conspicuous species, and this technique has been successfully used during surveys of nearshore sublittoral ecosystems in Britain. The separate habitat categories are detailed in Fig. 9.1.

Presence–absence surveys

The listing of conspicuous species present at sites is often used as part of the initial survey of an area or during rapid survey of large areas. Surveys using tugs, hydroplanes, or drift-diving can often be too rapid to allow for anything other than making records of the presence of a species. Presence–absence data are often adequate to detect gross trends in species distribution, for instance, in surveys at stations placed at regular intervals away from a toxic effluent.

> *Time.* One diver per site for general surveys or 5–10 minutes per station.
>
> *Equipment.* Writing board, telephone or tape recorder, check-list where appropriate, numbered plastic bags, towed hydroplane or tug for use over extensive flat areas.
>
> *Advantages.* Rapid.
>
> *Disadvantages.* Not sufficiently detailed to allow accurate comparison of sites in situations where species are widely distributed but present in very different numbers from site to site.

The method does not provide any indication of the ecological importance of species in terms of density or cover.

Semi-quantitative surveys

In many situations, accurate analysis of distributional patterns or comparison of communities in different habitats requires that the quantity of each species at the sites studied must be recorded. However, direct counting is extremely time consuming and some form of semi-quantitative recording is often most suitable. The degree of accuracy and the methods used will depend on the requirements of the survey, the methods of data analysis to be used, the time available, and the abilities of the personnel. Subjective estimates of the abundance of a species made by one worker

Table 9.3. *Abundance scale used for surveys of nearshore sublittoral areas in south-west Britain* (*Hiscock, 1981*)

Animals

1. Large solitary species and colonies (e.g., solitary sponges, *Alcyonium digitatum*, hydroid clumps, large anemones, *Pentapora foliacea*, *Cellepora pumicosa*, echinoderms, large solitary tunicates)

Abundant	one or more per 0.1 m²
Common	one or more per 1 m²
Frequent	less than 1 per m² but more than about 20 individuals observed
Occasional	about 3–20 observed
Rare	one or two observed

2. Small solitary species (e.g., *Grantia compressa*, small anemones, *Caryophyllia smithii*, *Antedon bifida*, small solitary tunicates)

Abundant	one or more per 0.01 m²
Common	one or more per 0.1 m²
Frequent	one or more per m², scattered patches
Occasional	less than one per m², scattered small patches
Rare	widely scattered individuals, one or two small patches

3. Small colonial species and crustose species (e.g., encrusting sponges, *Corynactis viridis*, small hydroids, *Polydora ciliata*, beds of *Mytilus edulis*, barnacles, Bryozoa, encrusting tunicates)

Abundant	large confluent colonies with more than 50% cover; more than 100 per 0.01 m²
Common	many small or a few large patches with 10% to 50% cover; one or more per 0.01 m²
Frequent	scattered patches less than 10% cover overall; one or more per 0.1 m²
Occasional	scattered small patches less than 1% cover overall; one or more per m²
Rare	widely scattered very small patches or individuals; less than one per m²

can often be converted to a three-point scale such as that used by Hiscock (1970). A five-point scale provides a basis for finer comparisons but the meaning of each part of the scale must be defined. Different scales are necessary according to the size of the organisms being studied, their growth form (e.g., solitary or colonial), and their habitat (some species are found only on particular substrata). The scale of abundance used for survey of conspicuous species in south-west Britain (Hiscock, 1981) is shown in Table 9.3. Boudouresque (1971) describes the use of a variety of scales for algae based on percentage cover and biomass.

Surveys using semi-quantitative methods of recording should be carried out systematically and with the use of reference quadrats, most conveniently 0.1 m² (31.6 × 31.6 cm) and 0.01 m² (10 × 10 cm). No time-limit should be specified for searching at particular stations or habitats, but the worker should be instructed to search until satisfied that all conspicuous or check-list species present at the station have been recorded and that the

Table 9.3 (*cont.*)

Algae	
4.	Kelps	
	Abundant	plants mostly less than 50 cm apart; difficult to swim between
	Common	plants 50 cm to 1 m apart
	Frequent	plants 1 to 2 m apart; easy to swim between
	Occasional	plants more than 2 m apart; zone still apparent
	Rare	few plants present
5.	Foliose or filamentous undergrowth species	
	Abundant	more than 20% cover over most of area
	Common	less than 20% cover but many plants present throughout zone
	Frequent	less than 20% cover and distribution patchy or scattered plants present throughout zone
	Occasional	scattered plants present
	Rare	few plants seen in dive
6.	Kelp stipe flora	
	Abundant	plants dense on most stipes
	Common	plants present on most stipes but not dense
	Frequent	distribution patchy; plants may be dense on some stipes, absent on others
	Occasional	few plants on many stipes
	Rare	only few plants seen during dive
7.	Crustose species	
	Abundant	more than 50% cover
	Common	more than 20% cover
	Frequent	more than 5% cover
	Occasional	less than 5% cover; few scattered large patches or many small patches
	Rare	few patches seen

Table 9.4. *Communities of conspicuous species present on horizontal (port side) and vertical (underside of hull) surfaces and in the hold of the wreck of the* MV Robert *off Lundy.*

Horizontal surfaces at 14 m	Vertical surfaces at 15–18 m	Hold at 15–17 m
Abundant		
Sabellaria spinulosa		
Common		
	Metridium senile	*Metridium senile*
		Ascidia mentula
Frequent		
Nemertsia antennina	*Nemertesia antennina*	*Urticina eques*
Nemertesia ramosa	*Pomatoceros triqueter*	*Filograna implexa*
Metridium senile	*Bugula plumosa*	*Pomatoceros triqueter*
Cellaria spp.	*Ascidia mentula*	*Asteria rubens*
Crisiidae		*Trisopterus minutus*
Occasional		
Rhodymenia pseudopalmata	*Dysidea fragilis*	*Tubularia larynx*
var. *ellisiae*	Encrusting sponges	*Caryophyllia smithii*
Antithamnion plumula	*Nemertesia ramosa*	*Aurelia aurita*
Antithamnion cruciatum	*Urticina felina*	(scyphistomae)
Ceramium tenuissium	*Eubranchus tricolor*	Encrusting Bryozoa
Hypoglossum woodwardii	?Jassidae (tubes)	*Bugula plumosa*
Myriogramme bonnemaisonii	Crisiidae	?*Protula tubularia*
Polyneura gmelinii	*Cellaria* spp.	*Antedon bifida*
Delesseria sanguinea	*Cellepora pumicosa*	*Diplosoma listerianum*
Radicilingua thysanorhizans	*Pentapora foliacea*	*Didemnum maculosum*
Dictyopteris membranacea	Encrusting Bryozoa	
Dictyota dichotoma	*Berenicea patina*	
?*Dysidea fragilis*	*Asterias rubens*	
Tubularia indivisa	*Antedon bifida*	
Sertularia argentea	*Botryllus schlosseri*	
Plumularia setacea	*Diplosoma listerianum*	
Aglaophenia tubulifera	*Didemnum maculosum*	
Sagartia troglodytes		
Urticina felina		
Sabella penicillus		
?Jassidae (tubes)		
Inachus sp.		
Eubranchus tricolor		
Polycera faeroensis		
Scrupocellaria sp(p.)		
Bugula plumosa		
Bugula turbinata		
Flustra foliacea		
Pentapora foliacea		
Omalosecosa ramulosa		
Amathia lendigera		
Antedon bifida		
Asterias rubens		

quantity of each has been accurately assessed. The worker will find it easier to record approximate numbers or percentage cover rather than try to determine the abundance category underwater. Raw percentage-cover data will enable the final data for each species to be fitted to an appropriate scale and will give more flexibility to data analysis.

The structure that has been used to present results from semi-quantitative surveys is illustrated in Table 9.4.

Time. An experienced diver can generally record from one habitat at a species-rich site in about 15 minutes. About three stations can be surveyed in one dive.

Equipment. Writing board or telephone or tape recorder, check-list where appropriate, numbered plastic bags.

Advantages. Rapid compared to quantitative counting or sampling. Records of abundance are adequate to compare the relative importance of different conspicuous species in the composition of communities. Data from encrusting, foliose, turf-forming, and solitary species are collected in a compatible form.

Disadvantages. Semi-quantitative data are unacceptable to many methods of statistical analysis. The use of only conspicuous species records a small part of the macrobenthos at a site, and on sediments this is unrepresentative of the community type.

Table 9.4 (*cont.*)

Horizontal surfaces at 14 m	Vertical surfaces at 15–18 m	Hold at 15–17 m
Luidea ciliaris		
Labrus bergylta		
Pollachius pollachius		
Rare		
Tubularia larynx	*Halecium halecinum*	*Alcyonium digitatum*
Hydrallmania falcata	*Abietinaria abietina*	*Munida rugosa*
Sertularella polyzonias	*Antennella secundaria*	
Sagartia elegans	*Caryophyllia smithii*	
Pomatoceros triqueter	*Corynactis viridis*	
Cancer pagurus	*Bugula turbinata*	
Liocarcinus puber	*Bugula flabellata*	
Parasmittina trispinosa	*Maia squinado*	
Alcyonidium gelatinosum		
Marthasterias glacialis		
Echinus esculentus		

Modified from Hiscock (1980).

Quantitative surveys and mapping using transects

The density of widely dispersed but easily recognised species can be surveyed along a line of known length (usually 30 or 50 m) stretched over the sea-bed and surveyed by a diver swimming along the line, counting all of the specimens that lie under a metre-long rod held at right angles to the line. The method has been used by Forster (1959, 1961) and by Larsson (1968), who reviews the technique. For recording the spatial distribution and aggregation of individuals, a tape measure is used together with a metre rule, and the co-ordinates of each specimen are recorded. Atkinson (1974) describes the use of a tape and rule to map burrow positions and also suggests methods for investigating aggregation in species. Lines and tapes are most easily deployed from a free-running reel by a diver swimming along a compass bearing or a depth contour.

> *Time.* Probably about 200 m² of open sea-bed could be surveyed for one large, widely dispersed species at 15 m during one dive. Larsson (1968) found about 20 minutes was needed for a thorough search of a 1 m × 10 m transect in order to collect almost all of two species of echinoderms in an area where it was necessary to turn stones for small specimens.

> *Equipment.* Non-floating line or tape measure on a free-running reel, measuring rod, and writing board or tape recorder.

> *Advantages.* Gives an accurate count of actual numbers. Rapid once the line is laid.

> *Disadvantages.* Considerable time is expended in laying the line. Only the largest species can be recorded.

Quantitative surveys using reference quadrats

The use of quadrats to record actual numbers of conspicuous species is particularly valuable in studies of one species, a small number of species, or for detecting statistically significant changes in the density of species (see, e.g., Larsson, 1968 on echinoderms; Gulliksen, 1972, 1973 on ascidians; Hiscock & Howlett, 1976 on *Caryophyllia smithii*). Underwater, a 0.1 m² quadrat is most easily handled. Quadrats should be placed at random locations (e.g., by using a tape measure and cursor to locate positions determined by random number tables). At least 30 quadrats should be sampled (but see Elliot, 1977 or a similar text on sampling methods for consideration of the requirements of later statistical tests).

> *Time.* Depends on the density and size of the species and the number of species included in the survey. Larsson (1968) found that 5 minutes was needed for a thorough search of a 1 m × 1 m

quadrat for *Echinus* on a substratum that included loose stones. On a rocky shore with dense algal cover, about 5 minutes was required to thoroughly search a 50 cm × 50 cm quadrat and tape-record numbers of about four species, approximate numbers of about seven species, presence of about five species, and percentage cover of live and dead barnacles. The time should be at least doubled for sublittoral work using a tape recorder.

Equipment. Quadrat; writing board or tape recorder.

Advantages. Actual numbers are recorded, enabling a detailed comparison between stations or accurate tracings of long-term changes. The study area is undisturbed since no collection is involved.

Disadvantages. Direct counting can be very slow.

Surveys using photographs

The biologist can derive a great deal of information by inspection of good-quality photographs, whether taken by the biologist in support of species recording, or by non-biologists. Photographs also provide illustrations to assist description in lectures and reports. Photographs taken from a defined angle or position, of easily identified features or areas marked by some means such as pitons, can be used for 'viewpoint monitoring'. Photographs with a picture width of more than 1 m usually lose detail to the extent that the conspicuous taxa cannot be identified. Photographs less than 10 cm across are usually of single species and are not very useful for description of communities. The photographer must provide details of site location, depth below chart datum, and scale for each photograph if the data are to be properly interpreted.

Time. About 5 minutes to take a good range of photographs.

Equipment. Camera, flashgun, appropriate supplementary lenses.

Advantages. Rapid, can be used where there is insufficient time for full recording; the recorder does not need to be a biologist. For monitoring projects the site does not have to be marked. Photography is non-destructive.

Disadvantages. Only a limited area is likely to be covered by photographs. Some species will be too small to recognise in wide-angle photographs. Some species will be missed in close-up photographs.

Quantitative surveys using photographs

The use of photography for quantitative survey and for the study of seasonal and long-term fluctuations in rocky sublittoral communities has been extensively developed in recent years, particularly in Sweden and Norway. Photography clearly offers a very rapid method of data collection in an environment where speed and efficiency are often essential. The Nikonos camera system fitted with supplementary lens and frame-finder provides the simplest readily available method of photography (e.g., see Gulliksen, 1980). Using a Nikonos and 28-mm lens, the picture area is *c*. 22 cm × 15 cm (0.033 m²). Bohnsack (1979) describes and assesses a technique using a 35-mm reflex camera. Several other fairly simple systems have been developed and single photographs are excellent tools for

Fig. 9.5. (*a*) A Nikonos III camera equipped for close-up photography. (*b*) The stereophotographic method used by Lundalv (1971) for following changes in sublittoral populations.

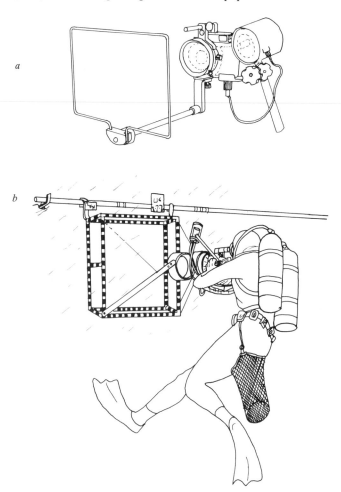

monitoring. However, stereophotography offers many advantages during analysis of photographs: species are easier to separate and identify, there is increased ability to view under canopy-forming species, and more accurate measurements can be made. Torlegard & Lundalv (1974) describe the use of a Hasselblad camera to follow changes on sublittoral rocks on the Swedish west coast (Fig. 9.5). Lundalv (1985) describes the results of some of the work and provides an assessment of sample area required to describe adequately the community present and to assess change. Recently, systems using paired Nikonos cameras with synchronised shutter release have been developed and these offer less expensive and less cumbersome equipment. Green (1980), in a limited circulation report, provides a thorough assessment of the technique. Christie, Evans & Sandness (1985) also describe the equipment and methodology together with an assessment of the time and costs involved. The picture area most often used is 0.25 m² (50 cm × 50 cm). However, despite the use of wide-angle lenses, the camera-to-subject distance would be too great for clear photography in many areas of the British Isles where water turbidity is high. The worker embarking on a new project should give careful consideration to the development of appropriate equipment and possible use of a 0.1 m² format. An assessment of the area that needs to be photographed to provide the basis for determining statistically significant change needs to be carried out for each project. Lundalv (1985) found that 1.5 m² was an adequate area for the analysis of data on large ascidians.

Analysis of photographs is done by counting individual organisms and measuring percentage cover by point sampling. Most workers have found that 100 points are adequate and there is no advantage in using random as opposed to systematically placed points. Points that are systematic make analysis much easier than wholly random points, although some workers use randomly selected points from a grid of a large number of systematically arranged points. Single photographs can be projected onto a screen for analysis. Photographs in stereo pairs need to be viewed in a stereo comparator or viewed using a linked pair of stereo microscopes with acetate overlay of the sampling grid on one of the photographs. Christie et al. (1985) suggest that organisms down to 2–3 mm may be identified, and Green (1980) suggests that size measurements of approximately 1.5 mm can be made using the Nikonos system.

In practice, photography has been found most useful for analysis of density and cover of a small number of conspicuous species in the total community, and the greatest problem has been the large amount of time needed for laboratory analysis of photographs. There is currently considerable development of underwater stereophotographic equipment for use in inspection of offshore installations, and this may prove useful to the biologist working in nearshore areas.

Time. Site preparation for surveillance work could be slow, possibly a day per site if no extensive searching or limit due to slack-water time is imposed. Using a small compressed-air drill powered by a 12–14-litre air tank, six to ten 3-cm-deep holes 6 mm in diameter could be drilled at between 5–25 m in one dive. Once established, the site can be photographed very rapidly and one dive should be adequate to photograph about three stations at one site.

Equipment. Camera or, for stereophotography, paired synchronised cameras, quadrat frame, electronic flash, equipment necessary for analysis (projector for single photographs, paired stereo microscopes for stereo pairs), point sampling grid.

Advantages. Surveys are rapidly carried out. 'Samples' remain undisturbed. Detailed analysis is possible in the laboratory and the standard of accuracy is much higher than for *in situ* survey. The photographs provide a permanent record so that possible errors can be checked and more detailed work can be carried out at a later date if required. Photographs enable the distinction of smaller organisms than *in situ* survey. Divers do not need to be biologists.

Disadvantages/limitations. Photographs do not record species or individuals that are obscured by overgrowth or silt. The consequent underestimate of abundance is particularly important if seasonal changes are being studied in the species that is occasionally obscured. Sampling is not possible in highly turbid water (Lundalv (1971) suggests 3 m as the limiting visibility for the Hasselblad system illustrated in Fig. 9.5). A halocline also makes sampling difficult because of optical distortion. Synchronous shutter release for flash on the Nikonos can be difficult to achieve. Where one camera is used in two positions for stereophotography, movement of organisms between photographs will make interpretation difficult. Large quadrats cannot be used in the kelp forest. It may be difficult, particularly in British waters, to locate a sufficiently extensive area of unbroken rock with the same inclination to provide an optimum sampling area or a sufficient number of replicate photographs. Analysis of photographs is very time consuming.

Measures of frequency

Point frames and cross-wire frames are very difficult to use underwater, particularly in the kelp forest or where there is wave surge, but they provide a means of recording the relative quantities of cover organisms such as foliose or encrusting algae, Bryozoa, and encrusting sponges. A cross-wire frame such as that described by Jones (1980) and Jones *et al.* (1980) (Fig. 8.8) could be used, but it is likely that great difficulty will be found in holding the apparatus on-station. Point frames and cross-wire frames often require a large number of 'strikes' to provide an optimum sampling number, and the time involved may be unrealistic. Measures of frequency of occurrence within divided frames (for instance a 50 cm × 50 cm frame divided into 25 squares 10 cm × 10 cm) provide an objective measure of abundance. However, great care should be taken where the distribution of a species is patchy. It may be very difficult to cover an adequate area to include even all of the common species.

Time. Not known.

Equipment. Cross-wire frame or divided quadrat; tape recorder or writing board.

Advantages. Gives an objective measure of abundance or cover. Particularly useful where it is difficult to estimate percentage cover.

Disadvantages. Cross-wire frames are difficult to use underwater, particularly where erect species, frame, and work are being swept back and forth by wave action. Species that might be abundant but do not occur in the chosen area are excluded.

Collection of samples

The removal of samples for analysis ashore or in the laboratory can be used to provide lists of the macrobenthos at a station and accurate counts or other quantitative measurement of individual species.

Non-quantitative removal of sessile or sedentary species

The scraping of an area of undergrowth on rock with a knife or paint scraper into a plastic bag can be carried out quickly and, on sorting, provide a useful list of the small species present. Similarly, a shovel or bucket full of sediment can be used to obtain a list of the species present and their relative numbers. By using numbered plastic bags, an accurate record of the location of each sample taken for identification can be made. The area that should be scraped will vary from site to site; minimum sampling areas have already been discussed.

Time. About 1 minute per sample.

Equipment. Knife, scraper, numbered plastic bags.

Advantages. Very rapid. Adequate for reconnaissance or presence–absence records.

Disadvantages. Not quantitative. Scraping does not collect crustose or some well-attached species. Collecting is difficult where there is water movement, especially wave surge – the sample may be dispersed before it can fall into the bag.

Rock samples

Careful inspection of collected rock samples will usually give a comprehensive list of the common undergrowth species present at each site. The problems of carrying bags full of heavy rocks can be alleviated by the technique detailed by Bailey, Nelson-Smith & Knight-Jones, (1967) (Fig. 9.6), or by the use of an adjustable buoyancy life jacket or inflation of a dry-suit. The collection of bedrock samples should be considered at each site in relation to the type of rock it is planned to remove – some rocks cannot be removed without great effort.

Time. Slate: about seven samples can be chiselled per dive at average depth 10 m. Other rock: considerably fewer samples per dive. Bailey *et al.* (1967) collected loose rocks and were able to take 12 samples along a 300-m line to a depth of 15 m in one dive. Time working up the samples: one day for inspection and recording the immediately recognised species from one dive's

Fig. 9.6. The technique described by Bailey *et al.* (1967) for collecting rock samples.

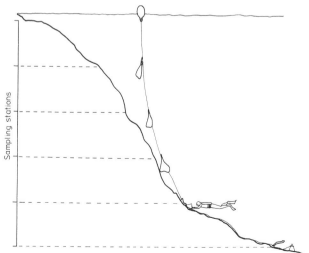

samples, or several days or weeks if all species require identification.

Equipment. Hammer, chisel, strong numbered net or polythene bags, lines and clips (Bailey *et al.*, 1967); reference quadrats if loose stones are being collected within a predetermined area.

Advantages. Almost all species present on the rock collected are included in the sample.

Disadvantages. Not completely quantitative. Most rock types are difficult to remove. Samples are heavy. It is probable that many mobile species migrate away from the area at the start of chiselling.

Quantitative sampling of flora and fauna from bedrock

The greatest difficulty in collecting sessile or sedentary species is ensuring that specimens are not lost due to water currents, to the force

Fig. 9.7. Frames and attached bags described by Drew (1971) (*a*) and by True (1970) (*b*) for catching quantitative samples from rock.

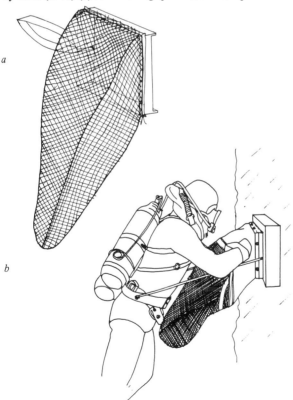

of scraping, or to floating before they can be caught in a bag. Drew (1971) describes a frame and attached bag that is held over the rock surface and a scraper placed through the side to remove algae which then fall into the bag (Fig. 9.7). A similar system which allows the sampling of large areas with the frame held steady by the diver's body and both hands available for manipulation is described by True (Fig. 9.7) The most easily used apparatus is an underwater suction sampler. A device in which the suction is provided by a hand pump is described by Gulliksen & Deras (1975) (Fig. 9.8). Hiscock & Hoare (1973) describe a portable sampler operated on an airlift principle by a compressed-air cylinder. The apparatus allows the collection of at least 0.5 m² of rock cover using 1.6 m³ (57 ft³) of air (Fig. 9.9). The airlift principle is very adaptable and size and capacity of equipment can be determined by the needs of the project.

> *Time.* Up to five 0.1 m² samples can be collected in one dive at a depth of 20 m, using the airlift sampler. A rich sample takes about three days to sort and count individuals, but this does not include the identification of all species.

> *Equipment.* Sampling equipment; scraper; spare sampling bags or tubes with lids; adjustable buoyancy life jacket or dry suit inflation.

> *Advantages.* Small species that cannot be observed *in situ* are

Fig. 9.8. A hand-operated suction sampler (redrawn from Gulliksen & Deras, 1975).

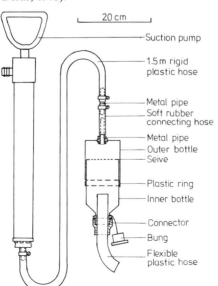

20 cm

Suction pump

1.5 m rigid plastic hose

Metal pipe
Soft rubber connecting hose
Metal pipe
Outer bottle
Seive
Plastic ring
Inner bottle

Connector
Bung
Flexible plastic hose

collected. Accurate counts can be obtained from the samples. If a method of catching the sample is used, particularly with a suction sampler, almost all organisms in a quadrat are collected.

Disadvantages. Scraping does not collect some organisms such as encrusting Bryozoa and crushes others such as serpulids and barnacles. Sorting and identifying are very time consuming. Only a small number of samples can be taken in each dive.

Quantitative sampling of the fauna of sediments using cores

Cores provide a means of rapid sampling of small areas of sediment. Cores are most useful in mud or muddy sand; on coarse sediments the sample is unlikely to be retained unless there is some means of closing the base before withdrawal. Corers can be constructed according to the area to be sampled and the materials available. Plastic pipes for building provide a cheap source of material, and screw-on caps are standard fittings. McIntyre (1971) notes that tubes of up to 4-cm diameter caused disturbance of the flocculent top layer of sediment, but 10-cm diameter tubes were satisfactory. A penetration of over 20 cm can be obtained easily in sediments without coarse material below the surface. The cores are deployed by pushing the open tube into the sediment, screwing

Fig. 9.9. An underwater airlift suction sampler (after Hiscock & Hoare, 1973) for collecting quantitative samples scraped from rock. The sample chambers are shown in section.

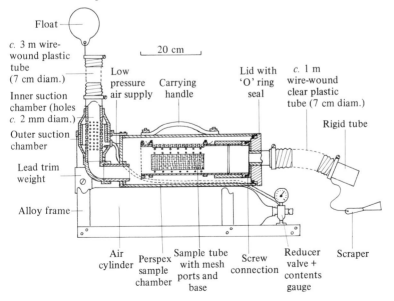

on a cap or placing a rubber bung in the top, removing the core, and placing a bung in the open end. Cores can also be constructed with a self-sealing flange which eliminates the need to remove, store, and re-find the bung or cap. If a large number of cores are to be taken, the contents can be pushed out into a plastic bag after each collection. Large cores may need to be hammered into the sediment and retrieval can be very difficult. A lever system may need to be developed to extract cores or the cores pulled out from a surface boat. The contents of large cores are also likely to be lost before a bung can be inserted.

> *Time.* One small core can be collected in about 1 minute. Sorting and identification of the species in each core take a number of days.
>
> *Equipment.* Plastic, Perspex, or metal coring tube, bungs, plastic bags, writing board.
>
> *Advantages.* Rapid. Upper sediment layers are much less disturbed than if gravity cores or grabs are used. The cores generally penetrate deeper than a grab.
>
> *Disadvantages.* Only a small area is sampled in each core. The corers do not work on clean, coarse sediments.

Quantitative sampling of the fauna of sediments using suction samplers

The usual and most rapid method of collecting samples from sediments is the deployment of a grab operated from a ship. Most grabs penetrate about 10 cm into the sediment depending on the weight of the grab, the coarseness of the sediment, and the presence of stones. The Knudsen corer and Reineck box sampler penetrate deeper into sediments, but considerable force is often required to retrieve them.

If it is required to sample a larger surface area than a core would provide, to sample deeper into the sediment than a grab would penetrate, or to sample at accurately placed locations (e.g., on a grid near to an outfall), a diver-operated suction sampler is most often used. Comparisons between the efficiency and effectiveness of diver-operated samplers versus remote samplers are given by Massé, Plante & Reys (1977). They found that the suction sampler is highly effective on sandy bottoms and has considerable advantages over the grab samplers used. However, the advantages of the suction sampler decrease as the mud content of the sediment increases, and on mud the effectiveness of the Smith–McIntyre grab and the suction sampler are almost identical. Air-lift suction samplers tend to damage soft-bodied organisms and the importance of this should be considered.

The depth of penetration is important. Ten centimetres is often considered adequate, but Christie (1976) found that on fine sand 40% of the species present to 60-cm depth occurred deeper than 10 cm. Keegan & Konnecker (1973) found that on maerl as much as 98% of the standing crop may be found 20–40 cm below the surface of the substratum. The results of Christie (1976) and Keegan & Konnecker (1973) indicate that samples should be collected to a depth of at least 50 cm to capture the majority of the macrofauna in coarse sediments.

The most widely used type of airlift suction sampler is based on the design of Barnett & Harvey (1967). Modifications to the first design have been made by various workers (e.g., Christie & Allen, 1972; Keegan & Konnecker, 1973). The alterations are generally minor and increase the ease with which the machine can be used. In particular, many workers have preferred to use a small compressed-air cylinder taken to the sea-bed rather than use large storage cylinders in a vessel at the surface. The difficulties of using the Barnett & Hardy type of sampler have encouraged the development of a new sampler where the sample is retained in a mesh bag before reaching the suction pipe. This also prevents samples being mixed with very turbulent air and water, and should reduce damage to specimens. Two suction samples for use on sediments are shown in Fig. 9.10.

The sampling area is most often defined by pushing a cylinder into the sediment and excavating the contents. A box quadrat is less useful since it cannot be twisted into the sediment, and pushing is very difficult underwater. The diameter of a cylinder to sample 0.1 m² is 35.7 cm. The

Fig. 9.10. Underwater airlift suction samplers for collecting quantitative samples from sediments. (*a*) Based on designs by Barnett & Harvey. (1967), Christie & Allen (1972), and J. M. Addy (personal communication). (*b*) Based on an original design.

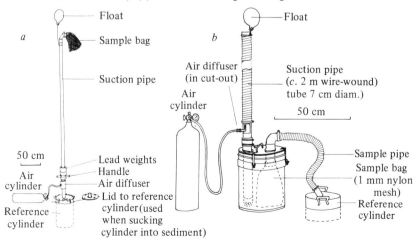

cylinder is usually 15 cm deep, but in many substrata the walls of a dredged hole remain firm and deeper samples can be collected. Barnett & Hardy (1967) and Christie & Allen (1972) found that compact sediments resist penetration by a frame, and they utilised the airlift system shown in Fig. 9.10 to drive the cylinder into the sediment. The operation of a suction sampler is described in detail by Christie & Allen (1972).

Deployment of samplers is assisted from a boat by the lowering and raising of the sampler on a rope.

> *Time and sampler capacity.* Christie & Allen (1972) report that the apparatus can be deployed and seven samples taken in 45 minutes; sinking the cylinder into fine mud can take as little as 15 seconds or up to 2 minutes in coarse sand. Keegan & Konnecker (1973) suggest that their sampling cylinder can be evacuated in seven minutes and that a single diving bottle permitted the taking of four to five 0.1 m^2 60-cm-deep samples. Barnett & Hardy (1967) report that a sample of medium sand at depth 10 cm can be collected using a 6-m-long suction tube with 0.5 m^3 of air. The new design of sampler shown in Fig. 9.10 can collect as many as four 0.1 m^2 samples to a depth of 20 cm using one air bottle; each sample takes about 5 minutes to collect, but further time is expended changing sample bags and preparing equipment.
>
> *Equipment.* Suction sampler, sample bags, support boat, writing board.
>
> *Advantages.* Sampling sites can be accurately located. Samples can be collected to depths greater than 10 cm in the sediment. The same size samples can be collected at each station.
>
> *Disadvantages.* Few samples can be collected in a certain time compared with grab sampling. Polychaete worms are often damaged. Depth of operation is limited to 30 m maximum.

Organisms as sampling units – the kelp holdfast

Widespread organisms that are themselves substrata for other species are found only on kelp plants and, in a detailed survey, *Laminaria* distribution of the associated flora and fauna. Kelp plants and, in particular, *Laminaria hyperborea* often have a wide range of algae and animals attached (see, e.g., Norton, Hiscock & Kitching, 1977). Many species are found only on kelp plants and, in a detailed survey, *Laminaria hyperborea* may need to be studied as a separate habitat.

The kelp holdfast is a particularly rich habitat and forms an easily collected sampling unit. Holdfasts have been used extensively in the study of pollution and turbidity on the north-east coast of England (Jones, 1971, 1972, 1973; Moore, 1971, 1973*a*, *b*, 1974) whilst Hoare & Hiscock (1974) used the holdfast as a sampling unit in studying the distribution of small species in the area of a chemical effluent in north Wales. A large number of species are found in holdfast samples, and considerable time is required in sorting and identification. Hoare & Hiscock (1974) recorded 120 species from 57 holdfasts, Jones (1973) used 101 species from 126 holdfasts, and Moore (1973*b*) recorded 389 species from 72 holdfasts (including 61 nematodes and 126 copepod species, groups not included by the other authors). The holdfast is collected most efficiently by: (1) removing the stipe and frond by cutting about 15 cm above the holdfast; (2) one diver holding open a large heavy-gauge polythene bag next to the holdfast; (3) the other diver pulling the holdfast off the rock and transferring it rapidly to the bag; (4) sealing the bag with an elastic band. Some of the problems of sorting from preserved holdfasts that become covered in mucilage or of transporting large volumes of sampled material can be reduced if preliminary sorting is carried out immediately after the collection. The polythene bags are opened and a small amount of formalin is introduced to encourage mobile species to desert the holdfast. The specimens can then be transferred to a small tube and the holdfast is preserved separately or discarded if the attached species have already been recorded or are not required. It is probable that five large holdfasts are sufficient to provide a representative sample. Moore (1972) considers that the following are of likely importance in determining the composition of the holdfast community:

1. sea-water turbidity
2. water movement
3. 'pollution'
4. holdfast age
5. holdfast height
6. holdfast weight
7. holdfast radius
8. holdfast volume
9. degree of silting
10. structure of holdfast (degree of branching)

Items 4–10 should be described in dealing with samples. The following can be controlled by sampling:

1. time of day
2. depth of water
3. holdfast size

Time. Five samples can be collected easily in 20 minutes at a depth of about 10 m. Sorting and identification take about two to three days per five samples. However, if the meiofauna groups are included, sorting and identification from one holdfast can take at least one week (P. G. Moore, personal communication).

Equipment. Knife, polythene bags, elastic bands or cord.

Advantages. Efficiency in collecting. The whole habitat is sampled. The habitat occurs almost all around the coast of Britain.

Disadvantages. The tedious nature of the sorting and the time involved in the identification of all species. Only a small part of the epibenthic fauna is collected. On some coasts (e.g., the east coast of Anglesey) *L. hyperborea* is absent. In areas of chronic pollution *L. hyperborea* may be absent.

Conclusion

To the person new to the use of diving for benthic surveys, this chapter might seem reasonably comprehensive. However, any project organiser should use it merely as a guide to the techniques and equipment that have been developed and should tailor the methods to his or her requirements. Much of the equipment described here can be improved and new equipment can be developed. Remember, always be clear about the objectives of your work before starting, and always assume that the weather will be against you and that equipment will fail from time to time; you then have a good chance of success.

References

Atkinson, R. J. A. (1974). Behavioural ecology of the mud-burrowing crab *Goneplax rhomboides*. *Mar. Biol.* **25**, 239–52.

Bailey, J. H., Nelson-Smith, A. & Knight-Jones, E. W. (1967). Some methods for transects across steep rocks and channels. *Rep. Underwater Ass.* 1966–67, 107–11.

Barnett, P. R. O. & Harvey, R. L. S. (1967). A diver-operated quantitative bottom sampler for sand macrofauna. *Helgolander wiss. Meeresunters* **15**, 390–8.

Bohnsack, J. A. (1979). Photographic quantitative sampling of hard-bottom benthic communities. *Bull. mar. Sci.* **29**, 242–52.

Boudouresque, C. F. (1971). Methodes d'étude quantitative du benthos (en particular du phytobenthos). *Tethys* **3**, 79–104.

Byers, G. J. (1977). A mini cassette recorder for use by divers underwater. In *Progress in Underwater Science* **2**, ed. K. Hiscock & A. D. Baume, pp. 131–4. London: Pentech Press.

Christie, H., Evans, R. A. & Sandness, O. K. (1985). Field methods for *in situ* subtidal hard bottom studies. In *Underwater Photography and Television for Scientists*, ed. J. D. George, G. Lythgoe & J. N. Lythgoe, pp. 37–47. London: Oxford University Press.

Christie, N. D. (1976). The efficiency and effectiveness of a diver-operated suction sampler on a homogeneous macrofauna. *Estuar. Coast. Mar. Sci.* **4**, 687–93.

Christie, N. D. & Allen, J. C. (1972). A self-contained diver-operated quantitative sampler for investigating the macrofauna of soft substrates. *Trans. R. Soc. S. Afr.* **40**, 299–307.

Coppejans, E. (1980). Phytosociological studies on Mediterranean algal vegetation: rocky surfaces of the photophilic infralittoral zone. In *The Shore Environment*, Vol. 2: *Ecosystems*, ed. J. H. Price, D. E. G. Irvine & W. F. Farnham, pp. 371–93. London: Academic Press.

Drew, E. A. (1971). Botany. In *Underwater Science*, ed. J. D. Woods & J. N. Lythgoe, pp. 25–68. London: Oxford University Press.

Earll, R. (1977). A methodology for primary surveys of the shallow sublittoral zone. In *Progress in Underwater Science* 2, ed. K. Hiscock & A. D. Baume, pp. 47–63. London: Pentech Press.

Elliott, J. M. (1977). Some methods for the statistical analysis of samples of benthic invertebrates. *Freshwater Biol. Ass. Sci. Pub.* **25**, 1–160.

Erwin, D. G. (1977). A cheap SCUBA technique for epifaunal surveying using a small boat. In *Progress in Underwater Science* 2, ed. K. Hiscock & A. D. Baume, pp. 125–9. London: Pentech Press.

Forster, G. R. (1959). The ecology of *Echinus esculentus* L. Quantitative distribution and rate of feeding. *J. mar. biol. Ass. U.K.* **38**, 361–7.

Forster, G. R. (1961). An underwater survey of the Lulworth Banks. *J. mar. biol. Ass. U.K.* **41**, 157–60.

George, J. D., Lythgoe, G. & Lythgoe, J. N. (1985). *Underwater Photography and Television for Scientists*. Underwater Association Special Volume No. 2. London: Oxford University Press.

Glover, T., Harwood, G. E. & Lythgoe, J. N. (1977). *A Manual of Underwater Photography*. Oxford: Clarendon Press.

Green, N. W. (1980). *Underwater Stereophotography Applied in Ecological Monitoring*, Report 1: *Methods and Preliminary Evaluation*. Oslo: Norwegian Institute for Water Research.

Gulliksen, B. (1972). Spawning, larval settlement, growth, variation of biomass, and distribution of *Ciona intestinalis* in Borgenfjorden, north-Trondelag, Norway. *Sarsia* **51**, 83–96.

Gulliksen, B. (1973). The vertical distribution and habitat of ascidians in Borgenfjorden, north-Trondelag, Norway. *Sarsia* **52**, 21–8.

Gulliksen, B. (1980). The macrobenthic rocky-bottom fauna of Borgenfjorden, north-Trondelag, Norway. *Sarsia* **65**, 115–38.

Gulliksen, B. & Deras, K. M. (1975). A diver-operated suction sampler for fauna on rocky bottoms. *Oikos* **26**, 246–9.

Hawkins, S. J. & Hartnoll, R. G. (1979). A compressed air drill powered by SCUBA cylinders for use on rocky shores. *Estuar. Coast. Mar. Sci.* **9**, 819–20.

Hiscock, K. (1970). Observations on the fauna of submerged rocks around Lundy. *Rep. Lundy Fld Soc.* **21**, 24–33.

Hiscock, K. (1979). Systematic surveys and monitoring in nearshore sublittoral areas using diving. In *Monitoring the Marine Environment*, ed. D. Nichols, pp. 55–74. London: Institute of Biology.

Hiscock, K. (1980). Marine life on the wreck of the M.V. "Robert". *Rep. Lundy Fld. Soc.* **32**, 40–4.

Hiscock, K. (1981). *South-West Britain Sublittoral Survey. Final Report.* Pembroke: Nature Conservancy Council, Huntingdon/Field Studies Council Oil Pollution Research Unit.

Hiscock, K. & Hoare, R. (1973). A portable suction sampler for rock epibiota. *Helgolander wiss. Meeresunters* **25**, 35–8.

Hiscock, K. & Howlett, R. (1976). The ecology of *Caryophyllia smithi* Stokes & Broderip on south-western coasts of the British Isles. In *Underwater Research*, ed. E. A. Drew, J. N. Lythgoe & J. D. Woods, pp. 319–34. London: Academic Press.

Hiscock, K. & Mitchell, R. (1980). The description and classification of sublittoral epibenthic ecosystems. In *The Shore Environment*, vol. 2: *Ecosystems*, ed. J. H. Price, D. E. G. Irvine & W. F. Farnham, pp. 323–70. London: Academic Press.

Hoare, R. & Hiscock, K. (1974). An ecological survey of the rocky coast adjacent to the effluent of a bromine extraction plant. *Estuar. Coast. Mar. Sci.* **2**, 329–48.

Jones, D. J. (1971). Ecological studies on macroinvertebrate communities associated with polluted kelp forests in the North Sea. *Helgolander wiss. Meeresunters.* **22**, 417–41.

Jones, D. J. (1972). Changes in ecological balance of invertebrate communities in kelp holdfast habitats of some polluted North Sea waters. *Helgolander wiss. Meeresunters.* **23**, 248–60.

Jones, D. J. (1973). Variation in the trophic structure and species composition of some invertebrate communities in polluted kelp forests in the North Sea. *Mar. Biol.* **20**, 351–65.

Jones, W. E. (1980). Field teaching methods in shore ecology. In *The Shore Environment*, volume 1: *Methods*, ed. J. H. Price, D. E. G. Irvine & W. F. Farnham, pp. 19–42. London: Academic Press.

Jones, W. E., Bennell, S., Beveridge, C., McConnell, B., Mack-Smith, S. & Mitchell, J. (1980). Methods of data collection and processing in rocky intertidal monitoring. In *The Shore Environment*, volume 1: *Methods*, ed. J. H. Price, D. E. G. Irvine & W. F. Farnham, pp. 137–70. London: Academic Press.

Keegan, B. F. & Konnecker, G. (1973). *In situ* quantitative sampling of benthic organisms. *Helgolander wiss. Meeresunters.* **23**, 256–63.

Larkum, A. W. D., Drew, E. A. & Crossett, R. N. (1967). The vertical distribution of attached marine algae in Malta. *J. Ecol.* **35**, 361–71.

Larsson, B. A. S. (1968). SCUBA-studies on vertical distribution of Swedish rocky bottom echinoderms – a methodological study. *Ophelia* **5**, 137–56.

Lundalv, T. (1971). Quantitative studies on rocky-bottom biocoenoses by underwater photogrammetry. A methodological study. *Thalassia Jugoslavia* **7**, 201–8.

Lundalv, T. (1985). Detection of long-term trends in rocky sublittoral communities. Representativeness of sites. In *The ecology of rocky coasts*, ed. P. G. Moore & R. Seed, pp. 329–45. London: Hodder & Stoughton.

McIntyre, A. D. (1971). Deficiency of gravity corers for sampling meiobenthos and sediments. *Nature*, **231**, 260.

Maggs, C. M. (1984). A seasonal study of seaweed communities on subtidal maerl (unattached coralline algae) in Galway Bay, Ireland. In *Progress in Underwater Science* 9, ed. J. C. Gamble & J. Shand, pp. 27–39. London: Pentech Press.

Main, J. & Sangster, G. I. (1978). A new method for observing fishing gear using a towed wet submersible. In *Progress in Underwater Science* 1, ed. J. C. Gamble & R. A. York, pp. 259–67. London: Pentech Press.

Massé, H., Plante, R. & Reys, J.-P. (1977). Etude comparative de l'efficité de deux bennes et d'une suceuse en fonction de la nature du fond. In *Biology of Benthic Organisms*, ed. B. F. Keegan, P. O'Ceidigh & P. J. S. Boaden, pp. 433–41. Oxford: Pergamon Press.

Moore, P. G. (1971). Ecological survey strategy. *Mar. Pollut. Bull.* **2**, 117–39.

Moore, P. G. (1973a). The kelp fauna of north-east Britain. I. Introduction and the physical environment. *J. exp. mar. Biol. Ecol.* **13**, 97–125.

Moore, P. G. (1973b). The kelp fauna of north-east Britain. II. Multivariate classification: turbidity as an ecological factor. *J. exp. mar. Biol. Ecol.* **13**, 127–63.

Moore, P. G. (1974). The kelp fauna of north-east Britain. III. Qualitative and quantitative ordinations, and the utility of a multivariate approach. *J. exp. mar. Biol. Ecol.* **16**, 257–300.

Mullett, J. C. & Mullett, J. A. J. (1980). The use of a grid to survey selected biotic and abiotic features of the rocky sublittoral. In *Progress in Underwater Science* 5, ed. H. M. Platt, pp. 129–36. London: Pentech Press.

Norton, T. A., Hiscock, K. & Kitching, J. A. (1977). The ecology of Lough Ine. II. The *Laminaria* forest at Carrigathorna. *J. Ecol.* **65**, 919–41.

Rowlands, P. (1983). *The underwater photographers handbook*. London: MacDonald.

Sigl, W., Von Rad, U., Oeltzschner, H., Braune, K. & Fabricius, F. (1969). Diving sled: a tool to increase the efficiency of underwater mapping by SCUBA. *Mar. Geol.* **7**, 357–63.

Torlegard, A. K. I. & Lundalv, T. (1974). Underwater analytical system. *Photogrammetric Engineering* **49** (3), 287–93.

True, M. A. (1970). Etude quantitative du quatre peuplements sciaphiles sur substrate rocheux dans la region Marseillaise. *Bull. Inst. Oceanogra.* Monaco **69**, No. 1401.

Turner, J. (1982). *Underwater Photography*. London: Focal Press.

Woods, J. D. & Lythgoe, J. N. (1971). *Underwater Science: An Introduction to Experiments by Divers*. London: Oxford University Press.

10
Bacteria and fungi

G. D. FLOODGATE and E. B. GARETH JONES

Introduction

The ecology of micro-organisms remains the least explored of all the aspects of marine biology, but it is becoming increasingly apparent that a substantial part of the flow of energy and nutrients in estuaries and sheltered coastal waters proceeds not through phytoplankton and herbivorous zooplankton, but through a food web based on particulate and dissolved organic material. This web includes bacteria, fungi, and heterotrophic protozoa, and rejoins the classical chain through crustaceans browsing on the protozoans (Pomeroy 1979). The role of fungi is particularly unclear, and though they are encountered much less commonly than bacteria, it may be speculated that their activity is important in degrading the larger detritus particles.

Organic substrates may be derived not only from natural sources, e.g., detritus from salt marshes (see Chapter 3) or macroalgae, but also from human activities. Examples are sewage, pulp mill wastes, oil discharges, and droppings from fish farms. In all these cases, the capacity (or otherwise) of the natural microbial systems to cope with the organic influxes is a matter of considerable practical significance.

An excellent general introduction to the microbiology of the sea is to be found in Rheinheimer (1974); whilst Mitchell (1972, 1978) describes the microbiology of polluted waters. Several handbooks dealing with practical methods and techniques are available for general microbiology (e.g., Gerhardt et al., 1981) and for marine and estuarine microbiology (Colwell et al., 1975). These should be consulted for details of media, sterilisation, and specialised techniques. Methods for surveys of bacteria and fungi are described in this chapter, and methods for plankton are described in the next chapter.

Bacteria and fungi may be free floating, saprophytic on dying plankton

238

or on small detritus particles such as faeces, or attached to various substrata on the sea-bed or shore. Benthic fungi may release spores that are planktonic for a while, and some, e.g., yeasts, may be truly free floating. This clearly has a bearing on sampling strategies. If floating bacteria and fungi are to be investigated, the reader is advised to consult the hydrographical section in Chapter 11. Examples of work on coastal and estuarine bacterioplankton are given by Ferguson & Rublee (1976) and Bent & Goulder (1981).

Similarly the growth and distribution of the bacteria and fungi associated with various substrata on the sea-bed and shore are regulated by physical factors, notably the sediment grain size and its absorptive power, the diffusion rate of gases through the sediment, and the overbearing pressure due to the tidal rise and fall. An example of a bacterial survey of estuarine sediments is that of Schröder & Van Es (1980).

Microbial surveys differ in a number of important ways from surveys of plants and animals. Whereas the macro-ecologist is usually searching for an organism that can be seen and recognised when it is found, the microbiologist can only examine a specimen or sample after removing it from the environment and examining it in the laboratory. This often involves culture work. In the field the activity of micro-organisms is deduced, for the most part, from the chemical changes that they mediate rather than by direct observation of the organisms themselves. Furthermore, many of the conclusions about these activities, and the nature of the organisms themselves, can only be arrived at in the laboratory where the organisms are studied under essentially artificial conditions. Inevitably inferences about the natural environment have to be drawn from these laboratory experiments, but this should always be done with a fair degree of circumspection. More than most ecologists, the micro-ecologists have to realise that in sampling the environment they necessarily disturb it, and so change it. Micro-organisms, especially the bacteria, respond very quickly to environmental change; hence the need to keep the shortest possible interval between sampling and processing.

There are hundreds of known species of marine bacteria and fungi and certainly many more species are uncharacterised as yet. They are ubiquitous and live in micro-environments that at the moment are impossible to monitor. Within these micro-environments, the various kinds of micro-organisms interact among themselves and with the macrobios, exhibiting such phenomena as competition and synergism. Nevertheless, although individually very small, micro-organisms are present on many occasions in such large numbers that they exert a considerable effect upon the environment, which is constantly changing because of their activities. It is also true that they are in turn affected by the chemistry of the environment. On the one hand it will govern whether they will grow or not and at what rate, but on the other hand, a feature of these organisms is that many are very adaptable and are able to adjust to a wide range of conditions. Because of the close relationship between the microbiology and chemistry of a body of water, for many purposes it is necessary to take samples for chemical analysis at the same time as taking the microbiological samples.

Much effort is still required to develop apparatus and techniques to explore adequately the bacterial and fungal worlds, and in almost all surveys some compromise has to be reached between what is desirable and what is practicable. Nevertheless, various basic techniques are available, and some general ground rules of procedure are mandatory. There is little point in attempting to carry out such a survey unless personnel have the necessary skills. For example, growing a pure culture requires a degree of proficiency in the preparation and sterilisation of media as well as the ability to carry out an aseptic transfer to a new medium. In addition, although few organisms harmful to humans are found in natural waters in any numbers, even the most 'harmless' of organisms may, if not treated with proper caution, cause unpleasant infections. Thus the common intestinal bacterium *Escherichia coli*, which is used as an indicator of faecal pollution of water systems, can cause cystitis or conjunctivitis if not handled with proper care.

BACTERIA *G. D. Floodgate*

Planning the programme

The first task in any survey is to sample the water or sediments under observation. This is more complicated than would at first appear, though much will depend upon the nature of the survey being undertaken. In tidal locations, for instance, it has to be decided whether to sample at a standard time of day or at a standard state of the tide. Seasonal variations are often found, and local temporary disturbances of the regime, e.g., caused by a sudden influx of storm water, can upset the most carefully laid plans. Accidental contamination of the sample, e.g., from the cooling water of a research ship's engines, the outboard of a dinghy, or the wire on the winch, can produce frustration and waste resources. The sample must be received into a vessel that is both sterile and chemically clean. If the same sample is being used for both chemical and microbiological analyses, then care must be exercised to ensure that the vessel is suitable from the chemical point of view as well. Thus for the most accurate results, samples for silicate analysis should not be collected in glass bottles. Samples for phosphate analysis should not be collected in plastic bottles as the plastic will absorb some of the phosphate; in this case glass only should be used. For further information on chemical sampling consult Riley (1975).

A further problem has to do with the distribution of sampling stations over the area and period to be studied. There is a natural tendency to extrapolate from one or two samples taken at a particular place, at a particular time, to a whole estuary or coastal area, but this temptation should be resisted. An adequate sampling pattern must extend both geographically and in time over the whole range of hydrographical and chemical conditions likely to occur in the area under investigation. Hence it is necessary to make physical and chemical studies along with the microbiological one. Sea water is neither physically nor chemically as homogeneous as might be thought. The temperature of the surface water will change with the time of year within a range of about 20 °C in temperate waters. There are also differences in density caused by temperature and/or salinity variation. These density changes do not in themselves affect bacterial growth, but set up a series of interfaces between the warm and cold water or the salt and fresh water. The interfaces, known as the thermocline and pycnocline respectively, tend to collect detritus and bacteria. At the air–water interface there is also a very thin layer that collects hydrophobic material such as fats and oils. Other forces generated by winds, waves, and tides and sometimes modified by the bottom topography, tend to mix the water and oppose the forces making for stratification. The result is that the hydrographical situation may be very complex and variable as the mixing and layering forces change in magnitude; see the hydrographical section of Chapter 11 for further information.

Bacterial activity is also dependent on the chemical environment. All micro-organisms require energy, carbon, nitrogen, and other elements, available in a suitable form, in order to grow. Depending upon the physiology of the micro-organism, the nutrient requirement may be for inorganic or organic substrates or both. In addition to low concentrations of easily assimilated organic substrates, all natural waters contain complex polymeric materials that are derived from plants and resemble the humic and fulvic acids found in soils. These substances are relatively inert to bacterial attack and account for a large proportion of the total organic matter. Total organic carbon and nitrogen analyses can, therefore, be misleading since they will include the recalcitrant substrates that the bacteria can deal with only slowly.

The chemistry of sediments is complex and is both affected by and affects the overlying water. When the amount of organic matter is high, bacterial activity reduces the oxygen in the mud faster than it can be replaced by diffusion. In this case the sediments become anaerobic and hydrogen sulphide is produced from the sulphate in sea water. This in turn leads to the precipitation of metallic sulphides, which gives rise to black muds.

In addition, many bacteria and some algae adhere to surfaces such as those that are formed from organic detritus, e.g., degenerating algae, faecal pellets, and inorganic sand or mud particles that have absorbed organic material. As a rule, the amount of heterotrophically available nutrients in particulate form is greater than in the dissolved form, and should therefore be included in the survey.

Clearly in any bacterial survey, the concurrent chemical programme will depend on what the survey is intended to achieve. For technical details of chemical methods of sea-water analysis, consult Strickland & Parsons (1972), Parsons, Maita & Lalli (1984), or Head (1985). Goldberg (1976) may be consulted for pollutants.

Finally, while the programme is still in the planning stage, thought should be given as to how the data that are generated are to be treated subsequently; see Chapter 1.

Obtaining the sample

Various pieces of apparatus for sampling sea water and sediments for bacteria have come into common use. Because the distribution of bacteria in the sea is often patchy, it is better to take large samples rather than small ones. A large sample can be defined as the maximum volume of water that is feasible to filter from any one sampling station. For some purposes it is advantageous to use a sampling pump rather than discrete samplers as this again tends to iron out the irregularities due to patchiness. However, the pump can also create considerable turbulance that generates shear forces that can destroy delicate organisms. For further information on pumping as a sampling method, see Chapter 11.

The commonest discrete samplers in general use are the Johnson–ZoBell (JZ) (ZoBell, 1941) (Fig. 10.1) and Niskin (Niskin, 1962) samplers. As already mentioned, the surface film on water has been found to be a region of intense bacterial activity, and it is sometimes desirable to sample it by removing a very thin film from the surface. Two suitable samplers for this purpose have been described in the literature (Garrett, 1965; Miget et al., 1974).

The problem of obtaining an undisturbed and indubitably uncontaminated sediment sample has not yet been solved. Where the sediment is accessible at low tide, sampling may be effected by using sterile spatulas

Fig. 10.1. The Johnson–ZoBell (JZ) bacteriological sampler. Procedure: (1) sterilise bottle in autoclave; (2) insert bung. A partial vacuum is created in the bottle as it cools; (3) mount bottle on carrier; (4) attach wire at X; (5) in the field, submerge to required depth and send messenger down wire to break glass tube. Water is then sucked into the bottle.

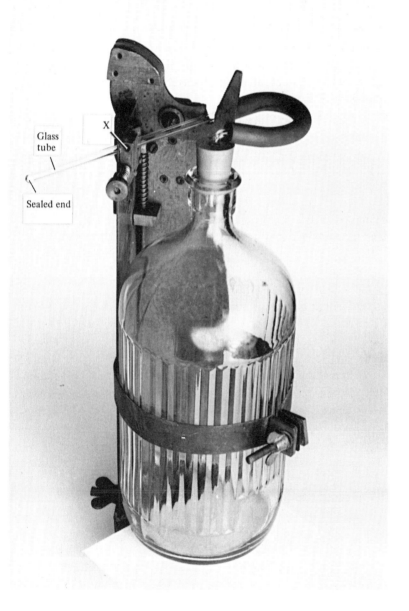

or spades, depending on the requirements. Simple corers can be made from lengths of plastic drain pipe (see Chapter 4). Schröder & Van Es (1980) used Perspex tubes (length 25 cm, inner diameter 24 mm), with subsequent cutting of the sample into 2-cm sections. For offshore work consult Chapter 5, also Taylor-Smith (1969) and Bailey (1971). Most of the samples obtained by these methods have to be sub-sampled for microbial investigation. This can be done conveniently by means of a sterile plastic syringe, the end of which has been sawn off with a small hack-saw whose blade has been sterilised by passing through a flame. The open cut-off end is pushed into the sediment and the plunger is pulled out slowly until the desired quantity of material is obtained. With practice, this method enables the investigator to collect the required quantity of sediment under adverse field conditions.

Methods of cleaning and sterilising equipment are dealt with in many texts, such as Elliott & Georgala (1969), Sirockin & Cullimore (1969) and Sykes (1969).

Processing a water sample

It is important to remember that once a sample is placed in a clean container it will start to change chemically and microbiologically. For example, organic matter will adsorb to the walls of the vessel. The microbiology will change, too. Sometimes these changes are irrelevant to the problem; at other times they must be taken into account. If possible, processing should begin at once. If storage is unavoidable, the sample should be kept cold to minimise change. Chemical samples should usually be deep-frozen and tightly corked. (Even ice can absorb enough tobacco smoke to invalidate an ammonia estimation.) However, freezing may rupture some organisms in the sample and so release organic compounds. It will be necessary to balance the loss of material caused by not freezing, on the one hand, with the gains due to cell rupture on the other. The water or sediment for chemical analysis should be dealt with as appropriate; for details see Strickland & Parsons (1972), Riley (1975), Parsons et al. (1984), and Head (1985) or, in the case of pollutants, Goldberg (1976). Samples for bacteriological analysis should not be frozen but kept at 1–2 °C above freezing. Bacteria can be killed and preserved by the addition of 1 ml of a 0.5% solution of formaldehyde to 25 ml of sea-water sample. Glutaraldehyde is probably a less-damaging preservative (Murchio & Allen, 1968). If 20 ml of 25% v/v solution glutaraldehyde and 50 ml distilled water are added to 140 ml sea-water sample, the resulting solution has the same osmolarity as sea water and so will not cause osmotic damage to delicate organisms (Nott & Parks, 1975).

Amount of bacteria present versus activity

In a very general way the number of bacteria present or their biomass is an indication of the amount of bacterial cell division and growth. However, bacteria can perform many chemical transformations without increasing their numbers. Hence it is common in micro-ecological studies to find that a few organisms may be very active under certain conditions, and conversely, many organisms, capable of carrying out a reaction, may be present but are, in fact, inactive. Hence it is necessary to draw a distinction between the biomass or numbers of organisms present in a certain area and their biochemical activity. Detailed critical reviews of the methods of determination of biomass and activity of bacteria in aquatic environments are available (Floodgate, 1980).

Estimation of bacterial numbers

Whatever method of estimating bacterial numbers is used, it is desirable to break up clumps of bacteria as far as possible, and to attempt to separate the organisms from the particles of suspended matter on which a high proportion of them are growing or to which they are simply attached. There is no one method that will separate all the individual organisms without damaging any in all circumstances. The simplest method is to 'shake the bottle' by hand, preferably a standard number of times to get good replication. Mechanical shakers may also be used, but the more violent agitation can cause cells to break up, and good replication becomes more of a problem. Low toxicity detergents, such as Triton-X 100, may be added to increase the amount of separation. Unfortunately, detergents can damage the cell walls of the delicate organisms, and excessive agitation will cause some cells to be ruptured. The most suitable compromise for any situation can only be found by trial and error.

In coastal and estuarine waters the number of bacteria is generally of the order of 10^5–10^7 or more/ml. Hence it is necessary to dilute the sample so that for a plate count (see section on viable count below) the number of colonies appearing is between 30 and 300; otherwise there will be too many colonies to count accurately or too few to make the count reliable. Also for total counts, dilution may sometimes be advisable, care being taken to use particle-free diluent. A $\times$ 10 dilution series is mostly adopted by placing 1 ml of sample into 9 ml of sterile diluent. Sterile sea or estuary water are used as diluents as appropriate. One millilitre of the diluted sample is added to another 9 ml of diluent to give a suspension that now contains one hundredth of the concentration of the original sample. This is repeated until it is judged that the sample has been diluted sufficiently. Care must be taken in measuring the volumes, and a fresh sterile pipette should be used for each operation to avoid carry over. Exactly the same amount of shaking for each tube is also important, otherwise mixing errors can be introduced.

The number of bacteria in a given volume can be estimated by either one of two ways. The methods are as follows.

Total Count

To make a 'total' count of bacteria in natural waters, the cells from a known volume are concentrated into a suitable filter whose effective area, i.e., the area through which the water actually passes, is known. After staining with a simple dye, e.g., crystal violet or safranin, the bacteria in a known area are counted, the area being measured by a micrometer in the microscope eyepiece. The number of bacteria on the filter, and hence in the sample, are then calculated. Suitable filters are made in a great variety of materials, pore size, solvent compatibility, and diameter. A pore size of 0.22 μm is required to remove all bacteria. Nucleopore (polycarbonate) filters are preferred for the total count as they can be stained to give a black background. If in doubt, the reader should consult the technical advisory service of the firm concerned. The disadvantage of the total count is that all the organisms are counted whether living or dead, and to make the count statistically sound the number of fields that have to be counted per sample can be high. A graphical method to determine the number of fields that should be examined to achieve a 90, 95, or 99% confidence limit for various values of mean count per field is given by Cassell (1965). Total counts are time consuming and can become tedious when many samples have to be analysed. In addition, it may not be easy to distinguish between small bacteria and small pieces of detritus, and there is the difficulty in deciding how many bacteria there are on clumps that have not been broken up, or that are attached to detritus on the facets that cannot be seen. Distinction between biological and abiological particles can be facilitated by using a UV-fluorescent dye (usually acridine orange) that stains nucleic acid; this is the most commonly used technique. The method as described by Zimmermann & Meyer-Reil (1974) is effective, though some flexibility is needed in staining and clearing times depending on the amount and nature of the suspended matter. The method can be used with both fresh and preserved samples. Because the material is on an opaque filter, an incident UV microscope has to be used.

An alternative method using phase-contrast microscopy has been described by Salonen (1977).

Viable Count

A viable count is one in which the bacteria from a known volume of a suitably diluted sample are cultured and the number of organisms in the sample calculated from the ensuing growth. A common viable count is a 'plate' count in which an aliquot of sample water may first be placed in a Petri dish and molten agar at just above the solidifying temperature mixed with it, or the aliquot may be added to the surface of a previously prepared plate and spread evenly over the surface with a sterile glass rod with a right-angle bend (i.e., shaped like a hockey stick). The first method, a 'pour plate', has the advantage of accurately dispensing the aliquot, but many marine bacteria are killed at the temperature of solidifying agar (around 42 °C), whereas the 'spread plate' avoids this problem and allows plates to be prepared some time beforehand, which is a great advantage when working at sea. The disadvantage lies in that the dispensing of the aliquot tends to be less accurate and is more liable to contamination. Gunkel (1964), and Gunkel & Trekel (1967) have described in detail a versatile procedure originally designed for a viable count of oil-degrading bacteria. This involves a high-speed blender (which breaks up clumps of bacteria) and pour plates, and has been used successfully many times on shore and at sea.

Alternatively, a nutrient surface may be provided by a membrane filter resting on a pad soaked in nutrient fluid. Counting bacteria grown on membrane filters has many advantages over the use of Petri dishes, especially under field conditions. Hand vacuum pumps can be used for filtration if electrical services are not available. The tins in which the filters and the nutrient pads are placed can be used repeatedly, and they store into a small space. For details on the use of membrane filters see Mulvaney (1969) and Burman, Oliver & Stevens (1969). The use of 'overdried' plates (Miles & Misra, 1938) has the advantage of enabling a degree of miniaturisation, but accurate pipetting of the aliquot onto the plate is required. Because of the dryness of the agar, the aliquots spread far less than normal, so allowing more aliquots per plate.

In all these methods, the colonies that develop are counted after a suitable period of incubation at an appropriate temperature. The growth on membrane filters can be detected at an early stage by staining the filter and examining under a binocular microscope. It is assumed that each colony consists of the progeny of a single bacterium so that it is possible to calculate the number of viable bacteria per unit volume. In fact, as pointed out above, the assumption is to some degree invalid due to aggregate formation. For this reason it has become the custom to report the results as the number of viable counting units (VCU) or colony-forming units (CFU) per unit volume which, while not increasing the information given by the count, makes the counter feel a little more honest. In addition, the method is limited by the medium and the cultural conditions employed. No one medium will support the growth of all marine bacteria, for each has a selective effect. The viable count therefore always underestimates the total number of bacteria that are present and, in fact, is frequently one or more orders of magnitude below the total count. This disadvantage can be turned to advantage. For example, the selectivity of plates containing chitin as sole carbon source can be used to count the number of bacteria that are able to digest this polymer, but will discourage the remainder.

A variant of the viable count is the most probable number (MPN) method, in which the organisms are cultured in liquid medium after being diluted serially. At a sufficiently high dilution, all the bacteria will have been diluted out so that none of the culture tubes (usually three to five replicates) of this dilution, will show any growth. By finding this end point and by the application of McGrady's statistical tables, it is possible to calculate the number of viable counting units in the original sample. The advantage of the MPN method is that it can be used for those organisms that do not grow easily on a solid medium, or where it is desirable to use a carbon source in the medium, such as crude oil, that will not easily incorporate into agar. Its major defect is that it is more statistically suspect than the plate count. For a discussion of viable count methods the reader should refer to Postgate (1969) who includes McGrady's probability tables for the MPN method, as does Report 71 (1969) and Rodina (1972). The American Public Health Association (1970) gives confidence limits as well.

The preparation of media is dealt with in many texts, such as Elliott & Georgala (1969), Sirockin & Cullimore (1969), and Sykes (1969).

Estimation of biomass

Sometimes the number of bacteria does not by itself supply sufficient information. An estimate of the amount of bacteria, that is, the biomass, is required.

Microscopic methods

If the mean volume of each size class of bacteria in the sample is determined by carefully measuring the dimensions of the cells, and the number in each class is found by the total count technique, then the volume of cells per unit volume of sample can be found. Frequently the size of the cells is measured using the acridine orange stained preparation as described in the section on total count. Dried fixed preparations are not suitable as the fixing process distorts the morphology of the cell. If the density of the cells can be ascertained, then the biomass, i.e., the weight of bacteria per unit volume of sample, can be calculated.

As the 'dry weight' often includes variable amounts of 'bound' water, the biomass is usually expressed in terms of weight of carbon. Either the bacteria are filtered off and then dried and the dry weight converted to weight of carbon by a suitable conversion factor (usually 20%), or the bacteria are both counted and sized under the microscope, and the total volume is converted to wet weight by the specific gravity (usually about 1.1) and thence converted to weight of carbon. The first method is easier, but in many circumstances the filtered weight will include particulate matter other than bacteria, while the second technique is time consuming and tedious. The conversion factors are uncertain, and some of the values quoted in the literature may seriously underestimate the biomass (Bratbak & Dundas, 1984).

Microscopic methods are set out in detail by Rodina (1972). It is easiest to obtain statistically significant data when the numbers of bacteria are low (not clumped) and they can be concentrated onto a filter from which a permanent mount is made.

A further adaptation of the UV-fluorescent technique to the problem of the rate of bacterial production is to note the frequency of dividing cells (FDC). The information obtained from the UV or light microscope can be supplemented by scanning electron microscopy (Hagstrom *et al.*, 1979). Bacteria that are actively synthesising new protoplasm can also be detected by the addition of naladixic acid. This compound specifically inhibits DNA synthesis so that division is prevented and the active cell become enlarged (Goss, Dietz & Cook, 1964).

Chemical methods

If the concentration of a single chemical substance typical of living bacteria can be measured, assuming that the amount of the substance is constant in all strains and does not vary significantly during the life cycle of the organisms, then the concentration of that substance will be an indication of the biomass. Adenosine triphosphate (ATP) comes close to having these desirable properties. It is found only in living cells since it is a product of active metabolism and decomposes very quickly once the bacterium is dead. Unfortunately, it is found in all living cells, so it is difficult to know whether the ATP that has been extracted is from bacteria or some other life form. The reaction involved is that between luciferase and luciferin, which is ATP dependent. The enzyme, which comes from fireflies, releases one photon of light for each molecule of ATP broken down to adenosine diphosphate (ADP). The light so generated is measured in a suitable apparatus that has been calibrated against an ATP standard. There are a variety of machines available ranging from portable field devices to sophisticated laboratory instruments. It is also possible to adapt some scintillation counters for light-measuring. The efficiency of extraction is important and varies with the method employed. Boiling Tris or glycine buffer are the most frequent extractants, the high temperature being required to destroy ATPase, an enzyme that rapidly breaks down ATP. Nitric and sulphuric acid are also used, but the extracted material has to be readjusted to pH 7.8 for the enzymic analysis; this causes dilution of the ATP and is also rather difficult in unbuffered solution.

However, the major problem with this technique is that pure enzyme preparations that give satisfactory results are costly. Lower-priced enzyme preparations are crude and give a high blank of 'inherent light'. The precise details of the method will depend upon the equipment used. For further details see Afghan, Tobin & Ryan (1977) and Deeming, Picciolo & Chapelle (1979).

Another approach uses some unique chemical features of the bacterial cell. Muramic acid is found only in the walls of prokaryotic 'cells' and is therefore found in bacteria and cyanobacteria but is not found in plant, fungal, or animal cells. The amounts per cell are very small so that high concentrations of cells are needed to accumulate sufficient muramic acid to measure. The process is lengthy, involving concentration of the bacteria, followed by acid hydrolysis for several hours. After this the muramic acid is separated by chromatography followed by further hydrolysis to release lactate, which is then estimated colorimetrically (Moriarty, 1978, 1980). The method is only of value when the number of samples to be processed is small.

Another substance found only in prokaryotes is poly-β-hydroxybutyrate. This substance is easily extracted from the bacteria by 5% sodium hypochlorate, and can be concentrated in chloroform and estimated spectrophotometrically (Herron, King & White, 1978). However the concentration does not correlate with biomass, but is an indication of the physiological status of the population since it is a storage product.

Recently, new techniques have been devised that make use of the analytical capabilities of gas–liquid chromatography, sometimes linked to mass spectrometry (White, 1983). Analysis of the lipid fraction has been particularly successful in estimating biomass and differentiating microbial consortia. However, a fair degree of chemical expertise is required, and the capital outlay is usually only justified if the equipment is well used.

Activity of bacteria

As mentioned earlier, the presence of a particular kind of bacterium does not necessarily indicate that the organisms are active nor does it give an indication of the kinetics of any activity that may be going on. Growth, that is, an increase in biomass, is the general response of bacteria to favourable chemical and physical conditions. A commonly used method of following bacterial production is based on the fact that bacteria take up radio-labelled thymidine and use it for DNA synthesis (Fuhrman & Azam, 1980). It is assumed that all the thymidine is incorporated into the DNA, and only negligible amounts are diverted to other pathways or nucleotide pools. This is disputed (Rosenbaum-Oliver & Zamenhof, 1972), and the method may overestimate growth.

However, bacteria may cause observable chemical changes in the environment with no change in the biomass. In recent years attempts have been made to devise ways by which the metabolic activity of the natural bacterial populations can be measured. Two important rules must be observed in all activity measurements. First, they must be of short duration. It is always necessary to enclose a sample in a container and, as stated above, this will cause rapid change, so that any observations made after more than a few hours must be considered suspect and not indicative of what goes on in the sea. Second, any chemical additions or variations in the physical parameters of the environment must be in the range that can be expected in the sea itself, otherwise interpretation becomes difficult because the organisms will be making a different response than the one they make in the sea. For example, bacteria differ in their ability to take up substrates at low dilution. If the concentration of a test substrate is made unnaturally high, then those bacteria that are poor scavengers are given an advantage, and the results will be biased.

The following approaches have been made to solve this problem.

Autoradiography

In principle, microautoradiography involves pipetting a few millilitres of the water sample into a bottle containing amino acids labelled with tritiated hydrogen. After a suitable incubation time, the cells are filtered off and, after drying, are covered with X-ray film. The radioactivity produces a 'spot' on the film so that the bacteria that have taken up the amino acids can be easily distinguished. The number of active cells can then be expressed as a percentage of the total. In practice, the method requires adequate controls and careful handling, and is rather slow. Nevertheless, the method has proved extremely useful (Hoppe, 1976).

Changes in the concentration of oxygen

Changes in the concentration of oxygen are followed over a few hours using the natural population and concentration of substrates. Oxygen uptake can be estimated by using an electrode sensitive to dissolved oxygen. This is undoubtedly the simplest method of oxygen determination, but unless care is taken to correct for the drift in readings due to the formation of films on the surface of the electrode, the value may be in error by quite considerable margins. Recent developments in electrode technology have improved their reliability but the good electrodes are expensive. A cheaper, reliable, but slow method is the classical Winkler titration. Details are available in many texts, e.g., Strickland & Parsons (1972). Although the method dates from the last century, it is still the most accurate and reliable method of estimating dissolved oxygen in sea water. The drawbacks to this technique are that the throughput is rather slow and the repetition of the same technique many times may lead to operator error. Direct oxygen-consumption determinations can be made using differential respirometers such as the Gilson respirometer (Burris, 1972).

Fate of added substrate

A known amount of substrate is added to a sample under controlled conditions and the fate of the added material is followed. To keep the concentration as close to the natural as possible, the obvious way to label the substrate is to use a radioactive isotope of high specific activity; carbon-14 is the most frequently employed. The use of radio-labelled chemicals requires sophisticated equipment, trained staff, and laboratory facilities that meet the legal requirements for their disposal and handling. The radio-labelled substrate is added to a freshly collected sample of sea water and incubated at a controlled temperature for a few hours (Wright & Hobbie, 1965). The reaction is then stopped by the addition of acid, which also releases the carbon dioxide that has been formed during the mineralisation of the substrate; the carbon dioxide is trapped by a suitable substance such as p-phenylethylamine. A scintillation counter is employed (often on both the substrate and the trapped carbon dioxide) to count the disintegrations in unit time; this, with the appropriate corrections for the particular instrument used, enables the operator to work out the rate at which the substrate is broken down and incorporated into the cells. By using a series of concentrations of the substrate within the range that might be expected in the environment, it is possible to compute the heterotrophic potential and the turnover time, and to ascertain if the uptake follows Michaelis–Menten kinetics. These are the normal kinetic patterns of enzymatic reactions (Campbell & Smith, 1982) and they are universally followed in pure enzyme preparations or pure cultures of bacteria. However, in the natural environment where, of course, the bacteria are of mixed species and many other factors play their part, the pattern frequently departs from that expected.

The heterotrophic potential is defined as V_{max} of the Michaelis–Menten plot and indicates the maximum rate at which the substance would be degraded under the conditions applied to the experiment providing that the concentration of the substrate is above the saturation values. The concentration of organic material in the sea is generally very low, so that saturation conditions may not be reached. Therefore it seems likely that V_{max} does not indicate what is actually happening in the sea, but what might happen under certain strictly limited conditions that do not occur very often.

Similarly, the turnover time can be a source of confusion. It is defined as the ratio of the substrate concentration at time t to the rate (i.e., the velocity) of the reaction. If the rate remained constant and independent of the concentration, the turnover time would represent the time taken for the concentration to reach zero. Unfortunately, the reaction velocity is dependent upon substrate concentration (i.e., first-order kinetics), particularly at the low concentration values found in the sea. So again, the turnover time is an interesting biochemical artefact rather than an ecological fact. Nevertheless, use of these concepts has enabled workers to distinguish water masses and to show differences with time, but precisely what the differences imply is not as clear as one would like.

It is quite common to combine several activity measurements in one investigation, e.g., autoradiography and uptake of radio-labelled substrates, or direct counts and thymidine incorporation; Hoppe, 1976, Newell & Fallon, 1982.

Reduction of tetrazolium salts (ETS)

The electron transport system (ETS) method essentially measures dehydrogenase activity by adding a substrate that acts as the terminal electron acceptor. Various derivatives of tetrazolium are the most frequently used; bacterial dehydrogenases reduce tetrazolium to effect a colour change (Iturriga & Rheinheimer, 1975). The most commonly used tetrazolium salt is 2-(p-iodophenyl)-3-(p-nitrophenyl)-5-phenyltetrazolium chloride, which is reduced to a water insoluble formazan which then has to be extracted with a solvent such as chloroform and measured spectrophotometrically. Unfortunately, the colour is affected by many factors such as population density, pH, substrate concentration, and the concentration of the indicator; thus, standardisation of the conditions is important and the method is more useful for plotting trends than for obtaining absolute values. Some of these difficulties can be overcome by the addition of buffers and quenching agents to stabilise the reduced electron acceptor (Christensen & Packard, 1979). The rate of tetrazolium reduction can be converted to an equivalent oxygen consumption by the method of Kenner & Ahmed (1975). One great advantage is that the method can be used immediately after the sample has been collected.

Adenylate energy charge

Another way of measuring the health of a microbial community is to determine the adenylate energy charge. This is defined as

$$\text{energy charge} = \frac{\text{molar concentration of } (ATP + \frac{1}{2}ADP)}{\text{molar concentration of } (ATP + ADP + AMP)}$$

$$\text{i.e.,} \quad \frac{\text{charged nucleotides}}{\text{total nucleotides}}$$

ATP is estimated by the luciferin–luciferase technique outlined above. The ADP and AMP are converted to ATP by enzymes, and the ATP is measured. The method therefore requires investigators with biochemical expertise and is limited to small-scale surveys. The values that have been obtained vary from about 0.9 for healthy active cultures to around 0.6 for those that are senescent. For details see Witzel (1979).

Processing a sediment sample

The methods used in processing samples of sediment are essentially the same as those used for sea-water samples. However, there are two major differences. First, the concentrations of both chemicals and micro-organisms are likely to be many times higher than in the water column, and second, there is liable to be some interference from the sediments themselves. This can take the form of the presence of inhibitors to reactions, as for example the presence of substances that inhibit the ATP estimations, or this interference can be due to the sorption capacity of the sediments. Some clay-like materials can virtually remove a substance from the system.

Some sediments are anaerobic and care must be taken to ensure that oxygen is not admitted until it is safe to do so, otherwise analyses for reduced components will be underestimated. For most routine work the traditional Macintosh–Fildes jar can be used, but for more extensive manipulation and for organisms requiring the virtual elimination of oxygen, an anaerobic cabinet is desirable (see Gerhardt *et al.*, 1981. A version of the Wright–Hobbie method of measuring activity using radio-labelled compounds in sediments is given by Harrison, Wright & Morita, (1971).

It should be remembered that some strictly anaerobic bacteria produce highly toxic products that cause death rapidly.

Growing aquatic bacteria

Many surveys of estuaries and coastal waters will call for the growth of bacteria at some stage for identification. Freshwater, brackish-water, and sea-water media will be required to take all eventualities into account (some freshwater bacteria may be washed into coastal waters down rivers, and may survive there for some time). Artificial sea water can be made by using dried sea-salts or by using a mixture of the major chemical components. The number of inorganic compounds in sea water is very large, and it would be tedious and generally unnecessary to add them all. For chemical composition of sea water and a recipe for artificial sea water, see Harvey (1957). Other recipes are given in Riley & Skirrow (1975). Another problem is that artificial sea water made from laboratory reagents may contain some organic matter. For many purposes this can be ignored; if necessary, it can be removed by incineration of the major components at 400 °C for several hours.

Natural sea water should be 'aged' before use. The water is first coarsely filtered to remove most of the suspended matter, but not the bacteria. The water is then left in the dark for several months so that the bacteria can digest the organic matter. The bacteria are then removed by filtration through a membrane filter. The drawback is that the water is not uniform from batch to batch, even when taken from the same area, but this does not matter for most culture work.

At present it is only possible to grow a fraction of the bacteria known to be present in the sea. Many media have been formulated for growing opportunistic heterotrophs that are easy to cultivate, but the rest are more difficult. Some will not grow on solid media, while others do not survive transfer onto fresh media. Since most marine bacteria live in cold, nutrient-poor water, the cultural conditions should reflect this situation. For a discussion on these and similar problems, the reader is referred to Oppenheimer (1968).

Some surveys concentrate on specific groups of bacteria such as those of the nitrogen or sulphur cycle. Details of the methods to cultivate many of these specialised organisms are available in Aaronson (1970), Rodina (1972), and Gunderson (1976).

Coliform bacteria

The commonest bacteriological survey in the marine environment does not concern marine bacteria at all, but is an enumeration of *Escherichia coli*, which is recognised as an indicator of human and animal faecal pollution. The number found will correspond to the rate of input minus the rate of loss by death and dispersal. The input may not be regular, and will depend on the disposal regime. Some small seaside towns, for example, only release sewage on certain states of the tide or at given intervals. The degree of maceration will greatly affect the count. The rate of *E. coli* death depends upon many chemical and physical factors, as does the rate of dispersion, so it is difficult to translate the number of faecal coliforms found in any particular situation into realistic terms of the risk to public health. Furthermore, there is no good epidemiological relationship between the incidence of enteric disease and bathing in polluted waters. All that can be safely asserted is that a potential danger exists, and the risk of disease is greater than usual, particularly for holiday-makers away from their normal environment. In the United States, the Environmental Protection Agency (1972) makes 'no specific recommendations concerning the presence of concentrations of micro-organisms in bathing water because of the paucity of valid epidemiological data', and notes that where there is gross microbiological pollution, the presence of foreign matter is of such a magnitude as to make the situation aesthetically unacceptable.

At present European countries vary considerably in their regulations, but those nations that form the European Economic Community now have to comply with the Council Directive of 8 December 1975 (Council of the European Community, 1976). A summary of this directive is given in Table 10.1. It is concerned with many aspects of the quality of water used for

Table 10.1. *European Community: water quality for bathing water, Council Directive 8 December 1975*

Bacterial type	Maximum number/100 ml		Minimum sampling frequency
	guide	mandatory	
Total coliforms	500	10000	fortnightly
Faecal coliforms	100	2000	fortnightly
Faecal streptococci	100	—	when necessary
Salmonella	—	0	when necessary
Enteroviruses	—	0	when necessary

From Council of the European Community (1976).

bathing, and lays down a mandatory maximum of 2000 faecal coliforms/100 ml in at least 80% of the samples. (Up to 20% of the samples may contain more than 2000.) Samples have to be taken fortnightly and the coliforms are enumerated by the MPN method or by membrane filtration using an appropriate medium. An excellent account of the sampling procedures recommended for water quality analysis has been provided by Gameson (1978) with EC regulations in mind.

Recently doubt has been cast on whether the standard methods of recovery of enteric organisms, including some pathogens, are foolproof (Huai-Shu et al., 1982). By using immunofluorescent microscopy, these authors claim that the organisms remain in a potentially dangerous state even though they are not 'recoverable'.

The water quality used for shellfish cultivation is also controlled; within the EC this is by the Council Directive of 30 October 1979. The faecal coliform content per 100 ml should not exceed 3000 in 95% of the samples. For shellfish flesh and intervalvular liquid, the limit is 500 coliforms in 100 g of sample. For United States shell fisheries, the recommendations of the United States National Shellfish Sanitation Programme are applied. These include an examination of the coliform bacteria present in the water under the most unfavourable conditions of time and tide, using the MPN (most probable number) count. The median value of the faecal coliform content must not exceed 70/100 ml water, and not more than 10% of the samples should exceed 230 viable counting units/100 ml for a five-tube replicated decimal dilution test or 330 organisms/100 ml for a three-tube replicated decimal dilution test. The standard bacteriological procedures used are those of the American Public Health Association (1970).

Bacteria as tracers

Besides giving data on water quality, an *E. coli* survey also provides information on the movement of water because the bacteria act as 'tracers'. This species tends to die off fairly quickly and therefore is not the most suitable organism for this purpose. Various dyestuffs and other conservative, i.e., not degraded, materials are more effective. However, a recent development in the use of trace organisms to monitor faecal pollution and the effects of sewage discharge sites has been to utilize a range of viruses known as bacteriophage. The phage chosen infect only specific host bacteria, and are therefore easily identifiable after recovery. The most widely used phage are those of the bacterium species *Serratia indica*. These phage are only rarely found in natural sea water, and show a good correlation with conservative tracers such as lithium chloride. Chloroform is added as a preservative since it kills the bacteria. The samples may be stored frozen until they can be analysed. The phage are counted using a soft agar overlay technique (Drury & Wheeler, 1982).

The advantages of using phage, compared with using bacteria such as *E. coli*, are that the viruses are not pathogenic to human beings, the method has a high sensitivity, and the method is cheap and easy to carry out.

Identification

Guidance on identification is given in Chapter 14.

Acknowledgements

The author wishes to acknowledge the kind assistance of Mr E. Pike and Mr B. Egan in the preparation of the bacterial section of this chapter.

FUNGI *E. B. Gareth Jones*

Planning the programme

Nature and availability of substrata, salinity, depth of the water, and water temperature may all affect the distribution and frequency of occurrence of fungi, so these factors must be taken into consideration when planning a survey. Other factors, such as pH, flow of water currents, light, and oxygenation and turbidity of the water may also affect distribution, but less is known about them.

The substrata available for colonisation are of particular importance. Examples are microalgae, living or decaying seaweeds, *Spartina* culms, wood, worm tubes, base plates of barnacles, cast skins of crustaceans, and sand grains. Each of these will support its own fungal flora, though some fungi are found on more than one substratum. For example, compare the species lists of Rees, Johnson & Jones (1979) for submerged wood and wood in sand with those of Gessner (1977, 1978) for *Spartina*. In the case of *Spartina alterniflora*, Gessner (1977) found *Buergenerula spartinae* and *Phaeosphaeria typharum* on new shoots, *Leptosphaeria* and *Pleospora* species primarily on dead standing culms, and *Halosphaeria hamata* and *Lulworthia* sp. on the lower parts of the plant.

Salinity limits the occurrence of marine fungi in an estuary, as has been shown by Hughes (1960), Brooks (1972), and Shearer (1972). Fungi imperfecti predominate at low salinities or in brackish-water regions of an estuary, while ascomycetes dominate collections from fully saline waters. In brackish-water zones, freshwater fungi may also be collected (Jones & Oliver, 1964). Truly marine fungi may be defined as those species that are repeatedly isolated from the sea and are able to sporulate in marine conditions.

Depth at which substrata are exposed or recovered may also affect the fungi recorded. Kohlmeyer (1981) groups marine fungi into four vertical zones: obligate intertidal, facultative inter-or subtidal, obligate subtidal, and deep-sea species. However, great care must be exercised in this respect, especially when only one collection of the organism has been made, e.g., *Ceriosporopsis capillacea* (Kohlmeyer, 1981). Temperature can affect the rate of colonisation of a substratum, as well as the geographic distribution of a species. Our knowledge of geographical distribution is very limited, as the work of Jones (1968), Hughes (1974), Kohlmeyer & Kohlmeyer (1979), and Kohlmeyer (1983) indicates. Some fungi may also be seasonal in their occurrence, e.g., *Digitatispora marina*, a marine basidiomycete, has only been recorded in Langstone harbour, Portsmouth, England when the sea-water temperature was below 10 °C (D. J. Miller & E. B. G. Jones, personal observation), and this observation confirms the laboratory studies of Doguet (1964).

Detailed accounts on the collection, isolation, and enumeration of marine fungi include those of Johnson & Sparrow (1961), Morris (1968), Jones (1971a, b), Meyers (1971), Fazzani *et al.* (1975), Bremer (1976), and Kohlmeyer & Kohlmeyer (1979). Studies of particular groups include those in Table 10.2.

No single technique is suitable for a comprehensive study of fungi in a particular locality because of their diversity of form and nutritional requirements.

Table 10.2. *Key references to ecological groups of marine fungi*

Algicolous fungi	Jones (1976); Kohlmeyer & Kohlmeyer (1979); Haythorn, Jones & Harrison (1980)
Fungi on salt-marsh plants	Gessner (1977); Kohlmeyer & Kohlmeyer (1979)
Leaf inhabiting fungi	Cuomo *et al.* (1982); see Fig. 10.2 for an example
Lignicolous fungi	Jones (1971a, 1976); Hughes (1975); Kohlmeyer & Kohlmeyer (1979); see Fig. 10.3 for an example
Fungi on animal substrata	Alderman & Jones (1971); Kohlmeyer (1972); Alderman (1976); Porter (1982)
Fungi on synthetic materials	Jones & Le Campion-Alsumard (1970a, b)
Yeasts	Fell (1976)
Thraustochytriales	Gaertner (1968, 1972); Alderman *et al.* (1974); Bremer (1976); Miller & Jones (1983)

The main lines of approach are as follows:
1. Baiting
2. Examination of drift and intertidal substrata
3. Examination of foam samples
4. Direct plating of water and sediments
5. Examination of living material for parasitic and commensal forms

Fig. 10.2. Mycelium of *Corollospora maritima* growing on a leaf of *Posidonia oceanica*. Bacteria are also visible on the lower electron micrograph.

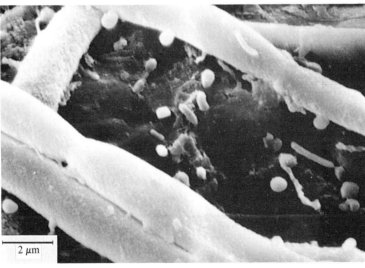

Baiting techniques

In the field

Apples, oranges, leaves, snake skins, ant egg cases, babys' hair, and wood panels are examples of the wide range of baits used to recover fungi with different nutritional requirements, e.g., keratonophilic, cellulolytic, or pectinolytic fungi. The baits are sterilised, e.g., in ethylene oxide fumes (Fazzani *et al.*, 1975), and then submerged in the sea for a time interval that will be determined by the temperature and the substrate used

Fig. 10.3. Branched conidium of *Orbimyces spectabilis* trapped on the scalariform pits of a section of wood. Scanning electron micrograph.

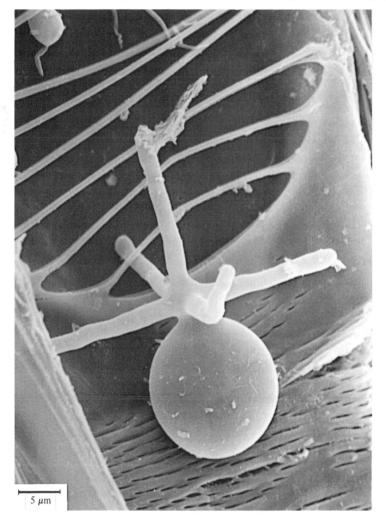

5 μm

(days for substrates such as apples, weeks for leaves, and months for wood panels in temperate conditions). Apples and oranges may be submerged in plastic mesh bass. Bags with a small mesh (litter bags) may be used for leaves and snake skins (Gilbert & Bocock, 1962; Suffling & Smith, 1974). Wood panels should be made into strings by drilling holes centrally for small panels (e.g., 5 cm × 2.5 cm × 0.5 cm) or at either end for large panels (e.g., 50 cm × 25 cm × 1.0 cm) and stringing them together with a nylon rope. Strings should be weighted so that the panels are always submerged regardless of the state of the tide.

After removal, the baits are placed in sterile polythene bags and returned to the laboratory for examination. They should be examined under a binocular microscope to determine if sporulating structures are present, then they should be carefully washed in sterile sea water to remove sediments and/or fouling organisms. Care should be taken to avoid dislodging reproductive structures, e.g., perithecia or pycnidia.

Incubation of baits

After cleaning test panels of fouling organisms, baits should be incubated under laboratory conditions. Incubation is required to enable fungi present in the substrate as mycelium to sporulate. Apples and soft fruits should be placed in sterile sea water in crystallising dishes. Wood panels, leaves, rhizomes, and culms of intertidal angiosperms should be incubated in sterile plastic boxes containing a layer of sterile Kleenex tissues moistened with sterile sea water. Suitable incubating temperatures may range between 5 and 25 °C according to the species of fungi present. In practice, several temperatures, e.g., 10, 20, and 25 °C, are usually used with each type of bait. Sterile distilled water should be added as necessary to prevent drying out. Incubated baits should be periodically examined for the presence of fungi and especially for sporulating structures that are required for identification. A succession of structures may be observed (Kane, 1980).

Sporulating material of marine fungi should always be mounted in the first instance in sea water. This is important to determine the number of flagella present on a zoospore, or the nature of the ascospore appendages in the Ascomycotina. Ascospores should be allowed to stand in sea water for up to 20 minutes to enable the appendages (if present) to fully dilate. Confusion and misidentification can result if spores are mounted directly into lactophenol or similar mounting media.

To prepare permanent mounts of spores of higher marine fungi, the water should be replaced gradually with lactophenol (with or without cotton blue) or glycerol, by placing a drop of the mounting fluid to one

Table 10.3. *Percentage occurrence of marine ascomycetes on driftwood collected from the foredune region of a Danish coastal sand dune system at Grønhøj in October 1976*

Fungi	Total no. of collections: 355	Occurrence (%)
Nereiospora comata (Kohlm.) Jones, R. G., Johnson and Moss	198	55.8
Kohlmeyeriella tubulata Kohlm.	99	27.9
Corollospora maritima Werdermann	79	22.3
Remispora pilleata Kohlm.	68	19.2
Amylocarpus encephaloides Currey	64	18.0
Arenariomyces trifurcatus Höhnk ex. Jones, R. G., Johnson and Moss	52	14.7
Nais inornata Kohlm.	44	12.4
Remispora stellata Kohlm.	30	8.5
Lulworthia sp.	24	6.8
Remispora maritima Linder	23	6.5
Halosphaeriopsis mediosetigera Cribb and Cribb	23	6.5
Carbosphaerella leptosphaerioides Schmidt	19	5.4
Corollospora lacera (Linder) Kohlm.	17	4.8
Eiona tunicata Kohlm.	5	1.4
Crinigera maritima Schmidt	5	1.4
Lophiotrema littorale Speg.	5	1.4
Lulworthia spp.	5	1.4
Grønhiella bivestia Koch, Jones and Moss	5	1.4
Nereiospora cristata (Kohlm.) Jones, R. G., Johnson and Moss	4	1.1
Leptosphaeria obiones (Crouan and Crouan) Sacc.	4	1.1
L. orae-maris Linder	3	0.9
Microthelia verruculosa Anastasiou	3	0.9
Ceriosporopsis halima Linder	2	0.6
C. tubulifera Kohlm.	2	0.6
Sporormia minima Auersw.	2	0.6
Lignincola laevis Höhnk	1	0.3
Haligena elaterophora Kohlm.	1	0.3
Haligena amicta Kohlm.	1	0.3
Lindra inflata Wilson	1	0.3
Myriangiales sp.	1	0.3
Nautosphaeria cristaminuta Jones	1	0.3
Pleospora sp.	1	0.3
Ceriosporopsis circumvestita Kohlm.	1	0.3

After Rees, Johnson & Jones (1979).

side of the cover slide so that it seeps in under the cover glass. Clean away any surplus fluid and seal the cover slide with nail varnish or proprietary sealants.

The procedure described will enable a list to be made of the fungi present on removal of baits from the sea, as well as on incubation under laboratory conditions. The method thus gives presence/absence data.

If sufficient samples are exposed, the percentage occurrences of different species can be compared.

$$\% \text{ occurrence of species} = \frac{\text{number of collections of a species}}{\text{total samples examined}} \times 100$$

An example is given in Table 10.3 with respect to marine fungi colonising wood in a sandy foredune.

The advantages of direct examination of substrata include: sporulating stages can be observed and identification to species is usually possible; the chemical composition of the substratum can be determined, as can loss of cellulose, loss in total weight, etc; to a limited extent, degree of colonisation can be estimated.

Disadvantages are that the method does not yield good quantitative data, as only those species that are sporulating can be counted; also, thick samples may be difficult to examine.

Quantifying fungi on baits
Bait blending and plating out
Place 1 g of bait (after removal from the sea) and 50 ml of sterile sea water in a Waring blender for 1–5 minutes, and make up to 1 l on completion of blending. It is important not to allow the material to become too hot (over 40 °C) in the blender. Plate out the suspension onto selective media (Jones, 1971b; Fazzani et al., 1975) in Petri plates. It is usual for the media to contain antibiotics (such as a mixture of penicillin and streptomycin) to kill bacteria (Jones, 1971b; Meyers, 1971). Incubate the plates over a range of temperatures, e.g., 10, 20, and 25 °C. A minimum of three replicates of each treatment should be made. Count the colonies that develop over a selected time period. Organisms develop at different rates and the time period has to be judged by experience. It is commonly up to 14 days. If the number of colonies is too high for counting, a dilution series of the blended bait should be prepared and plated out (see section on estimation of bacterial numbers). After counting, transfer the various colonies to new plates to obtain isolates in pure culture for identification.

This procedure can be applied to soft baits, e.g., leaves and apples, while for harder samples, e.g., wood, blending time may be extended to

10 minutes, or a ball and mill grinder may be used to break up the sample.

This method has the advantage that with replication, quantitative data can be accumulated. Results can be expressed as a percentage of the plates sampled or as a percentage of the total fungal count. The disadvantages are that many of the Ascomycotina do not sporulate readily on agar plates and identification of the isolates is not possible. Furthermore, this method favours the fast-growing Deuteromycotina, especially terrestrial forms, that may be present in marine samples as dormant spores. The supply of rich nutrient media may encourage these spores to germinate, and the data is not representative of the activity of these organisms in nature. Rees *et al.* (1979) and Rees & Jones (1985) found that by plating sea sand out onto cornmeal agar or malt agar, a wide range of terrestrial fungi grew on the plates. However, by baiting the same sand with 2 mm × 2 mm × 25 mm strips of balsa wood, typical marine fungi could be recovered, e.g., *Corollospora maritima* and *Arenariomyces trifurcatus*. In the former case, terrestrial fungi washed from land or air borne were present in the sand as dormant propagules, but on plating out onto agar media, they germinated. However, they are not considered to be part of the fungal flora of sand dunes.

Sub-sampling of bait
A core of the bait is removed with a sterile cork borer, sliced into 1-mm segments with a sterile scalpel, and plated out onto selective media (Meyers, 1971). Replication, incubation, and counting are as described above.

This approach is particularly suitable for isolation of fungi from wood (see Meyers, 1971; Cavalcante, 1981) and has the advantage that the depth of penetration of the fungus into the substratum can be determined if the core slices are plated out sequentially. However, it is subject to the disadvantages described in the previous section.

Aeration and collection of spores
Sub-samples such as slivers of wood, 15-cm segments of leaves, and culms of intertidal marsh plants are removed from baits, placed in 250-ml flasks containing 50 ml sterile sea water, and vigorously aerated. It is necessary for the pumped air to pass through a trap (e.g., sterile cotton wool) before entering the flasks. Spores produced after a selected time interval (e.g., 5, 10, 12, 24 hours to 7 days) are collected on a Millipore filter. The filters are flooded with lactophenol cotton blue to stain and fix the spores, which are then counted with the aid of a microscope. Filters should be left for

up to 5 hours before counting to ensure adequate staining of spores. These are semi-permanent mounts and may be left for a number of days, provided they do not dry out.

The method is particularly useful for the collection of estuarine hypho-mycetes and marine species such as *Varicosporina ramulosa, Clavatospora stellatacula, Flagellospora* sp., and *Sigmoidea* spp., and eliminates the dormant spores of terrestrial fungi, which are a problem with the two preceding methods. It gives quantitative data (but great care must be exercised in interpretation) and is fast and easy to employ, although the counting can be tedious. The samples may be kept for long periods. Disadvantages are that the spores of the lower fungi cannot be identified, and the method favours the freely sporulating hyphomycetes, whereas some other groups may not produce spores under these conditions.

Millipore filtration and plating out

The aeration method above is used to obtain spores on a Millipore filter. Spores are resuspended in 5–10 ml sterile sea water and plated out on selective media as outlined in the section on bait blending. Colony counts are made after incubation of the plates for the selected time period. The Millipore filters may also be placed directly on the agar plates (Bahnweg, 1973).

This method may result in a number of non-sporulating isolates. These can be tested for sporulation as follows. A 1-cm disc is removed from a 3-week-old agar culture, and the discs are placed in sterile sea water and aerated for 1–3 days. This technique will encourage some hyphomycetes to produce conidia. A disadvantage of the method is that a few terrestrial fungi may appear on the plates, but this is less of a problem than with the blending and sub-sampling methods.

Isolation of fungi

Fungi are isolated by removing a perithecium, zoosporangium, or mass of conidia (with fine forceps and under a dissecting microscope), and placing them in 5–10 ml of sterile sea water in a McCartney bottle. The sea water should have been treated with antibiotics (Jones, 1971*b*; Meyers, 1971). Perithecia should be crushed to ensure release of spores, and zoosporangia should release spores naturally. Shake the bottle vigorously to ensure uniform dispersal of spores. Drops of the spore suspension are plated (on average each drop should contain one spore; prepare a dilution series if each delivery contains more than one). Incubate the plates at 10 °C and follow the germination of the spore, then subculture the germinating spore onto an appropriate agar medium (Jones, 1971*b*; Fazzani *et al.*, 1975) in a Petri dish.

Sporulation of isolates

As noted above, many Ascomycotina species do not readily sporulate under laboratory conditions. Methods for overcoming this have been described by Jones (1971b). Two methods found to be particularly useful are described here.

Sand grain method

Slivers of sterile wood (beech, birch, balsa) 5 cm × 0.5 cm × 0.5 cm are placed in a McCartney bottle filled to a depth of 2 cm with sterile sand. Two millilitres of sterile sea water are added and the wood is inoculated with an agar disc from the culture of the non-sporulating fungus. The bottles are incubated, e.g., at 10 and 15 °C for 3 weeks to 3 months. Perithecia develop on the wood or on the sand grains.

Shearer method (Shearer & von Bodman, 1983)

Pieces of sterile alfalfa stems (2 cm long) are placed in 50 ml of sterile sea water in a 250-ml Erlenmeyer flask. The stems are inoculated with the vegetative mycelium from agar culture, and the flasks are shaken (100 rpm) for 2–3 weeks at 20 °C until the alfalfa stems are covered by mycelium. The stems are then transferred to a Petri dish containing a sterile filter-paper disc moistened with sterile sea water. The Petri dish is sealed to prevent desiccation and incubated, e.g., at 10 or 15 °C, in the dark or in an illuminated incubator for 3 weeks to 3 months. It is useful to try both the dark and the light regimes as different fungi may respond to these different conditions.

Sea-water baiting in the laboratory

Sea-water samples are collected in sterile bottles and returned to the laboratory. Willingham & Bucks (1965) discuss various techniques for the sampling of sea water at different depths. In the laboratory the sea water is poured into sterile crystallising dishes and baited with sterile baits, e.g., with small tomatoes, snake skins, ant eggs, larvae of *Artemia salina*, hawthorn fruits, babys' hair, hemp seeds, or pollen grains. These and other baits are discussed by Sparrow (1960) and Jones (1971b). Dishes are incubated e.g., at 10 or 15 °C or room temperature. The baits are observed under a microscope for the development of fruiting structures. This method is particularly useful for the collection of 'pure stands' of members of the Thraustochytriales, Haptomastigomycotina, and Diplomastigomycotina.

Quantitative data can be obtained using this technique, e.g., percentage colonisation of pollen grains or *Artemia* larvae by thraustochytrid species. Gaertner (1968) developed the 'lowest sure number' for the estimation of thraustochytrids in sediments and sea water. For this a set of bottles containing various dilutions of the sample (sediment, water, etc.) were baited with a constant volume of *Pinus* sp. pollen, incubated at 15 °C for 14 days, and then examined for fungi growing on the pollen grains. The lowest sure number calculation is made as follows, where

a is the sample size in the last dilution giving a positive result
b is the number of replicates at that dilution
n is the number of bottles yielding fungi at that dilution

the number of fungi/ml $= \dfrac{n}{a \cdot b}$

therefore, the number of fungi/l $= \dfrac{n \cdot 1\,000}{a \cdot b}$

However, this does not allow for the computation either of mean or variance (Bahnweg, 1973; Bremer, 1976). Most probable number (see bacteria section on viable count) or relative measure of abundance technique, based on the ratio:

$$\frac{\text{number of fungi found}}{\text{number of samples examined}}$$

have also been applied to baiting methods (Dick, 1976). This technique can only be used when sufficient true replicates have been made to enable the data to be statistically analysed.

Sand baiting in the laboratory

Sand can be collected from the shore, particularly from under pieces of driftwood (Rees, Johnson & Jones, 1979). Samples are taken with a sterile spatula and transferred to a sterile McCartney bottle containing a sliver of sterile balsa wood 5 cm × 0.5 cm × 0.5 cm moistened with sterile sea water. On return to the laboratory, bottles can be incubated for up to 15 months. A number of marine Pyrenomycetes can be isolated by this method and terrestrial fungi are not generally recovered.

Examination of drift and intertidal substrata

Collection of decaying wood and rotting algae along the shore line has been a common method of obtaining marine fungi. Wood collected from the shore has been categorised as (1) driftwood, that is, wood that is floating or capable of floating at the time of collection; (2) intertidal wood, that is, wood that has been trapped between rocks, or cannot float because it is waterlogged; and (3) fixed intertidal wood such as that used in pilings and groynes. Each type of wood yields a slightly different marine mycota for various reasons (Hughes, 1975). For a survey of indigenous marine fungi, it is best to concentrate on (2) and (3) above (Hughes, 1975).

On return to the laboratory, material should be examined for sporulating structures. Collections, if heavily contaminated by sediments or fouling organisms, should be washed with sterile sea water and incubated as described in the section on incubation of baits. Enumeration procedures are as for baits.

A greater diversity of species has been reported from drift or intertidal substrata than baits submerged in the sea (Schaumann, 1968; Hughes 1969; Kohlmeyer & Kohmeyer, 1979). A disadvantage of the method is that the origin and period of submergence of the material is frequently not known. Fungi encountered are likely to be both marine and terrestrial.

Examination of foam samples

White foam seen at the water's edge frequently contains the propagules of aquatic fungi. Foam can be scooped into sterile Universal bottles with a little of the water. On examination under the microscope, spores and mycelia of fungi can be seen. These spores can be isolated, as described in the section on isolation of fungi.

Kirk (1983) has devised a technique using a neuston screen with a 1.6-mm mesh for the collection of foam from surface layers of water, and quantitatively estimating the species present.

Direct plating of water and sediments

Direct plating of sea water, filtered sea water, mud, and sand grains onto selective media has been widely used for the isolation of fungi from the sea (Nicot, 1958a, b; Borut & Johnson, 1962; Roth, Orput & Ahearn, 1964; Fell, 1967; Steele, 1967; Pugh, 1968; Kumar, 1973; Gessner & Kohlmeyer, 1976). The species recovered by these techniques are largely terrestrial and it is generally agreed that most are not active in sea water and marine sediments (Roth et al., 1964; Pugh, 1974; Miller & Whitney, 1981). Kohlmeyer & Kohlmeyer (1979) exclude these species in their treatise on the higher marine fungi because 'of the uncertainty of the marine activity of most of the fungi isolated by plating and dilution plates'. This aspect is also discussed by Jones (1976). However, for many free-floating fungi, e.g., some Thraustochytriales and yeasts, direct plating seems to be the best method for their isolation and accurate enumeration.

For all three methods outlined below it is important that the surfaces of the plates do not dry out, as this may affect the germination of the spores.

Sea water

Samples of sea water are filtered through Millipore filters. A suspension is made by transferring the filter to 5 or 10 ml sterile sea water and shaking vigorously. The suspension is then plated out onto selective media (Jones, 1971*b*; Fazzani *et al.*, 1975). Colony counts are made following incubation. If counts are high, a dilution series of the spore suspension may be necessary.

Millipore filters

Sea water is filtered as above and the filters are then transferred to agar plates containing selective media. Media should contain bacterial inhibitors, e.g., lactic acid or HCl (Fell, 1976) or antibiotics (Jones, 1971*b*).

Sediments

Sediment samples are plated out directly onto agar plates, or the pour plate method is used (see bacteria section on viable count). Incubation of the plates at 10–25 °C follows, and colonies present are counted at daily intervals.

Examination of living material for parasitic and commensal forms

Many fungi are found growing parasitically on algae but only a few have been grown in culture as many of the fungi are host specific. Algicolous fungi have received little attention in comparison to lignicolous fungi and this in part is due to the difficulty of obtaining infected material. Parasitic marine fungi are discussed in the texts by Jones (1976) and Kohlmeyer & Kohlmeyer (1979).

Similarly, little is known of pathogenic fungi on marine animals. Thraustochytrids are implicated in the death of octopuses in England (Polglase, 1980), squid in Nova Scotia (Gwyneth Jones, unpublished), and the nudibranch *Tritonia diomedea* (McLean & Porter, 1982). Marine pathogenic fungi are reviewed by Alderman (1976, 1984).

Commensal fungi belonging to the class Trichomycetes have been reported from 17 species of marine Crustacea (Hibbits, 1978). The intact digestive tract must be removed from the host for examination for fungi, few of which have been cultured (Jones, 1971*b*). Lichtwardt (1976) reviews their morphology and life cycles.

Estimation of biomass

Techniques described above have concentrated on the isolation and enumeration of specific groups of fungi from a variety of substrates. None have been concerned with the measurement of fungal productivity and this is an area that has attracted little attention from marine mycologists. It results from lack of suitable techniques, although White *et al.* (1980) have suggested the use of biochemical analyses, measuring pentadecanoic and heptadecanoic acids for prokaryotes, and C_{18} and C_{22} fatty acids for fungi. Miller *et al.* (1985) did not find the latter to be effective markers for fungi but found that the levels of ergosterol gave a good indication of fungal activity in wood. The concentration of the fungal sterol ergosterol was correlated with weight loss of wood panels ($r = 0.99$, $P < 0.01$) submerged in Langstone harbour, UK. They concluded that the data indicated that ergosterol is a useful indicator of higher fungal biomass in marine ecosystems.

Identification

Guidance on identification is given in Chapter 14.

Acknowledgements

This paper was written during a study visit to the Friday Harbour Marine Laboratories, San Juan Island, of the University of Washington. I am grateful to the Royal Society for financial support from the Marshall and Orr Bequest that enabled this visit to take place. I am grateful to Dr J. David Miller for reading the manuscript.

References

Aaronson, S. (1970). *Experimental Microbial Ecology*. London: Academic Press.

Afghan, B. K., Tobin, R. S. & Ryan, J. F. (1977). An improved method for quantitative measurements of ATP and its application to measure microbial activity in natural waters, activated sludge and sediments. In *Second Biannual ATP Methodology Symposium*, ed. G. A. Borun, pp. 349–89. San Diego, Ca: SAI Technology Co.

Alderman, D. J. (1976). Fungal diseases of marine animals. In *Recent Advances in Aquatic Mycology*, ed. E. B. G. Jones, pp. 201–49. London: Elek Science.

Alderman, D. J. (1984). In *Fungal Diseases of Aquatic Animals*, ed. J. Roberts, pp. 189–242, London: Academic Press.

Alderman, D. J., Harrison, J. K., Bremer, G. B. & Jones, E. B. G. (1974). The taxonomic revisions in the marine biflagellate fungi: the ultrastructural evidence. *Mar. Biol.* **25**, 345–57.

Alderman, D. J. & Jones, E. B. G. (1971). Shell disease of oysters. *Fishery Investigations*, London, Ser. II, 26, 1–18.

American Public Health Association. (1970). *Standard methods for the examination of water and waste water*, 13th ed. New York: American Public Health Association, 1740 Broadway, New York, NY 10019.

Bahnweg, G. (1973). 'The Occurrence, Distribution and Taxonomy of Fungi: in particular Lower Phycomycetes, in the Subantarctic and Antarctic Marine Ecosystems.' Unpublished Ph.D. Thesis, University of Michigan, Ann Arbor.

Bailey, R. J. (1971). Geological sampling of the sea floor. *Underwater J.*, June, 110–19.

Bent, E. J. & Goulder, R. (1981). Planktonic bacteria in the Humber Estuary; seasonal variation in population density and heterotrophic activity. *Mar. Biol.* **62**, 35–45.

Borut, S. Y. & Johnson, T. W. (1962). Some biological observations on fungi in estuarine sediments. *Mycologia*, **54**, 181–93.

Bratbak, G. & Dundas, I. (1984). Bacterial dry matter content and biomass estimations. *Appl. Environ. Microbiol.* **48**, 755–7.

Bremer, G. B. (1976). The ecology of marine lower fungi. In *Recent Advances in Aquatic Mycology*, ed. E. B. G. Jones, pp. 313–33. London: Elek Science.

Brooks, R. D. (1972). 'The Occurrence and Distribution of Wood-Inhabiting Marine Fungi in Point Judith Pond.' Unpublished M.Sc. Thesis, University of Rhode Island.

Burman, N. P., Oliver, C. W. & Stevens, J. K. (1969). Membrane Filtration techniques for the isolation from water of coli-aerogenes, *Escherichia coli*, faecal streptococci, *Clostridium perfringens*, actinomycetes and micro-fungi. In *Isolation methods for microbiologists*, The Society for Applied Bacteriology Technical series No. 3, ed. D. A. Shapton & G. W. Gould, pp. 127–34. London: Academic Press.

Burris, R. H. (1972). Constant pressure manometry. In *Manometric and Biochemical Techniques: a Manual Describing Methods Applicable to the Study of Tissue Metabolism*, 5th edn, ed. W. W. Umbreit, R. H. Burris & T. F. Stauffer, pp. 100–110. Minneapolis: Burgess.

Campbell, P. N. & Smith, A. D. (1982) *Biochemistry Illustrated*. London: Churchill-Livingstone.

Cassell, A. A. (1965). Rapid graphical method for estimating the precision of direct microscopical counting data *Appl. Microbiol*, **13**, 293–6.

Cavalcante, M. S. (1981). 'The Role of Actinomycetes in Timber Decay.' Unpublished Ph.D. Thesis, CNAA (Portsmouth Polytechnic).

Christensen, J. P. & Packard, T. T. (1979). Respiratory electron transport actvities in phytoplankton and bacteria: Comparison of methods. *Limnol. Oceanogr.* **24**, 576–83.

Colwell R. R., Sizemore R. K., Carnay J. P., Morita, R. Y., Nelson, J. D., Pickar, J. H., Schwartz, J. R., van Valkenberg, S. D., Walker, J. D. & Wright, R. T. (1975). *Marine and Estuarine Laboratory Manual*. Baltimore, Md: University Park Press.

Council of the European Community (1976). Council directive of 8th December 1975 concerning the quality of bathing water. *Official Journal of the European Community*, No. L31/1, 5.2.76.

Cuomo, V., Vanzanella, F., Fresi, E., Mazzella, L. & Scipione, M. B. (1982). Micoflora delle fanerogame marine delli isola D'Ischia: *Posidonia oceanica* (L.) Delile e *Cymodocea nodosa* (Ucria). *Boll Mus. Inst. Biol. Univ. Genova*, **50** (suppl.), 162–166.

Deeming, J. W., Picciolo, G. L. & Chapelle, E. W. (1979). Important factors in ATP determinations using firefly luciferase; applicability of the assay to studies of native aquatic bacteria. In *Native Aquatic Bacteria*:

Enumeration, Activity, Ecology, ASTM Special Publications 694, ed. R. R. Colwell & J. W. Costerton, p. 89–98. Philadelphia: American Society for Testing and Materials.

Dick, M. W. (1976). The ecology of aquatic phycomycetes. In *Recent Advances in Aquatic Mycology,* ed. E. B. G. Jones, pp. 513–42. London: Elek Science.

Doguet, G. (1964). Influence de la température et de salinité sur la croissance et la fertilité du *Digitatispora marina* Doguet. *Bull. Soc. Fr. Physiol. Veg.* **10**, 285–92.

Drury, D. F. & Wheeler, D. C. (1982). Application of a *Serratia marcesens* bacteriophage as a new microbial tracer of aqueous environments. *J. Appl. Bact.* **53**, 137–42.

Elliott, E. C. & Georgala, D. L. (1969). Sources, handling and storage of media and equipment. In *Methods in Microbiology,* volume 1, ed. J. R. Norris & D. W. Ribbons, pp. 1–20. London: Academic Press.

Environmental Protection Agency (1972). *Water Quality Criteria.* E.P.A. Report No. R3.73.033. Washington: Superintendent of documents, U.S. Government Printing Office, Washington D.C. 20402. Stock No. 5501–00520.

Fazzani, K., Furtado, S. E. J., Eaton, R. A. & Jones, E. B. G. (1975). Biodeterioration of timber in aquatic environments. In *Microbial Aspects of the Biodeterioration of Materials* Appl. Bacteriol. ed. D. W. Lovelock & R. J. Gilbert, pp. 39–57. London: Academic Press.

Fell, J. (1967). Distribution of yeasts in the Indian Ocean. *Bull. mar. Sci. Gulf Caribb.* **17**, 454–70.

Fell, J. (1976). Yeasts in oceanic regions. In *Recent Advances in Aquatic Mycology,* ed. E. B. G. Jones, pp. 93–124. London: Elek Science.

Ferguson, R. L. & Rublee, P. (1976). Contribution of bacteria to the standing crop of coastal plankton. *Limnol. Oceanogr.* **21**, 141–5.

Floodgate, G. D. (1980). Methods of Assessment of Microbial Biomass and activity in Aquatic Environments. *Microbiology* 1980, 355–60.

Fuhrman, J. A. & Azam, F. (1980). Bacterioplankton secondary production estimates for coastal waters of British Columbia, Antarctic and California. *Appl. Environ. Microbiol.* **39**, 1085–95.

Gaertner, A. (1968). Eine Methode des quantitauven Nachweiss Niederer, mit Pollen Köderbarer pilze im Meerwasser und im Sediment. *Veröff. Inst. Meeresforsch. Bremerh.* **3**, 75–92.

Gaertner, A. (1972). Characters used in the classification of thraustochytriaceous fungi. *Veröff. Inst. Meeresforsch. Bremerh.* **13**, 183–94.

Gameson, A. L. H. (1978). *Application of Coastal Pollution Research. 2. Sampling Coastal Waters for Bacterial Analysis.* Technical Report TR 77. Water Research Centre, Stevenage Laboratories, Herts, England.

Garrett, W. D., (1965). Collection of slick forming materials from sea surface. *Limnol. Oceanogr.* **10**, 602–8.

Gerhardt P., Murray, R. G. E, Costilow, R. N., Nester, E. W., Wood, W. A.,

Kries, N. R. & Phillips, G. B. (1981). *Manual of Methods for General Bacteriology*. Washington: American Society for Microbiology.

Gessner, R. V. (1977). Seasonal occurrence and distribution of fungi associated with *Spartina alterniflora* from a Rhode Island estuary. *Mycologia*, **69**, 477–91.

Gessner, R. V. (1978). *Spartina alterniflora* seed fungi. *Can. J. Bot.* **56**, 2942–7.

Gessner, R. V. & Kohlmeyer, J. (1976). Geographical distribution and taxonomy of fungi from salt marsh *Spartina*. *Can. J. Bot.* **54**, 2023–37.

Gilbert, O. J. & Bocock, K. L. (1962). Some methods of studying the disappearance and decomposition of leaf litter. In *Progress in Soil Zoology*, ed. P. W. Murphy. London: Butterworths.

Goldberg, E. (1976). *Strategies of Marine Pollution monitoring*. London: Wiley Interscience.

Goss, W. A., Dietz, W. H. & Cook, T. M. (1964). Mechanism of naladixic acid on *Escherichia coli*. *J. Bact.* **88**, 1112–80.

Gunderson, K. (1976). cultivation of micro-organisms. In *Marine Ecology* volume III, Part 1; *Cultivation*, ed. I. Kinne, pp. 310–5. London: John Wiley & sons.

Gunkel, W. (1964). Die Verwendung des Ultra-Turrax zur Aufteilung von Bakterien-aggregaten in marinen Proben (The use of Ultra Turrax for the separation of bacterial aggregates in marine samples). *Helgoländer wiss. Meeresunters.* **11**, 287–95.

Gunkel, W. & Trekel, H. H. (1967). Zur methodik der quantitativen Erfassung Ölabbauender Bakterien in verölten Sedimenten und Boden Öl-Wassergemischen Ölen und teerartigen Substanzen. (On the method of quantitative determination of oil decomposing bacteria in oil polluted sediments and soil, soil–water mixture and oils and tarry substances. *Helgoländer wiss. Meeresunters.* **16**, 336–48.

Hagstrom, A., Larsson, U., Horsted, P. & Normark, S. (1979). Frequency of dividing cells; a new approach to the determination of bacterial growth rates in aquatic environments. *Appl. Environ. Microbiol.* **37**, 805–12.

Harrison, M. J., Wright, R. T. & Morita, R. Y. (1971). Methods for measuring mineralisation in lake sediments. *Appl. Microbiol.* **21**, 698–702.

Harvey, H. W. (1957). *The chemistry and fertility of sea water*, 2nd edn. Cambridge University Press.

Haythorn, J. M., Jones, E. B. G. & Harrison, J. L. (1980). Observations on marine algicolous fungi, including the hyphomycete *Sigmoidea marina*, sp. nov. *Trans. Br. mycol. Soc.* **74**, 615–23.

Head, P. C. (ed.) (1985). *Practical Estuarine Chemistry*. Estuarine and Brackish-Water Sciences Association Handbook. Cambridge University Press.

Herron J. S., King, J. D. & White, D. C. (1978). Recovery of poly-β-hydroxybutyrate from estuarine microflora. *Appl. Environ. Microbiol.* **35**, 251–7.

Hibbits, J. (1978). Marine Eccrinales (Trichomycetes) found in crustaceans of the San Juan Archipelago, Washington. *Syesis*, **11**, 213–61.

Hoppe, H.-G. (1978). Determination and properties of actively metabolising heterotrophic bacteria in the sea investigated by means of autoradiography. *Mar. Biol.* **36**, 291–302.

Huai-Shu, X. A., Roberts, N., Singleton, F. L., Attwell, R. W., Grimes, D. J. & Colwell, R. R. (1982). Survival and viability of nonculturable *Escherichia coli* and *Vibrio cholerae* in estuarine and marine environments. *Microb. Ecol.*, **8**, 313–23.

Hughes, G. C. (1960). 'Ecological Aspects of some Lignicolous Fungi in Estuarine Waters.' Unpublished Ph.D. Thesis, Florida State University, Tallahassee.

Hughes, G. C. (1969). Marine fungi from British Columbia: occurrence and distribution of lignicolous species. *Syesis*, **2**, 121–40.

Hughes, G. C. (1974). Geographical distribution of the higher marine fungi. *Veröff. Inst. Meeresforsch. Bremerh.*, Suppl. 5, 419–41.

Hughes, G. C. (1975). Studies of fungi in oceans and estuaries since 1961. I. Lignicolous, caulicolous and foliicolous species. *Oceanogr. Mar. Biol. Annu. Rev.* **13**, 69–180.

Iturriga, R., & Rheinheimer, G. (1975). Eine emfache Methode zur Auszahlung von Bakterien mit Aktiven Elektronen transportsystem in Wasser und Sediment proben. *Kieler Meeresforsch.* **31**, 81–6.

Johnson, T. W. & Sparrow, F. K. (1961). *Fungi in Oceans and Estuaries*. Weinheim: Cramer.

Jones, E. B. G. (1968). The distribution of marine fungi on wood submerged in the sea. In *Biodeterioration of Materials*, ed. A. H. Walters & J. J. Elphick, pp. 460–85. Amsterdam: Elsevier.

Jones, E. B. G. (1971*a*). The ecology and rotting ability of marine fungi. In *Marine Borers, Fungi and Fouling Organisms of Wood*, ed. E. B. G. Jones & S. K. Eltringham, pp. 237–58. Paris: OECD.

Jones, E. B. G. (1971*b*). Aquatic Fungi. In *Methods in Microbiology*, vol. 4, ed. C. Booth, New York & London: Academic Press.

Jones, E. B. G. (1976). Lignicolous and algicolous fungi. In *Recent Advances in Aquatic Mycology*, ed. E. B. G. Jones, pp. 1–51, London: Elek Science.

Jones, E. B. G. & Le Campion-Alsumard, T. (1970*a*). The biodeterioration of polyurethane by marine fungi. *Int. Biodeterior. Bull.* **6**, 119–24.

Jones, E. B. G. & Le Campion-Alsumard, T. (1970*b*). Marine fungi on polyurethane covered plates submerged in the sea. *Nova Hedwigia*, **19**, 567–82.

Jones, E. G. B. & Oliver, A. C. (1964). Occurrence of aquatic hyphomycetes on wood submerged in fresh and brackish water. *Trans. Br. mycol. Soc.* **47**, 45–8.

Kane, D. G. (1980). 'The Effect of Sewage Effluent on the Growth of Microorganisms in the Marine Environment.' Unpublished Ph.D. Thesis, CNAA (Portsmouth Polytechnic).

Kenner, R. A. & Ahmed, S. I. (1975). Measurements of electron transport in marine phytoplankton. *Mar. Biol.* **33**, 119–27.

Kirk, P. W. (1983). Direct enumeration of marine arenicolous fungi. *Mycologia* **75**, 670–82.

Kohlmeyer, J. (1972). Parasitic *Haloguignardia oceanica* (Ascomycetes) and hyperparasitic *Sphaceloma cecidii* sp. nov. (Deuteromycetes) in drift *Sargassum* in North Carolina. *J. Elisha Mitchell Sci. Soc.* **88**, 255–9.

Kohlmeyer, J. (1981). Marine fungi from Martinique. *Can. J. Bot.* **59**, 1314–21.

Kohlmeyer, J. (1983). Geography of marine fungi. *Aust. J. Bot.* Suppl. Ser. **19**: 67–76.

Kohlmeyer, J. & Kohlmeyer, E. (1979). *Marine Mycology: The Higher Fungi.* New York: Academic Press.

Kumar, S. P. (1973). Marine lignicolous fungi from India. *Kavaka*, **1**, 73–86.

Lichtwardt, R. W. (1976). Trichomycetes. In *Recent Advances in Aquatic Mycology*, ed. E. B. G. Jones, pp. 651–71. London: Elek Science.

McLean, N. & Porter, D. (1982). The yellow-spot disease of *Tritonia diomedea* Bergh, 1894 (Mollusca, Gastropoda: Nudibranchia): encapsulation of the thraustochytriaceous parasite by host amoebocytes. *J. Parasitol.* **68**, 243–52.

Meyers, S. P. (1971). Isolation and identification of filamentous marine fungi. In *Marine Borers, Fungi and Fouling Organisms of Wood*, ed. E. B. G. Jones & S. K. Eltringham, pp. 89–113. Paris: OECD.

Miget, R., Kator, H., Oppenheimer, C. H., Laseter, J. L. & Ledet, E. J. (1974). New sampling device for recovery of petroleum hydrocarbons and fatty acids from aqueous surface films. *Anal. Chem.* **46**, 1154–7.

Miles, A. A. & Misra, S. S. (1938). The estimation of the bacteriocidal power of blood. *J. Hyg. Camb.* **38**, 732–42.

Miller, J. D. & Jones, E. B. G. (1983). Observations on the association of thraustochytrid marine fungi with decaying seaweed. *Botanica Marina*, **26**, 345–51.

Miller, J. D., Jones, E. B. G., Moharir, Y. E. & Findlay, J. (1985). Colonization of wood blocks by marine fungi in Langstone harbour. *Botanica Marina* **28**, 251–7.

Miller, J. D. & Whitney, N. Y. (1981). Fungi from the Bay of Fundy. II. Observations on fungi from living and cast seaweed. *Botanica Marina*, **24**, 405–11.

Mitchell, R. (1972, 1978). *Water Pollution Microbiology*, vol. 1 & 2. London: Wiley Interscience.

Moriarty, D. J. W. (1978). Estimations of bacterial biomass in water and sediments using muramic acid. In *Microbial Ecology*, ed. M. W. Loutit & J. R. Miles, pp. 31–3. New York: Springer Verlag.

Moriarty, D. J. W. (1980). Measurement of bacterial biomass in sandy sediments. In *Biogeochemistry of Ancient and Modern Environments*, ed. P. A. Trudiser, M. R. Walter, & B. J. Ralph, pp. 131–8. Canberra: Australian Academy of Science.

Morris, E. O. (1968). Yeasts of marine origin. *Oceanogr. Mar. Biol.* **6**, 201–30.

Mulvaney, J. G., (1969). Membrane filter techniques in microbiology In *Methods in Microbiology, vol. 1*, ed. J. R. Norris & D. W. Ribbons, pp. 205–54. London: Academic Press.

Murchio, J. C. & Allen, M. B. (1968). Preservation of nannoplankton. In *Unresolved Problems in Marine Microbiology: Proceedings of the Fourth International Interdisciplinary Conference*, Princeton 1966, ed.

C. H. Oppenheiner, pp. 111, 453. New York: New York Academy of Science.

Newell, S. Y. & Fallon, R. D. (1982). Bacterial productivity in the water column and sediments of the Georgia (USA) coastal zone. Estimates via direct counting and parallel measurements of thymidine incorporation. *Microb. Ecol.* **8**, 33–46.

Nicot, J. (1958*a*). Remarques sur la mycoflore des sols sableux immergés à marée haute. *C.R. Hedb. Seances Acad. Sci.* **246**, 451–4.

Nicot, J. (1958*b*). Une moisissure arénicole du littoral atlantique: *Dendryphiella arenaria* sp. nov. *Rev. Mycol.* **23**, 87–99.

Niskin, S. J. (1962). A water sampler for microbiological studies. *Deep Sea Res.* **9**, 501–3.

Nott, J. A. & Parks, K. R. (1975). Calcium accumulation and secretion in the serpulid polychaete *Spirorbis spirorbis* L. at settlement. *J. mar. biol. Ass. U.K.* **55**, 911–25.

Oppenheimer, C. H. (1968). *Unresolved Problems in Marine Microbiology: Proceedings of the Fourth International Interdisciplinary Conference, Princeton 1966.* New York: New York Academy of Science; Interdisciplinary Communication Program.

Parsons, T. R., Maita, Y. & Lalli, C. M. (1984). *A Manual of Chemical and Biological Methods for Seawater Analysis.* Oxford & New York: Pergamon Press.

Polglase, J. L. (1980). A preliminary report on the Thraustochytrid(s) and Labyrinthulid(s) associated with a pathological condition in the lesser Octopus *Eledone cirrhosa. Botanica Marina*, **23**, 699–706.

Pomeroy, L. R. (1978). Secondary production mechanisms of continental shelf communities. In *Ecological Processes in Coastal and Marine Systems*, ed. P. J. Livingston, pp. 163–86. New York: Plenum Press.

Porter, D. (1982). The appendaged ascospores of *Trichomaris invadens* (Halosphaeriaceae), a marine ascomycetous parasite of the tanner crab, *Chionoecetes bairdi. Mycologia*, **74**, 363–75.

Postgate, J. R. (1969). Viable counts and viability. In *Methods in Microbiology*, vol. *1*, ed. J. R. Norris & D. W. Ribbons, pp. 611–28, London: Academic Press.

Pugh, G. J. F. (1968). A study of fungi in the rhizosphere and on the root surfaces of plants growing in primitive soils. In *Methods of Study in Soil Ecology*, ed. J. Phillipson, pp. 159–64. Paris: UNESCO.

Pugh, G. J. F. (1974). Fungi in intertidal regions. *Veröff. Inst. Meeresforsch., Bremerh.*, Suppl. **5**, 403–18.

Rees, G., Johnson, R. G. & Jones, E. B. G. (1979). Lignicolous marine fungi from Danish sand dunes. *Trans. Br. mycol. Soc.* **72**, 99–106.

Rees, G. & Jones, E. B. G. (1985). The fungi of a coastal sand dune system. *Botanica Marina* **28**, 213–320.

Report 71 (1969). *The bacteriological examination of water supplies.* Reports on Public Health and Medical Subjects No. 71. London: Her Majesty's Stationary Office.

Rheinheimer, G. (1974). *Aquatic Microbiology.* London: J. Wiley & Sons.

Riley, J. P. (1975). Analytical chemistry of sea water. In *Chemical*

Oceanography, 2nd edition, vol. 3, ed. J. P. Riley & G. Skirrow, pp. 193–514, London: Academic Press.

Riley, J. P. & Skirrow, G. (1975). *Chemical Oceanography*, 2nd edn. London: Academic Press.

Rodina, A. G. (1972). *Methods in aquatic microbiology*, translated, edited, and revised by R. R. Colwell & M. S. Zambruski. Baltimore: University Park Press & London: Butterworths.

Rosenbaum-Oliver, D. & Zamenhof, S. (1972). Degree of participation of exogenous thymidine in the overall deoxyribonucleic acid synthesis in *Escherichia coli*. *J. Bact.* **110**, 585–91.

Roth, F. J., Orpurt, P. A. & Ahearn, D. G. (1964). Occurrence and distribution of fungi in a subtropical marine environment. *Can. J. Bot.* **42**, 375–83.

Salonen, K. (1977). The estimation of bacterioplankton numbers and biomass by phase contrast microscopy. *Ann. Bot. Fenn.* **14**, 25–8.

Schaumann, K. (1980). Marine höhere Pilze (Ascomycetes und Fungi-imperfecti) aus dem Weser-Ästuar. *Veröff. Inst. Meeresforsch. Bremerh.* **11**, 93–117.

Schröder, H. G. J. & Van Es, F. B. (1980). Distribution of bacteria in intertidal sediments of the Ems-Dollard estuary. *Neth. J. Sea Res.* **14**, 268–87.

Shearer, C. A. (1972). Fungi of the Chesapeake Bay and its tributaries. III. The distribution of wood-inhabiting Ascomycetes and Fungi Imperfecti of the Patuxent River. *Am. J. Bot.* **59**, 961–9.

Shearer, C. A. & von Bodman, S. B. (1983). Patterns of occurrence of Ascomycetes associated with decomposing twigs in a mid-western stream. *Mycologia*, **75**, 518–30.

Sirockin, G. & Cullimore, S. (1969). *Practical Microbiology*. London: McGraw-Hill.

Sparrow, F. K. (1960). *Aquatic Phycomycetes*, 2nd ed. Ann Arbor: University of Michigan Press.

Steele, C. W. (1967). Fungus populations in marine waters and coastal sands of the Hawaiian, Line and Phoenix islands. *Pac. Sci.* **21**, 317–31.

Strickland, J. D. H. & Parsons, T. R. (1972). *A practical Handbook of seawater analysis*. Bulletin 167. Ottawa: Fisheries Research Board of Canada.

Suffling, R. & Smith, D. W. (1974). Litter decomposition studies using mesh bags: spillage inaccuracies and the effects of repeated artificial drying. *Can. J. Bot.* **52**, 2157–63.

Sykes, G. (1969). Methods and equipment for sterilisation of laboratory apparatus and media. In *Methods in Microbiology*, vol. 1, ed. J. R. Norris & D. W. Ribbons, pp. 77–120, London: Academic Press.

Taylor-Smith D. (1969). *Remote Sampling and in situ testing of the sea floor.* Society for Underwater Technology & Technical Report. London: Society for Underwater Technology.

White, D. C. (1983). Analysis of micro-organisms in terms of quantity aand activity in natural environments. In *Microbes in their Natural Environments*, Society for General Microbiology Symposium 34, ed. J. H. Slater, R. Whittenbury & J. W. T. Wimpenny, pp. 37–68. Cambridge University Press.

White, D. C., Bobbie, R. J., Nickels, J. S., Fazio, S. D. & Davis, W. M. (1980).

Non selective biochemical methods for the determination of fungal mass and community structure in estuarine detrital mycoflora. *Botanica Marina*, **23**, 239–50.

Willingham, C. A. & Bucks, J. D. (1965). A preliminary comparative study of fungal contamination in non-sterile water samples. *Deep-Sea Res.* **12**, 693–5.

Witzel, K. P. (1979). The adenylate energy charge as a measure of microbial activities in aquatic habitats. *Arch. Hydrobiol. Beih.* **12**, 146–65.

Wright, R. T. & Hobbie, J. E. (1965). The uptake of organic solutes in lake water. *Limnol. Oceanogr.* **10**, 22–8.

Zimmermann, R. & Meyer-Reil, L. A. (1974). A new method for fluorescence staining of bacterial populations on membrane filters. *Kieler Meeresforsch.* **30**, 24–7.

ZoBell, C. E. (1941). Apparatus for collecting water samples from different depths for bacteriological analysis. *J. Mar. Res.* **4**, 173–88.

11

Plankton

P. B. TETT

Introduction

Plankton, taken from the Greek for 'wandering', is the collective name for the animals, plants, and micro-organisms that live in and drift with the waters of the sea. They cannot be investigated in the same way as the attached benthos or the active swimmers of the nekton. It is simple to define a fixed point for benthic sampling; but the sea itself is constantly in motion. Throw a dozen oranges into the water: where will they be tomorrow?

Each fruit moves in a complex path: bobbing with the waves; drifting and returning with the tide; or progressing steadily in a non-tidal current. The random eddying of turbulence disperses the group. If plankton behave like these oranges, they cannot properly be sampled without an understanding of the physics of the sea.

But plankton do more than drift. They grow, reproduce, and die, at rates that depend on food supply, predation, and physical and chemical conditions. The young of benthic animals may join or leave the plankton, and some animal plankton carry out daily vertical migrations. Are the effects of these biological factors important compared with what happens to plankton as passive contaminants of moving water? The question can often be answered by comparing the time-scales of the relevant physical and biological processes, as discussed, e.g., by Steele in Steele (1978) and Lewis & Platt in Kennedy (1982), and as further examined below. Only when the answer is 'yes' is it worth sampling plankton intensively: in other cases their distribution may largely be predicted from physical observations.

Thus, this chapter stresses the intimate relation between plankton and its physical environment, and the need to understand local hydrography before planning a plankton survey. Furthermore, it is concerned only with *survey* methods. Investigation of processes of the study of the biology of a single organism requires more specialised advice than can be given here. My aim in what follows is limited to suggesting efficient ways to investigate and explain the amount, distribution, and general composition of plankton in coastal seas and estuaries.

Five works are particularly useful in giving more information than can be provided in this chapter. UNESCO handbooks edited by Steedman (1976) and Sournia (1978) deal in detail with methods for zoo- (animal) and phyto- (plant) plankton. Ketchum (1983) is an account of the hydrography and ecology of estuaries and some enclosed seas. Morris (1983) covers the sampling and analysis of zooplankton in estuaries in particular. Finally, Newell & Newell (1977) provides a short introduction to the plankton and methods of sampling and identifying it.

Hydrography
The movements of the sea
The causes of water movement include wind, tide, the rotation of the planet, and density differences due to the addition of fresh water or heat to the sea. They are explained by Duxbury (1971) and Knaus (1978), and, in more detail in relation to coastal oceanography, by Bowden (1983). Water movements in coastal seas can be turbulent due to mixing by wind and tidal streams, rhythmic due to tidal displacements, or unidirectional when averaged over several tidal cycles. These mean currents are often slow, like the northwards drift of Irish Sea water, which carries radioactive caesium from the nuclear installations at Sellafield in NW England up the Scottish coast (Mauchline, 1980*a*; McKinley *et al.*, 1981), taking one to two years to round Britain and reach the southern North Sea (Kautsky, 1973). Tidal oscillations can transport water and plankton several kilometres away from a sampling position, and back, within a few hours. Winds blowing over the surface of the sea can also cause small-scale circulatory patterns, resulting in the accumulation of floating material into windrows, long streaks parallel to the wind and 5–300 m apart (Barstow, 1983). Horizontal turbulence disperses patches of plankton or pollutants; vertical turbulence might remove the plants of the plankton from the illuminated region near the surface of the sea, or bring up from deeper waters the mineral salts that the plants need. Although the structure of turbulence is non-directive, it can cause a net transfer of substance from a source (such as a region of plant growth) to a sink (such as filter feeders grazing phytoplankton).

In many shallow coastal seas the turbulence caused by friction between strong tidal streams and the sea-bed strongly influences the distribution of plankton. Examples are provided by the continental shelf seas of north-western Europe and North America. But even here the effects of wind- and density-driven currents are important, and some idea of the physical complexity of the coastal environment, and its effects on marine organisms, may be had from the proceedings of a meeting on 'Circulation and Fronts in Continental Shelf Seas', edited by Swallow *et al.* (1981).

Where continental shelves are narrow, as on the western shores of Africa and South America, wind-driven upwelling is sometimes the dominant process, enhancing coastal productivity by injecting nitrates and silicates into the illuminated layer of the sea. See, e.g., Boje & Tomczak (1978), Richards (1981), and Hempel (1982).

The vertical structure of the water column

The density of sea water is reduced by fresh water and solar heating, with the result that the sea is often layered. The stratifying effect of these factors is opposed by wind or tidal turbulence, which mixes warm or reduced-salinity water away from the sea surface. Stratification is shown by profiles of temperature, salinity, and density (Fig. 11.1). In estuaries and

Fig. 11.1. Profiles of temperature, salinity, density and chlorophyll. Examples are presented from western British coastal waters. The temperature and salinity scales are roughly in proportion to relative effects on density, which is expressed as σ_T. The chlorophyll scale is geometric, the corresponding graphs having initially been plotted against $\log_{10}$ (mg chl m^{-3}) Filled circles represent single chlorophyll samples taken at depths chosen after considering the relevant physical profiles. Temperature and salinity (or in some cases temperature and conductivity) were measured using electronic probes, in some cases

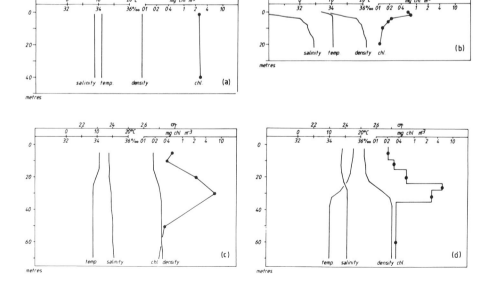

some coastal waters, salinity is the main factor controlling layering, whereas temperature often dominates offshore during the summer. In temperate latitudes a difference of 1 ppt in salinity has roughly the same effect on density as a temperature difference of 5 °C. Appendix 11.1 contains an algorithm for calculating density from temperature and salinity.

Phytoplankton need light and mineral nutrients for growth. Stratification can enable phytoplankters to remain in the illuminated region near the surface of the sea, from which turbulence might otherwise remove them. Conversely, stratification might isolate near-surface phytoplankters from nutrients regenerated near the sea-bed. 'Fronts' in shelf seas are places where mixed and stratified waters meet, and are often regions of high plankton biomass (e.g., Holligan in Swallow et al., 1981). A strong density gradient (or *pycnocline*) might act as a barrier to the vertical migration of

---

read directly at depth increments of between 1 and 5 m, in other cases digitally recorded and averaged over 5 m intervals. $\Delta\sigma_T$ refers to the density difference over the specified depth range.

(a) Almost completely mixed (as a result of strong tidal streams): station J9 of Jones, Gowen & Tett (1984) in Sound of Jura, Scotland, 6 July 1982; profiled to only 40 m because of ship drifting in current; bottom depth 110 m, $\Delta\sigma_T$ (0–40 m) = 0.03 kg m^{-3}.

(b) Strongly salinity stratified (as a result of freshwater input to a small fjordic estuary) : station C5 of Raine & Tett (1984) in Loch Creran, Scotland, 29 November 1983; bottom depth 23 m, $\Delta\sigma_T$ (0–20 m) = 6.3 kg m^{-3}. The downwards increase in density that was due to increasing salinity more than outweighed the slight decrease in density that was due to increasing temperature.

(c) Moderate temperature and salinity stratification at station X8.25 east of Barra Head in the Scottish Outer Hebrides; unpublished data of J. H. Simpson & D. G. Bowers from cruise 9/82 of RRV *Shackleton*; 24 May 1982; bottom depth 132 m, $\Delta\sigma_T$ (5–125 mm) = 0.70 kg m^{-3}. The salinity layering was associated with the mean northwards transport by the Scottish Coastal Current of freshwater runoff on western Britain. Part of the current flows around Barra Head, mixing with and overlying Atlantic water. By this time in late spring the superficial layer of the sea had absorbed sufficient solar heat to show thermal layering whose effect on density reinforced that of the salinity stratification.

(d) Strong temperature stratification (due to summer insolation): station FGO of Simpson et al. (1982) near Scilly Isles, England, 26 July 1979; bottom depth 108 m, $\Delta\sigma_T$ (1–100 m) = 1.80 kg m^{-3}. Some extra stabilisation provided by superficial water of slightly reduced salinity (perhaps resulting from runoff from the Scilly Isles). Isopycnal deep water resulted from strong tidal mixing. To interpolate between chlorophyll samples, the water column has been notionally divided into layers, the boundary between each pair of layers being placed at a temperature half-way between that of the relevant pair of samples.

zooplankton (e.g., Hansen, 1951); it may also provide a region where phytoplankton can enjoy adequate amounts of both light and nutrients (see, e.g., Pingree *et al.*, 1975). Finally, stratification in an estuary often gives a clue to water movement, as discussed below.

Circulation and exchange in estuaries and enclosed seas

The principles of water circulation and mixing in estuaries are described by Bowden in Lauff (1967), Dyer (1973; and in Dyer, 1979), and Officer (1976; and in Ketchum, 1983). Some estuaries are dominated by tidal mixing. These 'well-mixed estuaries' show little vertical stratification but strong horizontal gradients of salinity. A segment of such an estuary can be treated as a box and the rate of replacement of its contents calculated from tidal or salinity data (see Appendix 11.2). The 'flushing time' thus calculated may be compared with the appropriate biological time-scale (see Table 11.1).

Other estuaries show salinity stratification and may be dominated by advection. On tidal ebb and flow, and dispersive turbulence, is superimposed a pattern of directional water movement (see Fig. 11.9) that is driven by density differences and the head of fresh water entering the estuary. The 'two-layer circulation' of such 'partially mixed estuaries' transports plankton or nutrients landwards in the deeper layers and seawards near the surface. A flushing time may be calculated from salinities in the deep and surface layers and information on river input.

Fjords are glacially deepened estuaries, often salinity stratified near their heads and mixed over a shallow entrance sill. They sometimes contain stagnant deep water enriched in nutrients, depleted in oxygen, and avoided by most plankton. See Saelen in Lauff (1967), Edwards & Edelsten (1976), and Gade & Edwards in Freeland, Farmer & Levings (1980).

The salinity layering that can be observed in many fjords (e.g., Fig. 11.9) is usually taken to suggest the presence of a two-layer circulation. This circulation (overlying any stagnant layer) may give way to a tidally alternating flow over sills shallower than the pycnocline depth. In some cases (generally those of fjords with substantial river inflow, such as the Scottish Loch Etive (Wood, Tett & Edwards, 1973)), current measurements have directly confirmed the presence of a seawards flow near the surface and a landwards flow in deep water. Sometimes however the two-layer circulation exists only as a weak flow that is easily lost in the recurring pattern of tidal movement, and a strong wind from the sea can temporarily reverse its direction.

Some outer estuaries behave like coastal seas; others are more complex. Thus, the Firth of Clyde in western Scotland is in some ways fjordic, having

Table 11.1. *Some physical and biological time-scales*

A. Flushing time-scales for estuaries and enclosed seas

Name	Greatest dimension (km)	Flushing time-scale	Reference
Loch Ardbhair, Scotland	1	1–2 days	Gowen, Tett & Jones (1983)
Loch Creran, Scotland	10	6 days (at 2 m)	Landless & Edwards (1976)
Western Dutch Wadden Sea basins	50	5–7 days	Zimmerman (1976)
Bristol Channel, England	120	250 days	Radford (in Joint & Pomeroy, 1981)
Bay of Fundy, North America	250	76 days	Ketchum & Keen (1953)
North Sea	1000	1–2 years	Kautsky (1973)
Mediterranean Sea	3600	80 years	Miller (in Ketchum, 1983)

B. Biological time-scales

Organism	Greatest adult dimension	Time for one generation	Reference
Microplankton	1–200 μm	1–10 days	—
Copepod (Calanus)	4 mm	70 days	Marshall & Orr (1972)
Euphausiid (Meganyctiphanes)	30 mm	1–2 years	Mauchline & Fisher (1969)

'Dilution rate' as defined in Appendix 11.2 has meaning only for a well-mixed body of water. 'Flushing time-scale' is a looser term, and may be thought of as a typical transit time for a packet of water containing some identifiable tracer, such as radio-caesium in the case of the North Sea.

an entrance sill and a substantial input of fresh water at its head, yet it has only weak tidal mixing and its main stratification is thermal during the summer. Dooley (1979) describes it as a 'coastal embayment'. The hydrography of the Baltic Sea (described by Kullenberg in Ketchum, 1983) also shows fjordic features. The Mediterranean Sea is often described as a 'reverse estuary' because it loses more water by evaporation than it gains by freshwater inflow. There is a deep outflow of dense water through the Straits of Gibraltar and a compensatory surface inflow of Atlantic water (Miller in Ketchum, 1983).

Many estuaries are longer than they are wide, and their longitudinal salinity gradients shift with the tide. Lagoons (Barnes, 1980) are another sort of coastal environment, typically being wider than they are long and having a relatively small entrance in relation to their volume. Their longitudinal salinity gradients are generally unperturbed by tides, although tidal mixing may sometimes bring about good flushing, as in the case of the Dutch Wadden Sea (Zimmerman, 1976, 1981). A detailed account of lagoonal mixing theory is provided by Dronkers & Zimmerman (1982).

Flushing times for estuaries, fjords, and lagoons vary from one to several hundred days, and those for coastal seas vary from one to a hundred or more years. Examples are given in Table 11.1, which also cites some relevant biological time-scales. It is apparent that the zooplankton of small and medium-sized estuaries are unlikely to complete their life cycles before they are washed out to sea, unless they can exploit countercurrents (Ketchum, 1954; Barlow, 1955). All but the smallest estuaries flush slowly enough to allow the development of resident phytoplankton populations if other factors are suitable.

Estuaries often contain convergences where flows of sea water and reduced-salinity water meet. Like shelf-sea fronts, such regions may stimulate the growth of plankton, or they may accumulate plankton and detritus by simple physical concentration. Incze & Yentsch (1981) give an example for a New England estuary; see also Simpson & Nunes (1981) concerning the hydrography of small, tidally varying convergences.

Temperature–salinity and related diagrams

When the effects of local heating, cooling, or evaporation are insignificant, temperature and salinity are 'conservative' properties of sea water and can be used as labels. A water *type* is identified by its temperature and salinity, and a water *mass* is the result of mixing between two water types. A temperature–salinity (T–S) diagram serves to identify water types and masses, to which plankton amount and composition can often be related. T–S diagrams are most often applied to sub-surface water masses

Fig. 11.2. Temperature–salinity and chlorophyll–salinity diagrams. The examples use data from a survey by C. Douglas of Loch Creran, a two-basin Scottish sealoch (or small fjordic estuary) on 9 August 1979. (a) A temperature salinity (T–S) diagram : the co-ordinates of each point are the temperature and salinity of individual water samples from the stations whose positions are given in (c). The T–S

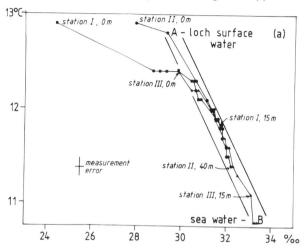

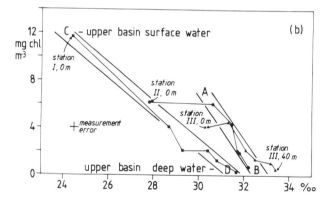

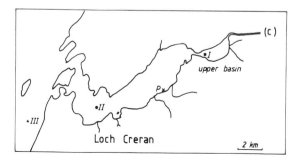

in the open ocean (see, e.g., Johnson & Brinton (1963) on water masses and zooplankton), but are also useful inshore and in estuaries. However, due allowance must be made for the probable lower precision of measurements made with simple equipment, and for some nonconservatism, especially of temperature, in surface waters. In principle all the water in an estuary results from the mixing of just two water types: fresh water and sea water. In practice there are complications, especially if the residence time of water is greater in some parts of the estuary than in others. Fig. 11.2 includes a T–S diagram for a Scottish sea loch. It suggests that most of the water in the loch results from mixing between cold salty water from the sea outside the loch (B) and warm reduced-salinity water from near the surface of the main basin of the loch (A). Some of the points lie off the main sequence, probably as a result of the inflow of cooler river water. Analogous diagrams, e.g., for phytoplankton biomass measured as chlorophyll (see subsequent section), can provide insights, as discussed in the legend to Fig. 11.2.

---

characteristics of most of the water in the loch, and that immediately outside, plot within a single T–S relationship (making due allowance for measurement imprecision). This water is thus held to result from mixing between water type A, found near the surface in the main basin of the loch, and water type B, found at depths of between 20 and 40 m outside the loch. Only water from 0 m depth in the main basin, and 0–3 depth in the upper basin, showed anomalous T–S properties, probably as a result of inflow into the immediate surface water of relatively cold freshwater from rivers and streams. Extra information is provided by the analogous chlorophyll–salinity (chl–S) diagram (b), where each point has co-ordinates corresponding to the chlorophyll concentration and salinity of a single water sample. A chl–S plot is harder to interpret than a T–S diagram; because phytoplankton can grow or die, chlorophyll is not necessarily a conservative property. The plot suggests, however, that there were at least two populations of phytoplankton in the loch at this time. The population exhibiting the CD relationship perhaps resulted from the growth of phytoplankton in upper basin surface water whilst mixing with upper basin deep water (itself ultimately derived from the main basin but presumably remaining long enough in darkness for phytoplankton biomass to decline). Other studies show this mixing to have a time-scale of a few days. The population exhibiting the AB relationship perhaps resulted from the growth near, but not at, the surface of the main basin, whilst mixing with main basin deep water that was supplied ultimately from intermediate depths outside the loch. An observation from the surface at station II fell within the CD relationship, suggesting that this surface water derived from the outflow of the upper basin, although perhaps with some warming, since (a) shows station II to have been warmer than station I at the corresponding salinity. AB and CD populations might be expected to differ in species composition.

Investigating hydrography in relation to plankton

The preceding sections point to the need to understand the often complex hydrography of an estuary or coastal sea before commencing a survey of the plankton. In addition to the scientific literature, charts, tidal atlases, and tide tables should be consulted. Given tidal velocities, it may be possible to use the model of Simpson & Hunter (see Simpson, Hughes & Morris, 1977; Pingree & Griffiths, 1978) to predict regions of stratification and mixing. In conjunction with estimates of volume, tidal data can be used to estimate a flushing time for an estuary (see Appendix 11.2). Maps of the land catchment should also be consulted, and can be used in conjunction with rainfall data, corrected for evaporation, to estimate freshwater inflow into the estuary, if the main river is not routinely gauged.

Furthermore, hydrographic observations should be made routinely as part of a plankton survey. Standard oceanographic methods are reviewed in Pickard & Emery (1982), and Kjerfve (in Dyer, 1979) describes the measurement of temperature, salinity, and currents in estuaries. In many estuaries there are large gradients of salinity and temperature, and in these cases inexpensive, battery-operated, temperature–salinity probes allow physical observations to be made prior to biological sampling at each station. The readings of these probes should be checked occasionally against a good mercury-in-glass thermometer and a salinity standard (e.g., 35 g of analar sodium chloride per litre of water to make enough salt solution to cover the probe).

In outer estuaries and in some fjords and coastal seas, salinity gradients are less, but their determination by simple probes is still possible if the probes are frequently calibrated against salinities of discrete samples determined in the laboratory with a precision salinometer. Because such probes compute salinity from measurements of conductivity and temperature, it will probably be found that the relationship between true salinity and that determined by the probe is complex and temperature dependent. Calibration data should thus be examined thoughtfully.

The construction of density profiles for, or the identification of water types in, many coastal seas requires salinity and temperature measurements of a precision and accuracy that exceeds the specification of simple probes. It is unlikely that a biological survey will be able to maintain and deploy the sophisticated conductivity–temperature–depth measuring instruments needed for such precise work, except through collaboration with physical oceanographers. However, an alternative is to use reversing thermometers for *in situ* temperature and to return water samples to the laboratory for precision salinometer measurement.

Biological surveys are also unlikely to be able to deploy recording current meters at the sites of their investigation. Although it may be necessary to deduce mean flows from salinity distributions, free-floating or tethered drogues provide a simple alternative for estimating short-term currents. Their use is described by Pipkin *et al.* (1977) and by Landless & Edwards (1976). The latter also describe other simple means for studying hydrography in nearshore waters.

Information on flushing and tidal movement can be used to estimate the best temporal and spatial intervals for sampling. There is little point in siting stations closer together than the horizontal tidal amplitude, unless it is possible always to sample at the same state of the tide. Frequency of sampling should be determined by the fastest time-scale of interest. Thus, an estuary with a flushing time of 7 days should be sampled at least once a week. In larger estuaries and coastal seas, sampling frequency is more often set by the time taken for an interesting organism to grow to maturity and reproduce; several samples should be taken during this period.

Further help in locating stations can be gained from maps of salinity and temperature distribution. Stations should be closer together in regions of stronger gradient. Finally, water samples should not be taken at equal depth intervals, but should relate to the density structure of the water column, more samples being taken in gradient than in mixed regions.

Much of the advice in this section follows from the premises that physical data can be collected more easily and cheaply than most biological data, and that the distribution of plankton depends largely on physical processes. Taken to the limit, this approach would use biological observation only to calibrate some physical yardstick, which would then be used for the majority of measurements.

Plankton

General

Hardy (1970) gives a non-technical introduction to marine plankton and its ecology; more advanced accounts are given by Raymont (1980, 1983), and the plankton of estuaries is reviewed by Miller and by Smayda (in Ketchum, 1983).

The plankton is conventionally divided into plant and animal categories: phytoplankton and zooplankton. This distinction, carried through into research philosophy and sampling methods, has led to the neglect of creatures that nowadays are increasingly thought of importance in marine ecology and especially in coastal and estuarine waters. These are the microscopic organisms that feed on the smallest members of the phytoplankton; also, their relatives that exploit the abundance of particulate and dissolved organic materials in estuaries. 'Microplankton' will be used to refer loosely to these pelagic protists, as well as to planktonic algae and microzooplankton of a size (less than a few hundred micrometres) that is better sampled with a water bottle than a net.

Phytoplankton

The marine phytoplankton include at least eight classes of the algae. The classes are distinguishable by photosynthetic pigment content and by fine structure, and recent advances in pigment methods and electron microscopy have both clarified and complicated their taxonomy. Consult Raymont (1980) for an introduction. Despite this diversity, the algae of the phytoplankton have in common their small size (most are less than 100 μm; many are less than 20 μm; some are less than 1 μm) and their ability to obtain their energy supply from light through photosynthesis mediated by chlorophyll *a* and to obtain their supply of carbon, nitrogen, and phosphorus almost entirely from inorganic sources. Unlike seaweeds and land plants, the cells of phytoplankton rarely specialise. Instead they float singly or in short chains or small colonies, held together by threads, spines, or jelly. Planktonic algae reproduce mainly asexually, each cell dividing into two once a day, or faster, when conditions are favourable. Such doubling produces rapid and exponential growth of phytoplankton populations, leading, if sustained, to a 'bloom' or visible discolouration of the sea. Generally, however, shortage of light or mineral nutrients slows growth, and thus blooms are uncommon.

For survey purposes it is convenient to adopt categories based mainly on ecology (see Fig. 11.3). Diatoms such as *Skeletonema* (see Fig. 11.6) and *Thalassiosira* are common in temperate coastal waters in spring and at other times of year when the water column is mixed. Diatoms require silicate for their cell walls, which are often spiny. In many cases cells are linked into short chains. Dinoflagellates are characterised by a pair of flagella, generally one transverse and one longitudinal, and some can swim at 1–2 m/hour. They are usually larger than diatoms, and more varied in their nutrition. Some, such as *Gonyaulax*, contain photosynthetic pigments and can, except for a need for organic vitamins, grow like other phytoplankton on sunlight, carbon dioxide, and mineral salts. Those that lack chlorophyll are discussed in a later subsection. Many dinoflagellates possess an obvious covering or 'theca' of plates of cellulose, often drawn out into horns or spines; others, however, have no obvious theca, and are called 'naked'. Special features of dinoflagellates include their ability, in some cases, to form 'red tides' (Ryther, 1955), or to bioluminesce (Tett & Kelly, 1973),

Fig. 11.3. Typical phytoplankton from coastal and estuarine waters. Drawn as far as possible from living material. (a) Diatoms : (1) *Rhizosolenia fragillima*; (2) *Thalassiosira nordenskioldii*; (3) *Chaetoceros* sp. (probably *cinctum*); (4) *Chaetoceros didymum*; (5) *Eucampia zodiacus*; (6) *Nitzschia delicatissima*; see also *Skeletonema costatum* in Fig. 11.6. (b) Dinoflagellates (note smaller scale) : (7) *Ceratium furca*; (8) *Gonyaulax spinifera*; (9) 'spiniferites' cyst of *Gonyaulax* sp.; (10) *Prorocentrum micans*; (11) *Katodinium rotundatum*; (12) *Gyrodinium aureolum*. (*c*) Flagellates and other small phytoplankters; (13) the silicoflagellate *Dictyocha specula*; (14) two euglenoids, *Eutreptiella* sp.; (15) a red cryptomonad, possibly *Plagioselmis* sp.; (16) the flagellate *Tetraselmis* sp.; (17) various small unidentified flagellates, 2–5 m in size; (18) small coccoid phytoplankters similar in appearance to the chlorophyte *Nannochloris*

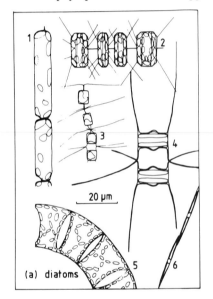

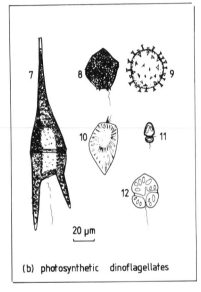

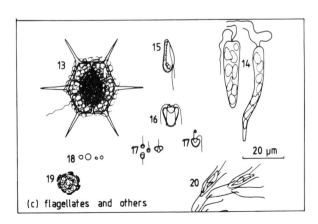

and some produce substances toxic to wild and farmed marine animals, not to mention humans (see Taylor & Seliger, 1979; for more recent examples see, Jones *et al.*, 1982 and Roberts *et al.*, 1983). Many of the remaining groups of planktonic algae have in common small size, fragility, and the possession of one to four flagella at some stage in their life; these are conveniently lumped together as 'small flagellates'. Some species or groups stand out from the tiny monads that often pass unnoticed in many phytoplankton samples. A silicoflagellate such as *Dictyocha* has a six-rayed silicified skeleton; coccolithophorids such as *Coccolithus* have a covering of calcareous plates; the flagellate *Dinobryon* occupies colonies of siliceous vase-like cases, and *Phaeocystis* forms gelatinous colonies; euglenoids such as *Eutreptiella* are larger than most other flagellates and are common in estuaries.

Blue-green algae or cyanobacteria are prokaryotes, organisms without well-defined nucleus or chloroplasts (Fay, 1983). Their taxonomy is problematic and their identification is difficult. Only a few truly marine species are known, most of which are reviewed by Humm & Wicks (1980). *Oscillatoria* and *Trichodesmium* are typical examples of filamentous marine and brackish-water blue-greens. Some of these colonial forms can obtain organic nitrogen by the direct reduction of dissolved nitrogen gas, and thus may bloom when phosphorus alone is enhanced.

It has recently been discovered that very small, coccoid cyanobacteria (species of *Synechococcus*) are abundant in many oceans and some coastal seas. Equally small eukaryotes, both coccoid and flagellated, may also be important in this 'picoplankton' (Johnson & Sieburth, 1979, 1982).

Being photosynthetic, phytoplankton can grow only in the illuminated region near the surface of the sea. The 'euphotic zone' extends to the depth at which the plants respire in 24 hours the same exact amount of organic material as they manufacture during daytime photosynthesis. Where the euphotic zone extends to the sea-bed, as in many shallow coastal and estuarine areas, or where the shore is exposed by the retreating tide, benthic microalgae (see Chapter 4) grow in addition to seaweeds. Thus, the phytoplankton of estuaries and coastal waters often includes benthic diatoms swept into the plankton by tidal or storm turbulence. It has only recently been appreciated that phytoplankters sometimes sojourn on the sea-bed; thus many dinoflagellates are now known to possess long-lived benthic cysts (Dale, 1983). Anderson & Morel (1979) describe the seeding of red tides by such cysts.

---

sp. or the cyanobacterium *Synechococcus* sp.; (19) the coccolithophorid *Emiliana huxleyi*; (20) a chain of cases, some with cells, of the chrysophyte *Dinobryon* sp., perhaps originating from freshwater.

Zooplankton

Almost all animal phyla have members that pass some part of their lives in the water column. It is, however, necessary to distinguish between zooplankton, whose swimming ability is absent or limited to swarming or diurnal vertical migration, and 'nekton', larger animals that can swim

Fig. 11.4. Typical zooplankton from coastal and estuarine waters. (a) The euphausiid *Thysanoessa raschi*; (b) the mysid *Leptomysis*; (c) the chaetognath *Sagitta setosa*; (d) the ctenophore *Pleurobrachia*; (e) egg of cod, *Gadus morhua*; (f) the copepod *Acartia clausii*; (g, h) planktonic larvae of the barnacle *Semibalanus balanoides* and a brittle-star *Ophiothrix*. (After Sars, 1903; Einarsson, 1945; Newell & Newell, 1977; and various ICES (International Commission for the Exploration of the Sea) Fiche d'Identification.)

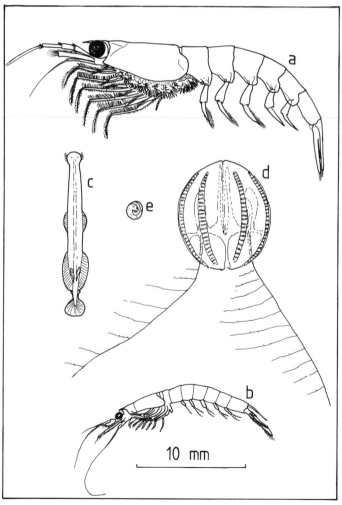

10 mm

significant horizontal distances. In principle the distribution of zooplankton should be governed by water movements, and that of nekton by their swimming behaviour, but in practice, and especially in estuaries, the distinction is often blurred. The important features of zooplankton, when compared with phytoplankton, are their feeding and migratory behaviour, and their life histories. These features are associated with the larger size and longer lives of zooplankton. Five ecological categories are worth distinguishing.

The copepod *Calanus* (see Marshall & Orr, 1972) is typical of the permanent plankton of near-surface waters. Feeding on phytoplankton, adults (4 mm) and young stages are found in or near the euphotic zone at night, sometimes migrating deeper during the day. In British waters *Calanus* goes through two generations in a year, overwintering in small numbers as the last larval stage. In early spring these young copepods mature and lay eggs, giving rise to the next generation. This feeds on the

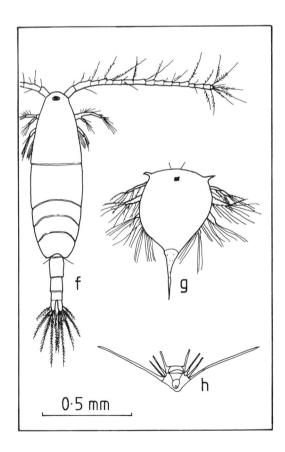

diatoms of the spring bloom, grows to maturity in about 70 days, and produces the generation that survives the next winter. *Calanus* or *Calanus*-like copepods are common in the plankton of coastal seas; in estuaries they are replaced by the related genera *Acartia* and *Eurytemora*. These lay resting eggs that sink to the sea-bed, thus avoiding being flushed out of the estuary during winter (C. Miller in Ketchum, 1983). Also found in the permanent plankton of the euphotic zone is the arrow-worm *Sagitta* (up to 10 mm), a transparent carnivore able to seize its copepod or fish larval prey with the ring of hooked bristles around its mouth (see Fig. 11.4).

Sound-scattering layers in the deep sea are made up of large crustaceans and small fish and squid that migrate vertically, perhaps over hundreds of metres, in response to diel changes in illumination. Such larger zooplankton are uncommon in most shelf seas, but some species occur abundantly in fjordic regions where water depths often exceed 100 m and sometimes 500 m. These include euphausiids such *Thysanoessa* and *Meganyctiphanes*, whose larvae may sometimes be abundant in near-surface plankton. Euphausiid biology is reviewed by Mauchline & Fisher (1969) and Mauchline (1980*b*).

The large jellyfish and smaller hydromedusae, the sea-gooseberries and other ctenophores, are planktonic carnivores that take prey with tentacles and have bodies that are 'blown up' with jelly to aid buoyancy. Most planktonic coelenterates have a benthic stage in their life cycle. Coastal waters of high salinity – and many fjords fall into this category – often contain many small jellyfish, released by the benthic phase, in early summer. The larger jellies are found later, further out to sea. Ctenophores are fully pelagic, but species of *Pleurobrachia*, *Mnemiopsis*, and *Bolinopsis* are common in the plankton of coastal waters, large estuaries, and fjords. See, e.g., Kremer & Nixon (1976).

During spring in temperate coastal waters the zooplankton is augmented by the larvae of benthic animals and fish. Excluding the young fish, these temporary zooplankton are less than 1 mm in size, and usually metamorphose and settle to the sea-bed within a few weeks. At this stage in their lives their main control over their fate is their ability to postpone metamorphosis if conditions are unfavourable. Unless they are able to exploit a two-layer circulation, temporary zooplankton released into the waters of small estuaries must often be swept out to sea before settlement. They are replaced by planktonic stages carried into the estuary from the coastal sea. Ketchum (1954) contains an early discussion of this problem, and particular accounts of larval recruitment in estuaries are given by Wood & Hargis (1971) Sandifer (1975), Boicourt, Cronin & Forward and Epifania & Dittel (both in Kennedy, 1982), and Johnson & Gonor (1982).

The final category of zooplankton includes many mysid, amphipod, and decapod crustaceans. These euryhaline animals, 2–20 mm long, dominate the plankton of estuaries and the plankton over sandy beaches. They live on or in the sediment during the day or when the tide is out, swimming into the water at night or when the tide returns. This, and their swimming behaviour, makes sampling very difficult. Mauchline (1980*b*) reviews the biology of mysids.

Small heterotrophs

Heterotrophs get their energy and organic material from sources other than sunlight and inorganic compounds. All metazoan zooplankton, feeding as they do on each other or on protists, are particle-ingesting heterotrophs; however, a wider range of nutritional types is found amongst micro-organisms. Protozoans such as ciliates take food particles into vacuoles and digest them there; some zooflagellates are capable of extracellular digestion, and many fungi and bacteria are nourished by dissolved organic substances. The bacterial and fungal plankton are dealt with elsewhere in this handbook, but it is necessary here to describe briefly the role that marine planktonic bacteria and protozoans (and metazoans of similar sizes and habits, such as rotifers) play in coastal and estuarine food webs.

Recent investigations have shown that algae less than 2 μm in size, collectively termed 'picoplankton', are common in both oceanic and estuarine waters. It is thought that they may be responsible for a substantial part of pelagic primary production, a part that is grazed mainly by particle-eating protozoans including zooflagellates and ciliates (see, e.g., Landry, Haas & Fagerness, 1984). Some protozoans are also known to eat larger phytoplankton. See Fig. 11.5.

In the open sea bacteria may be nourished by the dissolved organics that are excreted by phytoplankton during photosynthesis or leaked when the algal cells are smashed by a grazer. A more plentiful supply of dissolved and particulate organic material is provided in estuaries and lagoons by the decay of terrestrial and littoral plants. In these environments much energy and nutrients flow through the bacteria and protozoans of the 'detrital food-chain', probably rejoining the classical marine food web through estuarine crustaceans that feed on the protozoans. Newell, Lucas & Linley (1981) describe the way that bacteria might channel material into the food chain. Fenchel (1982*b*) describes the importance of small heterotrophic flagellates, including the collared choanoflagellates, as grazers of bacteria. Williams (1981) discusses the ideas associated with food webs that involve dissolved organic matter and bacteria; an important point is that the biomass in this 'microcyle' can turn over very quickly, perhaps in less than a day.

At the apex of protozoan food webs are ciliates and the larger heterotrophic dinoflagellates. Tintinnids are cased ciliates that are typical of high salinities and feed mainly on phytoplankton. Naked oligotrich ciliates, characterised by specialised ciliary fields and rounded bodies, are

Fig. 11.5. Typical planktonic protozoa from coastal and estuarine waters. (a) The naked dinoflagellate *Gyrodinium*; (b) the tintinnid ciliate *Heliocostomella* with animal retracted inside its case; (c) the ciliate *Mesodinium* with symbionts; (d, e) the choanoflagellates *Diaphanoeca and Codosiga*; (f, g) the zooflagellates *Pseudobodo* and *Paraphysomonas*. (From living and preserved material, and after Taylor, Blackburn & Blackburn, 1971 and Fenchel, 1982a.)

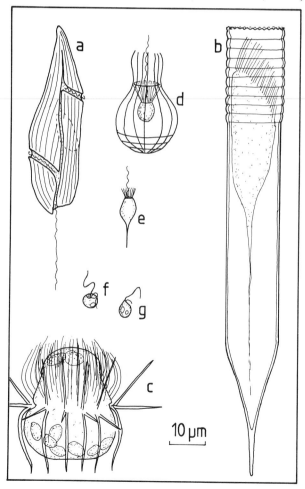

common in estuaries with a high organic loading, and probably feed on zooflagellates and bacteria. Benthic ciliates are sometimes found in the plankton of disturbed estuaries; they are characteristically flattened, sometimes elongated, and often more uniformly ciliated. The common pelagic ciliate *Mesodinium* is worth noting: it contains symbiotic algae and can perhaps obtain food by photosynthesis as well as phagotrophy. It occurs in a wide range of near-shore environments, and sometimes forms red tides (e.g., Holm-Hansen, Taylor & Barsdate 1970).

The proceedings of a symposium on 'Marine pelagic protozoa and microzooplankton ecology', edited by Bougis (1982), contains much useful information on microheterotroph biology and on methods for their observation and identification.

The plankton of estuaries and coastal waters

The plankton of coastal seas is, typically, greater in biomass and lower in diversity than that of the open ocean. It contains few large, vertically migrating zooplankton but more benthic larvae and young fish. The microzooplankton is probably richer in ciliates exploiting the detritus food chain, and there are probably fewer species of photosynthetic dinoflagellate and of the pelagic protozoan radiolarians and foraminiferans. Various authors have listed species of phytoplankton and zooplankton considered to be 'neritic' or typical of nearshore waters, as opposed to 'oceanic', and some of these (including members of the arrow-worm genus *Sagitta*) are used as 'indicator species' for water masses (see Fraser, 1973 or Newell & Newell, 1977, concerning British waters). But in general the plankters of coastal waters are a mixed lot, some originating in the ocean and some in estuaries, in addition to those that pass their entire lives in shelf seas. See, e.g., Cox & Wiebe (1979) concerning the origin of plankton in the middle Atlantic Bight of North America.

The plankton of deep fjords may be richer than that of adjacent coastal seas. However, the density of estuarine zooplankton is usually reduced by the stresses imposed by low and fluctuating salinities, shallow waters, and high turbidities. Flushing both removes estuarine forms and injects coastal species, but the latter may not survive estuarine conditions. Finally, a change in food type may be as important as the changes in other factors in regulating the species composition of estuarine plankton. The open sea is dominated by phytoplanktonic production, but in many estuaries the main source of organic material is detritus of terrestrial or marine macrophytic origin. In most estuaries the relative contribution of phytoplankton to total primary production is low; in some turbid estuaries, such as the inner part of the Bristol Channel (Joint & Pomeroy, 1981), the absolute contribution of phytoplankton is also small. Further out to sea, where tidal mixing is less strong and turbidity and the supply of detritus is reduced, the relative contribution of phytoplankton increases, and their absolute contribution may be enhanced by mineral nutrients from the inner estuary.

Matthews & Heimdal (in Freeland et al., 1980) discuss the differences between the food chains of small and large fjords, which in some ways mimic, respectively, those of estuaries and the open sea. The phytoplankton of estuaries and small fjords is often dominated by small euryhaline diatoms such as *Skeletonema*, by photosynthetic euglenoid flagellates such as *Eutreptiella*, or by small photosynthetic dinoflagellates such as *Heterocapsa*. Heterotrophic flagellates and ciliates are often important. The zooplankton (see McLusky, 1981) is often dominated by copepods like *Acartia* and *Eurytemora*, which probably exploit the detritus food chain, by benthic larvae, and by amphipods and mysids, which may be exploiting benthic microalgae and detritus in addition to planktonic food.

At the head of estuaries is a zone variously called or comprising the 'freshwater–brackish interface' or the 'turbidity maximum'. It is a region of concentration of detritus as well as of inorganic particulate material. The large microbial populations sometimes found in this zone may channel energy to estuarine zooplankton through bacteria-feeding ciliates.

The phytoplankton of some low-salinity 'inland seas', such as the northern Baltic and the Gulf of Finland, is dominated by blue-green algae. See Smayda (in Ketchum, 1983).

Seasonal cycles

It is well known that most temperate coastal waters show an annual cycle of plankton standing crop and production. This is explained by the requirements of phytoplankton for light and mineral nutrients. The plants grow little in winter because of dull illumination. At this time, however, storms mix nutrients as well as phytoplankton throughout the water column. In spring, increasing illumination, decreasing mixing, and ample nutrients provide ideal conditions for the 'spring increase'. When nutrients run out the extra phytoplankton biomass is grazed down or washed out. If the water column stratifies during the summer (because of surface heating or freshwater inflow), the euphotic zone may remain depleted of nutrients and hence support little phytoplankton production. Any physical process that brings, or any anthropogenic input of, nutrients to the near-surface waters might cause summer blooms. However, as discussed by Pingree et al. (1975) in the context of frontal production, the

Fig. 11.6. Seasonal cycles of autotrophs and heterotrophs. The autotroph is the common nearshore diatom *Skeletonema costatum*, which like many other planktonic diatoms forms auxospores as a means of increasing cell size. The heterotrophs are pelagic ciliates, probably mainly the oligotrichs *Strobilidium* spp. and *Lohmaniella* spp. Water samples were taken weekly from depths of 1–2 m from a pier (marked P in Fig. 11.1c) in Loch Creran, Scotland, whose flushing time is about a week. They were preserved with acidic Lugol's iodine and counted by the sedimentation method described in the text. Each point represents one sample, except where there are several points for one day – these represent replicate counts. The curves were drawn from Fourier series fitted to the data using programs supplied by Hewlett Packard for their 9825 microcomputer. Each series has ten pairs of coefficients, and so high-frequency variation is smoothed out; the fastest cycle that can be represented has a period of about 35 days. See also Tett & Edwards, 1984. Note the geometric scale for abundance. The ciliates show little trace of seasonality, probably because they tap a detritus food chain, in this case augmented by organic waste from a seaweed-processing factory. *Skeletonema* has displayed a marked spring peak in each of the 10 years that I have sampled the loch; the exact time-course of the peak varies however from year to year, and in some years (as in 1979) the diatom has also bloomed during the summer.

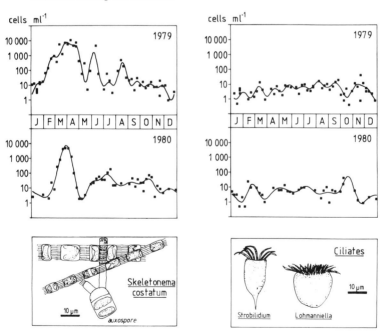

balance among mixing, illumination, and nutrient supply is a delicate one, and needs to be understood in detail if such blooms are to be predicted.

Zooplankton often follows this phytoplankton cycle. Few herbivorous plankters overwinter successfully. In early spring their eggs hatch and larvae grow; benthic and fish larvae join the plankton, perhaps triggered by, or in some way timed to coincide with, the ample food provided by the spring bloom. In summer, zooplankton biomass falls below spring levels, for benthic larvae have settled and fish larvae have grown up. Many of the remaining herbivores have been eaten by carnivores such as jellyfish and sea-gooseberries. Raymont (1980) has a fuller account of the seasonal cycles of phytoplankton and the impact of grazing upon them, and Raymont (1983) describes zooplankton cycles.

Seasonal cycles may be less obvious, or may peak at a different time of year, in estuaries dominated by the detritus food chain. Thus Fig. 11.6 compares the annual cycle in a Scottish sea loch of the phototrophic diatom *Skeletonema* with that of ciliates presumed to be feeding on heterotrophic flagellates and bacteria.

Strong tidal mixing and turbidity in nearshore waters and estuaries can delay the start of the spring bloom, or may altogether prevent it. In the relatively clear, salinity-stratified waters of Scottish sea lochs, however, the bloom begins 1–2 months earlier than in other coastal waters of the British Isles (Tett & Wallis, 1978).

Many estuaries and fjords experience seasonal variations in flushing as a result of seasonal variations in rainfall or snowmelt. These changes may strongly influence the seasonal cycles of plankton composition, biomass, and production, as demonstrated in the reviews by Smayda and by Miller (in Ketchum, 1983).

Identification

Many genera, and some species, of plankton are widespread in their distribution, and the number of known species is small compared with, say, insects. Nevertheless, identification and taxonomy can be one of the most difficult areas of plankton research. Diatoms, dinoflagellates, tintinnid ciliates, and crustacean zooplankton can be identified from hard parts, are well described in identification guides, and belong to groups whose taxonomy is substantially agreed upon by the relevant experts. However, many protozoans and phytoflagellates are too small and fragile for proper study with the light microscope and are the subjects of much taxonomic dispute. As a result these are described mainly in a scattered literature. Even where the general taxonomy of a group is stable, specific and sometimes generic names are changed from time to time, and hence names should always be checked in the most recent publications. Regional check-lists and taxonomic catalogues play a useful role in confirming identification.

A guide to identification literature is given in Chapter 14.

Measuring plankton
General

Plankton are, in general, thinly and heterogenously spread through a complex environment. How can one obtain representative samples containing just the right amount of plankton for efficient and effective analysis?

Sampling might be avoidable. For a number of years satellites have provided synoptic maps of sea-surface temperatures, and undulating recorders have provided near-synoptic vertical sections of temperature. Using sensors of sea colour, or sensors that respond to chlorophyll fluorescence, these devices can sometimes provide detailed pictures of phytoplankton distribution (see, e.g., Denman & Mackas in Steele, 1978; Smith & Baker, 1982; Le Fevre *et al.*, 1983). But for biological purposes the techniques remain experimental and expensive, and require calibration against simpler methods involving sampling. The measurement of *in situ* chlorophyll fluorescence, from ships underway or in water pumped from a profile of the euphotic zone, may be possible in surveys. It is discussed on p. 313. Pugh (in Steele, 1978) describes a particle counter for shipboard use in plankton surveys.

Once taken, samples must be analysed. Preservation is necessary if this is delayed. Analysis may involve physical or chemical determinations of biomass or composition, or identification and enumeration of species. Finally, the results of analysis must be related back to the sea from which the samples were taken, with due attention to the effects of sampling and measurement errors and artefacts. Some of the problems arising from these effects are discussed in this section and some are discussed in the next section.

Two handbooks, both in the UNESCO series of Monographs on Oceanographic Methodology, are essential works of reference when measuring plankton. They are the guide *Zooplankton Fixation and Preservation* compiled by SCOR (Scientific Committee on Ocean Research) Working Group 23 and edited by H. F. Steedman (1976), and the *Phytoplankton Manual* compiled by SCOR Working Group 33 and edited by A. R. Sournia (1978). In addition, the conclusions of earlier SCOR working parties in *Zooplankton Sampling*, edited by D. J. Tranter & J. H. Fraser (1968) are useful, although they are becoming outdated. These

SCOR-UNESCO handbooks should always be consulted when further details are necessary. Morris (1983) contains a useful and detailed account of methods for use with zooplankton of larger estuaries, and Barnes (1980) describes simple methods for use in shallow lagoons. Finally, the handbooks of chemical methods by Strickland & Parsons (1972) and Parsons, Maita & Lalli (1984) are also useful.

Fig. 11.7. Nets and their operation. (a) A modified Working Party 2 (WP-2) net used for vertical tows from depths of less than 200 m to the surface. Hoisting rope or wire (*a*) attaches by swivelling shackle (*b*) to net bridle (*c*) which in turn is shackled to ring (*d*) with internal diameter 0.57 m (giving mouth area of 0.5 m²); non-filtering collar (*e*) attaches net to this ring; the net itself is made of nylon mesh with 200-μm aperture and comprises tubular (*f*) and conical (*g*) sections; the latter attaches by a collar (*h*) to a detachable bucket (*i*) with several filtering windows. See Tranter & Fraser (1968) for further details. (b) A Gulf III net, used for horizontal or oblique tows at 2–3 m sec⁻¹. Wire (*j*) attaches to the net's metal case, which comprises a main part (*k*) and a detachable rear part (*l*). A 20-kg depressor, shaped to give negative lift, balances the upwards force on the net resulting from the drag of the water and the pull of the towing cable. The case contains a net (*n*) of non-corroding metal mesh with 200-μm aperture; volume filtered is measured by front (*o*) and rear (*p*) flowmeters. (After Gehringer, 1952.)

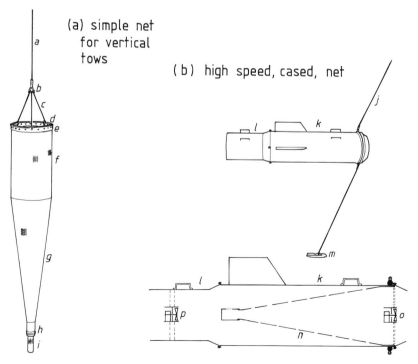

(a) simple net
for vertical
tows

(b) high speed, cased, net

Sampling

Sampling devices include nets, pumps, or water-bottles, all of which can be avoided by nervous animals. Apart from such losses, water-bottles and pumps capture everything present in the volume trapped within the bottle or sucked into the pump inlet. Water-bottles take an instantaneous sample of limited volume at a fixed depth; pumps can be used to acquire large volumes of water, from which the plankton must, however, be extracted using netting or filters. Pumps can be used to profile the distributions of organisms in the water column; this may be time consuming if the residence time of water in the tubing that connects the sampling inlet with the surface is long. Nets are convenient to use and filter large volumes of water; however, what they catch depends not only on their mesh size but also on how quickly they clog.

Simple conical nets (Fig. 11.7) can be used for qualitative sampling of the smaller zooplankton or larger phytoplankton. For the former, a net of diameter 0.5 metre and mesh size 0.1–0.2 mm is adequate; for the phytoplankton a net of diameter 20–30 cm and mesh 30–60 μm will serve. For the phytoplankton, the net can be towed by hand, from a pier perhaps, for a few metres. For the zooplankton, the net should be towed behind a boat for 5–20 minutes at a speed of 20–50 cm/sec, or hoisted vertically at the same speed. Larger zooplankton, such as euphausiids, are best taken in a coarser net of diameter 1–2 m and mesh 1–2 mm, towed at about 1 m/sec.

A water-bottle is the simplest device for quantitative sampling of phytoplankton and microzooplankton; bottle types are shown in Fig. 11.8. Simple 'opening' bottles are adequate for sampling down to about 20 m; the bottle is lowered with the bung(s) in place, and a tug on the rope removes them. Landless & Edwards (1976) describe a sampler that can be constructed with the simplest of facilities. 'Closing' bottles are lowered clamped to a smooth wire; a metal weight that is slid down the wire triggers spring-loaded stoppers to close the bottle at a suitable depth. A closing bottle may itself drop a weight, thus triggering bottles further down the wire. Bottles of 0.5–2 l are convenient for phytoplankton work; larger bottles of up to 20 l can be obtained, but are unwieldy. For samples of more than a few litres, a pump is best. Sampling depths should be related to water layering, as discussed in the hydrographic section (p. 281).

Quantitative sampling of zooplankton poses many difficulties, which are discussed by Tranter & Fraser (1968) and in Morris (1983). In coastal waters a medium-mesh tow-net of the design recommended by SCOR–UNESCO Working Party 2 (Tranter & Fraser, 1968, pp. 152–9) or the IMER (Institute of Marine Environmental Research) Estuarine Ecology

Group (Morris, 1983, p. 147) can be used to sample the copepods, arrow-worms, temporary plankton, and jellyfish of the euphotic zone. These nets have mesh apertures of 0.2–0.3 mm and mouth diameters of 45–50 cm. Since they can rapidly become clogged with phytoplankton, their filtering performance should be monitored by a flowmeter placed eccentrically inside the mouth of the net. The propellers of such meters complete one turn when moved through the water a distance L specified by the manufacturer's calibration. If at the end of the tow the meter records

Fig. 11.8. Water sampling bottles. (a) A 'closing' bottle of the UK National Institute of Oceanography pattern. The bottle is fastened to a wire cable by clamp (a) and spring-loaded clip (b), and lowered with the end-caps (d) raised. A messenger weight striking the upper arm (c) releases the spring-loaded caps, which close, sealing the water-bottle. The lower arm (e) falls, dropping a second messenger that may have been resting on it. The cable is unwound from a winch (f), which may be hand- or power-driven, and passes over a measuring wheel (g) indicating length of wire out and hence depths of sampling. Bottle (h) has been closed and has released a messenger (i) which is travelling towards the next (and still open) bottle (j). (b) An 'opening' bottle of the Collins Laboratories pattern. The bottle is lowered with stoppers (b) in place, a weighted chamber (d) ensuring that the sampler is heavier than water. A tug on rope (e) (which should be marked at metre intervals) extends spring (c) against the inertia of the water-bottle and hence, via strings (a), pulls out the stoppers and allows water to enter. The unstoppered holes are small and, after filling, the bottle exchanges an insignificant amount of sample as it is pulled rapidly to the surface.

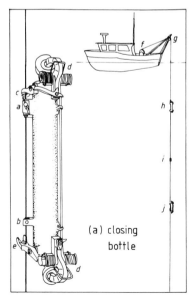

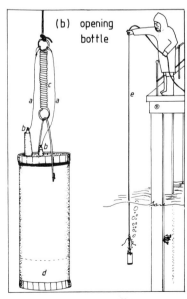

N turns and the net's mouth area is A, the volume filtered is NAL. NL is often less than the linear distance towed. Flowmeter technology and calibration is further discussed in Morris (1983).

Figure 11.7 illustrates such a net and possible towing arrangements. Towing speed should be 0.5–1 m/sec when towed horizontally or obliquely, and as close to this as possible when hoisted vertically. Oblique tows are achieved by steadily reducing the length of towing cable. Unless the net can be fitted with a recording or acoustic transmitting depth sensor (e.g., Baker, Clarke & Harris, 1973), the depth of tow must be estimated from the angle and length of the towing cable. This can rarely be done accurately, and to avoid the net striking the bottom, its depth should always be overestimated.

Cased high-speed nets, such as the Gulf III (Gehringer, 1962; Southward, 1962) or the Lowestoft sampler (Beverton & Tungate, 1967), can be used for quantitative sampling of larger and more active zooplankton, including larval fish. Rectangular midwater trawls (e.g., Baker *et al.*, 1973) have been increasingly used for this purpose; however, they are often so big as to be usable only from vessels with heavy lifting gear.

Nets can be fitted with closing devices, as in the case of the Working Party 2 net, the Bongo net of McGowan & Brown (1966), or the widely used Clarke-Bumpus sampler (Clarke & Bumpus, 1940; see also Morris, 1983). The Hardy–Longhurst sampler (Longhurst *et al.*, 1966) replaces the cod-end of a net by a continuously moving gauze, and thus allows multiple and serial sampling. But as net technology grows more sophisticated, its cost and complexity puts it beyond the reach of many surveys. Pumps suitable for surface or submerged operation have, however, become smaller, cheaper, and more reliable of recent years, and now offer a better way of sampling the small and medium-sized zooplankton of coastal waters and estuaries. Sample volumes and depths can be measured precisely; however, sufficient pumping time must be allowed before collection of material from the surface outlet, in order to flush the submerged tubing. A simple pumping system for use from a small boat could employ a lead-acid accumulator powered pump that sucked water through reinforced garden hose, the outflow being passed through netting of suitable mesh and the water being collected in a larger container to estimate the volume sampled. Such pumps deliver a few litres per minute, a flow rate suitable for sampling microplankton and most larval zooplankton. Ships with a good electricity supply can operate powerful submersible electric pumps that are capable of sending many litres per minute from depths of 50–100 m, and are thus adequately able to sample most zooplankters. The main difficulties with such a system will probably stem not from the pump but from the need to deploy lengths of wide-bore hose tubing from a ship at sea. Pump sampling systems are discussed by Beers (in Sournia, 1978), with particular reference to that system of Beers, Stewart & Strickland (1967). Waite & O'Grady (1980) describe a lightweight, battery-operated system that combines a pump and a tow-net in a single submersible unit, and Miller & Judkins (1981) describe two high-flow systems for coastal studies.

Sample treatment

It is always desirable to examine living material but it is usually necessary to preserve material for later analysis. Analysis may involve physical or chemical analysis of total biomass or some component thereof, or the identification and enumeration of the components of the plankton. Although these alternatives will be discussed in more detail below, it is necessary to anticipate the method of analysis when deciding on sample treatment.

One-litre plastic-jacketed vacuum flasks are good for transporting living material from water-bottle or pump samples; net-concentrated plankton should be copiously diluted with sea water. Phytoplankton and planktonic protozoa for microscopic analysis can be preserved with a small amount of buffered formalin (enough to bring the sample to 1% formalin or 0.4% formaldehye; good for coccolithophorids and many dinoflagellates) or with acidic Lugol's iodine (1%, or enough to turn a sample golden-brown; good for diatoms and small flagellates). Acidic Lugol's is made by adding 50 g of iodine and 100 ml of glacial acetic acid to a solution of 100 g potassium iodide in 1 l of distilled water. See below concerning formalin.

Preserved microplankton should be kept cool and in tightly closed glass jars with little air space. Lugol-preserved material should be kept in darkness, to prevent photo-oxidation of the iodine. See Sournia (1978) for further discussion of phytoplankton preservation.

Zooplankton can be preserved with buffered formalin, using 1 part of the commercial 40% solution of formaldehyde in water to 9 parts of sea water. This strength of preservative is usually called '10% formalin', although it is only 4% formaldehyde. The plankton should take up no more than a tenth of the volume of liquid, and are best added to the sea water mixture after the formalin, to avoid direct contact between animals and concentrated preservative. Formaldehyde solutions are hazardous to health and should be kept in tightly closed containers. When preserved material is examined, it should be washed free of formalin, and returned to fresh preservative for continued storage. Preservation is improved and handling is rendered more pleasant if, after a few days of fixation, the plankton is transferred to a mixture of 9 parts of sea water and 1 part of the following preservative: 50 ml propylene phenoxatal, 450 ml propylene glycol, and 500 ml of buffered 40% formaldehyde. Formalin is best buffered with borax (excess, or about 20 g/l).

Further details of zooplankton and microplankton preservation are given at length in Steedman (1976).

Finally, zooplankton samples may be conveniently stored frozen if destined for chemical or biomass analysis, and phytoplankton may be frozen on glass-fibre filters for later measurement of chlorophyll; see below. Division of the sample into two or more size classes, by passing it through one or more filters (netting, wire-mesh, or membrane), may be useful at this stage.

Microscopical analysis of microplankton samples

No single method is suitable for all kinds of phytoplankton and microzooplankton. The following sedimentation method is simple in routine use and is adequate for diatoms, most small flagellates, and some armoured dinoflagellates. It requires an inverted microscope.

Twenty to fifty millilitres of water from a sampling bottle or pump are preserved with acidic Lugol's iodine in a small screw-capped glass jar labelled with date, position, and depth of sampling. Although it is best to examine the material within a few weeks of sampling, it may be kept for several years in cool, dark conditions. If opened for sub-sampling, more iodine solution should be added to replace that photo-oxidized. Loss of colour does not necessarily indicate deterioration of the contents, so long as the jar is kept tightly sealed.

Twenty-four hours before analysis, the sample is shaken and a 10 ml sub-sample is pipetted into a sedimentation chamber, whose essential feature is a bottom made of thin, optically plane glass. The chamber is covered to prevent evaporation and placed on or near the stage of an inverted microscope, to allow the microplankton to sink onto the glass bottom. The chamber should be moved subsequently only with great care.

Suitable inverted microscopes are made by Leitz and Olympus, amongst others, specifically for plankton counting. They are constructed so that the sedimentation chamber may be viewed from beneath, to examine the concentrated phytoplankton. In addition they have long-working distance optics, designed to function efficiently with 1–2 cm of water in the light path. Phase-contrast optics are not essential but are a great help in examining small flagellates. A range of magnifications from × 100 to × 800 is desirable.

The microscope should have a movable stage, so that the entire bottom of the sedimentation chamber can be viewed. If some species are abundant, they may be examined in randomly selected parts of the chamber.

It is at this stage that problems of identification and biomass estimation arise. These can become particularly severe if aims of the survey are not kept firmly in view. Thus for many purposes it suffices to identify, and to record as dominant, the most abundant species. If details of relative abundance are required, each taxon must be enumerated, and the count must be converted to cells per litre of sea water. Conversion factors will be large if only a small part of the sedimentation chamber has been examined, and the resulting magnification of errors must be borne in mind when interpreting microplankton concentrations. Thus, if cells of one species are distributed randomly after sedimentation (an assumption that should be checked), and 50 are counted in an area that represents 1/20 of the bottom of the chamber, on which have sedimented the cells from 10 ml, the estimated concentration in the sea is 100 000/l, with a likely error of 14%, or ± 14 000 cells/l. (This error is one standard deviation on either side of the mean, assuming a Poisson distribution of frequency of cell counts in sub-areas of the chamber.)

How many cells to count depends upon the purpose of the survey, and is discussed by Venrick (in Sournia, 1978). For most purposes it is enough to count between 20 and 100 of the units (cells, chains, or colonies) of the more abundant taxa. Given a random distribution of counted units in the sedimentation chamber, the error at 20 is 22% and at 100 is 10%.

Phytoplankton cell volumes range from less than 1 μm^3 to more than 1 000 000 μm^3, and thus good estimates of total biomass, or of the relative biomass of each species, require cell measurements as well as counts. Smayda (in Sournia, 1978) discusses methodology. However, such approaches to biomass are not only microscopically tedious and subsequently demanding in data processing, but are also subject to large errors. For survey purposes, therefore, it is usually best to employ chemical methods for determining biomass, using the microscope only to identify dominants and to enumerate cells of selected species.

Whatever the procedure adopted in respect to counting and measurement, the Lugol-sedimentation technique does not work well for many dinoflagellates, or for coccolithophorids or ciliates. Buffered formalin-preserved samples should be examined when coccolithophorids are likely to be abundant, or when it is necessary to identify armoured dinoflagellates to species. In some cases 10 ml is too little to sediment. Larger sub-samples may be conveniently concentrated by gravity-driven filtration through a large (8–15 μm) pore size membrane filter. The filter should not be allowed to dry out, and the cells concentrated onto it may be gently brushed or washed into a little filtered sea water for transference to a sedimentation chamber. The method is quantitative for most armoured dinoflagellates and other robust microplankton if all the washing water is transferred. This concentration method also works well with living armoured dinoflagellates. For more fragile organisms, centrifugation of fresh material is sometimes useful. When the microplankton is abundant, 10 ml of untreated sea water may be put into a sedimentation chamber and viewed within a few minutes; the heavier organisms, such as armoured dinoflagellates, coccolithophorids, and tintinnid ciliates, sink quickly to the bottom. This may be the only way to observe naked ciliates such as *Mesodinium*. However, living ciliates are hard to identify because of their movement, and Lindholm (1982) suggests narcotizing them with EDTA.

Most of these methods can, in principle, be used with a conventional high-power microscope, so long as the concentrated sample can be transferred without losses to a suitable counting slide such as a Sedgewick–Rafter chamber. This is a rectangular slide holding up to 1 ml beneath a coverslip. Only low-power objectives can generally be brought to focus on the bottom of the chamber because of the overlying thickness of water. Guillard (in Sournia, 1978) gives further details of counting slides.

I have counted the larger dinoflagellates, after membrane concentration from 1 l of sample, in a grooved Perspex block (a 'Bogorov tray') beneath a stereo microscope. Living dinoflagellates are often easy to identify by their movements, and individual cells may with practice be sucked into a fine pipette and transferred to a slide beneath a high-power microscope for more-precise identification.

Epifluorescence techniques (see Varga in Sournia, 1978) have recently come into use for counting flagellates as well as pelagic bacteria. In an epifluorescence microscope an excitation light is shone onto the material through the object lens itself. An optical barrier filter excludes excitation light from, but transmits fluorescence through, the eyepiece. Sherr & Sherr (1983) have recently described a method for microflagellates that includes epifluorescence and other techniques. Samples preserved with buffered formalin are concentrated onto a small (0.8 μm) pore size membrane filter. The filter is then flooded with a solution of fluorescein isothiocyanate, which fluoresces green and binds to proteins. Finally the filter is mounted on a slide and examined using an epifluorescence microscope. The authors claim to be able to distinguish heterotrophs, which fluoresce only green, from autotrophs, whose chlorophyll, even after formalin preservation, fluoresces red. Fenchel (1982b) and Davis & Sieburth (in Bougis, 1982) describe similar epifluorescence techniques.

Epifluorescence can also be used with living material, perhaps after semi-quantitative concentration by filtration or centrifugation, into a drop of water beneath a coverslip on a regular slide. Chlorophyll-containing organisms appear red when illuminated with blue (430 nm) light, but the colour quickly fades as the pigment photo-oxidizes. The phycoerythrin pigments of blue-green algae fluoresce orange, and this provides a simple means of distinguishing in the picoplankton amongst cyanobacteria, eukaryotic algae, and true bacteria. Although cryptomonads also contain phycoerythrin, all known species are larger than 2 μm.

Methods for microplankton biomass

Strickland & Parsons (1972) and Parsons *et al.* (1984) give several chemical methods for the biomass of plankton retained on a suitable (usually glass-fibre) filter, the method for particulate carbon being the most useful. Automatic analysers are available for particulate carbon (and for some other elements, such as nitrogen). Calorimetry offers a possible method for organic material; Scott & Marlow (1982) describe a microbomb calorimeter that can be used with less than 100 μg of carbon (5 J or less; 1 mg C = 48 J for typical microplankton). This could be obtained by filtering a few hundred millilitres of sea water; a difficulty is that the instrument requires a small (4 mm) filter. In all cases involving filters, it may be necessary to apply a correction for dissolved organic material retained during filtration. There is often, in unit volume of sea water, ten times as much dissolved as particulate organic carbon.

These chemical and calorific methods do not, however, discriminate between the organic matter in phytoplankton and that in small zooplankton and organic detritus. The latter often make up more than half, and sometimes 90%, of the particulate organic carbon in sea water. Coulter-type particle counters (see Sheldon in Sournia, 1978) do not distinguish algal from other material, either, but since they size as well as count, it is sometimes possible to relate peaks in the particle size/abundance spectrum to microscopically identified phyto- or microzooplankters. However, their main use is in laboratory experiments with one or a few species of microplankton, not in survey work.

Leftley, Bonin & Maestrini (1983) review other possible but still largely experimental methods for phytoplankton biomass, including those intended to separate and enumerate the main components of the microplankton. Nevertheless, the most practically effective method for the estimation of phytoplankton biomass is still that of measurement of photosynthetic pigments. It is quick and easy compared with microscopic analysis, and, in the version described here, it excludes heterotrophic microplankton and detritus. There are disadvantages. The chlorophyll:biomass ratio is variable, ranging from 20–100 mg carbon/1 mg of chlorophyll, and although chlorophyll and cell counts can be equated (for example one million cells of the diatom *Skeletonema costatum* contain roughly 1 μg of chlorophyll), there is, because of variation in cell size amongst species and samples, often only weak correlation between chlorophyll and phytoplankton numbers.

Precise chlorophyll determination requires the concentration of waterborne particulates onto glass-fibre filters, and the extraction of the planktonic pigments into 90% acetone. The concentration of photosynthetic pigments in the extract can be estimated by spectrophotometric measurement of optical density at the wavelength (663 nm) of maximum extinction of chlorophyll, or by fluorometry. When exposed to blue light (430 nm), chlorophyll and its derivatives emit a red fluorescence (peaking at about 670 nm in the case of chlorophyll *a*), whose amount is proportional to the exciting irradiance and the pigment concentration. Fluorometry is more specific and more sensitive than spectrophotometry, but it does require a specialised instrument and must be calibrated against a chlorophyll solution whose concentration has been determined spectrophotometrically.

An acetone extract contains a mixture of pigments. Those that appear green, due to strong absorption of the red light, and emit a red fluorescence include chlorophyll *a* and its breakdown products chlorophyllide *a*, pheophorbide *a*, and pheophytin *a* (the last two termed 'pheopigments'), plus chlorophyll(ide) *c* and its derivatives. Measurement of fluorescence using narrow-band optical filters, or optical density at precisely defined wavelengths, before and after acidification of the extract, which converts the mixture of chlorophylls and pheopigments entirely to pheopigments, allows the latter to be distinguished, and thus 'chlorophyll' can be measured free of contamination. Detailed methods are given in Appendex 11.3; they derive from Holm-Hansen *et al.* (1965), UNESCO (1966), and Strickland & Parsons (1972). As Gowen, Tett & Wood (1983) point out, these methods do not distinguish chlorophyll *a* from chlorophyllide *a*. Although the latter cannot participate in photosynthesis, both pigments are associated only with living or recently dead phytoplankton, and the methods may thus be considered adequate for surveying the distribution of phytoplankton biomass.

The fluorescence of chlorophyll in living algae can be used to estimate their biomass by pumping sea water through a suitable fluorometer (Lorenzen, 1966). This *in vivo* fluorescence must be calibrated with chlorophyll extracted from water sampled at the fluorometer outflow. The ratio of *in vivo* fluorescence to phytoplankton biomass may vary by several orders of magnitude. Pheopigments and dissolved substances also fluoresce, and in some cases *in vivo* fluorescence has no discernable relationship to phytoplankton biomass. In other cases it can be used only to draw attention to the most obvious features of phytoplankton distribution. For examples of its effective use in mapping horizontal or vertical distributions of phytoplankton, see Pingree *et al.* (1982) and Simpson *et al.* (1982). Leftley *et al.* (1983) review some of the physiological problems in the interpretation of *in vivo* fluorescence.

Analysis of zooplankton samples

Beers (in Steedman, 1976) discusses the determination of zooplankton biomass. As with phytoplankton and microzooplankton there is a choice between physical or chemical measurements of gross biomass and the identification and enumeration of each zooplankton component, perhaps down to the level of sex or age-group within species. The results of analysis reflect not only the method but also the catching properties of the sampling device.

A rapid but crude measure of biomass can be obtained by allowing a preserved zooplankton sample to settle in a measuring cylinder, and recording the volume occupied by the animals. A better method is to remove all surplus water from the sample and then to measure the volume displaced when the animals are introduced into a suitable apparatus. In either case, large gelatinous animals should be removed and measured separately.

Ash-free dry weight is probably the best simple measure of zooplankton biomass. Fresh or frozen material is dried to a constant weight either in an oven at 60 °C or by freeze-drying. The material is then combusted in an oven for 12 hours at 450 °C, thus leaving a mineral ash. The change in weight is equal to the weight of the dry organic material. Carbon, nitrogen, or calorific content can be determined on replicate samples, but for many purposes it suffices to assume that 100 g of ash-free dry weight is equivalent to about 40 g carbon or about 4800 kJ. Parsons, Takahashi & Hargrave (1977) discuss these ratios further.

Because of the variety of animals present in the plankton, identification of all organisms to species is usually difficult, and is often unnecessary for survey purposes. It generally suffices to sort the animals in a sample into their main taxonomic groups and to seek to identify to species level only the dominants and indicators. Such sorting requires a low-power stereo microscope, a set of small dishes, and items such as small tea-strainers, teaspoons, forceps, needles, and pipettes.

In the procedure used by the UK Institute of Marine Environmental

Research (see Morris, 1983), zooplankton samples containing much detrital and inorganic material are first treated with a 1% aqueous solution of the dye rose bengal. This stains most zooplankton pink and thus makes the animals easy to distinguish from other material. Large organisms are then picked out and stored separately for later identification, counting, and measurement. Sub-sampling is necessary when the remainder are numerous; the IMER group recommend the use of a stainless steel ladle first to stir and then to sub-sample from material in a wide-mouth beaker. The zooplankters can then be examined microscopically in a Bogorov tray, i.e., a grooved Perspex block with a capacity of 5–25 ml. A good-quality binocular microscope is needed, with a range of magnifications up to × 50; individual animals may need to be further transferred for final identification onto a slide under a high-power standard or inverted microscope. Because the distribution of animals in the tray may not be uniform, the whole of the sub-sample should be analysed, and it is important to adjust the proportion sub-sampled so that about 100 individuals are counted from the commonest species; this will give a precision (plus or minus one standard deviation) of about $\pm 10\%$, assuming random distribution in the original sample when mixed for sub-sampling.

As with microplankton, counting and recording is aided by the use of standard analysis sheets and tally counters. It may be possible to program a microcomputer so that each of its keys corresponds to a single taxon (Cunningham & Purewal, 1983), and perhaps in the near future, cheap and effective speech recognition technology will further ease the time-consuming task of sample analysis.

Biomass estimates for each zooplankton group can be made from counts, provided that the average weight or calorific or carbon content of an individual is known. The commonest method is to prepare length–weight relationships for each important taxon by removing, measuring, and assaying individuals or groups of similar individuals, and thereafter measuring only the lengths of counted animals. Further details are given in Morris (1983). This laborious approach should be employed only if knowledge of the biomass contribution of each taxon is important.

SCOR (Scientific Committee on Ocean Research) Working Group 23 recommended (in Steedman, 1976) that samples should not be split for biomass and composition analysis, since zooplankton sub-sampling devices are unreliable and may damage the more-delicate animals. Although the zooplankton of estuaries is probably sufficiently robust for this precaution to be unnecessary, it is desirable to carry out chemical analyses on fresh or frozen material and usually necessary to make identifications on preserved samples. Fresh samples cannot be properly divided, and so replication may be necessary. The twin 'Bongo' nets of McGowan & Brown (1966) would seem especially suited for this purpose, but they do not seem to have been used much on the eastern side of the Atlantic. Only smaller nets can easily be employed in pairs, and repeated tows of single nets are unlikely to provide suitable replication because of zooplankton patchiness. Pump sampling is thus clearly superior when repeated samples are needed, since the pump outflow can easily be divided.

Strategy and interpretation
Don't change the questions
In designing a sampling programme it is necessary to decide what questions the survey is intended to answer; what variables should be measured, where, and how often; and what resources are available. The design should not be inflexible. Results should be analysed as they are obtained, and if it begins to seem that the questions will not be answered, the sampling scheme should be changed. Avoid, however, changing the questions!

Resources
A laboratory that carries out routine work on plankton needs the following: water-bottles; electronic means of measuring salinity and temperature; equipment for analysis of dissolved nutrients; a quantitative net with a flowmeter, or a pump system, for zooplankton; stereo low-power and inverted high-power microscopes; and a filter fluorometer for chlorophyll measurement.

For sampling, it is useful to have a boat equipped with a winch that can be precisely controlled, and that has standard hydrographic (6 mm diameter) wire cable passing over a metre wheel to measure length of wire out. A shipboard laboratory in which water can be filtered and then frozen for subsequent chemical and chlorophyll analyses, and in which plankton samples can be preserved, is desirable. However, much sampling can be done from boats, including, in sheltered waters, small open boats, without such equipment, so long as sample treatment can take place soon afterwards.

Labour can replace specialized equipment. Using an 'opening' bottle, or small, battery-driven pumps, sampling can take place from a pier or small boat. Chlorophyll extracts can be measured spectrophotometrically, and phytoplankton can be examined using a conventional high-power microscope. However, the hydrography must not be neglected even when resources are scarce; much can be learned from charts and a few calculations, or with the aid of simple drogues. Water temperature can be profiled with a simple electronic probe, or even with a good thermometer in the outflow of a pump system. Salinity can be measured by titration, or, with less precision, with a sensitive hydrometer or refractometer. The zooplankton of shallow estuaries can be, and is perhaps best, sampled with a hand-held net or a battery-operated pump in a backpack, working in waders or a wet-suit in areas where a boat cannot easily be taken. Particular thought should be given to safety under these conditions: estuaries are notoriously places of shifting banks and rapidly changing water level.

Whatever their availability, resources should not determine the sampling programme, and, in particular, should not influence the frequency and spatial intensity of sampling. It is, for example, likely to be fruitless to sample phytoplankton once a year, given the much faster time-scales of algal growth and water movement. Shortage of resources may properly influence the questions that are asked and the variables that are measured. Thus, since chlorophyll measurements are easier than microscopic analysis of phytoplankton species composition, it is often sensible to put the effort into sampling chlorophyll, determining species composition only occasionally and as a check on the main components of biomass.

Nutrient chemistry

Given the importance of mineral nutrients in phytoplankton growth, it will probably be necessary to investigate the distribution of at least one nutrient. Nitrate is probably the most important nutrient controlling algal growth in the sea. Ammonia should be measured where there is anthropogenic nutrient input. Phosphorus is the more usual limiting nutrient in fresh water, and thus in estuaries both dissolved nitrogen and phosphorus should be measured, since it may not be apparent which nutrient is limiting productivity. Silicate data may be needed to interpret diatom distribution.

Dissolved and detrital organic material provides the food source for heterotrophic microplankton, and should thus be measured when these organisms are under investigation. Butler, Knox & Liddicoat (1979) and others have argued that organic compounds may supply the nitrogen and phosphorus needs of phytoplankton during the summer when inorganic nutrients are scarce in the euphotic zone. There is no doubt that phytoplankton can utilise small organic molecules such as urea, but there remains considerably uncertainty over the concentrations of such compounds, and the extent to which algae can use larger organic molecules. Thus, it is best to measure total organic nitrogen and phosphorus, perhaps using a photo-oxidative method.

The subject of nutrient chemistry is too large for proper discussion here, and is dealt with in Head (1985). Strickland & Parsons (1972) and Parsons *et al.* (1984) provide a guide to many of the methods.

Designing a sampling programme

What questions is the survey intended to answer? Once these are known the hydrography of the region can be assessed from charts, tidal data, and the calculations discussed in the hydrographic section and Appendix 11.2, and used, with information on the biology of the relevant organisms, to choose appropriate scales for sampling. As emphasised previously, bodies of water that flush rapidly should be sampled at least once every flushing time. In other cases, frequency should relate to the life cycle of the organisms investigated. It is desirable to sample more frequently sometimes, to assess the extent of more-rapid variation and so help in putting error limits to the results of the main survey.

Sampling positions should reflect the hydrography of the region. If boats are not available it may be possible, by sampling over a tidal cycle from a fixed point such as a pier, to sample effectively over a range of a spatially varying condition such as salinity. Conversely, it may be desirable always to sample at the same state of the tide, to avoid such effects. The hydrographic section suggested that sampling stations should be placed at equal increments of relevant variables, such as salinity or intensity of vertical mixing, not at equal spatial intervals. Equal increments of density provide the best guide to vertical sampling intervals.

Aliasing arises when sampling frequency differs slightly from a dominant natural frequency. If, for example, samples are taken at the same clock time each day, their timing will retreat in relation to the time of high water, until after 14 days the original relationship is restored. Such sampling might appear to demonstrate a fortnightly cycle, when the major variation in fact takes place over a tidal cycle. Thought should thus be given to the potential causes, and the avoidance, of aliasing.

In the case of phytoplankton a knowledge of hydrography alone is generally adequate to design a sampling programme. In the case of zooplankton the animals' behaviour must often be taken into account. Samples should initially be taken by night as well as day, and, in shallow waters, at different states of the tide, in case of migration or aggregation on a solar or lunar diel basis. Net sampling cannot discriminate finely between depths, but pump sampling can, and, where possible, the depth distribution of zooplankton should be examined in relation to water-column structure. Do the animals, and especially the microzooplankton, concentrate at a pycnocline? Does a pycnocline separate layers of different zooplankton biomass or species composition?

The nature of the gear clearly determines what is sampled, as Angel (1977) points out forcefully for oceanic midwater zooplankton. It is important that the limitations of the equipment be known and that sampling programmes be designed to stay within them. Otherwise the results will tell more about the properties of the sampler than of the organisms sampled.

Hammerton, Newton & Leatherland (1981) discuss the design of surveys carried out to monitor the changes caused by pollution. Ryther & Dunstan (1971) discuss the basis of cultural eutrophication in coastal waters, predicting that increased discharges of nitrogen should lead to enhanced algal production. In general, there is no doubt that estuarine phytoplankton biomass and production increases with increasing nutrient loading (Boynton *et al.* in Kennedy, 1982). Yet, in large estuaries and in coastal waters, such eutrophication rarely leads to an obvious increase in algal blooms, and even on average eutrophication may be difficult to discern in a single estuary against a background of other changes. It may be that in many inner estuaries phytoplankton growth is light limited because of high turbidity (e.g., Joint & Pomeroy, 1981), so that nutrient enrichment has little local effect. Sullivan & Hancock (1977) concluded that it was difficult to find unambiguous evidence of effects of point-source pollution on coastal and estuarine zooplankton. Gabriel, Dias & Nelson-Smith (1975) could find no clear changes in the plankton of the Milford Haven estuary in Wales despite the establishment of a major oil port. Thus, although exceptions to these conclusions might be expected in poorly flushed basins and in inner estuaries where the organic loadings create substantial extra biological oxygen demand in the water column, the effects of pollution on plankton have rarely been unambiguously demonstrated.

A general explanation may be sought in water movements; pollutants, and the water-borne organisms that absorb them, are diluted and dispersed, so that visible effects on plankton are moderate and widespread rather than local and acute as in the case of effects on benthos. Thus, in designing a survey to investigate some anthropogenic effect on plankton, two points must be borne in mind. The first is that perturbations are likely to be hidden by natural short- and long-term variation and the effects of spatial patchiness. Many data may therefore be needed to demonstrate (or refute) any effect. The second point is that effects on plankton are likely to take place on a larger scale than those on benthos. Plankton surveys should thus be designed independently of those on the benthos, and will in general require spatially less, but temporally more, intense sampling.

There are discussions of spatial and temporal variability in plankton in Steele (1978). Table 11.2, from Tett & Grantham (in Freeland *et al.*, 1980) analyses the source of variability in measurements of chlorophyll concentration made in a Scottish sea loch. Method error was responsible for only a very small part of total variation. Small-scale patchiness contributed more, but most of the variability about the generalised annual cycle of phytoplankton biomass came equally from year-to-year variation and from spatial variability on a scale of a few kilometres. These data again suggest that it is better to put extra effort into collecting samples than into improving measurements on individual samples.

Data analysis and presentation

For an introduction to data analysis and presentation see Chapter 1. A few types of diagrams serve for the presentation of most of the results of a plankton survey. Profiles may be drawn against depth for any variable or group of variables for which sufficient measurements have been made at a station. Fig. 11.1 gives examples. Given an adequate amount of data, contoured maps and sections are useful for showing the distribution of single variables in the horizontal or vertical plane. Fig. 11.9 gives examples. Sections are often more useful than maps, since the main structure of a plankton distribution lies most often in the vertical plane. The contour intervals should be at least twice the standard error of sampling, and it is best, in the interests of clarity, to have no more than six contours. Where logarithmic transformation of the data has been necessary, contour values should form a geometric series. Finally, sections drawn for shallow waters should take account of the state of the tide at the time of sampling.

Fig. 11.6 shows plankton concentrations graphed against time. The points could be replaced by perpendicular lines or bars, making a histogram, and this might be the best form of presentation when sampling

Table 11.2. *Sources of variability in chlorophyll measurements*

Source of variation	Variance	Proportion
1. Total variation (all samples)	0.33	3.8
2. General annual cycle	0.24	2.8
3. Variation about the general annual cycle	0.087	1.00
4. Variation between years	0.037	0.43
5. Variation over a few days and the loch	0.038	0.44
6. Small-scale patchiness	0.009	0.11
7. Measurement error	0.002	0.02

The units of variance are $(\log_{10}$ mg chlorophyll$/m^3)^2$.
The model employed in the analysis of variance assumed that variance due to source 1 = that due to 2 + 3, and that variance due to 3 = that due to 4 + 5 + 6 + 7. Based on 1832 chlorophyll samples taken in Loch Creran between 1972 and 1979. See Tett & Grantham (in Freeland *et al.*, 1980).

took place at widely spaced and irregular intervals, since it does not suggest to the eye any particular relationship between successive results. When sampling and measurement errors are small and sampling is frequent compared with the relevant physical and biological time-scales, points may be joined by straight lines. If the vertical scale is logarithmic, a straight line implies exponential growth or decline. Does this seem realistic? When sampling is regular but the data are subject to substantial

Fig. 11.9. Results of a survey of Loch Spelve, Scotland. The sections (b) to (d) are drawn through the stations 2, 4, 7, and 9 shown on the map (a). The north arm receives most of the loch's fresh-water from the river entering near station 9, and displays lower surface salinities (see (a)) and a brackish wedge (see (b)), from which is deduced the presence in this arm of a two-layer circulation (see (c)). The south arm generally shows little salinity layering and is presumed to exchange mainly by tide-driven mixing. The sections (b) and (d) were drawn from measurements made from a small boat between 1 and 3 hours after high water during the morning of 3 September 1982, using an electronic temperature–salinity probe and a water-bottle; depths sampled for chlorophyll are shown by dots in (d). A larger vessel was anchored at station 0 outside the loch and recorded changes in salinity associated with the ebb tide outflow; these are suggested in the map (a) by the dashed contours, which indicate isohalines at low water. On the subsequent flood tide, water of gradually increasing salinity flowed into the loch from the sea, sinking to a depth corresponding to its density once past the entrance sill, which has a minimum depth of 5 m below chart datum (CD). On 3 September there were spring tides, reaching about 3.2 m above CD.

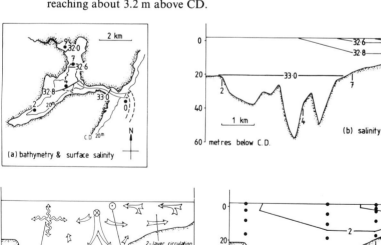

sampling or measurement errors, some form of smoothing procedure may be used to fit a curve. My preference (as in Fig. 11.6) is to use a Fourier series derived from spectral analysis of the data. Suitable programs are available for many microcomputers. The number of coefficients used in plotting the series can be chosen according to the degree of smoothing required. This approach is particularly suitable for establishing general annual cycles, because smoothing by reduction of the number of coefficients of the Fourier series leads to the elimination of high-frequency variation. Time-series analysis can be valuable in itself, as a means of assessing variability and its causes. See Chatfield (1980).

Given frequent profiles at a station, a useful method of presentation is through a diagram whose axes are depth and time, contoured for the variable of interest. Fig. 11.10 shows such a contour diagram for chlorophyll in a sea loch. The chlorophyll peaks have been labelled with the names of the dominant phytoplankters. Much relevant information can thus be economically presented.

Finally, useful insights into relationships can often be obtained, and presented, by plotting one variable against another. The use of temperature/salinity diagrams to identify water masses and mixing processes has been discussed in the hydrographic section. Officer (1979) has discussed the use of plots against salinity of a nonconservative property, such as the concentration of a nutrient, which may be altered by remineralization or uptake by phytoplankton. A graph of chlorophyll against salinity (as in Fig. 11.2b) may indicate whether a distribution of phytoplankton results

Fig. 11.10. A depth–time diagram contoured for chlorophyll. From a station near the head of Loch Striven, Scotland, in 1980. Marks on horizontal axis show sampling dates; chlorophyll contours, which are in mg m⁻³, based on four to seven samples on each visit. The names of phytoplankton are those dominating biomass during periods when chlorophyll exceeded 5 mg m⁻³.

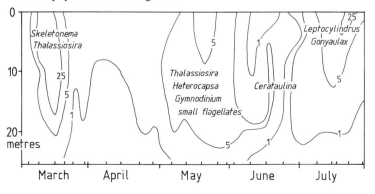

mainly from physical processes, such as mixing between two water masses of differing salinities and chlorophyll concentrations, in which case the graph will be a straight line, or whether local growth or grazing are important, in which case there will be deviations from a straight-line plot. Graphs of chlorophyll versus nutrient concentration, or phytoplankton versus zooplankton biomass, may also prove rewarding.

Patchiness

The topic of patchiness, much discussed in the literature, has been played down in this account. There seems little evidence to contradict the hypothesis that on most size scales, most of the variability in the distribution of microplankton – and perhaps also of much zooplankton – is due to physical variability (Tett & Edwards, 1984). Features of plankton behaviour such as swarming or vertical migration, and the results of zooplankton grazing on phytoplankton, may however cause patchiness whose mechanism is essentially biological and hence not predictable from physical distributions. Parsons *et al.* 1977 discuss the topic further. For most practical purposes small-scale patchiness can be treated as 'noise', to be estimated and as far as possible diminished by appropriate statistical methods. Sometimes however the patch is the signal, as in the case of the narrow regions of enhanced plankton biomass found at tidal-mixing fronts (Pingree *et al.*, 1975). In such cases biological patchiness almost always relates clearly to physical gradients, such as those in sea surface temperature or salinity, or degree of water-column stratification.

Example of a survey

Loch Spelve (Fig. 11.9a) is a shallow-silled fjord containing several fish-farms. The phytoplankton ecology of the loch was investigated in 1981 and 1982 (1) to assess the occurrence and distribution of species of plankton known to be toxic to salmon, shellfish, or their consumers; and (2) to find the place with the greatest phytoplankton biomass as a guide to resiting a mussel farm. For the sake of this example, the following may be supposed to have been part of the survey aim: (3) to discover when and where collectors of mussel spat should best be exposed. Points 2 and 3 are commonly determined pragmatically, by growing test mussels and exposing test collectors, but there are long-term advantages in understanding the distributions of the phytoplankton food, and the larvae, of the shellfish.

Examination of charts and maps, and some preliminary measurements of salinity distribution showed that the north (N) arm of Spelve receives a substantial freshwater inflow and normally has the stratification pattern typical of a partially mixed estuary. The entrance sill and south (S) arm of the loch are normally well mixed by tidal currents. Given a semi-diurnal tide, a mean tidally exchanged volume of 17 million m³ and a segment mean high-water volume of 125 million m³, the calculated flushing time of the S arm is about 4 days. Since there was evidence of imperfect exchange with the sea, the flushing time was taken as a week. The catchment of the N arm is 54 km²; it receives a rainfall of 1800 mm/year; allowing for 35% evaporation suggests a freshwater inflow of 170000 m³/day. The mean salinity of the near-surface layer in the N arm is 32.0 ppt, and that of the deeper water is 33.0 ppt. The mean-tide volume of the N arm is 40 million cubic metres, and the flushing time is thus about 7 days. These flushing times set the basic time-scales for sampling, and it was thus arranged that two fish-farmers would use 'opening' bottles to take weekly water samples from a depth of 1 m at their farms, these samples being used for the determination of chlorophyll and microplankton species composition. A pier near the entrance of the loch seemed suitable for sampling for mussel spat, and it would have been possible for a metered tow-net to have been streamed each week from this pier for a few minutes during the maximum flood and again during the maximum ebb.

Mussel spat could have been counted, if necessary after sub-sampling, using a stereo low-power microscope. The microplankton was preserved with Lugol and analysed, using the sedimentation method described previously, for dominants and known toxic species. Chlorophyll was determined fluorometrically to provide the main measure of phytoplankton biomass.

To investigate the spatial distribution of plankton, Spelve was visited at times chosen to represent different seasons and weather conditions. During the summer a small open boat was used within the loch; but during other seasons, and for work in the sea outside, a larger vessel was used. Vertical profiles were made, with electronic probes and water-bottles, of temperature, salinity, chlorophyll, and nitrate at the stations shown in Fig. 11.9a, and these were used to construct sections of the loch such as those shown in Fig. 11.9b and c. Most sections reflected the normal circulation within the loch, which includes a presumed two-layer circulation in the N arm, but some drogue and salinity measurements showed that persistent northerly winds could strip the reduced-salinity layer from the N arm and blow it into the S arm of the loch, thus changing physical and biological conditions there.

The tow-nets taken in the entrance channel might have suggested that mussel spat were not produced in the loch but instead entered on the flood tide, fewer being carried out by the ebb. Once the season of greatest spat abundance had been ascertained, a survey of the loch for spat could have been carried out by pump sampling, and a spat/salinity diagram could have been used to confirm that there were more spat at higher salinities. A deviation from linearity at the lowest salinities might suggest that the spat tend to avoid the brackish surface layer in the N arm.

Finally, the reliability of the results of weekly sampling and of the occasional sectioning of the loch was investigated by short periods of intensive study. The pier and fish-farm rafts provided sites for sampling over a tidal cycle, and on several occasions duplicate sections of the loch for salinity and chlorophyll were made at high and low water.

Conclusions

Other examples include the account by Hammerton *et al.*, (1981) of a pollution survey of the Firth of Clyde in western Scotland, and Southward's (1962) survey of the larger zooplankton of the English Channel. It should be clear that each plankton investigation requires a sampling programme adapted both to the specific aims of that investigation and to local conditions. However, a few general points are worth re-emphasising here:

1. Investigate plankton in relation to hydrography.
2. Choose spatial and temporal sampling patterns appropriate to the hypotheses under investigation and the relevant physical and biological time-scales.
3. Carefully select the variables to be measured in relation to the aims of the survey and the efficiency of their measurement. If appropriate, use physical and chemical techniques for most measurements, employing time-consuming biological analyses only to calibrate the simpler measurements or to indicate the composition of biomass.

Acknowledgements

I am grateful to all those who, by sharing in surveys or discussions, have helped define the ideas in this chapter. They include Open University and Stirling University students who took part in practical courses at Dunstaffnage, fish-farmer participants in the Scottish Marine Biological Association's Phytoplankton & Mariculture programme, staff of the Clyde River Purification Board, D. Boyd, C. Douglas, M. Drysdale, R. Gowen, B. Grantham, K. Jones, D. McLusky, and J. Shaw. A. Edwards provided my hydrographic education. I am also grateful to J. Baker, J. Mauchline, and W. J. Wolff for comments on earlier drafts. The Scottish Marine Biological Association is grant aided by the (UK) Natural Environment Research Council. Some of the examples derive from work funded by the

Aquacultural Insurance Service Ltd, the Department of Agriculture and Fisheries for Scotland, Golden Sea Produce Ltd, the Highlands and Islands Development Board, and the Ministry of Agriculture, Fisheries and Food.

APPENDIX 11.1

Calculation of density

Because water is compressible, its density is affected by pressure (and hence depth), as well as by temperature and salt content. The depth effect is neglible in shelf seas, and it is usual to express the density (ρ) of sea water as the variable 'sigma-T', which specifies the excess mass over the same volume of distilled water at 4 °C and normal atmospheric pressure:

$$\sigma_T = 1000(1-\rho) \quad \text{kg m}^{-3}$$

Table 11A.1 contains a UCSD (University of California at San Diego) Pascal function for the calculation of σ_T from temperature and salinity. The function may be used in a computer program or worked through by hand, starting at 'BEGIN'.

Table 11A.1. *A Pascal function for σ_T*

```
(*:::::::::::::::::::::::::::::::::::::::::::::::::::::::::::::::::::::::::::*)
     FUNCTION SIGMAT(SAL,TEMP : REAL) : REAL;
(*                                                                         *)
(* TEST VALUES : SAL = 35 P.P.TH, TEMP = 10 DEG. C  :                      *)
(*                    SIGMAT = 26.97                                       *)
(*:::::::::::::::::::::::::::::::::::::::::::::::::::::::::::::::::::::::::::*)

VAR
  B1,B2,E1,S1,T1 : REAL;

BEGIN
  T1:=TEMP + 4.4E-06 * TEMP * (100 - TEMP);
  S1:=((6.7678614E-06 * SAL - 4.8249614E-04) * SAL + 0.81487658) * SAL
       - 0.093445863;
  E1:=(((-1.438031E-07 * T1 - 1.982484E-03) * T1 - 0.5439391) * T1
       + 4.53164843) * T1;
  B1:=((-1.0843E-06 * T1 + 9.8185E-05) * T1 - 4.7867E-03) * T1 + 1.0;
  B2 :=((1.677E-08 * T1 - 8.614E-07) * T1 +1.803E-05) * T1;
  SIGMAT := (E1/(T1 + 67.26)) + (S1 * (B2 * S1 + B1));
END;

(*:::::::::::::::::::::::::::::::::::::::::::::::::::::::::::::::::::::::::::*)
```

APPENDIX 11.2

Estimation of a flushing time-scale for an estuary

A well-mixed body of water, volume V, from which a small volume dV is removed, and replaced by new water, in each time interval dT, has a dilution rate $D = (dV/dT)(1/V)$. It can be shown formally that the specific growth rate ($\mu = $ (rate of change of biomass)/(biomass)) or organisms in that water body must exceed the dilution rate of the body if a population is to sustain itself therein by adequately replacing losses in the outflow. The proof of this requires assumptions of perfect mixing of water and organisms, and perfect disposal of any water and organisms that are removed, that is, they must not re-enter the water body on some later occasion.

These assumptions are rarely satisfied in nature. It is thus better to make a looser comparison between a 'flushing time-scale' $1/D$ and a biological time-scale given by $1/\mu$, a typical division time for microplankton, or a generation time for relevant metazoan zooplankton.

There are two simple methods for estimating a flushing time-scale for an estuarine segment of mid-tide volume V. Each requires that the head of the segment is the head of the estuary, although the segment mouth need not be that of the estuary. The equations give dilution rate per tide; the flushing time-scale in days is given by $1/nD$, where there are n tides per day. R refers to river flow per tide.

Bowden (in Lauff, 1967) and Edwards & Edelsten (1976) present versions of a tidal exchange method, giving:

$$D = (V_h - V_l)/V_h \qquad (1)$$

where V_h is the segment's high-water volume and V_l is its low-water volume. The difference between these volumes is the tidal exchange. The equation is inaccurate unless $V \gg (V_h - V_l) \gg R$. The method requires that there be good mixing within the segment and no return of water leaving the segment on the ebb tide. It is best used with well-mixed estuaries.

Bowden and Saelen (both in Lauff, 1967) give a method based on river flows and salinities:

$$D = (R \cdot S_o)/[V \cdot (S_o - S)] \qquad (2)$$

where S_o is the mean salinity of water entering the segment and S is the mean salinity of the outflow. These parameters can be estimated, in the cases of well-mixed and partially mixed estuaries, from salinity observations at the mouth of the segment during a tidal cycle. Alternatively, S may be taken as the mean salinity of the segment and S_o as that of the sea immediately outside. D can be obtained for the top layer of a well-stratified estuary by taking S as the mean salinity and V as the volume of that layer. S_o is then the salinity of the deep layer. In each case, mean salinities must take account of the different volumes in each depth segment in an estuary with sloping sides, or of the different volumes entering and leaving the estuary at different stages of the tidal cycle. Considerable care must be taken with observations and averaging when the difference $(S_o - S)$ is small. Equation (2) is inaccurate unless $D \gg R/V$.

If the main rivers are not gauged, mean R may be estimated from:

$$R = (A \cdot r \cdot (1 - e))/(365 \cdot n) \tag{3}$$

where A is the catchment area of the estuarine segment, r is the annual rainfall, and e is the proportion of rainfall lost as evaporation. As before, n is the number of tides per day.

The river flow/salinity method assumes a steady state, that is, one in which the salinities remain constant over several flushing times. When there is evidence that this is not the case, the ratio $S_o/(S_o - S)$ should be averaged over a number of occasions. Landless & Edwards (1976) present a method that estimates flushing time by relating the variability in S to that in R; this requires a good series of observations at intervals equal to or less than the flushing time.

The tidal exchange method often gives a shorter flushing time than the river flow/salinity method, because the latter relies on estimating the rate at which fresh water is flushed from the estuary and so takes account of imperfect disposal of the ebb water. The advantages of the tidal exchange method is that flushing time can be computed from charts and tide tables. An initial estimate made in this way may be taken as setting a lower limit to flushing time, and the estimate may be revised later when salinity data become available.

Other methods for estimating flushing times are given by Bowden (in Lauff, 1967) and Officer (1976).

APPENDIX 11.3

Measurement of chlorophyll

Introduction

As discussed in the main text, chlorophyll can be extracted into an organic solvent such as acetone, determined by measurements of optical density or fluorescence, and used as a measure of phytoplankton biomass.

Such extracts contain a mixture of pigments. Those with extinction or fluorescence spectra different from chlorophyll *a* can be eliminated by a careful choice of measurement wavelength. An acidification step distinguishes between the primary pigments and their breakdown products, the pheopigments, with similar wavelengths of peak extinction or fluorescence.

A more-detailed account of the method follows. It derives from Holm-Hansen *et al.* (1965), UNESCO (1966), and Strickland & Parsons (1972), and is given in spectrophotometric and fluorometric versions. For recent discussions of pigment measurement, see Rai & Marker (1982).

For reasons explained below, the variable measured by the methods in this Appendix and the references given above is hereafter called 'chlorophyll', not 'chlorophyll *a*'.

Extraction of pigments

Filter a known amount (V, litres) of sample through a glass-fibre filter: Whatman GF/C are suitable, generally retaining at least 90% of coastal phytoplankton. GF/F grade filter more slowly but are to be preferred when there are many very small algae. Membrane filters of 0.45 μm pore size can be used when the highest precision is needed, but these are more expensive than glass-fibre filters and some types partially dissolve in acetone. A convenient filter diameter is 47 mm. Suck the filter dry, fold it, and place it immediately in a stoppered centrifuge tube after adding about 10 ml of neutralized 90% acetone. This is prepared by adding 1 part of distilled water to 9 parts of analytical quality acetone, and storing the liquid over a little sodium bicarbonate.

If extraction cannot be performed immediately, the filter may be rapidly frozen and stored if necessary for several months. It should thereafter be placed in acetone without thawing.

Leave the centrifuge tube for a minimum of 18 hours and a maximum of 72 hours in darkness in a refrigerator whilst extraction occurs. Centrifuge for a few minutes to take the filter to the bottom of the tube; shake to destroy pigment gradients; and recentrifuge. Record exact extract volume (E, ml).

This method extracts at least 90% of the pigment from most phytoplankton samples, but it is not suitable for many benthic or freshwater algae, whose pigments should be extracted either with acetone after grinding or with boiling methanol. See Rai and Marker (1982) for further discussion of extraction technique.

Measurement of pigments with spectrophotometer

If using a spectrophotometric method, V should be 0.5–5 l, depending on phytoplankton abundance. Smaller volumes can be used with longer path-length spectrophotometer cells, but the method described here requires a matched pair of 1-cm cells. Carefully clean these cells with 90% acetone, and fill one with 90% acetone as a blank. Fill the other cell with the extract and carefully wipe the optical surfaces. Measure optical density (o.d.) of sample and blank at 750 nm and then at 663 nm. The latter is the red extinction peak of chlorophyll a in acetone. (Since the wavelength reading of many spectrophotometers is subject to errors of several nanometres, and since the chlorophyll peak has a narrow bandwidth, it is desirable to check the wavelength accuracy of the instrument. If the pigment extract derives from healthy phytoplankton, and thus contains little pheopigment, this can be done by finding the wavelength between 655 and 670 nm at which the extract has the greatest o.d.)

Add 2 drops of 2N (roughly 8% by volume concentrated HCl) to each spectrophotometer cell, shake, and wipe clean. Measure o.d. at the nominal wavelength 663 nm, and then at 750 nm. Best results are obtained if the wavelength setting is not altered during the acidification step.

Take care to rinse the cells well before the next sample, to avoid any transference of acid.

Each o.d. reading should be corrected for the equivalent blank. From the pre- or post-acidification sample o.d. at 663 nm, subtract the pre- or post-acidification sample o.d. at 750 nm. The corrected results are, respectively, e_o and e_a. Calculate the sample 'chlorophyll' concentration (C) from:

$$(C) = K_e(e_o - e_a) \cdot E/V \quad (\mu g \text{ chl } a \text{ equivalent) l}^{-1} \tag{1}$$

If needed, pheopigment concentrations (P) can be computed from:

$$(P) = K_e(H_e \cdot e_a - e_o) \cdot E/V \quad (\mu g \text{ chl } a \text{ equivalent) l}^{-1} \tag{2}$$

Values of the constants K_e and H_e are discussed below.

Measurements of pigments with fluorometer

When illuminated with blue light of about 430 nm, many of the extracted pigments emit red light. In the case of chlorophyll a and some of the pheopigments, the emission peak is at about 670 nm. Several instruments are available that have been especially designed for the measurement of chlorophyll fluorescence. (Barker, Smith & Nelson (1983) discuss the selection of filters and lamps for fluorometers.) They regulate wavelengths of exciting and emitted light with optical filters, and are thus called filter fluorometers to distinguish them from spectrofluorometers in which exciting-light and emission-detector wavelengths may be varied continuously. The method described here applies to the Turner Designs model 10 and the Sequioa–Turner models 111 and 112, in which the relative amount of exciting light can be varied in steps of roughly $\sqrt{10}$ and is specified by the range factor R. Blanks are measured using the same cuvette as the sample. The instruments should be equipped for chlorophyll measurement as specified by the manufacturer.

When using a fluorometric method it suffices to filter between 50 and 500 ml of sample.

Rinse the cuvette well with 90% acetone. Add extract and place in fluorometer. Select range so that fluorescence reads between 0.3 and 0.9 of full scale. Read the fluorescence ($f_o{}^*$ in instrument units). Add 2 drops of 2N (roughly 8% conc. HCl by volume), shake the cuvette gently, and read fluorescence again after 30 seconds ($f_a{}^*$) *without changing range*. Rinse the cuvette thoroughly before the next sample, to avoid transferring acid. At intervals, measure 90% acetone blanks before ($f_{o(b)}$) and after ($f_{a(b)}$) acidification on all the ranges used. Correct the sample fluorescences for the appropriate blanks and for the range used:

$$f_o = (f_o{}^* - f_{o(b)})/R \tag{3}$$
$$f_a = (f_a{}^* - f_{a(b)})/R \tag{4}$$

'Chlorophyll' (C) and, if needed, pheopigment (P) concentrations can be calculated from:

$$(C) = K_f(f_o - f_a) \cdot E/V \quad (\mu g \text{ chl } a \text{ equivalent}) \, l^{-1} \tag{5}$$
$$(P) = K_f(H_f \cdot f_a - f_o) \cdot E/V \quad (\mu g \text{ chl } a \text{ equivalent}) \, l^{-1} \tag{6}$$

The values of the constants K_f and H_f are discussed below.

Theory

The pigment mixture in the extract includes chlorophyll a and its derivatives chlorophyllide a, pheophytin a, and pheophorbide a, plus other chlorophylls and their derivatives, and carotenoids. The other chlorophylls and the carotenoids have peak extinction at shorter wavelengths than that of chlorophyll a, and the fluorescence of the other chlorophylls is emitted at shorter wavelengths. Carotenoids do not fluoresce significantly under the conditions used for chlorophyll. Choosing the correct wavelength at which to measure o.d., or the correct excitation and emission filters (see the fluorometer manufacturer's specifications for chlorophyll measurement) thus excludes from consideration all pigments except chlorophyll a, chlorophyllide a, and some of the pheopigments – especially pheophytin a and pheophorbide a. Chlorophyllide a is probably naturally present in algal cells, perhaps as a precursor in the synthesis of chlorophyll; in addition, chlorophyllide a is formed from chlorophyll a by the action of chlorophyllase when the cell contents are disrupted. Pheopigment concentration is generally taken as an index of the amount of dead plant material present.

The acidification step converts chlorophyll a into pheophytin a and chlorophyllide a into pheophorbide a. Since chlorophyll a can be distinguished from chlorophyllide a only by chromatography, the two pigments must be lumped together; although chlorophyllide a has a lower molecular weight than chlorophyll a, they have similar molar extinction and fluorescence coefficients. Chlorophyllide a probably does not participate in photosynthesis, but it seems to be associated with living or only recently dead cells, and thus for survey purposes its confusion with chlorophyll a is tolerable (see Gowen, Tett & Wood, 1983). Thus, 'chlorophyll' concentration (C) refers in fact to (chlorophyll a + chlorophyllide a).

Expressing all concentrations in terms of the weight of chlorophyll a from which they have been derived:

$$e_o = E_c \cdot (C) + E_p \cdot (P) \quad cm^{-1} \tag{7}$$

$$e_a = E_p \cdot (C) + E_p \cdot (P) \quad cm^{-1} \tag{8}$$

where E_c and E_p are the specific extinction coefficients for 'chlorophyll' and pheopigments (chlorophyll a equivalent weight) in 90% acetone at 663 nm. Also:

$$f_o = F_c \cdot (C) + F_p \cdot (P) \quad \text{fluorometer units} \tag{9}$$

$$f_a = F_p \cdot (C) + F_p \cdot (P) \quad \text{fluorometer units} \tag{10}$$

where F_c and F_p are the specific fluorescence coefficients for 'chlorophyll' and pheopigments (chlorophyll a equivalent weight) in 90% acetone for the particular emission filters in use, and on the fluorometer range providing the least exciting light.

Given that:

$$H_e = E_c/E_p \tag{11}$$

$$H_f = F_c/F_p \tag{12}$$

and:

$$K_e = 1/(E_c(1 - 1/H_e)) \quad (\mu g \text{ chl } a \text{ equivalent}) \text{ cm ml}^{-1} \tag{13}$$

$$K_f = 1/(F_c(1 - 1/H_f)) \quad (\mu g \text{ chl } a \text{ equivalent}) \text{ ml}^{-1}$$
$$(\text{fluorometer unit})^{-1} \tag{14}$$

equations (7) and (8) may be solved to give equations (1) and (2), and equations (9) and (10) may be solved to give (5) and (6).

The specific extinction for chlorophyll a in 90% acetone at 663 nm is

87.67 l g^{-1} cm^{-1}, according to Jeffrey & Humphrey (1975). According to Strickland & Parsons (1972) the 'acidification factor' H_e is 1.7. The value of K_e is thus 27.7 (μg chl a equivalent) cm ml^{-1}. K_f and H_f must be determined (and checked from time to time) for each fluorometer used.

Fluorometer calibration

Obtain pure chlorophyll a either by chromatography or from a reputable supplier. Make up a solution of about 4 μg ml^{-1} in 90% acetone and determine its exact concentration using the spectrophotometric procedure given above. Take especial care to make the $o.d.$ measurements at a true wavelength of 663 nm. Check that the acidification step gives a ratio of e_o/e_a of between 1.7 and 1.8, and that the ratio of blue (430 nm) to red (663 nm) peak extinctions is 1.1 to 1.2. If not, the chlorophyll a solution is not pure and should not be used. If it is pure, the following simplified equation may be used to calculate its concentration, given 1-cm cells:

$$(C) = e_o \cdot 1000/87.67 \quad \mu\text{g ml}^{-1} \tag{15}$$

Prepare a series of dilutions of this standard solution, ranging from 1:100 to 1:10000, and measure the fluorescence of these dilutions before and after acidification, using all the ranges on the fluorometer. Correct for blanks. Use these results to:

1. Check on the manufacturer's value of the range factor R.
2. Plot fluorescence against concentration to check that the relationship is linear. Significant self-absorption of fluorescence may occur in the more-concentrated solutions. If that is the case, those fluorometer ranges should be avoided and pigment extracts should be prepared from smaller volumes of sample. Values of the range factor R should relate to the least sensitive range in use.
3. Calculate the values of F_c and F_p for the least-sensitive range in use, and thus determine H_f and K_f from equations (12) and (14). For the Turner Designs model 10 fluorometer that I use, the value of H_f is 2.02 and the value of K_f is 0.083 (μg chl a equivalent) (ml extract)$^{-1}$ (instrument unit)$^{-1}$. K_f depends, however, on the settings of the instrument's sensitivity and backing-off controls.

Finally, it should be noted that F_c and F_p decrease, and that therefore K_f increases, with increasing temperature. The effect is small, but it should be investigated and allowed for if measurements are made at room temperatures more than 2 °C different from those of calibration.

Discussion

In the procedure described above the fluorometer is calibrated with a pure pigment solution whose concentration has been determined spectrophotometrically; the calibration is then applied to a pigment mixture. Why, then, use a fluorescence method? The main reason is convenience. The problems arising from a mixture of pigments are equally acute in spectrophotometric measurement, and there is little evidence that F_c for chlorophyllide a is significantly different from that for chlorophyll a. Fluorometer calibration can be infrequent, given the long-term stability of many filter fluorometers. Pigment extracts for fluorescence measurement can be prepared from smaller volumes of sample than those needed for spectrophotometric measurement, and this is helpful because of the amount of filter-clogging sediment in many estuarine water samples. Spectrophotometric measurements of optical density rely on small transmission differences between the sample and reference beams; it is therefore necessary to clean spectrophotometer cells very carefully. This is not necessary with fluorometry, because there are very few substances that might contaminate the cuvette and that are excited by 430-nm light to fluoresce at 670 nm. Because $H_f > H_e$ it is possible to distinguish more exactly between 'chlorophyll' and pheopigments, and thus fluorometric estimates for a mixed-pigment extract are potentially more precise than the corresponding spectrophotometric estimates. Errors in calibration add inaccuracy to the fluorometric method, and thus the error total for each method is probably about the same.

In general, fluorometric measurement is less demanding, and faster, than spectrophotometric measurement, and so is advised in any survey in which measurement of 'chlorophyll' carries the main load of biomass investigation.

References

*Denotes multi-authored volumes referred to by the name of the editor(s) in the interests of brevity and containing several articles cited in the text.

Anderson, D. M. & Morel, F. M. M. (1979). The seeding of two red tide blooms by the germination of benthic *Gonyaulax tamarensis* hypnocysts. *Est. Coast. Mar. Sci.* **8**, 279–93.

Angel, M. V. (1977). Windows into a sea of confusion: sampling limitations for the measurement of ecological parameters in oceanic mid-water environments. In *Oceanic Sound Scattering Prediction*, ed. N. R. Andersen & B. J. Zahuranec, pp. 217–48. New York: Plenum Press.

Baker, A. de C., Clarke, M. R. & Harris, M. J. (1973). The N.I.O. combination net (RMT 1+8) and further developments of rectangular midwater trawls. *J. mar. biol. Ass. U.K.* **53**, 167–84.

Barker, K. S., Smith, R. C. & Nelson, J. R. (1983). Chlorophyll determinations with filter fluorometers: lamp/filter combinations can minimize error. *Limnol. Oceanogr.* **28**, 1037–40.

Barlow, J. P. (1955). Physical and biological processes determining the distribution of zooplankton in a tidal estuary. *Biol. Bull. mar. biol. Lab. Woods Hole,* **109**, 211–25.

Barnes, R. S. K. (1980). *Coastal lagoons.* Cambridge University Press.

Barstow, S. F. (1983). The ecology of Langmuir circulation: a review. *Mar. Env. Res.* **9**, 211–36.

Beers, J. R., Stewart, G. L. & Strickland, J. D. H. (1967). A pumping system for sampling small plankton. *J. Fish. Res. Bd. Canada,* **24**, 1811–18.

Beverton, R. J. H. & Tungate, D. S. (1967). A multipurpose plankton sampler. *J. Cons. perm. int. Explor. Mer,* **31**, 145–57.

Boje, R. & Tomczak, M. (eds) (1978). *Upwelling ecosystems.* Berlin: Springer-Verlag.

*Bougis, P. (ed.) (1982). Marine pelagic protozoa and microzooplankton ecology. CRNS/NATO symposium, Villefranche-sur-Mer, May 1981. *Ann. Inst. Oceanogr.* **58** suppl., 1–350.

Bowden, K. F. (1981). *Physical oceanography of coastal waters.* Chichester: Ellis Horwood Ltd.

Butler, E. I., Knox, S. & Liddicoat, M. I. (1979). The relationship between inorganic and organic nutrients in seawater. *J. mar. biol. Ass. U.K.* **59**, 239–50.

Chatfield, C. (1980). *The analysis of time series: an introduction,* 2nd edn. London: Chapman & Hall.

Clarke, G. L. & Bumpus, D. R. (1940). The plankton sampler – an instrument for quantitative plankton investigations. *Spec. publ. Amer. Soc. Limnol. Oceanogr.* **5**, 1–8

Cox, J. & Wiebe, P. H. (1979). Origins of oceanic phytoplankton in the middle Atlantic Bight. *Est. Coast. Mar. Sci.* **9**, 509–27.

Cunningham, C. R. & Purewal, J. S. (1983). A microcomputer based aid for counting plankton samples. *J. Plankt. Res.* **5**, 783–6.

Dale, B. (1983). Dinoflagellate resting cysts: "benthic plankton". In *Survival Strategies of the Algae,* ed. G. A. Fryxell, pp. 69–136. Cambridge University Press.

Dooley, H. D. (1979). Factors influencing water movements in the Firth of Clyde. *Est. Coast. Mar. Sci.* **9**, 631–42.

Dronkers, J. & Zimmerman, J. T. F. (1982). Some principles of mixing in tidal lagoons. *Oceanol. Acta,* 4, suppl., 101–17.

Duxbury, A. C. (1971). *The Earth and its oceans.* Reading, Mass.: Addison-Wesley.

Dyer, K. R. (1973). *Estuaries: a physical introduction.* London: John Wiley and Sons.

*Dyer, K. R. (ed.) (1979). *Estuarine hydrography and sedimentation.* Estuarine and Brackish-Water Sciences Association Handbooks. Cambridge University Press.

Edwards, A. & Edelsten, D. J. (1976). Marine fish cages – the physical environment. *Proc. R. Soc. Edinb. B.* **75**, 207–21.

Einarsson, H. (1945). *Euphausiacea.* I. North Atlantic species. Dana-Rep. 27. Copenhagen: Carlsberg Foundation.

Fay, P. (1983). *The Blue-Greens.* Studies in Biology, 106. London: Edward Arnold.

Fenchel, T. (1982*a*). Ecology of heterotrophic microflagellates. I. Some important forms and their functional morphology. *Mar. Ecol. Progr. Ser.* **8**, 211–23.

Fenchel, T. (1982*b*). Ecology of heterotrophic microflagellates. IV. Quantitative occurrence and importance as bacterial consumers. *Mar. Ecol. Progr. Ser.* **9**, 25–42.

Fraser, J. H. (1973). Zooplankton of the North Sea. In *North Sea Science*, ed. E. D. Goldberg, pp. 267–289. Cambridge Mass.: MIT Press.

*Freeland, H. J., Farmer, D. M. & Levings, C. D. (eds) (1980). *Fjord Oceanography*. New York; Plenum Publishing Co.

Gabriel, P. L., Dias, N. J. & Nelson-Smith, A. (1975). Temporal changes in the plankton of an industrialized estuary. *Est. Coast. Mar. Sci.* **3**, 145–51.

Gehringer, (1952). An all-metal plankton sampler (model Gulf III). *U.S. Dept. Int. Spec. Sci. Rept. Fish.* **88**, 7–12.

Gehringer, J. W. (1962). The Gulf III and other modern high-speed plankton samplers. *Rapp. P.-V. Réun. Cons. perm. int. Explor. Mer*, **153**, 19–22.

Gowen, R. J. Tett, P. & Jones, K. J. (1983). The hydrography and phytoplankton ecology of Loch Ardbhair: a small sea-loch on the west coast of Scotland. *J. exp. mar. Biol. Ecol.* **70**, 1–16.

Gowen, R. J., Tett, P. & Wood, B. J. B. (1983). Changes in the major dihydroporphyrin plankton pigments during the spring bloom in two Scottish sea-lochs. *J. mar. Biol. Ass. U.K.* **63**, 27–36.

Hammerton, D., Newton, A. J. & Leatherland, T. M. (1981). The design and interpretation of marine pollution surveys. *Water Pollut. Control*, **80**, 189–203.

Hansen, K. V. (1951). On the diurnal migration of zooplankton in relation to the discontinuity layer. *J. Cons. perm. int. Explor. Mer*, **17**, 231–41.

Hardy, A. C. (1970). *The Open Sea: its natural history*, Part I: *The world of plankton*. London: Collins New Naturalist.

Head, P. C. (ed) (1985). *Practical Estuarine Chemistry*. Estuarine and Brackish-Water Sciences Association Handbook. Cambridge University Press.

Hempel, G. (ed.) (1982). The Canary Current: studies of an upwelling system. *Rapp. P.-v. Reun. Cons. int. Explor. Mer*, **180**, 1–455.

Holm-Hansen, O., Lorenzen, C. F., Holmes, R. W. & Strickland, J. D. H. (1965). Fluorometric determination of chlorophyll. *J. Cons. perm. int. Explor. Mer*, **30**, 3–15.

Holm-Hansen, O., Taylor, F. J. R. & Barsdate, R. J. (1970). A ciliate red tide at Barrow, Alaska. *Mar. Biol.* **7**, 37–46.

Humm, H. J. & Wicks, S. R. (1980). *Introduction and guide to the marine blue-green algae*. New York: Wiley Interscience.

Incze, L. S. & Yentsch, C. M. (1981). Stable density fronts and dinoflagellate patches in a tidal estuary. *Est. Coast. Shelf Sci.* **13**, 547–56.

Jeffrey, S. W. & Humphrey, S. F. (1975). New spectrophotometric equations for determining chlorophylls a, b, c_1 and c_2 in higher plants, algae and natural phytoplankton. *Biochem. Physiol. Planzen.* **167**, 191–4.

Johnson, G. E. & Gonor, J. J. (1982). The tidal exchange of *Callianassa californiensis* (Crustacea, Decapoda) larvae between the ocean and the Salmon River estuary, Oregon. *Est. Coast. Shelf. Sci.* **14**, 501–16.

Johnson, M. W. & Brinton, E. (1963). Biological species, water-masses and currents. In *The Sea*, Vol. 2, ed. M. N. Hill, pp. 381–414. New York: Wiley-Interscience.

Johnson, P. W. & Sieburth, J. McN. (1979). Chrococcoid cyanobacteria in the sea: a ubiquitous and diverse phototrophic biomass. *Limnol. Oceanogr.* **24**, 928–35.

Johnson, P. W. & Sieburth, J. McN. (1982). In-situ morphology and occurrence of eukaryotic phototrophs of bacterial size in the picoplankton of estuarine and oceanic waters. *J.Phycol.* **18**, 318–27.

Joint, I. R. & Pomeroy, A. J. (1981). Primary production in a turbid estuary. *Est. Coast. Shelf. Sci.* **13**, 303–16.

Jones, K. J., Ayres, P., Bullock, A. M., Roberts, R. J. & Tett, P. (1982). A red tide of *Gyrodinium aureolum* in sea lochs of the Firth of Clyde and associated mortality of pond-reared salmon. *J. mar. biol. Ass. U.K.* **62**, 771–82.

Jones, K. J., Gowen, R. J. & Tett, P. (1984). Water-column structure and summer phytoplankton distribution in the sound of Jura. *J. exp. mar. Biol. Ecol.* **78**, 269–89.

Kautsky, H. (1973). The distribution of the radio nuclide caesium 137 as an indicator for North Sea watermass transport. *Dt. hydrogr. Z.* **26**, 241–6.

*Kennedy, V. S. (ed.) (1982). *Estuarine comparisons*. New York: Academic Press.

Ketchum, B. H. (1954). Relations between circulation and planktonic populations in estuaries. *Ecology*, **35**, 191–200.

*Ketchum, B. H. (ed.) (1983). *Ecosystems of the world, 26: Estuaries and Enclosed Seas*. Amsterdam: Elsevier Scientific Publishing Co.

Ketchum, B. H. & Keen, D. J. (1953). The exchange of fresh and salt waters in the Bay of Fundy and in Passamaquoddy Bay. *J. Fish. Res. Bd. Canada*, **10**, 97–124.

Knaus, J. A. (1978). *Introduction to Physical Oceanography*. Englewood Cliffs, New Jersey: Prentice-Hall.

Kremer, P. & Nixon, S. (1976). Distribution and abundance of the ctenophore *Mnemiopsis leidyi* in Narragansett Bay. *Est. Coast. Mar. Sci.* **4**, 627–39.

Landless, P. J. & Edwards, A. (1976). Economical ways of assessing hydrography for fish farms. *Aquaculture*, **8**, 29–43.

Landry, M. R., Haas, L. W. & Fagerness, V. L. (1984). Dynamics of microbial plankton communities: experiments in Kaneohe Bay, Hawaii. *Mar. Ecol. Progr. Ser.* **161**, 127–33.

*Lauff, G. H. (ed.) (1967). *Estuaries.* Publication 83. Washington, D.C.: American Association for the Advancement of Science.

Le Fevre, J., Vollier, M., Le Corre, P., Dupouy, C. & Grall, J.-R. (1983). Remote sensing observations of biological material by LANDSAT along a tidal thermal front and their relevancy to the available field data. *Est. Coast. Shelf. Sci.* **16**, 37–50.

Leftley, J. W., Bonin, D. J. & Maestrini, S. Y. (1983). Problems in estimating marine phytoplankton growth, productivity and metabolic activity in nature: an overview of methodology. *Oceanogr. Mar. Biol. Ann. Rev.* **21**, 23–66.

Lindholm, T. (1982). EDTA and oxalic acid – two useful agents for narcotizing fragile and rapid microzooplankton. *Hydrobiologia,* **86**, 297–8.

Longhurst, A. R., Reith, A. D., Bower, R. E. & Seibert, P. L. R. (1966). A new system for the collection of multiple serial plankton samples. *Deep Sea Res.* **13**, 213–22.

Lorenzen, C. J. (1966). A method for the continuous measurement of *in vivo* chlorophyll concentrations. *Deep Sea Res.* **13**, 223–7.

McGowan, J. A. & Brown, D. M. (1966). *A new opening–closing paired zooplankton net.* La Jolla, California: Scripps Institute of Oceanography. Ref. 66–23.

McKinley, I. G., Baxter, M. S., Ellett, D. J. & Jack, W. (1981). Tracer applications of radiocaesium in the Sea of the Hebrides. *Est. Coast. Shelf Sci.* **13**, 69–82.

McLusky, D. S. (1981). *The Estuarine Ecosystem.* Glasgow: Blackie.

Marshall, S. M. & Orr, A. P. (1972). *Biology of a marine copepod: Calanus finmarchicus* (Gunnerus). Berlin: Springer-Verlag.

Mauchline, J. (1980*a*). Artificial radioisotopes in the marginal seas of North-Western Europe. In *The North-West European Shelf Seas: The Sea Bed and the Sea in Motion,* vol. II: *Physical and Chemical Oceanography, and Physical Resources,* ed. F. T. Banner, M. B. Collins & K. S. Massie. Amsterdam: Elsevier.

Mauchline, J. (1980*b*). The biology of mysids and euphausiids. *Adv. Mar. Biol.* **18**, 1–677.

Mauchline, J. & Fisher, L. R. (1969). *The Biology of euphausiids.* Advances in Marine Biology 7. London: Academic Press.

Miller, C. B. & Judkins, D. C. (1981). Design of pumping for sampling zooplankton with descriptions of two high capacity samplers for coastal studies. *Biol. Oceanogr.* **1**, 29–56.

*Morris, A. W. (ed.) (1983). *Practical procedures for estuarine studies.* Plymouth: Natural Environment Research Council, IMER.

Newell, G. E. & Newell, R. C. (1977). *Marine Plankton: A Practical Guide.* London: Hutchinson Educational Ltd.

Newell, R. C., Lucas, M. I. & Linley, E. A. S. (1981). Rate of degradation and efficiency of conversion of phytoplankton debris by marine micro-organisms. *Mar. Ecol. Progr. Ser.* **6**, 123–36.

Officer, C. B. (1976). *Physical oceanography of estuaries and associated coastal waters.* New York: Wiley-Interscience.

Officer, C. B. (1979). Discussion of the behaviour of non-conservative dissolved constituents in estuaries. *Est. Coast. Mar. Sci.* **9**, 91–4.

Parsons, T. K., Maita, Y. & Lalli, C. M. (1984). *A Manual of Chemical and Biological Methods of Seawater Analysis*. Oxford & New York: Pergamon Press.

Parsons, T. R., Takahashi, M. & Hargrave, B. (1977). *Biological Oceanographic Processes*, 2nd edn. Oxford: Pergamon.

Pickard, G. L. & Emery, W. J. (1982). *Descriptive physical oceanography*, 4th enlarged edn. Oxford: Pergamon.

Pingree, R. D. & Griffiths, D. K. (1978). Tidal fronts on the shelf seas around the British Isles. *J. Geophys. Res.* **83**, 4615–22.

Pingree, R. D., Holligan, P. M., Mardell, G. T. & Harris, R. P. (1982). Vertical distribution of plankton in the Skagerrak in relation to doming of the seasonal thermocline. *Cont. Shelf. Res.* **1**, 209–19.

Pingree, R. D., Pugh, P. R., Holligan, P. M. & Forster, G. R. (1975). Summer phytoplankton blooms and red tides along tidal fronts in the approaches to the English Channel. *Nature, Lond.* **258**, 672–77.

Pipkin, B. W., Gorsline, D. S., Casey, R. E. & Hammond, D. E. (1977). *Laboratory exercises in oceanography*. San Francisco: W. H. Freeman and Co.

Rai, H. & Marker, A. F. H. (eds (1982). The measurement of photosynthetic pigments in freshwaters and standardization of methods. *Ergebn. Limnol.* **16**, 1–130. Stuttgart.

Raine, R. & Tett, P. (1984). *SMBA int. rept.* 106. Oban: Scottish Marine Biological Association.

Raymont, J. E. G. (1980). *Plankton and productivity in the oceans*, 2nd edn, vol. 1: *Phytoplankton*. Oxford: Pergamon.

Raymont, J. E. G. (1983). *Plankton and productivity in the oceans*, 2nd edn. vol. 2: *Zooplankton*. Oxford: Pergamon.

Richards, F. A. (ed.) (1981). *Coastal Upwelling*. Washington: American Geophysical Union.

Roberts, R. J., Bullock, A. M., Turner, M., Jones, K. & Tett, P. (1983). Mortalities of *Salmo gairdneri* exposed to cultures of *Gyrodinium aureolum*. *J. mar. biol. Ass. U.K.* **63**, 741–53.

Ryther, J. H. (1955). Ecology of autotrophic marine dinoflagellates with reference to red water conditions. In *The luminescence of biological systems*, ed. F. H. Johnson, pp. 387–414. Washington D.C.: American Association for the Advancement of Science.

Ryther, J. H. & Dunstan, W. H. (1971). Nitrogen, phosphorus and eutrophication in the coastal marine environment. *Science*, **171**, 1008–13.

Sars, G. O. (1903). *An account of the Crustacea of Norway. IV. Copepoda Calanoida*. Bergen: Bergen Museum.

Sandifer, P. A. (1975). The role of pelagic larvae in recruitment to population of adult decapod crustaceans in the York River Estuary and adjacent lower Chesapeake Bay, Virginia. *Est. Coast. Mar. Sci.* **3**, 269–79.

Scott, J. M. & Marlow, J. A. (1982). A microcalorimeter with a range of 0.1–1.0 calories. *Limnol. Oceanogr.* **27**, 585–90.

Sherr, B. & Sherr, E. (1983). Enumeration of heterotrophic microprotozoa by epifluorescence microscopy. *Est. Coast. Shelf Sci.* **16**, 1–7.

Simpson, J. H., Hughes, D. G. & Morris, N. C. G. (1977). The relationship of seasonal stratification to tidal mixing in the continental shelf. In *A Voyage of Discovery*, ed. M. Angel, pp. 327–40. Oxford: Pergamon.

Simpson, J. H. & Nunes, R. A. (1981). The tidal intrusion front: an estuarine convergence zone. *Est. Coast. Shelf Sci.* **13**, 257–66.

Simpson, J. H., Tett, P. B., Argote-Espinoza, M. L., Edwards, A., Jones, K. J. & Savidge, G. (1982). Mixing and phytoplankton growth around an island in a stratified sea. *Cont. Shelf. Res.* **1**, 15–31.

Smith, R. C. & Baker, K. (1982). Oceanic chlorophyll concentrations as determined by satellite (Nimbus-7 Coastal Zone Color Scanner) *Mar. Biol.* **66**, 269–79.

*Sournia, A. (ed.) (1978). *Phytoplankton Manual*. UNESCO Monographs on Oceanographic Methodology, 6. Paris: UNESCO.

Southward, A. J. (1962). The distribution of some plankton animals in the English Channel and approaches. II. Surveys with the Gulf III high speed sampler, 1958–60. *J. mar. biol. Ass. U.K.* **42**, 275–375.

*Steedman, H. F. (ed.) (1976). *Zooplankton fixation and preservation*. UNESCO Monographs on Oceanographic Methodology, 4. Paris: UNESCO.

*Steele, J. H. (ed.) (1978). *Spatial Pattern in Plankton Communities*. New York: Plenum Press.

Strickland, J. D. H. & Parsons, T. R. (1972). *A Practical Handbook of Seawater Analysis*, 2nd edn. Bulletin 167. Ottawa: Fisheries Research Board of Canada.

Sullivan, B. H. & Hancock, D. (1977). Zooplankton and dredging: research perspectives from a critical review. *Water Res. Bull.* **13**, 461–8.

*Swallow, J. C., Currie, R. I., Gill, A. E. & Simpson, J. H. (eds) (1981). *Circulation and Fronts in Continental Shelf Seas*. London: The Royal Society.

Taylor, D. L. & Seliger, H. H. (eds) (1979). *Toxic dinoflagellate blooms*. New York: Elsevier/North Holland.

Taylor, F. J. R., Blackbourn, D. J. & Blackbourn, J. (1971). The red-water ciliate *Mesodinium rubrum* and its "incomplete symbionts": a review including new ultrastructural observations. *J. Fish. Res. Bd. Canada*, **21**, 391–407.

Tett, P. & Edwards, A. (1984). Mixing and plankton: an interdisciplinary theme in oceanography. *Oceanogr. Mar. Biol. Ann. Rev.* **22**, 99–123.

Tett, P. & Kelly, M. G. (1973). Marine Bioluminescence. *Oceanogr. Mar. Biol. Ann. Rev.* **11**, 89–173.

Tett, P. & Wallis, A. C. (1978). The general annual cycle of chlorophyll standing crop in Loch Creran. *J. Ecol.* **66**, 227–39.

*Tranter, D. J. & Fraser, J. H. (eds) (1968). *Zooplankton sampling*. UNESCO Monographs on Oceanographic Methodology 2. Paris: UNESCO.

UNESCO (1966). *Determination of photosynthetic pigments in seawater*. UNESCO Monographs on Oceanographic Methodology, 1. Paris: UNESCO.

Waite, S. W. & O'Grady, S. M. (1980). Description of a new submersible filter-pump apparatus for sampling plankton. *Hydrobiologia*, **74**, 187–91.

Williams, P. J. LeB. (1981). Incorporation of microheterotrophic processes into the classical paradigm of the planktonic food web. *Kieler Meeresforsch.*, Sonderh. **5**, 1–28.

Wood, B. J. B., Tett, P. B. & Edwards, A. (1973). An introduction to the phytoplankton, primary production and relevant hydrography of Loch Etive. *J. Ecol.* **61**, 569–85.

Wood, L. & Hargis, W. J. (1971). Transport of bivalve larvae in a tidal estuary. In *Fourth European Marine Biology Symposium*, ed. D. J. Crisp pp. 29–44. Cambridge University Press.

Zimmerman, J. T. F. (1976). Mixing and flushing of tidal embayments in the Western Dutch Wadden Sea. 1. Distribution of salinity and calculation of mixing time scales; 2. Analysis of mixing processes. *Neth. J. Sea Res.* **10**, 149–91. 397–439.

Zimmerman, J. T. F. (1981). The flushing of well mixed tidal lagoons and its seasonal fluctuation. *UNESCO tech. Pap. mar. Sci.* **33**, 15–26.

12

Fish

G. W. POTTS and P. J. REAY

Introduction

Many fish are large, long-lived, mobile, and of direct commercial importance. Such characteristics, either individually or in combination, have a dominant influence on survey techniques. On the other hand, part of every fish community consists of small organisms, either small species or early life history stages, which can often be surveyed by the techniques used for benthic and planktonic invertebrates (see Chapters 5, 11).

Clearly a large range of techniques are available for fish studies. The choice in any particular situation will depend on a variety of factors (see, e.g., Allen, 1977). For investigating distribution and abundance, the choice will depend on:

1. the precise survey objectives;
2. environmental characteristics (e.g., water depth);
3. fish characteristics (e.g., vertical distribution);
4. human resources and the time available.

These points will be developed further in relation to the techniques described in this chapter.

Clear definition of the survey objectives (including units required and level of precision) and careful planning of the survey are particularly important in fish work where the characteristics of the organisms tend to generate time-consuming and costly research effort. Typically, the immediate objectives of fish surveys relate to one or more of the following topics:

1. distribution (vertical and/or horizontal) and abundance within a prescribed area;
2. changes in abundance with time – typically from year to year but changes over short time periods are relevant to topic 1;
3. population and community structure, typically in terms of cohorts and species respectively. Subsequent objectives (involving compu-

tation and modeling using data from the above types of survey) may be related to

4. production of a population or community throughout a year;
5. optimum yields obtainable from an exploited population or community.

Once the objectives are identified, the next important step is to determine ways of quantifying the information in a way that will render the results easy to understand by other workers in the field and yet at the same time enable the results to be compared with existing data or proposed future results. This need to standardise quantitative procedures cannot be stressed too strongly if the work is to have any long-term significance.

The emphasis on behavioural aspects in this review is concomitant with the influence that high mobility and complex behaviour patterns have in fish studies (Herrnkind, 1974). Behavioural research is often of course, an end in itself, but in the present context it is seen as complementary to the primary survey objectives (Merdinyan, Mortimer & Melbye, 1980). Examples include the effects of seasonal and diel migrations on the design of sampling programmes; the interactions between fish behaviour and the design and operation of sampling gear (Parrish, 1969; Hemmings, 1973; Wardle, 1976); and the effect behavioural interaction between fish and their environment (including interspecific and intraspecific components) has on the analysis of changes in abundance and community composition.

Some of the most useful and comprehensive information on fish survey techniques in relation to fisheries has come from FAO publications (e.g., Laevastu, 1965; Gulland, 1969, 1971; Holden & Raitt, 1974; Saville, 1977; Ulltang, 1977; Jones, 1979), but these are not always readily available. Bagenal's (1978) handbook on freshwater fish production is more accessible, and much of the material is as applicable to marine fish as it is to freshwater fish. Nielsen & Johnson (1983) have also recently provided a comprehensive review of fisheries techniques that is of value to those working in estuarine and coastal ecosystems. Ricker (1975) has produced the definitive work on computational procedures relating to the assessment and management of fish stocks; this work contains numerous worked examples. Lackey & Hubert (1977) cover similar ground but in abbreviated form, and Gulland (1983) has brought many of these techniques further up to date. For other reviews, the works of Cochran (1960), Cushing (1973), Rounsefell (1975), Kelley (1976), and Holme & McIntyre (1984) should be consulted. Cushing (1982) and Pitcher & Hart (1982) provide useful theoretical background on many of the aspects covered in this chapter.

Planning considerations

Relative and absolute abundance

Abundance data have their own intrinsic value but are also used to estimate mortality rates, production, and optimum yield. They are of central importance, therefore, in most ecological and fishery-oriented studies. Abundance may be expressed in either numerical or biomass terms, which can be interconverted if the (geometric) mean weight of fish is known.

Relative and absolute abundance need to be distinguished. Relative abundance is expressed in relation to units of effort, such as a trap-day (a trap set for 24 hours), an hour's standard trawl, a SCUBA dive along a transect line, or horizontal distance on a sonar plot. In some case these can be directly related to area or volume of sea and hence to absolute abundance, which is the actual number or biomass of fish in a population, community, or specified area. Alternatively, absolute abundance can be arrived at independently, e.g., by using mark–release methods. However it is important to recognise that some survey objectives can be attained using only relative abundance, which is usually more easily measured.

Environmental effects on fish behaviour

Fish behaviour is controlled by internal genetic factors and external environmental factors. With any type of fish survey it is a great advantage to have a good knowledge of the behavioural ecology of the species being studied (Herrnkind, 1974). Such information enables the fish researcher to make predictive statements about the environment and the influence it may have on the availability and distribution of fish; with this, the researcher has the ability to assess the most suitable survey and catching methods.

Estuaries provide a changeable environment in which factors such as salinity, turbidity, and current speed undergo diurnal and seasonal changes. Relatively few species are tolerant of the osmotic stress imposed by these conditions, although bass, mullet, flounder, and gobies are commonly found. Some species, most notably the salmonids, undergo migrations (Harden Jones, 1968) from the sea to estuaries and rivers to spawn. Other fish use estuaries as nursery grounds (Dando, 1984). Surveys must bear these considerations in mind.

Intertidal fish need to be especially tolerant of a changeable environment. Tidal cycles and climatic extremes all have considerable influence and often result in a series of physiological and behavioural adaptations among the inhabitants of this zone (Gibson, 1982) Examples of the importance of tidal cycles are those of Rijnsdorp *et al.* (1985) for plaice larvae and Wirjoatmodjo

Table 12.1. A Classification of Fishing Gear and Survey Methods

	Requirements					Substratum		Areas			Fish			Fish stages			Auxiliary equipment			
	Shore access	Diver	Dinghy	Boat (large)	Fixed structure	Soft	Hard	Intertidal	Close inshore	Offshore	Pelagic	Benthopelagic	Demersal	Eggs/Larvae	'Small fish'	'Large fish'	Hooks, spears, etc.	Anaesthetics	Light	Electric
Hand-gathering																				
No net	++	++					++	++	++		+	+	++		++		+	++		
Hand net	++	++	+			+	++	++	++		+	+	+	+	++			++	+	
Towed nets																				
'Plankton'			+	+		+	+		+	+	+	+	+	+	+				+	
Bottom trawl and dredges			+	+		+			+	+		+	++		+	+				
Midwater trawl				+		+	+		+	+	+				+	+			+	
'Flounder sampler'[a]		+				+		+					+		+	+				
Push net	+		+			+		+	+				+		+					+
Encircling & vertical nets																				
Beach seine	+		+			+		+	+		+	+	+		+	+			+	
Purse seine				+		+			+	+	++	+			+	+				
Danish seine			+	+		+			+	+		+	+		+	+				
Cast net	+		+			+	+	+	+		+	+			+				+	
Lift net			+		+	+		+	+		+				+	+			++	
Drop-net quadrat		+	+		+	+		+	+				+	+	+			+	+	
Set nets & traps																				
Gill net			+	+		+	+	+	+	+	+	+	+		+	+				
Trammel net			+	+		+	+		+	+		+	+		+	+				
Fixed trap			+		+	+	+	+	+			+	+		+	+				
Fyke net			+			+			+			+	+		+	+				
Baited traps						+	+		+				+		+	+			+	
Baited hooks																				
Long lines				+		+			+	+	+	+	+			+	+			
Hand lines			+			+		+	+		+		+			+			+	
Angling	+		+			+	+	+	+		+		+		+	+	+			
Pumping																				
Plankton pumps	+					+	+	+	+	+	+	+	+	+	+				+	
Power stations	+			+	+	+	+		+		+	+	+	+	+	+			+	
Cores, grabs & dredges																				
Cores		+	+	+		+		+	+					+						
Grabs			+	+		+	+		+				+	+		+				
Animals																				
Predator stomachs	+		+	+		+			+	+	+	+	+	+	+	+				

[a] Diver-operated, see Walton & Bartoo (1976).

& Pitcher (1984) for adult flounders. Clarke & King (1985) give an example
of semilunar behaviour changes.

Selectivity of observation and capture techniques

All methods and techniques of observation and capture are
selective to some degree, and unless such selectivity is taken into account,
errors will arise. The selectivity may relate to species or to sex, size, and
other groups within species (Pope *et al.*, 1975). It is brought about by both
the relative distribution of, and the interaction between, the fish and the
catching or recording gear. Variation in the response of fish to gear can
arise from variation in experience, e.g., towards baited hooks (Fernö &
Huse, 1983).

Choice of methods

Choice of methods will depend upon many factors including
species and stages of fish to be sampled, water depth, and substratum type.
A guide is given in Table 12.1.

Fish handling

Most fish are readily harmed by excessive handling, which should
be kept to a minimum if physical, physiological, and behavioural damage
are not to occur. Most capturing methods involve the physical restraint
of the fish, and it is at this stage that the most damage may result. It is
therefore advisable to use capturing methods of short duration and to
remove the specimens at frequent intervals. Special procedures or modifications to gear may be needed to prevent damage to specimens; these may
include rings in the cod end to prevent it collapsing, short trawls, barbless
hooks, and specially designed traps. Fish are rapidly stressed if removed
from water and it is advisable that some provision be made to keep them
in water at all times.

Surveys using observation techniques

Considerable progress has been made in recent years with the
development of sonar, underwater photography, SCUBA diving, and
submersibles; the techniques are now of considerable value in work on fish
and fisheries. In general terms, observational techniques produce quicker
results and can cover larger areas than capture techniques, but relative
merits among and within the major groups of techniques are only relevant
in the particular context in which they are to be used.

In addition to being used on their own, observational techniques often
give support to catching techniques and vice versa. They are important in

examining the relationship of fish to their natural environment and should, where possible, be attempted before the more routine fishing techniques are employed. Indeed, if elaborate and expensive catching gear is to be used, it is usually wise to carry out some form of observational pilot survey to check not only that the fish population to be sampled is in fact present, but also that the environment is suitable for the effective use of the gear and that the gear is performing adequately.

Visual observation techniques are very hard to use in poor light, turbid water, for camouflaged flatfish, or for dull-coloured fish. Sonar, radiotelemetry, and electronic fish recorders are immune from the problems imposed by low visibility, but all techniques suffer from problems of accurate identification of the species being counted. Again, all techniques select for the fish that are most conspicuous: surface fish for the aerial observer; pelagic fish with swim-bladders for sonar equipment.

Aerial observations

Surface-swimming fish can often be seen by aerial observations and it is possible to record their presence and movements with some accuracy. Schools of fish can often be seen from high vantage points on land, but further away from the coast it may be necessary to resort to light, mobile spotter aircraft (Cram & Hampton, 1976). The technique of using high vantage points for recording the presence of migrating tuna is important in controlling Mediterranean fisheries (Sund, 1981).

Aerial photography (using a polarising filter to reduce surface glare) may be possible in some cases, and satellite imagery indicating climatic and hydrographical conditions is likely to be useful for planning and interpreting large-scale surveys (see Chapter 2). The use of Polaroid spectacles may help the fish watcher to observe surface-living mullet or rock pool species (Aronson, 1951) or, if water conditions are suitable, long-shore migrations or even predatory activity can be followed (Potts, 1970). In calm conditions, observation boxes with Perspex or glass window can be used from a small boat (Gibson, 1980), or glass-bottomed boats provide a similar facility and permit the observer to watch and record the activity of fish. Under these conditions notes may be taken, books referred to, and electronic recording equipment used, activities which may not be possible for divers. The main drawback of this technique is that it is restricted to calm conditions and it is difficult to determine the influence of the boat and its shadow on those fish under observation.

Direct observations underwater

For shallow-water work (down to 10 m) in clear, calm conditions, snorkelling may be adequate for following and recording fish and has the advantage of presenting the minimal disturbance (Potts, 1973, 1980). At greater depths (10–50 m) SCUBA diving must be used, which also permits an observer to operate below the turbulent surface conditions.

For diving techniques see Chapter 9, and also Woods & Lythgoe (1971) and Drew, Lythgoe & Woods (1976).

In areas (such as rocky reefs) that are difficult to sample by conventional methods, SCUBA diving can provide the means of observing and collecting shallow-water fish. This may form part of large commercial programmes of fishing systems evaluation (High, 1969; Wickham & Watson, 1976) or flatfish abundance studies (Walton & Bartoo, 1976; Gibson, 1980) or relatively small-scale sampling at a highly selective level using poisoning stations or suction samplers (Randall, 1963; Wilcox, Meek & Mook, 1974; Gilligan, 1976).

Direct observations by divers have been an important part of developing our understanding of fish behaviour and the way fish associate with the environment (Hemmings, 1971). However there are drawbacks and it has been shown that fish may be sensitive to the noise of an aqualung from a considerable distance (Chapman *et al.*, 1974). The use of hides can help reduce the visual impact of a diver, although the construction and siting of such hides can provide considerable disturbance to residential fish populations. The use of oxygen rebreathing sets may avoid the noisy bubbles from demand valves (Losey, 1971). Usually it is better to accept the fact that the diver imposes himself upon the environment and to allow an acclimatisation period for the fish to become used to the presence of the diver before making quantitative observations. By doing this and by using fish response patterns as a guide, it is possible to make meaningful observations with the minimum of disturbance (Potts, 1973, 1980, 1983).

Where large areas are to be surveyed in shallow depths, a diver can be towed behind a boat using a simple board as a hydrofoil (see chapter 9). Such simple equipment can be used to survey flat areas at slow speeds, but if larger areas are to be examined, then free flooding towed vehicles (Foulkes & Scarratt, 1972) which permit the diver some protection against water drag (Woods & Lythgoe, 1971) should be used. If for any reason cables are not wanted, self-propelled diver vehicles or tugs can be used. However these generally have the drawback that the power sources, such as dry batteries, have a limited operational life (Potts, 1974).

Underwater photography

With the development of new technology and with improved optical equipment, underwater photography is having an increasing role in the study of fish biology. The equipment ranges from simple hand-held cameras operated by divers to elaborate pressurised systems capable of being operated in very deep water. Still cameras may be used with or without supplementary lighting and either singly or in pairs to provide stereoscopic pictures. Using motorised cameras with time-lapse control mechanism, series of pictures can be taken along set transects and these provide valuable data on the nature of the environment.

Water pressure necessitates that great care must be taken in designing pressure housings for cameras and photographic equipment. Further, the power source to the camera and flash units must either be sealed in the housing with the flash or be provided with special waterproof and pressure-resistant cables and sockets. With increasing depth, the amount of incident light decreases until, in clear water, very little remains at about 200 m depth. To film under these conditions demands special pressure-housed lights. Bright lights will affect the behaviour of mobile species like fish, which are either attracted to them or repelled, and thus lights can create an artificial estimation of abundance or scarcity. At shallower depths where enough incident light is available, the use of TV cameras has proved valuable, and with image intensifiers these can operate and produce workable images at very low light levels. Further, the use of modern fibre-optics systems, such as the silicone diode cameras, gives sensitivity to low light intensities; the camera of these systems is more robust and has a faster reaction time than the conventional 'Vidicon' tube.

Apart from fixed station TV cameras it is likely that underwater photographic equipment will disturb and influence the behaviour of the species that are under investigation. This is particularly true of artificial light sources. A further problem relates to the mobility of fish and, apart from diver-held cameras in shallow water, it is unlikely that remote-controlled cameras can record useful records of more than a very few fish and species. Lighted or baited lures can be used to attract fish to remote cameras; however, the overall interpretation of such data is limited.

There are many reviews of the use of cameras both by divers and remote ship-borne control and in conjunction with sample equipment, and the following references should be consulted: Livingstone (1962), Craig & Priestley (1963), Engel (1968), Mertens (1970), Holme & McIntyre (1971), Hemmings (1972), Strickland (1973), Myrberg (1974), Serebrov (1974), Gusar & Kupriyanov (1975), Ray (1977).

Acoustic surveys

The use of echo sounders for depth finding is now widespread. Echo sounding depends upon the time taken for a signal to travel from a ship-borne transducer to the sea-bed and back again (Cushing, 1978). The frequency of the signal depends upon the depth of water being measured; generally, deep water requires large transducers with a low frequency (10–12 kHz). The use of higher frequencies of between 20 and 50 kHz allows fish to be detected, and with more-sophisticated equipment the abundance of these fish can be estimated. This is now an essential part of most fishing operations; before setting nets, fishermen usually carry out a sonic search to determine the nature of the bottom and the presence of adequate fish stocks. The advanced forms of sonar such as side scan and sector-scanning sonar enable a quick and efficient assessment of the abundance of fish stocks, such as the mackerel in the English Channel (Lockwood, 1976), and can be used for tracking schools of fish at distances of up to 15 km (Rusby *et al.*, 1973).

The methodology is reviewed by Newton & Stefanou (1975). The application of acoustic survey techniques in stock assessment is reviewed by Thorne (1980) for tropical small-scale fisheries. The main disadvantage is the poor discrimination of species, but this would be less of a problem in inshore temperate waters where schooling fish are usually easy to recognise.

Surveys using capture techniques

Capture techniques can be used in the same way as observational ones (to give relative estimates of abundance, which may or may not be converted into absolute estimates), but there are additional methods of utilising catch data, such as mark–recapture and cohort analysis. In addition, of course, samples of either live or dead fish become available for further analysis.

Capture techniques all rely on catching gear of which a great variety exists, and within which there is something suitable for almost any objective, type of fish, and type of habitat. Probably the most widely used gear is the bottom trawl, but this can only be used over soft substrata. Other gear, or observational techniques, must be used over rough ground such as rocks and reefs.

There are many ways of classifying fishing gear types and some are very detailed (e.g., Laevastu, 1965), but a basic division into hand nets, traps, hook and line, set nets, seines, and trawls is adequate for most purposes (see Table 12.1). Further details of their construction and operation are provided by von Brandt (1984) and Rounsefell (1975). Some of the basic

Fig. 12.1 Fishing methods. (*a*) Fish trap for small sedentary species; (*b*) estuarine fixed trap; (*c*) purse-seine; (*d*) otter trawl.

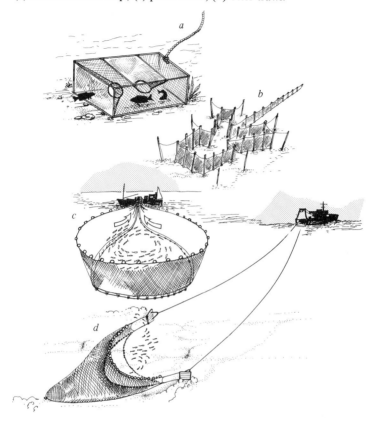

Fig. 12.2. Fishing methods. (*a*) Beach seine; (*b*) Riley type push net for shallow water; (*c*) simple bottle trap made from a disused plastic bottle; (*d*) simple lift net.

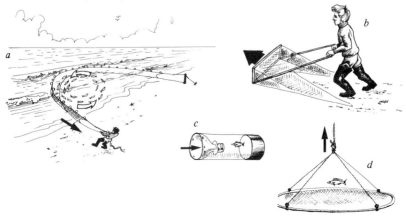

types are illustrated in Figs. 12.1 and 12.2, and brief notes on their relative merits are given in the next section.

Catching gear
Hand nets and associated techniques

By themselves hand nets are of limited use in fish survey work because of the small area that can be covered and because of the evasive action taken by all but the most sluggish species. The latter problem can, however, be overcome by the use of anaesthetics and poisons, so that the hand net in these cases is simply used to scoop up narcotised or dead fish.

The use of fish narcotics and poisons is mostly restricted to small-scale research programmes. Such methods are mostly carried out with divers in attendance and enable a wide range of fish to be caught. Best used for collecting species restricted to reef situations, they have the disadvantage of being non-selective and should only be used under very controlled conditions. For offshore poison stations, Rotenone is the most widely used poison (Randall, 1963; Smith, 1973; Russel et al., 1978).

The technique providing the best results is to enclose a reef in fine netting and swamp the area in Rotenone. The fish of the reef are killed and, with care, some kind of quantitative assessment of the fish fauna can be seen. The fish narcotics such as Quinaldine (Gibson, 1967) are best used in the intertidal situation where pools are narcotised by the addition of a mixture of 1 part Quinaldine and 4 parts acetone. The fish rapidly succumb to the narcotic but will quickly recover if transferred to fresh sea water. With reasonable care there is no danger associated with the use of Rotenone in coastal sampling stations, provided it is not ingested. However, Quinaldine may cause severe irritation of the skin and must at all times be kept clear of the face, the eyes in particular. It is wise to wear some form of protective rubber gloves when using Quinaldine.

While for the most part electrofishing techniques have been confined to fresh water, in the last ten years there has been an increase in the research looking into its potential for use in marine and brackish waters (Seidel & Klima, 1974; Stewart, 1975, 1977; Lamarque, 1977). The aim is not to stun the fish with an electric shock (a.c.) as is often used in fresh water fisheries techniques, but to exploit the tendency of some schools of fish to move along an electrical gradient (d.c.) towards the cathode where they may be caught in nets or suction pipes. The basic problem with electrofishing in sea water is that the conductivity of the medium is higher than that of the fish, so that the current tends to flow around the fish giving no voltage gradient (Nielsen & Johnson, 1983). There are considerable risks involved

with using electrical currents with salt water, owing to its greater conductivity compared with fresh water. It is therefore best not to use such
techniques without being fully aware of the necessary precautions and their
use should only be undertaken with very experienced personnel.

Traps
These range from minnow or bottle-traps through small cages of the
crab-pot type (Fig. 12.1*a*) to large semi-permanent structures such as weirs
or corrals designed to exploit the migration patterns of inshore and
estuarine fish (e.g., Bay of Fundy herring fishery) (Fig. 12.1*b*). Minnow
traps, constructed of an inverted funnel inserted into disused plastic
bottles, are effective for sampling small fish in rock pools and other inshore
locations (Fig. 12.2*c*). Traps may be made from any materials that will
prevent the escape of fish, and the essential feature is to have an opening
that will allow the fish to enter but not escape easily. The size of this and
any other openings influences the size selectivity of the gear. Traps are often
baited to attract feeding fish, but fish may also be guided physically into
the trap by 'wings' (Fig. 12.1*b*), or may enter in search of cover, or out
of curiosity. This type of trap can be worked over any type of ground
(Beamish, 1972).

Hook and line
Baited hooks can be used individually, as in angling, or on floating or
bottom long lines which may well have several hundred hooks. Both
natural and artificial baits can be used, the fish responding to either visual
or olfactory stimuli. Baited hooks can be worked almost anywhere and
a great variety of species can be caught depending on type of bait, location,
and size of hook.

Set nets
These are vertical walls of netting with a floated head rope and weighted
foot rope that can be fished at the surface (drift nets) or on the bottom.
They are usually set across the direction of water/fish movement. Many
set nets rely on the fish being caught by the gill covers or other
protuberances (hence a given mesh size will not retain fish very much
smaller or larger than the mesh). Tangle nets and trammel nets are
variations whose selectivity does not depend simply on mesh size, but on
the fish getting tangled or falling into net pockets, respectively. These nets
can be set over rough or smooth ground, on the bottom, or at the surface
and tend to catch the most-mobile fish species.

Seines

Together with trawls, these constitute active fishing gear in comparison with the passive methods described so far. All seines basically consist of a wall of netting which is set in such a way that it encircles an area containing fish, all of which are large enough to be retained by the meshes are caught. Seines may be ring nets, purse-seines (Fig. 12.1c), Danish seines, or beach seines (Fig. 12.2a). Beach seines have the greatest utility in estuarine and inshore waters, and although they cannot be used over rough ground or far from the shore, they are capable of catching a considerable variety of inshore species. The lower limit of size is determined by the mesh size. Large fish can avoid being caught in the closing net by swimming fast or by jumping. Beach seines can be simply operated in tidal and estuarine areas by staking a vertical net in a semicircle, the diameter of which is perpendicular to the tidal flow of the water. On the falling tide, fish are trapped by the net and can be collected at low tide. Such permanent structures go on fishing tide after tide and should be visited frequently to remove the catches and avoid attracting predators such as seabirds.

Trawls

Trawls are similar to seines, but rather than encircling an area, they are dragged in a linear direction; the area fished is therefore a long, thin (determined by the width of the trawl mouth) rectangle. Trawls are usually fished demersally (bottom trawls) but midwater trawls are also available. Beam trawls (Muus, 1967; Kuipers, 1977) or otter trawls may be used (Fig. 12.1d). The former uses a rigid beam to spread open the mouth of the net, whereas the latter uses two otter boards acting as hydroplanes to keep the trawl mouth open. Although trawls cannot be used over rough ground, they are the most commonly used gear in survey work. The mesh size in the cod-end determines the minimum size of fish caught. Large meshes elsewhere will still retain small fish because of the herding effect. Tickler chains across the mouth of the net are often used to disturb fish buried in the substratum (e.g., Pleuronectidae, Ammodytidae) so that they become accessible to the gear. Electrical ticklers have been used (e.g., Stewart, 1977).

Lift, drop, and push nets

Lift and drop nets have sometimes been used by workers in shallow water and estuarine situations (Hellier, 1958; Muus, 1967; Gilmore, 1978). They have the advantage of enclosing and retaining fish from an area of known size (Fig. 12.2d). Push nets are relatively cheap, easy to make, and useful for local investigations of small species of fish and young fish in shallow water (about 10–70 cm). The Riley push net is described by Holme & McIntyre (1984), and is illustrated in Fig. 12.2b.

Intake screens of cooling water systems
Coastal electricity generating stations and some types of industrial installation such as oil refineries have cooling systems requiring the intake of large volumes of water. Valuable data can be obtained from the fish retained on the intake screens (filters) of these cooling water systems. Some details are given by Hardisty & Huggins (1975) and Langford (1983).

Catch per unit effort surveys
Precision
The concept of precision, with associated practical decisions concerning numbers of samples, applies of course to both relative and absolute estimates. Fish populations show a highly aggregated distribution and this is particularly true for schooling pelagic species. Barnes & Bagenal (1950), Atsatt & Seapy (1974), and Pitcher (1981) have discussed the significance of such aggregations for the design and operation of fish surveys. More generally it is a problem of increasing the number of samples when variance is high, to give acceptable levels of precision. Saville (1977) has analysed this problem and, with examples, demonstrated the clear value of the stratified sampling approach whereby sampling effort is concentrated in the high density areas.

An example of a study on the distribution and abundance of estuarine fish communities using a trawl survey is given by McErlean *et al.* (1973).

Calculation of absolute abundance
It is possible to calculate absolute abundance only where the size of the area fished by the gear can be reasonably estimated. This therefore applies to trawls, seines, lift nets, drop nets, and push nets. Generally, the use of all other gear will give only relative abundance, but recently Eggers *et al.* (1982) have developed techniques for estimating the areas fished by baited traps and hooks. This now provides an important method for estimating population densities over the rough grounds that cannot be trawled or seined.

Estimating the area fished is most straightforward for beam trawls, where the area is given by the width of the trawl (length of beam) multiplied by the distance trawled. This ignores the fact that not all fish in the path of the trawl will be caught. This is taken into account by including a catchability coefficient, q, which is the proportion of fish in the path that are caught; a value of 0.5 (50%) is commonly used. The concept of catchability has two components: accessibility and vulnerability. Accessibility describes the proportion of fish that are over the strip of sea-bed fished by the trawl and that are actually in the path of the mouth of the trawl; it thus depends on the vertical distribution of the fish. Vulnerability describes the proportion of accessible fish that are actually caught; those not caught escape either from the path of the trawl or through the meshes. Not all fish are of course equally accessible and vulnerable, and within a species there is a strong size-selective component. For example, older fish tend to occur in deeper water than younger ones, and, being larger (and more experienced?) are better able to escape from the path of an oncoming trawl. Conversely, small fish will be more likely to escape through the meshes. Catchability is clearly an important concept, but is not easy to estimate: either it can be inferred if independent estimates are available, or it can be derived from data on the distribution and behaviour of the fish species being investigated, or it can be calculated from data on fishing effort and fishing mortality collected over a time period. Details can be found in Cushing (1982) and Pauly (1979).

Otter trawls are more complicated than beam trawls in relation to estimating the area fished, but a formula is given by Pauly (1979) as follows:

$$d = \frac{c}{Z \cdot H \cdot S \cdot q}$$

d = density, kg km^{-2}

c = catch-rate, kg h^{-1}

Z = a coefficient adjusting headline length to spread of towed net (0.67)

H = length of headline, m

S = trawling speed, km h^{-1}

q = catchability coefficient (e.g., 0.5)

The problems outlined above are concerned with the accuracy of the estimate of abundance. Obviously errors will arise if catchability is ignored, or is inaccurately calculated, in estimates of absolute abundance. For relative abundance, catchability does not strictly have to be known, but in not incorporating it, the assumption is being made that it is constant for all situations under study. This is a rash assumption which cannot always be justified.

Mark–recapture methods

These methods are well described in general by Begon (1979) and Blower, Cook & Bishop (1981), and for fish by Ricker (1975). A wide range of tagging or marking techniques are employed (Fig. 12.3). These are described in a number of important reviews (ICES, 1953; Laird & Stott, 1978; Stonehouse, 1978). The simplest tags are numbered discs or small flags that are fitted through the dorsal muscle by a stainless wire or nylon thread. Other ways of labelling individual fish include internal tags, telemetric tags (Mitson, 1978), freeze branding with liquid nitrogen (Dando & Ling, 1980), injection of rubber latex into juvenile fish (Riley, 1966), radioactive isotope injections, fin clipping or coded magnetic tags (Krieger, 1982) injected from hypodermic needles into the nasal cavities, and many others. The choice of tagging method will depend upon the purpose of the study, the species, its size, and what information is needed. A tag needs to be small enough not to irritate or damage the fish or impede its freedom of movement, and yet at the same time must be conspicuous enough to be recognised easily by non-scientific personnel (Jones, 1976, 1977, 1979).

While tagging technology is well advanced, it is not always recognised that tagging is stressful to fish and that it may affect their behaviour for several days after the operation. Further, if fish are removed from water, their survival rate upon return is reduced. It has been shown that if the fish are tagged by divers underwater without bringing them to the surface, the survival rate may be as high as 90%, while of surface-tagged individuals only 19% survived (Hislop, 1969; Matthews & Bell, 1979; Wilson, 1982). In addition to differential mortality and catchability of marked and

Fig. 12.3. Fish tagging methods.

unmarked fish, sources of error include the non-random dispersal of marked fish, mark loss, and the non-reporting of marked fish, particularly if fishermen are being relied upon.

A particular problem of the mark–recapture method was described by Beukema & De Vos (1974) in their studies on carp (*Cyprinus carpio*) populations of known size. Using traps (fyke nets), seine nets, and baited hooks, they found that very poor estimates were obtained if the same gear was used for both initial capture and recapture, but that good estimates could be obtained if different gear was used. This arises because of (a) differences in vulnerability between individuals (e.g., trap-prone and trap-shy fish in the population) and (b) learning (e.g., learned discrimination between baits and natural food). These results should be carefully studied by anyone contemplating the use of mark–recapture for fish.

Mark–recapture methods can be used for any species of fish and give absolute estimates of abundance. However, they are better suited to enclosed bodies of water rather than the open sea, where the movements of fish in and out of the study area can generate large errors.

Egg and larval surveys

There is typically a large and variable mortality in fish during the early life history and particularly during the transition from yolk-sac to exogenous feeding. As a result, the number of eggs laid, while being a good indication of the size of the parent stock that spawned them, is a very poor index of the strength of the resulting year-class. Therefore, to estimate the latter, surveys of post-larvae or juvenile fish are usually used (Russell, 1976). Fluctuations in year-class strength generate fluctuations in the abundance of fish populations, and monitoring the size of incoming year-classes is an important aspect of predictive fishery research.

The back-calculation of parent stock size from egg abundance is a technique usually applied to species with pelagic eggs which can readily be sampled with plankton nets (see Chapter 11). It has, however, also been applied to herring (*Clupea harengus*) which lay demersal eggs which are counted by divers, remote cameras, or grabs (Schweigart & Fournier, 1982). The principle is that the estimate of the total number of eggs laid in a spawning season is divided by the mean fecundity of the females and their proportion in the whole stock to obtain the estimate of stock size. However, there are real problems in getting precise estimates of the abundance of eggs at even one point in time, and the difference between the number of ovarian eggs and the number in the plankton (a result of incomplete fertilisation and early mortality) can give rise to large errors.

To estimate seasonal egg production, counts of fertilised eggs in a recognisable early developmental stage are made at intervals throughout the season. Daily production is obtained by dividing the numbers counted by the duration of the development stage at the prevailing temperatures. The method is discussed by Saville (1977) and a good example and analysis is provided by Lockwood, Nicholas & Dawson (1981) for mackerel (*Scomber scombrus*). Techniques for sampling fish eggs and larvae are reviewed by Bailey (1975), Nicholas & Wood (1978), and Smith & Richardson (1977).

Indirect methods

It may be possible to make estimates of the size of a prey population from a study of the stomach contents and feeding frequency of its predators. It is also possible to estimate the size of a trophic level or perhaps a dominant species by extrapolating from measurements of primary production, chlorophyll concentrations, or zooplankton abundance. These methods are discussed by Saville (1977). The morpho-edaphic index is used to predict fish production in freshwater lakes but equivalent indices may have application in other aquatic systems (Ryder *et al.* 1974).

Soutar & Isaacs (1974) estimated the historical population sizes of various pelagic species in the bay of California by counting fish scales in the different layers of anoxic sediment (each layer representing a year's deposition).

Sample analysis

Deck sampling, catch recording, and preservation

Procedures for deck sampling and catch recording are given by Saville (1977) and Pauly (1980). It is often necessary to preserve all or part of the catch for analysis; some details are given in Bagenal (1978). Either freezing or chemical preservation (neutralised formalin, alcohol, or phenoxetol) may be used but it should be noted that significant colour change, shrinkage, and weight loss are associated with all preservation techniques; see, e.g., Lockwood & Daly (1975).

Identification

Identification guides are given in Chapter 14. Additionally, the concept of a unit stock or population is an important one in fishery management (Cushing, 1982) and is, or should be, equally important in any biological study. The subject has recently been covered by the Stock Concept Symposium (Fetteroff, 1981). Stocks can be separated by sample analysis (e.g., meristic counts, scale and otolith patterns, parasite fauna, and serological/biochemical characteristics) as well as by studies on distribution and migration.

Length, weight, and condition

Length data are particularly valuable (Pauly, 1980) and are likely to be the most commonly collected information from fish samples. A decision has to be made between total, fork, and standard lengths (Laevastu, 1965) and it is important to standardise between studies on the same species: the shape of the tail fin, the extent to which it is damaged in capture or preservation, and the precedent set by earlier work will largely determine which length measurement is used (Schnute & Fournier, 1980).

Weight data will usually be in the form of total weight, gutted weight, or (gutted) dried weight depending on the objectives of the study. A weight–length regression is commonly fitted after log transformation of the raw data. This relationship can be used to convert length (L) to weight (W) (e.g., for use in production or yield models). The weights of individual body organs or tissues may be included in sample analysis to give some index of 'condition'. The weight or a subjective estimate of the extent of the mesenteric fat deposits appears to be particularly useful in this context (Iles, 1984).

Sex, maturity, and fecundity

In some cases, sex and sexual maturity can be determined from an external examination of fish in the samples. It is usual, however, to open up the body cavity and examine the gonads to determine these and other aspects of reproductive biology. Information on sex ratio, spawning season, age at maturity, and fecundity is essential in connection with the egg survey method of estimating abundance, but aspects of reproductive biology are also routinely collected in general survey work.

Gonad ripeness, and hence age at maturity and spawning season, may be determined by the gonadosomatic ratio (gonad weight as a percentage of either total body weight or somatic weight) by maturity stages based on the size and colour of the gonads, or by histological studies. The latter, involving the determination of oocyte size and the presence of vacuoles and yolk, may also be particularly important in assessing the fecundity of batch-spawning fish; an example is provided by Macer (1974).

The determination of fecundity (the number of ovarian oocytes potentially released during the current spawning season) is usually based on sub-samples of preserved ovarian tissues. Counting is facilitated if the ovary has been preserved in Gilson's fluid which causes the oocytes and remaining ovarian tissue to separate (Bagenal, 1978). Automatic egg counters (e.g., Boyar & Clifford, 1967) or mechanical-digit colony counters (Dodgshun, 1980) can improve the speed and efficiency of counting eggs.

Diet determination

Diet can be obtained by observation in either the natural or captive environment, but quantitative estimates are almost invariably based on stomach contents analysis. Information on stomach contents is primarily used to construct food webs, to investigate feeding tactics (optimal foraging), and to compute the input term in energy budgets.

It is not necessary to kill fish to obtain their stomach contents; for example, Strange & Kennedy (1981) describe a stomach flushing technique for use on anaesthetised salmonids. However, whether live or dead fish are used, care should be taken in the collection of the fish sample to minimise regurgitation, feeding under abnormal conditions (e.g., on other fish in the trawl or trap), digestion after capure, and diel or tidal bias between samples. Numerical, volumetric, or gravimetric analysis of the contents may be carried out depending on the objectives of the study and the discreteness and ease of identification of the food organisms. It must always be remembered that the proportions of food in the stomach are unlikely to reflect exactly the proportions ingested.

Good reviews of diet determination and the estimation of food consumption are provided by Bagenal (1978) and Hyslop (1980). A useful study of flounder (*Platichthys flesus*) food selection in an estuarine environment is given by Moore & Moore (1976).

An alternative to visual examination analysis of stomach contents is provided by serological techniques. These have been used with mixed success in fish (Westcott, 1980) but overcome some of the disadvantages encountered with the standard techniques.

Age determination

The description of a population's age-structure, cohort analysis, the construction of life-tables, and the determination of growth rates, mortality rates, age at first capture, and age at maturity, all depend on the ability to determine the age of fish. Aging techniques are therefore a fundamental part of ecological and fishery survey work, and have attracted considerable attention (see, e.g., Bagenal, 1974, 1978).

Fish are normally aged on an annual basis (with January 1 birthdays) and are described as 0-group, I-group, etc. The two basic techniques used are length-frequency analysis and the counting of growth rings in skeletal structures such as scales, otoliths, opercular bones, spiny fin rays, and vertebrae (Fig. 12.4). In both cases fish from the less seasonal environments of the tropics present the most problems, but careful attention to length-frequency analysis (Pauly, 1980) and diel rather than annual banding in the otoliths (Brothers, 1980; Pannella, 1980) may help in some cases. Macdonald & Pitcher (1979) briefly review length-frequency analysis and describe a mixture analysis technique that overcomes some of the difficulties normally encountered with visual identification of modal groups.

Length-frequency analysis is based on quick and easy data collection and is usually successful for separating at the youngest age-classes (which account for the bulk of biological production in most populations). However, large samples are required (minimum of 50 for each age-group, and polymodality within a group, missing year-classes, and overlap between groups can give rise to errors. To some extent these problems can be overcome by the use of skeletal structures; this method depends upon a permanent record of intermittent body growth appearing as structural discontinuities that can be related to a time-scale. Validation of the latter is achieved by examination of seasonal series of samples, by injection of chemical markers, or by the use of tagged or captive fish. Further details are given in the references quoted.

Scales or otoliths are the main skeletal structures used in aging (Fig. 12.4). Not all species have accessible scales, and loss and subsequent replacement of scales and marginal resorption can give rise to errors in age determination (Ottaway & Simkiss, 1979). However, scales require virtually no preparation and they can be removed from live fish (as can fin rays) which may be an advantage in some situations. All teleosts have

Fig. 12.4. Two methods by which fish are aged. Scales taken from the sides of the body show annual growth checks. Otoliths may be obtained by taking a horizontal slice from the top of the head exposing the brain and otoliths. Held up to a strong light or examined under the microscope, they show annual opaque and hyaline bands.

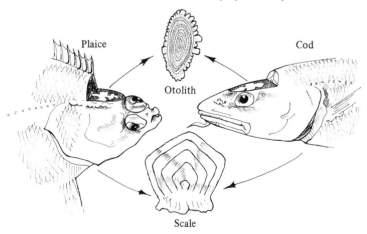

otoliths; if these do not initially show a pattern of alternate opaque and hyaline zones, grinding, sectioning, staining, and burning techniques are available to enhance zone appearance. In most elasmobranch fish the only skeletal stuctures of use in aging are the vertebrae.

Data processing

General information is available in Chapter 1. Additionally, the following techniques are of particular importance in fisheries studies. A full treatment of these computations is well beyond the scope of this chapter, however, it is relevant to indicate how raw survey data may be used in the context of fisheries management.

Cohort analysis

This is a fundamental method used in modern fishery management, and is based on the catch data obtained for the different cohorts (age-groups) of the population in successive years. It generates estimates of absolute abundance. Requirements apart from the catch data are assumed values or calculated values for natural mortality and for the fishing mortality being applied to the oldest cohort. The method is described in simple terms by Pope (1982), and a brief explanation is provided by Pitcher & Hart (1982).

Estimating growth and mortality rates

These are fundamental both to production studies and to yield computations involving dynamic pool fishery models and cohort analysis. Techniques are described by Ricker (1975), Bagenal (1978), and, for tropical species which are difficult to age, by Pauly (1980).

Estimating production

Estimating the production of fish populations and communities is of course basically the same as that for other animals. Most methods require input data on growth rate, mortality rate, and abundance at at least one point in time, but it is possible to derive the production of groups of species (trophic levels or communities) from production estimates of other parts of the food web, notably the primary producers. Production and its estimates are well covered by both Bagenal (1978) and Gerking (1978).

Single-species yield models

Most fishery management to date has involved the use of single-species yield models of which there are two basic types: the surplus production model, and the dynamic pool or yield-per-recruit model.

Further details, including the development and operation of the models may be found in Ricker (1975), Saila & Roedel (1980), Cushing (1982), and Pope (1982).

Multi-species yield models

Very few fisheries exploit single species and it is increasingly being recognised that management should be based on communities or multi-species assemblages rather than the traditional single-species approach. The latter usually ignores the biological interactions between species and the effects that the exploitation of one species unintentionally has on others (e.g., in generating by-catch).

The multi-species approach is discussed further, for example, by Anon. (1978) and Saila & Roedel (1980). It is sufficient, in the present context, to emphasise the value of taking a community rather than a population view of fish survey work, and to note the way in which fish surveys can benefit from surveys on other components of the ecosystem.

Use of fishery statistics

Information on catches and landings are available for global (FAO Yearbooks of Fishery Statistics), regional (e.g., ICES Bulletin Statistique for the NE Atlantic), and national (e.g., MAFF Statistical Tables for England and Wales) levels, and also for individual ports, landing places, and even individual fishing boats. It is at the latter levels that all fishery statistics are initially collected, and their validity depends entirely on the reliability of fishermen in providing information, and the efficiency of those concerned with its collection.

It is well known that most statistics underestimate the amount of fish landed and certainly the amount caught. Collecting statistics is most difficult for small-scale fisheries where landing places are scattered, false reporting is common, and much of the catch does not pass through a market. Gulland (1980) has suggested that in these cases a frame survey should be carried out to obtain a complete enumeration of landing places from which a *sample* is selected for detailed collection of statistics. By concentrating the recorded effort in this way there is likely to be a considerable gain in accuracy for an acceptable loss of precision; for most purposes, quite rough estimates, within $\pm 10\%$, are adequate. Further details on the collection and compilation of fishery statistics are given by Brander (1975).

The main advantage of using commercial fishery statistics is the good coverage they often provide of both area and time. Many now span several decades and in a few cases much longer periods (e.g., Cushing & Dickson, 1976). However, even if reasonably accurate and precise estimates of landings are available, there still exist two main problems affecting the use of such data. First, fishing activities select for the most valuable species and the areas where these are concentrated; this is an addition to the inherent selectivity of the gear used. Secondly, unless effort can be assumed to be constant through time or from area to area, the catch/landing data must be expressed in relation to the effort applied if they are going to be an adequate index of abundance. Effort can be expressed most simply in terms of numbers of boats or hours fished, but the estimation of standard effort in a mixed and/or developing fishery is notoriously difficult. The general procedure for using catch and effort data to monitor fish stock abundance is given by Anon. (1976). Rothschild (1977) has drawn attention to the problems of estimating effort.

Some individual fishermen keep detailed logs of their catches and activities; these logs may be more valuable than the official statistics for a particular port or area (e.g., Harden Jones & Scholes, 1980). In addition, where sport fishing occurs, the records of individual anglers or angling clubs may be of some value. The records of club competitions are often very detailed (giving the weights and numbers of fish caught, the number of anglers, and the time spent fishing) and may go back many years. Gee & Milner (1980) provide an example of a study of a salmon population from a 70-year record of catches.

References

Allen, M. J. (1977). Field methods for sampling demersal fish populations and observing their behaviour. In *Fish Food Habits and Studies*, ed. C. A. Simenstad & S. J. Lipovs, pp. 56–72. Pullman: Washington State University Press.

Anon. (1976). *Monitoring of Fish Stock Abundance: The Use of Catch and Effort Data*. FAO Fisheries Technical Paper 155. Rome: FAO Fisheries Dept.

Anon. (1978). *Some Scientific Problems of Multispecies Fisheries*. FAO Fisheries Technical Paper 181. Rome: FAO Fisheries Dept.

Aronson, L. R. (1951). *Orientation and Jumping Behaviour in the Gobiid Fish Bathygobius soporator*. American Museum Novitates No. 1486. New York: American Museum of Natural History.

Atsatt, L. H. & Seapy, R. R. (1974). An analysis of sampling variability in replicated midwater trawls off southern California. *J. exp. mar. Biol. Ecol.* **14**, 261–73.

Bagenal, T. B. (1974). *The Ageing of Fish.* London: George, Allen and Unwin.

Bagenal, T. B. (ed.) (1978). *Methods for Assessment of Fish Production in Fresh Waters*, 3rd edn. IBP Handbook No. 3. Oxford: Blackwell.

Bailey, R. S. (1975). Observation on the diel behaviour patterns of North sea gadoids in the pelagic phase. *J. mar. biol. Ass. U.K.* **55**, 133–42.

Barnes, H. & Bagenal, T. B. (1950). A statistical study of variability in catch obtained by short repeated hauls taken over an inshore ground. *J. mar. biol. Ass. U.K.* **29**, 649–60.

Beamish, R. J. (1972). *Design of a Trapnet for Sampling Shallow Water Habitats.* Technical Report 305. Ottawa: Fisheries Research Board of Canada.

Begon, M. (1979). *Investigating Animal Abundance: Capture–Recapture for Biologists.* London: Edward Arnold.

Beukema, J. J. & De Vos, G. (1974). Experimental tests of a basic assumption of the capture–recapture method in pond populations of carp, *Cyprinus carpio. J. Fish. Biol.* **6**, 317–31.

Blower, J. G., Cook, L. M. & Bishop, J. A. (1981). *Estimating the Size of Animal Populations.* London: George, Allen & Unwin.

Boyar, H. C. & Clifford, R. A. (1967). An automatic device for counting dry fish eggs. *Trans. Am. Fish. Soc.* **96**, 361–3.

Brander, K. (1975). *Guidelines for Collection and Compilation of Fishery Statistics.* FAO Fisheries Technical Paper 148. Rome: FAO Fisheries Dept.

Brandt, A. von (1984). *Fish Catching Methods of the World*, 3rd edn. Farnham, Surrey: Fishing News Books Ltd.

Brothers, E. B. (1980). Age and growth studies in tropical fish. In *Stock Assessment for Tropical Small-scale Fisheries*, ed. S. B. Saila & P. M. Roedel, pp. 119–36. Kingston: University of Rhode Island.

Chapman, C. J., Johnstone, A. D. F., Dunn, J. R. & Creasey, D. J. (1974). Reactions of fish to sound generated by divers' open-circuit underwater breathing apparatus. *Mar. Biol.* **27**, 357–66.

Clarke, D. R. & King, P. E. (1985). Spawning of herring in Milford Haven. *J. Mar. Biol. Ass. UK*, **65**, 629–35.

Cochran, W. G. (1960). *Sampling Techniques.* Chichester: John Wiley.

Craig, R. E. & Priestley, R. (1963). Photographic studies of fish populations. *Nature, Lond.* **188**, 333–4.

Cram, D. L. & Hampton, I. (9176). A proposed aerial/acoustic strategy for pelagic fish assessment. *J. Cons. perm. int. Explor. Mer*, **37**, 91–7.

Cushing, D. (1973). *The Detection of Fish.* Oxford: Permagon Press.

Cushing, D. H. (1978). The present state of acoustic survey. *J. Cons. perm. int. Explor. Mer*, **38**, 28–32.

Cushing, D. H. (1982). *Fisheries Biology: A Study in Population Dynamics*, 2nd edn. Madison: THe University of Wisconsin Press.

Cushing, D. H. & Dickson, R. R. (1976). The biological response in the sea to climatic changes. *Adv. mar. Biol.* **14**, 1–122.

Dando, P. R. (1984). Reproduction in Estuarine Fish. In *Fish*

Reproduction – Strategies and Tactics. ed. G. W. Potts & R. J. Wootton, pp. 155–70. London: Academic Press.

Dando, P. R. & Ling, R. (1960). Freeze-branding of flatfish: flounder (*Platichthys flesus*) and plaice (*Pleuronectes platessa*). *J. mar. biol. Ass. U.K.* **60**, 741–8.

Dodgshun, T. J. (1980). Simple accurate method of counting fish eggs. *Progr. Fish-Cult.* **42**, 237–8.

Drew, E. A., Lythgoe, J. N. Woods, J. D. (eds) (1976). *Underwater Research.* London: Academic Press.

Eggers, D. M., Rickard, N. A., Capman, D. G. & Whitney, R. R. (1982). A methodology for estimating area fished for baited hooks and traps along a ground line. *Can J. Fish. aquat. Sci.* **39**, 448–53.

Engel, C. E. (ed). (1968). *Photography for the Scientist.* London: Academic Press.

Fernö, A. & Huse, I. (1983). The effect of experience on the behaviour of cod towards a baited hook. *Fish. Res.* **2** (1), 19–28.

Fetteroff, C. M. (ed.) (1981). Stock Concept Symposium. *Can. J. Fish. aquat. Sci.* **38**, 1457–921.

Foulkes, T. J. & Scarratt, D. J. (1972). Design and performance of TURP – a diver controlled tower underwater research plan. *Tech. Rep. fish. Res. Bd Can.*, No. 285, 1–11.

Gee, A. S. & Milner, N. J. (1980). Analysis of 70-year catch statistics for Atlantic salmon in the River Wye and implications for management of stock. *J. appl. Ecol.* **17**, 41–58.

Gerking, S. D. (1978). *Ecology of Freshwater Fish Production.* New York: Halstead Press.

Gibson, R. N. (1967). The use of the anaesthetic quinaldine in fish ecology. *J. Anim. Ecol.* **36**, 295–301.

Gibson, R. N. (1980). A quantitative description of the behaviour of wild juvenile plaice (*Pleuronectes platessa* L.). *Anim. Behav.* **28**, 1202–16.

Gibson, R. N. (1982). Recent studies on the biology of intertidal fishes. *Oceanogr. Mar. Biol. Ann. Rev.* **20**, 363–414.

Gilmore, R. J. (1978). Portable tripod drop net for estuarine fish studies. *Fishery Bull. natn. oceanic atmos. Adm. U.S.* **76**, 285–9.

Gilligan, M. R. (1976). Small marine animal collector for use by divers. *Progr. Fish-Cult.* **38**, 40–1.

Gulland, J. A. (1969). *Manual of methods for fish stock assessment.* Part 1: *Fish population analysis. FAO Manuals in Fisheries Science* 4. Rome: FAO Fisheries Dept.

Gulland, J. A. (1971). Science and fishery management. *J. Cons. perm. int. Explor. Mer.* **33**, 471–7.

Gulland, J.A. (1980). Stock assessment in tropical fisheries past and present practices in developing countries. In *Stock Assessment for Tropical Small-scale Fisheries*, ed. S. B. Saila & P. M. Roedel, pp. 27–34. Kingston: University of Rhode Island.

Gulland, J. A. (1983). *Fish Stock Assessment: a Manual of Basic Methods.* FAO/Wiley Series on Food and Agriculture, vol. I. Chichester: John Wiley & Sons.

Gusar, A. G. & Kupriyanov, V. S. (1975). Use of underwater television to study the behaviour of fishes in light fields. *J. Ichthyol.* **15** (3): 519–21.

Harden Jones, F. R. (1968). *Fish Migration.* London. Edward Arnold Ltd.

Harden Jones, F. R. & Scholes, P. (1960). Wind and the catch of a Lowestoft trawler. *J. Cons. perm. int. Explor. Mer*, **39**, 53–69.

Hardisty, M. W. & Huggins, R. J. (1975). A survey of the fish populations of the middle Severn estuary based on power station sampling. *Int. J. Env. Studies*, **7**, 227–42.

Hellier, T. R. (1958). The drop-net quadrat, a new population sampling device. *Publs. Inst. mar. Sci. Univ. Tex.* **5**, 165–7.

Hemmings, C. C. (1971). Fish Behaviour. In *Underwater Science – An Introduction to Experiments by Divers* ed. J. D. Woods & J. N. Lythgoe, pp. 141–74. Oxford University Press.

Hemmings, C. C. (1972). Underwater photography in fisheries research. *J. Cons. perm. int. Explor. Mer*, **34**, 466–84.

Hemmings, C. C. (1973). Direct observation of the behavior of fish in relation to fishing gear. *Helgoländer wiss. Meeresunters.* **24**, 348–60.

Herrnkind, W. F. (1974). Behavior: *in situ* approach to marine behavioral research. In *Experimental Marine Biology*, ed. R. N. Mariscal, pp. 55–98. London: Academic Press.

High, W. L. (1969). Scuba diving, a valuable tool for investigating the behavior of fish within the influence of fishing gear. In Fisheries Report FAO, No. 62, vol. 2, pp. 253–67.

Hislop, J. R. G. (1969). Investigations by divers on the survival of tagged haddock. *Underwater Ass. Rep.* 1969, 86–90.

Holden, M. J. & Raitt, D. F. S. (ed.) (1974). *Manual of Fisheries Science:* Part 2: *Method of Resource Investigation and their Application.* FAO Fisheries Technical Paper 115 (Rev. 1). Rome: FAO Fisheries Dept.

Holme, N. A. & McIntyre, A. D. (eds) (1971). *Methods for the Study of Marine Benthos.* IBP Handbook 16. Oxford: Blackwell Scientific Publications.

Holme, N. A. & McIntyre, A. D. (eds) (1984). *Methods for the Study of Marine Benthos*, 2nd edn. IBP Handbook No. 16. Oxford: Blackwell.

Hyslop, E. J. (1980). Stomach contents analysis – a review of the methods and their application. *J. Fish. Biol.* **17**, 411–29.

ICES (Internation Council for the Exploration of the Sea) (1953). A guide to fish marks. *J. Cons. perm. int. Explor. Mer.* **19**(2), 241–89.

Iles, T. D. (1984). Allocation of resources to gonad and soma in Atlantic herring, *Clupea harengus* L. In *Fish Reproduction – Strategies and Tactics*, eds. G. W. Potts & R. J. Wooton, pp. 331–47. London: Academic Press.

Jones, R. (1976). *The Use of Marking Data in Fish Population Analysis.* Fisheries technical Paper 153. Rome: FAO Fisheries Dept.

Jones, R. (1977). Tagging: theoretical methods and practical difficulties. In *Fish Population Dynamics*, ed. J. A. Gulland, pp. 46–66. Chichester: Wiley.

Jones, R. (1979). *Materials and Methods Used in Marking Experiments in Fishery Research.* FAO Fisheries Technical Paper 190. Rome: FAO Fisheries Dept.

Kelley, J. C. (1976). Sampling the sea. In *The Ecology of the Seas*, eds. D. H. Cushing & J. J. Walsh, pp. 361–87. Oxford: Blackwell.

Krieger, K. J. (1982). Tagging herring with coded-wire microtags. *Mar. Fish. Rev.* **44** (3), 18–21.

Kuipers, B. (1977). On the ecology of juvenile plaice on a tidal flat in the Wadden Sea. *Neth. J. Sea Res.* **11** (1), 56–91.

Lackey, R. T. & Hubert, W. A. (1977). *Analysis of Exploited Fish Populations*. Charlottesville, Virginia: Sea Grant, Extension Division, Virginia Polytechnic Institute and State University.

Laevastu, T. (1965). *Manual of Methods in Fisheries Biology*, Fascicule 9, Section 4: *Research on Fish Stocks*. FAO Manuals in Fisheries Science 1. Rome: FAO Fisheries Dept.

Laird, L. M. & Stott, B. (1978). Marking and tagging. In *Methods for Assessment of Fish Production in Fresh Waters*, IBP Handbook 3, ed. T. B. Bagenal, pp. 84–100. Oxford: Blackwell.

Lamarque, P. (1977). Un appareil de pêche a l'électricité pour les eaux de forte conductivité (eaux saumâtres et marines) *Cybium*, 3rd Ser., 1977 (1), 75–81.

Langford, T. E. (1983).'Electricity Generation and the Ecology of Natural Waters.' Ph.D. thesis, University of Liverpool.

Livingstone, R. (1962). Underwater television observations of haddock (*Melanogrammus aeglefinus* (L.)) in the cod end. *J. Cons. perm. int. Explor. Mer*, **27**, 43–8.

Lockwood, S. J. (1976). The use of the von Bertalanffy growth equation to describe the seasonal growth of fish. *J. Cons. perm. int. Explor. Mer*, **35**, 175–9.

Lockwood, S. J. & Daly, C. de B. (1975). Further observations on the effects of preservation in 4% neutral formalin on the length and weight of O-group flatfish. *J. Cons. perm. int. Explor. Mer*. **36**, 170–5.

Lockwood, S. J., Nichols, J. H. & Dawson, W. A. (1981). The estimation of a mackerel (*Scomber scombrus* L.) spawning stock size by plankton survey. *J. Plankton Res.* **3**, 217–33.

Losey, G. S. (1971). Communication between fishes in cleaning symbiosis. In *Aspects of the Biology of Symbiosis*, ed. T. C. Cheng, pp. 45–76. London: Butterworths.

Macdonald, P. D. M. & Pitcher, T. J. (1979). Age-groups from size frequency data: a versatile and efficient method of analysing distribution mixtures. *J. Fish. Res. Bd Can.* **36**, 987–1001.

Macer, C. T. (1974). The reproductive biology of the horse mackerel (*Trachurus trachurus* (L.)) in the North Sea and English Channel. *J. Fish. Biol.* **6**, 415–38.

McErlean, A. J., O'Connor, S. G., Mihursky, J. A. & Gibson, C. I. (1973). Abundance, diversity and seasonal patterns of estuarine fish populations. *Estuar. Coast. mar. Sci.* **1**, 19–36.

Matthews, J. & Bell, J. D. (1979). A simple method for tagging fish underwater. *Calif. Fish Game*, **65**, 113–17.

Merdinyan, M. E., Mortimer, C. D. & Melbye, L. (1980). *Bibliography: The*

Relationship between the Development of Fishing Gear and the Study of Fish Behavior. Mar. Memo. University of Rhode Island, Kingston.

Mertens, L. E. (1970). In-water Photography: Theory and Practice. Chichester: Wiley.

Mitson, R. B. (1978). A review of biotelemetry techniques using acoustic tags. In Rhythmic Activity of Fishes, ed. J. E. Thorpe, pp. 269–83. University of Stirling, 4–8 July 1977, London: Academic Press.

Moore, J. W. & Moore, I. A. (1976). The basis of food selection in flounder (Platichthys flesus (L.)) in the Severn estuary. J. Fish Biol. 9, 139–56.

Myrberg, A. A., Jr. (1974). Underwater television – a tool for the marine biologist. Bull. mar. Sci. 23, 823–36.

Muus, B. J. (1967). The fauna of Danish Estuaries and Lagoons. Distribution and Ecology of Dominating Species in the Shallow Reaches of the Mesohaline Zone. Meddr Danm. Fisk.-og Havunders. 5, 1–314.

Newton, R. S. & Stefanou, A. (1975). Application of side-scan sonar in marine biology. Mar. Biol. 31, 287–91.

Nichols, J. H. & Wood, R. J. (1978). Sorting and identification techniques for clupeoid larvae. J. Cons. perm. int. Explor. Mer, 38, 48–53.

Nielsen, L. A. & Johnson, D. L. (eds) (1983). Fisheries Techniques. Bethesda, Maryland: The American Fisheries Society.

Ottaway, E. M. & Simkiss, K. (1979). A comparison of traditional and novel ways of estimating growth rates from scales of natural populations of young bass (Dicentrarchus labrax). J. mar. biol. Ass. U.K. 59, 49–59.

Pannella, G. (1980). Growth patterns in fish sagittae. In Skeletal Growth of Aquatic Organisms, ed. D. C. Rhoads & R. A. Lutz. London: Plenum Press.

Parrish, B. B. (1969). A review of some experimental studies of fish reactions to stationary and moving objects of relevance to fish capture processes. In Fisheries Report FAO No. 62, vol. 2.

Pauly, D. (1979). Theory and management of tropical multispecies stocks: a review with emphasis on the S.E. Asian demersal fisheries. ICLARM Studies and Reviews 1. Manila, Philippines: International Centre for Living Aquatic Resources Management.

Pauly, D. (1980). A Selection of Simple Methods for the Assessment of Tropical Fish Stocks. FAO Fisheries Circular 729. Rome: FAO Fisheries Dept.

Pitcher, T. J. (1981). Some ecological consequences of fish school volumes. Freshwater Biol. 10, 539–44.

Pitcher, T. J. & Hart, P. J. B. (1982). Fisheries Ecology. Beckenham, Kent: Croom Helm.

Pope, J. G. (1982). Background to Scientific Advice on Fisheries Management. Laboratory Leaflet, Fisheries Laboratory, Lowestoft, 54. Lowestoft: MAFF.

Pope, J. G., Margetts, A. R., Hamley, J. M. & Akyuz, E. F. (1975). Manual of Methods for Fish Stock Assessment, Part III. Selectivity of Fish gear FAO Fisheries Technical Paper 41. (Rev. 1). Rome: FAO Fisheries Dept.

Potts, G. W. (1970). The schooling ethology of Lutianus monostigma (Pisces) in the shallow reef environment of Aldabra. J. Zool. Lond. 161, 223–35.

Potts, G. W. (1983). The ethology of *Labroides dimidiatus* (C. & V.) (Labridae, Pisces) on Aldabra. *Anim. Behav.* **21**, 250–91.

Potts, G. W. (1974). A diver-controlled plankton net. *J. mar. biol. Ass. U.K.* **56**, 959–62.

Potts, G. W. (1980). The predatory behaviour of *Caranx melampygus* (Pisces) in the channel environment of Aldabra Atoll (Indian Ocean). *J. Zool. Lond.* **192**, 323–50.

Potts, G. W. (1983). The predatory tactics of *Caranx melampygus* and the response of its prey. In *Predators and Prey in Fishes*, ed. D. L. G. Noakes, D. G. Lindquist, G. S. Helfman & J. A. Ward, pp. 181–91. The Hague: Dr W. Junk Publishers.

Randall, J. E. (1963). Methods of Collecting Small Fishes. *Underwater Nat.* **1** (2), 6–11.

Ray, B. (1977). Advanced underwater television and photographic systems. *Underwater Ass. Rep.* **2** (n.s.), 121–4.

Ricker, W. E. (1975). Computation and interpretation of biological statistics of fish populations. *Bull. Fish. Res. Bd. Can.* **191**, 1–382.

Rijnsdorp, A. D., Stralen, M. van & Veer, H. W. van der (1985). Selective tidal transport of North Sea plaice larvae *Pleuronectes platessa* in coastal nursery areas. *Trans. Amer. Fish. Soc.* **114**, 461–70.

Riley, J. d. (1966). Liquid latex marking techniques for small fish. *J. Cons. perm. int. Explor. Mer*, **30**, 354–7.

Rothschild, B. J. (1977). Fishing effort. In *Fish Population Dynamics*, ed. J. A. Gulland, pp. 96–115. Chichester: Wiley.

Rounsefell, G. A. (1975). *Ecology, Utilization and Management of Marine Fisheries*. St. Louis: The C.V. Mosby Company.

Rusby, J. S. M. Somers, M. L., Revie, J., McCarney, B. S. & Stubbs, A. R. (1973). An experimental survey of a herring fishery by long-range sonar. *Mar. Biol.* **22**, 271–92.

Russell, B. C., Talbot, F. H., Anderson, G. R. V. & Goldmann, B. (1978). Collection and sampling of reef fishes. *Monogr. Oceanogr. Methodol.* **5**, 329–45.

Russell, F. S. (1976). *The Eggs and Planktonic Stages of British Marine Fishes*. London: Academic Press.

Ryder, R. A., Kerr, S. R., Loftus, K. H. & Regier, H. A. (1974). The morphoedaphic index, a fish yield estimator – review and evaluation. *J. Fish. Res. Bd Can.* **31**, 663–88.

Saila, S. B. & Roedel, P. M. (eds) (1980). *Stock Assessment for Tropical Small-scale Fisheries*. International Center for Marine Resource Development, University of Rhode Island, Kingston.

Saville, A. (ed.) (1977). *Survey Methods of Appraising Fishery resources*. FAO Fisheries Technical Paper 171. Rome: FAO Fisheries Dept.

Schnute, J. & Fournier, D. (1980). A new approach to length-frequency analysis: growth structure. *Can. J. Fish. aquat. Sci.* **37**, 1337–51.

Schweigart, J. F. & Fournier, D. (1982). A model for predicting Pacific herring spawn density from diver observations. *Can. J. Fish. aquat. Sci.* **39** (10), 1361–5.

Seidel, W. R. & Klima, E. F. (1974). In situ experiments with coastal pelagic fishes to establish design criteria for electrical fish harvesting systems. *Fishery Bull. Natn. Oceanic Atmos. Adm. U.S.* **72**, 657–69.

Serebrov, L. I. (1974). Application of underwater photography to study ecology and stocks of bottom commercial objects (fishery species). Extract in, *Ocean 74: International Conference on Engineering in the Ocean Environment*, Halifax, Nova Scotia, 21–23 August 1974, vol. 1, pp. 147–51. New York: Institute of Electrical & Electronic Engineers.

Smith, C. L. (1973). *Small Rotenone Stations: a Tool for Studying Coral Reef Fish Communities.* American Museum Novitates No. 2512. New York: American Museum of Natural History.

Smith, P. E. & Richardson, S. L. (1977). *Standard Techniques for Pelagic Fish Egg and Larva Surveys.* FAO Fisheries Technical Paper 175. Rome: FAO Fisheries Dept.

Soutar, A. & Isaacs, J. D. (1974). Abundance of pelagic fish during the 19th and 20th centuries as recorded in anaerobic sediments off California. *Fish. Bull. natn. oceanic atmos. Adm. U.S.* **72**, 257–73.

Stewart, P. A. M. (1975). Catch selectivity by electrical fishing systems. *J. Cons. perm. int. Explor. Mer*, **36**, 106–9.

Stewart, P. A. M. (1977). A study of the response of flatfish (Pleuronectidae) to electrical stimulation. *J. cons. perm. int. Explor. Mer*, **37**, 123–9.

Stonehouse, B. (ed.) (1978). *Animal Marking: Recognition Marking of Animals in Research.* London: MacMillan Press.

Strange, C. D. & Kennedy, G. J. A. (1981). Stomach flushing of salmonids: a simple and effective technique for the removal of the stomach contents. *Fish. Mgmt.* **12** (1), 9–16.

Strickland, C. L. (1973). Underwater television – its development and future. *Underwater J.* **5**, 244–9.

Sund, P. N. (1981). *Tunas, Oceanography and Meteorology of the Pacific, an Annotated Bibliography, 1950–78.* Special Scientific Report of the National Oceanic and Atmospheric Administration, U.S. (Fisheries), No. NMFS SSRF–744. Seattle: NOAA.

Thorne, R. E. (1980). The application of hydroacoustics to stock assessment for tropical small-scale fisheries. In *Stock Assessment for Tropical Small-Scale Fisheries.* ed. S. B. Saila & P. M. Roedel, pp. 110–18. Kingston: University of Rhode Island.

Ulltang, Ø. (1977). *Methods of Measuring Stock Abundance Other Than by the Use of Commercial Catch and Effort Data.* FAO Fisheries Technical Paper 176. Rome: FAO Fisheries Dept.

Walton, J. M. & Bartoo, N. W. (1976). Flatfish densities determined with a diver-operated flounder sampler. *J. Fish. Res. Bd Can.* **33**, 2834–6.

Wardle, C. S. (1976). Fish reactions to fishing gears. *Scott. Fish. Bull.* No. 43, 16–28.

Westcott, K. A. (1980). 'A Comparison of a Serological and Visual Technique for Fish Gut Content Analysis.' Unpublished Ph.D. Thesis, University of Exeter.

Wickham, D. A. & Watson, J. W., Jr (1976). Scuba diving methods for fishing systems evaluation. *Mar. Fish. Rev.* **38**, 15–23.

Wilcox, J. R., Meek, R. P. & Mook, D. (1974). A pneumatically operated slurp gun. *Limnol. Oceanogr.* **19**, 354–5.

Wilson, T. C.(1982). An underwater fish tagging method. *Calif. Fish. Game*, **68**, 47–50.

Wirjoatmodjo, S. & Pitcher, T. J. (1984). Flounders follow the tides to feed: evidence from ultrasonic tracking in an estuary. *Estuar. Coast. Shelf Sci.* **19**, 231–41.

Woods, J. D. & Lythgoe, J. N. (1971). *Underwater Science: An Introduction to Experiments by Divers.* Oxford University Press.

13

Birds

A. J. PRATER and C. S. LLOYD

Introduction

Birds are one of the more abundant, larger forms of wildlife that occur on the coast. Many species use different coastal habitats during at least part of their life cycle. In the last 35 years, surveys have been carried out and others are still under way on wildfowl, waders, gulls, auks, and other species that use the coasts of Europe for breeding, feeding, or roosting. Anyone endeavouring to survey the birds of a particular stretch of coast should first investigate whether this area is already covered in a survey scheme.

With a few exceptions, birds are relatively easy to census as they are large, readily identified without being collected, and easy to see. Nevertheless, surveys do need careful planning. The greatest problem concerns the birds' mobility. Whilst on migration they are quite capable of moving 500 km in a single night, and similar sudden movements can be made by otherwise sedentary flocks in relation to short-term climatic variables such as cold weather. Numbers present in a coastal area may depend on many different factors and each group of species must be assessed separately. The main variations are related to annual, seasonal, tidal, and diurnal rhythms, which are discussed later in this chapter. For these reasons, surveys of birds should be related to the national and possibly the international picture.

Addresses of some of the organisations that co-ordinate surveys are given in Appendix 13.1.

Numbers and distribution of non-breeding coastal birds
Estuaries

The main groups of species occurring on estuaries are waders, wildfowl, gulls, and terns, and they may be found there during winter or summer or while on migration. In general, wintering birds are present for the longest period of the year, sometimes for eight or nine months. In autumn and spring, migrant birds use estuaries as staging posts where they are able to feed and renew their energy reserves before departing to wintering or breeding grounds. This use, although of enormous conservation importance, is essentially short-term as few of the birds remain for more than a month. Indeed, co-ordinated monthly counts can only observe the birds present on a single date in each month, and while this should be adequate to assess the west European population, the numbers at any one site must be regarded as dynamic. Such counts give a representation of the typical numbers present at any one time. In major west European estuaries the number of birds passing through may be 25–30% higher than the single day's count, while in some coastal sites, especially Baltic coasts, during migration periods there may be an almost total change of individuals each day. Some species use the larger estuaries as moulting grounds where they can renew their flight feathers in areas with abundant food and minimal disturbance (Goethe, 1961; Boere, 1976). In the larger species, some of which do not breed until their third year, immature birds may be present on an estuary during the summer months. Although numbers are usually relatively small, these concentrations, primarily on the larger estuaries, represent the future breeding stock.

Ringing recoveries have shown that the wintering and migrant birds that occur on European estuaries breed in a wide zone of the arctic and subarctic regions that stretches from 90° W in north-east Canada to at least 130 °E in eastern Siberia. Several of the arctic wader species have discontinuous breeding distributions, with morphologically distinct races. Each species has a characteristic seasonal pattern of occurrence on an estuary, and this is also true of its races.

Since 1969, the 'Birds of Estuaries Enquiry' has collected information on the bird population of many of the estuaries in Britain; this joint British Trust for Ornithology, Nature Conservancy Council, and Royal Society for the Protection of Birds survey is organized by the BTO. The closely related 'Wetlands Enquiry', organized by the Irish Wildbird Conservancy, has gathered similar data in Ireland. Other countries have started similar surveys in their estuaries, and presently counts are organized in the majority of estuaries in Europe.

The main aim of these surveys is to provide an assessment of the national and international importance of each estuary. The second aim is to provide an index of annual changes in numbers of birds using the estuaries, and the third aim is to study migration by combining counts with ringing data.

Methods

Between August 1969 and May 1975, monthly counts of the birds (mainly waders and wildfowl) on all British and Irish estuaries were made by a team of up to 1000 voluntary observers. From 1976 to 1980, three international counts were made annually in the months of December, January, and February. Since 1980, regular counts from September to March have been made each winter. The counts are co-ordinated by regional and estuary organisers and are made on the weekend spring tide that is nearest to the middle of the month. On all larger estuaries, the birds are counted in roosting flocks during the two hours either side of high water. This is the only time that birds that feed on the intertidal areas are concentrated on a few, relatively accessible sites. Birds on small or narrow estuaries are usually counted during the low tide period as they disperse when forced off the mud. Details of methods are described in Prater (1981), Meltofte (1981), and Hustings *et al.* (1985).

Each species has its own pattern of behaviour and this may be different in different sites. Thus, each counter must design the counting technique to suit both the site and the species. Low tide censuses may be used as a check on the reliability of high tide counts. Low tide counts are often the only way to accurately count birds on rocky or mixed habitat beaches because of the difficult access at high tide when most beaches with cliffs behind are inaccessible or because birds may disperse widely inland to roost. Off-lying skerries or islets at low tide may, however, complicate the counting of such areas, as may the short day-length and the often poor weather in northern latitudes (da Prato & da Prato, 1979; Summers *et al.*, 1984).

Sampling errors and accuracy

There are four main types of potential errors in the information. They are: (1) failure to count important estuaries; (2) many birds occurring on rocky/sandy coasts or inland; (3) failure to find all birds on counted estuaries; (4) accuracy of counting observed individuals. These are briefly discussed below but a fuller discussion is in Prater (1981) and Rappoldt, Kersten & Smit (1985).

    1. Failure to count important estuaries. Of the 133 estuaries and bays in Britain with at least 1 km² of intertidal flats, only two or three in north-western Scotland were not counted regularly in the 'Birds of Estuaries Enquiry'. They, and many smaller areas, were visited occasionally during the survey. Of the approximate total of 1.5 million shore waders wintering in Britain between 1969 and 1976, the estimated number not found is in the order of 100 000 to

200000. This is obtained by extrapolation from the relationship between the size/number of birds in well-counted estuaries in the same area (Prater, 1981).

2. Birds in other habitats. Waders do occur on rocky shores or sandy beaches between estuaries, and inland. Generally, it is estimated that estuaries support 80% of the total numbers of shore waders in Britain. Few species of wader regularly occur inland, apart from species such as Lapwing, Golden Plover, and Snipe; in some locations others such as Curlew or even Turnstone may utilise coastal fields. Many species (e.g., Knot, Black-tailed Godwit, Bar-tailed Godwit, and Dunlin) are restricted almost completely to estuaries, and probably less than 5% of their total population occurs in other habitats. By comparison, in Britain and Ireland about 70000 Oystercatchers (23% out of a total population of about 300000) are known to occur away from estuarine sites in winter, and a survey of Sanderling in Britain (a species that normally prefers sandy beaches) showed 6000 birds out of a total of 12000 (50%) outside regularly counted areas, mostly estuaries (Prater, 1981; M. Moser, personal communication). A count of all of the shoreline of Britain in January 1985 has emphasised that rocky coasts support a very substantial proportion of Turnstone and Purple Sandpiper populations, while many Ringed Plovers may be present on sandy bays. The species composition and abundance depends on a number of factors, principally substratum type, weed cover, tidal range, slope, and exposure (M. Moser, personal communication).

3. Location of all birds on a count. Finding all the birds presents a problem, especially on large estuaries. However, after five or ten visits at high tide, ideally on the days preceding the count date, usually all the main and most of the small subsidiary roosts can be located. The species least likely to be fully located are ubiquitous birds such as Dunlin, Redshank, and Curlew (Prater, 1981), as well as the less common species (Rappoldt et al., 1985).

4. Counting accuracy. It is very difficult to count densely packed flocks of small waders, especially on the ground. The accuracy of different observers' counts have been tested using photographs of wader flocks of known size and by comparing estimates made by independent observers in the field. The errors involved vary with the conspicuousness and size of the bird and with its abundance. Numbers are consistently underestimated by less than 10% for small numbers (flocks of less than 200) of small waders or larger

numbers (up to 4000) of large waders. However, for large flocks of small waders the error can be 20–25%. As there is a high level of consistency both within and among individual observers, especially with the more experienced observers, counts usually can be compared (Atkinson-Willes, 1963; Prater, 1979*a*, Kersten, Rappoldt & Smit, 1981; Rappoldt *et al.*, 1985).

Ducks, Brent Geese, and other estuarine waterfowl are usually easier to count than waders as they are larger and roost in fairly dispersed flocks close to the shore.

Special wader counts
Between 1978 and 1985 a number of special surveys of coastal waders in west Europe and western and southern Africa have been carried out. Frequent counts at weekly intervals or less at a number of sample sites have been made during migration periods to document in detail, in combination with ringing techniques, the migration routes and timing of many species (e.g., Piersma, 1984*a*).

Related wetland surveys: Wildfowl Counts organised by the Wildfowl Trust
There is another counting scheme for ducks, geese, and swans in Britain that also involves birds on estuaries. Between 1948 and 1978 'Wildfowl Counts' covered a large sample of British wetlands, both coastal and inland, each month between September and March. Subsequently, as many sites as possible have been included in these monthly counts. Such counts have now been introduced in many other parts of Europe.

The methods are similar to those already described, but the date chosen is fixed at the Sunday nearest to the 15th of the month. The main aims of the monthly counts are to provide a site assessment, the national population level and to obtain a monthly index of abundance for each species (Atkinson-Willes, 1963, 1976). A special effort is made in January to try to cover all sites as part of the international count which provides a population estimate and index for north-west Europe. International counts have also been made in November (for five years) and March (six years); these help to provide more detail on the changing international distribution between seasons. The international assessment of both the wetland and the estuaries surveys is made by the International Waterfowl Research Bureau (IWRB) (Atkinson-Willes, 1976; Prater, 1976).

Special counts took place in Britain in late July and August 1985 to document concentrations of moulting wildfowl. Similar counts have been made in several areas of north-west Europe in the past.

There is a considerable danger of drawing conclusions on the patterns of abundance of birds from studies, however detailed, on a single estuary. Even adjacent estuaries may play different roles in the migration cycle of a species. This is illustrated in Fig. 13.1.

Units of national and international assessment
The IWRB counts, averaged over a three to five year period, provide an estimate of the west European population of waders and wildfowl. At the International Waterfowl Conferences at Heiligenhafen, Federal Republic of Germany in 1974 (Atkinson-Willes, 1976) and Cagliari, Sardinia, Italy in 1980 (Atkinson-Willes, Scott & Prater, 1982), scientists and government representatives agreed that either of two numerical criteria could be used to assess if any wetland was of international importance. These criteria are

Fig. 13.1. *Left*: Average number of Knot in each month in Britain and Ireland. Based on summation of average monthly counts in each estuary 1960–75. *Right*: Number of Knot in each month on the principle British estuaries. Filled circles, mean numbers; vertical bars, standard errors; based on 3–6 counts. From Prater (1979*b*).

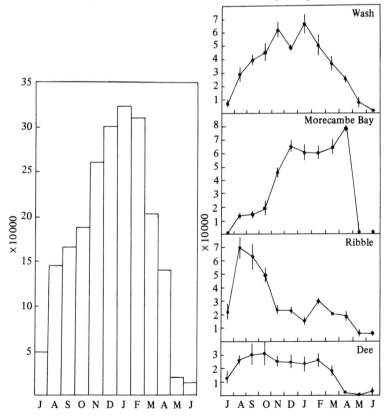

that the site holds 1% or more of the regional population of a species or that it supports at least 10000 ducks or coots or at least 20000 waders. Special criteria apply to rare species and to certain other aspects of wetland conservation. National importance is also based on these criteria; for example, in Britain it can be assessed by 1% of the national total of a species or 5000+ ducks or 10000+ waders.

Results

Using these criteria, it is possible to assess the importance of sites objectively. The distribution and abundance of different species in each month can also be mapped. Bird numbers change both seasonally and annually for many reasons and long-term surveillance of populations is vital.

Between 1948 and 1984 the wildfowl counts have shown that many wildfowl populations have increased by 50–100%. Populations do not usually fluctuate wildly; however, very cold weather can cause substantial, even dramatic changes in numbers in any individual country. As most species are relatively long lived, if other survival factors are favourable, they can increase in numbers fairly rapidly (Fig. 13.2). In general, mild winters during the 1970s and the decrease in hunting pressure in Western Europe have probably also been important factors in maintaining the increase in numbers in several different species of wildfowl. The breeding success of arctic and subarctic species is variable. For example, between 1961 and 1984 the Dark-bellied Brent Goose, which breeds in north central Siberia, had 11 good breeding seasons (with 30–53% young surviving to reach the wintering grounds) and 11 unsuccessful years (when less than 7% young survived; in five of these years there was nearly total failure) (Ogilvie & St. Joseph, 1976; Owen, Atkinson-Willes & Salmon, 1986).

Inshore waters

A number of birds occur regularly in large numbers on the shallow inshore waters off the European coasts. The divers, grebes, cormorants, and most diving ducks (with the exception of Tufted Duck, Pochard, Goosander, and Smew, which are primarily inland birds) fall into this category. These birds have much in common with estuarine birds, especially as there are large seasonal variations in their occurrence, and to some extent they have diurnal rhythms related to tidal fluctuations. In many places these birds can be observed from suitable vantage points on the shore. Apart from the ubiquitous problem of accuracy, there are a number of difficulties in counting them. Only the birds close in to the shore can be seen and identified. The sea is often rough and, unless an observation height of *c*. 18 m is reached, it may be impossible to make even an approximate estimate of numbers. Eider, Long-tailed Duck, scoters, and divers occur further out from land than Scaup and Goldeneye, for example, and are therefore more difficult to count accurately. In Britain, seaducks and divers are most abundant in northern and western parts; these are often remote areas where access can be difficult or even impossible. Seaduck have been counted successfully by boat and by fixed

Fig. 13.2. (*a*) Changes in the January index of Shelduck and Wigeon in Britain, 1961–83. 1971 is taken as 100. From Owen *et al.* (1986). (*b*). Changes in the world population level of Dark-bellied Brent Geese 1956–85. All winter in west Europe.

(preferably high-winged) plane or helicopter. Prearranged transects are followed to ensure the whole of an area (e.g., a firth or bay) is covered. Flights are carried out between 30 m and 130 m, usually 100–130 m so that the observer is low enough to see all birds but high enough to minimise panic flights or crash diving among them. The optimal height for aerial surveys depends both on the species involved and weather conditions: the optimum speed is usually about 60–80 knots. The accuracy of the estimates obtained depends on the skill and experience of the observers; ideally there should be two observers using a tape recorder to dictate counts. Where possible, simultaneous air and ground (boat) counts should be carried out, so that the proportion of each species in the flocks that are seen from the air can be determined to calibrate the observations; this is particularly important when counts involve scoters and divers (Joensen, 1968; Milne & Campbell, 1973).

There is no regular international count of all seaduck and divers although the 'Wildfowl Counts' do encompass many of the more accessible concentrations of the former.

Gulls

Although only a few species of gulls occur frequently in European estuaries, they can form a significant component of the bird fauna. All species are found during the day, feeding or loafing, and counts are relatively easy to make. The largest numbers, however, occur when inland-feeding gulls move to the coast to roost for the night (many also roost at inland lakes and reservoirs). Roosts may be found in estuaries, in relatively sheltered bays, or even on open coastlines. The only satisfactory way to count them is to count birds flighting into the roost. Gull flight lines from the feeding grounds to the roosting site are traditional in almost all areas. After counting the numbers present on the roost area during the late afternoon, a series of observers are stationed on each flight line, or in sectors if there is movement into the roost on a broad front. Gulls fly in relatively small flocks, which are usually easy to count. The observers have to remain until it is dark as the roosting movement continues well past sunset. Some counts have been made at the morning departure, but many birds leave before first light and numbers are usually lower than those obtained in the evening (Hickling, 1977).

There can be considerable difficulty in identifying gulls, particularly in immature plumages, and often they have to be broken down into two categories: small (Black-headed and Common) or large (Herring, Lesser Black-backed, and Great Black-backed). The best way to overcome identification problems is to have several observers at each observation point, each having responsibility for a single species or size group.

Infrared or light-intensifying binoculars have been used with some success at night on roosting flocks, but their efficiency tends to be limited by lack of definition at long range and difficulty in identifying the species involved.

Numbers of breeding seabirds

The coasts of Europe provide nesting places for many millions of pairs of seabirds. A major problem in estimating their breeding distribution or counting their numbers is the frequent inaccessibility of the colonies or of the nests themselves. For example, the Manx Shearwater only visits the breeding colony at night and nests underground in a burrow, often on steep cliffs of offshore islands. However, because many seabirds only come to land to breed and spend most of their time, perhaps up to nine or ten months a year, at sea, a survey of breeding numbers is the only way known at present to assess their populations.

During 1969 and 1970 a complete survey of all the coastal seabird colonies in Britain and Ireland was carried out by more than one thousand volunteers (Cramp, Bourne & Saunders, 1974). This provided invaluable baseline information on the distribution and approximate numbers of seabirds. As an annual survey of this scale is impossible, in 1970 two groups of seabirds, i.e. cliff-nesters and terns, were chosen for long-term population monitoring by annual counts of birds breeding in a sample of colonies.

Cliff-nesting seabirds

These include the Fulmar, the Kittiwake, and two auks – the Razorbill and the Guillemot. A third auk, the Puffin, lays eggs in cliff-top burrows and is also considered in this section. Many auk colonies in the 1980s are considerably smaller than they were in the 1930s and all the birds are currently under threat from oil pollution at sea, toxic chemicals they receive via their food, and industrial fishing of food species, the true effects of which are not yet fully understood. Natural ocean changes may also have an effect. Because of these factors, continuous monitoring of population levels is considered important. Kittiwakes and Fulmars, which by comparison have been increasing both in numbers and in breeding range, are included in these surveys as they tend to share breeding colonies with the auks.

A survey of this kind is essentially of a long-term nature to detect population trends. Most seabirds do not breed for the first time until at least their third or fourth summer of life, and once they enter the breeding population, annual survival is high. These characteristic features of a seabird's population dynamics also made it exceptionally vulnerable to increases in mortality. For example, an auk like the Guillemot lays a clutch of a single egg and, as breeding success is generally good, it has a relatively high chance of producing a fledged young. If the proportion of the fledged birds that die before reaching maturity (at the age of four or five years) suddenly increases, too few of them may survive and enter the breeding population to balance the current adult mortality, so that the population will decline. Similarly a relatively small increase in the numbers of adult breeding birds that die in a year can result in a doubling of the overall annual mortality with a serious deficit of breeding birds the following season.

Methods
A sample of about 50 seabird breeding colonies throughout Britain and Ireland are visited more or less annually for the survey. The original selection of these study colonies depended mainly on the distribution of available observers so that few of the colonies in remote areas of Ireland and Scotland are covered. The presence of suitable colonies containing some or all of the five relevant species was also considered and, as a result, few colonies are covered in south-east England.

In 1979 a total of 23 000 pairs of Kittiwakes were counted in 25 study colonies; this is 5% of the total population estimate for 1969. Similarly in 1979 the survey included an estimated 3% of the Razorbills (*c.* 5000 birds), 7% of the Guillemots (*c.* 40 000 birds), and 2% of the Fulmars (*c.* 6300 pairs) nesting in Britain and Ireland.

Coverage is relatively low because observers are strongly recommended to make accurate repeat counts following specified methods, if necessary for only part of the colony, rather than inaccurate coverage of wider areas. The method used to collect seabird numbers, especially in the case of the auks, determines the accuracy of the count and hence its resulting value.

Counting units
Kittiwakes build nests in which to lay their eggs, and Fulmars, though they make no nests, occupy specific sites on a cliff. The counting unit for these species is the 'apparently occupied' nest site.

Census counts and their interpretation are complicated by the fact that not all Fulmars occupying sites are breeding birds. Some non-breeders sit in nest sites almost continuously throughout the breeding season. To some extent, these sites can be excluded from the census by making several counts, on successive visits to the colony; not all the non-breeders will be present on land on every occasion. Counts relatively late in the season, after the chicks have hatched, can also exclude non-breeders' sites as Fulmar chicks are large and conspicuously fluffy. However, eggs or small chicks may have been lost from some sites. Similarly, not all Kittiwakes that occupy nests are breeding birds. Pairs of non-breeders often repair or build nests and spend much time displaying and standing on them. Census counts should include only nests in which eggs, chicks, or continuously sitting birds are visible.

Auks also pose special problems such as the following.

1. They make no nest.
2. They are usually found in confusingly high densities.
3. They can lay their eggs out of sight, e.g., in a burrow (Puffin), under boulders (Razorbill, Puffin), or in caves (Guillemot).

For these species, the recommended counting unit is the individual bird on a breeding ledge of the colony. One exception is the Puffin, for which occupied burrows are also counted at certain special study colonies.

Harris, Wanless & Rothery (1983) recommend that the population to be monitored should be delimited and unambiguously marked on photographs or maps. Also, as many sample plots as can be counted in the available time should be randomly selected.

Timing

Attendance at a seabird colony is extremely variable – both seasonally and hour by hour throughout the day (Lloyd, 1975). Birds arrive and depart, new nests are built or sites are adopted. The ideal time for census counts of auks is at the stage of the breeding season when the eggs have hatched, but before the first chicks leave the ledges at fledging, about 18–20 days after hatching in both Guillemots and Razorbills. This is usually during the month of June in much of Britain and in Ireland, but may be slightly later in north Scotland.

Generally, Kittiwakes and Fulmars also have young chicks at this time. Counts that are timed to coincide with this period of the breeding season should give results that will be comparable from one year to the next. If counting is left too late in the season, i.e., after mid-July, many birds (except Fulmars) will have deserted the colony with their chicks. In addition, Puffins must be counted late in the evening at the time of their peak colony attendance on land, and it is advisable to avoid Razorbill and Guillemot counts soon after dawn or at dusk. Wanless *et al.* (1982)

reported that for multi-species counts, numbers were less variable between 06.30 and 16.00 GMT, while for guillemots, Harris *et al.* (1983) recommend counts between 07.00 and 12.00 GMT.

Frequency of counts

Because of the day-to-day variations in attendance at auk colonies, it has been consistently recommended to count the birds on at least five different days (in June) each year (Lloyd, 1975; Birkhead & Nettleship, 1980; Evans, 1980; Harris *et al.*, 1983). Counts based on fewer visits to a colony can give inaccurate results (Table 13.1), and will therefore be useless for detecting change in numbers from one year to the next.

Kittiwake and Fulmar counts are also much improved by more than one visit to the colony.

Sampling errors and accuracy

Of the five species covered by this survey, adult Razorbills and Guillemots are known to be almost entirely faithful to their breeding colony; they also usually return to the same colony, sometimes nearly to the same nest site, where they were fledged. Although the Puffin is generally faithful to its colony and nest site once it starts breeding, it may move away from its natal area. Comparatively large-scale inter-colony movements have been detected in birds breeding on the east coast of Britain (Harris, 1976). Movement between colonies in Kittiwakes and Fulmars is mainly associated with the population expansion, although Kittiwakes very occasionally move locally between colonies for no obvious reason, and Fulmars sometimes change their preferred nesting locations within a colony. Wherever possible, careful mapping and a photographic record of the distribution of nesting birds both within the study colony and in adjacent breeding colonies are recommended so that, in at least some of the cases, any movement can be detected.

Because the annual surveys cover only part of the total populations of the species concerned, the results are useful only in providing long-term population trends. Kittiwake counts are generally considered to be accurate enough to detect small population fluctuations (e.g., less than 5%). This is not true of the auks and Fulmar, however. An index of change in numbers at a Puffin colony can be obtained by separate counts of individuals present on land and adjacent sea in the late evening in successive years, but these are more accurate if the average of a minimum of five evenings' observations are available, as attendance is extremely variable in this species. The maximum count of birds on land can be assumed to approximate the number of breeding pairs. A more accurate assessment of Puffin population change in a study colony can only be made by counts of occupied burrows, either a complete count or a sample count of the area. This is clearly not feasible at inaccessible colonies and is generally outside the scope of the annual seabird survey work. For the Guillemot and Razorbill, single annual counts give a potentially very inaccurate assessment of numbers, and wherever possible the average of at least five, preferably ten, counts on different days in June are used to assess change in numbers (see Table 13.1). Trends of small magnitude can be detected in numbers of Guillemots at a study plot by current methods of census and analysis (Stowe, 1982a), especially where data exist for a number of preceding years.

Results

The results of the annual seabird surveys between 1970 and 1979 (Stowe, 1982a) show that Fulmars have continued to increase at about 4% per year, compared with the annual increase of c. 7% reported for the total population of Britain and Ireland up to 1969. Their breeding range has also continued to grow, especially in south-east England, but more gradually than in the first half of this century.

Kittiwakes have been increasing at 3–4% a year for the whole of this century. However, both the annual seabird surveys at selected sites and a national survey of British and many Irish colonies in 1979 (Coulson, 1983) have shown that the increase has slowed to 1% per year, and that numbers are even declining at some sites around the Irish Sea, in north-east England, and the Orkney Islands.

Due to the variable accuracy of counts, no such confident statement can be made for auk population change (but see Stowe, 1982a). Undoubtedly

Table 13.1. *Amount of error to be expected from different numbers of counts of birds in the breeding colony in June*

Numbers of counts	Razorbill	Guillemot
1	41–56%	14–25%
5	11–25%	6–11%
10	8–17%	4–8%

Thus single visits to a Razorbill colony, for example, in successive years will produce counts accurate enough to detect only major population changes. But if an average of ten counts is available for each year, changes of about 10% can be detected. Percentages are errors with 95% confidence limits.
After Lloyd (1975).

numbers of all three species are at present considerably lower than in the 1930s, but early records are at least as inaccurate as some of the more recent ones. However, few actual declines in numbers of either Guillemots or Razorbills were recorded between 1969 and 1975. At colonies for which reliable (i.e., averaged), comparable counts were available, Guillemots showed either no change in numbers, or increases of between 2 and 16% per year. Razorbills mostly have increased by between 4% and 14%, although there was no change in numbers at some colonies, and at others in south Wales and the west of Ireland numbers had decreased by up to 7% in the same time (1972/3 to 1979).

The recent apparent decline in Puffins has mainly taken place at small colonies on the southern edge of the species range. Detailed burrow counts at seven Scottish colonies have shown a halt in the earlier decline of the species and a spectacular increase at colonies on the east coast.

Continuing surveys of the kind outlined here is necessary if a baseline of relatively accurate, comparable annual counts is to be established, against which future population changes can be assessed.

Terns

Seven species of terns nest along European coasts. The Little, Roseate, and Sandwich Terns are coastal breeders and tend to concentrate in relatively few sizeable breeding colonies. The Common Tern breeds in scattered colonies throughout Europe, sometimes far inland, whilst a large proportion of the Arctic Tern is found along the coasts of Scotland and Scandinavia, where some colonies contain several thousand pairs each. Gull-billed and Caspian Tern are rare species, occurring in widely isolated colonies.

Between 80% and 90% of the total north-western Europe breeding Roseate Terns bred in Britain and Ireland in 1979, and the majority of these (90%) were found in only nine colonies. Because numbers of this species have decreased by 80% since 1969/70 and are currently threatened by human hunting in their wintering areas, population surveillance is considered especially important (Bibby, Bourne & Merne, 1974). The drastic decline in Sandwich Tern numbers in the Netherlands during the 1960s following contamination of their food by toxic chemicals, has increased the international importance of the other breeding populations. The Dutch population has now partially recovered. As terns often nest in mixed colonies, annual tern surveys of all species in the main breeding colonies are carried out in several countries; these surveys are aimed at monitoring population changes. The methods described below for terns, in general, may also be used for the monitoring of breeding colonies of gulls.

Methods
Each year counts of breeding birds and other data are collected from coastal tern colonies. As terns are relatively scarce seabirds, most of their colonies, including nearly all the Roseate and Sandwich Terns, are now protected on nature reserves, usually manned by wardens. In addition to giving protection from casual and deliberate disturbance during the breeding season, this facilitates an annual population survey and enables an assessment of possible causes for changes in breeding numbers to be made by people familiar with each colony.

Units, timing, and frequency of counts
The counting unit for all tern species is the 'apparently occupied' nest site, ideally a nest with eggs. Visits to a breeding area early in the season (early to mid-May) should be avoided because before a majority of the birds have laid and incubation is underway, they are extremely vulnerable to disturbance. Sandwich Terns, especially, will sometimes completely desert a breeding colony if disturbed during laying or early in incubation.

The optimum time to count terns is when a majority of the birds have nests with eggs (sitting firmly when the colony is undisturbed). This is usually the last week of May and early in June in the Netherlands, southern Britain, and Ireland, and a little later in Scotland. Laying can be spread over up to four or five weeks; birds may leave other neighbouring colonies, perhaps due to disturbance, and settle to breed in established colonies. This often occurs at colonies on reserves that gradually collect birds from more-disturbed adjacent areas. Some terns, notably the Roseates, tend to lay later in the season (mid-June to July) after the other birds have begun incubation. For these reasons several visits to a colony, e.g., once every week or ten days, or perhaps until no more new nests are being found, gives the best breeding census. When the eggs start to hatch, visits should be made with extreme care, as disturbance of a colony with large numbers of young leads to increased loss of chicks. Counting of occupied nests is also made impossible at this time because the chicks leave the nest site soon after hatching.

In most colonies, with careful mapping subdivision of the nesting area, it is feasible to count all nest sites. If the colony is large, disturbance should be limited to periods of 10–15 minutes at hourly intervals, or less if there is a threat of egg predation by gulls.

With very large colonies professional help should be sought on developing a suitable census technique and avoiding disturbance to nesting birds. This usually relies on accurate mapping of the colony with reference to areas of different nest densities and on nest counts within sample areas (quadrats or transects) to measure these densities. Using the techniques outlined above, breeding censuses can be achieved at most colonies, though accuracy depends upon the terrain in the colony, frequency of visits, and the previous experience of the observer.

Results

In the ten years following the national survey of all British and Irish coastal tern colonies in 1969/70, numbers of both Common and Arctic Terns in the colonies covered by the annual tern surveys remained approximately stable, whilst both Sandwich and Little Terns increased in numbers, by about 30% and 10% respectively. Roseate Terns decreased by about 61%, while in 1984 their number stood at just 20% of the 1969 level. Coverage of all main colonies has been found to be especially important because terns, and in particular Sandwich and Arctic Terns, move readily between colonies in successive seasons. Their local population changes must be considered on a regional, national, or sometimes even international scale (Lloyd, Bibby & Everett, 1975; Thomas, 1982).

Beached-bird surveys

One of the most practicable methods at present to obtain some index of mortality in birds in estuaries and at sea is finding and recording those washed ashore dead or dying (e.g., Stowe, 1982*b*; Camphuijsen, 1984; Danielsen & Skov, 1984; Reineking, 1984). A related method frequently used is analysis of recoveries of ringed birds in which the number of birds found dead is compared with the number of birds actually ringed to estimate mortality and survival (Mead, 1974; Baillie & Mead, 1982; Baillie & Stowe, 1984; Hudson & Mead, 1984). Large-scale beached-bird surveys started on a casual basis in Britain during the 1920s in an attempt to monitor the effects of oil and other forms of marine pollution on bird-life. The first beached-bird surveys in the Netherlands were carried out from 1947 onwards (Mörzer Bruijns, 1959). These two countries were the first ones where these surveys became more or less regular.

This kind of survey must be both long-term and widespread in coverage if a realistic assessment is to be made, and if the effect of biases in the data are to be reduced. Today's beached-bird survey methods and standardised reporting forms were first established in 1971, so that at least in Britain from that time onwards comparable information could be collected annually. After the first reports on beached birds in the Netherlands in the 1950s (Mörzer Bruijns, 1959; Tanis & Mörzer Bruijns, 1962), more-comprehensive surveys covering practically the entire coastline were carried out from 1965 onwards at the end of each winter (Camphuijsen,

1984). These February surveys were organised on an international level. Britain participated in these from 1968 onwards and most other countries from 1969 onwards. Among these countries are the Republic of Ireland, Denmark, the Federal Republic of Germany, Belgium, France (Bourne & Bibby, 1975) and, more recently, Spain. In at least Ireland, Denmark, Germany, The Netherlands, Belgium, and France regular surveys at other times of the year are carried out as well (e.g., Kuyken, 1978; Camphuijsen, 1981; Danielsen & Skov, 1984; Reineking, 1984). In Britain and Ireland, too, regular surveys are made throughout the winter months. These surveys have been organised nationally since 1971, while the Republic of Ireland started in 1977 with similar work in cooperation with the British. All the information gathered this way forms a baseline against which recent and future trends in mortality can be measured.

Methods

In the Beached-Bird Survey in Britain, about 2000 km of beaches all over the country are covered regularly by up to 650 volunteer observers who are co-ordinated by the Royal Society for the Protection of Birds (RSPB) and the Seabird Group through local (county) organisers. A rather similar structure co-ordinates the survey in the Netherlands (e.g., Camphuijsen, 1981), while in the Federal Rupublic of Germany the organisation of the counts is more decentralized. There the acquired data are re-collected from the various local observers and bird protection groups to be analysed and published by the Institute für Vogelforschung, Vogelwarte Helgoland (Reineking, 1984). In these three countries the coverage is good except for some remote areas such as north and west Scotland.

The dead birds found on a particular, well-defined stretch of beach are counted and identified; some additional information on age and sex may be recorded whenever possible. In recent years some corpses have been collected for external and internal examination to obtain more information on possible causes of death, physical condition, age, sex and biometrics (e.g., Hope Jones *et al.*, 1984; Osborn, Young & Gore, 1984). An assessment is also made, if possible, of the amount of oil on the bird's plumage. This can only be done with corpses that are still reasonably complete. Normally three categories are used:

'Heavy': corpse nearly or completely covered
'Slight': less than half the surface covered
'Clean': no trace of oil

In fact the latter may also have died as a result of oil pollution, because ingested oil, swallowed accidentally or while preening, can be fatal (cf.

Bourne & Bibby, 1975), though in at least some cases birds may successfully clean themselves (Birkhead, Lloyd & Corkhill, 1973). On the other hand, birds that died of other causes might get oiled after death (Kuyken, 1978) and thus complicate the interpretation of these data.

In some cases, however, it is possible to tell, from the amount and distribution of oil patches on the body together with evidence of preening, whether a bird has been oiled before or after death, either while floating at sea or on the beach. Dead birds can be collected, thrown above high-tide mark, or marked (cutting off the wingtips with a pair of scissors) to be able to distinguish between corpses recorded before and new corpses washed up.

Frequency of surveys

Each participant in the British Beached-Bird Survey undertakes responsibility for a certain stretch of beach of known position and length. Prior to 1982, counts were made in at least five months each winter and on many sites counts were made monthly throughout the year, but from the 1982/83 winter, four counts (in December, January, February, and March) are carried out by each observer. Counts take place on pre-arranged weekends. The data are submitted on special postcards.

The priority survey at the end of February coincides with the annual International Beached-Bird Survey during which large parts of the western European coastline are checked for dead birds. The results of these surveys provide valuable comparison of bird mortality and oil pollution in the 1960s with the present day (cf. Stowe 1982b; Camphuijsen, 1984).

On the European mainland, organisation of the other beached-bird surveys is not as strict as in Britain and Ireland. For example, in the Netherlands every regular observer is allowed to count any stretch of beach at any time of the year. The data asked on each occasion are length of the stretch covered and the actual dead bird data. Because of the relatively easy access to practically all Dutch beaches, the total coverage is excellent. Nevertheless, since 1984/85 a second centrally organised national survey at the end of October has been introduced in addition to the one at the end of February to facilitate interpretation.

Emergency arrangements

The regular beached-bird survey teams provide extra coverage of beaches during incidents of unusually heavy mortality, such as that caused by an oil spill or stormy weather (Camphuijsen, 1981; Danielsen & Skov, 1984; Reineking, 1984; Underwood & Stowe, 1984). In this way, few incidents that involve birds go undetected, and information is obtained on the extent of the mortality, total numbers and species involved, and the apparent cause of death. If the cause of the incident is not evident, specimens are collected for post-mortem examinations, chemical analyses, and pathological tests (Hope Jones *et al.*, 1984; Osborn *et al.*, 1984).

Biases in beached-bird survey data

Experiments with marked gull corpses dropped at known positions in the northern Irish Sea have shown that, in different conditions, anything from 11% to 59% of the dead birds drifting at sea can be washed ashore and found. However, the distribution and timing of recoveries in these experiments indicated that, while the birds were offshore, the direction and speed at which they moved was largely determined by prevailing winds. The corpses drifted at an average of 2.55% wind speed. Whether or not they were finally beached appeared to depend mainly on the inshore tides and currents, but the type of beach also played an important part in their subsequent recovery, i.e., being discovered and reported (Bibby & Lloyd, 1977). Only 10% of the corpses dropped in a similar experiment in the North Sea were recovered, and this was over a longer time period than in the Irish Sea. Recoveries were made along the Norwegian coast as far north as the Lofoten Islands, and this thinly populated, heavily indented coastline evidently reduced the birds' chance of being beached or discovered (Bibby, 1981). Drifting experiments were also used to obtain an estimate of the actual bird mortality during the later phases of the *Amoco Cadiz* oil pollution incident on 30 March 1978. Only 30% of 144 corpses dropped at points 30 km, 15 km, or 7.5 km offshore were recovered at a time when great attention was being paid to the collection of oiled birds (Hope Jones *et al.*, 1978).

Regional results of the Beached-Bird Survey can be affected by stormy weather or long periods of onshore wind. The first seems to cause exhausted birds to swim towards land so that many of them are beached after death; the second produces large numbers of beached corpses at varying stages of decomposition by the scouring effect it has on offshore waters. When the birds come under stress, possibly through starvation in rough weather or the physiological demands of the moulting period, toxic chemicals that they have obtained through their food supply and that normally have sub-lethal physiological effects, combine with other factors to cause exceptionally heavy mortality. Hence the Beached-Bird Survey results have to be interpreted with caution and used only as indices to measure changes in mortality levels (Underwood & Stowe, 1984).

Results

Routine surveys

The Beached-Bird Survey records collected throughout the year show that winter is the period of heaviest mortality for birds (Bourne & Bibby, 1975). In addition, many dead seabirds are sometimes found on beaches near the breeding colonies during summer (e.g. Hope Jones, 1980), and also during the immediate post-fledging period when young and inexperienced birds succumb to starvation and autumn storms. The five priority surveys each year between 1971 and 1980 show that, on average, mortality increases from four to six birds per 10 km stretch of beach covered from September to January/February. The proportion of oiled corpses also rises to a mid-winter peak (Fig. 13.3).

The exact reasons for this heavy winter mortality are not clear. Oil decomposes more slowly at sea in low temperatures and hence has more time in which to contaminate birds (Bourne & Bibby, 1975). The distribution of the birds themselves also increases their vulnerability to oiling. In the breeding season most seabirds stay close to land and the breeding colony because of the demands of eggs and young. For many species, the main feeding grounds at this time are close to the colonies and often inshore, although both the Fulmar and Manx Shearwater may range long distances.

Fig. 13.3. Seasonal variation in percentage oiled of (*a*) all birds (*N* = 47711) and (*b*) auks (*N* = 14024) found on Beached-Bird Survey routine counts 1971 to March 1979. After RSPB (1979).

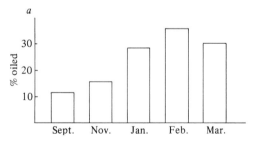

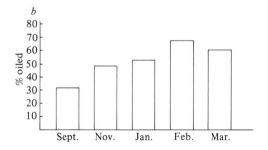

After breeding, the birds disperse away from land or migrate, and many of the seabirds tend to gather at rich fishing grounds offshore during the winter. These areas may coincide with busy shipping routes, such as the English Channel, Irish Sea, or Kattegat, where oil pollution is likely to be relatively heavy, and the birds' winter mortality rises accordingly. Other reasons may be that oil patches at sea can be detected by eye and accordingly avoided much easier in summer when there are obviously more hours of light. For the same reason, illegal oil spills may be frequent in winter with less risk of being discovered. Finally, during the cold winter season birds that lose the water-resistant properties of their plumage by oil contamination are much more vulnerable to large energy losses than in summer.

The priority surveys in Britain indicate regional variations in the amount of seabird mortality as shown, for example, by the numbers of auks (Razorbill, Guillemot, and Puffin) found around the coasts of Britain (Fig. 13.4). The stretches where most dead birds are found are the north-east coast of Britain and the Irish Sea coast of north-west England, the latter bordering a relatively enclosed sea area that is subject to high levels of pollution by toxic chemicals other than oil (Lloyd et al., 1974). Oil appears to cause most of the mortality on the east and south coasts of England where it accounts for 74% to 93% of all dead birds found. Along the beaches of the European mainland more than 80% of the corpses are oiled in normal winters (Kuyken, 1978; Camphuijsen, 1981, 1984; Van Gompel, 1981; Danielsen & Skov, 1984; Reineking, 1984). In severe winters many birds may die because of cold-stress and starvation (cf. Piersma, 1984b).

The information collected during the annual International surveys makes it possible for regional indices of mortality to be examined on a wider scale. In both Denmark and the Netherlands, corpse counts regularly exceed those on British beaches, and at least two-thirds of all corpses found in these countries are oiled. Finds on beaches of Belgium and northern France were also high (average of four dead birds/km of beach surveyed) in the late 1960s and early 1970s, but these have since dropped to about one corpse/km, which is similar to that on British beaches, although still higher than that on the relatively unpolluted Irish beaches. In the early 1980s, however, a huge rise in numbers of oiled corpses has been established in all these countries from Denmark down to Belgium (Camphuijsen, 1984; Danielsen & Skov, 1984; Reineking, 1984).

Results from other countries follow a similar trend. The Beached-Bird Survey finds in the late 1960s and early 1970s usually averaged two to three corpses/km in northern Europe, or up to eight dead birds/km in the

Netherlands (1969–72). At least three quarters of these birds were oiled. Since 1973 the normal mortality has been only one or two dead birds/km, and even on Dutch beaches on average only four dead birds/km were found, with correspondingly fewer oiled. Since 1981, however, the average mortality here has increased again to some six to eight birds/km (Camphuijsen, 1984).

The species of birds at greatest risk from oil at sea are also shown up by the Beached-Bird Survey. The high-risk species in Britain, for which about half to two thirds of those found dead are oiled, are the divers,

Fig. 13.4. Regional variations in the numbers of auks found on routine Beached-Bird Survey counts, 1971–79, showing proportions oiled. After RSPB (1979).

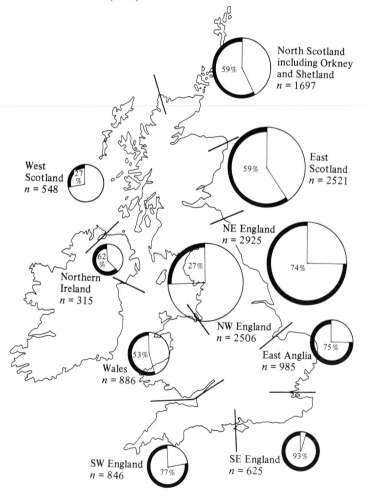

seaducks and auks. Percentages of these birds oiled are much higher on the Continent. Auks as well as divers hardly ever show less than 80% oil casualties. Kittiwakes seem to be much more at risk here, too. Large numbers of auks are always found in surveys on British coasts, and the group usually account for a third or, in early years, up to a half of all the corpses counted (Stowe, 1982*b*). The seaducks (eiders and scoters) are more important in the International Beached-Bird Surveys where lately they have accounted for a quarter to a third of all birds found. They appear to have become increasingly susceptible to oiling in recent years, especially

Fig. 13.5. Oiling incidents, January 1971 to June 1979. After RSPB (1979).

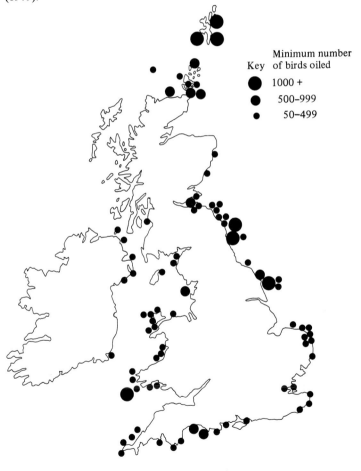

Key

Minimum number of birds oiled

● 1000 +
● 500–999
• 50–499

● (Channel Islands)

off Danish, German, and Dutch coasts (e.g. Joensen, 1972). More recently, the seaducks have become less important in the Netherlands (Camphuijsen, 1984), but in Denmark and Germany they still suffer high mortalities (Danielsen & Skov, 1984; Reineking, 1984). The divers make up only 1–3% of all dead birds found, but 80% or more of them are oiled. Two of these high-risk species groups (auks and seaduck) have in common a tendency to gather into large flocks during autumn and winter, and all three groups feed entirely by diving from the surface to swim and hunt underwater. This behaviour means they spend a lot of their time swimming on the sea and this increases their vulnerability to pollution from oil slicks. According to Blake *et al.* (1984), Kittiwakes often join these flocks, and this may very well be the reason why this species has become, at least on the mainland, one of the most frequent oil victims (Camphuijsen, 1984; Reineking, 1984). By contrast, the groups considered to be at comparatively low risk from oil are the other gulls, waders, and pelagic species such as the petrels (Fulmars and shearwaters), which spend most of their time far offshore. Usually about 10–12% of all these corpses found are oiled, although the gulls usually constitute at least a third of beached-bird survey finds on European coasts.

Fig. 13.6. Distribution of oiling incidents by month, January 1971 to June 1979. After RSPB (1979).

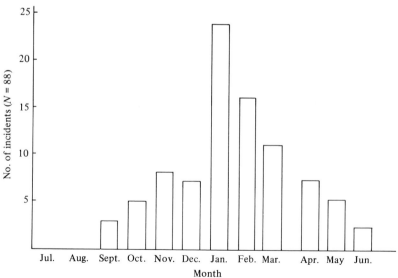

Oil pollution incidents

Between 1966 and 1983, the British Beached-Bird Survey recorded 144 oil pollution incidents involving 50 or more birds. These are known to have killed a minimum of 89, 213 birds and the true total is likely to be far higher. Unlike the declining levels of mortality and oiling shown by the routine beached-bird surveys, the toll due to specific oil pollution incidents rose steadily during the 1970s (Stowe & Underwood, 1984). Like the day-to-day mortality caused by chronic pollution, these oiling incidents are more frequent in the east and south of Britain (Fig. 13.5) and also occur more regularly in the winter months (Fig. 13.6).

Acknowledgements

We would like to thank our colleagues in the RSPB for their help in the production of this chapter, in particular Lesley Underwood, Tim Stowe, and Gareth Thomas. Mike Moser of the BTO and David Salmon of the Wildfowl Trust also provided most useful comments on the text. The comments from Wim Wolff and Maarten Platteeuw were invaluable. The chapter, however, is based on the accumulated knowledge of very many amateur and professional birdwatchers and their role should not be overlooked.

APPENDIX 13.1

Some Organisations Responsible for Co-ordinating Bird Surveys

International

Wildfowl and wader co-ordinated surveys: International Waterfowl Research Bureau, Slimbridge, Gloucestershire, GL2 7BT, UK

Special wader surveys: Wader Study Group, c/o Dr S. R. Baillie, 44 The Pastures, Edlesborough, Dunstable, Bedfordshire, LU6 2HL, UK

United Kingdom

Wader counts: British Trust for Ornithology, Beech Grove, Tring, Hertfordshire, HP23 5NR

Wildfowl counts: Wildfowl Trust, Slimbridge, Gloucestershire, GL2 7BT

Beached bird surveys, seabird monitoring: Royal Society for the Protection of Birds, The Lodge, Sandy, Bedfordshire, SG19 2DL

Seabird surveys and monitoring: Institute of Terrestrial Ecology, Hill of Brathens, Banchory, Kincardineshire, Scotland

Seabird Group, c/o Dr T. Birkhead, Zoology Department, University of Sheffield, S10 2TN

Belgium
Laboratorium voor Oecologie der Dieren, Zoogeografie en Natuurbehoud, K.L. Ledeganckstraat 35, 9000 Gent

Denmark
Vildtbiologisk Station, Kalø, Rønde
Beached bird surveys: Dansk Ornithologisk Forening, Vesterbrogade 140, 1620 Copenhagen V

Federal Republic of Germany
Wader counts: World Wildlife Fund Germany, c/o Dr. P. Prokosch, Norderstrasse 22, 2250 Husum
Beached bird surveys: Vogelwarte Helgoland, An der Vogelwarte 21, 2940 Wilhelmshaven

France
Station Biologique de Bailleron, Séné, 56000 Vannes
Ligue pour la Protection des Oiseaux, La Corderie Royal, B.P. 263, 17305 Rochefort Cedex

Netherlands
Rijksinstituut voor Natuurbeheer, P.O. Box 59, 1790 AB Den Burg, Texel
Beached bird surveys: Nederlands Stookolieslachtoffer Onderzoek, c/o C. J. Camphuijsen, Perim 127 Zaandam

Portugal
CEMPA, Rua Filipe Folque 46, Lisbon

Republic of Ireland
Irish Wildbird Conservancy, Southview, Church Road, Greystones, Co. Wicklow

Spain
Spanish Ornithological Society, c/o Dept. de Zoologia, Faculdad de Biologia, University of Leon, Leon

References

Atkinson-Willes, G. L. (1963). *Wildfowl in Great Britain.* Nature Conservancy Monograph No. 3. London.

Atkinson-Willes, G. L. (1976). Numerical distribution of ducks, swans and coots as a guide in assessing the importance of wetlands. In *Proceedings of the Fifth International conference on Conservation of Wetlands and Waterfowl*, Heiligenhafen 1974, ed. M. Smart, pp. 199–254. Slimbridge: IWRB.

Atkinson-Willes, G. L., Scott, D. A. & Prater, A. J. (1982). Criteria for selecting wetlands of international importance. In *Proceedings of the Conference on Conservation of Wetlands of International Importance especially as a Waterfowl Habitat*, Cagliari 1980, Suppl. Ricerche di Biol. della Selvaggina VIII, No. 1, pp. 1017–42. Bologna: Instituto Nazionale di Biologia della Selvaggina.

Baillie, S. R. & Mead, C. J. (1982). The effect of severe oil pollution during the winter of 1980–81 on British and Irish auks. *Ringing & Migration*, **4**, 33–44.

Baillie, S. R. & Stowe, T. J. (1984). A comparison between the percentage of seabirds reported as oiled from ringing recoveries and from the Beached Bird Survey. *Seabird Report*, **7**, 47–54.

Bibby, C. J. (1981). An experiment on the recovery of dead birds from the North Sea. *Orn. Scand.* **12**, 261–5.

Bibby, C. J., Bourne, W. R. P. & Merne, O. J. (1974). Roseate Terns in trouble. *BTO News*, **63**, 809.

Bibby, C. J. & Lloyd, C. S. (1977). Experiments to determine the fate of dead birds at sea. *Biol. Cons.* **12**, 295–309.

Birkhead, T. R., Lloyd, C. & Corkhill, P. (1973). Oiled seabirds successfully cleaning their plumage. *Brit. Birds*, **66**, 535–7.

Birkhead, T. R. & Nettleship, D. N. (1980). *Census Methods of Murres Uria Species: a Unified Approach.* Occasional Paper No. 43. Ottawa: Canadian Wildlife Service.

Blake, B. F., Tasker, M. L., Hope Jones, P., Dixon, T. J., Mitchell, R. & Langslow, D. R. (1984). *Seabird distribution in the North Sea.* Huntingdon: Nature Conservancy Council.

Boere, G. C. (1976). The significance of the Dutch Waddenzee in the annual cycle of arctic, subarctic and boreal waders. 1. The functions as a moulting area. *Ardea*, **64**, 210–91.

Bourne, W. R. P. & Bibby, C. J. (1975). Temperature and the seasonal and geographic occurrence of oiled birds on west European beaches. *Mar. Poll. Bull.* **6**, 77–80.

Camphuijsen, C. J. (1981). Olieslachtoffers op de Nederlandse kust, winter 1980/81. *Het Vogeljaar*, **29**, 232–8.

Camphuijsen, C. J. (1984). Twintig jaar stookolieslachtoffers op de Nederlandse kust: veranderingen in de zeevogelbevolking? *Limosa*, **57**, 157–9.

Coulson, J. C. (1983). The changing status of the Kittiwake (*Rissa tridactyla*) in the British Isles, 1969–1979. *Bird Study*, **30**, 9–16.

Cramp, S., Bourne, W. R. P. & Saunders, D. (1974). *The Seabirds of Britain and Ireland.* London: Collins.

Danielsen, F. & Skov, H. (1984). Olie pä vandere – og pä fuglene! *Fugle*, **3**, 14–15.

Evans, P. G. H. (ed.) (1980). *Auk Censusing Manual*. Sheffield: Seabird Group.

Goethe, F. (1961). The moult gatherings and the moult migration of the Shelduck in north-west Germany. *Brit. Birds*, **54**, 145–61.

Gompel, J. Van (1981). De massale zeevogelsterfte aan de Belgische kust tijdens de voorbije winter. *Wielewaal*, **47**, 137–42.

Harris, M. P. (1976). The present status of the Puffin in Britain and Ireland. *Brit. Birds*, **69**, 239–64.

Harris, M. P., Wanless, S. & Rothery, P. (1983). Assessing changes in the numbers of Guillemots *Uria aalge* at breeding colonies. *Bird Study*, **30**, 57–66.

Hickling, R. A. O. (1977). Inland wintering gulls in England and Wales, 1973. *Bird Study*, **24**, 79–88.

Hope Jones, P. (1980). Beached birds at selected Orkney beaches 1976–8. *Scot. Birds*, **11**, 1–12.

Hope Jones, P., Barrett, C. G., Mudge, G. P. & Harris, M. P. (1984). Physical condition of auks beached in eastern Britain during the wreck of February 1983. *Bird Study*, **31**, 95–8.

Hope Jones, P., Monnat, J-Y., Cadbury, C. J. & Stowe, T. J. (1978). Birds oiled during the *Amoco Cadiz* incident – an interim report. *Mar. Poll. Bull.* **9**, 307–10.

Hudson, R. & Mead, C. J. (1984). Origins and ages of auks wrecked in eastern Britain in February–March 1983. *Bird Study*, **31**, 89–94.

Hustings, M. F. H., Kwak, R. G. M., Opdam, P. F. M. & Reijnen, M. J. S. M. (1985). *Vogelinventarisaties. Achtergronden, Richtlijnen en Verslaglegging*. Wageningen: Pudoc.

Joensen, A. H. (1968). *Wildfowl Counts in Denmark in November 1967 and January 1968. Methods and results*. Danish Rev. Game Biol. vol. 5, No. 5. Kalø: Vildtbiologisk Station.

Joensen, A. H. (1972). *Oil Pollution and Seabirds in Denmark. 1935–1968 and 1969–1971*. Danish Rev. Game Biol., vol. 6, Nos 8 & 9. Kalø: Vildtbiologisk Station.

Kersten, M., Rappoldt, C. & Smit, C. (1981). Over de nauwkeurigheid van wadvogeltellingen. *Limosa*, **54**, 37–46.

Kuyken, E. (1978). Beached bird surveys in Belgium. *Ibis*, **120**, 122–3.

Lloyd, C. S. (1975). Timing and frequency of census counts in cliff-nesting auks. *Brit. Birds*, **68**, 507–13.

Lloyd, C. S., Bibby, C. J. & Everett, M. J. (1975). Breeding terns in Britain and Ireland in 1969–74. *Brit. Birds*, **68**, 221–37.

Lloyd, C. S., Bogan, J. A., Bourne, W. R. P., Dawson, P., Parslow, J. L. F. & Stewart, A. G. (1974). Seabird mortality in the north Irish Sea and Firth of Clyde early in 1974. *Mar. Poll. Bull.* **5**, 136–40.

Mead, C. J. (1974). The results of ringing auks in Britain and Ireland. *Bird Study*, **21**, 45–87.

Meltofte, H. (1981). *Danske rastepladser fur Vadefugle. Vadefugle-tuellingen i Danmark 1974–1978*. Fredningsstyrelsen. Copenhagen.

Milne, H. & Campbell, L. H. (1973). Wintering sea-ducks off the east coast of Scotland. *Bird Study*, **20**, 153–72.

Mörzer Bruijns, M. F. (1959). Stookolievogels op de Nederlandse kust. *De Levende natuur*, **62**, 172–8.

Ogilvie, M. A. & St. Joseph, A. K. M. (1976). Dark-bellied Brent Geese in Britain and Europe; 1955–76. *Brit. Birds*, **69**, 422–39.

Osborn, D., Young, W. J. & Gore, D. J. (1984). Pollutants in auks from the 1983 North Sea bird wreck. *Bird Study*, **31**, 99–102.

Owen, M., Atkinson-Willes, G. L. & Salmon, D. (1986). *Wildfowl in Great Britain*, 2nd edn. Cambridge University Press.

Piersma, T. (1984a). International wader migration studies along the East Atlantic flyway during spring 1985. *Wader Study Group Bull.* **42**, 5–9.

Piersma, T. (1984b). Estimating energy reserves of Great Crested Grebes *Podiceps cristatus* on the basis of body dimensions. *Ardea*, **72**, 119–26.

Prater, A. J. (1976). The distribution of Coastal Waders in Europe and North Africa. In *Proceedings of the Fifth International Conference on Conservation of Wetlands and Waterfowl*, Heiligenhafen 1974, ed. M. Smart, pp. 255–71. Slimbridge: IWRB.

Prater, A. J. (1979a). Trends in accuracy of counting birds. *Bird Study*, **26**, 198–200.

Prater, A. J. (1979b). Shorebird census studies in Britain. In *Shorebirds in Marine Environments*, ed. F. A. Pitelka, pp. 157–66. Studies in Avian Biology No. 2. Los Angeles: Cooper Ornithological Society.

Prater, A. J. (1981). *Estuary birds of Britain and Ireland*. Poyser: Calton.

Prato, E. S. da & da Prato, S. R. D. (1979). Counting wintering waders on rocky shores in East Lothian, Scotland. *Wader Study Group Bull.* **25**, 19–23.

Rappoldt, C., Kersten, M. & Smit, C. (1985). Errors in large-scale shorebird counts. *Ardea*, **73**, 13–24.

Reineking, B. (1984). Zum Seevogelsterben durch Oelpest an der deutschen Nordseekuste im Winter 1982/83. *Seevogel*, **5**, 43–9.

RSPB (Royal Society for the Protection of Birds) (1979). *Marine Oil Pollution and Birds*, 126 pp. unpubl. booklet.

Stowe, T. J. (1982a). Recent population trends in cliff-breeding seabirds in Britain and Ireland. *Ibis*, **124**, 502–10.

Stowe, T. J. (1982b). *Beached Bird Surveys and Surveillance of Cliff-breeding Seabirds*. The Lodge, Sandy: RSPB.

Stowe, T. J. & Underwood, L. A. (1984). Oil spillages affecting seabirds in the United Kingdom, 1966–1983. *Mar. Poll. Bull.* **15**, 147–52.

Summers, R. W., Corse, C. J., Meek, E. R., Moore, P. & Nicoll, M. (1984). The value of single counts of waders on rocky shores. *Wader Study Group Bull.* **41**, 7–9.

Tanis, J. J. C. & Mörzer Bruijns, M. F. (1962). Het onderzoek naar stookolievogels van 1958–1962. *De Levende Natuur*, **65**, 133–40.

Thomas, G. J. (1982). Breeding terns in Britain and Ireland 1975–79. *Seabird Report*, **6**, 59–69.

Underwood, L. A. & Stowe, T. J. (1984). Massive wreck of seabirds in eastern Britain, 1983. *Bird Study*, **31**, 79–88.

Wanless, S., French, D. D., Harris, M. P. & Langslow, D. R. (1982). Detection of annual changes in the number of cliff-nesting seabirds in Orkney, 1976–80. *J. Anim. Ecol.* **51**, 785–95.

14

Identification

W. J. WOLFF

Introduction

In most surveys of estuaries and coastal waters, identification of the organism found is aimed for. Several techniques for the analysis of survey data commonly in use today (diversity indices, log-normal distribution, ordination, and classification) require, or are rendered more sensitive, by the distinction of all species of the samples.

For the analysis of a particular survey it is not strictly necessary to know (all) the names of the organisms encountered. Identification by numbers or another code may be sufficient for several forms of data analysis. However, for comparison with literature data or previous and subsequent surveys, it is necessary to know the scientific names or organisms encountered. Nichols (1973), for example, reported that the results and conclusions of several of the benthic surveys of San Francisco Bay were of limited value because inadequate identifications meant that comparisons between surveys could not be made. These identification problems were attributed to the taxonomic inexperience of personnel and the use of incomplete literature.

This chapter mentions some of the problems encountered in the identification of organisms from estuaries and coastal waters and contains some recommendations on literature to be used. However, it is not a taxonomic treatise. If real taxonomic problems are met with, one has to consult a specialist. National centres of taxonomic expertise (e.g., National Museum of Natural History) exist in the majority of European countries.

The literature recommendations are meant for European waters with a focus on the East Atlantic shelf. Introductions to flora and fauna of other parts of the world include the works by Morton & Miller (1973: New Zealand), Carefoot (1977: Pacific coast of North America), Gosner (1978:

Atlantic coast of North America), Day (1981: South Africa), and Meinkoth (1981: Atlantic coast of North America).

Although flora and fauna of European waters may be regarded as well known, identification handbooks are rarely fully comprehensive, since in many taxonomic groups new taxa are described from the area each year. Also many taxonomic puzzles are still being solved.

There are several guides of an introductory nature for European coastal waters. These may be helpful to get a first impression of the flora and fauna of a particular region. They include Barrett & Yonge (1976: Britain), Campbell (1976: Britain, Europe), Luther & Fiedler (1976: Mediterranean), Prud'homme van Reine (1980: Netherlands, Belgium), and Riedl (1983: Mediterranean). However, one should be aware that field guides never cover all species of a particular area. Moreover, attempts to identify specimens by matching them with illustrations often go wrong.

Even when identifications are made carefully, one should be aware of possible personal bias. In dubious cases different investigators may be consistent in making different choices. Hence, whenever possible, continuity in sample sorting and species identification in a monitoring scheme should be maintained by using the same personnel on each survey. If staff changes are inevitable, a comprehensive collection of reference specimens is indispensable. Reference specimens do not, of course, guarantee that adequate identification of samples has been made. For this reason it is useful to retain the original samples so that subsequent queries concerning the species composition or abundance in samples may be answered.

It is to be expected that the number of taxa from a site will increase with subsequent surveys. In at least some cases this is explained by increasing staff expertise and familiarity with the organisms. Comparability with earlier surveys can be maintained by 'lumping' of species to previously used (and usually broader) taxonomic groups or by retaining the samples and 'splitting' the earlier 'species'.

Anybody with a biological training will recognise the majority of the organisms found as far as the main taxonomic groups are concerned. Sometimes, however, one encounters organisms for which it is unclear to which class or even phylum they belong. In such cases textbooks on general botany or zoology may be consulted for guidance.

Species identification by taxonomic groups
General

Sims (1980) gives a useful reference guide to the bewildering abundance of literature available for the identification of marine and brackish-water animals from all over the world. Kerrich, Hawksworth &

Sims (1978) published a similar volume for the north-west European flora and fauna. It is, however, dominated by British literature.

The following series of identification works may be recommended. They cover a large part of Europe and are, in part, relatively recent.

> *Fiches d'Identification du Zooplankton* (English). Published by the Conseil Permanent International pour l'Exploration de la Mer, Palaegade 2–4, 1261 Copenhagen K, Denmark.
>
> *Faune de France* (French). Librairie de la Faculté des Sciences, Paris; also available as Kraus reprints.
>
> *Synopses of the British Fauna*: New Series (English). Nos. 1–18 available from the Linnean Society (Burlington House, Piccadilly, London W1V OLQ, England); nos. 19–28 from Cambridge University Press; nos. 29 and following from E. J. Brill Publishing Company, Leiden.
>
> *Flora Europaea* (English). Cambridge University Press.
>
> The Comité International Permanent pour la Recherche sur la Préservation des Materiaux en Milieu Marin has published a useful series under the general title of *Catalogue of Main Marine Fouling Organisms*, with the following volumes:
>
> Vol. 1: *Barnacles*
>
> Vol. 2: *Polyzoa*
>
> Vol. 3: *Serpulids*
>
> Vol. 4: *Ascidians*
>
> Vol. 5: *Sponges*
>
> Vol. 6: *Algae*
>
> This series is available from the Office d'Etudes Marines et Atmosphériques (ODEMA), 64 rue Gabrielle, 1180 Bruxelles, Belgium.

In the following sections an attempt has been made to list for each taxonomic group some works that can be used in a relatively large part of Europe, are as complete as possible, and are of good taxonomic standing. If comprehensive works in English do not exist or are out of date, works in other languages are given as well. Not all taxonomic groups are covered, but entries to several minor groups are to be found in Sims (1980) and Kerrich *et al.* (1978). Parasitic groups have been omitted.

Bacteria

The identification of marine bacteria, except for certain highly specialised groups, is very difficult and time consuming. For details the reader should consult Buchanan, Holt & Lessel, (1966), Gibbs & Skinner (1966), Gibbs & Shapton (1968), Rodina (1972), and *Bergey's Manual of*

Systematic Bacteriology (Krieg, 1984). Standard 'type' strains of bacteria are maintained at the UK National Collections of Industrial and Marine Bacteria, and named strains for comparison with fresh isolates can be obtained from the Curator (National Collections of Industrial and Marine Bacteria Ltd., Torry Research Station, PO Box 31, 135 Abbey Road, Aberdeen, Scotland AB9 8DG). Fortunately, aquatic microbiologists do not always find it necessary to identify their isolates as far as the specific or even the generic level. For many purposes it is sufficient to describe them in terms of a particular function such as proteolytic or saccharolytic.

Fungi
Some groups of marine fungi are well monographed with good keys to aid their identification to species level. For the filamentous higher marine fungi, the reader is referred to the monographs by Johnson & Sparrow (1961) and Kohlmeyer & Kohlmeyer (1979). Ninety species are beautifully illustrated in the *Icones Fungorum Maris* by Kohlmeyer & Kohlmeyer (1964–69).

There are no keys specifically for the identification of the marine Mastigomycotina, yeasts, and the Thraustochytriales, and more general texts should be used – Sparrow (1960) for the Mastigomycotina and Lodder (1970) for the yeasts. Gaertner (1972, 1977) and Bremer (1976) provide an introduction to the Thraustochytriales. Olive (1975) provides an introduction to the Labyrinthulales.

Algae
Newell & Newell (1977) provide an introductory guide to plankton identification; their illustrations of phytoplankton may be supplemented by the photographs of living diatoms and dinoflagellates in Drebes (1974). Estuarine plankton sometimes includes freshwater algae, and Belcher & Swale's (1976) beginner's guide is useful for provisional identification to genus. Another useful introductory guide is provided by Sykes (1981; British diatoms). Dodge's (1982) guide to dinoflagellates and Hendey's (1964) guide to diatoms in British waters replace earlier works. Humm & Wicks (1980) give two taxonomies for marine blue-green algae, and an indication of the systematic and identification difficulties likely to be encountered with this group. The works of Drouet & Dailey (1956) and Drouet (1968) on blue-green algae may be used if only a relatively rough separation into the main forms is required for material collected in the field. A useful but incomplete series (Butcher, 1959, 1961, 1967) deals with some of the important groups amongst the smaller algae of British coastal waters. A recent account of Flemish brackish-water phytoplankton

(Caljon, 1984) contains illustrations of many freshwater, brackish-water, and marine microalgae, including small flagellates. Sournia (1978) should be consulted for a fuller list of phytoplankton identification literature. George (1976) contains a guide to algal keys, including both marine and freshwater forms.

There is a large variety of identification works for marine macroalgae. Rueness (1977) describes the algal flora of Norway (in Norwegian). Kornmann & Sahling (1977) made a well-illustrated algal flora (in German) for the German island of Helgoland. Pankow (1971) describes the algae of the Baltic Sea (in German). Stegenga & Mol (1983) is a complete survey (in Dutch) of the macroalgae of the Dutch coast. A major series of volumes for the British Isles was started by Dixon & Irvine (1977) and Irvine (1983), but no other volumes have been published yet. Useful British keys are Jones (1962), and Hiscock (1979, 1986). Coppejans & van der Ben (1982) have written a flora (in Dutch) for the coast of Belgium and northern France. Gayral (1966) is another illustrated guide (in French) to the algae of the French Atlantic coasts.

For the study of algae of tidal flats the monographs on *Vaucheria* (Blum, 1972), *Cladophora* (Söderström, 1963; Van den Hoek, 1963), and *Ulva, Monostroma, Enteromorpha* etc. (Bliding, 1963, 1968) are relevant. Unfortunately the works by Bliding do not have any keys, which makes them difficult to use. It must also be pointed out, for the latter five works cited, that concepts concerning the taxonomy of these groups are going through a period of rapid change at present.

Lichenes
Fletcher (1975a, b) give keys for the identification of coastal lichens from the British Isles. Dahl & Krog (1973) give keys to all Scandinavian species.

Spermatophyta
Den Hartog (1970) described the seagrasses of the world. A comprehensive account of the Spermatophyta of Europe is presented in the *Flora Europaea* by Tutin et al. (1964, 1968, 1972, 1976, 1980). The various national and regional floras, however, are more practical to use for most purposes.

Protozoa
Euglenoid flagellates may be identified with Leedale (1967). Murray (1979) provides a key to British nearshore foraminiferids. Beers in Sournia (1978) discusses literature for identification of the protozoan

zooplankton. Patterson (1978) has published a translation of the keys in the ciliate monograph by Kahl (1932). Zooflagellate identification is not well served; a paper on flagellate ecology by Fenchel (1982) provides perhaps the best available way into the literature.

Porifera

Arndt (1935) gives an account (in German) of the sponges of the Baltic and the North Sea. Van Soest (1976) gives a key to the species of the Netherlands (in Dutch).

Coelenterata

Russell (1953, 1970) is a useful work on hydromedusae and scyphomedusae. Siphonophores and velellids may be identified with Kirkpatrick & Pugh (1984); Anthozoa or sea-anemones may be identified with Manuel (1981). Kramp (1935) (in Danish), Vervoort (1946) (in Dutch), and Leloup (1952) (in French) may be consulted for identification of Hydrozoa.

Clausen (1971) contains a useful bibliography on interstitial coelenterates.

Platyhelminthes

Ball & Reynoldson (1981) and Prudhoe (1982) describe and give keys to the British triclad and polyclad turbellarians, respectively. Dörjes (1968) describes (in German) the Turbellaria Acoela of the German coast. Karling (1974) presents a key to the Baltic species.

Since the taxonomy of Turbellaria is still evolving rapidly, the Newsletter of the International Association of Meiobenthologists *Psammonalia* should be consulted for recent additions to the literature.

Nemertini

Nemertini are difficult to identify; however, when alive, several species can be identified on the basis of their external features. For preserved specimens, histological studies are essential. Brunberg (1964) and Gibson (1982) may be recommended for identification.

Nematoda

Gerlach & Riemann (1973) enumerate more than 5000 species in the Bremerhaven check-list of aquatic nematodes. Nematode taxonomy is mainly based on differences in size and shape of the buccal cavity, the buccal armature, the male genital apparatus, and the cuticular ornamentation. Those authors cited below and prior to 1973 may be found in

Gerlach & Riemann (1973). The others are in the References at the end of this chapter. De Coninck (1965) gives extensive information on the fundamentals of nematode morphology and taxonomy. Platt & Warwick (1983) give an excellent key to the Enoplida of British waters, which also may be used in other European areas. Two more volumes, covering the remaining nematode species, are planned in the same series. The following authors are of particular importance for various taxonomic groups: Gerlach (1950 (genus *Microlaimus*), 1951 (subfamily Metachromadorinae), 1951 (family Chromadoridae), 1951 (genus *Theristus*), 1963 (genus *Haliplectus*), 1963 (family Linhomoeidae), 1964 (family Choniolaimidae)); Jensen (1978 (families Microlaimidae and Molgolaimidae), 1979 (family Comesomatidae)); Kreis (1934 (family Oncholaimidae)); Lorenzen (1966, 1969, 1973 (entire phylum), 1969, 1972 (family Desmoscolecidae), 1971a, b (orders Araeolaimida, Monhysterida, Desmodorida, and Chromadorida), 1972 (family Cyatholaimidae), 1972 (genus *Leptolaimus*), 1977 (family Xyalidae)); Platt (1982 (family Ethmolaimidae)); Riemann (1966 (genus *Trefusia*)), Timm (1970) (order Desmoscolecidae)); and Warwick (1971 (family Cyatholaimidae)).

Since the nematode literature is rapidly evolving it is also useful to consult *Psammonalia*, the Newsletter of the International Association of Meiobenthologists.

Sipuncula, Echiura, Annelida

Stephen & Edmonds (1972) give an account of the sipunculans and echiurans of the world. Gibbs (1977) may be used for identification of sipunculans from the larger part of the East Atlantic shelf.

Fauchald (1977) gives a useful key to the orders, families, and genera of polychaetes of the world, although his classification deviates to some extent from those by others.

For the identification of European polychaetes the relatively old works of Fauvel (1923, 1927) are still very useful. More recent are Hartmann-Schröder (1971) (in German) on the polychaetes of the North Sea and Baltic and Rioja (1977) (in Spanish) on those of Spain.

Specific groups are covered by Knight-Jones & Knight-Jones (1977: Spirorbidae), Nelson-Smith (1967: Serpulidae), Gidholm (1966: Autolytinae), Hamond (1974: Autolytinae), Pearson (1969: Terebellidae), Zibrowius (1968: Mediterranean Serpulidae), Muus (1953: pelagic species and larvae), and Hannerz (1961: larvae of Spionidae, Disomidae, and Poecilochaetidae).

Marine and estuarine oligochaetes may be identified with Brinkhurst (1982). More species are described in Brinkhurst & Jamieson (1971).

Pycnogonida
A fairly recent key to pycnogonids or sea-spiders is that of King (1974), now revised (King, 1986).

Ostracoda
Klie (1938) is still a useful guide (in German) to the Ostracoda.

Copepoda and other zooplankton
Newell & Newell (1977) provide a convenient introductory guide to the zooplankton of temperate seas, and give references to more-advanced works on identification. Tregouboff & Rose (1957) deal at greater length with the Mediterranean plankton. The International Council for the Exploration of the Sea (ICES, Palaegade 2–4, DK 1261 Copenhagen K, Denmark) publishes a series of Fiches d'Identification, each dealing with the identification and distribution of a selected group of zooplankton from the North Atlantic.

Cirripedia
Keys to barnacles are provided by Southward (1963, 1976) and Rainbow (1984).

Mysidacea, Euphausiacea
A still very useful account of the British (and north-west European) mysids is Tattersall & Tattersall (1951). Borghouts-Biersteker (1983) produced a key (in Dutch) to the species of the Netherlands. Mauchline (1984) gives keys to north-west European euphausiid, stomatopod, and leptostracan crustaceans. Einarsson (1945) provides a guide to North Atlantic euphausiids and their larvae.

Cumacea
Keys to European cumaceans are given by Fage (1951) (in French) and Jones (1976).

Tanaidacea and Isopoda
Keys to Tanaidacea and/or Isopoda are given by Huwae (1977) (in Dutch) for the Netherlands, Gruner (1965) (in German) for the Baltic and the North Sea, and Naylor (1972) and Holdich & Jones (1983) for British waters.

Amphipoda

Schellenberg (1942) is the most recent comprehensive account of the amphipods of the North Sea and Baltic. Lincoln (1979) covers the gammaridean species of the British Isles.

Decapoda: Natantia

Holthuis (1955) gives keys to all genera of shrimps and prawns of the world. Lagardère (1969, 1971) has produced (in French) accounts of species occurring off Morocco and the Bay of Biscay; see Zariquiey Alvarez (1968) for the Iberian peninsula, Holthuis & Heerebout (1976) (in Dutch) for the Netherlands, Bacescu (1967) (in Rumanian) for the Black Sea, and Smaldon (1979) for the British Isles.

Decapoda: Reptantia

Accounts of the lobsters and crabs of various parts of Europe are given by Bacescu (1967) (in Rumanian) for the Black Sea, by Zariquiey Alvarez (1968) for the Iberian peninsula, by Christiansen (1969) for Scandinavian waters (Brachyura only), by Holthuis & Heerebout (1976) (in Dutch) for the Netherlands, and by Ingle (1980, 1983) for British waters (Brachyura only). Crothers & Crothers (1983) provide a well-illustrated key to the crabs and crab-like animals of British inshore waters.

Insecta

Reviews of the major groups of marine insects are given in Cheng (1976).

Mollusca

Nordsieck (1968, 1969, 1972) describes European prosobranch, bivalve, and opisthobranch molluscs (in German). Tebble (1976) gives an account of the British bivalve molluscs, whereas Graham (1971) and Thompson & Brown (1976) do so for prosobranch and opisthobranch molluscs respectively. A series of supplements to *The Journal of Molluscan Studies* (Fretter & Graham 1976, 1977, 1978, 1980, 1981) describe different groups of prosobranch molluscs of Britain and Denmark. Smith (1982) reviews the genus *Littorina* in British and Atlantic waters. Some brackish-water species are described by Macan (1977).

Ziegelmeier (1957, 1966) gives accounts (in German) of the species of the German coasts; Grossu (1956, 1962) gives those of the Rumanian Black Sea coast (in Rumanian). Schmekel & Portmann (1982) describe Mediterranean opisthobranchs (in German).

Bryozoa

Ryland & Hayward (1977) and Hayward & Ryland (1979) published accounts of various groups of British Bryozoa. Prenant & Bobin (1956, 1966) give an account of the French species (in French). Fouling species are described by Ryland (1965), whereas keys to intertidal species are given by Ryland (1962). Nielsen (1962), describes the species from Danish waters.

Echinodermata

Mortensen (1927) is still a very useful account of the echinoderms of NW Europe. Tortonese (1965) (in Italian) gives an account of Italian and Mediterranean species.

Tunicata

Monniot & Monniot (1972) give a key (in French) to the ascidian genera of the world. Millar (1966) gives an account of the Ascidia of Scandinavian waters, and also (Millar, 1970) for British waters. Buizer (1983) gives a key to the species of the Netherlands (in Dutch). Monniot (1965) describes the interstitial ascidians of Europe (in French), and also (Monniot, 1969) covers the family Molgulidae (in French).

Fraser (1981) gives keys to British pelagic tunicates.

Pisces

Hureau & Monod (1973) published a check-list of the fishes of the north-eastern Atlantic and the Mediterranean. Wheeler (1969, 1978) is to be recommended for identification of fishes in northern Europe. Other useful titles are Muus & Dahlstrom (1964) (in Danish, but translated into many other languages), Duncker & Ladiges (1960) (in German), Nijssen & de Groot (1980) (in Dutch), and Poll (1947) (in French).

Russell (1976) produced an excellent account of the eggs and planktonic stages of fishes of British waters.

Aves

There are numerous field guides for European birds, several of them translated into many languages. Useful guides are Peterson, Mountford & Hollom (1954) and Bruun & Singer (1974).

A field guide to the sea birds of the world is Tuck & Heinsel (1978). A detailed account of all aspects of European birds is given in the *Handbuch der Vogel Mitteleuropas* (Bauer & Glutz von Blotzheim, 1966, 1968, 1969; Glutz von Blotzheim, Bauer & Bezzel, 1973, 1975, 1977; Glutz von

Blotzheim & Bauer, 1982), as well as in the *Birds of the Western Palearctic* (Cramp *et al.*, 1977, 1983, 1985).

Mammalia

Van den Brink (1967) produced a field guide to the mammals of Europe, whereas Mörzer Bruyns (1971) did so for the cetaceans of the world. Fraser (1976) gives keys to British cetaceans, and Duguy & Robineau (1973) do so for the species occurring along the coasts of France. The seals of the world are described by King (1983).

Acknowledgements

This chapter is to a large extent based on information provided by the authors of the previous chapters, in particular Dr. J. H. Crothers. I would also like to thank Mr R. Dekker for his suggestions.

References

Arndt, W. (1935). *Porifera*. Die Tierwelt der Nord-Und Ostsee 3a. Leipzig: Akademischer Verlag.
Bacescu, M. C. (1967). *Decapoda*. Fauna Republic Populare Romîne. Bucharest: Academiei Populare Romîne. 4 (9), 356 pp.
Ball, I. R. & Reynoldson, T. B. (1981). *British Planarians*. Linnean Society Synopses of the British Fauna (NS) 19. Cambridge University Press.
Barrett, J. H. & Yonge, C. M. (1976). *Collins' Pocket Guide to the Seashore*, 9th ed. London: Collins.
Bauer, K. M. & Glutz von Blotzheim, U. N. (1966, 1968, 1969). *Handbuch der Vogel Mitteleuropas*, vols. 1, 2, 3. Frankfurt: Akademische Verlagsgesellschaft.
Belcher, H. & Swale, E. (1976). *A Beginner's Guide to Freshwater Algae*. London: HMSO.
Bliding, C. (1963). A critical survey of European taxa in Ulvales. I. Capsosiphon, Percursaria, Blidingia, Enteromorpha. *Op. bot. Soc. bot. Lund.* **8**, 1–160.
Bliding, C. (1968). A critical survey of European taxa in Ulvales. II. Ulva, Ulvaria, Monostroma, Kornmannia. *Bot. Notiser* **121**, 535–629.
Blum, J. L. (1972). Vaucheriaceae. *North Am. Flora Ser.* (3) **8**, 1–64.
Borghouts-Biersteker, C. H. (1983). *Aasgarnalen* (*Mysidacea*). Tabellenserie Strandwerkgemeenschap 23. Hoorn: Koninklijke Nederlandse Natuurhistorische Vereniging.
Bremer, G. B. (1976). The ecology of marine lower fungi. In *Recent Advances in Aquatic Mycology*, ed. E. B. G. Jones, pp. 313–33, London: Elek Science.
Brink, F. H. van den (1967). *A Field Guide to the Mammals of Britain and Europe*. London: Collins.
Brinkhurst, R. O. (1982). *British and Other Marine and Estuarine Oligochaetes*. Linnean Society Synopses of the British Fauna (NS) 21. Cambridge University Press.

Brinkhurst, R. O. & Jamieson, B. G. M. (1971). *Aquatic Oligochaeta of the World.* Edinburgh: Oliver & Boyd.

Brunberg, L. (1964). On the nemertean fauna of Danish waters. *Ophelia* 1, 77–111.

Bruun, B. & Singer, A. (1974). *The Hamlyn Guide to Birds of Britain and Europe.* London: Hamlyn.

Buchanan, R. E., Holt, J. G. & Lessel, E. F. (1966). *Index Bergeyana.* Baltimore: Williams & Wilkins.

Buizer, D. A. G. (1983). *De nederlandse zakpijpen (manteldieren) en mantelvisjes. Tunicata, Ascidiacea en Appendicularia.* Wetenschappelijke Mededelingen KNNV. Hoorn: Nederlandse Natuurhistorische Vereniging.

Butcher, R. W. (1959). An introductory account of the smaller algae of British coastal waters. I. Introduction and Chlorophyceae. *Fish. Invest. Lond.* ser. 4, 1–74.

Butcher, R. W. (1961). An introductory account of the smaller algae of British coastal waters. VIII. Euglenophyceae (Eugleninae). *Fish. Invest. Lond.* ser. 4, 1–17.

Butcher, R. W. (1967). An introductory account of the smaller algae of British coastal waters. IV. Cryptophyceae. *Fish. Invest. Lond.* ser. 4, 1–54.

Caljon, A. (1984). *Brackish-water Phytoplankton of the Flemish Lowland.* Developments in Hydrobiology 18. The Hague: Dr W. Junk.

Campbell, A. C. (1976). *The Hamlyn Guide to the Seashore and the Shallow Seas of Britain and Europe.* London: Hamlyn.

Carefoot, T. (1977). *Pacific Seashores: A Guide to Intertidal Ecology.* Vancouver: J. J. Douglas.

Cheng, L. (ed.) (1976). *Marine Insects.* Amsterdam: North-Holland Publishing Co.

Christiansen, M. E. (1969). *Crustacea Decapoda Brachyura.* Marine Invertebrates of Scandinavia 2. Oslo: Universitetsforlaget.

Clausen, C. (1971). Interstitial Cnidaria: present status of their systematics and ecology. *Smithsonian Contrib. Zool* 76, 1–8.

Coppejans, E. & Ben, D. van der (1982). *Zeewierengids voor de Belgische en Noordfranse Kust.* Gent: Belgische Jeugdbond voor Natuurstudie.

Cramp, S., Brooks, D. J., Dunn, E., Gillmor, R., Hollom, P. A. D., Hudson, R., Nicholson, E. M., Ogilvie, M. A., Olney, P. J. S., Roselaar, C. S., Simmons, K. E. L., Voous, K. H., Wallace, D. I. M., Wattel, J., & Wilson, M. G. (1977, 1983, 1985). *Handbook of the Birds of Europe, the Middle East and North Africa. The Birds of the western Palearctic,* vols. 1, 3, 4. Oxford University Press.

Crothers, J. H. & Crothers, M. (1983). A key to the crabs and crab-like animals of British inshore waters. *Field Studies* 5, 753–806.

Dahl, E. & Krog, H. (1973). *Macrolichens of Denmark, Finland, Norway and Sweden.* Oslo: Universitetsforlaget.

Day, J. H. (1981). *Estuarine Ecology with Particular Reference to Southern Africa.* Rotterdam: Balkema.

Dixon, P. S. & Irvine, L. M. (1977). *Seaweeds of the British Isles. I. Rhodophyta. 1. Introduction, Nemaliales, Gigartinales.* London: British Museum of Natural History.

416   W. J. WOLFF

Dodge, J. D. (1982). *Marine Dinoflagellates of the British Isles*. London: HMSO.
Dörjes, J. (1968). Die Acoela (Turbellaria) der deutschen Nordseeküste und ein neues System der Ordnung. *Z. Zool. Syst. Evol. Forsch.* **6**, 54–452.
Drebes, G. (1974). *Marines Phytoplankton*. Stuttgart: George Thieme Verlag.
Drouet, F. (1968). *Revision of the Classification of the Oscillatoriaceae*. Monograph 15. Philadelphia: Academy of Natural Sciences.
Drouet, F. & Dailey, W. A. (1956). *Revision of the coccoid Myxophyceae*. Butler University Botanical Studies 12.
Duguy, R. & Robineau, D. (1973). Cetacés et phoques des côtes de France. Guide d'identification. *Annls. Soc. Sci. nat. Charente-maritime*, Suppl. 1973, 1–93.
Duncker, G. & Ladiges, W. (1960). Die Fische der Nordmark. *Abh. Verh. naturw. Ver. Hamburg* (NF) Suppl. 3.
Einarsson, H. (1945). Euphausiacea. I. North Atlantic species. *Dana-Reports* 27.
Fage, L. (1951). Cumacés. *Faune de France* **54**, 1–136.
Fauchald, K. (1977). The polychaete worms. Definitions and keys to the orders, families and genera. *Nat. Hist. Mus. Los Angeles City, Sci. Ser.* **28**, 1–140.
Fauvel, P. (1923). *Polychètes Errantes*. Faune de France 5. Paris: Lechevalier.
Fauvel, P. (1927). *Polychètes Sédentaires*. Faune de France 16. Paris: Lechevalier.
Fenchel, T. (1982). Ecology of heterotrophic microflagellates. IV. Quantitative occurrence and importance as bacterial consumers. *Mar. Ecol. Progr. Ser.* **9**, 25–42.
Fletcher, A. (1975a). Key for the identification of British marine and maritime lichens. I. Siliceous rocky shore species. *Lichenologist* **7**, 1–52.
Fletcher, A. (1975b). Key for the identification of British marine and maritime lichens. II. Calcareous and terricolous species. *Lichenologist* **7**, 73–115.
Fraser, F. C. (1976). *British Whales, Dolphins and Porpoises*. London: British Museum of Natural History.
Fraser, J. H. (1981). *British pelagic tunicates*. Linnean Society Synopses of the British Fauna (NS) 20. Cambridge University Press.
Fretter, V. & Graham, A. (1976–81). The Prosobranch Molluscs of Britain and Denmark. Supplements to *The Journal of Molluscan Studies*. Part 1 (1976) Pleurotomariacea, Fissurellacea and Patellacea. Part 2 (1977) Trochacea. Part 4 (1978) Marine Rissoacea. Part 5 (1980) Marine Littorinacea. Part 6 (1981) Cerithiacea, Strombacea, Hipponicacea, Calyptracea, Naticacea, Tonnacea, Heteropoda.
Gaertner, A. (1972). Characters used in the classification of thraustochytriaceous fungi. *Veröff. Inst. Meeresforsch. Bremerh.* **13**, 183–94.
Gaertner, A. (1977). Revision of tthe Thraustochytriales (lower marine fungi). I. *Ulkenia* nov. gen., with description of three new species. *Veröff. Inst. Meeresforsch. Bremerh.* **16**, 139–57.
Gayral, P. (1966). *Les Algues des Cotes Francaises*. Paris: Ed. Doin.
George, E. A. (1976). A guide to algal keys (excluding sea weeds). *Brit. Phycol. J.* **11**, 49–55.

Gerlach, S. A. & Riemann, F. (1973). The Bremerhaven checklist of aquatic
    nematodes, 1, 2. *Veröffentl. Inst. Meeresforsch. Bremerhaven Supple.* **4**,
    1–736.
Gibbs, B. M. & Shapton, D. P. (1968). *Identification methods for microbiologists.*
    Part B. The Society for Applied Bacteriology Technical Series No. 2.
    London: Academic Press.
Gibbs, B. M. & Skinner, F. A. (1966). *Identification methods for microbiologists.*
    Part A. The Society for Applied Bacteriology Technical Series No. 1.
    London: Academic Press.
Gibbs, P. E. (1977). *British Sipunculans.* Linnean Society Synopses of the
    British Fauna (NS) 12. London: Academic Press.
Gibson, R. (1982). *British Nemerteans.* Linnean Society Synopses of the British
    Fauna (NS) 24. Cambridge University Press.
Gidholm, A. (1966). A revision of Autolytinae (Syllidae, Polychaeta) with
    special reference to Scandinavian species and with notes on external
    and internal morphology, ecology, and reproduction. *Ark. Zool.* (2)
    19, 157–213.
Glutz von Blotzheim, U. N., Bauer, K. M. & Bezzel, E. (1973, 1975, 1977).
    Handbuch der Vogel Mitteleuropas, vols 5, 6, 7. Frankfurt:
    Akademisches Verlagsgesellschaft.
Glutz von Blotzheim, U. N. & Bauer, K. M. (1982). *Handbuch der Vogel
    Mitteleuropas,* vol. 8. Frankfurt: Akademisches Verlagsgesellschaft.
Gosner, K. L. (1978). *A Field Guide to the Atlantic Seashore from the Bay of
    Fundy to Cape Hatteras.* Boston: Houghton Mifflin Company.
Graham, A. (1971). *British prosobranchs and other operculate gastropod
    molluscs.* Linnean Society Synopses of the British Fauna (NS) 2.
    London: Academic Press.
Grossu, A. V. (1956). *Gastropoda prosobranchia si opisthobranchia.* Fauna
    Republicii Populare Romine, vol. 3, fasc. 2 Bucharest: Academiei
    republicii socialiste România.
Grossu, A. V. (1962). *Bivalvia.* Fauna Republicii Populare Romine, vol. 3, fasc.
    3. Bucharest: Academiei republicii socialiste România.
Gruner, H. E. (1965). Krebstiere oder Crustacea. V. Isopoda. 1. Lieferung.
    Tierwelt Deutschlands, **51**, 1–160.
Hamond, R. (1974). The culture, experimental taxonomy, and comparative
    morphology of the planktonic stages of Norfolk autolytoids
    (Polychaeta: Syllidae: Autlytinae). *Zool. J. Linn. Soc.* **54**,
    299–320.
Hannerz, L. (1961). Larval development of the polychaete families Spionidae
    Sars, Disomidae Mesnil, and Poecilochaetidae n. fam. in the
    Gullmarfjord (Sweden). *Zool. Bidr. Uppsala* **31**, 1–204.
Hartmann-Schröder, G. (1971). Annelida, Borstenwurmer, Polychaeta. *Tierwelt
    Deutschlands,* **58**, 1–594.
Hartog, C. den (1970). The sea-grasses of the world. *Verh. Kon. Ned. Akad.
    Wet. Afd. Natuurk.* (2) **59**, 1–275.
Hayward, P. J. & Ryland, J. S. (1979). *British Ascophoran Bryozoans.* Linnean
    Society Synopses of the British Fauna (NS) 14. London: Academic
    Press.

Hendey, N. I. (1964). *An Introductory Account of the Smaller Algae of British Coastal Waters.* Part V. *Bacillariophyceae (Diatoms).* London: HMSO.

Hiscock, S. (1979). A field key to the British brown seaweeds (Phaeophyta). *Field Studies* **5**, 1–44.

Hiscock, S. (1986). A field key to the British red seaweeds. *Occasional Publication of the Field Studies Council* No. 13. London: Field Studies Council.

Hoek, C. van den (1963). *Revision of the European species of Cladophora.* Brill, Leiden.

Holdich, D. M. & Jones, J. A. (1983). *Tanaids.* Linnean Society Synopses of the British Fauna (NS) 27. Leiden: E. J. Brill.

Holthuis, L. B. (1955). The recent genera of the caridean and stenopidean shrimps with keys for their determination. *Zool. Verh. Leiden* **26**, 1–157.

Holthuis, L. B. & Heerebout, G. R. (1976). *De nederlandse Decapoda (Garnalen, Kreeften en Krabben).* Wetenschappelijke Mededelingen KNNV 111. Hoorn: Koninklijke Nederlandse Natuurhistorische Vereniging.

Humm, H. J. & Wicks, S. R. (1980). *Introduction and guide to the marine blue-green algae.* New York: Wiley Interscience.

Hureau, J. C. & Monod, T. (1973). *Check-list of the Fishes of the North-Eastern Atlantic and of the Mediterranean (CLOFNAM).* Paris: UNESCO.

Huwae, P. H. M. (1977). *De isopoden van de nederlandse kust.* Wetenschappelijke Mededelingen KNNV 118. Hoorn: Koninklijke Nederlandse Natuurhistorische Vereniging.

Ingle, R. W. (1980). *British Crabs.* Oxford University Press.

Ingle, R. W. (1983). *Shallow-water Crabs.* Linnean Society Synopses of the British Fauna (NS) 25. Leiden: E. J. Brill.

Irvine, L. M. (1983). *Seaweeds of the British Isles,* vol. 1: *Rhodophyta,* part 2: *Cryptonemiales sensu stricto, Palmariales, Rhodymeniales.* London: British Museum (Natural History).

Jensen, P. (1978). Revision of Microlaimidae, Erection of Molgolaimidae fam. n. and Remarks on the Systematic Position of Paramicrolaimus (Nematoda, Desmodoriada). *Zool. Scr.* **7**, 159–73.

Jensen, P. (1979). Revision of Comesomatidae (Nematoda). *Zool. Scr.* **8**, 81–105.

Johnson, T. W. & Sparrow, F. K. (1961). *Fungi in Oceans and Estuaries.* Weinheim: Cramer.

Jones, W. E. (1962). A key to the genera of the British seaweeds. *Field Studies* **1**, 1–32. Reprinted in 1964 with revisions.

Jones, N. S. (1976). *British Cumaceans.* Linnean Society Synopses of the British Fauna (NS) 7. London: Academic Press.

Kahl, A. (1932). Urtiere oder Protozoa. I: Wimpertiere oder Ciliata (Infusoria), 3. Spirotricha. In *Die Tierwelt Deutschlands* 25, ed. F. Dahl, M. Dahl & H. Bisschoff, pp. 399–650. Jena: Gustav Fischer.

Karling, T. G. (1974). Turbellarian fauna of the Baltic proper. Identification, ecology and biogeography. *Fauna Fennica* **27**, 1–101.

Kerrich, G. J., Hawksworth, D. L. & Sims, R. W. (1978). *Key Works to the*

Fauna and Flora of the British Isles and North-Western Europe. London: Academic Press.

King, J. E. (1983). *Seals of the World,* 2nd edn. London: British Museum of Natural History.

King, P. E. (1974). British Sea Spiders. *Linnean Society Synopses of the British Fauna* (NS) 5. London: Academic Press.

King, P. E. (1986) Revised key to Sea Spiders. *Field Studies* 6.

Kirkpatrick, P. A. & Pugh, P. R. (1984). *Siphonophores and velellids.* Linnean Society Synopses of the British Fauna (NS) 29. Leiden: E. J. Brill.

Klie, W. (1938). *Ostracoda, Muschelkrebse.* Tierwelt Deutschlands 34. Jena: Gustav Fischer.

Knight-Jones, P. & Knight-Jones, E. W. (1977). Taxonomy and Ecology of British Spirorbidae (Polychaeta). *J. mar. biol. Ass. U.K.* **57**, 453–99.

Kohlmeyer, J. & Kohlmeyer, E. (1964–69). *Icones Fungorum Maris.* Weinheim and Lehre: Cramer.

Kohlmeyer, J. & Kohlmeyer, E. (1979). *Marine Mycology: The Higher Fungi.* New York: Academic Press.

Kornmann, P. & Sahling, P. H. (1977). Meeresalgen von Helgoland. *Helgol. wiss. Meeresunters.* **29**, 1–289.

Kramp, P. L. (1935). Polypdyr (Coelenterata) I. Ferskvandspolypper og Goplepolypper. *Danmarks Fauna* **41**, 1–207.

Krieg, N. R. (ed.) (1984). *Bergey's Manual of Systematic Bacteriology.* Baltimore: Williams and Wilkins.

Lagardère, J. P. (1969). Les crevettes du Golfe de Gascogne (region sud). *Tethys* **1**, 1023–48.

Lagardère, J. P. (1971). Les crevettes des côtes du Maroc. *Trav. Inst. scient. cherifien* **36**, 1–140.

Leedale, G. F. (1967). *Euglenoid Flagellates.* Englewood Cliffs: Prentice-Hall.

Leloup, E. (1952). *Coelentères.* Faune de Belgique. Brussels: Institut Royal des Sciences naturelles.

Lincoln, R. (1979). *British Marine Amphipoda. Gammaridea.* London: British Museum of Natural History.

Lodder, J. (ed.) (1970). *The Yeasts: a Taxonomic Study,* vols. 1, 2. Amsterdam: North-Holland Publishing Company. 1385 pp.

Lorenzen, S. (1973). Freilebende Meeresnematoden aus dem Sublitoral der Nordsee und der Kieler Bucht. *Veröff. Inst. Meeresforsch. Bremerh.* **14**, 103–30.

Lorenzen, S. (1977). Revision der Xyalidae (freilebende Nematoden) auf der Grundlage einer kritischen Analyse von 56 Arten aus Nord- und Ostsee. *Veröff. Inst. Meeresforsch. Bremerh.* **16**, 197–261.

Luther, W. & Fiedler, K. (1976). *A Field Guide to the Mediterranean Sea Shore.* London: Collins.

Macan, T. T. (1977). *A Key to the British Fresh- and Brackish-water Gastropods.* Ambleside: Freshwater Biological Association.

Manuel, R. L. (1981). *British Anthozoa.* Linnean Society Synopses of the British Fauna (NS) 18. London: Academic Press.

Mauchline, J. (1984). *Euphausiid, Stomatopod and Leptostracan Crustaceans.*

Linnean Society Synopses of the British Fauna (NS) 30. Leiden:
E. J. Brill.

Meinkoth, M. A. (1981). *The Audubon Society Field Guide to North American Seashore Creatures.* New York: Knopf.

Millar, R. H. (1966). *Tunicata: Ascidiacea.* Marine Invertebrates of Scandinavia 1. Oslo: Universitetsforlaget.

Millar, R. H. (1970). *British Ascidians.* Linnean Society Synopses of the British Fauna (NS) 1. London: Academic Press.

Monniot, C. (1969). Les Molgulidae des mers européens. *Mem. Mus. nat. Hist. nat. Paris,* Ser. A **60**, 171–272.

Monniot, C. & Monniot, F. (1972). Clé mondiale des genres d'ascidies. *Arch. Zool. exp. gen.* **133**, 311–67.

Monniot, F. (1965). Ascidies interstitielles des côtes d'Europe. *Mem. Mus. natn. Hist. nat. Paris,* Ser. A **35**, 1–154.

Mortensen, T. (1927). *Handbook of the Echinoderms of the British Isles.* Oxford: Clarendon. Reprinted 1977 by Backhuys, Rotterdam.

Morton, J. & Miller, M. (1973). *The New Zealand Seashore.* London: Collins.

Mörzer Bruyns, W. F. J. M. (1971). *Field Guide of Whales and Dolphins.* Amsterdam: Tor.

Murray, J. W. (1979). *British nearshore foraminiferids.* Linnean Society Synopses of the British Fauna (NS) 16. London: Academic Press.

Muus, B. J. (1953). Polychaeta. Families Aphroditidae, Phyllodocidae and Alciopidae. Families Tomopteridae and Typhloscolecidae. *Fiches d'Identification du Zooplankton* **52**, 1–6; **53**, 1–6.

Muus, B. J. & Dahlstrom, P. (1964). *Havfisk og Fiskeri i Nordvest Europa.* Copenhagen: GEC Gadsforlag. (Translated into several other languages).

Naylor, E. (1972). British Marine Isopods. *Linnean Society Synopses of the British Fauna* (NS) 3. London: Academic Press.

Nelson-Smith, A. (1967). *Serpulids.* Catalogue of Main Marine Fouling Organisms vol. 3. Paris: OECD.

Newell, G. E. & Newell, R. C. (1977). *Marine Plankton: a Practical Guide.* London: Hutchinson Educational Ltd.

Nichols, F. H. (1973). A review of benthic faunal surveys in San Francisco Bay. *U.S. Geol. Surv. Circ.* **677**, 1–20.

Nielsen, C. (1964). Studies on Danish Ectoprocta. *Ophelia* **1**, 1–76.

Nijssen, H. & Groot, S. J. de (1980). *Zeevissen van de nederlandse kust.* Wetenschappelijke Mededelingen KNNV 143. Hoorn: Koninklijke Nederlandse Natuurhistorische Vereniging.

Nordsieck, F. (1968). *Die Europäischen Meeresgehauseschnecken (Prosobranchia).* Stuttgart: Gustav Fischer Verlag.

Nordsieck, F. (1969). *Die Europäischen Meeresmuscheln (Bivalvia).* Stuttgart: Gustav Fischer Verlag.

Nordsieck, F. (1972). *Die Europäischen Meeresschnecken (Opisthobranchia mit Pyramidellidae, Rissoacea).* Stuttgart: Gustav Fischer Verlag.

Olive, L. S. (1975). *The Mycetozoans.* New York: Academic Press.

Pankow, H. (1971). *Algenflora der Ostsee.* 1. *Benthos.* Stuttgart: Gustav Fisher Verlag.

Patterson, D. J. (1978). *Kahl's keys to the Ciliates.* University of Bristol.

Pearson, T. H. (1969). *Scionella lornensis* sp. nov., a new terebellid (Polychaeta: Annelida) from the west coast of Scotland, with notes on the genus *Scionella* Moore, and a key to the genera of the Terebellidae recorded from European waters. *J. nat. Hist.* **3**, 509–16.

Peterson, R., Mountford, G. & Hollom, P. A. D. (1954). *A Field Guide to the Birds of Britain and Europe.* London: Collins. (Many editions and many translations in other languages).

Platt, H. (1982). Revision of the Ethmolaimidae (Nematoda: Chromadorida). *Bull. Br. Mus. nat Hist. (Zool.)* **43** (4), 185–252.

Platt, H. M. & Warwick, R. M. (1983). Free-living marine Nematodes. Part 1. British Enoplids. *Linnean Society Synopses of the British Fauna* (NS) 28. Cambridge University Press.

Poll, M. (1947). *Poissons marins.* Faune de Belgique. Brussels: Institut royal des Sciences naturelles de Belgique.

Prenant, M. & Bobin, G. (1956). Bryozoaires, 1. *Faune de France* **60**, 1–398.

Prenant, M. & Bobin, G. (1966). Bryozoaires, 2. *Faune de France* **68**, 1–647.

Prudhoe, S. (1982). *British Polyclad Turbellarians.* Linnean Society Synopses of the British Fauna (NS) 26. Cambridge University Press.

Prud'homme van Reine, W. J. (1980). *Wat vind ik aan't strand?* 8e druk. Zutphen: Thieme.

Rainbow, P. S. (1984). An introduction to the biology of British littoral barnacles. *Field Studies* **6**, 1–51.

Riedl, R. (1983). *Fauna und Flora des Mittelmeeres.* Hamburg: Parey.

Rioja, D. E. (1977). *Estudio de los Poliquetos de la Peninsula Iberica.* Madrid: Nuevas Graficas.

Rodina, A. G. (1972). *Methods in aquatic microbiology.* Translated, edited, and revised by R. R. Colwell & M. S. Zambruski. Baltimore: University Park Press. London: Butterworths.

Rueness, J. (1977). *Norsk Algeflora.* Oslo: Universitetsforlaget.

Russell, F. S. (1953, 1970). *The Medusae of the British Isles.* 1. *Anthomedusae, Limnomedusae, Trachymedusae and Narcomedusae.* 2. *Pelagic Scyphozoa, with a Supplement to the First Volume on Hydromedusae.* Cambridge University Press.

Russell, F. S. (1976). *The Eggs and Planktonic Stages of British Marine Fishes.* London: MacMillan.

Ryland, J. S. (1965). *Polyzoa.* Catalogue of Main Marine Fouling Organisms, vol. 2. Paris: OECD.

Ryland, J. S. (1962). Biology and identification of intertidal Bryozoa. *Field Studies* **1**, 33–51. (Revised key in prep.).

Ryland, J. S. & Hayward, P. J. (1977). *British Anascan Bryozoans.* Linnean Society Synopses of the British Fauna (NS) 10. London: Academic Press.

Schellenberg, A. (1942). Flohkrebse oder Amphipoda. *Tierwelt Deutschlands* **40**, 1–252.

Schmekel, L. & Portmann, A. (1982). *Opisthobranchia des Mittelmeeres. Nudibranchia und Sacoglossa.* Berlin: Springer Verlag.

Sims, R. W. (1980). *Animal Identification. A Reference Guide.* 1: *Marine and Brackish Water Animals.* Chichester: John Wiley.

Smaldon, G. (1979). *British Coastal Shrimps and Prawns.* Linnean Society Synopses of the British Fauna (NS) 15. London: Academic Press.

Smith, S. M. (1982). A review of the genus *Littorina* in British and Atlantic waters. (Gastropoda: Prosobranchia). *Malacologia,* **22,** 535–9.

Soest, R. W. M. van (1976). *De nederlandse mariene en zoetwatersponzen.* Wetenschappelijke Mededelingen KNNV. Hoorn: Koninklijke Nederlandse Natuurhistorische Vereniging.

Söderström, J. (1963). Studies in Cladophora. *Botanica Gotheburg.* **1,** 1–147.

Sournia, A. (ed.) (1978). *Phytoplankton Manual.* UNESCO Monographs on Oceanographic Methodology 6. Paris. UNESCO.

Southward, A. J. (1963). *Barnacles.* Catalougue of Main Marine Fouling Organisms. Paris: OECD. 46 pp.

Southward, A. J. (1976). On the taxonomic status and the distribution of *Chthamalus stellatus* (Crustacea, Cirripedia) in the north-east Atlantic region; with a key to the common intertidal barnacles of Britain. *J. mar. biol. Ass. U.K.* **56,** 1007–28.

Sparrow, F. K. (1960). *Aquatic Phycomycetes,* 2nd ed. Ann Arbor: University of Michigan Press.

Stegenga, H. & Mol, I. (1983). *Flora van de Nederlandse Zeewieren.* Hoorn: Koninklijke Nederlandse natuurhistorische Vereniging.

Stephen, A. C. & Edmonds, S. J. (1972). *The phyla Sipuncula and Echiura.* London: British Museum of Natural History.

Sykes, J. B. (1981). An illustrated guide to the diatoms of British coastal plankton. *Field Studies,* **5,** 425–68.

Tattersall, W. M. & Tattersall, O. S. (1951). *The British Mysidacea.* London: The Ray Society.

Tebble, N. (1976). *British Bivalve Seashells,* 2nd ed. London: British Museum (Natural History).

Thompson, T. E. & Brown, G. H. (1976). *British Opisthobranch molluscs.* Linnean Society Synopses of the British Fauna (NS) 8. London: Academic Press.

Tortonese, E. (1965). *Echinodermata.* Fauna d'Italia. Bologna: Calderine.

Tregouboff, G. & Rose, M. (1957). *Manuel de Planctonologie Mediterranéenne.* Paris: Centre National de la Recherche Scientifique.

Tuck, G. S. & Heinsel, H. (1978). *A Field Guide to the Seabirds of the World.* London: Collins.

Tutin, T. G., Heywood, V. H., Burges, N. A., Moore, D. M., Valentine, D. H., Walters, S. M. & Webbs, D. A. (1964–80). *Flora Europaea,* vols. 1–5. Cambridge University Press.

Vervoort, W. (1946). Hydrozoa. Hydropoliepen. *Fauna Nederland* **14,** 1–336.

Wheeler, A. (1969). *The Fishes of the British Isles and North-West Europe.* London: MacMillan.

Wheeler, A. (1978). *Key to the Fishes of Northern Europe.* London: Frederick Warne.

Zariquiey Alvarez, R. (1968). Iberian Decapod Crustacea. *Invest. Pesq.* **32,** 1–150.

Zibrowius, H. (1968). Etude morphologique, systematique et écologique des

Serpulidae (Annelida, Polychaeta) de la region de Marseille. *Rec. Trav. Stat. mar. Endoume H.S.* Suppl. 59, 81–253.

Ziegelmeier, E. (1957). *Die Muscheln der deutschen Meeresgebiete.* Hamburg: Biol. Anstalt Helgoland.

Ziegelmeier, E. (1966). *Die Schnecken der deutschen Meeresgebiete.* Hamburg: Biol. Anstalt Helgoland.

15

Safety

COMPILED FROM INSTITUTE OF BIOLOGY
AND NATURAL ENVIRONMENT RESEARCH
COUNCIL SAFETY GUIDANCE NOTES

Introduction

Assessment of potential dangers, choice of safe working procedures, acquisition and checking of relevant equipment, and instruction of staff are essential steps to be carried out *before* a survey is conducted. All organisations engaged in survey work should have codes of practice within which their members must work and that take into account national health and safety legislation. This chapter does not replace any such codes of practice, but is intended as a basic guide, supplement, reminder, or reinforcement.

Anyone carrying out survey work is responsible for ensuring or not endangering their own safety, that of their colleagues, and that of members of the public. The ultimate responsibility for matters of safety lies with directors, heads, and others in overall authority; they must ensure that any person about to supervise or undertake survey work is not only trained in the basic techniques and practices appropriate to the work, but also passes on an appreciation of the safety practices down the line of authority to the individual worker.

General Procedures

Assessment of potential dangers

Hazards and dangers will vary according to the locality and type of work to be carried out. The level of hazard or danger must be assessed before survey work begins, and suitable methods of working must be agreed. National and local sources of detailed knowledge on the working area should be consulted (e.g., coastguards, harbour masters, local fishermen, colleagues).

A HAZARDOUS locality or task in the context of this chapter is one in which potential dangers may arise in the course of the work to be performed.

A DANGEROUS locality or task is one in which dangers are always present.

While workers may go alone into hazardous localities, or perform a hazardous task, *no field-worker should go alone into a dangerous locality or undertake a dangerous task*, unless there are special reasons for doing so. Work in any habitat at night should be regarded as potentially *dangerous*, and should be carried out in pairs.

Field-workers should ascertain the nature and extent of any possible *health hazards* in the proposed locality. Advice should be sought, if appropriate, to ensure that the worker or party is guarded against such hazards as industrial or sewage outfalls.

Preparation for a field excursion

Any person or group planning a field trip of a hazardous or dangerous nature more than a short distance from base should leave some record of each trip in the laboratory, institute, or centre. This should contain the following information.

1. Date and time of departure.
2. Method of travel to the site and around the site.
3. Proposed itinerary to be followed. The Natural Environment Research Council (NERC) (Thomason, 1983) recommended that the working area be indicated by a circle of diameter not more than 1.5 km, drawn in pencil on a 1:50 000 map, and dated. The map should also show the route to be used to and from the vehicle to the working area.
4. Any potentially hazardous technique to be used.
5. Expected time of leaving the site and return to the laboratory, or the expected duration of the trip.

Before departure for such longer trips, a person (or group) must inform a *designated person* at his place of work or home that he is leaving and has recorded the details of his trip.

Procedure after an excursion

A 'sign off' procedure must be agreed for longer trips or short trips to a dangerous locality, and carried out on return to the institution or to home. This may involve informing a designated person, and will normally be done before the pre-arranged time of return previously recorded. It is the responsibility of those remaining at base to initiate a search-and-rescue procedure when certain pre-arranged criteria have not been met.

Records should be kept of incidents that have occurred during field-work, and used for up-dating safety procedures.

Clothing and field equipment
Field-workers must ensure in advance that suitable clothing and equipment are available to them for the time that the trip is planned. The following check-lists cover most eventualities, but see also the specialist procedures sections.

Clothing check-list
1. Warm and waterproof clothing
2. Wellingtons or waders
3. Waterproof boots that give a good grip
4. Extra, or thick, socks – spare pair(s)
5. Strong gloves
6. Rubber gloves for wet work
7. Hat, cap, balaclava, etc.
8. Change of clothes
9. High-visibility clothing
10. Wet-suit

Equipment check-list
1. Maps, charts, recent aerial or satellite photographs
2. Compass
3. Tide tables
4. Accurate waterproof watch, alarm clock (?)
5. Portable radio communicator, spare batteries
6. Whistle
7. Torch and/or lantern, spare batteries
8. Flares, heliograph
9. Wading pole
10. Rope for rescue
11. Sun-glasses, polarizing (?), safety spectacles, goggles
12. Survival knife
13. Sleeping bag – good quality
14. Survival bag – vacuum. packed
15. Life-jacket
16. Hard hat – check date of manufacture, reject if over 4 years old
17. Protecting shoes

18. Ear defenders
19. First-aid kit, personal
20. First-aid, car
21. First-aid kit, major accident
22. Food and drink (warm), water
23. Binoculars
24. Firearms, ammunition
25. Fire extinguisher
26. Warning flags, tapes, red triangle, flashing beacon
27. Mud-flat sledge
28. Tin of lifeboat matches

International distress signals

Before undertaking field-work in any area, leaders should ensure that those of whom they have charge know the distress codes appropriate to that area.

The INTERNATIONAL DISTRESS CODE at SEA is as follows:

1. *Whistles and torches*
   The Morse-code signal 'SOS', that is:
   Three SHORT blasts/flashes – three LONG – three
   SHORT – pause – (repeat)...
2. *Red* flares or orange smoke
3. *Outstretched* arms, raised and lowered slowly and repeatedly
4. An oar with a cloth tied to it, waved slowly from side to side

The INTERNATIONAL DISTRESS CODE on LAND:
SIX long flashes/blasts/shouts/waves in succession, repeated at 1-minute intervals.

INTERNATIONAL SIGNALS from DIVERS on the surface are:

1. Arm held up with thumb and forefinger tip-to-tip:
   I AM O.K.
2. Arm held up and waved from side to side:
   I NEED HELP

First aid

In the event of an accident, first aid must be rendered at once, and medical and relief help should be sought if necessary. It is the duty of directors and heads to ensure that appropriate first-aid skills are understood by those who might need them and that the procedures for enlisting help are known.

First-aid boxes should be made of suitable material and designed to protect the contents from damp and dust. They should be clearly identified as first-aid containers.

First-aid kits check-list
1. Card giving first-aid guidance
2. Individually wrapped sterile adhesive dressings
3. Sterile eye pads, with attachment
4. Triangular bandages (these should if possible be sterile; if not, sterile coverings appropriate for serious wounds should also be included)
5. Safety pins
.6. A selection of sterile unmedicated wound dressings
7. Packets of sterile cotton wool
8. Splints
9. Antiseptic fluid and a small dish
10. Scissors, tweezers
11. Crepe bandages, $2\frac{1}{2}$ inch or 60 mm
12. Pain-relieving tablets

Hypothermia is a condition resulting from dangerous loss of body heat. A drop in body temperature of only 2 degrees from the normal 37 °C indicates the onset of hypothermia and a drop of 4 °C is life threatening. The early stages of hypothermia are insidious in that they are lassitude with a lessening of critical faculties and will to live. The main causes of hypothermia are wind chill through inadequate clothing or total immersion in cold water. In both cases, the first choice remedy is a hot bath (40 °C) kept up to temperature by the addition of hot water. In locations where a bath (or shower) is not available, provide extra clothing, use a survival bag and move the victim to shelter, and subsequently obtain professional treatment. Encourage shivering and other muscular activity. Provide hot food and drink whenever possible, shelter from wind, and keep dry.

Special procedures
Intertidal flats and salt marshes
The period available for work is usually limited by the tides; knowledge of the state of the tide and of the time is essential. Because of the time limitations, the dangers of becoming lost or sustaining accidents or injury during the work are greater. Field-work should not be carried out alone in these environments. Local exceptions may be made where work is confined to the bank. Always carry a compass, in case mist or fog develops suddenly and obscures the shoreline.

Intertidal flats and salt marshes are, in general, very exposed and can be very cold; the limitations on working time, due to tides, may also result in work having to be carried out early in the morning or late in the evening. Suitable clothing and footwear are essential.

A knowledge of the day's tides is essential, but allowance must also be made for local conditions and changes in the weather, e.g., a change to an onshore wind can bring forward the time of high tide. When the terrain is flat the tide advances quickly, and work should be planned to allow ample time for exit *before* the flood-tide starts to advance across the work area.

Obtain a detailed local weather forecast immediately before departure. Do not attempt any work if the weather forecast is unsatisfactory, including risk of being caught in fog, mist, or thunderstorms.

Check your watch immediately before departing, e.g., against the radio or telephone 'clock' service.

Intertidal areas are often crossed by deep creeks or channels, and the depth and the nature of the bottom of any such feature should be determined using a stout pole before any attempt is made to wade across.

The conditions underfoot are often highly variable and can be dangerous, e.g., quicksands, soft mud. When traversing soft mud, test before each footstep, probing ahead with a pole.

If the mud becomes too soft and one's feet sink in, it is essential not to make violent movements to try to get free, as this inevitably makes the situation worse. If one's boots or waders become stuck, gradually slip one foot out and rest the leg on the surface and gradually free the other foot. When lying on the surface, the weight distribution is such that one does not usually sink. Proceed to firm ground using a 'leopard crawl' (spread-eagle face down, keeping the maximum area of your body in contact with the ground all the time).

Do not prepare too heavy a load to carry. Use a mud-flat sledge.

Avoid quicksands, but if caught in one, call for help and use the 'leopard crawl' to return to firm ground.

Land mines and unexplored bombs may be present on some coasts. In known danger areas the local bomb disposal unit should be consulted so that, if thought necessary, they will 'sweep' the area with mine detection equipment. On no account touch anything suspect.

The featureless nature of much of this type of terrain makes navigation difficult, and distances and travel times may be difficult to judge. As a result it is easy to become lost. Surface form, location, and course of creeks change frequently; do not rely on those features for location.

Because of the time limitation and tides, any injury that slows down progress can become fatal. Do not attempt work in these areas if you already have an injury or illness that slows you down, e.g., a twisted ankle.

Above all else, the main considerations are *tides and time*. Always have a detailed knowledge of the tides and always allow ample time for access to and exit from the site – several short work spells on successive days are preferable to one or two sessions, which leave no margin of error with tides. Take up-to-date tide tables with you.

Always have some means of attracting attention in case of difficulty (see section on international distress signals).

Rocky shores and cliffs

Rocky shores are always potentially hazardous, because of their uneven surfaces, slippery weed cover, and fissures; exposed headlands are dangerous because of their steepness and liability to violent wave action.

Clothing should be suitable for the worst potential conditions, including spray from waves, and the soles of any footwear should have adequate tread. In colder weather a pair of diving or domestic rubber gloves can prevent excessive heat loss from the hands whilst, for example, handling wet algae.

In situations such as steeply shelving shores or stations near the water's edge that may be affected by large waves, any worker should be roped to another person higher up the shore, or to a stable fixture such as projecting rock. Where work has to be carried out on or below cliffs, a hard hat must always be worn, and any essential climbing must be carried out with a companion, using ropes and proper belaying procedures and safe climbing techniques. Care should be taken not to dislodge loose rocks or other objects.

Small boats

Small boats are those carrying up to 12 people, in addition to any crew members. Boats with motors, inboard or outboard, will require different preparation and equipment from rowing boats. Working in boats must be regarded as a dangerous activity.

If a boat is hired with crew, the responsiblity for safety rests with the operator, but the survey leader should satisfy himself that adequate precautions are being taken.

As usual for work in situations where adverse weather conditions are likely to be encountered, the clothing of all members of the group must be effectively waterproof and must anticipate the worst conditions likely to arise.

Life-jackets must be worn at all times by all persons on board, and the operation of the jackets should be explained before departure. Life-jackets must be tested and serviced at least once a year.

At sea, carry charts of the area of operation, and try to obtain local information, pencilled onto the chart, of tidal conditions, races, rocks, wrecks, and other hazards likely to be encountered.

When used at sea, a boat should be equipped with the following:

1. Navigational aids, including compass
2. Fire extinguisher
3. Distress signals, such as flares and fluorescent dyes
4. Anchor, with substantial line, properly secured
5. Baler, or hand-operated pump for inboard-engined boats
6. A set of oars or paddles
7. Torch and spare batteries
8. A box of engine and boat spares, including spark-plugs
9. Contact breakers, gaskets, cables, shear-pins, a set of tools for the engine, and spare bungs
10. Bellows or inflator for inflatables
11. Emergency food supply and water
12. Survival suits
13. Spare engine
14. Radio communication

Before using the boat, the survey leader must judge if the boat is safe and adequate for the job, if it is crewed by people who are competent, fit, and suitably prepared, and that it is not overfilled, either by personnel or equipment. In many circumstances a leader may need to insist that all members of the party must be competent swimmers.

When intending to use boats at sea, inform the coastguard of details of the work to be undertaken. See also the section on international distress signals. For further information, see HM Coastguard (1981).

Research vessels

A research vessel may be a ship of any size, having a master or crew whose sole duty while at sea is the running of the ship. The ultimate responsibility for safety on board rests with the master, and his instructions should be complied with at all times. The scientific activities to be carried out should be planned, in detail, and agreed with the master beforehand. Before embarking, a basic knowledge of seamanship should be acquired; training in the use of machinery to be operated should be obtained, and no other ship's equipment should be operated or interfered with unless specific authority is obtained. If any doubt arises during the work while at sea, the officer of the watch should be consulted; in any case, the scientist in charge should ensure that the duty officer is kept informed of the work underway. Work on research vessels should always be regarded as hazardous, and in some situations, such as poor weather, when working aloft, and when handling certain equipment, it should be regarded as *dangerous*. Good housekeeping is essential for safety on board ships.

Adequate clothing that anticipates the worst conditions must be worn while working, and effective waterproofs should be worn when necessary.

At all times non-slip footwear should be worn, and when working with deck lifting gear, protective industrial shoes or boots should be worn.

Hard hats should be worn when gear is being lifted above the deck. Heavy equipment swinging from a boom or A-frame can present a considerable hazard.

Industrial gloves should be worn when handling lines or ropes.

For working on deck in an exposed position or aloft, a safety harness, life-line, and life-jacket must be worn. For routine work on deck, a life-jacket must be worn.

Electrical equipment, particularly that to be used on deck, must be adequately protected against ingress of water. A check should be made to make sure that interconnected electrical equipment is on the same phase.

All loose items of equipment both on deck and in laboratories should be secured at all times. Toxic materials must be stored securely and should be handled in safety cabinets. The arrangements for the storage of materials with low flash points, such as solvents, and of concentrated formaldehyde must be agreed with the master, so that emergency drills in case of fire or other accidents can be organised. When using formaldehyde, protective glasses should be worn, and eye-washing facilities should be available in case of splash.

The master must be assured that all tackle to be used on board carries a current test certificate.

For further information see Department of Trade (1979).

Diving

The use of SCUBA diving techniques to undertake scientific work has increased considerably in recent years, and the record for safety among biologists is good. Nonetheless, by its very nature, the technique must be regarded as potentially *dangerous*, requiring special skills and care.

Since projects will vary so markedly, only broad guidelines are set out here. Most research establishments have their own codes of practice or 'diving rules', which may differ in certain respects from this summary. Such codes must always be adhered to by workers, either permanent or visiting, at these institutions.

Anyone considering diving work should be fully aware of national regulations concerning scientific diving; there may be differences in regulations according to whether divers are professional divers, scientists, or unpaid assistants.

Any employee who intends to undertake or supervise diving work *should consult his institution's insurers* to make certain that he has adequate cover. Individuals should additionally take out their own personal accident insurance, suitably endorsed for professional or amateur diving activities, as appropriate.

It is particularly important that all members of a diving team working from a boat should have a high level of skill in boat handling.

The following are requirements of the Health and Safety Executive (UK) (1981) for professional diving.

Personnel

A diving contractor must be appointed in writing by the institution in which the project team is based. He/she shall have ultimate control of all diving operations undertaken by the team, wherever carried out.

Diving supervisors must be appointed in writing by the diving contractor for a series of operations, such as the duration of a research contract or project. A diving supervisor takes charge of a single dive, and while thus employed *shall not dive*. After the underwater team has surfaced, there can be a change-over to another nominated supervisor, so that the first supervisor may dive. The hand-over of responsibility shall have been previously determined in *Diving Operations Log Book* (see below). A diving supervisor who remains on the surface must have experience of diving operations, but need not be a practising diver medically 'in date' (see below).

Divers must:
1. be in possession of a valid certificate of professional training (see below);
2. have a valid certificate of medical fitness, issued by a doctor from an approved list (see below);
3. be considered by the supervisor for the dive as competent to carry out the work.

Certified amateur divers, such as students, or members of a sub-aqua club, may accompany a diving team on a task, and must at all times comply with the code of practice laid down by the institution, and be subject to the control of the supervisor(s). Such amateurs shall not be appointed as supervisors or stand-by divers.

Log-books

Two types of log-books must be kept by any professional diving team:

1. A *Diving Operations Log-book*, in which the supervisor shall list details of personnel and equipment to be used on each dive, including the nomination of supervisors for each dive or each part of the operation. This log-book must be lodged with a designated person at work or at home prior to departure, and collected again after completion of the operation.
2. Each diver shall keep his/her own *Diver's Log-book* of an approved design. In this are recorded all details of training and medical certification, together with details of every dive and simulated dive.

Medical certification

Each professional diver or diver paid to take part in a diving operation shall be examined annually by a doctor approved by the Health and Safety Executive. The certificate shall be filed in the *Diver's Log-book*. If a diver is judged fit to dive subject to limitations, this shall be made known to the diving contractor and supervisor.

Equipment certification

All air cylinders, including those used in conjunction with life-jackets, all demand valves, and any other equipment used in supplying air to a diver, must be inspected annually by a competent authority and a certificate must be issued. The certificates shall be filed in the *Diving Operations Log-book*.

The diving team

There shall be a minimum of THREE divers for each dive where the depth of water exceeds 1.5 m but does not exceed 30 m, and divers shall normally descend in pairs. One fully kitted diver, the supervisor for that dive, shall remain on the surface. Where the diving contractor is satisfied that diving in pairs or a group would jeopardise the successful completion of a task, he may permit a diver to descend alone, provided that a fully kitted stand-by diver, in addition to the supervisor, is available at the surface, and that the diver undertaking the work is in contact with the surface by line. The stand-by diver in this instance must not act as line-tender. Where the depth of water exceeds 30 m, there shall be an extra stand-by diver at the surface, in addition to the supervisor, i.e., a team of FOUR. A stand-by diver must not be carrying an inhibitive time penalty in case he/she is required to descend in an emergency.

Procedure for Each Dive

1. A diving operation starts from the time the equipment and personnel are being prepared, and it finishes after completion of all necessary therapeutic procedures and checking of equipment afterwards.

2. Details of each dive, including nomination of supervisor(s) and names of team members for each dive, equipment to be used, and the tasks to be undertaken, shall be entered in the *Diving Operations Log-book*, which, after being signed by the contractor, must be lodged with a designated person at work or at home. A call-out procedure must be agreed with that person, and details entered in the *Log-book*, in case the diving team fails to return by a specified time.

3. Less than six hours before the commencement of the diving operation, all equipment for use on that dive must be examined by a competent person or persons nominated to do so by the contractor or supervisor; if the contractor or supervisor so decide, that person can be the diver him/herself.

4. Compressed air for cylinders must be obtained from a reputable source, known to conform to approved standards of purity.

5. The supervisor must be satisfied that all divers are fit; if not satisfied, he may refuse to permit a diver to enter the water. It is also the duty of each diver to ensure that he/she is fit to dive, and to tell the supervisor if he/she has reason to suspect that his/her health is in any way impaired.

6. The supervisor shall outline the programme of work to be carried out, equipment to be used, and the allocation of duties during the operation. Each diver shall record his specific duties in his personal *Diver's Log-book*.

7. The supervisor must record in the *Diving Operations Log-book* the time each team entered the water, the bottom-time, the time of reaching the surface again, the maximum depth reached, the tasks carried out, and any decompression schedule implemented.

8. Diving must normally be carried out in pairs (but see section *The diving team*, above), and if individuals of a pair become separated during a dive, then both shall surface to re-establish contact. Surface marker buoys must be used by each pair underwater, except where their use would cause additional danger to the operation, such as during the inspection of salmon nets, etc.

9. All wet-suit divers, including those standing-by, must wear adjustable buoyancy life-jackets capable of being filled from an

integral air cylinder; dry-suit divers must satisfy the supervisor that buoyancy can be satisfactorily controlled.

10. On surfacing after a dive, all divers must signal that all is well, to each other and to the supervisor. Teams should bear in mind that accidents and diver distress mostly occur at the surface rather than underwater. The surface cover should be alert at all times during a dive, and not just when the diving team are expected to surface. It should be assumed that the team members are cold and tired after a dive, and they should be recovered quickly.

11. If an emergency situation develops, proceed quickly with first aid, such as expired air resuscitation or dealing with injuries. If decompression sickness or ruptured lung are suspected, telephone or radio the nearest coastguard or other relevant authority and contact a nearby doctor as soon as possible. Telephone numbers and addresses of nearby doctors should be noted before the start of each diving operation, and also telephone numbers of available decompression chambers.

For further information consult Underwater Association (1979) and Health and Safety Executive (UK) (1981).

Electric fishing

Electric fishing is safe if properly carried out, but its nature requires that it be regarded as dangerous, in two respects: first, there is danger from electric shocks from the equipment, and, secondly, there are the normal hazards of the aquatic environment itself.

The technique uses the physiological effect of an electric field in the water to act upon the nervous systems of fish so that they can be caught.

The equipment most commonly in use operates at about 240 volts, either a.c. or d.c. A d.c. system is preferable, because the electrodes are widely separate, and the cathode need not be handled while the generator is operating.

All operators must be *medically fit*, and have no known heart or respiratory defect, since an electric shock may have a more serious effect on operators with certain medical conditions.

All electric cables must be carefully run to eliminate loops or coils which may trip operators.

All equipment within the boat must be carefully stowed and securely lashed in position.

Anybody undertaking electric fishing should notify the laboratory steward, or other responsible person, of the time and location at commencement and of their safe return.

Nobody should undertake electric fishing alone.

Any group of people undertaking electric fishing must have one member with previous experience and adjudged to be competent by his officer in charge.

The most experienced person will be nominated the person in charge of the exercise.

The principal safeguard in electric fishing is experience and a well-briefed party. Particular attention should be paid to novices and any inexperienced visitors.

If buckets form part of the ancillary equipment, they must be plastic with plastic handles, and all pond nets must have non-conducting handles.

All operators must wear dry rubber boots in good condition.

No electric fishing should be carried out in the rain.

Electric fishing apparatus must not be tampered with, modified, or changed during the course of an operation.

Each party member should be assigned a specific duty and be fully conversant with the requirements of that duty before the work commences. One person should be stationed at the generator with specific instructions and the capability to switch it off if an emergency threatens. Another person should have the duty of housekeeping the boat with particular reference to loops and coils in cables.

Care must be taken to ensure the stability of the boat due to loading and disposition of personnel at all times.

Electric shocks can injure or kill directly, but they can also injure indirectly by causing the operator to recoil involuntarily. Direct effects also induce electrical burns, heart failure, and interference with breathing.

The principal causes of electric shocks when electric fishing may be:
1. contact with the two energised electrodes at the same time;
2. contact with the water within the radius of the electric field where there is a dangerous voltage gradient;
3. shocks from inadequately insulated equipment.

Members of the team competent in first aid must be able to recognise the possibility of the following medical conditions, and take appropriate action AT ONCE.
1. Electrocution, in which case heart message and artificial resuscitation must be started,
2. Respiratory arrest, when the respiratory control centre in the brain has been affected, in which case artificial resuscitation must be started,
3. Asphyxia from chest cramp caused by an electric shock, in which case artificial resuscitation must be started.

In any case, medical help should be obtained AT ONCE.

For further information consult Hartley (1975) and National Joint Health and Safety Committee for the Water Industry (1983).

Formalin

Solutions of formalin (formaldehyde, methanal) are irritating to the nose, throat, eyes, and skin, and should be used with caution. Protective glasses should be worn if there is any danger of splashing (e.g when working on a research vessel). A carcinogen (Bis-chloromethyl ether) can be formed spontaneously from the vapours of formalin and hydrochloric acid (Department of Education and Science, 1978). Precautions must be taken to reduce the chances of the two vapours mixing and of subsequent inhalation.

Acknowledgements

This chapter is largely based on guidelines given in two publications, *Safety in Biological Fieldwork – Guidance Notes for Codes of Practice* (Institute of Biology, London) (Nichols, 1983) *Guidance Note – Safety in Fieldwork* (Natural Environment Research Council, Swindon) (Thomason, 1983).

The editors are grateful to the Institute of Biology and the Natural Environment Research Council for permission to use material from these publications.

References

HMSO publications can be obtained from HMSO Government Bookshop, 49 High Holborn, London WC1V 6HB.

Department of Education and Science (1978). *Safety in Science Laboratories.* DES Safety Series No. 2. London: HMSO.

Department of Trade (1979). *Personal Safety on Ships.* London: HMSO.

Hartley, W. G. (1975). 'Electrical fishing apparatus and its safety'. *Fish. Manag.* **6**, (3): 73–7.

Health and Safety Executive (UK) (1981). *A Guide to the Diving Operations at Work Regulations 1981.* Health and Safety series booklet HS (R) 8. London: HMSO.

HM Coastguard (1981). *Seaway Code – a Guide for Small Boat Users*, 2nd ed., revised. London: HMSO.

National Joint Health and Safety Committee for the Water Industry (1983). *Safety in Electric Fishing Operations.* Health and Safety Guidelines 6. London: NJHSCWI.

Nichols, D. (ed.) (1983). *Safety in Biological Fieldwork — Guidance Notes for Codes of Practice*, 2nd (revised) ed. Institute of Biology, 20 Queensway Place, London.

Thomason, J. G. (ed.). *Guidance Note – Safety in Fieldwork*. Swindon: Natural Environment Research Council.

Underwater Association (1979). *Code of Practice for Scientific Diving*, 3rd ed. Swindon: Natural Environment Research Council.

Index

The number in *italics* refers to the figure on the page indicated.
The suffix 't' refers to the table on the page indicated.